W9-AKY-551

54

AMERICAN WRITERS

AMERICAN WRITERS

A Collection of Literary Biographies

LEONARD UNGER
Editor in Chief

VOLUME IV
Isaac Bashevis Singer

to

Richard Wright

Index

Charles Scribner's Sons, New York

ISBN 0-684-13673-2 (Vol. I)   ISBN 0-684-15797-7 (Supp. I)
ISBN 0-684-13674-0 (Vol. II)   ISBN 0-684-16482-5 (Supp. II)
ISBN 0-684-13675-9 (Vol. III)   ISBN 0-684-17322-0 (Set)
ISBN 0-684-13676-7 (Vol. IV)

Acknowledgment is gratefully made to those publishers and individuals who have permitted the use of the following materials in copyright.

Introduction
from "Mr. Apollinax," *Collected Poems 1909-1962*, by T. S. Eliot, by permission of Harcourt Brace Jovanovich, Inc. and Faber and Faber Ltd.
from "Sweeney Agonistes," *Collected Poems 1909-1962*, by T. S. Eliot; copyright 1936 Harcourt Brace Jovanovich, Inc.; copyright © 1963, 1964 T. S. Eliot, by permission of Harcourt Brace Jovanovich, Inc. and Faber and Faber Ltd.

"Henry Adams"
from Henry Adams, "Prayer to the Virgin of Chartres," *Letters to a Niece and Prayer to the Virgin of Chartres*, by permission of Houghton Mifflin Company

"James Agee"
from "Draft Lyrics for Candide," *The Collected Poems of James Agee*, ed. Robert Fitzgerald, by permission of Houghton Mifflin Company and Calder and Boyars Ltd.
Part of this essay first appeared, in a different form, in the *Carleton Miscellany* and is used by permission.

"Conrad Aiken"
from *Collected Poems*, copyright 1953 and *Selected Poems*, copyright © 1961, by permission of Oxford University Press

"John Barth"
from John Barth's unpublished lecture "Mystery and

Tragedy: The Two Motions of Ritual Heroism," by permission of Mr. Barth

"John Berryman"
from *Short Poems: The Dispossessed*, copyright 1948 John Berryman; *His Thoughts Made Pockets & the Plane Buckt*, copyright © 1958 John Berryman; *Formal Elegy*, copyright © 1964 John Berryman; *Berryman's Sonnets*, copyright 1952, © 1967 John Berryman; *Homage to Mistress Bradstreet*, copyright © 1956 John Berryman; *His Toy, His Dream, His Rest*, copyright © 1964, 1965, 1966, 1967, 1968 John Berryman, by permission of Farrar, Straus & Giroux and Faber and Faber Ltd.
from "The Lovers" and "The Imaginary Jew," first published in *The Kenyon Review*, by permission of Mrs. Berryman

"Randolph Bourne"
from letters and manuscripts of Randolph Bourne, by permission of Columbia University Libraries

"Van Wyck Brooks"
material drawn from William Wasserstrom, *The Legacy of Van Wyck Brooks*, copyright © 1971, by permission of Southern Illinois University Press

"James Fenimore Cooper"
material drawn from Robert E. Spiller, Introduction to *Cooper: Representative Selections*, copyright 1936, by permission of the American Book Company

"James Gould Cozzens"
from James Gould Cozzens, *Men and Brethren, Ask Me Tomorrow, The Just and the Unjust, Guard of*

AMERICAN WRITERS

Isaac Bashevis Singer

1904-

A RECENT literary surprise has been the incursion into American letters of a Polish-born Yiddish novelist only a few years younger than the century. Alone of Yiddish writers, Isaac Bashevis Singer has caught the fancy of critics, teachers, students, and public. His closest rival for this distinction would be Sholem Asch, whose novels sold widely in the United States in the 1930's and 1940's. But Asch never garnered Singer's critical acclaim.

Singer's fame was overdue. For two decades only a dwindling Yiddish readership knew he existed. He lived in America for fifteen years before having a book, *The Family Moskat* (1950), published in English. His new audience formed with *Satan in Goray* (1955) and *Gimpel the Fool and Other Stories* (1957). Now even his earliest works are in paperback. He has won several awards, the quarterlies run articles on his fiction, and the weeklies review him as an important "American" writer. One month in the late 1960's saw five of his tales in as many major magazines and journals. Each new book broadens, even when it doesn't enhance, his literary reputation. Five novels, four collections of tales, four slender volumes for children, and one series of autobiographical sketches are now in English. Two long novels (*Shadows by the Hudson*, *A Ship to America*)

await translation, as do three shorter ones (*Enemies—A Love Story*, *The Certificate*, and *The Charlatan*).

Wary of his new fame, Singer views the Yiddish writers in America as living in the past, "a ghost . . . [who] sees others but is himself not seen." This is hard to refute. Yet his own fiction evokes a past rich in the sufferings and joys, shapes and sounds of the Jewish exile's last four centuries. His dybbuks and beggars, rabbis and atheists, saints and whores are bound by common spiritual ties, an expressive common tongue, a common destiny, and frequently a common martyrdom. Together they constitute the most varied and coherent cavalcade of Jewish life in modern fiction.

Singer is no primitive. Despite exotic materials and idiomatic style, he is a sophisticated craftsman with the easy fluency attained by only the finest writers in any culture. He is a born storyteller, with sure insight and an outrageous compulsion to create. Fable and fantasy, chronicle and saga, tale and essay issue from his pen. His least inspired tales have a tender, gusty, tragic vitality derived from a sensitive fusion of Yiddish and Western traditions. His little people's pieties and lusts evoke the stark realities not only of Gogol and Dostoevski, Isaac Babel and Isaac Loeb Peretz, but of Nathaniel Hawthorne and William Faulkner. He rejects any claim that imagination cannot compete with reality. All men are hedonists, he declares, and they expect literature to provide enjoyment and information; thus a writer does well to concentrate on "real stories" while avoiding mood pieces and obscurities. "One Kafka in a century is enough," he states. "A whole army of Kafkas could destroy literature." A veteran journalist, Singer has a healthy respect for the hard fact and objective report. Yet he sees perversity and originality in all existence; "everything alive," he points out, is unique, singular, and non-repeatable. Those "realistic" writers who reduce all creation to the near and familiar only end up sounding alike. Fiction mirrors God's artistry, Singer believes, only when facts are extended and enlarged by images from the unconscious or supernatural. This fusion of fact and image, of objective report and subjective fancy, he terms chronicle—"external chronicle and psychological chronicle."

Singer's knowledge of Jewish psyche and culture is deep, certain, ancestral. One of the few writers to have mastered the entire Judaic tradition, he can enter and articulate it at any point without a discordant note. So true are eye, ear, and verbal touch that tone and mood are often the major conveyors of meaning. Viewing traditional concepts and values with an ambiguous mixture of love, pride, and doubt, he finds no easy answers to the eternal questions. What few answers there are, he makes clear, each must glean for himself. His refusal to champion group, philosophy, or commandment bothers many. For Singer all mankind constitutes the human reality; hence he spares neither Jew nor Christian, code nor attitude.

From an Orthodox background, with rabbis on both sides of the family, Singer (born in 1904) read no secular literature until he was twelve. His older brother was Israel Joshua Singer, author of *Yoshe Kalb* and *The Brothers Ashkenazi*. Both rejected rabbinical careers to champion the *Haskala* or Jewish Enlightenment. Their sister, Esther Kreitman, was also a novelist. Singer leans heavily on this rich heritage. His literary world is the circumscribed but rich one of Polish Jewry from the seventeenth to the twentieth century. Now gone, its vestiges cremated or obliterated, this world has been reshaped in his fiction by an adroit mingling of Hasidic and cabalist thought, demonology and Cossack massacres, the Sabbatian heresy and the Enlightenment.

Singer writes only in Yiddish, a language experiencing steady attrition if not extinction. Most of his work appears first in the *Jewish Daily Forward*, to which he has contributed since his arrival in America in 1935. He has been a *Forward* staff member since 1944 and also writes sketches for the paper's radio program on New York station WEVD. Singer enjoys thoroughly the "very good profession" of newspaper work, but he signs his journalistic fiction Isaac Warshawsky and does not publish it in book form. His more serious work (appearing in the *Forward*'s weekend literary supplement) he signs Isaac Bashevis. When a journalistic piece turns out well, he may revise and publish it under his own name. His fiction rarely reveals concern over his shrinking Yiddish audience; personal views are reserved for essay and lecture. If in these he admits the future of Yiddish appears "very black," he still insists the language is like the Jews themselves —who "die all the time and yet go on living."

Singer weaves into his fiction the motions, idiom, and humor of ghetto and small-town Jewish life, the *shtetl* life which was—if little else—integrated and coherent. His precise images lay bare the Jewish grain without pretense or shout. No aspect of life is too trivial or solemn to be reduced to bare motive. "I am," he confesses, "more fascinated by page four of the *Daily News* than I am by the front page of the *New York Times*." Aware of everything, he disdains little. Singer's characters do not perform great deeds; the world has crushed or bypassed them. Yet despite terror, suffering, disappointment, they accept and even love life, being determined to endure. Singer refuses to apologize for his material. His stance is that of the traditional tale-spinner whose listeners grasp every outlandish allusion, nuance, and inflection. East Europe's Jewish world becomes a familiar, continuing culture and its complex structure of beliefs, customs, and loyalties understandable commonplaces. Distance, time, and cultural change are bridged without forced reverie or nostalgia. Yet Singer feels keenly his peculiar situation. "When I sit down to write," he states, "I have the feeling that I'm talking maybe to millions and maybe to nobody." He need have little fear. The modern reader, non-Jew and Jew, finds himself responding to that strange, departed clime and becoming intensely involved with Singer's embattled little people who now seem very much like all men everywhere.

Singer's tough, intimate, earthy prose conveys the rhythms of Yiddish folk speech—its human beat and stress, intonations and embodied gestures. His frequently archaic, at times obsolete, Yiddish (discernible even in translation) reinforces a complex interweaving of fact and fantasy, comedy and terror. Like that of the last century's Yiddish masters—Mendele, Sholom Aleichem, Peretz—Singer's language exudes the verbal spontaneity and improvisation of a long oral tradition. Lucid, exact, penetrating, it conveys a human voice—"the swift, living voice," as Ted Hughes puts it, "of the oral style"; thus it proves a prime medium for expressing the Jewish communal code with its memories, hopes, and defeats. Above all, Singer's prose gives lie to the legend

that Yiddish does not translate into English. He is pleased to be read in English, to have a "very real" audience rather than the "near-imaginary" Yiddish one. Still, forty percent of each book's value, Singer feels, is lost in translation, despite his personal involvement. He has translated Russian and German fiction into Yiddish and is aware of the difficulties. "Translation is an endless process," he states, with every work posing a unique problem. "Nevertheless, good translation is possible, but it involves hard work for the writer, the translator, and the editor. I don't think that a translation is ever really finished. To me the translation becomes as dear as the original."

His appalled conviction that English translators had mutilated Sholom Aleichem's writings precipitated a deep concern for his own work. His collaboration helps explain why early translators proved sensitive enough to his subtle nuances to attain unity of style and tone. To say Singer's lucid, pithy Yiddish finds ready English equivalents takes nothing from able craftsmen like Saul Bellow, Jacob Sloan, and Isaac Rosenfeld. Together they brought Singer to a large, appreciative audience and demonstrated the value of competent literary translation—an endeavor not lacking in deriders. His more recent successes in English, however, have been due to Singer himself: in the past few years he has translated his own works and stories. Those listed as "translators" merely edit his English syntax and grammar; most do not know more than a few Yiddish words.

Ironically, Yiddish critics do not rate Singer as high as do the English-speaking critics. American readers find appealing his offbeat themes and rejection of social philosophies—in short, his existential stance; Yiddish readers, however, often view him with an uneasiness akin to suspicion. Several Yiddish critics have attacked his tales of "horror and eroticism," his "distasteful blend of superstition and shoddy mysticism," and his "pandering" to non-Jewish tastes. What merit these criticisms may have is vitiated by the obvious resentment accompanying them—a resentment that develops in some literary corners whenever a writer wins recognition beyond the Yiddish pale. Sholem Asch proved a similar target.

Yet Singer does have a perverse, if not morbid, taste for violence, blood, and animal slaughter, not to mention rape, demons, and the grave—all gothic horror story elements. He relishes those medieval superstitions and fears that clung to *shtetl* life into the twentieth century. His devils, demons, and imps may represent a partial deference to the strong contemporary taste for "black humor" in its myriad forms. But primarily his demonology enables Singer to expose the demons driving us all. His devils and imps symbolize those erratic, wayward, and diabolic impulses that detour men from their fathers' piety and morality. Singer's popularity is the more understandable at a time when such practitioners of the gothic and macabre as William Faulkner, William Styron, Flannery O'Connor, Tennessee Williams, and Edward Albee have won strong acceptance.

Many young readers today lack rapport or patience with the "traditional" novel, or with any adherence to the older themes and values. Singer's skepticism, his spiritual and psychological openness, seem attuned to their own intellectual restlessness. But Singer's integrity and imagination transcend mere fad or fashion. His vision is as tragic as that of the Greek dramatists. He too sees a universe governed by forces lying beyond reason or justice. For man this often means neither certainty on earth nor concern in heaven. "From a cabalistic point of view," he states, "I am a very realistic writer. Cabalists believe there are millions of worlds, but the worst is this one. Here is the very darkness itself." Singer therefore is as convinced as

were Hawthorne and Faulkner that evil is so near and constant a danger no one can avoid profaning life's most sacred aspects. Not for Singer, then, a facile romantic optimism. He has few illusions about man's ability or desire to better the world or himself. "My judgment is that good does not always triumph," he asserts, "that this is very far from the best of all possible worlds. That's why my Jews are not all good Jews. Why should they be different from anybody else?"

Certainly few of the driven souls in *The Family Moskat* contribute much to society's betterment. Singer's first novel to appear in English, it sprawls through the years 1911 to 1939 and three generations of Warsaw's brawling, disoriented Jews. Here (and occasionally elsewhere) he borrows several characters and expands incidents from the fiction of Joshua Singer, whom he credits with having taught him much of the writer's craft. But then both draw from the same fund of people and memories; both also utilize Gogol's sharp, kaleidoscopic detail and Flaubert's disciplined detachment to cut deeply into Jewish life.

The bleakness and nihilism so characteristic of European literature before World War II frame the painful encounter of traditional Judaism and the twentieth century. A disorderly array of new Jewish bohemians here mire themselves in emotional misdeeds and misjudgments just when Eastern Jewry is losing its social and religious coherence and Hasidism its wholeness and joy. They reveal little of the humanity, courage, or spirituality of the ghetto fighters in John Hersey's *The Wall*, published the same year. Nor are they the familiar Jewish stereotypes isolated in an alien setting. Torn between reason and flesh, orthodoxy and secularism, they form a vigorous, clamoring community hungry for good food, sex, wealth, and learning. Not for Singer are the pallid nuances of so much modern psychological fiction. Old and young struggle for moral perspective in a world shattered not only by war but by exposure to Western ideology and culture. With mounting uncertainty and disillusionment, Orthodox Hasidim bitterly debate Zionists, socialists, cosmopolites, and an increasingly aggressive middle class. Oblivious to the forthcoming catastrophe, all dissipate their energies in internecine quarrels, succeeding only in losing God without winning the world. Relying little upon introspection, less upon nostalgia or pathos, Singer keeps his people moving and talking.

Wealthy, stubborn, patriarchal Reb Meshulam Moskat dominates the early chapters and the small army of heirs waiting impatiently as he lives on into his eighties. Linked to their discarded pieties by social and emotional ties, the Moskats are denied full participation in Polish life not only by laws and prejudices but by their own religious taboos, intrigues, and delusions. In Singer's world few receive what they expect. When finally Reb Meshulam dies, the Moskats experience not quick riches but rapid disintegration of individual and family life. Most would agree with Heine's wry comment that Judaism is less a religion than a misfortune.

Exemplifying not only the Moskats' moral and spiritual decay but that of all Poland's Jewry is Asa Heshel Bannet, who has married into the clan. Asa Heshel has impossible dreams, a disbelief in God or man, and a flair for failure and running away. A descendant of Hasidic rabbis, he rejects Orthodoxy for Spinoza while striving for a university degree, divine truth, and earthly happiness. He attains only an obsessive cynicism and a determination to shield his individuality—by running from problems, family, and self. His talent for failure is matched only by his knack for survival. Asa Heshel survives war, prison, hunger, typhoid, and pogroms. But in a final act compounded equally of inertia, courage, and surrender, he rejects escape from Warsaw and rejoins family and friends to await the Nazis. In thus accepting death he again overcomes it. He proves one more avatar of that pervasive historical symbol the Wandering Jew—that introverted, rootless intellectual fated never to reach those whom he loves or who love him.

Singer makes it clear that philosophical abstractions mean little when confronted by physical deprivation and brutality. He rejects, with existential finality, all formulas and panaceas —including Zionism, Marxism, material wealth, religious orthodoxy, and romantic love; he emphasizes instead man's essentially tragic fate. No better life or Messiah exists. As Hitler's legions approach, Hertz Yanover, Asa Heshel's philosopher-friend, declares: "The Messiah will come soon. . . . Death is the Messiah. That's the real truth." So those who rely upon the world's philosophies to reject or soften death's inevitability are deluded. Those who preach such philosophies are innocents or frauds. Self-delusion is for Singer a cardinal sin.

Many have misread *The Family Moskat* as a bitter indictment of Poland's prewar Jews. Singer omits none of their flaws, tragic or pathetic; on the other hand, he unfailingly endows his embattled spirits with compensatory flashes of generosity and courage. Failing to win our admiration, they evoke compassion and understanding. At their worst they contain those biological juices which nourished their ancestors down the dark centuries. No outraged prophet, Singer avoids commentary or opinion and depends on "facts," forcing the reader to pass judgment. Seeing no solutions to man's dilemmas, he offers none, advising his fellow writers to do the same. What the writer considers profound and new, he has stated, is likely to be for the reader "already self-understood and banal." He thus differs sharply from novelists like Sartre and Camus, whose thinly disguised parables dramatize ideas expressed more explicitly in essay form.

The Family Moskat represents one of Singer's two major fictional modes. Like *The Magician of Lublin, The Slave,* and *The Manor,* it is essentially direct, realistic narrative. But Singer's earliest novel, *Satan in Goray,* and many of his short tales embody the demonic and supernatural. Realism and fantasy are not for Singer mutually exclusive categories but only, as he puts it, "two sides of the same coin. The world can be looked at one way or another, and the theme of a story determines its style." Whereas *The Family Moskat* has been undervalued, *Satan in Goray* has been overpraised. Written in 1932, the latter launched its twenty-eight-year-old author's "black-mirror" concern with Satan. A miracle-and-cabala narrative indebted to Yiddish gothics like S. Ansky's *The Dybbuk* and H. Leivick's *The Golem, Satan in Goray* is less novel than loosely linked vignettes. Singer here probes deeply the Jewish Messianic dream and the moral gap between the ideal and real. Borrowing from history, he chronicles the spiritual annihilation of a seventeenth-century community by the followers of a false Messiah. Viewing man's nature even more darkly than in the Moskat saga, he emphasizes that to expect on earth purity without corruption, the sacred without the profane, is sheer delusion.

From the chaos produced by the 1648 Cossack pogroms emerged a curious Messianic pretender named Sabbatai Zevi. Igniting Europe's exhausted Jews with promises of spiritual peace and earthly pleasures, he delivered only disunity and suffering. Convinced by wandering Sabbatian cultists of the Messiah's imminent arrival, entire communities abandoned not only Mosaic law but social decorum. Singer begins with Goray's isolated survivors excitedly receiving the year 1665–66; cabalist calcula-tions have marked it as presaging the Messiah's return and the exile's termination. But Satan, not the Messiah, now appears to transform the community into a hotbed of gossip, vice, and expediency. His agents are newly arrived Sabbatians carrying word of their master's miracles and his boast to overthrow the Turkish Sultan. Disorders erupt in the prayer house as cultists and Orthodox struggle for control. Gaining the upper hand, the Sabbatians reject rabbinic law; the Messiah's arrival, they insist, invalidates the Commandments.

Goray prospers and excitement is high. But days pass without a miracle. Enthusiasm gives way to panic, shame, and bitterness; the exile of centuries is not over. Then shattering news: faced with martyrdom or conversion, Sabbatai Zevi has led a multitude into apostasy. The Sabbatian movement is shattered. The sacred have defeated the profane. Yet the victory is at best temporary and limited—with human vision and wisdom again revealed as flawed. An unnamed cabalist underscores this by summarizing briefly for posterity the entire tale—in Yiddish rather than Hebrew. (Tradition stipulates only the vernacular be used for themes of profanation.) For Singer, then, man is at once the noblest and most vulnerable of creatures. Any claim of having penetrated life's dark complexities, of having distinguished between reality and illusion or good and evil, marks one as fraud or fool. True wisdom lies in recognition of personal weakness, acceptance of sin, and patience. Goray's Jews, in their folly, would have hurried the Messiah to end their worldly pains. They learn instead that they can hasten the Messiah only by curbing their own appetites—and that the only certain Messiah is, again, death.

In this book Singer reveals virtuosity as a Yiddish stylist, employing the archaic Hebraic Yiddish of the Hebrew *pinkassim* (community chronicles). Jacob Sloan's English translation must inevitably fall short of the original, yet it does convey Singer's verbal dexterity. But despite such obvious artistry, and a deft blend of the historic, demonic, and psychological, *Satan in Goray* is one of Singer's rare aesthetic failures. Reducing his narrative to its most suggestive essentials, he allows economy to become sketchiness and overlooks some surprisingly loose ends. The insertion of demons into Goray's harshly realistic setting is so sudden and late that it jars. As events wax fantastic and abstract, Singer relies for credibility on cultural and theological details; these remain more veneer than essential. The central characters prove merely striking caricatures; only externally visible, they reveal little consistency. Several who throughout seem ignobly motivated suddenly reverse themselves. Singer here may intend irony. But without a glimpse into the protagonists' inner thoughts the reader can only feel cheated. Other characters simply are dropped. Thus much intended irony and subtlety culminate in confusion rather than coherence.

Still no other modern writer mirrors so clearly man's urge toward the sacred and yielding to the profane. Singer has read not only Freud but such Freudian precursors as Spinoza and Schopenhauer, as well as Dostoevski, who formulated for literature man's "satanic" aspects. But Singer's judgments are implicit rather than explicit, and his stories are not so much "morality tales," he insists, as narratives "constructed around a moral point of view." Whether good or evil wins out depends in his fiction on individual character as much as on events beyond human control. His refusal to condemn evil directly troubles those who miss or misread his moral concern.

A religious man rather than an observant Jew, Singer believes in God, "but not in man insofar as he claims God has revealed Himself to him." He shuns organized prayer for the more personal form, rejecting dogmas as man's handiwork. Man has free choice to believe or doubt; Singer chooses to believe, describing his credo as "a sort of kasha of mysticism, deism, and skepticism," composed as it is of near-equal parts Schopenhauer, Spinoza, and the cabalist Isaac Luria. He is convinced God is with man always and everywhere, "except, perhaps, at the meetings of Marxists and other left-wingers. There is no God there; they have passed a motion to that effect." God's presence, however, is no guarantee of His intervention. A more certain intruder is Satan or one of his myriad agents, who prevent life from being neutral by forcing man to do either right or wrong. Blessed with an imagination given to sacred visions and profane apparitions, Singer draws occasionally upon Jewish mystic lore for angels but more frequently for demons, imps, and spirits. Sporting names like Samael, Asmodeus, Ketev Mriri, and Lilith, they serve as a "compositional shorthand" or "spiritual stenography"—enabling Singer to embody quickly his conviction that the thinnest line separates truth from appearance, the supernatural from the natural, virtue from sin. "I am possessed by my demons," he declares, "and they add a lot to my vision and my expression." Another world exists just beyond ours, he tells interviewers, a world not so much different from this one as its extension, projection, or mirror image. Anything is possible, therefore, in a world that may be imaginary and without substance. Certainly reason is woefully inadequate; merely passion's agent, it is incapable of extending beyond the here and now to the future and unseen. (He invites *Forward* readers to submit to him their experiences with psychic phenomena but dismisses most psychic practitioners as liars and charlatans. Still, he finds "their lies interesting. If nothing else, they are revealing fantasies.")

Singer gave shape to his views in *Gimpel the*

Fool and Other Stories. These are eleven compassionate fables of Jews who otherwise interest no one but God, the devil, and themselves. God's concern is never certain. When He does make a belated appearance, He punishes not Satan, who is merely plying his trade, but a sinfully weak human. Satan and his imps move unimpeded through Polish forest, swamps, and *shtetl*, debauching the vulnerable. The *shtetl*, with its muddy streets, shabby houses, and cluttered prayer house, was at the core of East Europe's Jewish life. It has proved modern Yiddish literature's dominant image and symbol. Rabbis, scholars, and students steeped in Talmud were its important men; newspapers, radios, and automobiles were nonexistent there. Shattered by Western thought, its very traces obliterated, the *shtetl* is removed just enough in time and space to render plausible the most mythical events or legendary figures; it also is close enough to embody reality. The real and unreal fuse there convincingly. Far from romanticizing the *shtetl*, Singer presents its peculiar beauty and shabbiness, its spirituality and vulgarity. Few have seen it more clearly, felt it more intensely, expressed it more tellingly. *Shtetl* life, he emphasizes, offered compensations as well as hardships. Confronted repeatedly by hostility and uncertainty, it imposed law and decorum upon its cohesive, intimate, vulnerable community. Group and family came first. The individual was not ignored, but neither was he exalted. Forced to subordinate his idiosyncrasies to the communal pattern, he had to derive his joys from within.

In a society so firmly stable, subtle human relationships can be exposed with a precision impossible in more turbulent contexts. As a novelist of manners Singer ranks with Jane Austen, Henry James, and Edith Wharton. But his tales transcend the regional and parochial to explore men's moral fiber under testing circumstances and their varied stratagems as they withstand or succumb to temptation. Most sorely tried here is Gimpel of Frampol, the town baker and recognized "fool." A lineal descendant of such famed "sainted fools" as Yoshe Kalb and Bontsha Schweig, Gimpel willingly accepts every jibe and cruel prank; he believes everything, even that which common sense rejects. Why? Well, after all, he reasons, anything is possible. Further, to accuse another of falsehood is to diminish his dignity. So when all Frampol conspires to marry him to Elka, the coarse-mouthed village slut, he agrees. When he becomes a father four months after becoming a husband, he accepts the child as "premature." Finding a man in his wife's bed, he views his discovery as a "hallucination"— such things do happen. His neighbors mock his gullibility, but Gimpel stands fast. Neither mistreatment nor trickery sour him. When his wife dies, Gimpel takes to the road. In his wanderings he hears many lies and falsehoods, yet he realizes there are no lies. "Whatever doesn't really happen," he declares, "is dreamed at night. It happens to one if it doesn't happen to another, tomorrow if not today, or a century hence if not next year." The physical world is for Gimpel but illusion and "once removed from the true world."

Thus Gimpel too joins the parade of Wandering Jews whose very lives testify that man's basic encounter is not between himself and God or Satan, but between self-discipline and inner needs. In this encounter Gimpel emerges triumphant. He is more fortunate, therefore, than most of the harassed little people in the collection's other tales. Satan's legions are everywhere, waiting to pounce at first hint of frailty or slackened obedience to God. Like Dostoevski, Singer often directs reader sympathy toward the narrator-as-victim. But his narrators frequently are demons or imps. An unwary reader may find himself pulling for a charmingly adroit demon to snare his weak human prey. In "From the Diary of One Not Born," for instance, the demonic narrator's pleasure proves contagious as he reduces a proud man to begging, drives an honest woman to suicide, and returns to hell for a hero's welcome. But Satan's pride in seducing the best individuals does not compare to his joy at corrupting an entire community. In "The Gentleman from Cracow," Frampol's browbeaten Jews (who derived such pleasure from abusing Gimpel) are victimized more easily by Satan than were their Goray neighbors. Satan arrives in Frampol during a famine as a handsome young doctor and scatters gold among the starving. The growing lust for money gives way to baser desires, and the town bursts into flame. A new village rises from the ashes, but the shame lingers through generations. Frampol's later inhabitants remain paupers. A tradesman who dares ask too high a price is instructed: "Go to the gentleman from Cracow and he will give you buckets of gold."

Crushing loss causes some to become obsessed with death; others refuse to relax their grip on life, finding happiness is possible even in this the grimmest of worlds. Still no man should expect God to bestow arbitrarily so rare a gift. In "Joy," Singer makes it clear man first must be cleansed of arrogance by doubt and suffering. Rabbi Bainish's suffering approaches that of Job, but he lacks the Patriarch's unwavering faith. He curses God and deprecates creation: "There is no justice, no Judge," he cries. The world is not ruled. "A total lie! . . . In the beginning was the dung." Nothing exists beyond the moment. The rabbi may reject God's existence, but he does not doubt that of the poor. To them he gives his possessions. Nor does he, strangely enough, cease prayers, studies, or fasts. With God deed is more important than word; so despite his

heresies, the rabbi has earned his reward. His dead daughter appears in a dream to declare he is soon to be summoned. This sign of heaven's concern renews the rabbi's faith, reveals to him, finally, an inscrutable God's purpose, and enables him to voice the theme underlying all eleven tales. "Life means free choice, and freedom is Mystery." Man's greatest blessing, he decides, is that God forever hides His face. The wicked make this an excuse for denial and wickedness. But for the faithful the danger is small. "If the pious man loses his faith, the truth is shown to him, and he is recalled." So, concludes Rabbi Bainish, one has cause always to be joyous.

One who would seem to have much cause for joy is Yasha Mazur, the ingratiating, scapegrace hero of *The Magician of Lublin* (1960). Yasha savors all late nineteenth-century Polish life has to offer—fame, excitement, good food, and willing women. But he is a driving, restless being who does not satisfy easily; his devoted wife and comfortable Lublin home pall early. His social masks of confidence and sophistication are paper thin. Jew and magician, he feels doubly the outsider. To fend off self-doubt and melancholy, he seeks untiringly new tricks and acrobatic stunts, possessions, and mistresses. A complex maze of religious impulses and dark fantasies, good intentions and erotic entanglements, Yasha can neither stop sinning nor shrug off guilt.

On his seasonal trek from Lublin to Warsaw, Yasha unfailingly hobnobs with a group of unsavory Jewish criminals who might have stepped from the pages of Sholem Asch or Joseph Opatoshu. Awaiting him in Warsaw is the cultivated widow of a celebrated Polish university professor; she expects him to convert to Catholicism and elope with her to Italy. The move requires money, with robbery seemingly the obvious solution. But Yasha is reluctant. Despite his philandering he is proud of his honesty and his pious forebears. His halfhearted attempt at burglary goes awry, and Yasha escapes capture only by fleeing to a synagogue. There he gazes at the Ten Commandments, realizing he has broken, or planned to break, each one. His misfortunes continue. When his loyal servant-mistress, having sensed his planned elopement, hangs herself, he surrenders to guilt, remorse, and fear. The implacable inner demons he has for years repelled by will and cunning have won.

Yasha's "punishment" forms the epilogue. Three years have passed. A broken Yasha has imprisoned himself in a doorless brick cell outside his Lublin home. There he lives out his days punishing the flesh, reading holy books, and striving to regain a childhood faith in a God who sees and hears, pities and forgives. After years of self-indulgence, however, faith does not come easily. Even solitude is denied him. Word of Yasha the Penitent has spread through Poland, and the ill and unhappy flock to his barred window for advice or promise of intercession with God. When he explains he is no miracle rabbi but merely a repentant sinner, many pound, shriek, and curse their angry frustrations. Others offer bribes, flattery, or insults.

More deadly than external threats is the evil lurking in his own brain and heart. Yasha's redemption, after all, is more an act of human will than divine grace. He continues to lust, question, and doubt. But unceasing battle is as much as he, or any man, can expect. The Creator is not to be bought off; life's meaning, Yasha discovers, lies in freedom and therefore discipline. As for atonement and absolution, these come not from God but from one's victims. So peace will elude Yasha until his final breath. His single consolation is that God, being merciful and compassionate, will assure good's ultimate triumph in the next world.

Yasha is as much Western picaro as Yiddish folk hero. Rarely do Yiddish characters make what Irving Howe terms the Aristotelian "climb from *hybris* into humility." Most have little occasion for "pride." Yiddish writers traditionally have rejected worldly standards of greatness as mere expressions of physical appetite; they have focused instead upon the unheroic who "live and endure in silence" and whose endings lack dramatic climax or social impact. On the other hand, Yasha's hybris is alloyed always by a Yiddish awe of God and fear of inner drives and ambitions. But his world is broader than that of Mendele's Fishke or Sholom Aleichem's Tevye or Mottel, who are confined within Jewish boundaries. Yasha moves convincingly into the non-Jewish world and back. Singer thereby introduces a theme long popular among American-Jewish novelists: the love of their Jewish heroes for Gentile women, who symbolize not only sexual taboo but a world of social gentility too foreign to be entered successfully.

That *The Magician of Lublin* does not involve the reader as deeply and movingly as does *Gimpel the Fool and Other Stories* is hardly grounds for complaint. The novel's spare, sinewy language conveys effectively the familiar Singerian world wherein a distant God chooses not to interfere in man's eternal struggle with the dark powers. Here man's greatest fears need be not of others but of himself. He cannot for a moment indulge his inner cravings; within the hidden corners of his being demons of perversity and desire struggle for his soul by blocking him from self-discipline and compassion for others. No middle road exists: the single step from God plunges man into a moral abyss.

The Magician of Lublin evoked complaint from several critics that Singer overemphasizes the sexual; so strong a concern for the erotic, they have contended, is contrary to Yiddish tradition. But a reading of earlier Yiddish fiction reveals a persistent regard for the flesh. (A similar charge was leveled a generation earlier at Sholem Asch.) Still, the objection merits attention. Certainly Singer's desire to titillate is undeniable. "In my stories," he has stated, "it is just one step from the study house to sexuality and back again. Both phases of human existence have continued to interest me." His handling of the erotic, however, is the most effective in a Yiddish context since Asch's *God of Vengeance* or Zalman Schneour's *Jews of Shklov*. Singer's earthiness rings true. Fed on centuries of poverty and fear, East Europe's Jews had little use for asceticism or the Christian suspicion of the flesh. Recurrent pogroms made urgent the Biblical dictum to be fruitful and multiply.

Singer neither champions nor condemns man's physical cravings. He simply makes it clear that his Jews (especially the Hasidim, who stress joy, song, and dance) retain enough vigor after life's demands to satisfy fleshly yearnings—despite beard, earlock, or matron's wig. Never condoning license, he points repeatedly to the dangers implicit in excessive yielding to passion. Such excess is socially and emotionally dangerous, rendering man vulnerable and punishment inevitable. Singer has derived much of his earthy, colloquial immediacy from the Hasidic folktales. (Martin Buber's twice-told, "antiseptic" anecdotes are not for him.) Moving in and out of the realistic tradition, his tales take on a timeless quality. Their Jewish ceremony and folklore provide a framework for all humanity's dreams and desires. Dates are occasional and irrelevant; the action frequently could be shifted backward or forward without affecting character or setting. Wandering through ghetto and countryside, often denied the simple dignity of citizenship, their feverish little people feel themselves outside history; the world's calendar and events do not reach them. A day's passing means

only Messiah and redemption are that much closer. Not one is a symbolic abstraction. Lusty, insatiable, and absurdly human, they struggle briefly, frantically; then, bewildered and exhausted, they succumb. The lowest chimney sweeps, beggars, thieves, and prostitutes have a dignity no disaster can destroy.

Neither prophet nor reformer, Singer lays bare, without shock or outrage, the intensity of their struggles. More existential and modern than many writers dealing with today's familiar materials, he rejects convenient platitudes of alienation, loneliness, or defeat. No character is permitted to rely upon God alone for spiritual victory. God is no mere protector; He gives, as Yasha Mazur discovered, few hints of what is permitted or forbidden. Never denying God's existence, Singer's skeptics (often Spinoza disciples) insist only that no man knows the truth of His divine being. So he who expects a universe of pure justice and reason, of virtue without evil, is a fool. In Singer (as in much Yiddish fiction—and Shakespeare) only for the saintly innocent is there hope. A Gimpel, Yoshe Kalb, Bontsha Schweig, or Lear's fool expects so little from life that his total acceptance of deprivation and suffering becomes a protective shield denied the more worldly or wise.

Singer distinguishes between the true pietists (rabbis primarily) and those pious pretenders (cabalists frequently) who corrupt their learning for material ends. Still he has no quarrel with cabalist or other ideas sincerely held and moderately espoused. Common sense, discipline, occasionally learning, and always luck are needed to avoid personal disaster. Calamity may result from the lack of any one. If compassion is missing, for instance, piety, asceticism, and intellectualism are useless. Even his pietists recognize worldly rewards are more likely for the strong or lucky than the weak or unlucky, but for no one is reward certain.

Testing these truths is the bizarre array of merchants and beggars, scholars and prostitutes who enact the eleven tales compiled in *The Spinoza of Market Street* (1961). These discover quickly that they are their own worst enemies and that the merest misstep means loss of paradise. Most confuse the paths to heaven and hell in revealing, as one critic puts it, Singer's "infinitely tender and infinitely ruthless meditations on the human condition." They also prove Singer's imaginative powers are not inexhaustible. Here his familiar mixture of folklore, religion, and legend does not win that easy suspension of disbelief so vital in tales of fantasy. Formula too often replaces insight as characters and plots seem pale recastings of various *Goray* characters and *Gimpel* tales. Yet even second-level Singer is of a quality higher than that attained by most writers today. And each tale does test anew the eternal tensions between reason and emotion, denial and license. The title story, for instance, underlines again the folly of denying the flesh. Above Warsaw's bustling Market Street, Dr. Nahum Fischelson, a lonely old scholar, spends his nights contemplating the heavens and his days writing a commentary on Spinoza's *Ethics*. For this task he has neglected ambition, comfort, and feelings. He views disdainfully those in the noisy street below who do pursue such things. They satisfy not reason but their intoxicated emotions.

When World War I halts Fischelson's meager pension he is saved from starvation by Black Dobbe, an ugly, hard-bitten peddler whose street battles leave little time for the metaphysical. She plies Fischelson with food and attention; to his surprise, he discovers a joy in living. To his further amazement, he finds himself in a marital bed. Frightened by the corporeal, Fischelson protests to his blushing bride that he has promised nothing; he is an old man and weak. Black Dobbe has not

waited these many years to be fed dialectic on her marriage night; she silently embraces her trembling philosopher, who finally drops Spinoza's *Ethics* to the floor and consummates their union. Later Fischelson is guilt-ridden at having betrayed Spinoza by succumbing to bodily passion. He gazes skyward to declare: "Divine Spinoza, forgive me. I have become a fool." But the old man's real foolishness lies in failing to recognize his first act of true wisdom. Ignorance, Singer makes clear, lies in denying the essential unity of flesh and spirit.

Those who refuse to accept this basic truth, or to fulfill their mortal obligations, pay for such arrogance even after death. The line between this life and the next is too thin to offer escape. Thus neither life nor death guarantees peace. Yet in "The Beggar Said So" Singer does suggest that simple, unquestioning faith may make life meaningful and post-mortal serenity a possibility. Some, however, reject belief and kindness for lie and trick. These prove Satan's special delight. He enjoys nothing more, he explains in "A Tale of Two Liars," than the clever thief with a knack for self-destruction. He then describes how a pair of magnificent con artists destroy each other. Most humans, however, are neither very evil nor virtuous, merely weak or unlucky. Chance largely determines their fates, with the difference between fortune and disaster being small indeed. An accident, a momentary miscalculation or weakness alters their lives. The fortunate, several tales here make clear, have nothing to crow about but their undeserved good luck. The unlucky have the poorhouse, or worse.

One who has it much worse is Hindele, in "The Black Wedding," in whom family melancholy and eccentricities have given way to madness. She dies convinced she has succumbed to Satan. Real or imagined, Hindele's demons have won. Satan relishes his every conquest, even over so pitiful a victim as Hindele. But in "The Destruction of Kreschev" he can boast again of vanquishing not only an innocent bride but an entire community. He chooses his targets well. So squalid and barren is Kreschev that there God Himself "dozes among the clouds." After all, gloats Satan, "the Almighty is old; it is no easy task to live forever." So Satan indulges there his love of mismating the old and young, beautiful and ugly, good and corrupt. There he causes the innocent Lise to forsake "both this world and next between the saying of a 'yes' and a 'no.' " He has made his point: so interwoven are love and hate, mercy and cruelty, joy and pain that values are easily confused and perverted. With the world distorted, the soul can only be lost.

Natural order is reversed completely in the nether world of "Shiddah and Kuziba." Here light is evil, black is virtue, and Satan is the Creator. The she-devil Shiddah and her son Kuziba flee in terror at the approach of light, which betokens man—that God-mistaken "mixture of flesh, love, dung, and lust." Shiddah's worst fears are realized when her underground haven crumbles beneath heavy drills. Workmen enter amid glaring light, and mother and son retreat toward earth's hated surface. They will hide there in marshes and graves while awaiting that final dark victory when God and Satan become one. Man will then have proved a bad dream, a minor distraction in God's eternal life.

God does occasionally have the last word. Even so, He first extends man's patience and loyalty before displacing Satan to reveal His own holy plan. In *The Slave* (1962), Singer's best novel, Satan's final victory repeatedly seems imminent. Returning to the infamous Chmielnicki massacres, Singer drops both his chatty tale-spinner and malicious demon-narrator; he tells instead an old-fashioned tale of devoted lovers who withstand crushing societal pressures to achieve what Susan Sontag terms a "tearfully satisfying" reunion-in-death. Jacob of Josefov has learned early that to expect more joy than suffering is to deny reality. Jacob's sufferings enable Singer to explore the complexities of freedom and slavery, sin and redemption. Blending elements from the Biblical legends of Jacob, Job, and Ruth, he underscores man's tenacity and courage in terms that are by turn earthy and idyllic, compassionate and cruel. Jacob has lost wife and children to Cossack pogroms which decimated his village. Captured by brigands, he has been sold to a Polish farmer in a remote mountain village. Left alone to tend cattle for months at a time, he struggles to retain a Jewish identity. Self-discipline comes hard at twenty-nine, especially when eager peasant girls and carousing villagers offer temptation. He need only pretend to convert to be free, but God is watching.

Jacob's greatest temptation is Wanda Bzik, his master's beautiful daughter, who repeatedly saves his life. Jacob resists seduction for four hard years. But, like all Singer heroes, he learns that ultimately the flesh is not to be denied. Despite a crushing sense of guilt and eventual tragedy, he capitulates to Wanda. Before making love to her he insists she take an icy bath and immediately afterward declare herself a daughter of Israel. Their union violates Polish, as well as Jewish, law. Discovery means certain death. Still Jacob experiences his first happiness. Finally ransomed, Jacob returns for Wanda. She converts to Judaism, takes the matriarchal name of Sarah, and joins Jacob in a life of fearful wandering to escape detection. Their subsequent life together is filled with uncertainty and disappointment, with Wanda-Sarah playing mute to disguise her Gentile origin. Jacob retains his faith through it all. Like Yasha Mazur, Jacob learns man must accept the world as God has decreed it, that God's law and purpose require man to choose daily between good and evil. Such free choice, it is clear, cannot function without evil, nor can mercy exist without sorrow. No formulas will suffice. In time Sarah is exposed, dies in childbirth, and is buried in unsanctified ground. Jacob is arrested, escapes, and with his son begins an arduous trip to the Holy Land. He sadly considers how his life parallels that of the Patriarch Jacob. The ancient laws and griefs, he sighs, remain the same.

Twenty years later a white-bearded Jacob returns from Jerusalem to Pilitz, where Sarah is buried. With age has come the belief that everything God does is good, including His intermingling of sacred and profane, beautiful and ugly: "An eye was watching, a hand guiding, each sin had its significance." Jacob's story has grown into legend, and his return causes great excitement. But he dies without finding Sarah's unmarked plot. Yet God *has* been watching. The gravedigger shoveling out Jacob's grave uncovers a still recognizable Sarah. Pilitz's astounded inhabitants are convinced only a saint's body could have withstood two decades of worms and elements. God has proclaimed the lovers' innocence for all to see.

The Slave finds Singer at his most effective. Nowhere does he express so movingly man's undying concern for the spirit and unfailing surrender to the flesh. No reward, he again makes clear, should be expected on earth. Yet all need not despair, for there are those for whom even the most crushing defeats may serve as a means of exploring and elevating the human spirit. True holiness and love transcend time and tragedy, cruelty and injustice, to attain a higher, heavenly reward. Indeed, those few who—like Gimpel, Yasha Mazur, Jacob, and Sarah—accept not only suffering's inevitability but its necessity attain a measure of serenity on earth. But such beings are rare.

Singer's prose, always spare and controlled, is here lyrical, his imagery precise. He reveals again his flair for sustaining interest and concern in the bizarre and remote. And rare in Yiddish fiction is his easy blending of plot, structure, and physical nature.

Short Friday (1964), however, is not of like quality. It consists of sixteen standard, rather than vintage, Singer tales of the Lublin district. Several reveal an element of strain, of a craftsman struggling with his craft—or perhaps not struggling enough and writing from formula rather than excited imagination. Singer has repeatedly expressed his belief in demonic spirits—at least as accurate symbols of human behavior. *Short Friday* validates his claim while pointing up its danger. His devils and imps sometimes prove overly facile devices evoked —without adequate logic, motivation, or avoidance of repetition—to enliven a thin plot. Singer tries to extend his imagination farther than in the past, to stretch his special vision to include such acts of desperation as murder, animalism, and lesbianism. "Never fear the sensational, the perverse, the pathological, the mystical," he has stated. "Life has no exceptions." He seemingly sets out to prove this. Yet if no tale here is quite another "Gimpel the Fool," none is without Singer's special flair and flavor. Each is peopled by his slightly grotesque *shtetl* types, whose exotic speech, dress, and habits somehow encompass humanity's joys and dreams, sufferings and sins.

Concerned as always with the dark inner struggles between man's angels and demons, Singer is equally involved with those battles waged more openly and crudely by husbands, wives, and lovers. These too expose good and evil's interlocking unity and remind us that in the God-man dialogue God often remains silent and inscrutable. They remind us also that man's path is precarious in a world torn between God and Satan. One misstep, indulgence, breach of faith gives Satan's watchful legions their opening. "Blood," the volume's shocker, underscores this vividly in tracing the frantic degeneration of the sensual young Risha, who betrays her enfeebled husband with an unscrupulous ritual slaughterer. The two soon find sexual satisfaction only amid the warmly flowing blood of animals they have butchered. Such carnality would not have surprised the ancient cabalists; their sages had insisted "the passion for blood and the passion for flesh have the same origin." They had known also that "one transgression begets another." Risha slides from adultery and bloodletting to blasphemy, apostasy, and madness—until chased and killed as a werewolf. Stretching credibility, yet steering clear of fantasy, Singer anchors Risha's outlandish behavior in realistic detail and insight. Extending Singer's skill and judgment even farther is "Yentl the Yeshiva Boy," wherein he mixes quaintly the religious and erotic, lesbianism and homosexuality. Against a backdrop of student life, study, and talk, Singer unfolds a perverse comedy of a girl whose gender seems a mistake.

Yet mistakes are likely anywhere. That mortals sin is hardly surprise enough to raise eyebrows in heaven. But angels giving vent to evil impulses cause a stir on high. "Jachid and Jechidah" presents a Platonic heaven where souls exist before birth and man's world is a Miltonic hell for fallen spirits (with all humans viewed as heaven's rejects). Singer alters his angle of vision to present truth as relative— a matter of ironic perspective. He also reverses the life-death cycle—all this by means of a pair of freethinking angels (or "souls") who hold the blasphemous opinion spirits are not created but evolve. They even reject free will and ultimate good and evil. For their crimes the two are sentenced to death—this means earth, with its "horrors called flesh, blood, marrow, nerves,

and breath." Singer thus frames a second philosophical essay in slight, but exotic, fictional terms. ("Shiddah and Kuziba" had conveyed a demon's-eye view of earth and hell.) His effort proves imaginative and intriguing enough to override the strained imagery and unexpectedly preachy overtones. More substantial as narrative are two of his earliest forays into American life, "Alone" and "A Wedding in Brownsville." Here Miami and Brooklyn spawn events as nightmarish and demonic as any in Frampol or Lublin, events that force their confused protagonists to meditate on what lies behind appearance and reality and to recall the Nazi holocaust.

Even more biting than "Alone" and "A Wedding in Brownsville," however, is the wryly humorous "The Last Demon," whose verve and witty horror make it *Short Friday*'s most memorable tale. Here too past, present, and holocaust merge. The demon-narrator's insulated world consists solely of Jews and demons—no outsiders allowed. "I don't have to tell you," he declares, "that I am a Jew. What else, a Gentile? I've heard that there are Gentile demons, but I don't know any, nor do I wish to know them." Assigned to the "Godforsaken village" of Tishevitz to corrupt a pious young rabbi, he is defeated on the verge of victory. His failure dooms him to remain in Tishevitz for "eternity plus a Wednesday." Thanks to the Nazis, eternity proves shorter than expected and man crueler than any devil. Our narrator is not surprised; most demons find man terrifying. No true devil, he laments, could have conceived the Nazis' grandiose cruelty. Indeed, for mere demons the devout and learned (like the young rabbi) always have been tough adversaries—but pathetically easy victims for Hitler's troopers. These last have obliterated Jewish Poland, Tishevitz included, with its demon world. A lone survivor, the narrator is being forced into retirement. "Why demons," he asks, "when man himself is a demon?" Still he is a Jewish devil and shares the Jewish sorrow. "There are no more Jews, no more demons. . . . We have also been annihilated," he cries. "I am the last, a refugee."

No gory detail shows as Singer again mourns the holocaust's victims. He also departs from his rule of offering "neither judge, nor judgment" in his tales. He here speaks, albeit indirectly, to charges leveled by his more caustic critics—some of whom view him as Yiddish literature's "last demon." If things were not bad enough, his narrator laments wryly, he and his fellow demons are being displaced as corrupters of Jews—by Yiddish writers whose stories adulterate traditional beliefs and values. Jews of old fed mind, soul, and spirit on Hebrew law and alphabet; now they have only tales of "Sabbath pudding cooked in pig's fat." Even the narrator draws sustenance from a tattered Yiddish storybook. His book's words, our demon admits, not only form "gibberish" but parody Hebrew law. He is keenly aware his own behavior merely parodies that of the rabbis. Yet is not even a parody better than nothing? He shudders only at realizing that when his volume of Yiddish tales goes, so does he. "When the last letter is gone,/ The last of the demons is done." His critics, Singer seems to imply, might give thought to this grim eventuality.

Aging survivors and fading memories trace the Jewish world Singer remembers. Writing *as if* this world still lives, he rejects the charge that his literary stance is artificial. "After all," he asks, "what could be more artificial than marriage? . . . Every man assumes he will go on living. He behaves *as if* he will never die. . . . It's very natural and healthy. . . . We have to go on living and we have to go on writing." Time only intensifies his efforts to give his world new, enduring life by his fiction. He has

tried to reactivate its ghosts and sounds in a cluster of autobiographical sketches published collectively as *In My Father's Court* (1966). A three-level memoir that fills out the Singer family portrait outlined earlier in Joshua Singer's *Of a World That Is No More* (1946, Yiddish), these recollections reveal the deep human well from which both Singers have drawn their fiction. For the family of Rabbi Pinchos Menachem Singer life in the Warsaw ghetto a half-century ago was hardly dull. A frantic, bizarre array of butchers and bakers, drifters and tearful women, criminals and saints shuffled through their modest Krochmalna Street apartment, atop a reeking, garbage-strewn stairway. There Rabbi Singer conducted his rabbinical court, the Beth Din. Rooted in Jewish tradition, the court combined synagogue, law court, and psychoanalyst's consulting room. Isaac Singer recalls it was for him "the celestial council of justice, God's judgment . . . absolute mercy." He eavesdropped from infancy on those troubled pietists and penitents "for whom the supernatural was so real it was almost negotiable." Most acted out their foolish, desperate, or selfless lives to the Mosaic law's very letter, developing thereby a wide range of behavioral quirks and obsessions. Krochmalna Street teemed with life and energy. Evoking that life with warmth, humor, verve, and, assumedly, imagination, Singer retells some of its uncountable tales. These Krochmalna Street sketches even have a "hero": Pinchos Menachem Singer. Scholarly, shy, innocent, fearful of the world's corruptions, he obviously has served as prototype for his son's numerous rabbinical saints. "In our home, the world itself was *tref*—unclean," Singer recalls. "Many years were to pass before I began to understand how much sense there was in this attitude."

Other vignettes deal more directly with the

author's own escapades and encounters. Amid intermittent impressions of journalistic haste, Singer provides rich insights into his boyhood. A significant event was a trip with his mother, during World War I, from German-occupied Warsaw to remote Bilgoray, where generations of his family had lived. His maternal grandfather had been that *shtetl*'s longtime rabbi; his uncle was the present one. Both are recognizable from his fiction. Bilgoray had changed little in several centuries. Young Isaac literally was able to enter and relive his past, to penetrate layers of Jewish customs and values. "In this world of old Jewishness I found a spiritual treasure trove. I had a chance to see our past as it really was. Time seemed to flow backwards. I lived Jewish history." For a future novelist it was a find beyond price.

These sketches also trace, almost inadvertently, the intellectual collapse of Poland's six-century-old Jewish community. People and incidents echo those to be found in *The Family Moskat* and *The Manor*, as well as in Joshua Singer's *The Brothers Ashkenazi*. For the brothers Singer these experiences shaped a psychological pattern of spiritual rebellion, temporary exile, and final return. They were far from alone. This century's first two decades found young Jews rejecting Talmud for socialism and the rabbis for Dostoevski; many clipped their earlocks to become painters and writers rather than yeshiva students. Among these was Joshua Singer. To his parents' shocked dismay, he also drew young Isaac into his world of freethinkers and artists. The latter records his adolescent delight at visiting his brother's bohemian friends; wandering into a sculptor's studio he discovered a dazzling new world where body and mind were honored as fervently as the Orthodox reverenced soul and spirit. He was caught irretrievably.

In this feverish atmosphere the two Singers grew to manhood. Joshua was a joiner of bohemian movements. Isaac was and is a loner; no movement engages his deepest sympathies. In Bilgoray, the rabbi's younger grandson caused consternation by reading not only Yiddish secularists but such corruptive worldlings as Strindberg, Turgenev, Tolstoi, Maupassant, Chekhov, and the excommunicate Spinoza, whose writings created "a turmoil" in his young brain. Isaac Singer's comment about his brother soon was self-applicable: "he had deserted the old, but there was nothing in the new that he could call his own." Their experiences profile a figure prominent in their fiction—the spiritual outsider torn by the demands of mind, flesh, and spirit. A deeply felt testimonial to the world Hitler's crematoria reduced to ashes, *In My Father's Court* conveys the essence of a rich Yiddish culture now barely a memory. Singer underscores its humanity and eccentricities, its family warmth and angers, its iron-bound faith and custom. When he discusses his family, his usual irony is constrained. But in the tribute paid to Warsaw's Jews, who "lived in sanctity and died as martyrs," his muted, moving sorrow shades into bitter, laconic eloquence.

Impatient young Jewish intellectuals, much like those of his own Warsaw days, reappear in Singer's *The Manor* (1967). Written between 1953 and 1955, this novel is the first of a two-volume old-style family chronicle that, like *The Family Moskat*, can double as a political-intellectual history of Eastern Europe. Rich in incident, dialogue, and description, it moves back to 1863 to follow a small cluster of Jews and Poles through the quarter-century after Russia's crushing of the Polish insurrection. Singer had thought of calling this volume "The Beginning," since it describes early socialist and Zionist stirrings in Poland. The country's social values and forms here are scrambled. Polish noblemen flee the police while Jews enjoy a rare respite of freedom and prosperity. Emerging from ghettos and *shtetls*, the latter share in the new industrialism and radicalism. Older Jews cling to Torah and prayers, watching bewilderedly as their children turn revolutionaries to redeem mankind.

Events revolve around pious Calman Jacoby and to a lesser extent the decadent Count Wladislaw Jampolski. As Calman's fortunes rise, the Count's decline; leasing the dispossessed nobleman's estate or "manor," Calman becomes wealthy. On the manor he wins and loses a world; there he watches his children grow, leave his house, and fashion their own lives. Expanding enterprises force him into non-Jewish contacts; devout and disciplined, he prays hard and eats sparingly. He also makes mistakes. Ambition, lust, pride, and family concern drive him hard. Success and pleasure, he finds, exact a price steep in weakened moral values, traditions, and family ties.

Calman's four daughters share his risks. Two marry pious Jews and slip easily into the traditional ways. Another, Miriam Lieba, is a fantasizing romantic who converts to Catholicism to plunge into a disastrous marriage with Lucian Jampolski, the Count's unstable, dissolute son. Shaindel Jacoby seemingly makes a more tenable marriage to Ezriel Babad, son of a Hasidic rabbi. But Ezriel's earlocks and black gaberdine mask a skeptic less interested in God than in science, contradictions in Holy Writ, and Voltaire, Kepler, and Newton. Such things, his father warns, lead inevitably to modern dress, loss of faith, even apostasy. Rabbi Menachem Mendel Babad (modeled closely after the author's father) proves prophetic. With the years Ezriel outgrows both his Hasidic past and his dowdy wife; he also develops strong resemblances to Yasha Mazur, Asa Heshel Bannet—and Joshua and Isaac Singer

(even to living on Krochmalna Street). He finally becomes a successful neurologist, only to learn science offers no more "truth" or certainty than does religious faith. But for Ezriel's generation the old, fixed values are gone; fear of social failure or political arrest has replaced fear of God.

Missing neither group's soft spots, Singer sympathizes with both—the older generation's reluctance to relinquish the past and youth's clamor for rapid change. Calman Jacoby clearly reflects Singer's mixed feelings; Calman is as illogical as he is sincere; he cuts down a forest to provide ties for a railroad that can only accelerate the very changes he deplores. Nor is Calman's final retreat into his private synagogue any more meaningful beyond the individual level than was Yasha Mazur's into his cell. Retreat (religious or temporal) offers at best, Singer emphasizes, only the most tenuous escape. He rejects equally past dogmatism, present relativism, and the ever-popular philosophy of despair. Individual choice, action, and responsibility are what matter. Only by accepting the burden of his acts can man survive his self-created frustrations.

The Manor conveys more than it mentions. Hitler, Auschwitz, the Warsaw ghetto uprising are still far in the future. But with the new century's approach these catastrophes seem tangible and close enough to render near meaningless all this frenzied human striving. Indeed each character's unawareness of his world's eventual fate adds poignancy. Richly textured, tightly structured, lucidly written, *The Manor* still disappoints. Singer relies even more heavily than usual upon plot to reveal character; Aristotle might approve, but surface narrative and situation predominate at cost of motive, insight, and depth. Introspective monologues are few, brief, inconclusive. Events move in swift, chainlike sequence, with people emerg-

ing just long enough to reveal momentary inclinations. Some, like the Jampolskis, fade out
unexpectedly; others reappear only at long intervals. Author and characters seem poised for
the future and volume two; several figures, for
instance, are introduced so late as to imply
further development.

These flaws, however, merely lessen the
novel's potential without weakening its eloquent, sharply realized detail or dramatic
impact. Singer best sums up his intent by observing that "It is not child's play to be born,
to marry, to bring forth generations, to grow
old, to die. These are matters no jester's witticisms can belittle." Nor can a critic's carpings
diminish them. Singer again delineates with
authority and fidelity the ethos of a time and
people known and imagined and now irretrievably lost. Such qualities result only when
a creative imagination has utilized fully a sensitive insider's knowledge and a disciplined
artist's perspective.

In *The Séance* (1968), Singer concentrates
more on the old and dying than on babies or
brides. Most of the sixteen tales are recent,
several go back a few years, and one is a
quarter-century old. Their characters are
frenetically familiar: unworldly rabbis and
scheming upstarts, good men gone foolish, bu-
reaucratic angels and rebellious dybbuks, and
several corpses who dance between life and
grave. The Evil One, however, is less evident,
appearing primarily to insist neither judge nor
judgment exists; in fact, fewer demons generally are called upon than in the past. They
are not needed—enough devilish humans are
available for the inevitable mischief. God?
Seemingly He sits in His seventh heaven snapping His fingers at everything. Other changes
or "shifts" emerge. Recent tales are longer and
more dense in thought and detail. Women
narrators are more frequent, as are symbolic

or prophetic dreams. Most surprising is a les-
sening of authorial detachment. Singer's views
on psychic phenomena and man's abuse of
animals do not obtrude but repeatedly motivate the action. Singer makes clear, however,
that man's major cruelties are reserved still for
those fellow humans showing him the most
kindness. And so perverse is the human animal
that perpetrator and victim often reverse roles,
with the victim feeling the more guilty. In "The
Plagiarist," for instance, gentle Reb Kasriel
Dan Kinsker cannot resist a brief, angry wish
that harm befall a disciple who, after plagiarizing his manuscripts, schemes to displace
him as town rabbi. When the latter falls ill and
dies, the rabbi decides he has failed a divine
test of his moral strength; he has broken, he
declares, the Commandment not to kill. Re-
signing his position, he wanders off to do
penance. Somewhat reminiscent of Saul Bellow's *The Victim*, "The Plagiarist" provides
an evocative glance at the tangled roots of
guilt and innocence.

Equally relevant to today's moral confusion
is "The Slaughterer," a taut, mind-wrenching
variation on "Blood," Singer's earlier probing
of the psychological ties between slaughter and
worship. Sensitive, scholarly Yoineh Meir has
prepared to be the Kolomir rabbi, but no man,
it seems, escapes this world's sorrows. Instead
of rabbi, he is appointed ritual slaughterer.
Constant bloodletting moved the sensual Risha
(in "Blood") to deepening carnality and degeneracy; Yoineh Meir experiences revulsion,
guilt, and depression. "Even in the worm that
crawls in the earth," he cries, "there glows a
divine spark. When you slaughter a creature,
you slaughter God." Yet signs of slaughter are
everywhere; not only his phylacteries and holy
books are of animal skin, but the Torah itself.
Insanity or death alone promises escape.
Shouting God Himself is "a slaughterer . . .

and the whole world . . . a slaughterhouse," Yoineh Meir plunges into madness and the river. The community has little time to grieve; a new slaughterer must be summoned for the holidays.

Yoineh Meir may find even death lacks repose. Certainly none is exhibited by the deceased in "The Dead Fiddler," a long tale of twists, turns, and wild, sad humor. Heaven and earth conspire often to hide the truth, it seems, while reality hangs by a thread and delusion overshadows all. Equally bizarre is the "love" story of "Zeitl and Rickel," two orphaned girls who, having had more than their share of sadness, form a lesbian relationship. Driven by curiosity and concern over future punishment, they seek to hurry matters by a double suicide. Singer displays his usual tact, but the wit and point of "Yentl the Yeshiva Boy," his previous literary foray into lesbianism, is lacking. More memorable than these two pitiable misfits is Wolf Ber, thief-hero of "The Brooch." A skilled safecracker and occasional pickpocket, Wolf Ber attributes success to a strict personal code. Like many another underworldling, he separates home from profession. But life does not divide so easily or neatly. His adored Celia shatters their cozy world by stealing an expensive brooch and lying about it. When he forces a confession, she turns defiant. He is a thief—why not she? No, he replies, his family cannot hold two thieves. How much, after all, is God expected to stand? "If she is a thief, I must become an honest man."

When strong, clever thieves find life crushing, what chance have honest, less adroit mortals? Certainly life on this side of the Atlantic for the aging, uncertain Jewish writers Singer lately seems fond of portraying is no less harsh than in old Poland. He adds to a growing roster of disoriented scribblers three whose misadventures in New York and Montreal ex-emplify his repeated conviction that all metaphysical speculations pale before fleshly needs. More positively expressed here than in earlier novels and tales, this theme enables Singer to convey his varied—and sometimes varying—views on the occult, dreams, compassion, and the deterioration of Judaica (that "vanishing specialty") in America. He continues also to confront the holocaust's residual horrors and human vestiges.

Dr. Zorach Kalisher, in "The Séance," is one such vestige. A shabby refugee scholar without prospects, he sponges meals from Lotte Kopitzky, an inept student of the occult who brings him "messages" from his dead relatives and mistress. Long grown cynical, he regards her as ridiculous and her séances as a joke but goes along with her messages and automatic writings, paintings, and symphonies. His doubts are confirmed when, after an embarrassing comedy of errors, he discovers in her bathroom the woman hired to pose as his dead mistress. Chagrined but undaunted, Lotte Kopitzky cries: "You're laughing huh? There is no death, there isn't any. We live forever, and we love forever. This is the pure truth." Singer seems to agree with the kindly old fraud, thus veering sharply from his ringing conclusion to *The Family Moskat* that "Death is the Messiah. That's the real truth." But more important than glib generalities about life, death, or truth, Singer implies, is even the feeblest attempt to reach out—as has Lotte Kopitzky—to another human being.

One who would agree with her rejection of death is Herman Gombiner, the sickly, fiftyish protagonist of "The Letter Writer," the collection's longest tale. An editor in a Hebrew publishing house on New York's Canal Street, Herman lives alone and believes himself able to see "beyond the façade of phenomena," having experienced since childhood numerous apparitions, telepathic incidents, clairvoyant visions, and prophetic dreams. Miracles are for Herman a daily occurrence; one has to be blind, he insists, not to acknowledge the concern of God or Providence for man's most trivial needs. His faith in Providence and psychic phenomena is confirmed when he contracts pneumonia and Rose Beechman, a new pen pal, appears to nurse him. Her dead grandmother, she explains, has summoned her to his side. When he recovers, these two near-strangers realize they are sharing a new miracle: neither will face old age alone. Moving and suggestive despite excessive length, "The Letter Writer" provides Singer with an excuse not only to probe the occult but to describe life in a crumbling Hebrew publishing house; his unsparing profiles of its staff members must have drawn blood and mirth along Canal Street. He also probes here (as in "The Last Demon") the writer's contribution to Jewish life and survival. In "The Lecture" (a rather incongruous *Playboy*-award winner) he does so a third time, and his conclusions are no more reassuring than before.

Half of *The Séance*'s offerings are vintage Singer, and even these might have gained from judicious editing and compression. Undoubtedly he would strike oftener to heart and marrow were he to publish less. But Singer's tales, as mentioned above, occasionally disappoint primarily because of the expectations aroused by his better work. Critics given to labels and categories apply to Singer such terms as modernist, traditionalist, gothicist, or even demonist; they like relating him to noted storytellers like Dostoevski, Tolstoi, and Dickens. Each term or link may have validity. But Singer is essentially his own man as individual and artist. His dignity, compassion, incisive intelligence, and originality are as evident as is his deep dedication to his craft. His unique vision gives to Jewish tradition, history, and lore new meaning and application.

This vision is broad as well as unique. For Singer no intellectual mode suffices alone; none proves a panacea for man's doubts and fears. Finding asceticism and indulgence equally unappealing, he rejects pointless sensuality, intellectualism, or parochialism for universal values of moderation and generosity or sincerity of spirit. Neither optimist nor cynic, Singer never strikes poses through his characters to defy faith or to disclaim learning. He observes his struggling figures without intruding judgment or sympathy; both seem almost irrelevant, but they prove otherwise. Through every tale runs a clear line that divides good and evil and renders an implied moral verdict on every act.

Singer's intent, however, is less to criticize his bedeviled fellow beings than to understand and reveal them. Despite his meticulous depiction of setting, manner, and belief, he never allows these elements to become as important as each character's painful self-scrutiny. The historical moment also is secondary. Singer strives for those acts of revelation that catch his proud, lustful, deluded little people at points of great stress, acts that cut through the banalities of religion, culture, and setting to expose their common substance across the generations. Ultimately, their loneliness and longings, their painful awareness of self and inevitable self-doubts, constitute a penetrating inquiry not into Jewish but into universal existence.

Selected Bibliography

WORKS OF
ISAAC BASHEVIS SINGER

NOVELS AND COLLECTIONS OF SHORT STORIES
The Family Moskat, translated by A. H. Gross. New York: Knopf, 1950.

Satan in Goray, translated by Jacob Sloan. New York: Noonday Press, 1955.

Gimpel the Fool and Other Stories, translated by Saul Bellow, Isaac Rosenfeld, and others. New York: Noonday Press, 1957.

The Magician of Lublin, translated by Elaine Gottlieb and Joseph Singer. New York: Noonday Press, 1960.

The Spinoza of Market Street, translated by Martha Glicklich and others. New York: Farrar, Straus and Cudahy, 1961.

The Slave, translated by the author and Cecil Hemley. New York: Farrar, Straus and Cudahy, 1962.

Short Friday and Other Stories, translated by Joseph Singer, Roger Klein, and others. New York: Farrar, Straus and Giroux, 1964.

The Manor, translated by Joseph Singer and Elaine Gottlieb. New York: Farrar, Straus and Giroux, 1967.

The Séance and Other Stories, translated by Roger Klein, Cecil Hemley, and others. New York: Farrar, Straus and Giroux, 1968.

Published since the writing of this essay
The Estate. New York: Farrar, Straus and Giroux, 1969.

A Friend of Kafka and Other Stories. New York: Farrar, Straus and Giroux, 1970.

Enemies—A Love Story. New York: Farrar, Straus and Giroux, 1972.

A Crown of Feathers. New York: Farrar, Straus and Giroux, 1973.

Shosha. New York: Farrar, Straus and Giroux, 1978.

The Collected Stories of Isaac Bashevis Singer. New York: Farrar, Straus and Giroux, 1982.

The Penitent. New York: Farrar, Straus and Giroux, 1983.

Love and Exile. New York: Farrar, Straus and Giroux, 1986.

King of the Fields. New York: Farrar, Straus and Giroux, 1988.

The Death of Methuselah: And Other Stories. New York: New American Library, 1989.

UNCOLLECTED STORIES
"The Boudoir," *Vogue*, 147:148–49, 214 (April 1, 1966).

"The Courtship," *Playboy*, 14:145, 200–02, 204, 206–07 (September 1967). (Excerpt from *The Manor*.)

"Hail, The Messiah," in *Jewish Short Stories of Today*, edited by Morris Kreitman. London: Faber and Faber, 1938. Pp. 35–51. (An abridged, variant version of *Satan in Goray*'s first six chapters.)

"My Adventures as an Idealist," *Saturday Evening Post*, 240:68–73 (November 18, 1967).

"The Prodigal Fool," *Saturday Evening Post*, 239: 64–66, 68–69 (February 26, 1966).

MEMOIRS
"Dreamers," *Reporter*, 35:45–46 (July 14, 1966).

In My Father's Court, translated by Channah Kleinerman-Goldstein and others. New York: Farrar, Straus and Giroux, 1966.

"A Wedding," *Dimensions in American Judaism*, 2:15–16 (Fall 1967).

ARTICLES AND REVIEWS
"The Everlasting Joke," *Commentary*, 31:458–60 (May 1961).

"The Extreme Jews," *Harper's*, 234:55–62 (April 1967).

"Hagigah," *American Judaism*, 16:19, 48–49 (Winter 1966–67).

"Introduction" to *The Adventures of One Yitzchok* by Yitzchok Perlov. New York: Award Books, 1967. Pp. 7–12.

"Introduction" to *Hunger* by Knut Hamsun. New York: Noonday Press, 1968. Pp. v–xii.

"Introduction" to *Yoshe Kalb* by I. J. Singer. New York: Harper and Row, 1965. Pp. v–x.

"A New Use for Yiddish," *Commentary*, 33:267–69 (March 1962).

"Once on Second Avenue There Lived a Yiddish Theater," *New York Times*, April 17, 1966, Section 2, p. 3.

"Peretz' Dream," *American Judaism*, 15:20–21, 60–61 (Passover 1966).

"A Phantom of Delight," *Herald Tribune Book Week*, July 4, 1965, pp. 2, 7.

"The Poetry of Faith," *Commentary*, 32:258–60 (September 1961).

"Realism and Truth," *The Reconstructionist*, 28: 5–9 (June 15, 1962).

"Rootless Mysticism," *Commentary*, 39:77–78 (January 1965).

"The Ten Commandments and the Modern Critics," *Cavalier*, June 1965, p. 30.

"What It Takes to Be a Jewish Writer," *National Jewish Monthly*, 78:54–56 (November 1963).

"What's in It for Me?" *Harper's*, 231:172–73 (October 1965).

CRITICAL AND BIOGRAPHICAL STUDIES

Angoff, Charles. "Aspects of American Literature," *Literary Review*, 10:5–17 (Autumn 1966).

Ash, Lee. "WLB Biography: Isaac Bashevis Singer," *Wilson Library Bulletin*, 37:356 (December 1962).

Blocker, Joel, and Richard Elman. "An Interview with Isaac Bashevis Singer," *Commentary*, 36:364–72 (November 1963).

Buchen, Irving. *Isaac Bashevis Singer and the Eternal Past*. New York: New York University Press, 1968.

Chametzky, Jules. "The Old Jew in New Times," *Nation*, 205:436–38 (October 30, 1967).

Eisenberg, J. A. "Isaac Bashevis Singer—Passionate Primitive or Pious Puritan," *Judaism*, 11:345–56 (Fall 1962).

Elman, Richard M. "The Spinoza of Canal Street," *Holiday*, 38:83–87 (August 1965).

Feldman, Irving. "The Shtetl World," *Kenyon Review*, 24:173–77 (Winter 1962).

Fixler, Michael. "The Redeemers. Themes in the Fiction of Isaac Bashevis Singer," *Kenyon Review*, 26:371–86 (Spring 1964).

Flender, Harold. "Isaac Bashevis Singer," *Paris Review*, 11:53–73 (Fall 1968).

Frank, M. Z. "The Demon and the Earlock," *Conservative Judaism*, 20:1–9 (Fall 1965).

Glanville, Brian. "An Interview with Isaac Bashevis Singer," *Jewish News*, September 28, 1962, p. 28.

Glatstein, Jacob. "The Fame of Bashevis Singer," *Congress Bi-Weekly*, 32:17–19 (December 27, 1965).

Goodheart, Eugene. "The Demonic Charm of Bashevis Singer," *Midstream*, 6:88–93 (Summer 1960).

Hemley, Cecil. "Isaac Bashevis Singer," in *Dimensions of Midnight: Poetry and Prose*, edited by Elaine Gottlieb. Athens: Ohio University Press, 1966. Pp. 217–33.

Hindus, Milton. "Isaac Bashevis Singer," in *Jewish Heritage Reader*, edited by Morris Adler. New York: Taplinger, 1965. Pp. 242–52.

Hochman, Baruch. "I. B. Singer's Vision of Good and Evil," *Midstream*, 13:66–73 (March 1967).

Howe, Irving. "Demonic Fiction of a Yiddish 'Modernist,' " *Commentary*, 30:350–53 (October 1960).

Hughes, Catharine R. "The Two Worlds of Isaac Singer," *America*, 117:611–13 (November 18, 1967).

Hughes, Ted. "The Genius of Isaac Bashevis Singer," *New York Review of Books*, April 22, 1965. Pp. 8–10.

Hyman, Stanley Edgar. "Isaac Singer's Marvels," *New Leader*, 47:17–18 (December 21, 1964).

Jacobson, Dan. "The Problem of Isaac Bashevis Singer," *Commentary*, 39:48–52 (February 1965).

Kazin, Alfred. "The Saint as Schlemiel," in *Contemporaries*. Boston: Little, Brown, 1962. Pp. 283–91.

Leibowitz, Herbert. "A Lost World Redeemed," *Hudson Review*, 19:669–73 (Winter 1966–67).

Madison, Charles A. "I. Bashevis Singer: Novelist of Hasidic Gothicism," in *Yiddish Literature, Its Scope and Major Writers*. New York: Frederick Ungar, 1968. Pp. 479–99.

Malin, Irving, ed. *Critical Views of Isaac Bashevis Singer*. New York: New York University Press, 1969.

Mucke, Edith. "Isaac B. Singer and Hassidic Philosophy," *Minnesota Review*, 7:214–21 (Numbers 3 and 4, 1967).

Pondrom, Cyrena N. "Isaac Bashevis Singer: An Interview," *Contemporary Literature*, 10:1–38, 332–51 (Winter, Summer 1969).

Rexroth, Kenneth. "Alienated: Indomitable," *Commentary*, 26:458–60 (November 1958).

Roback, A. A. "The Singer Family," in *Contemporary Yiddish Literature: A Brief Outline*. London: Lincolns-Prager, 1957. Pp. 63–71.

Siegel, Ben. "Sacred and Profane: Isaac Bashevis Singer's Embattled Spirits," *Critique*, 6:24–47 (Spring 1963).

Sloan, Jacob. "I. B. Singer and His Yiddish Critics," *Congress Bi-Weekly*, 33:4–5 (March 7, 1966).

Sloman, Judith. "Existentialism in Par Lagerkvist and Isaac Bashevis Singer," *Minnesota Review*, 5:206–12 (August–October 1965).

Sontag, Susan. "Demons and Dreams," *Partisan Review*, 29:460–63 (Summer 1962).

Teller, Judd L. "From Yiddish to Neo-Brahmin," in *Strangers and Natives*. New York: Delacorte, 1968. Pp. 262–65.

Wolkenfeld, J. S. "Isaac Bashevis Singer: The Faith of His Devils and Magicians," *Criticism*, 5:349–59 (Fall 1963).

—BEN SIEGEL

Gertrude Stein

1874-1946

At least three Gertrude Steins have been accounted for in modern criticism, biography, and gossip: the formidably gracious and effective matron of modern American letters, expatriate mistress of ceremonies; the theorist of language and literature and of their fusion in "composition as explanation" of the thing seen; and the artist, author of two or three distinguished books and of a dozen or more provocative and puzzling others. The first of these has been abundantly described, testified to, and in one sense or another exploited. From the time she agreed to separate from brother Leo (1912), to set up her own literary shop in Paris, her prestige as an informal arbiter of special tastes in the arts grew and flourished. She posed for the role, and having succeeded in carrying it off, became convinced of its genuineness and worth. Subsequently the roles of hostess and critic were combined, and in her triumphant tour of America (1934–35) she was known both as an engaging and intriguing personality and as a person who had many penetrating things to say. At times vague, often apparently naive, she was nevertheless appreciated by those who knew her and troubled themselves to read her work as a dedicated spirit, narrowly intent upon expanding and illustrating her original views of language and its literary function.

The woman who invited gossip, superficial interest in her eccentricities, laughter and even ridicule, was a part of the ceremony that was her work. That she was received with enthusiasm in the 1920's by many of the postwar generation of writers is a testimony to the fascination she exercised over young talents looking for new forms and manners. When she settled in Paris (1903), at 27, rue de Fleurus, she was unknown and unpublished. With her brother she began to purchase modern paintings (Picasso, Matisse, Cézanne, Braque) and to encourage the careers of several artists. Her talent for judging the art may have been debatable, but her skill in making the artist indebted to her was not; and in a few years her *salon* featured a variety of paintings, vying for the honor of a position on its walls. They were dominated by Picasso's portrait of her, which looked down upon its subject at her desk, a memorable testimony to the beginnings of twentieth-century experiment in the arts.

The response to Miss Stein was not always respectful. The very nature of her insistence upon divergent forms and practices puzzled many and made them shy away from what seemed to them a clever game or a play for notoriety. As a dominating woman, she inspired trust in many at the start, then offended that trust or seemed to exploit it too selfishly.

The flowers of friendship often faded. The sponsors of "realistic decorum," who wanted their literature intelligible and overtly "purposeful," left her early; only *Three Lives* (1909) pleased them, and this not all. But even more tolerant contemporaries found her work wearisomely repetitive, formless, and offensively coy. While she seemed in the vanguard of the new literature and was for a time (in the 1920's especially) honored by its pundits and sponsors, her position as titular head of the *avant-garde* was often threatened and finally lost altogether. Harsh ridicule of her stubborn dowagership was not uncommon; and however simply honest and decorous her *ménage aux arts* proved actually to be, the spectacle of the mistress of ceremonies invited suspicion both of her motives and of the clarity of her intentions. Katherine Anne Porter, who on at least one other occasion had found her work formidably impressive, provided the most cleverly devastating of disparagements (in an essay, "The Wooden Umbrella," 1947). She described Miss Stein as "of the company of Amazons which nineteenth-century America produced among its many prodigies: not-men, not-women, answerable to no function in either sex, whose careers were carried on, and how successfully, in whatever field they chose: they were educators, writers, editors, politicians, artists, world travelers, and international hostesses, who lived in public and by the public and played out their self-assumed, self-created roles in such masterly freedom as only a few early medieval queens had equaled."

Miss Porter's suggestion of the female prodigy is not altogether unwise, though she does not appreciate sufficiently the facts of her subject's persistence and of her dedication to an art and the theory of an art. Gertrude Stein did not begin her career as a writer; when, after she had reached the age of fifteen and begun "to understand boredom" (as John Malcolm

Brinnin put it, in *The Third Rose*, 1959), she thought of the life of a scholar. At Radcliffe, which she entered in 1893, she had courses with George Santayana, Josiah Royce, William Vaughn Moody, and, most important, William James. Her first interest was experimental psychology, and with Leon Solomons she collaborated on a study of "Normal Motor Adjustment" (*Psychological Review*, September 1896). She then began a course in premedicine at the Johns Hopkins University, thinking that it would be the best preparation for the life of a psychologist.

The academic life did not last. In 1902, she and Leo traveled to England, where she sat for a while in the British Museum, "living continuously," as Brinnin says, "with the English language." In the next year, Leo found the Paris apartment where she was to live most of her life to the beginning of World War II. The years as a student, the time spent reading English classics, and the experiences of buying and defending contemporary art all fell quite neatly into the pattern that was her life and her career. She was very much the American artist; but, like many Americans of a later generation, she found Paris an ideal "second country" from which to observe and to describe her native land.

It almost seemed that Miss Stein's first years in Paris were intended as a way of preparing for modern literature. In *The Autobiography of Alice B. Toklas* (1933) she served as a historian of the new generation (or at least, an informal diarist of its affairs), but she was also actively engaged in sponsoring and directing its ambitions. Before World War I she was interested mostly in painting and, very much with Leo's help, learned to understand modernist painting and bought and displayed the new canvases; above all, she considered Cézanne and Picasso as closely identified with what she was trying to do in writing. When the younger generation of writers arrived from America (or stayed on, after the war), many of them headed for the rue de Fleurus and the author of *Three Lives* and *Tender Buttons* (1914). In the 1920's, she became the leader of an informal *salon*, in which she talked with and advised Hemingway, Fitzgerald, Sherwood Anderson, and scores of others, known and unknown, talented and mediocre. She shared this role of elder spokesman with another "pioneer expatriate," Ezra Pound (who was in Paris in the early 1920's), and with Ford Madox Ford, a British poet and novelist who edited the *Transatlantic Review* in 1924–25.

Her career as sponsor of bright young men was not without its difficulties, many of them of her own making; but despite personal squabbles, her reputation as an informal critic grew and she was soon asked to explain her methods on more formal occasions. The most famous of these were the trip in 1925 to Oxford and Cambridge universities, where she delivered the lecture "Composition as Explanation," which remains the key discussion of her literary practice; and the months spent in America a decade later. From the latter excursion came *Narration* and *Lectures in America* (both 1935), which are elaborations upon her theory, and especially show her skill in handling the give-and-take of semiformal audiences. But she was best at the improvised personal discussion of writing and art, which she carried on over the years in Paris with a succession of admirers and followers through the decades between the wars.

In 1937 Miss Stein moved to number 5, rue de Christine, also on the Left Bank; some years later, she and her companion Alice B. Toklas were caught in the confusions of World War II and remained in exile in Bilignin, in southern France; from the experiences there and with the liberation by American troops came *Wars I Have Seen* (1944) and *Brewsie and*

Willie (1946). When she returned to Paris after the war, she became an informal hostess to scores of American soldiers, who counted a visit to her teas and her "evenings" at the top of the list of tourist attractions. In 1946, she suffered a decline in health and was admitted to the American Hospital in Paris; there, after a futile operation, she died on July 27. In her last moments she summoned energy enough to say "What is the answer?" and, failing to get a response, concluded her life with this, its companion query: "In that case, what is the question?" It was a most suitable conclusion of a life devoted to the major questions and answers that had puzzled herself and her contemporaries.

The truth is that Gertrude Stein was a nineteenth-century American with a difference. Born in 1874, she spent twenty-six years in the nineteenth century, forty-six in the twentieth. She herself claimed that, with Henry James, she had initiated in literature the "twentieth-century way" of knowing and of writing. Brinnin claims that "while she spent a lifetime trying to escape the nineteenth century, her career belongs to its sunset phase—to the era of William James and John Dewey, George Bernard Shaw and the science of economic reform, of the 'Boston marriage' and votes for women, of the incandescent lamp and the Michelson-Morley experiment." The idea is in part persuasive, and particularly the superficially startling suggestion of her belief in the "enlightened, the rational mind." It is only that she pushed the rational modes so far as to produce apparently irrational results. But, while the impetus of her literary practice was nineteenth century, she was right in maintaining that its result was wholly consonant with the twentieth-century scene and that she provided a remarkably acute sense of its intellectual decorum and habitude. She was if anything more "modern" than Eliot and

Pound. What attracted such younger artists as Hemingway to her was her conviction not only that "the past did not matter" but that the present was overweeningly demanding and that its "spirit" and rhythms had to be continuously sustained in literature. Her primary contribution to twentieth-century literature was methodological. Except when she wrote reminiscences (and she did these superbly and with great popular success), her work was only indifferently related to context. Its major objective was to illustrate and to refine the manner of fusing the "seeing" and the re-creation of an importunate present moment.

This is both her major achievement and her principal concern. Her famous lecture "Composition as Explanation" (published as a book in 1926) contains the gist of her intention: "There is singularly nothing that makes a difference a difference in beginning and in the middle and in ending except that each generation has something different at which they are all looking. By this I mean so simply that anybody knows it that composition is the difference which makes each and all of them then different from other generations and this is what makes everything different otherwise they are all alike and everybody knows it because everybody says it." In her *Picasso* (1939) she remarks upon this—to her—essential truth again, but with a difference: "People really do not change from one generation to another . . . indeed nothing changes from one generation to another except the things seen and the things seen make that generation, that is to say nothing changes in people from one generation to another except the way of seeing and being seen . . ." Her lifework is a continuous illustration of this text, with many changes and variations, but with a remarkably dedicated consistency of attention to it.

It is a simple thesis, logical and rational, in the manner of Mr. Brinnin's nineteenth-century apostles of the rational: its very simplicity proved both its strength and its weakness. Miss Stein pushed it very far indeed. Her fight with the nineteenth century was motivated by a kind of subjectively classical dislike of "emotion"; to her the word meant *any* form of distracting implication that weakens the effectiveness of the conscious grasp of the thing seen at the moment in which it is seen.

In short, Miss Stein was engaged in an analysis of the mind in its precise function of apprehending and experiencing objects. Change for her was nuance, gradation, the gradual accretion of subtle qualifications of meaning. In literature, she was the sturdiest and the most persistent enemy of the "substantial" self (which is to say, the self independent and transcendent of conscious experience). For the initial push required of this task she was indebted primarily to William James, and especially to his *Principles of Psychology* (1890). As a student of James, she thought of herself for a while as a "scientist of the mind," but the practices and the methods were limited and fallible, and she herself was scarcely temperamentally suited to them. She was not to become a scientist; nor did she follow James beyond the implications of laboratory psychology and its rudimentary essays in definition. While she refers approvingly to such other James books as *The Will to Believe* (1897) and *The Varieties of Religious Experience* (1902), she was a faithful and on occasions a discerning pupil only of his exercises in practical and radical empiricism.

This is not to say that Miss Stein comprehended William James as a philosopher, or that she admired his later discussions of metaphysics and immortality. James's use of imagery was designed almost entirely to adorn a text or persuade a student. Language was to him necessarily precise, but not necessarily the substance of experience. In most respects,

James was the nineteenth-century scientist who puzzled at times over the discouraging inferences he might make of his insights. He excited Miss Stein most when he discussed the nature and the limits of consciousness; but while he took pride in his discovery of the "flow" or "stream" of consciousness, which seemed at least to rescue it from an impasse, Miss Stein was much more interested in the fact of an *arrested* consciousness, apparently static and fixed and sacrificing motion or flow to precision. James saw consciousness as process, Miss Stein as a cube or form or shape, to which the resources of the arts must be applied for most effective definition.

Nevertheless, the essential doctrine was there, with all of its modest cautions. James denied the possibility of a "substantial" or a transcendent self, or at least maintained that psychology could not account for it. Psychology was after all a "natural science, an account of particular finite streams of thought, co-existing and succeeding in time" (*Principles of Psychology*). We can *know* only about a state of consciousness as a particular situation, though it is possible to infer from it both time and will. The irreducible minimum of the conscious ego in the *process of being conscious* is the focus of real knowledge. It exists instantaneously, is then superseded by another instant. Assuming the metaphor of the "flow," these instants cohere, and if we wish to explore the psychology of willed decision and choice, they have as well a structure that is self-determined. But in the severely controlled passages of his *Principles*, James was able to say (was even forced to admit) that "the only states of consciousness that we naturally deal with are found in personal consciousnesses, minds, selves, concrete particular I's and you's." The minutiae of self-identity are strictly of the occasion, but definition of them involves the use of relational and qualifying words: "There is not a conjunction or a preposition, and hardly an adverbial phrase, syntactic form, or inflection of voice . . . that does not express some shading or other of relation which we at some moment actually feel to exist between the larger objects of our thought."

Gertrude Stein was fascinated by the substance of these relations. To her, they seemed to have the virtues of solid reality, to exist in a more than linguistic or logical sense, to be hard and three-dimensional. They were geometric forms of thought, and they fixed the meaning of the thing seen in the focus of its actually existing *as a thing*. Experience for her, then, was objective to the point of being indistinguishable from reality. In this sense, she was radically different from the naturalist, who (like Dreiser and Norris) saw things primarily in massive and relentless sequence and structure. She was also sharply independent of the scrupulous realism of such a man as Flaubert; she sought not *le mot* but *l'objet juste*.

She did not ignore "flow," but found it very difficult to attend to, and dangerous as well, for attention to it ran the risk of losing the integrity and precision of the word-object nexus. She generally agreed with James's suggestion that "Resemblance among the parts of a continuum of feelings (especially bodily feelings) experienced along with things widely different in all other regards, thus constitutes the real and verifiable 'personal identity' which we feel." The procession of resemblances constituted movement for her; they were the means of progressing from one instant of consciousness to the next. But the reality lay not in the "flow" (which was incidental and awkward), but in the objective condition of the word-object relation in each instant.

Miss Stein's flirtations with contextuality can be illustrated in any number of passages, and especially well in one from the portrait of "Miss Furr and Miss Skeene" (in *Geography and*

Plays, 1922). The rhythm moves gracefully enough in terms of central sounds and shades of meaning, circling about the focus, moving away and (with a slight variation) back toward it: "She was quite regularly gay. She told many then the way of being gay, she taught very many then little ways they could use in being gay. She was living very well, she was gay then, she went on living then, she was regular in being gay, she always was living very well and was gay very well and was telling about little ways one could be learning to use in being gay, and later was telling them quite often, telling them again and again."

The progress is discernible, but not prominent, and Miss Stein is concerned to preserve the essential experience from the accidents of flow. In another passage, this one from the more famous "Melanctha," the narrative progress is clear, and yet one has the impression that she is building solidly from center, that she is much more interested in determining a substance of character than in telling "what happened": "Jeff Campbell never knew very well these days what it was that was going on inside him. All he knew was, he was uneasy now always to be with Melanctha. All he knew was, that he was always uneasy when he was with Melanctha, not the way he used to be from just not being very understanding, but now, because he never could be honest with her, because he was now always feeling her strong suffering, in her, because he knew now he was having a straight, good feeling with her, but she went so fast, and he was so slow to her; Jeff knew his right feeling never got a chance to show itself as strong, to her."

William Carlos Williams, marveling at her skill, said that she has "taken the words to her choice . . . to emphasize further what she has in mind she has completely unlinked them from their former relationships to the sentence. . . .

She has placed writing on a plane where it may deal unhampered with its own affairs, unburdened with scientific and philosophic lumber." She herself spoke of the "feeling of words doing as they want to do and as they have to do when they have to live . . ." (*Narration*). The danger is that words, so scrupulously separated from familiar or suggestive contexts, come to have an abstract role and meaning, which they do not vividly and recognizably describe. But this is not only a risk Miss Stein is willing to take; it is substantially what she wants to do. For objects, she says, do not present themselves manageably to the consciousness in a riot of colorful detail; they are (as is experience) eligible to gradual change, in each successive detail preserving what they have had before altering it slightly and in minute degree. No more eloquent testimony of the shrewdness of her energy of attention is available than the famous play upon "pigeons" in *Four Saints in Three Acts*:

> Pigeons on the grass alas.
> Pigeons on the grass alas.
> Short longer grass longer longer shorter yellow grass. Pigeons large pigeons on the shorter longer yellow grass alas pigeons on the grass.
> If they were not pigeons what were they.

The risk of abstraction in this "ballet of words" is assumed in the interests of what she calls (in *The Autobiography of Alice B. Toklas*) her "pure passion for exactitude."

Miss Stein's fight against time, against the intrusions of the past and of extra-situational meaning, is a similarly important concern. On the basis of the relation of experience to before, after, and because, she judged it to be pure or adulterated. Being is not remembering, she said in *What Are Masterpieces* (1940): "At any moment when you are you you are you without the memory of yourself because if you remember yourself while you are you you are not for purposes of creating you." In *The Geographical History of America* (1936) she discussed a major distinction, which was to recur again in later writings, that between human nature and the human mind. The predominating characteristic of human nature is that it "clings to identity, its insistence on itself as personality," and this effort to assert identity distracts from the necessary, minimal function of the mind. The mind, however, knows only in the process of its knowing; pure mind is not distracted into wishing to know who it is that is knowing and in what sequence of remembering: "it knows what it knows and knowing what it knows it has nothing to do with seeing what it remembers. . . ."

The distinction is carried beyond these limits, into geography and history. One of the reasons why America is above all of the twentieth century, she said, is that there are larger spaces, much flat land which "is connected with the human mind." In 1934–35, when she traveled by plane for the first time, she saw how well suited America was to the exercises of the human mind. Up there, she said, there was no "remembering," the human mind worked entirely without depending upon past, and the geometrically "pure" landscape encouraged its functioning without interference from time. All of this speculation is closely associated with Miss Stein's views of identity. The reliance upon the clichés of tradition, the desire to have movement and progress in writing (a beginning, a middle, and an end whose relationships are obvious and predictable)— these inhibit the successful analysis of consciousness as she assumed James had defined it. Because of its geography, which did not encourage close, intimate "daily" living but in-

stead suggested adventure, America was most properly the country of the human mind, the most venturesome of all cultures, and the first to move into the twentieth century.

Spain also was appropriately landscaped; and Spain was quite naturally the birthplace of cubism, which was to Miss Stein the most important modern development in the visual arts to parallel hers in literature. In *The Geographical History of America* she had distinguished between the literary practices of "going on" and "staying inside," and had of course preferred the latter, for "there is not going on not in the human mind there is just staying within." The same distinction needs to be made in the other arts: in music, she was pleased only with the "ballet" repetition of sounds attached to words, like Virgil Thomson's score for her *Four Saints in Three Acts* (which she first published independently in *transition*, 1929); in painting, it was the fixed patterning of spatial relations, first of Cézanne and then of Picasso after the "Rose period." She had had many sittings for her portrait; then, when she went away, he had brushed in the face in a few hours. The lines and forms of the face are quite independently expressive of its objective nature; they mark an important break from color tones and representational sentimentalities that had characterized Picasso's painting to that time.

Three Lives was written from the dual incentives of Flaubert and Cézanne. As Elizabeth Sprigge puts it (in her *Gertrude Stein*, 1957): ". . . with Flaubert [of *Trois contes*] in the forefront of her mind and William James at the back of it, Cézanne before her eyes and Baltimore in memory, she began to write *Three Lives*." With the exception of James, each of these associations is halfway to being traditional, closely tied to the nineteenth century, and an invitation to "remembering." She thus *identified* herself with her literary and actual past, though she went beyond it as well, to establish the beginnings of a technique of separation. Shortly after her first two published books, she dropped subject matter, or context as such, and moved on to explore the nature of language itself, separated from memory and time, in the manner of James's definition of pure consciousness in the *Principles*. The words related to each other as the lines did in Picasso's art. She wished to make a space art out of an art that had been dominated by both time and associative meanings. It was quite radically different from Joyce's maneuverings of language, which were after all rich in allusion and association, and dominated by a number of ambitious and brilliant forms of schematic interpretation. It was also very different from the Proustian moment, rescued as that was from the past but indispensably associated with the memory. Both of these techniques assumed complex schemata of interrelationships of past and present and relied absolutely upon them. The Joycean epiphany, like the Proustian moment, gains its supreme value from associations not directly a part of the particular experience but a "sentimental" or an erudite or a philosophic expansion of it.

Miss Stein was engaged in nothing less than nonrepresentational writing. Its root sources were American, as Picasso's were Spanish. Both Spanish and American cultures, at least in her view, were linked to the character of the landscape and to the manner in which it encouraged a creative activity that was independent of tradition and cultural "remembering." Just how genuine her "literary cubism" was it is difficult to say. The question of the denotative and contextual values of words needs to be answered. She maintained that both context and denotation were properties of the moment of consciousness. As the architecture of Spain did not need to obey an enforced,

familiar context, neither did words have to mean what they had meant before. Words in relation to each other were also subject to the same independent usage; syntax was a matter of much concern. She developed a form of criticism that tried to protect usage from clichés and the risk of the familiar.

In many ways Miss Stein's critical volumes (*Lectures in America; Narration; How to Write; Composition as Explanation; Pissaco*) have often been received with more charity than her creative work; but this is at least partly because in them she explained what she was doing and there was (at least in many of them) a discursive line that one might, with some effort, follow to its conclusion. Her criticism is not distinct or separable from her other works; nor is it merely an explanation of what she does elsewhere. The two kinds of work are often interchangeable, and at any rate she did not contradict herself in the one in order to gain converts to the other.

Miss Stein was, first of all, a shrewd (though often an eccentric) observer of twentieth-century culture. *Lectures in America* contains many such deceptively simple observations of language and culture as these: "One century has words, another century chooses words; another century uses words and then another century using the words no longer has them"; ". . . in the nineteenth century what they thought was not what they said, but and this may sound like the same thing only it is not, they said what they thought and they were thinking what they thought." The essential difference between England and America is that because England is an island, there is always "daily living" and everything is therefore neatly put together and linked to precedent and custom and tradition. "Nothing is perplexing if there is an island," she said in *Geography and Plays*. "The special sign of this is in dusting."

Americans, however, who live on a huge continent where there is much space separating persons, do not have this decorum of "daily living": "The American not living every minute of every day in a daily way does not make what he has to say to be soothing he wants what he has to say to be exciting" (*Narration*). The root meaning of this distinction has much to do with Stein's central insistence upon the purely objective character of experiencing. Apparently, if one does have space, he is less likely to rely on precedent, tradition, the contrivances of "daily living," and is more inclined to take experience for what it is, even to venture into new experience. There is less search for "identity" in this case, less of what we have come to know in another context as "bad faith."

When Miss Stein defined the process of writing, she thought of it as a delicate balance of motion and form, the form providing the present context, the motion formally (and gracefully) described in terms of it. For Miss Stein was always striving for such balances, a balance such as is achieved in a ballet, where the dancer combines motion with the illusion of a fixed point within a formally described space. As she put it in *Lectures in America,* she was "achieving something that had neither the balance of a sentence nor the balance of a paragraph but a balance a new balance that had to do with a sense of movement of time included in a given space which as I have already said is a definitely American thing."

To perfect the balance of movement and form, there must be many repetitions, as there are for example in the play on "pigeons" and "grass" of *Four Saints in Three Acts*. Miss Stein set down as the second of her three "rules of composition" that to maintain a "continuous present" one must "begin again and again" (*Composition as Explanation*). Repetition is an essential strategy in composition; it guarantees

similarity and forces the consciousness upon the nature of the thing seen while at the same time it provides the avenue along which movement and change may occur. Hence Miss Stein's writing is often accused of being monotonous and wearisomely repetitious; but it is deliberately so, to preserve it from being superficial. Deliberate simplicities ("a rose is a rose is a rose is a rose") are an important characteristic of modern prose style. They are as effectively a rendering of experience and a scenic reflectiveness in the writing of Hemingway, for example, as the syntactic effusions of Faulkner are a means of recording his sensibility in relation to his material. Miss Stein compared what she was doing to the cinema— not to what was happening in it but to the way in which images are persistently there in a scenic sense while they are also subject to modulations of quality and shifts of position: ". . . it was like a cinema picture made up of succession and each moment having its own emphasis that is its own difference and so there was the moving and the existence of each moment as it was in me" (*Lectures in America*).

This is, in a sense, a solution to the problem posed much earlier to Miss Stein of preserving the *integrity* of the scene while allowing for change within it, or admitting qualitative variants that exist within it: the difference between pigeons on the grass and large pigeons on the shorter yellow grass alas. Narration, therefore, is a succession of these minute, subtle gradations of change; the image is substantially what it has always been, but it admits slowly accretions of variant meaning. This is not progress so much as it is an enriching of process. Miss Stein is of course much concerned over the necessities posed by narration. Throughout her career she avoided committing herself to the representation of abrupt changes (except occasionally to shift radically from century to century when she felt the need to do so). Her "novels" have a static quality; sometimes they are empty of overtly significant movement, even of conventional content. Her characters endure experience more often than they initiate it. And the major signs of development within her fiction are an increasing complexity of attitude and a change of relational terms. The fiction "develops" by accretion in much the same way as sentences move into paragraphs—neither situation calls for much movement in either space or time.

One of her enigmatic "definitions" is relevant in this connection. In that difficult and puzzling book *How to Write*, she shows how the *nature* of a definition actually contains the character of the thing defined: "A narrative of one of that one having met to repeat that one of that one replace one one replace one one of that one two replace two of that one there never having been two of that one one of that one." This is virtually a synopsis of "plot"; it quite adequately describes the limited maneuverings (in "Melanctha," for example) of persons in space. Narrative, as distinguished from succession, shows a variation and shading of persons, not from one into another, but from an aspect of one to an aspect of another. In a sense which she herself appreciated, there is a valuable suggestion here of the line of narrative development from Henry James to Hemingway. In the matter of niceties of discrimination, granted that they live in very different worlds indeed and have rather importantly differing views of both moral and cultural proprieties, there is really much to suggest of comparison in the basic technical maneuvers of James and Miss Stein. James's intense concentration upon the nuances and shades of meaning within a given moment of his novel has the quality of unique representation, of his having suspended context in a desire to operate imaginatively within a created convention. Miss Stein definitely set about at one

time to emulate James, in a short novel written in 1903 but not published until 1951, *Things as They Are* (originally called *Quod Erat Demonstrandum*); and, while this conscious affectation of another writer's poses results in many dreary banalities, there are several characteristics of manner that the two writers have in common: a tendency to stay within the consciousness of the characters as they "consider" their situations; suspension of the narrative from any involvement in the particulars of a scene; lack of interest in documentation with respect to space and time; and a sense of the narrated experience as an imagined, aesthetically controlled "convention."

This parallel should not be pushed too far. It is really a question of what is made of consciousness in a work of art. Henry James remained within the world of appearances, and if his sense of place was not often specified in his fictions, it at any rate yielded many symbolic meanings and contrasts that are an essential part of their design. One may say that Miss Stein, who might conceivably have become a novelist like Henry James, did not because she lacked his interest in the design of conventions and moral forms that gives substance to his fiction. She preferred William to Henry; and, in her case, the line of descent in modern literature is from the psychologist rather than from the novelist. Because it was so, her role in modern literature is quite different.

Except for a group of novels in the 1880's, Henry James's work opposed rather than altered the naturalism which is a major trend in our literature. Miss Stein, however, in her role primarily of critic, made a larger contribution to the modification of naturalism. Her curious insistence upon what she called "science," which should "explain and include everything," made several changes possible in postwar naturalism: in the conception of time and movement of narrative; in the matter of purifying language, making it more "responsible" to the situations to which it addressed itself; in the process of simplifying syntax, making the sentence the key of narration and allowing succession a larger role in fiction; and finally in making a reliance upon what Hemingway called "spiritual faking" seem simply ridiculous. It seems not unreasonable to assume that the great difference between Dreiser's *An American Tragedy* (1925), with its clumsy locutions and absurd involutions, and Hemingway's *The Sun Also Rises* (1926) is not altogether unrelated to Gertrude Stein's influence upon the younger artist.

She limited herself deliberately in the matter of subject, having a distaste for "subjects" as such, and worked often within a "scientifically pure," an isolated, situation. The result was a method repeated and refined, almost obsessively practiced, but above all immune from the worst gaucheries of naive naturalism. Whatever of it Hemingway took to himself served him immensely well—even though, as may have been, he did it "without understanding it" (as Miss Stein claimed in *The Autobiography of Alice B. Toklas*). John Peale Bishop has said of Hemingway that he had an abundance of material but lacked the refinements of a method; but, as Bishop adds, he "had known in his own person an experience for which Gertrude Stein had vainly sought a substitute in words" ("Homage to Hemingway," 1936). Which is rather as much as to say that Hemingway had a subject but lacked a method and somehow managed to borrow it from her. Whatever this may mean, Hemingway's indebtedness to Miss Stein should be obvious enough. It is as if she were working to perfect techniques for his use; though it is mainly to *Three Lives* and *The Making of Americans* (1925) that he is indebted.

The debt consists roughly of these essentials:

first, definitely a sense of looking at things in a "contemporary" way, working out a style consistent to "the thing seen"; a revision of time sense, so that (in the fiction of the 1920's at least) he avoided a simple chronological succession of events and paced his narrative, in a variation of her description of narrative progression, so that progress occurs in terms of clusters of personal relationships, considerably more complicated though no more sophisticated than those in "Melanctha"; a much more shrewd and accurate sense of movement and the exploitation of scene than the naturalists had, as though their crudities had been refined with her aid. In *Death in the Afternoon* (1932), Hemingway describes a literary style as "the sequence of motion and fact which made the emotion." It is true that Miss Stein would rather have inhibited the "motion" than not—she always objected to his obsession with violence; but the fundamental manner was there: of concentration upon the object at hand, attention to the precise language needed to make it come to life, a careful sense of timing and pacing, and a suppression of relational and qualifying words that may have been beyond his power to make genuinely expressive.

In many respects Miss Stein's concern over the limits of complication in writing seems overly anxious and fastidious. She cared little for punctuation of any kind, claimed that it interfered with the "going on"; a comma, for example, "by helping you along holding your coat for you and putting on your shoes keeps you from living your life as actively as you should lead it . . ." (*Lectures in America*). But she saved most of her attention for the risks a writer takes when he pushes beyond the securities of the sentence. She has rung many changes upon the famous remark "A sentence is not emotional, a paragraph is" (*How to Write*). When you push beyond the sentence, you also push beyond the genuine focus upon the object. Sequences of words and thoughts begin; movement begins. Paragraphs are threatened by the distractions of "beginning, middle, and end," and extraneous matter is bound to get into them. "A sentence has not really any beginning or middle or ending because each part is its part as its part," she said in *Narration*, "and so the whole exists within by the balance within but the paragraph exists not by a balance within but by a succession." A sentence is beautifully balanced (if it has the correct kinds of words within it): it is "inside itself by its internal balancing . . ." and gains its merit because of the tight, exact, clear interrelationship of parts. True knowledge, she maintained, depends upon an "immediate existing"; this is William James's pure sense of the "in-itself," beyond which he went a long way in both his psychology and his philosophy. Miss Stein did not follow him, but remained as if transfixed within the limits of "immediate existence." She deliberately wrenched words not only from familiar context but from almost any context at all. Yet the effects are intermittently extraordinary, though even the most dedicated follower at times admits to weariness.

Miss Stein was above all convinced that the twentieth century was interested, as she put it in *Lectures in America*, in *feeling a thing existing*: "we that is any human being living has inevitably to feel the thing anything being existing, but the name of that thing of that anything is no longer anything to thrill any one but children." And this leads us, finally, to her genuine value as a critic of modern literature: she is above all the most important sponsor of what we have called "presentational immediacy," of the integrity and the uniqueness of the "thing seen at the moment it is seen." Though she read widely and even exhaustively in the classics, they had no meaning for her except as they pointed to parallels with the present. Most importantly, it was the *visual* sense that intrigued her, the shape, color, depth, dimension, and texture of the thing seen. In the grain of that texture lie the differences from one generation to another. Her sense of time was limited to two things: the alterations (subtle as they may be) in the way of seeing things; the effect of force on surfaces. Of war she said that it speeds up change, that it makes spectacular differences not only in the arrangements of objects in space but also in the ways in which one "feels existence." In the case of World War II, which she described in *Wars I Have Seen* as an unheroic war, when the "nice heroic deeds" were no longer possible, it made a radical difference. In any case, the twentieth century was remarkably different from the nineteenth, and the difference simply emphasized the need for a radical change in sensibilities, so that it could be honestly and faithfully recorded.

The essential difference was fragmentation, or the separation of objects and persons from each other so that they could no longer feel securely dependent upon one another. This change the Americans understood far more clearly than the Europeans; Miss Stein was convinced that the twentieth century was American and that Europe was able only after World War II to break from the nineteenth. Partly this was because the American space enabled Americans to see things in a "cubist way," and their speed of movement above or along the landscape made them see reality as a disembodied, geometrical series of forms. But it was mostly because of that remarkable convergence of self-consciousness and science, which nourished each other, the one forcing analysis, the other reducing it to a study of pure and impersonal forms.

Gertrude Stein offers a remarkably interesting series of observations; they are all in these volumes of criticism, all of them united in her single and singular preoccupation with the elements of consciousness, in her version of William James's *Principles*. The effect upon her literary practice was to reduce its scope and to introduce one after another kind of abstraction and attenuation. She set about deliberately eliminating time from human consideration, moving from the idea of "history as generations" of *The Making of Americans* to the pure stasis of her late plays. Having been left with space, she tried to purify it, holding it in the syntactic balance of the carefully limited sentence and protecting it from the threat of superficial and destructive motion. She worked hard at the task of reducing connotation to the bare minimum necessary to suggest a context of any kind. In consequence, she was left with a very much reduced field of deliberation: not surrealistic or impressionistic, not at all realistic, a world of concepts all but deprived of percepts, providing an intellectual music of successions and echolalic improvisations. The story of how she traveled this long road from *Three Lives* is a fascinating one, and it ought to be given at least in outline.

Miss Stein was obviously making a bow to the great French tradition when she wrote *Three Lives*. Her first title was *Three Histories*, and she says she had tried a translation of Flaubert's *Trois contes* at the time of composing her own book. The epigraph is from Jules Laforgue: "Donc je suis malheureux et ce n'est ni ma faute ni celle de la vie" ("For I am an unhappy man, and it is neither my fault nor life's"). The book was published, at her expense, by the Grafton Press of New York in 1909. It had a long, slow struggle for success, but is the book to which almost all critics turn approvingly, no matter what they think of her other work.

It contains three "portraits," but they are narratives as well, two of them ("The Good Anna" and "The Gentle Lena") fairly simple and straightforward, the third ("Melanctha") a subtle analysis of the mind and temperament of its Negro heroine. Unlike *Things as They Are* (which preceded it by two years in date of composition), the major roles are taken by members of the servant or working class; Anna and Lena are German servants in upper middle-class households, Melanctha a daughter of a Negro workingman. One of the major contributions of *Three Lives* to American literature was its clear proof that such characters are susceptible to the same kind of analysis as James had used with his characters of high degree and undoubtedly superior status. In fact, at least in the case of Melanctha, Miss Stein seems to have set out to prove that the quality and complexity of a consciousness depend not at all upon status, that they are there and differ only in degree and kind of articulateness from the others. It is true that Anna's concerns are with the several members of the households she serves, that her standards are fairly easy to define, and that her fidelity to them makes the diagramming of her career a fairly simple task. Yet "The Good Anna" is generously provided with niceties of observation. The simplicities of Anna are after all based upon a complex set of social manners, which are supported and made vividly real by emotional attachments and tensions. The simplicities of Miss Stein's manner are deceptive; Anna emerges as "good" but also complexly real. She is viewed in terms of her consciousness of place, manner, and code. The "goodness" of Anna appears often to be wasted on lazy mistresses, or to have the contrary effect of "spoiling" the men whom she favors as masters; but goodness is in itself a convention that has many particular forms of expression, and the values of Anna's goodness are realized with a full appreciation of their pathos, occasional eccentricity, and ultimate soundness. "The Gentle Lena" is almost pure pathos. She suffers experience without really understanding what is happening to her. The manners of her world require of her decisions that she is scarcely able to comprehend. In both of these *histoires* a basic convention (of the servant class, of the German household, of ranks and sexes) is assumed; the narrative functions in terms of it, and the quality of portrait is measured against the limits it sets up and determines.

Miss Stein's originality comes in part from her sense of intimate understanding; the two figures are seen "from the inside," and their sensibilities determine both the style of presentation and its meaning. But the two sketches are relatively simple, if only because the relationship between temperament and convention provides for a minimum of tension. For the most part, Anna is able to meet an emotional crisis by enclosing it within the social and domestic convention to which she has been in the manner bred. Lena's pathos comes from her immaturity, her inability to appreciate any crisis personally; she dies without really understanding why she has lived. She is passively a victim of the failure of persons to respond to a convention and to live within it. Melanctha Herbert is different in two ways from Lena, whom she otherwise superficially resembles: she actively pushes herself into the society, struggling to understand it; the convention in her case is more flexible and allows for more subtly interesting experiments in personal experience.

"Melanctha" is also stylistically more interesting than the other two; we find in it the beginnings of Miss Stein's distinctive manner. She herself recognized that fact and referred to it on a number of occasions in her critical writings. In 1925 she said that in "Melanctha" there was "a constant recurring and beginning there was a marked direction in the direction of being in the present although naturally I had been accustomed to past present and future, and why, because the composition forming around me was a prolonged present" (*Composition as Explanation*). "Melanctha" was her first full experiment in the use of a "continuous present." Though here there is a definite sense of narrative progress, the style moves from a succession of centers, linking them and giving them an appearance of unity and centrality. The effect is of a succession of consciously apprehended moments of experience, to each of which fully complex states of "present" emotion, temperament, and convention (as they are presently sensed and understood) adhere. But it is also significantly true that Miss Stein presents these states in the idiom and within the range of articulation of her characters; the words used are those that they would and should use. As Donald Sutherland has said, in the best critical study of Gertrude Stein so far published, ". . . the word had to have not its romantic or literary meaning but the immediate meaning it had to the contemporary using it, a literal axiomatic meaning confined to the simple situations of the average life" (*Gertrude Stein: A Biography of Her Work*, 1951).

"Melanctha" is an intricate pattern of human conflicts, moving forward and back with the heroine as she forces herself into experience, hesitates at the edge of understanding it, moves back toward its beginnings. It is, as Miss Stein has said of it, a pattern of "beginning again and again." Melanctha Herbert must move into the violent world, to test her desire and to reach "understanding." She was always "seeking rest and quiet, and always she could find new ways to be in trouble." Each of the significant phrases is repeated, again and again, in slightly new contexts, until one is aware of change within a central pattern of conscious experience. When her desire for experience leads to violence, she "discovers wisdom," though she "never did or meant anything that was wrong." She "wandered on the edge of wisdom." Wisdom in this sense means a fulfillment for which Melanctha understands that she is in some way responsible, above all one in which she has actively participated.

The heart of the narrative is Melanctha's complex relationship with Jefferson Campbell, "a serious, earnest, good young joyous doctor." He suggests the promise of a "more refined" adventure in "wisdom" than she has had so far. They alternately reach and withdraw from "understanding." As her more volatile and passionate nature pushes forward, he retreats; her "real strong feeling" excites and puzzles him. He must "go fast" with her, and he doesn't understand how he can explain to her what it is she should want him to want. The most brilliantly effective passages of the tale describe the torture of their trying to decide what they mean to each other and what they mean by meaning it and what they might have meant if they had not meant it at the beginning. The temperamental clashes are too much for both of them; they come near to understanding, but never quite go all the way, and the frustration is an agony to both of them.

When she has finally taught him to be in love with her, she loses interest in him. It is not what she has wanted at all, or rather the realization of what she has vaguely sought proves to be less in quality and intensity than she has wished it to be. "I ain't got certainly no hot passion any more now in me." The agony of not understanding what one is wanting—of not wanting it when one has it—affects both with equal intensity. Jeff Campbell's shame is a complex and powerful feeling of both frustration and fear: "Only sometimes he shivered hot with shame when he remembered some things he once had been feeling." When they move away from each other, and Melanctha once more searches for "wisdom,"

the tale is all but finished. It has revealed fully what it had started to say. Melanctha's subsequent adventures are unsuccessful, because she has not adjusted emotionally to the apparently contrary necessities to "go slow" and to "go fast" at the same time. She cannot break away from passion or adjust to human circumstance. The burden of trying to understand is really too much for her; though she never killed herself because she was blue, she often thought "this would really be the best way for her to do." Instead she fades away, dies in a home for poor consumptives. Her passion spent and dispersed, she is no longer "herself," or the person who vigorously tried to realize the wisdom of being what she wanted to be.

The progress from vague desires to initial experiments in satisfaction, to major crisis and failure, is brilliantly intricate. The burden of movement is assumed by words and phrases. Miss Stein "begins again and again," she "uses everything," she maintains a "continuous present." The pattern is that of a spiral moving within and beyond several levels and stages of passion and knowledge. The language changes and remains the same; slight additions and qualifications indicate advances and retreats, and Melanctha's progress in "wisdom" is shown in a successively sharpened emphasis in the language. Perhaps the key word is "trouble"; it suggests a commitment to experience without a full understanding of it. Trouble occurs when passion is forced beyond the comprehension of those involved in its expression. Jeff Campbell, for example, "had never yet in his life had real trouble." Melanctha always "could only find new ways to be in trouble." Because neither is able to redeem "wisdom" from the menace of "trouble," the relationship fails. Miss Stein is similarly masterly in her development of their uncertainties: Jeff is never really "very sure about her"; at the critical moment, "All he knew was he wanted

Melanctha should be there beside him, and he wanted very badly, too, always to throw her from him"; he was always uneasy because "he knew now he had a good, straight, strong feeling of right loving for her, and yet he never could use it to be good and honest with her."

The style and substance are an immense advance beyond those of "The Good Anna" and "The Gentle Lena." The personal tensions are communicated naturally and easily, while in Miss Stein's first writing (*Things as They Are*), the language clumsily interferes and the conflicts are handled in an interplay of artificial and unreal poses. "Melanctha" strikes one as a peculiarly effective piece, whose place in modern literature is important in a wide variety of ways. It is, for one thing, a triumph of analysis of the kind that Henry James (who at the time of its writing was producing his most complex works) could never have achieved. This is in itself a fact of more than ordinary importance, since it suggests a broadening of perspective in the functions and uses of analysis. Its application to the minds of relatively "unlettered" persons pointed away from the clumsy assumptions of contemporary naturalists who seemed to think that subconsciously a person's emotional status was as complex as his background and social level dictated. It is infinitely superior, in analytic correctness and appropriateness at least, to Dreiser's fumbling attempts to define Sister Carrie's "vague yearnings for the ideal." Sherwood Anderson's sketches of lonely, inarticulate souls come closer both in type and in merit; but Anderson lacked Miss Stein's intensity, and his analyses often settled into formula characterizations.

"Melanctha" is also important in its relation to the Negro consciousness. Richard Wright said that reading it was one of the most important events of his career. Its importance has nothing to do with the Negro per se as belonging to a social or economic class; in fact,

"Melanctha" succeeds in part because it assumes an equality that underlies social discrimination, an equality of feeling and emotion.

Finally, it has done much—much more than the early naturalists were able to do—by way of breaking down artificial barriers of class, manner, "culture." The "simple soul," the "peasant complex," the "servant's mind" are all ruled out. Miss Stein may be said here to have initiated or shown the possibilities of an entirely new type of "novel of manners." Partly this is because manners are in themselves surface indications of personality; they are a group's simplest ways of identifying itself and of measuring forms and degrees of compliance and conformity. But "manners" in another sense are the external sign of social articulation. They may be understood at any level and in any context of human relationships. Such words as "wisdom," "passion," and "trouble" are universals, to which "manners" adhere as particular social expressions. This fact, which seems extraordinarily simple at this remove of time, was not at all easy to grasp at the beginning of the century. Class distinctions have always been a difficulty in the struggle to set up and to maintain fictional structures. The trouble is seen in gaucheries of style that get in the way of an author's full grasp of his characters. In a sense, Miss Stein's desire to emulate Flaubert (however actual the relationship can be proved to be) was here more appropriate than her rather stubborn and awkward attempt to set up a "Jamesian shop" in *Things as They Are*. She did present a *type* of Emma Bovary in "Melanctha," but she did not borrow Flaubert's Normandy for backdrop. The pathos of unachieved "wisdom," of the failure to find unobtrusive settings for emotional drives, exists in both works; but they are each happily self-sufficient.

The link between *Three Lives* and *The Making of Americans* is at first rather difficult to see; the two are so different in scope and length that they would appear to have nothing at all in common. Yet there is a means of seeing the one as an outgrowth of the other that becomes more convincing the more one attends to it. Miss Stein has herself described *The Making of Americans* (which she wrote in 1906–08) as an outgrowth of her interest in experimental psychology. The experiments themselves taught her nothing, but they started several kinds of curiosity in human types. She became "enormously interested," she says in *Lectures in America*, "in the types of their characters that is what I even then thought of as the bottom nature of them . . ." The "bottom nature" was revealed, as it is in *The Making of Americans*, by the way in which "everybody said the same thing over and over again with infinite variations but over and over again until finally if you listened with great intensity you could hear it rise and fall and tell all that that there was inside them . . ." Here it was not so much the words but the movement of thought, the circling back, the going over the same ground, the alternation of particulars and generalities.

The Making of Americans is in a sense a book about time, about history, particularly about American history. But there are no events, in the ordinary sense; nor are there heroes such as we find in political and social histories. To begin, we must sense what Miss Stein means by history and time. Time is the passing of generations; the span from grandfather to grandson is a long one, and it comprehends a full measure of historical parallels and variation. The quality of Miss Stein's history is a quality of observations repeated from generation to generation, of the cumulative wisdom of domestic generalities as they meet and are modified by particular circumstances. The death of generations is as important as the living in which they acquire identity. Identity is in itself dependent upon one's being

within a transition from death of the past generation to one's own death. Generations overlap, but they also succeed one another; and it is the repetition of "what they say," together with the variants upon "what has been said," that makes time and history. The true *modus operandi* of *The Making of Americans* is custom, as this is communicated from one generation to the next. So that what changes within a few months of the lifetime of Melanctha Herbert becomes in *The Making of Americans* a succession of family patterns. In the use of words, formulas, phrases, wisdom and its imperfect manifestations in human life are given form: "Nay they love to remember, and to tell it over, and most often to their children, what they have been and what they have done and how they themselves have made it all to be so different and how well it is for these children that they have had a strong father who knew how to do it so that youngsters could so have it."

The effect of this retelling and recasting of family wisdom is of course substantial and immense in the long account of the Herslands and the Dehnings, in a book of 925 closely printed pages. But it is not true, as B. L. Reid maintains (in *Art by Subtraction*, 1958), that the shorter version edited by Bernard Fay for Harcourt, Brace (1934) was better than the original and that Miss Stein had therefore no sense of proportion. In one sense at least the original is not long enough; it may be said that a "history" of this sort, to account for the minutiae of what people say when they seem to be repeating their father's saying it, must attend to infinitesimal variants. *The Making of Americans* is an "abstract" book, or it tends in the direction of abstractness; but this impression is only the result of its initial foundation in the scrutiny of types. Its primary effect is like that of the Old Testament, if the wars and the visitations were omitted. Generations follow one another without actually succeeding one another. They move in a stately procession of living and saying and believing and behaving, and they are concerned with specific variations of first and last things.

As in *Three Lives*, the style and movement rely upon the key of repetition. Repetition with variants upon text is the stylistic practice of all of Miss Stein's work. Here the pattern is set up to defeat the ordinary belief in time, to give time a biblical dignity, and to remove persons as far as possible from the exigencies of clocks. "There are many ways of being a man," she says; "there are many millions of each kind of them, more and more in ones living they are there repeating themselves around one, every one of them in his own way being the kind of man he has in him, and there are always many millions made just like each of them." This brings the idea of individual differences down to a basic generality; the 900-odd pages are used to define the differences, and the eventual impression is to emphasize the sameness-in-difference. "Every one then has in their living repeating, repeating of every kind of thing in them, repeating of the kind of impatient feeling they have in them, of the anxious feeling almost every one has more or less always in them."

This repetition of characteristics makes for a constant intermingling of universal and particular. Miss Stein is convinced that the general is realized, if one will but look, in the particular manifestation of it; and, if one is satisfied that this is true, time will seem to be absorbed in the shifting and slow groupings of particulars in a set of principles. Persons become absorbed in types, particulars in generalities. The particular hides in the world, but it also hides from it; the conflict between the two, once formulated, is the most one can make of time and history: "Being important to one's self inside one. Being lonesome inside one. Making the world small to one to lose from one the lonesome feeling a big world feeling can make inside any one who has not it in them to feel themselves as big as any world can be around them."

Between *The Making of Americans* and her next important work, Miss Stein wrote "portraits." She had hoped to write, in *A Long Gay Book*, something as long and as ambitious as the *Americans* volume, but it did not turn out that way, so she turned then to short exercises, responses to persons in relation to her and to situations. They were to the general design of her work what Hemingway's "chapters" of *In Our Time* (1925) were to the major themes of his first two novels. But the portraits were also a step in the direction of greater abstractness and of freeing herself from time and from what she called "remembering." The portraits had the visual impact that the words of *Tender Buttons* were to have, in relation to the objects with which they were associated. As she said (in *Lectures in America*), "I had in hundreds of ways related words, then sentences then paragraphs to the thing at which I was looking." The portraits were not so complete a removal from representation as were the majority of *Tender Buttons* sketches. The titles always served to direct the manner of understanding the context, as in "sitwell Edith Sitwell" (1925) and "He and They, Hemingway" (1923); in the latter case the following lines illustrate the conjunction: "How do you do and good-bye. Good-bye and how do you do. Well and how do you do." There are links, however, between the earlier portraits and *Tender Buttons*, which suggest that they are a move away from the two major books and in the direction of greater abstractness and experimental "purity." *Tender Buttons* is called by John Malcolm Brinnin "thought-in-the-process-of-being-recorded." The language is truly a move away from the area of familiar denotation, and toward an absolute objectivity. The objects contained here are not named; seldom do the words used to respond to them suggest them. The passages are, instead, creations in themselves, independent existences. They are the moments of consciousness which William James discussed, but without his suggestion of continuity and references beyond themselves. Miss Stein's language tends to fix attention entirely upon itself, not upon her or upon what context it might allusively suggest. This is an extreme way of putting it, of course; Miss Stein did not always remain so objectively pure. "Celery," for example, retains much of what celery is known to be and taste: "Celery tastes tastes where in curled lashes and little bits and mostly in remains." The slicing of a roast is suggested as a family ceremony, in "Roast-beef": "All the time that there is use there is use and any time there is surface there is a surface, and every time there is an exception there is an exception and every time there is a division there is a dividing."

But *Tender Buttons* shows her well launched in the new style: lean and abstract, playfully and eccentrically unconventional, erratic and unpredictable. Miss Stein's work following *Tender Buttons* can be seen in three classifications: the experimental works, in which attempts to create the greatest objectivity lead to usages and devices that are isolated from all traditional literature (there are plays, portraits, and novels in this group, each of them a radical departure from what its genre has customarily meant); the autobiographies, of which *The Autobiography of Alice B. Toklas* and *Everybody's Autobiography* (1937) are the major achievements; and "reflections," partly autobiographical and partly philosophical, in which her general stance as an unorthodox, unconventional writer is expanded to allow her to assume a position as commentator upon twentieth-century culture. All three of these classes

are closely interrelated. Miss Stein the artist of the first group makes possible the "celebrity" Miss Stein of the autobiographies, who in turn is listened to (though not always respectfully) in relation to the third class of books. In addition, we have the figure of Miss Stein the literary theorist whom we have already considered in some detail.

With respect to the first of these classes, the principal examples are portraits and plays. In the former case, the portraits sometimes expanded into "novels," like the much-worked-over *Ida* (1941), and some of the posthumous works published by the Yale University Press. In these cases the novel is a development out of the focus of attitude and character found in the portrait, or an expansion of it. "Ada" is self-contained within a fixed context; *Ida* moves geographically but remains static as a personality. The novel is often a fuller rendering of surfaces. At times, as in *Mrs. Reynolds* (written in 1946), it resembles somewhat the kind of technique used in "The Good Anna." At other times, as in *Two: Gertrude Stein and Her Brother* (written in 1910–12), there is of course an autobiographical basis and the piece is an extended, a lengthened portrait. There are many suggestions of Miss Stein in all these works—of her at work, seated in her chair, of her dogs and her place; the place intrudes upon the consciousness but it does not therefore make the work autobiographical.

The most revealing examples of her experiments are the plays. There is a great difference between so simple an arrangement of phrases and "characters" as "A Curtain Raiser" (*Geography and Plays*) and the elaborate ballet of sounds and phrases in *Four Saints in Three Acts*. Yet the same conception of the drama is maintained. Again, as in her other works, Miss Stein adapts the play structure to her needs and to her conception of art. She said several times that there was something distressing about the pace of ordinary drama. Audiences were always being required to "catch up" emotionally to the play, and there was always a disturbing gap between them and it. As in her other works, she hoped to close this gap by putting audience and work on an equal footing, by removing the necessities of plot, movement, "remembering" from the play. Because she helped them less (that is, she did not "put them into" a situation to which they would have to adjust emotionally), she helped them more.

All of this meant that she would have to be arbitrary in her selection and arrangement of words and phrases. There are no discernible relationships between characters and phrasing; there are no characters really, in the conventional sense. There are only persons speaking words, and occasionally numbers. The plays have the same intransigently nonrepresentational quality as abstract painting. "A Curtain Raiser" is a good example:

> Six.
> Twenty.
> > Outrageous.
> Late.
> Weak.
> > Forty.
> More in any wetness.
> Sixty three certainly.
> Five.
> Sixteen.
> Seven.
> Three.
> More in orderly.   Seventy-five.

Even when there appears to be a conventional dialogue (as in "Turkey and Bones and Eating and We Liked It," *Geography and Plays*), the dialogue is only apparently dramatic; it is actually static and has no relation to action real or imagined. As in her portraits-into-novels, the plays vary from simple struc-

tures of a few lines to elaborate interplays of sounds and words. "Not Sightly" (*Geography and Plays*) contains many Steinian plays upon sounds arranged in a form of order and structure that suggest the ballet rather than the drama: ". . . when similar and jointed and prized and quilted quietly quilted tights quietly quilted tight minds when three innerly expensive shrugs meant more . . ."

The most elaborate, and the most successful, of these experiments is *Four Saints in Three Acts*. The history of this play has to do with Miss Stein's love of Spain, with her having come upon a group of statuary in a Paris shop window, with her interest in "saintliness" as an especial maneuvering of the will and sensibility. It may be thought of as another "laboratory observation," though this time immensely expanded and lyrically enhanced by the use of some of her more tuneful juxtapositions of sounds and rhythms. Her saints are not religious in any theological sense. They are domestic and "living"; that is, they have the character of simple and unsophisticated souls engaged in an exchange of simple "beatitudes." Donald Sutherland has described Miss Stein's view of saints exceptionally well: they were "primarily useful to her as they afforded a stable metaphor on which to maintain her own generically poetic exaltation, her own vision of a world saturated with miracles." *Four Saints* lends itself especially well to the suggestion of music; her phrasing and repetitions are exceptionally "melodious," and they suggest as well the measures and pauses in music. She was interested in sounds, as she was in the visual impact of spaces; they were both necessary to the comprehension of the thing consciously apprehended. The play is a wonder of both sounds and meanings interwoven and in movement. None of these elements add up conventionally to a "plot"; nor is theology discussed. But the suggestion of the miraculous and of sanctity is nevertheless there. In the version with Virgil Thomson's music (first performed in Hartford, Connecticut, in 1934), it acquired an additional dimension, though it is possible to suspect that this addition went far toward making it more of a "traditional" play than Miss Stein had intended.

Four Saints in Three Acts is a play upon the will toward saintliness, and upon the quality of saintliness as a human disposition and temperament, as "Melanctha" was an analysis of passion in its move toward social complication. It is, therefore, as a whole, an aesthetic object without context except what the concept of abstract disposition of saintliness can give it. It makes an elaborate design out of a possible and a probable form or type of human disposition. Since this disposition is saintliness and neither passion nor convention, the effect is ceremonial and gay and colorful and—within Miss Stein's own scope of apprehension—beatific. These are all available to emotional response, but the play lacks what she always regarded as an "audience trap," the building of suspense through plot, the directing of the audience's sense of time and event, stimulating the need for the audience to reconstruct themselves in terms of the drama that was unfolding.

One way of appraising Gertrude Stein's value in modern literature is to say that she was preeminently a theorist (a "scientist" of sorts), who offered some illustrations of what she thought literature should be. It is true that we are always busy examining her creative work as demonstration, to "see if composition comes out as she says it should." There is no question of her value as a critic whose primary function was to define language and to examine its place in the work of art. Perhaps it is, after all, her main claim to eminence. It would be a false reading of her work, however,

to say that it served only to validate her theory. The work often stands by and for itself. It does not stand by itself in the manner of other contemporary masterpieces, however. Its merits are essentially those of a work designed to break new experimental ground. It is tendentious in the most useful and illuminating sense that word might have. Its limitations are a result of her virtues; one may truthfully say that the limitations are necessary to the virtues.

Of the three major values I see in Miss Stein's contribution to modern literature, one is intrinsic and the other two "historical" in the sense of their affecting the nature of contemporary work. As for the intrinsic value, some of her writings remain as substantial masterpieces, though of two kinds: *Three Lives* is a minor masterpiece of great significance to modern writing because it is intrinsically good and impressive as literature and was received as such by many of her sensitive contemporaries; *The Making of Americans* cannot be so regarded, but must be thought of as the most elaborate of all demonstrations, intrinsically great but valuable because its merits come from its elaborate illustration of a theory of time and history; *Four Saints in Three Acts* is similarly beautifully successful but never truly separable from the variety of theoretical convictions from which it emerged. There are other pieces that move somewhere between the level of demonstration and the status of *sui generis* masterpiece. Some of these, like the novel *Ida*, the little books *Paris France* (1940) and *Picasso*, and *The Geographical History of America*, have frequently a strong and persuasive identity as books of unaffected wisdom; they are original and characteristic of their author, but they are also, in the sense in which she was capable of being so, profound.

Of the other two kinds of merit she has demonstrated, one must point to her role as an informal teacher, a guide and a leader in the "new literature." This aspect is difficult to see clearly because it is confused by gossip and claims and counterclaims. Nor is it possible to determine exactly *what* it was she was able to do for others. It is certainly *not* true that, as Brinnin claims, her influence "has been all but nil," though the sense in which he makes that claim has some merit. Her influence is very difficult to determine, and it is furthermore hard to separate it from the kind of influence a person like Sherwood Anderson had upon his contemporaries. The personal charm, the awesome regard in which many have seemed to hold her, the impact of her personality in the matter of making an idea "seem right" at the time she was considering it: these have all to be considered as variable and ultimately doubtful conditions. Those critics who were her personal friends seem to have come away more than convinced, often enthusiastically moved. But her personality is now receding; she is, after all, dead. And the work itself must ultimately become the test of influence. Any true measure is impossible, but it is not unlikely that such works as *Three Lives* and *The Making of Americans* have already served as "writer's texts" and will continue to do so. Above all, in many little ways, the "argument" of Miss Stein's criticism, which we have examined, seems very probably destined to have a major effect, not so much upon any specific author or text, but upon the writer who seeks a way out of naturalist impasses (naturalism is pervasive in modern literature, but it seems also destined to lead to impasses) and does not wish to exploit currently popular ideologies as a means.

This position, of Miss Stein as critic or theorist or both, is distinctive and yet an important part of modern criticism. Despite Miss Stein's overwhelming "presence" on the modern literary scene, she actually asks for and even demands an impersonal literature. It is true that many of her works are gratuitously personal, and that often she coyly peeps out at the reader from behind whatever large object conceals her. But unless we wish to assume that most or all of her critical discourses are merely self-ingratiating, the appeal in them is to a literature divested not only of specific autobiographical meaning but of the traditional structural implications of literature. These virtues are considerable because the limitations are so enthusiastically admitted and so significantly assumed. There is nothing specious about Gertrude Stein; to call her a supreme egotist does not convict her of simply posing before her Picassos for personal gain. She has had much to say, and she has often said it with a stubborn (perhaps a naively truculent) persistence. When her manner of saying it is penetrable, and it often is, the ideas are worth the value that she has been able to give them. She will, at any rate, merit a position in literary criticism as the person who carried as far as it might go William James's analysis of consciousness. Beyond that, she has stared hard at the prospect of an art objectively hard and autonomously real, using its instruments in strangely new but often startlingly effective ways. Much of what she has done to prove her theoretic convictions falls far short of enabling her to do so. She has had many failures, and in any case the perspective of an old-maid eccentric can scarcely be expected to yield large truths consistently. There is a wide margin between her profound insights and her more obvious and banal observations.

These conditions limit her usefulness, but they do not destroy it. She has the undoubted strength of the creative person who is able to call upon her powers of imagination to prove what literature might be. The true value of her criticism lies in its applicability to her work as creative artist, and by extension to the problems of those who are stimulated to follow its example. Her "modernity" is a necessary corrective of that of others, as theirs is needed to keep her distinction within reasonable limits.

Selected Bibliography

PRINCIPAL WORKS OF GERTRUDE STEIN

Three Lives. New York: Grafton Press, 1909.

Tender Buttons. New York: Claire Marie, 1914.

Geography and Plays. Boston: The Four Seas, 1922.

The Making of Americans. Paris: Contact Editions, 1925. (Abridged Edition, New York: Harcourt, Brace, 1934.)

Composition as Explanation. London: Hogarth, 1926.

Useful Knowledge. New York: Payson and Clarke, 1928.

How to Write. Paris: Plain Edition, 1931.

The Autobiography of Alice B. Toklas. New York: Harcourt, Brace, 1933.

Portraits and Prayers. New York: Random House, 1934.

Lectures in America. New York: Random House, 1935.

Narration. Chicago: University of Chicago Press, 1935.

The Geographical History of America. New York: Random House, 1936.

Everybody's Autobiography. New York: Random House, 1937.

Picasso. New York: Scribners, 1939.

Paris France. New York: Scribners, 1940.

What Are Masterpieces. Los Angeles: Conference Press, 1940.

Ida, a Novel. New York: Random House, 1941.

Wars I Have Seen. New York: Random House, 1944.

Brewsie and Willie. New York: Random House, 1946.

Four in America. New Haven: Yale University Press, 1947.

Last Operas and Plays. New York: Rinehart, 1949.

Things as They Are. Pawlet, Vt.: Banyan, 1951.

Two: Gertrude Stein and Her Brother. New Haven: Yale University Press, 1951.

Mrs. Reynolds. New Haven: Yale University Press, 1952.

Bee Time Vine. New Haven: Yale University Press, 1953.

As Fine as Melanctha. New Haven: Yale University Press, 1954.

Painted Lace. New Haven: Yale University Press, 1955.

Stanzas in Meditation. New Haven: Yale University Press, 1956.

Alphabets and Birthdays. New Haven: Yale University Press, 1957.

A Novel of Thank You. New Haven: Yale University Press, 1958.

Selected Operas and Plays of Gertrude Stein, edited by John M. Brinnin. Pittsburgh: University of Pittsburgh Press, 1970.

Lucy Church Amiably. Hastings-on-Hudson, N.Y.: Ultramarine Pub., 1972.

Matisse, Picasso and Gertrude Stein, with Two Shorter Stories. Hastings-on-Hudson, N.Y.: Ultramarine Pub., 1972.

A Book Concluding with As a Wife Has a Cow: A Love Story. Hastings-on-Hudson, N.Y.: Ultramarine Pub., 1973.

Blood on the Dining-Room Floor: A Murder Mystery. Berkeley, CA: Creative Arts Books, 1982.

Lifting Belly. Tallahassee, Fl.: Naiad Press, 1989.

Money. New York: Stewart Tabori and Chang, 1989.

BIBLIOGRAPHIES

Haas, Robert B., and Donald C. Gallup. *A Catalogue of the Published and Unpublished Writings of Gertrude Stein.* New Haven: Yale University Library, 1941.

Sawyer, Julian. *Gertrude Stein: A Bibliography.* New York: Arrow Editions, 1940.

CRITICAL AND BIOGRAPHICAL STUDIES

Brinnin, John Malcolm. *The Third Rose: Gertrude Stein and Her World.* Boston: Atlantic, Little, Brown, 1959.

Miller, Rosamond S. *Gertrude Stein: Form and Intelligibility*. New York: Exposition Press, 1949.

Reid, B. L. *Art by Subtraction: A Dissenting Opinion of Gertrude Stein*. Norman: University of Oklahoma Press, 1958.

Rogers, W. G. *When This You See Remember Me*. New York: Rinehart, 1948.

Sprigge, Elizabeth. *Gertrude Stein: Her Life and Her Work*. New York: Harper, 1957.

Stein, Leo. *Journey into the Self*, edited by Edmund Fuller. New York: Crown, 1950.

Sutherland, Donald. *Gertrude Stein: A Biography of Her Work*. New Haven: Yale University Press, 1951.

Weinstein, Norman. *Gertrude Stein and the Literature of the Modern Consciousness*. New York: Ungar, 1970.

ARTICLES

Auden, W. H. "All about Ida," *Saturday Review of Literature,* 23:8 (February 22, 1941).

Burke, Kenneth. "Engineering with Words," *Dial*, 74:408–12 (April 1923).

Eagleson, Harvey. "Gertrude Stein: Method in Madness," *Sewanee Review*, 44:164–77 (1936).

Gass, W. H. "Gertrude Stein: Her Escape from Protective Language," *Accent*, 18:233–44 (Autumn 1958).

Haines, George, IV. "Forms of Imaginative Prose: 1900–1940," *Southern Review*, 7:755 (Spring 1942).

————. "Gertrude Stein and Composition," *Sewanee Review*, 57:411–24 (Summer 1959).

Hoffman, Michael J. *The Development of Abstractionism in the Writings of Gertrude Stein*. Philadelphia: University of Pennsylvania Press, 1966.

Moore, Marianne. "The Spare American Emotion," *Dial*, 80:153–56 (February 1926).

Porter, Katherine A. "Gertrude Stein: Three Views," in *The Days Before*. New York: Harcourt, Brace, 1952. Pp. 36–60.

Rago, Henry. "Gertrude Stein," *Poetry*, 69:93–97 (November 1946).

Riding, Laura. "The New Barbarism and Gertrude Stein," *transition*, 3:153–68 (June 1927).

Skinner, B. F. "Has Gertrude Stein a Secret?" *Atlantic Monthly*, 153:50 (January 1934).

Stewart, Allegra. "The Quality of Gertrude Stein's Creativity," *American Literature*, 28:488–506 (January 1957).

————. *Gertrude Stein and the Present*. Cambridge, Mass.: Harvard University Press, 1967.

Toklas, Alice B. *What is Remembered*. New York: Holt, Rinehart, and Winston, 1963.

Troy, William. "A Note on Gertrude Stein," *Nation*, 137:274–75 (September 6, 1933).

Wilson, Edmund. "Brewsie and Willie," *New Yorker*, 22:192 (June 15, 1946).

————. "Gertrude Stein," in *Axel's Castle*. New York: Scribners, 1931. Pp. 237–56.

—*FREDERICK J. HOFFMAN*

John Steinbeck

1902-1968

SOME AMONG the distinguished array of American novelists who volunteered as witnesses to what life was like in the half century after World War I now seem rather far removed from us. The writers who developed themes that were highly personal to their own experience stand apart. Ernest Hemingway, though he exercised enormous influence on the taste, and even the thinking, of the young in his time, has become an aloof presence only the more withdrawn from us because his gifts were so original and striking. His obsession was with crises of courage dramatized, in his best novels, against a background of foreign wars. He seems to be less a product of our tradition than a titan of ego and energy existing in a world all his own. William Faulkner saw his corner of the American world through a Gothic mist of shock and surprise and the high talents used to evoke this strange realm seem to belong to another age and to a place not quite our own.

Other of the novelists of this time have remained close to us because of their preoccupation with the continuing problems of American life, because of their ability to depict a physical, social, and psychological environment that quickens in us a sense of immediacy and recognition. Two such were F. Scott Fitzgerald and John Steinbeck. Between them they

divided up the American world of their era. Fitzgerald took as his share the domain inhabited by the rich, the sheltered, the frequenters of cafés, bootleggers' parties, and psychiatrists' consulting rooms. He found pity and terror among these people and had both moving and ominous things to say about his discoveries. Steinbeck, for his inheritance, took the orchards and growing fields of California, the wasteland of the Depression, the refugee camps of rebels and the slums of poverty. He helped himself also to a scientific laboratory and certain places into which men retire to meditate. He, too, found pity and terror among his fellow human beings but, like Fitzgerald, he also found beauty, charm, and wit. Though the two men would never have thought of themselves as collaborators, they shared the responsibility of presenting in fiction all the conflicts that have confused our time and yet confirmed its aspirations.

Steinbeck's work formulated and dramatized attitudes toward the human experience which anticipated those of young men and women born years after his time of literary ascendancy. Many of his characters seem to be the forerunners of rebels who gathered in centers of protest from Greenwich Village to the Haight-Ashbury district of San Francisco during the decades of the fifties and the sixties. What can the dissidents of *Tortilla Flat* and *Cannery Row* be called but dropouts from society, prompted by impulses of rejection similar to those that motivated members of the later hippie generation? On the negative side the credo of those revolutionaries seemed, like that of Steinbeck, to be influenced by a pervasive disillusionment with the gospel of success, by contempt for cynical commercialism, and by resentment of arbitrary authority. On the positive side the group-conscious residents of Cannery Row were in complete sympathy with the group-conscious members of the student communes in their preference for love over the destructive impulses of human nature. Steinbeck writing in the 1930's protested against tendencies in the American way of life which inspired the banners and drew the fire of campus rebels in the 1960's.

More than this, however, Steinbeck never forgot the crucial character of the confrontation between man and his destiny. In the least sober of his books, *Sweet Thursday*, he slipped in a statement which succinctly sets forth his own fundamental belief: "Men seem to be born with a debt they can never pay no matter how hard they try. It piles up ahead of them. Man owes something to man. If he ignores the debt it poisons him, and if he tries to make payments the debt only increases, and the quality of his gift is the measure of the man." The novels, plays, and short stories of this conscientious artist represent successive efforts to pay his debt to man. Wide in the range of their interests, diverse in mood, passionately concerned in their sympathies, they all celebrate the worth of man. For that integrity Steinbeck demands justice and respect; to that integrity he lends the support of his own conviction that all men everywhere are and must be inextricably identified with their kind. Much more clearly than in the instance of any other American writer of his time, Steinbeck's consistent

effort to establish the dignity of human life offers the measure of the man.

He was born (on February 27, 1902) into an environment that served well to develop his inclinations and to satisfy his needs. The Salinas Valley of California provided a physical setting in which majesty and menace were mixed. Its alternate promises of fertility and threats of drought woke wonder in a sensitive, plastic nature and stirred an alert intelligence. He developed a passion for all the sounds, scents, and tastes of things, animate and inanimate. These crowded in upon him making him conscious, as he once expressed it, of "how the afternoon felt." The sentient boy, recognizable in transfiguration as Jody in *The Red Pony*, was father to the sentient man. And it was in his youth that Steinbeck seized on the belief, which remained with him always, that he shared with all living things the same essence and the same destiny, that there is a oneness of man with men and man with nature.

Spontaneously investigative and responsive from the first, the young Steinbeck found himself in a family setting that he could enjoy. Its assets included many books from among which the boy chose what he needed to serve the purposes of his self-education: Malory, Milton, Shakespeare, Dante, Goethe, Dostoevski, and Thucydides. That he digested instruction well is evident in the enduring influence that many of these guides had on his own work. The oneness of human experience was real to Steinbeck in relation to time as well as to space. What he read seemed to be not about events and passions of far away and long ago but rather, as he observed, "about things that happened to me."

His family, neither rich nor poor, made up a comfortable community the members of which helped each other when they could but encouraged any show of initiative and independence. The father, always unobtrusively sympathetic to the younger Steinbeck's desire to become a writer, once paid, out of a small salary as an official of city government, a minute allowance which kept him in the bare necessities of life while he worked at his manuscripts. The mother as a girl had been a schoolteacher and, though she did not want her son to become a writer and would have preferred to see him established in a profession of acknowledged prestige, she set him on the long search for enlightenment through books.

Olive Hamilton Steinbeck appears briefly on the autobiographical periphery of the novel *East of Eden*, a creature of intense feeling, "as intuitive as a cat," but incapable of disciplined thought. Her theology, Steinbeck wrote, "was a curious mixture of Irish fairies and an Old Testament Jehovah." This naive effort to integrate unlike deities in a pantheon all her own dazzled the imagination of her son and Steinbeck's fiction was to receive great drafts of refreshment from mythology. He did not hesitate to give to a character of his own creation traits which he had first perceived in figures as unlike as Christ, Faust, and the lord of Camelot. From one or another of the great fables, read in his youth, he borrowed here an intimation, there an insight. These stories were for him myths "which have their roots in reality." In his tireless investigation of their roots, he refined and enriched what he had absorbed under his mother's unsophisticated instruction —and placed it in logical perspective. She had tried to obliterate any reality that threatened her whims either by refusing to believe in it or by raging blindly against it. Steinbeck's own reconciliation with reality became in the end complete. "Things are as they are," he wrote, "because they must be."

Though his logic was cool his temper was not. All his work steams with indignation at injustice, with contempt for false piety, with scorn for the cunning and self-righteousness of an economic system that encourages exploitation, greed, and brutality. What saved him from the helpless vexation against frustrating reality that characterized his mother was in part his humor, which exercised a sanative and corrective influence on all his judgments, and in part his belief in oneness, in "a kind of wholeness to sense and emotion": "Good and bad, ugly and cruel all [are] welded into one."

Throughout the five years of Steinbeck's intermittent attendance at Stanford University (where he did not in the end bother to earn a degree) he worked at odd jobs usually involving physical labor—rancher, road worker, hod carrier, deck hand, cotton picker. He found these occupations congenial because they brought him into intimate association with the great company of workers among whom he chose his friends long before he used them as models for characters in stories. These were men whose courage he admired, whose rejection of cant and hypocrisy he applauded, and whose "high survival quotient" became for him the essential proof of a human being's success.

The man was ready for his work at twenty-seven when he published his first novel, *Cup of Gold* (1929). During the next quarter of a century he produced copiously: eleven novels (*To a God Unknown*, 1932; *Tortilla Flat*, 1935; *In Dubious Battle*, 1936; *The Red Pony*, 1937; *The Grapes of Wrath*, 1939; *Of Mice and Men*, 1940; *The Moon Is Down*, 1942; *Cannery Row*, 1945; *The Wayward Bus*, 1947; *The Pearl*, 1947; *East of Eden*, 1952), as well as two collections of short stories (*The Pastures of Heaven*, 1932; *The Long Valley*, 1938), dramatizations of two of his novels (*Of Mice and Men*, 1940; *The Moon Is Down*, 1942) and a play in story form (*Burning Bright*, 1950), a documentary (*The Forgotten Village*, 1941), two volumes of reportage (*Bombs*

Away, 1942, and *A Russian Journal*, 1948), and a journal of travel and scientific research (*Sea of Cortez*, 1951). His performance from the start was accomplished and professional: his books were carefully designed according to artistic principles of his own. The results were often moving, always disturbing, and in several instances strikingly impressive.

There were still two novels to come (*Sweet Thursday*, 1954; *The Winter of Our Discontent*, 1961), and a variety of other publications. But the later phases of Steinbeck's work were largely disappointing to thoughtful critics. That they were disappointing to the writer himself is made clear by a confession which, with a total lack of histrionism, he introduced into *Travels with Charley* (1962). This account of a trip made across the United States with his pet dog is as much an experiment in self-discovery as it is an effort to rediscover America. It contains a scene in which the lonely traveler listens to a fire-and-brimstone sermon preached by an old-fashioned fundamentalist in a Vermont pulpit. Steinbeck reports that he took this indictment of human frailty to himself: "I hadn't been thinking very well of myself for some years." It was at this precise moment that the Nobel Prize for literature was belatedly and almost apologetically awarded him. The vehement protest that the selection roused from many commentators must have made the laurels weigh on his head like a crown of thorns.

Steinbeck did no more significant work. Because he had not lost his taste for the art of communication he took to writing journalistic pieces like *America and Americans* (1966). This study of the native scene is steadily appealing and often shrewdly, though generously, critical. But a tone of autumnal melancholy broods over its pages.

His private life cannot have been without conflict, for he was married three times and divorced twice. However, certain shy liftings of the veil upon his privacy which occur in *Travels with Charley* indicate that his last marriage was happy and that the way of life it brought him—complete with cabin boat on Long Island, town house in New York, and loyal friends—was congenial.

His outlook changed in many ways. A return to Salinas showed him that, as Thomas Wolfe had also found, "you can't go home again." The boys in the back room of his favorite bar were no longer the brothers in spirit that they once had been. And in one significant way Steinbeck was surprisingly out of sympathy with the young whose parents he had so articulately anticipated: he sided with the hawks on the issue of war in Vietnam. Despite these ironies of psychological change, the end of his life did not forget or reject its beginnings. Steinbeck's last intimate communication to his following, contained in a chapter of *Travels with Charley*, expresses, with a ringing echo of the old anger, the "weary nausea" he experienced as he watched a "demoniac" crowd in New Orleans baiting a frightened black child as she entered a previously all-white school. In the midst of momentary despair, his pity and pride were invested as deeply as ever in the fate of the miserable and the dispossessed.

John Steinbeck died on December 20, 1968, in New York City.

While he lived Steinbeck was regarded by many of his critics as a kind of perennial apprentice. He experimented with many forms and, as he once boasted a little boyishly, none of his books was like any other. He seemed always to be beginning anew and this suggested to some that he lacked a sense of direction. Doctrinaire critics tended to dismiss any claim that might be made for him as an artist of rank and even the most sympathetic of his contemporary appraisers temporized with a cautious attitude of "waiting to see." Now that the record is complete a dispassionate inspection of his work and an assessment of his accomplishment are in order.

It says something significant about the importance of Steinbeck's work that the testimony must be examined on several different levels of interest. The same can be said of comparatively few American writers up to the very recent phantasmagorical/psychedelic experimentation with forms of fiction. Earlier storytellers conformed to familiar methods, producing, like Edith Wharton, the novel of manners; like Sinclair Lewis, the novel of social satire; or more or less like the master Henry James, the novel of subtle inquiry into states of mind induced by exquisite crises of loyalty. Below such enduring figures as these stood the great mass of fictioneers who ground out replicas of the well-made novel all having similarly stupefying patterns of predictable climaxes.

In contrast, Steinbeck from the moment when he made his debut with *Cup of Gold* was ever an audacious creator of new worlds. Exploring as broadly as possible the secrets of the species man, he presented himself simultaneously as storyteller, fabulist, critic of social institutions, innovative stylist, and appraiser of experience in philosophical terms. In all these roles Steinbeck struggled to give the upper hand to the original over the banal, to fresh intuition over accepted doctrine or dogma, to generous values over shabby ones, and to personal observation over the clichés of image, emotion, or conviction. The degree of success that he attained must be examined separately for each of the roles he played.

That Steinbeck was a storyteller of persuasive power is clear. Always the quintessential dramatist, he demanded of a reader that he identify himself with a particular moment of crisis. Then, by selecting the most revelatory bits of evidence, he wooed his audience subtly but insistently into acceptance of whatever he wished the meaning of an incident, an event, or a passion to be.

The story called "The Chrysanthemums" (from *The Long Valley*) presents the problem of the artist in conflict with philistinism. It does so in a way that makes a familiar, but often drearily detailed, complaint seem immediate and moving because the storyteller has offered a small, unexpected, fully dramatized instance. A woman whose painstaking creativity has been invested in growing flowers is persuaded to give some of her precious sprouts to a man who, while he pretends to warm sympathy with her work, is in fact only exploiting her dedication to gain a petty advantage for himself. When she finds that he has thrown away her sprouts as worthless she suffers the shock of an encounter with insensate brutality. Imbedded in the narrative, which is tense despite its seeming casualness and powerful despite the modesty of its material, is the further implication that to be touched by meanness, even accidentally, is to be a little tainted by it. A struggle to maintain her integrity ends in failure for the once sturdy woman when she finds that vengeful hatred has transformed her into a feebly weeping victim.

André Gide was an admirer of Steinbeck's stories, likening some of them to the best of Chekhov. What these talents have in common is an economy of means which yields a wealth of implication. Steinbeck's attack on what he wished to unmask and to destroy was far more aggressive than that of Chekhov but equally effective. He knew how to touch the sensitive area.

It is one thing to be able to improvise telling incidents and quite another to build a solid narrative out of such materials. In *The Grapes of Wrath* Steinbeck demonstrated that he was indeed master of this technique. His expertness of craftsmanship was not, however, evident to some critics when the novel first appeared. One even said that *The Grapes of Wrath* was as formless as a novel could manage to be. To such critics this seemed to be a haphazardly charted odyssey unworthy of its classical model in that it lacked a hero, like Homer's, whose various adventures were held together by his compelling drive to escape danger and find his way home. Yet this is, in fact, precisely the pattern that *The Grapes of Wrath* does possess. Instead of one central figure there is the family of the Joads, dispossessed tenant farmers of Oklahoma who take to the highway in a collapsing truck. These people are in flight from danger even as Odysseus was; they, too, are trying to find their way home, to a new home which will give them a secure way of life and enable them to achieve dignity. The encounters they have along the way—across the desert, toward the orchards and growing fields of California—are not merely random adventures but the meaningful events of a vigorous struggle for survival.

Viewed from the perspective of time *The Grapes of Wrath* seems not to be merely a "proletarian novel," one having only a fleeting interest as a document of the Great Depression. Rather it presents itself as an admirably modeled work of art having impressive size and just proportion, movement, balance, symmetry, and power. Each incident representing the struggle of the Joads against time and fate is precipitated onto the stage with the persuasiveness of immediate crisis: the loss of a machine part essential to the operation of the truck; the perilous crossing of the desert in a decrepit vehicle; the betrayal of the workers by landowners who lower wages below subsistence level simply because there is a surplus of fruit pickers; the cynical parody of the rule of law and order in which men wearing badges as deputy sheriffs turn their guns on men who

want nothing but the right to support their families; the herding of itinerant workers into squalid camps; the cunning defense by the group of laborers against gross injustice, against the threat of extinction of their kind. Each event in this crucial series is precisely, dramatically defined; each is articulated into the next; the mass of happenings is formed into a climax; the climaxes gain in power until the significance of the group adventure is impressively clear.

The essential point made by this study of the plight of man under the conditions of the Great Depression is that, no matter how bitter the assault on its existence may be, the group will defend itself unyieldingly. It obeys what Steinbeck called in the *Sea of Cortez* "the one commandment for living things: Survive!"

This is what he is able, with the aid of a rich variety of demonstrations, to persuade us is true of the Joads and of the group that forms around them. The families seem to disintegrate; the old members die of hunger and exhaustion; those who expose themselves to special danger as leaders are beaten and one is killed; some of the young people defect through moral weakness or in the service of self-interest. But even as the old group falls apart, a new one is seen to be forming. Tom Joad will become the leader of a new and better trained army fighting for the survival of his kind.

A literary device used by Steinbeck to amplify the meaning of his story may have been what made the book appear formless to certain eyes. Not infrequently he interrupts the flow of narrative to introduce chapters of comment and generalization. One is reminded by them of the way in which the chorus of a Greek play intervenes in the action. These passages contain parables dealing with the problem of survival and with the intricacies of the economic system in which the Joads find themselves inarticulately enmeshed. Abstract though these discussions are, and theoretical, they preserve the tone of drama and parallel the concerns of the story itself.

One of these sections describes, with an air of tension that might be appropriate to the detailing of a performance of a high-wire circus act, the dogged behavior of a turtle crossing a road, evading the purgatorial horrors of highway traffic and finally achieving its goal in the dust of a sheltered place. This minute spectacle dramatized in essence the meaning of the struggle in which the Joads are engaged.

In another of these excursions into allegory Steinbeck dramatized the unending debate between man and a powerful institution which he himself has created but whose vast, impersonal power now threatens to destroy him. The bank which owns the land on which people like the Joads live must put it to more profitable use than tenant farming. The inadequate worker must be put off and his house bulldozed to the ground. "The bank," says the oracle of this ingenious side drama, is "something more than men . . . It's the monster. Men made it, but they can't control it." Thus, without indulging in the moralizing rhetoric of the more usual proletarian novel Steinbeck establishes his point. Man, as victim of his own technological skill, must learn patiently to unweave the noose around his neck.

The Grapes of Wrath does not stand alone as evidence of Steinbeck's storytelling skill. The earlier novel *In Dubious Battle* (still surprisingly neglected) is virtually a model for a certain kind of craftsmanship. Hard, tight-packed as a bullet in its form, its propulsive power matches its theme. *In Dubious Battle* is like *The Grapes of Wrath* in no way except that both books are concerned with workers in a California valley who test fate by defying the power of a growers' association. If *In Dubious Battle* had been intended as a strikers' hand-

book it could hardly have been more explicit about the tactics of conflict, more scrupulously factual in its concentration on the events of one crisis in full ferment. The novel's unity of time and its strict enclosure within the limits of a particular place give it a classical sharpness of design. Within that pattern the style is as native as the scene is peculiarly American. The language is blunt, colloquial, emphatic, the mood resolute and impersonal.

As the novel opens the wage scale in the apple orchards of Torgas Valley has been dropped in direct proportion to an increase in the number of available pickers. A Communist organizer, Mac, precipitates himself into the situation, assuming a proprietary right to any battlefield of frustration and discontent. Influenced by his delicate manipulation, the workers walk off the job. Mac sees little hope for this particular strike but foments its violence with dedicated zeal and with great skill in the strategy of disruption. In the interest of his party's war on capitalism he maneuvers this skirmish toward its foredoomed tragedy.

When this book was first published Steinbeck was accused of harboring Communist sympathies. Because his strikers are presented as men suffering from unbearable wrongs it was possible for a heedless or prejudiced reader to assume that the novel constituted an endorsement of any movement that promised to correct these wrongs. But the author of *In Dubious Battle* remains as coolly detached as his characters are hotly involved. He puts his own attitude into the mouth of a young doctor who has come voluntarily to this battleground simply to patch up broken heads. Doc is challenged by Mac to clarify his position. "If it rains good and hard tonight the men'll be sneaking out on us. They just won't take it, I tell you. It's a funny thing, Doc. You don't believe in the cause, and you'll probably be the last man to stick. I don't get it at all." And Doc responds: "I don't get myself. . . . I don't believe in the cause, but I believe in men. . . . I have some skill in helping men, and when I see some who need help, I just do it."

Steinbeck's realistic concept of society ("Things are as they are because they must be") had no room in it for any but a clinical interest in a system like that of communism. Its theories seemed to him not merely arbitrary but degrading. One of the most revealing scenes of *In Dubious Battle* exposes a professional revolutionary, the young apprentice, Jim, indulging in an almost orgiastic love of violence for its own sake. Steinbeck's distaste for such doctrinaire dedication is evident. Uncommitted to any cause but the affirmation of the dignity of man, he offered *In Dubious Battle* as a study of the way in which the compulsive behavior of a group may threaten its own survival. It threatens, he seems to insist, and yet cannot finally defeat. Like Doc, Steinbeck did not believe in causes but in men. His novel comments on the problem of man's conflict with his environment, suggesting with a kind of somber optimism that though a battle may end in stalemate the war itself is not lost. The end of *In Dubious Battle* implies a new beginning, satisfying the principle of catharsis.

East of Eden presents Steinbeck in a contrasting facet of his role as storytelling craftsman. The longest of his novels, it manages to be intimate and personal in tone, establishing itself as a kind of genial father-confessor among his books. The contrast with *In Dubious Battle* is complete; one is as diffuse in interest as the other is compact; the later is as full of conversational perambulations as the earlier is severely short of such devices. A diary Steinbeck kept for the benefit of his editor during the composition of *East of Eden*, and published posthumously, throws curiously little light on his creative method. But it is clear that in this effort he drew his inspiration from the symphonic form of which he was a devoted student. Into the novel he weaves three themes. Each is given its major and minor variations which play upon each other with harmonic intricacy, producing crescendos of cumulative power. The motifs reveal their interrelationships with ever increasing lucidity so that in the end the work is discovered to be a hymn to earth and to man as protector, expander, and fulfiller of its destiny.

The first motif may be identified by the word "westering." The compulsive movement of men and women across a sea and a continent, to establish a new society in a setting foreign to its origins but sympathetic to its needs, is dramatized in the chronicles of two families, the Hamiltons out of Ireland and the Trasks out of Connecticut. They come together in the Salinas Valley, there to enact the scenes that are vital to Steinbeck's story of a new creation, this time the creation by man of his own world. This is, however, no usual family record of getting and spending, begetting and dying. The events are numerous, spectacular, often violent. They involve all the inevitable crises of conflict ranging from personal feud to war itself. But these concerns of individuals are offered as evidence that a far more significant story is in the process of unfolding. Steinbeck defines westering as the impulse of the group to transform itself into "one great crawling beast" compelled by the secrets of its nature to move through perils, survive disaster, and "get there." This is, in effect, an account in allegorical terms of the great yearning of man ever and again to reenact the drama of Genesis.

The second motif searches out the personal compulsions which in each individual underlie the urgent thrust of the will to survive. In each generation of the family of Adam Trask the conflict of Cain and Abel is paralleled. This, Steinbeck suggests, is "the symbol story of the human soul" and he undertakes to explore the maze of hostilities through which each man must make his way in the inevitable struggle for dominance of brother over brother. The same fateful pattern of ambivalence is evident in the relationship of father and son. As Steinbeck's spokesman observes: "The greatest terror a child can have is that he is not loved, and rejection is the hell he fears. I think everyone in the world to a large or small extent has felt rejection. And with rejection comes anger, and with anger some kind of crime in revenge for the rejection, and with the crime guilt." Steinbeck's two versions of the passion of Everyman, dramatized in Adam Trask's struggle first with a violent brother and then with a difficult, demanding, sensitive son, play contrapuntally on each other until the significance of each phase is fully revealed. The "story of mankind" has been restaged, losing none of its complexity, in the homely setting of the Trask household. The purpose of the author in doing so is, again in the words of his spokesman, to show how many "pains and insanities" could be "rooted out if the causes were known."

The third motif is also a familiar one but it is given a new variation. What Steinbeck contributes to the discussion of humanity's Problem One—the conflict between good and evil —is his own concept of the doctrine of free will. Again he refers to the biblical story recalling that the Lord, in the severity of His love, says to Cain: "If thou doest well, shalt thou not be accepted? and if thou doest not well, sin lieth at the door. And unto thee shall be his desire, and thou shalt rule over him." Steinbeck became convinced that the King James version of the Bible erred in its translation of the significant word in this passage, the Hebrew verb *timshel*. His redefinition makes it a word not of command but of counsel: thou mayest, rather than thou shalt, rule over sin.

When the book first appeared a brisk con-troversy arose over Steinbeck's interpretation of the meaning of *timshel* and over his spelling of the word as well. Scholars challenged both and then a second group of scholars challenged the first. Steinbeck, beset and defended, held his ground with characteristic self-assurance. In the absence of divine guidance in the matter he may be allowed to accept responsibility for his philosophy and for his orthography as well.

For him the difference between thou shalt and thou mayest works a peaceful revolution in the world of morality. Man ceases to be the slave of unintelligible forces over which he has no control; he becomes master of his destiny when he is given "the glory of the choice" be-tween good and evil. It was Steinbeck's phi-losophy to the end of his life—as his Nobel address revealed—that three wills are operative in man's experience: the will of the group, the will of the individual, and the moral will which must in the end prevail over the lesser two.

East of Eden is parable, poem, and tale of action all in one. Like Melville's *Moby Dick* it finds a meeting ground for physical and spir-itual adventure, exploring skillfully the in-terests of both.

For contrast to this amplitude of design one may turn to an entirely different example of Steinbeck's technical skill. *Of Mice and Men* is so essentially dramatic in its structure that to adapt it to the requirements of the theater it was necessary only to compress its descriptive passages into stage directions and allow the remaining dialogue to take command. Here in the simplest possible terms Steinbeck offers a statement of his belief in the importance of a voluntary acceptance of responsibility. It re-minds us again that "man owes something to man."

The central character, George, is a typical Steinbeck figure, a man of the humble work-aday world who, as migrant worker, has shown a high survival quotient both in physical resourcefulness and in independence of mind. But his freedom is grotesquely limited by the fact that he has assumed guardianship over a creature of monumental ineptitude, a retarded child in a man's huge body. Lennie's great hands, not being under the control of an adult conscience, cannot resist the temptation to touch and caress any soft thing they encounter. A mouse will do but a girl is better. Inevitably he brings trouble down upon the ill-matched pair wherever they try to settle as workers.

On a ranch where George finds employment for both the fateful routine is enacted again. The provocative, amoral wife of the ranch boss's son attracts Lennie's limited but disastrous interest. What Lennie's weakness urges him to touch his strength compels him to kill. To run away from the fear of punishment is the only wisdom available to the totally inadequate creature and he obeys it. The search that follows must, if it is successful, end in a ritual murder of revenge. George is obliged to find his pitiful friend before the posse can do so and shoot him as an act of kindness.

The novel's climactic scene has been anticipated by one having exactly the same import. The stench of an old dog, owned by one inmate of the ranch barracks, has become intolerable to the other men. He is destroyed in all decency—even with respect for his blameless integrity as ranch animal—by one bullet aimed at the back of his head. The point of the parable is explicitly made: no life is unworthy of reverence, not that of an ailing dog, not that of an idiot. Life must be sacred even to a man who is obliged to destroy in order to save.

The small book of related sketches called *The Red Pony* has been overpraised as Steinbeck's best artistic achievement. One may well agree that this portrait of a sensitive boy is indeed distinguished without finding the work

as a whole satisfactory. Seldom has the identification of a fledgling artist with the natural scene that surrounds him been presented with a lyricism so innocently appealing. But the structure is topheavy. The one decisive act in this study of an approach to maturity occurs in the first episode, leaving the others to taper off in successive stages of anticlimax. When the boy, Jody, beats in frantic rage at the buzzards hovering over the body of his beloved dead pony, managing to kill one, he declares his sentiments and his loyalties with dramatic eloquence. In the other experiences of the story he is revealed with steadily less ingratiating poignancy. An interesting comment on Steinbeck's preoccupation with problems of technique is to be found in the fact that when he prepared his own scenario for a film version of *The Red Pony* he corrected his mistake by putting the climax where it belongs—at the end.

It is the vocation of the storyteller to communicate to readers a sense of life lived outside the confines of their own skins and beyond the limitations of their own intelligences. To respond to such an evocation is to become momentarily a new man, quickened in flesh, mind, and spirit to new awareness and alerted also to the powerful influence of a certain setting upon all the sensibilities. A world unlike one's own is all at once made intimately familiar.

A writer may be a genius without possessing this special gift of persuasion. Edith Wharton once—quite innocently as she insists in her memoirs—made the confidence of Henry James falter by asking: Why do your characters seem never to have any other place to go when they leave the printed page? James's abashed acknowledgment that he did not realize this was so made tacit confession to certain limitations in his art.

Another highly gifted novelist, John O'Hara, in his stories of conflict over crises in manners, ambitions, and loyalties made do with a similarly restricted realm of creativity. His characters exist tantalizingly, pugnaciously within the space of each well-contrived scene in which they play their parts. But absence from the next scene suggests only that they are being hastily repaired for the ardors of another passage in a love duel or for the rigors of a still more intense struggle for domination in the immediate situation.

The total environment of Steinbeck's world is quite different. Its physical manifestations—the menace of a desert, the peril of flood in a valley—are introduced not as mere stage effects; their impacts fall as awesomely on the reader as they do on the Joad family in *The Grapes of Wrath*. In *East of Eden* the unwritten scenes of Aaron Trask's yearning for identification with his father tug at the imagination with implications of an unappeased desire that grows even during the author's silence. It is the novelist's method to cut into the midst of a scene that seems to have been in progress before the factual report begins and to go on after it closes. The loyalties and hostilities of the hobo jungles that give the setting to *In Dubious Battle* constitute a way of life that seems to draw energy from forces far beyond the arbitrary control of a mere contriver of happenings. The variety, urgency—even the quirkiness—of the mental adventures of many of Steinbeck's characters suggest a richness of experience the like of which is to be found only in the work of the important Russian writers. Indeed it might be said of his novels, as Virginia Woolf said of Dostoevski's, that they are "composed of the stuff of the soul."

Because his creations seem to leap over the barriers of lines on a printed page into an existence of their own, Steinbeck must be cred-

ited with distinguished success not merely as storyteller but as reflector of the quality of contemporary American life.

Steinbeck's gift as fabulist contributed heavily to making his work unique among American writers of his time. His borrowings from literature's wealth of folklore and his evident desire to show a kinship between many of his chief characters and the towering figures of myth are evident in *The Grapes of Wrath* and *East of Eden*. But it is in a comparatively obscure early novel, *To a God Unknown*, that his concern with man's heritage from the past is most apparent. This is a book of striking interest, strewn tantalizingly with samples of what he himself described as "the harvest of symbols in our minds [which] seem to have been implanted in the soft, rich soil of our pre-humanity."

The novel may be read on its surface as another story of westering. Joseph Wayne finds the Vermont farm on which he has lived with his father and brothers too small to satisfy his land hunger and, with the blessing of his parent, leaves home. "After a time of wandering," he comes at last to a promising valley of California. He feels close to the land, nourishes its needs, sends for his brothers to join him, becomes the acknowledged patriarch of his clan, marries, loses his wife, faces disaster from drought, and literally gives his life to the soil he loves.

But Steinbeck means to imply much more in this allegory of man's unity with nature. Joseph Wayne is not merely a priest of natural religion; he is one of its demigods, feeling himself to *be* the land, to embody its urgencies, its trials, its failures, and its fulfillment. When at the end he dies by his own hand he regards the sacrifice as having ritualistic significance. Relief from drought immediately follows the use of a knife on the veins of his wrist and he thinks in triumph: "I am the land . . . and I am the rain. The grass will grow out of me in a little while."

Steinbeck did not edge timidly into this large-scale parable of man as "symbol of the earth's soul." He welcomed its challenges boldly. His Joseph Wayne insists upon believing that his dead father has come to live in a tree that stands beside his door; he puts his child into the tree's branches to receive its benediction; he accepts the death of the tree as warning of disaster to come. With these alliances to the occult he passes out of the realm of everyday reality into the realm of mysticism where he reveals his kinship to a cult of primitive deities. A novel must offer many demonstrations of its theme and Steinbeck with his virtuosity of invention finds no difficulty in dazzling a reader with references, back and forth through time, to precedents of wonder. His Joseph is related in the genealogy of letters to Joseph of the Bible who also brought his brothers into a new world, established his authority over the people of a country not his own, and created a society for the protection of all. But Joseph Wayne's ancestry may be traced back farther still to forebears in the primitive world. He is entirely at home among neighbors who engage in rites to propitiate the gods and who, when their incantations seemed to be answered in signs of benediction, erupt lustily into orgies. Even the blood sacrifices of animals in which another neighbor engages, with exquisite skill accompanied by sensations of joy, neither surprise nor appall him.

What must be accepted in order to receive the intended impression of this long prose poem to nature is that Joseph is a creature of earth belonging not to a particular moment in time but, like any figure in mythology, to all time. Or, as the spokesman for Steinbeck's mysticism says: ". . . he is all men. The strength, the resistance, the long and stumbling thinking of all men, and all the joy and suffering, too . . ." There is in him something of the majesty, the harshness, and the detachment of a natural element. What adds greatly to the surprise and high excitement of this conceit is that Steinbeck has been able to give to so extraordinary a being a local habitation and an American name.

A phrase which Steinbeck has used to describe this kind of exercise is "the working of atavistic magic." Surrender of disbelief may not be easy in the face of so unexpected a demand, but the reward of making the effort is a kind of pleasure that is also rare and unexpected. A haunting music flows from every page and the novel's many incantations are alive with what one of the Hindu scriptures calls "right rapture." There is evidence in *To a God Unknown* that, in devising a myth of his own out of a blend of old and new, familiar and remote, Steinbeck was under the influence of Eastern literature. The book's title is derived from a Hindu poem in which these lines occur:

He is the giver of breath, and strength is his gift.
The high Gods revere his commandments.
His shadow is life, his shadow is death;
Who is He to whom we shall offer our sacrifice?

This impulse to refresh imagination at whatever font world literature may offer was not unlike that of Emerson who, in his hymn to Brahma, celebrated the same esoteric faith that Steinbeck bespeaks in *To a God Unknown*. "Shadow and sunlight are the same . . . one to me are shame and fame."

It is the task of the novelist to capture the universal in the particular, revealing the elusive in intriguing incident. Working in *To a God Unknown* with materials of a peculiarly volatile kind, Steinbeck managed to reduce his favorite theme of unity to the explicit terms of dramatic parable.

A better known example of his skill at myth-making gives a droll turn to the enterprise. *Tortilla Flat* encloses a group of ironic anecdotes within the framework of a romance which claims kinship with the medieval spirit represented by the legend of King Arthur and his Knights of the Round Table. The preface offers this clue to the author's intention: "This story deals with the adventuring of [Danny and] Danny's friends, with the good they did, with their thoughts and their endeavors. . . . It is well that this cycle be put down on paper so that in a future time scholars, hearing the legends, may not say as they say of Arthur and of Roland and of Robin Hood—'There was no Danny nor any group of Danny's friends . . . Danny is a nature god and his friends primitive symbols of the wind, the sky, the sun.' This history is designed now and ever to keep the sneers from the lips of sour scholars." Obviously Steinbeck's fluent tongue is, for the moment, lodged snugly in his cheek. This is a grandiose joke. Out of his boyhood love of Malory he has fashioned, still in boyish temper, a good-natured parody of the chivalric tradition. Danny, King Arthur's comic counterpart, is a California paisano, recently returned from World War I. He takes into his house a group of strays ardently devoted to indolence who range through the neighborhood of Monterey seeking liquor, women, and whatever fight may help to while away the afternoon. Their "endeavors" are all exuberant parodies of the questing of Arthur's knights.

The loosely linked incidents are mildly bawdy and Steinbeck's treatment of each is ironically indulgent. It is his gleefully maintained pretense that every drunken bout is a grand ceremonial of comradeship and every buffoonish encounter between the sexes a fine display of chivalric spirit. The success of *Tortilla Flat* rests solidly on Steinbeck's complete savoir-faire in maintaining his own air of gravity. A comic miniature of heroic romance, the book keeps its proportions, its emphases, and its implications all in scale, corresponding neatly to those of the myth of the Round Table. Even when Danny dies, in a fall from a cliff after a drunken party, it is solemnly suggested that he has not been lost to humanity; rather, he has been "translated" to be forever, again like Arthur, "the once and future king."

What this parallel treatment of the Arthurian legend implies is that the first prerequisite for knighthood is generosity. And no matter how grotesque the vagaries of Danny and his friends, they are in lively possession of qualities that Steinbeck genuinely admires: virility, honesty, and comradeliness. They are able to make accommodation to circumstance and by that adaptability they manage to survive. Danny's house becomes the symbol of man's environment; the resourceful ways of its inhabitants offer suggestions which are by no means wholly frivolous about how that environment can be made livable.

Steinbeck's one failure in the realm of myth-making is the play in story form called *Burning Bright*. Here he attempted to re-create Everyman or, perhaps more nearly, the universal father. The central situation is that of a man who, though he does not know of his disability, cannot have a child of his own because he is sterile. In an effort to restore his self-esteem his wife enters into an otherwise meaningless relationship with another man so that she may become a mother. This so closely duplicates a crisis of Eugene O'Neill's *Strange Interlude* that Steinbeck must have believed it to be as legitimate to borrow from one's contemporaries as to borrow from the classics. To the appropriated material he adds something that is entirely his own: the idea that a mature intelligence must accept the oneness of humanity. At the close of the play the protagonist, having learned the truth about the child's paternity, is still able to say: "I love my son." This endorsement carries with it the implication that in a good society every man should consider himself to be the father to every son.

The difficulty with the experiment is simply that it does not come off. As in no other of Steinbeck's works the language is uninterruptedly high-flown and artificial. Even the structure seems labored and clumsy: to emphasize the universality of his characters Steinbeck gives them the same names throughout but in each act presents them in a different social setting, first in a circus, then on a farm, and finally against the background of the sea. Even so, Steinbeck's Everyman dwindles into Everystereotype. The interest of *Burning Bright* collapses under the burden of its moral purpose, which burns only too ardently.

Entirely successful, within the more modest limits of its intent, is the parable called *The Pearl*. In the *Sea of Cortez*, Steinbeck tells of hearing a story about a Mexican Indian pearl diver who found such a fine jewel that he knew "he need never work again." Possession of this rare object so poisoned the existence of the fisherman, however, that he cursed it and threw it back into the sea.

Steinbeck's comment on the story, made in *Sea of Cortez*, was that he did not believe it: "it is far too reasonable to be true." But this uncharacteristic literal-mindedness presently gave way to a realization that the legend cried out for elaboration and interpretation. Showing a fine respect for the special quality of the material, he produced a touching story of good in desperate struggle with evil. An infant becomes his symbol of innocence betrayed. The baby, born to a pearl fisherman, Kino, and his wife, Juana, is bitten by a scorpion and the local doctor refuses treatment because he knows the family to be poor. The situation is reversed when it becomes known that Kino has found "the Pearl of the World." Every-

one becomes eager to exploit his ignorance. The doctor tries to play on a father's fears for the child, hoping to get the pearl in payment for useless services. The dealer in pearls belittles the jewel thinking to get it for little. Thieves set upon Kino in the dark trying to rob him and beat him viciously in the attempt. His house is burned in the course of another invasion. Crises mount until Kino realizes that he must try to escape from a world that has turned into an implacable enemy. But there is no escape from the evil that has been loosed into this community. Kino is tracked into the mountains where he has taken wife and child to hide. Bullets from the gun of the trackers hit and kill the child. The irony is complete; the pearl which should have been the means of helping to fulfill Kino's ambitions for his son actually has been an agent of disaster, producing only suffering, despair, and finally death. Back it goes into the sea, flung by Kino's hand.

The unfolding of incident presents Kino always as the angry, frightened, but resolute man, determined to keep what he has earned. This establishes the human element with satisfying dramatic emphasis while the allegorical element envelops the child in a miasmic cloud of evil. A pattern of symbols draws the delicate complexity of the parable into a tight design. The sea—Kino's environment—gives and takes away like a superbly indifferent minister of destiny. The pearl itself represents the wonder, the mystery, the maddening, fateful beauty of the world, all in one luminous sphere.

As well as in any other of his stories, major or minor, Steinbeck matches manner to matter in *The Pearl*. The style has a subdued, foreboding lyricism which communicates easily with a reader's sympathies and never wavers toward elegiac excess. Because his people are inarticulate Steinbeck must tell their story in the language of the heart and he is able to keep its idiom warm, believable, and touching. This is perhaps the best of his achievements in the role he liked best, that of fabulist.

Steinbeck, the analyst and critic of society, had in his time to refute many charges of bias against democracy and "the American way of life." Consideration of his work on this level of its interest may well begin with a listing of the kinds of influence he did not aspire to exert. He was never a radical thinker, pamphleteer, agitator, Communist, or fellow traveler.

If evidence is needed that he entertained neither overt nor disguised sympathies with the Soviet system this may be readily found in his *Russian Journal.* The book is not one of his impressive accomplishments. It contains no striking insights and is content to offer merely a rambling account of casual encounters with bureaucrats, fellow writers, students, shop keepers, official guides, Ukrainian farmers, stage performers, and mighty drinkers of vodka. The tone is relaxed to the point of being flaccid but what it conveys inescapably is a distaste for nearly everything that a repressive government does to its likable victims. Men are good, their institutions dangerous, he seems to be repeating again and again with a kind of unsurprised sorrow. In *The Grapes of Wrath* he had stated explicitly and by implication his dissatisfaction with the status quo in American society. But his comments on his experience in Russia leave no doubt that he had far greater hope for the regenerative power of democratic processes of government than for the arbitrary authority of any totalitarian system.

As one who believed in a writer's duty to try to keep humanity's morale high, Steinbeck believed also in the duty to expose attacks on its well-being. His two most searching examinations of the social scene, *The Grapes of Wrath* and *In Dubious Battle,* reveal clearly his ideas of what had gone wrong with the principles of democracy during the 1930's. He had seen men uprooted, degraded, and finally destroyed by the ruthlessly mechanistic operation of the economic system. He became deeply convinced that the rule of law and order is perverted into tyranny whenever democracy yields supinely to the demands of oligarchy. As propagandist he wished to do no more than to indicate how society, by encouraging morbid growths of special privilege for the rights of property over the rights of men, endangers its own survival. When it allows human beings to starve democracy squanders its greatest asset, creative energy.

Steinbeck had no precise scheme of reform to expound, no nostrum to offer. As an artist he could only observe and record the struggle of man against himself, hoping, by a vivid presentation of a problem in human affairs, to awaken minds to its crucial character. Without assuming the responsibilities of a reformer he wished to influence the temper of the time simply by urging acceptance of sane attitudes in matters of economic opportunity and attitudes favoring equality in the administration of justice.

His first book showed the direction his work was to take. *Cup of Gold* undertakes to demolish the inflated notions about the splendor of derring-do which have always tended to glorify the conqueror. This free treatment of the life story of the British pirate Sir Henry Morgan is offered as the epitome of all tales of ruthless enterprise. Out of the welter of its savage happenings rises the conviction that the most fearful of all false beatitudes might read: Blessed be the arriviste for he shall inherit the earth. What such anti-heroes really inherit, Steinbeck insists, are the rewards of all emotionally retarded creatures: memories of mindless cruelty and visions of a world pointlessly laid waste.

The imaginary Henry Morgan of the novel appears first as a stolid, determined boy of fifteen who leaves his home in Wales to go—as Steinbeck puts it with sly irony—"a-buccaneering" in the flamboyant style of the seventeenth century. He ships to sea, is sold into slavery in Barbados, becomes actual master of his languid, ineffectual owner, enriches himself at the latter's expense, becomes "Admiral" of a fleet of pirate vessels, and accepts commissions for bloody enterprise in international conflicts at sea. His crowning victory in Steinbeck's version of the story comes to him when he captures, sacks, and utterly destroys a rich city of Panama, the "Cup of Gold." With characteristic presence of mind and absence of morality, he manages to leave his followers marooned in the wasteland he has made and sails off with all the booty.

Below the surface of this ravening tale lies a pattern of symbols used to emphasize its meaning as parable. The wisdom of the ages is concentrated in the mind of Merlin, revived out of Arthurian romance to appear as young Henry Morgan's mentor. The symbol figure of Faust is reborn in Morgan himself. The grandiosity of his ambitions matches that of Goethe's heroic sinner though he becomes Faust's antithesis in his utter lack of concern for humanity. Echoes of Goethe's tone keep recurring. In the final scene Morgan on his deathbed is confronted, as was Faust, by the accusing shades of his wasted opportunities, his cruelties, and his crimes.

The clues to Steinbeck's basic intent in presenting so blasted an image of dehumanization are many. It is Merlin who anticipates the moral even before the tale has been told. Morgan, the seer says, will always catch his fireflies—that is, realize his wayward ambitions—if he keeps the heart of a child. What Steinbeck means to suggest is that savagery and bloodletting—in general, heedless indifference to human rights—are the perverted pleasures of the immature. By implication he reaffirms the belief, expressed by Shaw in *Back to Methuselah*, that the race can save itself from its own destructive impulses only if it manages at last to grow up.

The man of aggressive, unapologetically acquisitive enterprise continued to be the target of Steinbeck's ironic temper throughout his career. In twentieth-century lore, and particularly on American soil, the buccaneer in the 1920's and 1930's often dwindled to the proportions of the excessively energetic businessman, the "go-getter" of the period's slang. Steinbeck never rested from the self-imposed task of shrinking this figure further still with his ridicule. The group of novels—*Cannery Row, The Wayward Bus*, and *Sweet Thursday* —which appear at first glance to be merely light entertainments actually have the purpose of challenging the values of a society that seeks to make a merit of one of its worst defects. A willingness to prey on others in the interest of self-aggrandizement is, in Steinbeck's code, the bleakest of sins.

The figures of *Cannery Row* and of its companion piece, *Sweet Thursday*, are idlers and drunkards, escapists from all the stern realities that control the lives of devotees of the gospel of success. The only rewards they want are those of the moment and their hedonistic activities as well as their buffoonish practical jokes conspicuously flout accepted ideas of proper behavior. But if they do no good, in the sense that dominates the thinking of conventional men and women, they do no harm either, which, Steinbeck says by implication, is more than can be said of many an enterprise of the righteous. The anti-heroes of *Cannery Row* are at least concerned with the happiness of one another. Like their brothers of *Tortilla Flat* they direct their "endeavors" toward the well-being of the group.

Steinbeck's jovial endorsement of this conduct is not to be taken as evidence of capriciousness. When he stands the accepted virtues and acknowledged vices on their heads—making conformity seem stuffily absurd if not altogether vicious and nonconformity somehow estimable in and of itself—he wishes to remind us that, after centuries of combining puritanical sanctimoniousness with Yankee cunning in our philosophy of getting on, we need to reexamine all our presuppositions about morality in the light of generosity and sanity.

Literary quality varies widely from scene to scene in each of these novels. *Cannery Row* contains anecdotes as amusing and as lethal as the best of his short stories offer; it indulges also in parodies of sentiment that seem more waggish than adroit. *Sweet Thursday* constantly threatens to collapse into a completely conventional boy-meets-girl romance, arbitrarily forced into a rowdy setting.

Best of the light entertainments is *The Wayward Bus*, which Henry Seidel Canby likened to *The Canterbury Tales*. Here the reader follows the events of a journey and learns the life stories of the accidentally assembled men and women who make it. Under one kind of stress or another each reveals the animating impulse of his nature. A boy, called Pimples in callous recognition of his affliction, touchingly acknowledges his yearning for dignity and acceptance. A smug woman cannot restrain from opening the door on the untidy alcove of fantasy in which she lives. A petty man of affairs exposes the wasteland of his mean ambitions and feeble desires. A dying martinet compulsively uncovers the abject fear that has lurked in the background of his effort to be a tyrant. A prostitute testifies by her behavior to the fact that to be amoral in matters of sex is not necessarily to be lacking in sensibility or personal integrity.

It is not difficult to understand why Steinbeck chose sometimes to present in the form of raucous comedy his deeply felt protest against the false values of a property-minded, profit-obsessed world. The clown is permitted to make severe judgments which, had they been spoken in all earnestness by a declared reformer, would have brought the accusation of lese majesty down on his head. Steinbeck, when he championed the cause of the Okies in *The Grapes of Wrath*, had been subjected to just such vituperation. Though he was ever ready to fight for his opinions and his various literary presentations of them, it satisfied his ironic temper now and again to mask sympathies in ribald hilarity. What he is saying in *Cannery Row* quite clearly and unapologetically is that a society that permits, even encourages, high crimes against humanity and then makes a great show of niggling priggishness in the face of venial sin is a fatuous society.

It was appropriate that Steinbeck ended his career as he began it with a novel of social protest. *The Winter of Our Discontent* presents a crisis in the life of a man of sensibility, intelligence, and humor who undertakes willfully to live by the code of a modern buccaneer. The only reward that comes to him out of this adventure in open-eyed obliquity is a self-disgust so grim as to make him suicidal.

The novel is disarming in many ways. It introduces a new Steinbeck, entirely at home in a New England setting but even more critical of its mores than he had previously been of the blunted conscience of his native place. The central figure is a complex product of an old society and his sophisticated graces make him the complete antithesis of the typical pseudo-primitive of *Cannery Row*. The pervasive wit welling up out of the many soliloquies of the protagonist, instead of being of the locker-room variety characteristic of the lively farces, is mental and intricately involuted.

The intention of *The Winter of Our Dis-*

content, like that of *Cannery Row*, is to show how false the values of society may be. In the earlier book the theme of protest is treated lightheartedly, with an air of frivolous irresponsibility; in the later the tone becomes progressively more severe until in the end it seems almost grim.

Ethan Hawley, the central figure of Steinbeck's last novel, is out of sorts with his world in many ways. In part his discontent springs from the fact that though he bears a fine family name the society of which he is a member has provided him with no money to support the flimsy benefits of his prestige. His own ill-fortune has reduced him to the status of manager-clerk in a modest grocery store. His wife and children want more than they seem to be getting from their lives. He decides, on his family's account, to transform himself into a ruthless activist. The examples before him of a world that rewards cunning no matter how low its compromises with conscience may be seen to justify an attempt to enrich himself without concern for the suffering his manipulations may cause others.

Ethan's scheme is intricate and has several facets. With characteristic resourcefulness in the invention of incident, Steinbeck explores every aspect of the story's lurid interest. Crime and cruelty are involved, acts of shocking, degrading kinds. Ethan even betrays to his death a friend whom he professes to love. Steinbeck, one must believe, chose these instances not because he believed them to be sensationally extreme but rather because they seemed to him to be altogether too usual in the workaday world of enterprise. Loathing the mischief he has done, Ethan is almost persuaded to pay for it with his own life. The decision is reversed when he realizes that he still owes a duty to life. Only if he survives can his sensitive daughter be expected to do so.

Many symbolic presences reveal themselves intriguingly in the background of the novel. Its title suggests that Steinbeck was thinking of Shakespeare's Richard III, who, like Ethan, is "subtle, false and treacherous," frivolously making evil his good. The dates of the book's events are significant. One cluster of events center around preparations for Easter. If Steinbeck's implication is that society is forever re-enacting the drama of the Passion, Ethan is appropriately cast as its Judas. The rest of the happenings occur on the Fourth of July. Ethan's betrayal of his own principles is glaringly highlighted by memories of the day on which American democracy made its bold affirmation of the rights of man. The problem which Steinbeck faced in *The Winter of Our Discontent* was to make Ethan's tragedy seem somehow worthy to stand in the shadow of events so portentous. He did not wholly succeed. Likable though the novel is, it betrays—even as Ethan does—its own intent. The gravity of the situation is covered by a froth of frivolity. The tone of the storytelling is too light to bear the weight of its implications.

But the final comment on Steinbeck's work as critic of society must be that no other writer of our time has found so many ways of reminding us that man should be the beneficiary of his institutions, not their victim. His best work dramatizes the plight of man—now tragically, now humorously, with the aid of challenge, irony, homely eloquence, and subtle insight—as he indomitably struggles to make his environment a protective garment, not a haircloth shirt.

A curious view of Steinbeck, expressed by some of his early critics, presented him as a kind of naive natural genius who, having limited resources of technique and an even more severely limited vocabulary, blundered occasionally into displays of impressive, if brutal, power. Closer examination of his way with words should help to dispel that illusion. He was, in fact, a stylist of originality and grace. Just as he set up the structure of each of his best books in accordance with a well-planned architectural design, so he brought together the elements of his sentences with an artist's disciplined awareness of his own values. He expressed his attitudes, his sympathies, and his ideas in figurative language that remains fresh because his metaphors were entirely his own.

This was not true at the beginning. Steinbeck had his mentors. Some were good; it is not difficult to discern in *Cup of Gold* and *To a God Unknown* reverberations of the stately music of the King James version of the Bible. But the recommendation of others can have been only that they enjoyed, at the moment, wide popularity. One finds, again in *Cup of Gold*, imitations of the verbal tricks of James Branch Cabell and echoes of the self-conscious melodiousness of Donn Byrne. As he became more secure in awareness of his own identity, however, Steinbeck found his own voice.

It is in *The Grapes of Wrath* that the tone of the experienced artist declares itself with quiet confidence. The language of the narrative chapters is that of the people involved—simple, urgent in the expression of primal needs and desires, fresh and colorful within the limitations of the Joads's experience, powerful and poetic in implication. The chapters of comment presented temptations to a writer of Steinbeck's facility. Here and there a momentary lapse threatens the modesty of the style and the organ tones of omniscience swell out fortissimo. But for the most part these passages are kept in harmonic sympathy with the rest of the work. Steinbeck's lucid, generally unpretentious style enables him to present *The Grapes of Wrath* as a grave and respectful celebration of the dignity of man, a homely yet eloquent eulogy of the anonymous great who were his heroes.

Examples of his verbal skill reveal the secret of his method which was to make the simplest words and phrases flash into significance with seeming spontaneity. The quality of patience in one of his characters is established by use of the graphic simile "as enduring as a sea-washed stone." When he describes a woman as being "humorless as a chicken" one immediately sees the skitterings and hears the feeble, repetitive complaints of a creature ridiculously, yet pathetically, at war with a frustrating environment. The same genius for making pictures of mental attitudes reveals itself in the suggestion that the mind of another character—a Chinese shopkeeper who has forever to protect himself against the connivers of Cannery Row— "picked its way as delicately as a cat through cactus." One of Steinbeck's many eager digesters of experience defines himself unforgettably when he says, "I eat stories like grapes." As easily recognizable as an elderly female relative of one's own is the woman who has "a collection of small round convictions." The idiot in the story "Johnny Bear" has only one interest in life, which is to cadge drinks at a bar; he keeps reiterating the sounds "Whis-key . . . Whis-key," as Steinbeck says, "like a bird call." By such small touches Steinbeck quickens his men and women into life.

He is equally successful with metaphor in creating landscape. Every season when the drenching rains came at last to his valley, the land, Steinbeck is inspired to say, "would shout with grass." A solitary visitor to a pool frequented by frogs remembers that "the air was full of their song and it was a kind of roaring silence." The modest poetry of surprise leaps out of such phrases as it does even more strikingly in descriptions of wild weather. An observer is warned of an approaching storm when he sees "a black cloud eating up the sky." In another such moment "a bristling, officious wind raked the valley." The device of making pictures of doleful situations is used to underscore tragedy: "Poverty sat cross-legged on the farm." Mood is established, the nature of a man defined, drama propelled by verbal devices so skillfully suited to their purpose as to be almost unnoticeable in themselves. Yet unobtrusive as these inspirations are they haunt the memory of the reader ever after.

The faults and limitations of Steinbeck's style have to do with matters of taste. Here, indeed, he did sometimes falter. It must be pointed out, however, that certain charges of grossness brought against books like *Cannery Row* would suggest themselves only to readers of parochial sensibility. The candor of the light entertainments belong as surely to their themes as the bluntnesses of Rabelais, Sterne, and Swift belong to their satiric material. To have turned away in timidity from the obligatory scenes of grotesquerie would have amounted to artistic irresponsibility. Yet it is true that Steinbeck was capable of strewing a page or two with ribaldries that are conspicuously inappropriate to character and mood. *The Winter of Our Discontent* puts into the mouth of a cultivated man, Ethan, bits of verbal outrageousness that would have shocked the outspoken residents of Cannery Row.

The charge that Steinbeck's style is heavily laced with sentimentality should be examined closely on suspicion of bias. Some readers of *The Grapes of Wrath* brought it against him disingenuously, hoping to discredit his social attitudes by demeaning his way of expressing them. Disinterested analysts of his work were more perceptive even amid the near hysteria that greeted the book's appearance. Still, one must admit that he yielded to the temptation to be extravagant, at crucial moments, in presenting scenes of sentiment. Though he often used the word "gently" with ironic intent he used it far too often as he also overworked the even more lush "tenderly." And if sentimentality may be defined as the deliberate distortion of the probable in the interest of what is strikingly picturesque, then it is true that Steinbeck is sometimes sentimental, twisting his characters into dubious postures of nobility. The last scene of *The Grapes of Wrath* provides an example. In it a girl who has just lost her child at birth gives her breast, charged as it is with milk, to a man who has collapsed of starvation. Humanity, one understands, owes something to humanity which it must cross any gap to pay. But the symbolic act fails of its own excessive strain. It is patently a theatrical gesture used to bring down the curtain on an artificially composed tableau.

But, considering Steinbeck's temperament and the abundance of his imagination, it is remarkable that such excesses were few. His style contributed warm benefits of sympathy and spontaneity to each important book. Reappraising his work one is reminded that style is the man and that this was a remarkably whole and wholesome man.

A special dimension is evident in Steinbeck's work when it is compared with that of most of the writers of his time. He was not content to be merely an observer of mores and recorder of the movements of the moment. His books were all products of a speculative intelligence. The writing of fiction was for him a means of trying, for his own benefit and that of his readers, to identify the place of man in his world. His conception of that world included not merely the interests of economics and sociology but those of science and the realm of the spirit as well. Into the bloodstream of his work he released a steady flow of ideas to enrich its vigor.

An apprentice chemist in his youth and, in his middle years, part owner of a laboratory of marine biology, Steinbeck had always a semiprofessional interest in science. The scientific studies he engaged in, which were guided by a highly trained friend, Ed Ricketts, reinforced his belief in the oneness of all life—organic and inorganic, animal, vegetable, and aquatic. The book *Sea of Cortez*, written in collaboration with Ricketts, is in part a statement of that belief. It is also an account of a voyage up and down the Gulf of California to take specimens for a collection which, it was hoped, would constitute in itself a history of the marine life of the region.

What the investigators felt that they found in each tide pool they visited was "a world under a rock," a tiny microcosm of the universe. They comment: ". . . it is a strange thing that most of the feeling we call religious . . . is really the understanding and the attempt to say that man is . . . related inextricably to all reality, known and unknowable. This . . . profound feeling . . . made a Jesus, a St. Augustine, a St. Francis, a Roger Bacon, a Charles Darwin, and an Einstein. Each . . . reaffirmed . . . the knowledge that all things are one thing and that one thing is all things—plankton, a shimmering phosphorescence on the sea and the spinning planets and an expanding universe, all bound together by the elastic string of time."

Such passages have baffled some of Steinbeck's readers, leading them to the conclusion that his personal philosophy amounted to nothing but animalism, the denial that man has a spiritual nature. It is curious that his testimony should have been so misread. In his Nobel address he made two significant declarations: first, that he lived, as a writer, to "celebrate man's proven capacity for greatness of heart and spirit, courage, compassion and love"; second, that "a writer who does not believe in the perfectability of man" cannot claim to have a true vocation. These might be dismissed as the afterthoughts of an elderly convert, apologizing for the heresies of his youth, if Steinbeck had not anticipated such affirmations many years before in *Sea of Cortez*. There he made it clear that a sense of man's oneness with the universe should not drug the mind into passivity. Man is not merely the creature of an unknowable pattern of existence. He has made himself unique among animals by accepting responsibility for the good of others. Only he has this "drive outside of himself," that is, toward altruism. It is the "tragic miracle of consciousness" that has re-created him. "Potentially man is all things" and his impulses urge him often to be greedy and cruel. But he is also "capable of great love." His problem is to learn to accept his cosmic identity, by which Steinbeck means: to become aware of himself as an integral part of the whole design of existence. Tom Joad said it for him more succinctly in *The Grapes of Wrath*: "Well, maybe . . . a fella ain't got a soul of his own, but on'y a piece of a big one."

The theme of oneness is developed in *Sea of Cortez* with illustrations drawn from scientific observation. In an illuminating passage he describes the phenomenon of interdependence among aquatic creatures: "The schools swam, marshaled and patrolled. They turned as a unit and dived as a unit. . . . We cannot conceive of this intricacy until we are able to think of the school as an animal itself, reacting with all its cells to stimuli which perhaps might not influence one fish at all. And this larger animal, the school, seems to have a nature and drive and ends of its own . . . a school intelligence." His sense of unity stirred once more, Steinbeck pushes the speculation on: "And perhaps *this* unit of survival [the school of fishes] may key into the larger animal which is the life of all the sea, and this into the larger of the world." This is the same concept which animated

Steinbeck's imaginative re-creation in *The Red Pony* of the movement which he calls westering. As the old man who has been the "leader of the people" remembers: "It wasn't Indians that were important, nor adventures, nor even getting out here. It was a whole bunch of people made into one big crawling beast . . . Every man wanted something for himself, but the big beast that was all of them wanted only westering. . . . We carried life out here and set it down the way those ants carry eggs. . . . The westering was as big as God, and the slow steps that made the movement piled up and piled up until the continent was crossed." So, as he might have said, the movement of westering keyed into the life of the continent and that into the life of the world.

It was the readiness to search behind the facts of life for a philosophical resolution of their complexity that gave depth and a rich texture to Steinbeck's picture of the life of his time. He had the rare ability to blend speculation into his fiction, making it an integral part of a narrative plan. Only a few of his contemporaries attempted to establish so broad a rapport with the minds of readers. Of such writers Thomas Mann offers the century's most brilliant example. As Joseph Wood Krutch once pointed out, Steinbeck's name must be linked with that of his European counterpart in any discussion of the novelist as thinker. Mann explored his magic mountain and Steinbeck his shimmering sea of contemplation but in doing so neither sacrificed the authority of his voice as storyteller.

Alexander Cowie has suggested, thinking of Steinbeck: "Perhaps this is the final responsibility of the novelist: he must be true to his time and yet save himself for Time."

Steinbeck was certainly true to his time in his eagerness to be identified with scientific enterprise and his willingness to take the guiding principles of science as his own. He might be called a moral ecologist, obsessively concerned with man's spiritual struggle to adjust himself to his environment. It is significant that this storyteller, conscious of a mission, undertook to popularize theories about the salvation of man's total environment long before public attention focused on the discipline of ecology.

He also nourished within himself the attitudes toward social reform that were growing slowly in the national consciousness of his time. His protests, his rejections as well as his affirmative convictions about the hope for regeneration, were exactly those that have been taken up by leaders of opinion in a later day enabling them, as teachers, theorists, and legislators, to change our minds in the direction of greater sensibility concerning human rights. Always the artist, never a practicing reformer, Steinbeck dramatized situations in American life and espoused beliefs about the need of room for growth in a way that helped to awaken the conscience of his fellow Americans.

Steinbeck was in addition a kind of working Freudian in the broad sense that he used the novel to remind readers that the myths of the past contain the wisdom of the race, that they tell us more about ourselves than sources of factual information can convey. Many, perhaps most, of the novelists of the 1930's and 1940's were deeply imbued with the same idea. But Steinbeck, consciously and conscientiously exploring the suggestions of Freud (and of Frazer, whose work he may have known even better), covered a far broader field than did his fellow writers. His was an ambitious and inclusive effort to relate contemporary evidence about "the human condition" to that of the great witnesses of the past. His work suggests again and again that the story of humankind is a steadily continuing one, full of passions that seem as familiar in a setting of two thousand years ago as they do in our own time. It is a sense of the past made present that gives Steinbeck's best books their universality of tone. Old perils the like of which still surround us, old aspirations renewed as commitments by our restatement of them—these are the elements that contribute the essence of drama to his stories and give them distinction.

Steinbeck said that the one commandment of life is "to be and survive." His work may be said to fulfill that commandment.

Selected Bibliography

WORKS OF JOHN STEINBECK

NOVELS

Cup of Gold. New York: Covici-Friede, 1929.
To a God Unknown. London: Heinemann, 1932.
Tortilla Flat. New York: Covici-Friede, 1935.
In Dubious Battle. New York: Covici-Friede, 1936.
The Red Pony. New York: Covici-Friede, 1937.
The Grapes of Wrath. New York: Viking Press, 1939.
Of Mice and Men. New York: Viking Press, 1940.
The Moon Is Down. New York: Viking Press, 1942.
Cannery Row. New York: Viking Press, 1945.
The Wayward Bus. New York: Viking Press, 1947.
The Pearl. New York: Viking Press, 1947.
East of Eden. New York: Viking Press, 1952.
Sweet Thursday. New York: Viking Press, 1954.
The Short Reign of Pippin IV. New York: Viking Press, 1957.
The Winter of Our Discontent. New York: Viking Press, 1961.

COLLECTIONS OF SHORT STORIES

The Pastures of Heaven. New York: Covici-Friede, 1932.
The Long Valley. New York: Viking Press, 1938.
Acts of King Arthur and His Noble Knights. New York: Ballantine, 1986.

PLAYS

Of Mice and Men (dramatic version with George Kaufman). New York: Viking Press, 1940.
The Moon Is Down (dramatic version). New York: Viking Press, 1942.
Burning Bright. New York: Viking Press, 1950. (A play in story form.)

NONFICTION

The Forgotten Village. New York: Viking Press, 1941.
Bombs Away. New York: Viking Press, 1942.
A Russian Journal. New York: Viking Press, 1948.
Sea of Cortez (in collaboration with Edward F. Ricketts). New York: Viking Press, 1951.
The Log from the Sea of Cortez. New York: Viking Press, 1951.
Once There Was a War. New York: Viking Press, 1958.
Travels with Charley. New York: Viking Press, 1962.
America and Americans. New York: Viking Press, 1966.
Journal of a Novel, The East of Eden Letters. New York: Viking Press, 1969.
Working Days: The Journals of the Grapes of Wrath. New York: Penguin USA, 1989.

CRITICAL STUDIES

Allen, Walter. *Tradition and Dream.* London: John Dent and Son, Phoenix House, 1961.
Beach, Joseph Warren. *American Fiction, 1920–1940.* New York: Macmillan, 1941.
Cowie, Alexander. *The Rise of the American Novel.* New York: American Book, 1948.
French, Warren. *The Social Novel at the End of an Era.* Carbondale: Southern Illinois University Press, 1966.
Geismar, Maxwell. *Writers in Crisis.* Boston: Houghton Mifflin, 1942.

Hoffman, Frederick. *The Modern Novel in America.* Chicago: Regnery, 1951.

Kazin, Alfred. *On Native Grounds.* New York: Reynal and Hitchcock, 1942.

Lewis, R. W. B. *The Picaresque Saint.* Philadelphia: Lippincott, 1959.

Lisca, Peter. *The Wide World of John Steinbeck.* New Brunswick, N.J.: Rutgers University Press, 1958.

Tedlock, E. W., editor. *Steinbeck and His Critics.* Albuquerque: University of New Mexico Press, 1957.

Watt, Frank William. *John Steinbeck.* New York: Grove Press, 1962.

Wilson, Edmund. *The Boys in the Back Room: Notes on California Novelists.* San Francisco: Colt Press, 1941.

—JAMES GRAY

Wallace Stevens

1879-1955

WALLACE STEVENS was an insurance man. That he was also a poet seems odd; for nowadays around here poets and businessmen seldom agree. Their agreement in one person, in Hartford, Connecticut, is so strange that some, trying to account for it, have guessed it less agreement than uneasy split.

Whether an uneasy or an agreeable composite, Stevens commonly kept his sides apart and, in Hartford, kept one dark. At home, tending his roses in the evening, or in the morning walking to his office on Asylum Street, he jotted poems down—but never on company time. Poetry was none of his business, which, as he announced in *Who's Who*, was "insurance." Few of his associates suspected his eccentricity. When told of it, a fellow insurance man of Hartford exclaimed: "What! Wally a poet?" At the door of the Hartford Canoe Club Stevens cautioned a literate luncheon guest: "We don't talk about poetry here." Talking of poetry in their groves, the literate were inclined to ignore insurance or else to dismiss it with wonder. "In any case," Stevens seems, like the sailor of "Sailing after Lunch," to have been

> A most inappropriate man
> In a most unpropitious place.

For Stevens himself it was not a question of "direct and total opposites" in conflict but of their happy, changing relationship. "It gives a man character as a poet," he said, "to have daily contact with a job." His ideal was the "all-round" or "many-sided" man—Benjamin Franklin, for example, man of affairs, philosopher, composer of words, and compositor. "Money," said Stevens, "is a kind of poetry," and it is a fact that both money and poetry are made. The man who can afford to buy pictures, he added, is a better judge of pictures than the man who can only talk about them. The ruler of Stevens' Platonic republic would be the man who could build bridges between all incompatibles: between theory and money, art and life, "fact and miracle." Indeed, such bridges connect two present worlds, one of which he liked to call "reality," the other "imagination," though both were real enough to him. Their consequent "interaction," becoming his theme, determined both the manner of his poems and their method. Interaction is his word for his peculiar virtue and the virtue of his poetry.

Mann's Tonio Kröger embodies the union of bourgeois and artist that Joyce's aesthetic Stephen may also have achieved after meeting Mr. Bloom, an advertising man. Tonio and Stephen had to leave home to present their union with it. No man, however, was less of an exile than Stevens. Let Henry James and

T. S. Eliot run as they would to better shores, here Stevens took his stand or walked, here in Hartford, the heart of American reality, confronting it, a "poet striding among cigar stores." There was no evasion on Asylum Street; yet like any asylum his chosen place, absurd and disconcertingly real at once, was a place for fictions.

Many, noting his elegance, have thought his odd asylum a kind of ivory tower. If so, it was ivory tower in vacant lot. Stevens accepted this metaphor: "The romantic poet now-a-days," he said, ". . . happens to be one who still dwells in an ivory tower," but this tower has "an exceptional view of the public dump and the advertising signs of Snider's Catsup, Ivory Soap and Chevrolet Cars; he is the hermit who dwells with the sun and moon, but insists on taking a rotten newspaper." Among such hermits Stevens also counted Marianne Moore of Brooklyn and William Carlos Williams of Rutherford. For all three the ivory tower seems a less appropriate metaphor than "The Man on the Dump." There he sits on the garbage of the past, rejecting it yet intent upon "the the" or what is here and now, garbage and all. "The the" was always the central concern of Wallace Stevens whatever his elegant airs.

Whatever those finical French airs, he was very American, descended on one side from Whitman. It may be that the lilacs of "Last Looks at the Lilacs" are not such as once in dooryard bloomed; but

Lightly and lightly, O my land,
Move lightly through the air again,

the last lines of "Imago," are Whitman himself, and it is he who, at the beginning of "Like Decorations in a Nigger Cemetery," strides "shouting the things that are part of him," his beard a flame. "Ploughing on Sunday" is a joyous celebration of freedom and space that Whitman, living now, might have written. Not Presbyterian maybe, and certainly not British, this secular exuberance on Sunday is American; and so is the dance of those children in "Life Is Motion." The significant landscapes in which Stevens delighted are not unlike those that Whitman, barbarously blaring, once delighted in: Oklahoma, Tennessee, Jersey City, Pascagoula, Schuylkill, and Neversink. Even the statues with which we adorn public parks and plazas fascinated Stevens. "The American Sublime," on General Jackson's statue at the White House, may show sublimity coming down to "empty spirit and vacant space," but mockery and despair are attended by affection; for

> . . . the panorama of despair
> Cannot be the specialty
> Of this ecstatic air.

No poet since Whitman has loved America more, or more ambiguously. Even that finical elegance in which Stevens departs from his good, gray master is a product of our land— like furniture of the Gilded Age or the prose of Henry James. Maybe "slovenly wilderness" and "nigger cemetery" call for such decoration.

That Stevens was singer and decorator of America is plain. That he was romantic, too, is another question, one that teased him continually. He found no final answer. Certainly his concern with the imagination is that of Coleridge and Baudelaire. Adding strangeness to beauty occupied Walter Pater no more than it was to occupy Stevens, whose irony and insistence upon personality are equally romantic. Yet he was no transcendentalist nor was he devoted to fragments of the past. Aware of mixture (as T. S. Eliot, amorous of classicism, was also aware), Stevens was uneasy. On the one hand the romantic belonged on the dump with other garbage of the past: Mozart's music, Plato's paradigm, and Aristotle's skeleton. On the other hand, both vital and exploratory, the romantic pleased. Sometimes he, Marianne Moore, and William Carlos Williams seemed romantic; sometimes everything romantic seemed "vapidest fake." The labels do not matter. But it is plain that Stevens, singing "the present, its hoo-hoo-hoo," partly conforms to the tradition he sometimes rejected. This would not be worth mentioning had he not worried so much about it. Enough that he was an American poet, singing the here and now.

More than curiously named landscape and strangely decorated park, America was social and political scene as well, seen, however, by "the man that is rich and right"—and Republican. Stevens, caught in the depression, was aware of the novels of the poor, the inordinate demands of workers, the picket lines around the auto works, the swarming of Polacks in Jersey City, and, above all, the menace of communism, bad business for businessmen. Regarding these aspects of a "leaden time" without sympathy or hope, he devoted "Owl's Clover" (an unfortunate, long thing, wisely excluded from *The Collected Poems*) to his fears for order and art. "Logical lunatics" of a "grubby faith," those Russians, dictating to artists, keep Shostakovich down. *Pravda* (that "damned rag") and the mass of men constitute "the pressure of reality" that poets must resist or evade. Without social, moral, or political obligation, the true poet refuses to confuse the values of life and art. Far from committed, still less *engagé*, he is true to himself alone and to pure form.

Stevens was a Republican, a Taft Republican, who thought Eisenhower a dangerous radical. It may be that few poets have occupied this position. But there is something austere, something fine and private—indeed, something heroic about it. All the romance of lost causes finds its happiest concentration here.

This extraordinary Republican was born in Reading, Pennsylvania, in 1879. Surrounded by farms, Reading is full of factories. There is a gallery of pictures there and an orchestra; and in the middle distance is the peak of Neversink:

Unsnack your snood, madanna, for the stars
Are shining on all brows of Neversink.

As suits one born near Neversink, Stevens was a Pennsylvania Dutchman—not German Dutch, he insisted, but Holland Dutch. Though Zeller, his mother's name, is German, Stevens is a Dutch name. (His father was a lawyer, a poet, a Presbyterian, and a Democrat.) An impressive Pennsylvania Dutchman, Stevens was "tall and of a port in air." Undemonstrative and shy, he was, nevertheless, among congenial people, genial.

Leaving Harvard without a degree in 1900, he went to the New York Law School. He was admitted to the bar in 1904, and in 1916 joined the legal department of the Hartford Accident and Indemnity Company, of which, in 1934, he became vice president. One daughter blessed his marriage to Elsie Kachel of Reading. Stevens did not keep a Cadillac. Indeed, he had no car; and the estate he left (in 1955) was small, considering his probable salary. But, more than most, he was in love with living and all good things: wine, pictures, and roses. An agent in Paris sent him the pictures.

To remain in America is what one expects of an American poet; but it may seem strange that one who was also the poet of lions in Sweden never visited Europe. He did go to Key West and Jersey City, but probably not to Tennessee, Tallapoosa, or Oklahoma. Voyaging around his chamber was enough for this mental traveler, and his office an adequate asylum. "I was the world in which I walked," says Hoon in his Palaz, his beard dripping ointment; and "what I saw," he adds, "came not but from myself."

The earliest verses of Stevens-Hoon, set down before the titivation of that beard, appeared in the *Harvard Advocate* before 1900. Of them, he said years later, "They give me the creeps." In New York, practicing law, he went around with William Carlos Williams, Marianne Moore, Alfred Kreymborg, and Carl Van Vechten. At this time, under the spell of Ezra Pound, who was intent on haiku, Noh, and Chinese décor, the Imagist movement was in full career. Free verse, accurate words, bright analogies, and eagerness to astound the conventional occupied Stevens and his Imagist companions, who also dared experiment beyond Imagist limits. From 1914 Stevens contributed to Harriet Monroe's *Poetry* and from 1915 to Kreymborg's *Others*. The two more or less Chinese or Japanese poetic plays that Stevens attempted around this time are "wrong as a divagation to Peking." Both lack, as he implied later on, the "terrible genius" a poetic play must have before it is more than a "literary relic." But the New York verses (now in *Opus Posthumous*) display the themes and manners that were to distinguish *Harmonium*:

> All over Minnesota,
> Cerise sopranos . . .

Such verses, as he observed in one of them, are "fecund in rapt curios." Yet this curious poet marked, sometimes, "the virtue of the common-place."

However conservative in politics, Stevens was daring in poetics. However bourgeois, he was out to outrage the bourgeoisie. Many of his poems, like Mencken's essays, seem designed to dismay high-toned old Christian women. His gaiety rebuked their stuffiness; his youth, persisting into middle age, rebuked the middle age of those who never had been young.

Their suburb was full of white nightgowns. None was "purple with green rings."

Harmonium, a selection of these poems, appeared in 1923, when Stevens was forty-four. It attracted little notice; but *The Man with the Blue Guitar* (1937), *Transport to Summer* (1947), and other dazzling volumes established him as "virtuoso." He won prizes, among them the Bollingen and the Pulitzer; and universities bestowed honorary degrees. None of his books before *Collected Poems* (1954) enjoyed wide sale. But, as he said, he wrote for an "*élite*," by which he was judged one of America's finest poets—as he certainly is. To read his poems in the little reviews where they appeared made one, as he put it, "one of the gang." As for general readers: he was either too odd or too bare to read generally. Or too obscure: the secretary of the Ice Cream Manufacturers' Association, having come across "The Emperor of Ice-Cream," wrote to Stevens, asking if he was for ice cream or against it.

The Necessary Angel (1951) consists mostly of speeches on the nature of poetry delivered without inflection before academic audiences. Easier to read than to hear as he delivered them, these essays are dense, intricate, and unsystematic, filled with contradictions; and sometimes, disconcertingly, they are full of fun: "The accuracy of accurate letters," he begins, "is an accuracy with respect to the structure of reality." Surely he is speaking through the persona of the scholar and mocking him—mocking himself too and his audience. It is as if, addressing Weisheit, his rabbi, he said: "We'll give the weekend to wisdom." Passionately devoted to poetry, he was an amateur of ideas. Other essays or speeches appear in *Opus Posthumous* (1957). (Would not *Posthumum* or *Postumum* be more seemly?)

His poems are of two kinds: the one strange

and imagistic, the other lean and discursive. Both are odd and both persist from start to end of his career. There is little real development in theme or method. Analogy and interaction remain his principles.

From start to finish there are manners, each from a persona or mask, at once expressive and defensive. Sometimes the mask is that of the dandy, sometimes of the magnifico, sometimes of the rabbi. These masks are absurd, but so is he who speaks through them, so those who listen, and so the nature of things. Behind each mask is the poet-insurance man, obsessed by ideas that excited him, and what excited him produced his poems. These poems unite mask, man, and idea in forms that consist of rhythm, sound, tone—of words, in short —and their interaction. To single one element out is a mistake, and the commonest mistake to take Stevens as a philosopher. To do that is to get more and more of the same thing, and a pretty elementary thing. Not philosophies, his poems are poems; but it is easier to say what poems say than what they are.

His themes are limited. Despite an insistence on personality, Stevens is rarely personal. However lyrical, he seldom deals with love. Over and over again, excited by those few ideas, he deals with imagination and fact or subject, object, and the nature of reality. You can write poems about anything if you can.

What strikes one on looking into *Harmonium* is an air of florid elegance. Plainly, Stevens has his mask of dandy on. In the later volumes, instead of gallant artifice, fastidious gaudiness, and "quirks of imagery," we commonly find the elegance of severity. The "final elegance," he says, is "plainly to propound."

Stevens was a burgher, and burgher as dandy is a burgherly phenomenon. His "Weeping Burgher," lamenting "sorry verities," finds consolation in "excess" and in the "strange

malice" with which he distorts the world— distorts by imposing, composing, transfiguring, and decorating: "I come as belle design / Of foppish line." The Restoration fop, Regency Brummell, Aubrey Beardsley, Oscar Wilde in Piccadilly, and Whistler at 10 o'clock in Chelsea—all these were dandies and all decorators of something like a "nigger cemetery." Dandyism, a comment on the commonplace and the quotidian, reveals these by their opposites. Revealing time and place, reworking fact, dandies display "the unreal of what is real" and, conversely, the real of what is unreal.

Keeping things as they are in mind, the dandy of our time responds not only to bourgeois society but to the nature exposed by science. Unnatural decorations suit this black continuum. But dandyism is unsuitable, too, as the deportment of Fragonard, all right at Fontainebleau, would violate Asylum Street. At once inappropriate and appropriate, dandyism depends on the interaction of opposites.

Not only a mask, dandyism is a dress and a style. The poem is its style, says Stevens, the style is the poet, and a change of style is a change of subject. Adjusting ruffle and cravat in vacant lot or, better, on the dump, Stevens displays Stevens and dump and Stevens on dump. (*Chacun à son égout.*) Whatever his style, he was always a realist and never more than when most elegant.

He came by artifice naturally; but the postwar period brought it out. Despair drove young Edith Sitwell to erect a rococo façade. Ronald Firbank responded to the aftermath of war by the precious and the bizarre, and even young Aldous Huxley found the air of a decadent Roman congenial. All were terribly gay, as Dame Edith said, all were funny, all serious, and however decadent in appearance, all were full of life. Stevens was their American counterpart:

Natives of poverty, children of malheur,
The gaiety of language is our seigneur.

There is always a French air—something a little foreign—about English or American elegance.

Example: "Le Monocle de Mon Oncle," one of the most precious poems of *Harmonium*. This poem is a traditional dramatic monologue, but, falling untraditionally into twelve sections of eleven lines, it mimics the sonnet sequence it misses being. Lordly blank verse upholds tradition as irregular rhyme and half-rhyme violate it. Coherence depends on the manner and tone of a single speaker.

Unlike Prufrock, this French uncle has lived and is still alive. His monocle, elegant and aristocratic, keeps distance between himself and life and between himself and self, as with mocking eye he regards love, age, and loss. His monocle is mask and he enjoys wearing it. Yet, however jaunty his tone, his feelings are mixed. Debonair, he is a little sad.

He displays his complexity by odd juxtapositions: of feeling and tone, of manner and matter, of the extravagantly poetic with the blandly ironic. "Saltier well" and "basic slate" are of one verbal kind; "bravura," "clippered," and "Cupido" of another; and "damsel" of a third. As for matter: the hair of part III is of two kinds, elaborately arranged or naturally disordered. As classical Chinese and Japanese or the ladies of eighteenth-century Bath once studied hairy artifice, so from sleep a present or remembered girl comes disheveled. From a romantic "pool of pink" in part XI a frog booms "from his very belly odious chords."

Part XII, the triumph toward which the sequence moves and its justification, depends on the relationship of two birds and two rabbis, all four of distinct shades. Whether soaring aloft or fluttering down, pigeons are appropriate to sentiment, be they blue or white; but putting rabbis next to them is the unlikeliest thing in the world, particularly when the old rabbi is "rose." Uncle is both rabbis; but, when young, he should have been rose, not dark. When young, instead of observing, he should have pursued. Here, blue and white, dark and rose, passive and active are curiously mixed. Things mixed and missed and white fluttering things bring age and death to mind. But eleven meditations, at once moving and distant, have led to this.

From a concert of elements (tone, feeling, metaphor, diction), from agreements and disagreements among them, comes the effect: how it feels to be forty or, at least, how a dandy of forty feels. Maybe, however, the feeling and idea of elegance itself, exceeding such particulars, are the ultimate effect. We have looked at life through a monocle awhile.

The strangely assorted diction, a principal element, is accurate in the senses of careful and precise. "My dame," said Stevens, addressing his Muse, "sing for this person accurate songs." His words for such songs are "fastidious," "immaculate," and "scrupulous." However precious, inappropriate, and affected in appearance, such songs, he said, are of an "exquisite propriety." Their gaiety, too, is a value, and, as he said in "Adagia" (*Opus Posthumous*), "Gaiety in poetry" is "a characteristic of diction."

At a time when poets were commonly descending to common speech the speech of Stevens was uncommon, "besprent" with archaisms, foreign intrusions, neologisms, and insolent hoo-hoos. Rejecting the logical positivists, lamenting those who, prejudiced against perfection, demand plain English for all occasions, Stevens announced that poems may require a "hierophantic phrase." For the poet there is no common speech. Consisting of the right words in the right places, poems sometimes call for the "gibberish of the vulgate," sometimes for a "lingua franca et jocundissima." Whatever the words, Anglo-Saxon or Latin, they must be exact. " '*Je tâche,*' " he quotes Jules Renard, " '*en restant exact, d'être poète.*' "

"Not British in sensibility," says Stevens in "Adagia," Americans find the British tradition "inappropriate." Not so the French tradition. "Ach, Mutter," says the Pennsylvania Dutch girl in "Explanation":

> This old, black dress
> I have been embroidering
> French flowers on it.

French embroidery on a commonplace dress—there is the habit of young Stevens, on familiar terms with French poets from Baudelaire to Valéry and Laforgue.

Though Stevens explains one of Baudelaire's poems, he seems to have preferred the master's prose: his essays on dandyism, artifice, imagination, and painting. "Supreme fiction" comes from Baudelaire's "plus haute fiction." Plainly "Esthétique du Mal" owes something to Baudelaire. To Laforgue Stevens may owe the nonchalance and jauntiness that attend his complaints about the "malady of the quotidian." From Paul Jean Toulet, a gentleman of letters, come the elegant *maximes* and *pensées* of "Like Decorations in a Nigger Cemetery":

> Serve the rouged fruits in early snow.
> They resemble a page of Toulet
> Read in the ruins of a new society,
> Furtively, by candle and out of need.

These poets and others contributed something, often no more than airs and hints, but the most formidable debt was to the Verlaine of *Fêtes galantes.*

Verlaine's bizarre poems embody a dandy's nostalgia in a bourgeois time and place for the faded artifice of Watteau and Fragonard, "*élégants*" both, according to Stevens, who admired their paintings as much as he admired Verlaine's response to them. "Messieurs," says Verlaine, regard

> Le chevalier Atys, qui gratte
> Sa guitar, à Chloris l'ingrate.

The place is Versailles or Fontainebleau, the time "un soir équivoque d'automne." "Fardées," the ingénues trail "longues jupes" along the avenues of the park,

> Et la mandoline jase
> Parmi les frissons de brise.

These lines from "Mandoline" reappear in *The Necessary Angel.* However faded now, says Stevens in "Study of Images," the "terraces of mandolins" are "inextricably there." His cortège, his colloquy, his ingénue, his *fantoche,* and all his mandolines and guitars are Verlaine's. Even the Doctor of Geneva is Verlaine's "excellent docteur Bolonais" with variations. The ordinary women of Stevens' poem rise from the poverty of the quotidian, "from dry catarrhs, and to guitars" go visiting Verlaine's Versailles with its "lacquered loges," its "girandoles" and "civil fans." How explicit their coiffures there. That those women must return to the old catarrhs improves the elegance of their evening out. As death is the mother of beauty, so reality of elegance.

Young Verlaine was a Parnassian, but most of Stevens' Frenchmen were "Symbolists." Plainly in a French tradition, was Stevens in the Symbolist tradition? Attempts to answer this question raise others. Take "Lions in Sweden." These stone lions of Stockholm, allegorical images of bourgeois virtues (Fides, Justitia, Patientia), are suitable for savings banks. Absurd perhaps, yet somehow the soul hankers after such "sovereign images." If the fault of these lions is theirs, Stevens tells Swenson, "send them back / To Monsieur Dufy's Hamburg whence they came. / The vegetation still abounds with forms." This calls for explanation. Raoul Dufy illustrated Guillaume Apollinaire's *Le Bestiaire*. Hamburg, a supplier of zoological specimens, stands for bestiary here; and a bestiary is commonly allegorical. Yet Apollinaire, author of a bestiary, is in the Symbolist tradition, whatever that is; and vegetation abounding with forms suggests Baudelaire's "forest of symbols."

The essays are of little help. There Stevens sometimes prefers the image without meaning; yet he praises the significant images of Bunyan and La Fontaine. Sometimes he calls an emblem or a sign a symbol. By his prose you can prove anything you like. It is a fact that however much he loved analogy, he hated the Hermetic transcendentalism on which the Symbolists based their analogies. Of no more help, his poems abound in allegorical signs with definite meanings, in allegorical personifications, and in unassigned symbols. His recurrent blue and green, north and south, moon and sun are signs for imagination and fact, not symbols. Many of his creatures (woman, giant, and ephebe) are allegorical. Yet many, "not too exactly labelled," are symbols. And his poems as significant forms are as symbolic as any. Was he, then, a Symbolist or an allegorist? The question is unprofitable. Like any good poet he used the analogies he required and all the other means.

Less elegant than bizarre, "The Virgin Carrying a Lantern" is his closest approach to the Symbolist manner. This picture of bears, roses, Negress, and virgin finds parallel—not necessarily source—in Mallarmé's

Une negresse par le démon secouée
Veut goûter une enfant. . . .

An odd desire, but no odder than the situation here. Stevens praised the "clear enigmas" of Mallarmé. In Stevens' little scene the details, which have the clarity of dream, share dream's darkness despite that lantern. What are the virgin and her observer doing there? Why are there no bears among the roses? Like a metaphor of Stevens' magnifico, this situation "will not declare itself yet is certain as meaning." Evading analysis, "The Virgin Carrying a Lantern" is indefinitely suggestive. It is a picture —like something by Rousseau, *le douanier*. It is a strange experience, and its meaning, like that of a picture, is what it is. "A poem," says Stevens in "Adagia," "need not have a meaning and like most things in nature often does not have."

His most elegant poems are a little bizarre. This, too, is in the French tradition. "Le beau," said Baudelaire, "est toujours bizarre." The passion for clowns that Stevens shared with Laforgue, Verlaine, and Baudelaire adds an element of the grotesque, which, Stevens said, is part of things as they are.

"The Emperor of Ice-Cream" owes its effect to unions of the grotesque and the quotidian, seeming and being, compassion and fun. However grotesque, death and the wake are part of life. The image of ice cream concentrates these meanings. At once cold and agreeable, ordinary and festive, it is a symbol of life and death. Imperative mood and the finality of the final rhyme add as much to this strange composition as the commonplace details: last month's newspapers in the first stanza and, in the second, the dresser lacking three glass knobs, the horny feet.

Call the roller of big cigars,
The muscular one, and bid him whip
In kitchen cups concupiscent curds.
Let the wenches dawdle in such dress
As they are used to wear, and let the boys

Bring flowers in last month's newspapers.
Let be be finale of seem.
The only emperor is the emperor of ice-cream.

Emperor and ice cream, though not opposites, have the effect of opposites. The interaction of such elements, as we have noticed, is one of Stevens' constant means. Let "Analysis of a Theme" serve as example. The theme, stated in prose, is poetic and mad: "How happy I was the day I told the young Blandina of three-legged giraffes." The analysis, stated in verse, is prosaic and logical in spite of diction and metaphor at odds with the habit of prose. Juxtaposed, verse and prose, logic and madness, are reversed. The verse of the more or less prosaic analysis deals with grotesques from the unconscious. But this quiet verse suddenly explodes into Herr Gott, "ithy oonts, and long haired plomets." As Herr Gott to Blandina so ithy oonts to those giraffes.

Putting two elements together results in a third thing, their radiance. In "The Ordinary Women," as we have seen, the effect comes from the contrast of catarrh and guitar, linked by sound. In "Floral Decorations for Bananas" the effect is from the contrast of blunt bananas, at home in jungles "oozing cantankerous gum," and eighteenth-century bijouterie. In "Cortège for Rosenbloom" heavy rhythm and insistent repetition support ritual action. A cortège is elegantly French and active. Poor Rosenbloom is ordinary, Germanic, and passive. The "finical carriers" bear him to the sky, as if poets transfiguring the commonplace, making "the intense poem of the strictest prose of Rosenbloom." But other possibilities crowd the grotesque ceremony. In "The Plot against the Giant" this giant replaces Rosenbloom and three aesthetic girls replace his carriers. The third girl will undo him by French sounds, "heavenly labials in a world of gutterals," and by a "curious puffing."

Even the titles, conflicting with texts sometimes, are little dramas. "Hymn from a Watermelon Pavilion" combines three incompatibles. Phrases too, like seventeenth-century "conceits," make concords of discords, "icy Élysée," for example, or "beau caboose." *Beau* is French, *caboose* American. Last car on the freight train, a caboose suggests bums and the dry, summer loneliness of sidings. The two words are united, yet divided, by dissonance. In conjunction with caboose, elegance (as Mrs. Alfred Uruguay says) "must struggle like the rest."

Perhaps the most splendid example of harmony and contrast is "Peter Quince at the Clavier." This imitation of symphonic form has four movements, each related to the others by theme and motif, each different from the others in rhythm and key. The first movement, quiet and meditative, is a thought process, logical in frame, yet consisting of two analogies to be elaborated: that of music and that of Susanna and her red-eyed elders. Odd rhymes and "pizzicati," interrupting sobriety at the end, promise another development. The second movement, an andante, reveals Susanna bathing in green water. A dramatic intrusion of cymbal and horn introduces the third movement, a scherzo. Elegant couplets and absurd rhymes suit tambourines and "simpering Byzantines." The last movement, returning to the meditative mode of the first, renders "on the clear viol of her memory" the composer's ruminations about body, death, and beauty. His composition is at once musical, logical, and brightly imagistic. Rhythm, curious diction and rhyme, the interaction of contrasting movements, and, above all, those two elaborated analogies produce the strange radiance.

Suggestive of music, maybe, the poem is not music. An approximation in shape and rhythm, it is as close to music as one whose genius was pictorial and meditative could get.

In spite of title and many aural felicities, *Harmonium* appeals less to ear than to eye. Stevens, who thought himself "*chef d'orchestre*," lacked the high musical abilities of Milton or T. S. Eliot. Music for Stevens was another analogy; and a harmonium, after all, is a little organ.

"Peter Quince" is an elegant picture, but the triumph of elegance in *Harmonium* is "Sea Surface Full of Clouds," another picture, which, like most of Stevens' *elegantiae*, is as suave as *Fêtes galantes* and as malign. The ostensible theme is his constant obsession: the relations between inner and outer, observer and object. His object here is clouds in the sky and their reflections in the water. Of their relationship the inconstant observer, confronting inconstant object, makes five things; for he finds five ways of looking at the thing. These are the parts of his poem, each different in feeling from the others, but each like the others in tone and structure.

Parallel structure, persisting through changes of inner and outer climate, is an important element. Each part begins with the "slopping" of the sea. In the second triplet of each part is a caesura separating the recurrent but changing analogy of chocolate and umbrella from the changing appearance of the sea. The third and fourth triplets pose a question. The fourth answers it in elegant French that varies according to its circumstances. In the quiet remainder of each part the tensions of "the tense machine" are relaxed. The poem begins and ends with a concert of opposites. At the beginning Stevens puts November next to tropical Tehuantepec. At the end the opposites of sea and sky, now transfigured, are one; and subject, at last, is one with object. Green and blue, his customary tags for nature and imagination, carry the sense, but other colors (yellow, mallow, and clownish motley) seem more important.

The telling elements of the form are chocolate and umbrella, the French refrain, the tone, and the insistent structure. Affected by these, the ostensible theme, becoming an element with the rest, yields to the real theme: a vision of suave civility or what it feels like to be civilized. The effect is like that of dinner at Le Pavillon with a bottle of Montrachet.

His poem "Montrachet-le-Jardin," which seems to have nothing to do with this great wine, has to do with its opposite. The bottle is empty. Good-bye, says Stevens, to the "bastard chateaux and smoky demoiselles" in which he once delighted. Now let facts fall "through nakedness to nakedness." Ascetic poems on emptiness, interacting with their bizarre companions, occur even in *Harmonium*, where one kind sets the other off. The bizarre, creating feelings in which ideas play a part, are florid; the ascetic, devoted to expressing ideas in which feelings play a part, are bare. In the later volumes austere poems outnumber the florid. "No turban walks across the lessened floors. . . . A fantastic effort has failed." If nabob at all, now, Stevens is "nabob of bones." Yet, however much the two kinds differ—the one concrete, the other more or less abstract, the one imagistic, the other more or less discursive—there is less difference than there seems. Each kind offers immediate experience, and each is elegant. The first has the elegance of abundance, the second the elegance of severity.

Of this second kind "The Snow Man" is the earliest expression. Unadorned, the poem sweeps in one sentence to a shocking finality. There are symphonic effects and descriptions, but no metaphor intervenes until the end, where the snow man, there by aid of the title, embodies the "mind of winter" and the reality on which this mind casts a cold eye. Not only this snow man but the entire poem is an analogy for these. "Nothing that is not there and the nothing that is" concentrates the austerities that have led to it. This concentration, at once felicitous and terrible, proves the capacity of naked discourse. Winter words for wintry matter, as elegant as any decoration, involve our feelings as directly as image can, and, like epigram or wit itself, involve our minds. And, as Stevens says, naked discourse can imply the images it lacks.

The nothingness embodied and revealed by this poem is not the same as the poverty of those ordinary women, who, though like John Donne's "ordinary nothings" in one sense, have catarrhs; and catarrhs are something. Like Eliot's "female smells," catarrhs, however unseemly, are not extraordinary. The nothingness the snow man sees makes ordinariness and customary elegance alike irrelevant. Under lacquered loge and girandole is a dark cellar, over them an empty attic, and poverty to right and left. The nothingness Stevens looks at in "The Snow Man" is that of mathematical abstraction, the universe of twentieth-century science, emptier and even more discouraging than Hardy's nineteenth-century universe. The nothingness Stevens looks at is emptier than the darkness and deprivation of sitting Eliot, at the end of whose negative way is a chorus of martyrs and virgins.

The realist must choose not only things as they are but things as they are not, "the dominant blank" that underlies "device." The bare poem is a steady look at "the the," such as it is and is not. But such looking has its pleasures, too. A bare things has its proper beauty. Autumn and winter with black branches in bleak light, all dapple gone, and, below these, even below the snow, the rock—such images, abounding in the later poems, are good, but plain statement is better: "Bare earth is best. Bare, bare."

Virtues of bareness are integrity, shape, and radiance. Autumn has its auroras and those of

winter are flashier. As for nothingness, not only our fate, it is our climate. We are natives there. Its virtues are challenge and space for the constructions it invites. As the poem "makes meanings of the rock" so that "its barrenness becomes a thousand things," so genius, entering the emptiest nothing, will inform it and build towers. The poet's job is to create shapes in nothingness and of it. Elegance, no longer evasive, is the property of structures raised in the void with full awareness of their place. Such elegance is severe, but even the lacquered loge and the girandole are fictions, or things made, good as such and reminders of their surroundings.

Creation from nothing is God's power and the poet's—and that of any man. Hence aesthetics or the study of shapes and their making is the proper study. Writing poems about poems, Stevens was writing about mankind. This brings us to the jar in Tennessee, a strange bare thing in the middle of nowhere. "Anecdote of the Jar" is an anecdote of a jar, a shape made by man and placed by him in a "slovenly wilderness." The theme is interaction: the effect of the round jar on its surroundings and of them on it. This artifact composes nature, but not entirely; for the slovenly place still sprawls. Wilderness of bird and bush makes jar stand out, gray and bare, "like nothing else in Tennessee." Jar and wilderness, art and nature, need each other. But, however serious this theme, the story of the jar is absurd.

The structure of this poem on structure is exemplary. Unrhymed couplets lead up to two end-stopped lines, set off by rhyme. This premature finality lends an air of unfinality to the end, another unrhymed couplet, which, however, by returning to "Tennessee" joins end to beginning, rounding things out. Internal rhymes and repetition, assuring coherence, emphasize the interacting contraries. "Round" and "ground," pointing central meanings out by sound, are confirmed by "around" and "sur-round." The climactic end-rhymes, "every-where" and "bare," restate the conflict. "It made . . . to it," a chiasmus, provides a rhetorical shadow of interaction. The shape is tight and bare, the diction lean; but questions arise. Why Tennessee? Is the jar empty or full? The raising of questions is a virtue of shape.

Stevens wrote three long poems on aesthetics and several short ones, all longer, however, than his "Anecdote," the first great statement of the theme. Of the long poems "The Come-dian as the Letter C" is the earliest and the least successful. Yet, fascinating as document, it is a comprehensive display of the things that teased him.

Crispin, the hero of "The Comedian," is a philosopher, poet, and clown—or so he is labeled—and, as his name implies, he is also valet and saint. Overtly, the poem is about his journey from Bordeaux to Carolina. Less like that of Candide than of Bunyan's Christian, this voyage is an allegorical "pilgrimage." Places and people are insistently significant. At journey's end, for example, Crispin, an abstrac-tion, cultivates a garden and raises four al-legorical daughters. Like any allegory, this "anecdote" is a "disguised pronunciamento . . . invented for its pith"—"not doctrinal in form but in design." The end of Bunyan's Christian is a place in heaven. By no means trans-cendental, that of Stevens' Crispin is a place on earth. His quest is for an "aesthetic." Chris-tian's pilgrimage is up moral hills and down moral valleys. Crispin's is an "up and down between two elements," imagination and fact or intelligence and soil, until he finds their point of balance. The poles between which he oscillates bear allegorical tags: moon and sun, north and south, blue and green. Their con-flict and synthesis are dialectical. Controlling theme, Stevens' principle of interaction con-trols manner and method, too.

His style, the outstanding element, is rococo fustian, an elaborate clowning at odds with the serious matter. Not Crispin but his author is the clown, whose "portentous accents" are also at odds with the bareness that sometimes in-trudes. Ambiguity vies with fustian to conceal the doctrine the poem seems designed to offer. "The words of things entangle and confuse," and so do things of words.

Nobody knows exactly what the title means. Is that "Comedian" the narrator or Crispin or both? And what of "the Letter C"? Does it imply denudation, abstraction, or simple ab-breviation? Is it a small letter, as "miniscule" implies, or a capital? The third letter, does it suggest third class, like an academic grade, or does it refer to the third stage of a develop-ment? The last line, "So may the relation of each man be clipped," is no less ambiguous. In context, "relation" may mean story or relative, a daughter in this case. "Clipped" may mean cut short, as by the third fatal sister or by an offhand author, clipped out, as from a news-paper, or clipped as hair is. Crispin has "a barber's eye," his daughters have curls, and hair has figured throughout, as importantly as those coiffures of "Le Monocle." As for tone: the last line may be deflationary or triumphant. In one sense it dismisses the matter as no mat-ter; in another it affirms the synthesis it in-cludes. On the one hand, a daughter represents nature, her hairdo, artifice. On the other hand —but, as the narrator jauntily says, "So much for that."

In the first part of the poem there is reason for the precious style. "Silentious porpoises," whose mustachios seem "inscrutable hair in an inscrutable world," will do as reflections in a barber's eye; and, what is more to the point, they represent a "civil" European's attempt at evading the sea, the "quintessential fact" that doctors of Geneva and connoisseurs of jupes and salad-beds must face at last. Triton, an evasion from the past, is dead; but rococo elegance may still do as reality's opposite, working as well in the "green barbarism" of Yucatan, the sea's exotic equivalent.

This will do, but inkhorn inflation, though abating after arrival in middling Carolina, still persists. "Pampean dits" for songs of the Pampas are a little too much for there and then, as are "palankeens" for baby carriages. Such residues of former elegance may be what realists must struggle against. Out of them, anyway, a realist's plainness begins to emerge. Example: "For realists, what is is what should be." The docks of Carolina and the "quotidian" welcome such "sinewy nakedness." Yet, even at the beginning of the journey "Nota" and "Sed quaeritur," absurd apart from the medieval manuscripts where they belong, surround "man is the intelligence of his soil," a prosaic proposition.

Failing to follow the transformation of Crispin from traditional European to bare American, the style remains more "poetic" than prosaic. Though he achieves a kind of "harmony" or "liaison," the style does not. "Trinket pasticcio" exceeds "veracious page on page, exact," and "the florist asking aid from cabbages" asks in vain. In a context between the elegance of abundance and the elegance of severity, abundance wins. This, after all, is early Stevens. But maybe—and we are left with buts and maybes—pomposity is the narrator's comment on himself. Far from representing imagination in conflict with sense, the style represents fancy alone.

The story of Crispin is a portrait of the artist—as a young man. As we ask if Stephen is Joyce, so we ask if Crispin is Stevens. Naturally there are resemblances between author and hero in each case; but in each the hero, distanced by irony, is also a figure of fun. Like Stephen, Stevens' unheroic hero evolves an aesthetic. Mann's Tonio Kröger, whose aesthet-

ic adjustment involves the contraries of north and south, blond and dark, offers an even closer parallel. But Stevens chose to write his novel in blank verse. Not prose, not quite poetry, this work of fancy and reason misses being the thing of words a poem must be. Perhaps the poet's "appointed power," like Crispin's own, was "unwielded through disdain." Unlike Crispin, perhaps, the poet preferred gloss to text.

"Illuminating, from a fancy gorged by apparition, plain and common things" was not enough for Stevens, older now. In "The Man with the Blue Guitar," his second long poem on aesthetics, he reviews the themes of the first, but with more assurance and greater success. A product of what we call the creative imagination, "The Blue Guitar" is poetry, we say. This composition is a suite of thirty-three short parts in four-beat couplets, sometimes rhymed, commonly unrhymed. These parts are variations on a theme.

Bright, clear images strike one first, and after this an air of tidiness and the gaiety that Stevens prized. The last of these effects comes from imagery in part, an imagery both familiar and strange, and in part from quick rhythms, neat structure, and a diction that successfully combines exactness with ambiguity. Order plays a part and so does drama. Each of the parts is a little drama with its conflict, climax, and appeasement, a drama not only of ideas but of structure, rhythm, and tone. In the conflict between clarity and obscurity that serves as underplot, clarity, after many trials, triumphs, for the play is a comedy. Among the personae, subtly masked, are a marionette and a clown. Though sedentary, the man with the guitar is more of an actor than either.

The first part seems a debate between player and audience. Their preferences, plainly stated, state the theme of the suite: actuality and imaginative transformation. The rhyme of "are" with "guitar" concentrates both the agreement and the disagreement of these contenders, both of whom are right. Their contest reveals two aspects of art, one from the player's point of view, the other from the listeners'. But, as subsequent poems show, this debate is internal. The speaker's head is the stage. Structure, also embodying the drama, suits the sense it reinforces. The first couplet, broken and unrhymed, sets the scene. "The day was green" is at once strange and natural. Day's green, moreover, contends with blue instrument. Then two rhymed, end-stopped couplets stage the conflict. "Guitar" and "are" in the first become "are" and "guitar" in the second, a significant reversal. These stopped and interlinked couplets are the climax. Following this come four run-on lines, the first two unrhymed, creating a momentary suspense. The second two, echoing "guitar" and "are," are for the moment final.

The last part brings all conflicts to an end— as usual, in Stevens, by an agreement of opposites; for he had looked into Hegel. Here, Sunday over, we put up with "Monday's dirty light." Both Sunday and Monday know bread and stone. The bread of Sunday is the daily bread of the Lord's Prayer; that of Monday is daily bread. The stone, Peter's rock on Sunday, is bedrock on Monday or the world itself. The "wrangling of two dreams" that has occupied us through the suite is brought to an end not only by bread and stone, composite opposites, but by the final phrase, "The imagined pine, the imagined jay," played now and again on the guitar. Pine is green, jay blue. Both are actual, both imagined, and both, being projections of our minds, are dreams. Rhyme, the only one in this part, makes the union certain. But "That's it" in the second couplet proves this end a sudden illumination, passing rather than final. We have shared a process of thought with its excitement and immediacy.

Of parts between last and first, most are good. Take xxv, in which the artist as juggling clown twirls a world on his nose. In the second part, as shearsman or tailor, unable to perfect his world, he has faced Mallarmé's penultimate. Now he brings something round or, shouting in his robes and symbols, thinks he does. Meanwhile liquid cats and graying grass remind us of Bergson's flux—if not that of Heraclitus. Nose and world, this juggler implies, beating time with fat thumb, are out of time and change, eternal. He is bizarre; his actions are gay and a little saddening. We know as well as he that his control of things is a moment's illusion, as unstable as liquid cats. The world he twirls "this-a-way" (or even that) is his, but he is in another.

In xxx the player evolves an "old fantoche," Verlaine's marionette as well as something more. This thing, responding to the strings of "Oxidia, banal suburb," could be the audience or Stevens in Hartford. Oxidia owes its name to *accidia*, medieval torpor, and to modern oxide or the soots and crusts of "stacks above machines." Here, surveying a "cross-piece on a pole," this *fantoche* sees three things at once: an actual telephone pole, the crossed stick that regulates marionettes, and Christ on cross, the last confirmed by "Ecce." By triple vision Oxidia, emerging from itself, seems not only soot but seed.

Other parts of the suite concern the artist's relation to art and its relation to society. The tenth poem, about art and politics, is suitably imperative in mood. A dictator is coming, his party indicated by the redness of columns and by consignment of bourgeois documents to the dump. Should the guitar celebrate such redness or assert blue individuality against it? Though the answer is clear enough, ambiguities of syntax leave details uncertain. Who is "hooing the slick trombones," dictator or adversary? In xii "Tom-tom, c'est moi." No more than opening gambit, this proposition confuses the issue. A tom-tom, though primitive, is a musical instrument, hence artificial. Being French, "c'est moi" is civilized, but, being the self, "moi" is natural. Part XXIII ironically proposes "a few final solutions." But the duet between an undertaker and a voice in the clouds settles nothing although, seeming to unite the above and the below, their song involves "Dichtung und Wahrheit." If art, the speaker asks in XV, is a " 'hoard of destructions,' " as Picasso says, does it depict or destroy society and self? The mood is interrogative. Nota: Stevens said he did not have Picasso's picture of the guitarist in mind. This picture (at the Chicago Art Institute) is generally blue, but the guitar is brown.

Interrogative or imperative, the parts of this suite solve none of the problems they raise. Poems, not dissertations, they question the nature of things. They feel things out. The ideas that excited Stevens may detain the reader. But, as Stevens reminds him in XXII, "Poetry is the subject of the poem." The "thinking of art" in VI is not thinking about art but art's radiant activity, for which the metaphor of thought is fitting. Radiantly embodying encounters, these poems make them "for a moment final." Structures, feelings, tones, ideas, and textures work together to this end. What poems say, we say, is but a part of what they are.

Excited again by these ideas, Stevens rearranged them in "Notes toward a Supreme Fiction." Again it is their arrangement that counts. The last poem of *The Collected Poems* is named "Not Ideas about the Thing but the Thing Itself." Of "Notes toward a Supreme Fiction," as of "The Man with the Blue Guitar," we could say, not ideas in the thing but the thing itself.

The title is important. "Notes toward," suggesting the penultimate again, is tentative. Toward a theory of a "Fiction" or toward in the sense of attempting the thing itself? To answer this question we must consider the meaning of fiction. "Poetry is the supreme fiction, madame," Stevens had told the high-toned old Christian woman of *Harmonium*, who would have found Baudelaire's religion as the highest fiction more to her taste, but only a little more. She would have thought a fiction something false or feigned, as, in one sense, it is. But the first meaning of fiction, as we know from its origin in Latin *fingere*, is something shaped, formed, or imagined. To Stevens a fiction meant a work of art, what Clive Bell called "significant form" or Ernst Cassirer "symbolic form." Through such forms we encounter reality and present it. Such forms or "fictive things," both radiant and disturbing, "wink most when widows wince." Aware of widows and his limitations, Stevens modestly proposes a preliminary draft of the great poem he will never write. Yet he thought this approximation his masterpiece.

The matter he chose to shape into a work of art is the work of art—or it seems so on first reading. Choice of subject reveals the poet's personality, said Stevens, and what is poetry but a transaction between a person and something else? The poet writes about what he must. The subject Stevens had to choose for his "Notes" is not so remote from our general interests as it seems. If the work of art is an arrangement of reality, he is writing about ways of accosting reality. The ostensible subject, however, is not the real one. Not the formulation of an aesthetic but the experience of trying to formulate it is the subject here: how it feels to think things out. "Not to impose," he says, but "to discover." When he wanted to announce his aesthetic he wrote an essay or made a speech. This poem is an essay only in the sense of being an attempt to fix the feeling and quality of an experience. Less rational than it seems, this poem is not philosophy; for nothing here approaches systematic thought. Rather, it is a meditation and a drama of thought in progress with all its hesitations, failures, and triumphs.

The dramatic meditation is divided into three parts of ten poems each. Each of these constituent poems consists of seven tercets or triplets. The development, like that of "The Comedian," is dialectical. This process, borrowed from philosophy, provides firm structure and adds philosophical flavor. Moreover, a structure of process suits a poem of process. This poem proceeds on two levels: that of idea and that of method and manner. The thesis, dealing with abstraction, is suitably bare—for the most part. The antithesis, dealing with time and change, is suitably concrete. The third part attempts a synthesis of these ideas, methods, and manners.

Dialectical opposition and union appealed to a poet whose working principle was interaction. Providing general structure, interaction controls the parts. Stevens gets his particular effects by surprising conjunctions of discourse and image, of the bare and the bizarre. The discursive austerity that claims our notice first in the first part proves to be an element working with its opposite. Discourse as neighbor of absurd concretion serves a nondiscursive end. Note the fruitful juxtaposition of the plainly discursive with the outrageously odd in the third poem of the first part. Into the soberly established climate of thought, an Arabian suddenly intrudes "with his damned hoobla-hoobla-hoobla-how." Such violent contrasts, useful for drama and fun, are there to create a third thing by cooperation, and what they create we feel. In the poem of "hoobla-how" there is a subsidiary interaction of serious matter with frivolous manner. "Two things of opposite natures seem to depend/On one another, as a man depends on a woman," Stevens says in the fourth poem of the second part. Marriage, in the third part, becomes his symbol of this interdependence.

Crispin, coming to terms with the soil, comes to see the virtues of a prose that "should wear a poem's guise at last." In the later poems, poetry often seems to wear the guise of prose. Increasingly fascinated by the bareness of reality, Stevens found bare prose a fitting instrument, Crispin's "fecund minimum." In "Notes," however, the poet of ice cream and the poet of barren rock are one. The two faces of elegance put on a single mask, that of the aesthetician in his chair, a mask less tragic than comic. "To have nothing to say and to say it in a tragic manner," says Stevens in "Adagia," "is not the same thing as to have something to say," or, he might have added, to say it with a sense of its absurdity.

An air of the prosaic, like the flavor of philosophy, was useful for this meditation, the commonest device of which is the proposition. Each of the three parts has a proposition for title; many of the constituent poems begin with a proposition; and most include one. Not a statement, a proposition is a gambit, something to be accepted or denied. Either true or false, it allows choice while embodying the interaction of possibilities. Whitehead, the philosopher of process, found propositions the cousins of symbols and like them in effect upon our feelings. Stevens in his "Notes" is the poet of process and proposition. "Life," he says in "Men Made Out of Words" (his poem on "castratos of moon-mash"), "consists of propositions about life." "It Must Be Abstract," a proposition, begins the process here. Beginning a poem with a metaphor, John Donne proceeds to elaborate it by logic. Beginning a poem with a proposition, Stevens proceeds to elaborate it by metaphor. Their procedures are not dissimilar.

In the first part of "Notes" Stevens tells his "ephebe" about the abstract and general elements of poetry. The "first idea" is no longer transcendental: "Phoebus is dead, ephebe." Even harder to define, the notion of "major man" (from Hobbes?) calls for particulars:

The MacCullough must become MacCullough to be conceived. Both abstract and general ideas are fictions, imagined things. This conclusion is intuitive, for "truth depends on a walk around a lake." In structure the tenth poem is typical. Beginning, as if Cassirer, with a proposition ("The major abstraction is the idea of man . . ."), Stevens proceeds by qualification and description. The question that follows (and questions are forms as significant as propositions) is strange and, after so pedestrian an approach, surprising. An intruding rabbi sees all men in a bum with baggy pants, "Looking for what was, where it used to be." That this shining line, a triumph of economy, is the climax of the process and its final elegance is indicated by the concluding proposition.

What rabbi, grown furious with human wish,
What chieftain, walking by himself, crying
Most miserable, most victorious,

Does not see these separate figures one by one,
And yet see only one, in his old coat,
His slouching pantaloons, beyond the town,

Looking for what was, where it used to be?
Cloudless the morning. It is he. The man
In that old coat, those sagging pantaloons,

It is of him, ephebe, to make, to confect
The final elegance, not to console
Nor sanctify, but plainly to propound.

The particulars of part II, contending with the abstractions of part I, are fittingly concrete to illustrate the other element of poetry. Strange scenes and curious stories, such as Nanzia Nunzio's, prove metaphor the agent of imaginative "transformation."

For "It Must Give Pleasure," the proposition that announces the third part, Stevens has the authority of Aristotle and Horace. What pleases seems the fecund marriage of abstraction and metaphor in a fiction. That the marriage of the maiden Bawda (reality) to her great captain (the artist) occurs in Catawba is more than verbally pleasing; for Catawba is in Carolina, where Crispin found harmony of intelligence and soil. The no less allegorical "fat girl" of the final poem ("a more than natural figure") is not only the earth-mother ("my green, my fluent mundo") but a great composite, uniting earth and art. She also serves as Muse, the "dame" invoked in part I as directress of "accurate song."

Stevens had addressed his Muse reverently in "To the One of Fictive Music," a poem of *Harmonium*. The fat girl, more convincing and attractive than this predecessor, claims a place beside the "Sister of the Minotaur," his Muse in *The Necessary Angel*. Not altogether reverent, his attitude toward her here is as enigmatic as she is ambiguous. Is the Minotaur's sister a half-sister, Ariadne, let us say— a real woman in a myth? Or is she an unknown sister, half-woman and half-cow? In either case, for a poet of interacting opposites that is a good Muse. But back to the fat girl: she is also a "crystal," a transparent shape and product of a process. Not only the Muse, she embodies the fiction.

"Notes toward a Supreme Fiction" is a poem on the poem. Many poets have written poems on this—Yeats and Dylan Thomas among them; for creation, whether of world or poem, fascinates creators. Stevens devoted poem after poem to the poem and its parts: "Imago," "The Motive for Metaphor," "A Primitive like an Orb," and more. But little here that was not said in "Notes," and little here so shapely.

"Notes toward a Supreme Fiction" is a shape concerning shape or order. Never through with ideas of order, Stevens also devoted "Connoisseur of Chaos" to them. "The Idea of Order at Key West" introduces Ramon Fernandez. Though Stevens claimed he picked this name out of a hat, the context makes Fernandez seem the neoclassicist, whose "rage for order" was as notable as that of Henri Focillon, author of *The Life of Forms*, one of Stevens' favorites.

Painting was his other art. Convinced that painting and poetry are alike, that what is said of one applies to the other, Stevens devoted poems to the sister art. Some are imitations of painting, some commentaries on it, and some are both. "The Apostrophe to Vincentine," who is "figured" nude between monotonous earth and sky, may be composed of the sounds and senses of words; yet it is an early Matisse, as *fauve* as the work of the master. "The Bouquet" is at once a still life, a commentary on it, and a comment on the commentary. For "meta-men" this object in a jar becomes a "para-thing" or symbol, "the real made acute by an unreal." That both elements are impermanent is proved by a soldier dumping their arrangement on the floor.

"So-and-So Reclining on Her Couch" is a transaction between a painter and his model or, at least, between her and his idea of what he is doing. There she is on that couch, "reclining on her elbow." He calls this pleasing sight "Projection A"; for he holds with Kant the idea that we project what we see. So projected, she is an anonymous thing of curves, a "motionless gesture." But the mind connects her with other things that complicate Projection A with Projections B and C:

If just above her head there hung,
Suspended in air, the slightest crown
Of Gothic prong and practick bright,

The suspension, as in solid space,
The suspending hand withdrawn, would be
An invisible gesture. Let this be called

Projection B. To get at the thing
Without gestures is to get at it as
Idea. She floats in the contention, the flux

Between the thing as idea and
The idea as thing. She is half who made her.
This is the final Projection, C.

The arrangement contains the desire of
The artist. But one confides in what has no
Concealed creator. One walks easily

The unpainted shore, accepts the world
As anything but sculpture. Good-bye
Mrs. Pappadopoulos, and thanks.

Anonymous no more, the thing in itself, evading all projections, emerges, shockingly.

Speaking to his "ephebe," Stevens exchanges the mask of aesthetician for that of teacher. Going further in some poems, he puts the mask of lecturer on to deliver "academic discourse" in Havana or elsewhere. Of the "Three Academic Pieces" in *The Necessary Angel* one is in prose, two are in verse, and all were delivered from a lectern. The verse develops from the prose. Each piece concerns "resemblance," his current word for metaphor, central to reality and poetry alike.

The difference between his most poetic prose and his driest poetry emerges from a comparison of these parallel specimens. The prose is more or less sober and straightforward. The poetry, both dense and intense, has a "particular tingle" and a few "whirroos and scintillant sizzlings such as children like" to vex "the serious folds of majesty." Far more metaphorical than the prose, the poetry is brighter, odder, gayer, and, as he says in "Man Carrying Thing," "it resists the intelligence almost successfully." This resistance, occupying our minds, allows the rhythms, images, oddities, and the sounds of words to work upon our feelings. Discourse, transfigured, becomes "bright excellence."

"Someone Puts a Pineapple Together," the second of these three academic pieces, is in verse. "O juventes, O filii," the lecturer begins. Still the aesthetician, he proceeds to examine the object before him, a pineapple on the table, another still life. There it is, and here is what we make of it. Once a pineapple was enough without a scholar's "enlargings and pale arrondissements." Now it invites "false metaphor." (The lecturer lists twelve resemblances or exfoliations, duly numbered.) "How thick this gobbet is with overlays . . . the sum of its complications, seen/And unseen." That his depreciation of metaphor is highly metaphorical is no more than academic humor demands. This excellent lecture, which is also one of Stevens' most joyous poems, was delivered at Harvard. With the same mask on, Stevens also addresses the Academy of Fine Ideas. "Messieurs . . ." he begins. What follows is what he calls "the intense poem of the strictest prose."

The mask of lecturer off, Stevens put on the mask of rabbi, a man who, whether dark or rose, is a philosopher; but a Hartford poet as rabbi is bizarre. Stevens put his mask on when, more than aesthetician, he confronted a wider reality; and above the mask he wore a hat. A philosopher's hat is square, as "aquiline pedants find," and part of the mind. The Doctor of Geneva wears a stovepipe hat, and the Pastor Caballero, a sombrero with sweeping brim, an image of a mind with bravura. Marianne Moore's "very big hat" in "The Prejudice against the Past" is that of a fastidious poet, whose poems are not to be confused with articles in *The Encyclopaedia Britannica.* Whether masked as philosopher or as hidalgo with guitar, Stevens had a hat on. The one he wore for "An Ordinary Evening in New Haven" was that of the rabbi from Hartford.

In this poem of thirty-one parts of six tercets each, New Haven serves as occasion and object. It is an autumn night there. Wind blows leaves and old newspapers about. Sitting in his hotel, at the window, or walking the streets, Stevens thinks about the nature of reality, or what he has always thought about: subject, object, and their uncertain relations. Reduced to this, his thinking seems monotonous; but, as he says, the imagination never touches the same thing twice in the same way. Another "search for reality," this poem is as new as sunrise or love. New thinking of old things is a theme as good for poets as sunrise or love— though less customary. The poem of New Haven is a fresh attempt to "conceive," a word, Stevens said, pointing to "A Pastoral Nun," that embodies his intention. Each of the "resemblances" with which his nun is concerned "matters only in that which it conceives." The poem of New Haven is an adventure in conceiving through proposition and metaphor.

Beginning with a proposition, the sixth part, descending immediately to metaphor, compares naked Alpha with hierophantic Omega. A is reality; O or Z is what the mind does with it. Alpha is always beginning; Omega, like Stevens' thought, "is refreshed at every end." In one sense Omega is the poem; in another, like New Haven itself, the poem is a union of A and Z, whose contention here is more exciting than what they stand for. Walking "the metaphysical streets of the physical town," Stevens conceives "a total double-thing," at once New Haven and its poem, which is "part of the res itself and not about it."

"Le Cimetière Marin" is the closest parallel. Here Valéry's thinker, sitting in a graveyard, thinks about the nature of reality, death, and life. He is commonly metaphorical. His occasional abstractions and references to philosophy are there, said Valéry, only to lend a flavor of philosophy to the thinking of this particular *moi.* Indeed, the matter of the poem is no more than something to fill a shape. Stevens, in his later years, is closer to the Valéry of "Le Cimetière" and "La Jeune Parque" than to any other poet.

The "pseudo-statements" of I. A. Richards and his "music of ideas," which Stevens quotes, apply to him. Not his statements but their composite shape is the point of his poem. A little odd and like nothing else in New Haven, it is another shape for the feeling of trying to know what one has tried to know again and again. Not only the feeling of an endless affair ("It can never be satisfied, the mind, never") but the feeling of facing time and death emerges from this shape.

Autumn leaves, bare branches, and all the intimations of the rock become more eloquent here than ruminations about subject and object. "The robins are lâ-bas." Gaiety, hardly here except for the "gaiety of exactness," is gone with those robins. Yet relics of old oddness remain and a few grotesques. Professor Eucalyptus, keeping his analytic eye on the object, seems a critic at Yale. The scholar whose "Segmenta" come from "Adagia" seems Stevens himself.

His arrangement of "the eye's plain version" and the mind's improvements, though visual on the whole, has a rhythm depending on the possibilities of the tercet, in which syntactical structure may violate prosodic structure freely in a kind of counterpoint. More flexible than couplet or quatrain, the tercet seems more shapely than blank verse. In the thirty-first poem, for example, this form, at once self-contained and uncontained, permits a long syntactical sweep of five tercets and the suddenness of two short periods in the last.

"An Ordinary Evening" is what in "Of Modern Poetry" Stevens calls "the poem of the mind in the act of finding." "Metaphors of a Magnifico" in *Harmonium* proves this theme an old one. Trying to fix reality here, a metaphysician looks, comes to his limit, and begins again. Frustrated again, he is left with a white wall and the fruit trees. This little poem (in imagistic free verse) seems to do more economically and intensely what "An Ordinary Evening" does. The theme of the feeling of thinking is the same; but, another shape, this poem offers another conception. Stevens' poems of the same thing are never the same poem.

"Sunday Morning," in which blank verse of the civilest kind establishes the quality of the experience, is another early adventure of the mind in the act of finding. Here the thinker is a woman at breakfast on a sunny terrace while her neighbors are at church. Coffee, oranges, and "green freedom" are here and now; but she is troubled, like all of Stevens' metaphysicians, with thoughts of a conflicting opposite, in this case, heaven and the "holy hush of ancient sacrifice." The contention in her mind between life and death, present and past, earth and heaven is the structure of the poem.

"We live in an old chaos of the sun," where it is good to be alive; but this woman longs for some "imperishable bliss." Living wins by death's assistance, for life's beauty depends on death. Sinking like a tired bird into blackness is inevitable, but the "ambiguous undulations" of the descent redeem it:

She hears, upon that water without sound,
A voice that cries, "The tomb in Palestine
Is not the porch of spirits lingering.
It is the grave of Jesus, where he lay."
We live in an old chaos of the sun,
Or old dependency of day and night,
Or island solitude, unsponsored, free,
Of that wide water, inescapable.

Deer walk upon our mountains, and the quail
Whistle about us their spontaneous cries;
Sweet berries ripen in the wilderness;

And, in the isolation of the sky,
At evening, casual flocks of pigeons make
Ambiguous undulations as they sink,
Downward to darkness, on extended wings.

Her thought has proceeded from complacency to awareness. Death and its "winter branch," before us here as in New Haven, are comfortably remote, and we are left with bright, green wings.

To enjoy the sun and bright wings without thought was the constant desire of thinking Stevens. Elegant rhetorician, poet of double vision, he longed to see things with a single eye, without monocle; and he longed in vain. But sometimes, like some of his thinkers, he approached success. His poems of the thing itself are among his brightest, whether announcements of his desire or its approximate achievements. In "The Sense of the Sleight-of-Hand Man" one's "grand flights," soulful "tootings," and "Sunday baths . . . occur as they occur." So clouds in a blue sky, so bluejays. To mate one's life with these one must be ignorant as the dawn. The wise man's difficulty is a subject of "Angel Surrounded by Paysans." This angel, without wing or aureole, comes for a moment and is gone:

I am the necessary angel of earth,
Since, in my sight, you see the earth again.

With angelic help in "Of Bright & Blue Birds & the Gala Sun" we see for a moment the gaiety of things as things, as if there were a "bright scienza" outside ourselves, "a gaiety that is being, not merely knowing." The roses of "Bouquet of Roses in Sunlight," exceeding the rhetorician's scope, are "too much as they are to be changed by metaphor." But for Lady Lowzen of Hydaspia by Howzen, fond of "feen masquerie" and of skimming the "real for its unreal"—for this lady "what is was other things." This was the trouble for Stevens, too,

although "reality" is the last word of his *Collected Poems*.

"A Lot of People Bathing in a Stream," an all but pure celebration of being, has something of the green and golden glory of Dylan Thomas' "Fern Hill," without its nostalgia. Not here once, we are here now in "the sun-filled water, brightly leafed," in today's "yellow green and yellow blue . . . floating without a head," natural grotesques and companions of the comic sun. Here is all summer in a day, and here the fitting introduction to "Credences of Summer."

About the feeling of a summer's day, "Credences of Summer" is also about how hard it is to feel the day as it is, without mind's intervention, and to put the feeling down in words. The season is important. More or less indifferent to romantic spring, Stevens turned more and more to autumn, which, in spite of its auroras, brings final nothingness to mind. But summer, static and fully there, was his darling. What Byzantium was to Yeats, summer was to Stevens—with this difference: Yeats's timeless city was out of nature, but Stevens' summer fields are as natural as ultimate cold and more pleasing. Threatening autumn is the mother of summer's beauty. A major poem of *Transport to Summer*, "Credences of Summer," transporting us, fulfills the promise of the volume.

"Now," the first word, and recurrent "this" are his keys to thisness. "Let's see the very thing and nothing else." Recurrent "see" and "look" are keys to the visible. Look at the sun "in its essential barrenness" and set it down "without evasion by a single metaphor." In the first two of the ten parts of this poem, metaphorical Stevens approaches his ideal of plain words for essential things: "This is the barrenness of the fertile thing that can attain no more." But metaphor, intruding in the third part, remains to plague him. Summer becomes a tower ("green's green apogee"), a mountain, and a ruddy old man. In the sixth part, summer becomes the rock, green below and blue above. Not the hidden, chilly rock of winter, "the rock of summer" is visible, solid and majestic—"As if twelve princes sat before a king." The summer day in the fifth part becomes a vital youth, an ephebe, no doubt, and one of the boys of summer.

Such images, bastards of the mind, failing to embody the feeling that the poet intends, put it off. But plain description, faithful to the eye, brings it back. The fourth part, on "a land too ripe for enigmas, too secure," makes us "accept what is as good. . . . The utmost must be good and is." Fields of hay, baked in the sun, recall Oley, a town near Reading. It may be that memory of youth gets between the poet and the view; but "Credences of Summer" plays memory against eye and metaphor against plain speech.

"It was difficult to sing in face of the object." This difficulty, replacing immediate summer, becomes the subject. Deep in the woods, in VII, poets try to sing of summer in the fields. Whereas the "concentered self," out of the woods, grips the object "in savage scrutiny," grips, subjugates, and proclaims "this hard prize." In VIII, a trumpet announces the visible by sound. This instrument, replacing the old guitar, may make the visible more than visible, but that is better than the invisible, which the mind of man, "grown venerable in the unreal," prefers. The bright cock on the bean pole in IX seems the poet in our time. Summer is over:

The gardener's cat is dead, the gardener gone
And last year's garden grows salacious weeds.

In this wasteland, the cock observes the decay of old arrangements with all their *douceurs* and *tristesses*. Soft and civil, this polished bird, now on the barest bean pole, once sat in a "suave bush." Their "complex" has fallen apart. Yet, considering the possibility of another order, not so soft and civil as his first, the old cock makes an ambiguous sound. Life was once "an old casino in a park." Once civil and polished in a suave bush, Stevens sits on his bean pole. Still cocky, he looks at the barrenness around him and does his best.

After this wintry interlude summer returns to the stage, observing its "huge decorum." The "personae of summer," playing their parts as an "inhuman author" directs, wear costumes of blue and yellow, red and green, the motley of the sun. Fat and roseate, these personae, as their name proclaims, were once masks. A persona of summer now, Stevens has no mask or hat on.

In "Thirteen Ways of Looking at a Blackbird," among the earliest of his variations on a theme, Stevens found, or perfected, what was to be his agreeable structure and accosted the strange relations of idea and things that were to be his care. "Looking at" in thirteen ways means not only seeing but conceiving and imagining or having ideas about. The thing looked at or the blackbird itself, a far from simple thing, may be a black bird of ill omen or the ordinary blackbird of Haddam and the other regions of Connecticut. Contrast, interferences of outer with inner or of inner with outer, their interpenetrations, and elegant economy attend the development of this suite from its likely origin in Pound's haiku or Williams' "red wheel barrow" to more important arrangements than the limits of Imagism allow. The fifth look, passing through the bird, is at poetry and the thirteenth, with its décor of night, snow, and cedar, at death. The "glass coach" in Connecticut, an artifice suitable for "bawds of euphony" or even for displaced insurance men, may be transparent; yet it casts a shadow that the troubled looker-out mistakes for substance.

Art, like that coach, may be a thing, a shadowing thing, but blackbirds are the thing, the thing that in his later years Stevens, coachless now, tried to look at, not through or around. Williams said: "No ideas but in things." For Joyce with his significant bathtub and Eliot with his Chinese jar things also are embodiments of ideas or, at least, objects that, within a traditional frame of reference, carry ideas. No less detained by bodies, Stevens found his idea of man in a man; "It Must Be Abstract" comes to mean It Must Be Concrete. But trying to see things without the interference of mind and its overlays, Stevens belongs less with Williams, Eliot, and Joyce than with later men, Beckett, for example, and Robbe-Grillet. Beckett said: "No symbols where none intended." Stevens said: "Not Ideas about the Thing but the Thing Itself." This echo of Williams goes beyond him. But Beckett, Robbe-Grillet, and Stevens, trying to see their bananas plain—bananas or blackbirds, who cares which?—saw something else; for however empty of meaning bananas are meant to be and are, they invite ideas as residents or neighbors. Desire for the meaningless particular—for the ultimate thisness—is always frustrated by a looking mind. The ultimate banana, interfered with, becomes penultimate, an object less possessed than desired; and desire, as Stevens knew, is "not to have" or "to have what is not." To desire is to have ideas about. It was desire for "the things of August" that kept Stevens from them.

Selected Bibliography

WORKS OF WALLACE STEVENS

POETICAL WORKS
Selected Poems. London: Faber and Faber, 1953. (Selected by Stevens.)
The Collected Poems. New York: Knopf, 1954.

Wallace Stevens, Mattino Domenicale de Altre Poesie, translated by Renato Poggioli. Torino: Giulio Einaudi, 1954. (Selected poems with translations into Italian, and notes on the poems by Stevens.)
Opus Posthumous, edited, with an Introduction, by Samuel French Morse. New York: Knopf, 1957. (Contains plays, "Adagia," early, late, and rejected poems, and miscellaneous prose.)
Poems by Wallace Stevens, selected, with an Introduction, by Samuel French Morse. New York: Vintage (Knopf), 1959.
The Palm at the End of the Mind. Hamden, Ct.: Shoe String Press, 1984.

LETTERS AND MISCELLANY
Letters of Wallace Stevens, edited by Holly Stevens. New York: Knopf, 1966.
Sur Plusieurs Beaux Sujects: Wallace Stevens' Commonplace Book, a Facsimile and Transcription. Stanford, Calif.: Stanford Univ. Press, 1989.

BIBLIOGRAPHY

Morse, Samuel French. *Wallace Stevens, A Preliminary Checklist of His Published Writings: 1898–1954*. New Haven: Yale University Library, 1954.

CRITICAL AND BIOGRAPHICAL STUDIES

Blackmur, R. P. *The Double Agent*. New York: Arrow, 1935.
Borroff, Marie, ed. *Wallace Stevens: A Collection of Critical Essays*. Englewood Cliffs, N.J.: Prentice-Hall, 1963.
Brown, Ashley, and Robert S. Haller, eds. *The Achievement of Wallace Stevens*. Philadelphia: Lippincott, 1962.
Bryer, Jackson R., and Joseph N. Riddel. *Wallace Stevens Checklist and Bibliography of Stevens Criticism*. Denver, Colo.: Swallow Press, 1963.
Enck, John J. *Wallace Stevens: Images and Judgments*. Carbondale: Southern Illinois University Press, 1964.
Fuchs, Daniel. *The Comic Spirit of Wallace Stevens*. Durham, N.C.: Duke University Press, 1963.
Gregory, Horace. *A History of American Poetry, 1900–1940*. New York: Harcourt, Brace, 1946.

Kermode, Frank. *Wallace Stevens*. Edinburgh: Oliver and Boyd, 1960.

Kreymborg, Alfred. *Troubadour, an Autobiography*. New York: Boni and Liveright, 1925.

Monroe, Harriet. *A Poet's Life*. New York: Macmillan, 1938.

Moore, Marianne. *Predilections*. New York: Viking, 1955.

Morse, Samuel French. "The Native Element," *Kenyon Review*, 20:446–65 (Summer 1958). (Contains letters and comments by Stevens. Mr. Morse is preparing a biography.)

O'Connor, William Van. *The Shaping Spirit, A Study of Wallace Stevens*. Chicago: Regnery, 1950.

Pack, Robert. *Wallace Stevens, An Approach to His Poetry and Thought*. New Brunswick, N.J.: Rutgers University Press, 1958.

Riddle, Joseph N. *The Clairvoyant Eye: The Poetry and Poetics of Wallace Stevens*. Baton Rouge: Louisiana University Press, 1966.

Rosenfeld, Paul. *Men Seen*. New York: MacVeagh, 1925.

Tate, Allen. *Sixty American Poets*. Washington, D.C.: Library of Congress, 1945.

Taupin, René. *L'Influence du symbolisme français sur la poésie américaine (de 1910 à 1920)*. Paris: Champion, 1929.

Vendler, Helen H. *On Extended Wings: Wallace Stevens' Longer Poems*. Cambridge, Mass.: Harvard University Press, 1969.

Walsh, Thomas F. *Concordance to the Poetry of Wallace Stevens*. University Park: Pennsylvania State University Press, 1963.

Wells, Henry W. *Introduction to Wallace Stevens*. Bloomington: Indiana University Press, 1964.

Williams, William Carlos. "Wallace Stevens," *Poetry*, 87:234–39 (January 1956).

Winters, Yvor. *In Defense of Reason*. Denver, Colo.: University of Denver Press, 1947.

SPECIAL ISSUES OF MAGAZINES

Harvard Advocate, vol. 127, December 1940.

Historical Review of Berks County (Reading, Pennsylvania), vol. 24, 1959.

Trinity Review, vol. 8, May 1954.

—WILLIAM YORK TINDALL

William Styron

1925-

*I*N DISTINGUISHING the experience of his generation for *Esquire*, William Styron gives us a key to his fictional perspective and development:

In 1944, as a Marine recruit, I was shanghaied into the "clap shack," the venereal-disease ward of the Naval Hospital at Parris Island, South Carolina. There at the age of eighteen, only barely removed from virginhood, I was led to believe that blood tests revealed I had a probably fatal case of syphilis—in those pre-penicillin days as dread a disease as cancer—and was forced to languish, suicidal, for forty days and forty nights amid the charnel-house atmosphere of draining buboes, gonorrhea, prostate massages, daily short-arm inspections, locomotor ataxia, and the howls of poor sinners in the clutch of terminal paresis, until at last, with no more ceremony than if I were being turned out of a veterinary clinic, I was told I could go back to boot camp: I would not die after all, *it was all a mistake*, those blood tests had turned up a false reaction to an old case of trench mouth. I could have wept with relief and hatred. Such experiences have given our generation, I believe, both the means and the spirit to bridge the generation gap.

Having come of age during World War II, Styron saw his situation as radically different from that of the writers who influenced him most—Faulkner, Fitzgerald, Wolfe, and Hemingway. They were initiated by the Spanish Civil War, which, no matter how ferocious, was nevertheless remote. It left Americans disillusioned but intact. Styron's generation was not left intact. And its experience was not so much the failure or impotence of old values. For it was initiated by the atomic bomb and the senseless and overwhelming destruction of Hiroshima. It was "traumatized" by the war experience, by the "unimaginable presence" of the bomb, and by the feeling that the war was perpetual, was, in fact, the condition of life. World War II turned into the Cold War, whose "clammy presence oozed into our nights and days." And the Cold War turned into the Korean War, for which Styron, like so many of his contemporaries, was recalled to duty. The work which captures this situation most explicitly is *The Long March*, where the central characters, recovered from their experiences in Okinawa and fattened by the postwar prosperity, are recalled to train for the Korean battlefront, and Lieutenant Culver, the novella's narrator, realizes that "for six years they had slept a cataleptic sleep, dreaming blissfully of peace, awakened in horror to find that, after all, they were only marines, responding anew to the old commands." But the feeling of war as the condition of life pervades all of Styron's works: in *Lie Down in Darkness*, Peyton Loftis commits suicide on the day the bomb is dropped on Nagasaki; in *Set This House on Fire* Cass Kinsolving traces the beginning of his self-destructive striving to his experiences in World War II, which drove him to the psychiatric ward. And even *The Confessions of Nat Turner*, although set a full century earlier, is informed by the spirit of the battlefield.

Besides being inescapable, war is outrageously unreasonable. The enemy is undefined; heroic action becomes clownish and self-destructive. And Styron's early experience as a marine recruit "shanghaied into the 'clap shack' " is a paradigm. There is the ambush or senseless surprise, the absurd humiliation, and finally the realization that "it was all a mistake." What Styron shows in his most convincing fiction is, first, that beneath the calm and affluent exterior of modern life lies a violent potential, and, second, that this violence has a capricious life of its own and erupts as a senseless surprise, often in the form of an accident. He was feeling his way toward this vision in *Lie Down in Darkness* where, despite the influence of Faulkner, his characters are moved not by the logic of history but by ahistorical, irrational, and undefinable energies which burst through the mannered and manicured surface of their lives to drive them apart, frustrate connection, and deny psychological and aesthetic resolution. He realizes this vision most clearly in *The Long March*, by opening it with a senseless surprise: eight young marines are blown up in the misfiring of two mortar shells on a cloudless summer afternoon. In *Set This House on Fire*, Peter Leverett is initiated into the world of Sambuco by an accident with a crazy motorscooterist; and Cass Kinsolving is brought to his tragic awakening by a senseless surprise and a mistake: the accidental murder of Francesca by the hitherto harmless village idiot, and Cass's mistaken revenge and murder of Mason Flagg. The novel ends with Luciano having inexplicably recovered from his motorscooter accident and then, just as senselessly, falling down a flight of stairs to break his collarbone. And the senselessness of violence is even carried into the world of Nat Turner, when the revolutionary leader, in what could almost be seen as a cartoon caricature, bounces his mishandled ax or his dull sword off the heads of several victims, to have the job finished by the half-crazed Will, who emerges late in the novel, almost gratuitously.

Styron has not focused directly on the war experience which initiated him into manhood, but this experience informs all of his major fiction. Those who wrote of World War II saw it from one of two perspectives. James Jones, Norman Mailer, indeed most of the novelists who went through the war, viewed the battlefield from the prewar perspective. They still operated within naturalistic· conventions and defined the social and psychological causes of their protagonists' condition. Joseph Heller, although he too fought in the war, viewed the battlefield from the postwar perspective and was quickly taken up by the new generation. He showed his world to be dominated by a runaway logic, and within his world there is no way to distinguish madness from sanity, reason from irrationality, selfishness from selflessness, nor is the mad destructiveness attributable to any social or psychological causes. Styron, in dramatizing war as the condition of life, developed a postwar perspective close to that of Heller and the next generation. Or perhaps it would be more accurate to turn his own phrase and see him as a "bridge" between two generations. With most writers of his generation he shares a faith in literature as a way to knowledge and order, and a faith in Christian humanism as a way to salvation. With the later generation he shares an apocalyptic, or neo-apocalyptic, view which denies the possibility of knowledge, order, or salvation.

The traditional apocalyptic view was dualistic or Manichean; it pictured a struggle between good and evil cosmic powers and revealed the present, irretrievably evil period of history headed for violent and complete destruction, to be followed by a new period, beyond history, of eternal harmony. The modern experience of apocalypse lacks a temporal or linear dimension. It is ahistorical and nonrational. It does not follow from anything, cannot be explained causally, cannot be justified morally, and does not look forward to a golden age of peace. It is an experience of violent and perpetual ending. Such an experience pervades the worlds of Peyton Loftis and Cass Kinsolving; both of these novels are charged with violent and irrational energies. *The Long March*, while far more tightly controlled, still reveals a world dominated by indefinable capricious forces; but, more importantly, it dramatizes the impotence of reason in explanation and moral guidance. The universe of the novel is dualistic, but there is no way of telling the forces of good from the forces of evil; and this is epitomized in the confrontation between Colonel Templeton, whose orders are both capriciously destructive and morally necessary, and Captain Mannix, whose rebellion is at once profoundly humanitarian and necessarily dehumanizing. The weaknesses in Styron's writing, especially in parts of his otherwise powerful *Set This House on Fire* and in the primary conception of *The Confessions of Nat Turner*, seem to arise when Styron substitutes a traditional, rational, and, in context, simplified apocalypse for the terrifying one he imaginatively discovered.

Styron also shares with the earlier generation a desire to see the world in heroic proportions; hence his use of myth in evoking the downfall of the Loftis family in *Lie Down in Darkness*, the crucifixion of Mannix in *The Long March*, the hubris of Cass in *Set This House on Fire*, the martyrdom of Nat Turner in *The Confessions*. But in each case the subject of his fiction is denied its heroic potential. *Lie Down in Darkness* remains a domestic tragedy, Mannix is turned into a clownish perpetrator of the very violence he rebels against, Cass is humiliated and must finally renounce his strivings. Except for *The Confessions of Nat Turner*, where I think Styron was working counter to his best imaginative instincts, the forces against which his characters contend cannot be confronted heroically. This is just their malicious quality. They end by reducing the protagonist, comically, by humiliating him. They are just like the forces that "shanghaied" young Styron into the "clap shack."

The senseless surprise, the absurd humiliation, and the final realization that it was all a mistake effect the ultimate violation in Styron's world. We should remember that violation is the end result of violence; it is an unjustified infringement, transgression, desecration, profanation, defilement, ravaging—primarily physical but finally psychological. The violation of Styron as a marine recruit was an exercise of violence as accident, of physical force inflicting profound psychological injury because it was undefinable in its source, immeasurable in its strength, unaccountable in its means of attack, unreasonable in its mistake. And Peyton Loftis, Mannix, Cass, and perhaps even Nat Turner are all violated by such irrational powers.

The reaction to violence, unless one accepts it, is outrage. Outrage, Ihab Hassan reminds us, "implies excess, the passing beyond all bounds; it signals disorder, extravagance, fury, insolence; it refers to violent injury and gross and wanton offence. Outrage is rage without measure, but its secret rhythm is one of assault and protest, force and counterforce . . . an irrational dialectic of violence threatening the human form, the very nature of man. In this dialectic, action and reaction are compressed, beyond time, in a form of terrible unity." And according to Hassan, Styron's heroes follow in the tradition of Ivan Karamazov and Ahab, as "metaphysical rebels," struggling against a world God created as "perpetually unjust," and perpetuating the unjust violence in the dialectic of their rebellions. Metaphysical rebels, yes, but not quite in the mold of Ivan or Ahab, for there is an unreasonable and indefinable force in the modern world which undermines their kind of heroic rebellion. William Faulkner recognized this, and the outrage that energizes his most powerful novels is in response to such a force. It was Faulkner whom William Styron chose as his first model.

Styron was born in 1925, in the shipbuilding center of Newport News, Virginia, and expected to find a career in engineering. Although two of his stories written before his first three-year tour of duty in the marines were published in a collection of creative writing at Duke University, it was only when he returned to Duke that he began to think about writing seriously. William Blackburn encouraged Styron to take Hiram Haydn's course on the novel at the New School of Social Research in New York City, and it was there that he conceived his first novel. Published in 1951, after three years' work (Styron has always been a slow writer), *Lie Down in Darkness* was a remarkable achievement of imagination, observation, and control. A large cast of characters are, for the most part, fully imagined. The locale and manners of Tidewater society are sensitively observed and recorded. The novel, a collage of flashbacks from the day of Peyton Loftis' burial, is skillfully put together. And there is a rich range of style and pace in the narrative, the descriptions, and the dialogue, which includes a final tour de force in Peyton's interior monologue on the day of her suicide.

Lie Down in Darkness bears Faulkner's imprint, despite Styron's deliberate efforts to eliminate it. The structure, the key symbols, and many of the characters recall *The Sound and the Fury*, and the funeral procession seems to derive from *As I Lay Dying*. But Styron's novel takes on a life of its own, and its success, indeed a major element of the fictional experience, depends on Styron's movement away from Faulkner and the world view of the twenties. Faulkner was outraged at what had become of a tradition grounded in aristocratic and Protestant values, values which he was to discover were simultaneously and unreasonably humane and life-denying. And his outrage was focused on history, or the passing of time. In *Lie Down in Darkness*, despite the literary allusions, there is almost no sense of passing time, no real connection between the present and a past that contained its communal and sustaining values. And despite the preponderance of flashbacks the novel is all present. Unlike Faulkner, who shows us a present rising out of an ambiguous past, Styron shows us a past that is part of the ambiguous present.

"At precisely eleven o'clock on a weekday morning in August of 1945, a black, shiny hearse, whose motor was so soundless that the effect was that of no motor at all, slid to a stop on the station dock at Port Warwick." But the motor turns out to be not so soundless after all, for while there are innumerable narrative lines leading back to important moments in the lives of all the major characters, the hearse carrying Peyton's body to the cemetery will remain central: it will serve, in its realistic detail and comic irrelevancy, to ground remembrance and rhetoric in the chaotic and sweltering reality of the present moment. For instance, Milton Loftis is waiting in a limousine behind the hearse for the arrival of his daughter's body. He carries us back in time by recollecting his father, who, with echoes of Mr. Compson, admonishes, "*I do not propose to convince you merely through paternal advice which no doubt you in your willful notion of filial duty would abjure anyway. . . .*" And this rhetorical flight from the present leads us through Milton's university days, when at the age of nineteen he was "a sot even by fraternity standards," and through his career in the army to his enviable marriage with the colonel's daughter. We are then drawn back to the present by a boat whistle to see Loftis still in his reveries, looking "up through the dust, the slanting frames of light," and reaching for the hand of his wife, Helen, who is not there, and now trying to escape once more. " 'No!' he cried. 'I can't go through with it!' " But the reader is forced to go through with it, for he cannot escape. We are brought back to the insistent necessity of the present. "The hearse was parked near the coal elevator. Each time Mr. Casper bent over to explain to Barclay what was wrong with the motor, a gondola car was upturned on the tracks above them, and his words were lost in the furious roar of coal." And what follows is a realistic description of men repairing the hearse's radiator—realistic in its careful recounting of detail and in its comic irrelevancy to Loftis' preoccupations.

If the hearse continually brings us back to the present moment in time, it also brings us back to the present position in space. After a long flashback, which takes us through the suburbs where Helen discovers Milton's infidelity, confronts Dolly Bonner in a tea shop, and turns for relief to the Reverend Carey Carr, we see the hearse stalled in a long line of cars behind the stoplight at Thirty-Fourth and Virginia: "Barclay ground away on the starter, but the hearse didn't move, and from all sides came the noise of car horns, irreverent and frantic in the noonday heat." The hearse serves to stall us, to fix us, in the mundane present. And if, with its implacable reminder of Peyton's death, it begins to suggest a meaningful connection between past events and the present moment, the connections are never made for us in the fabric of the novel and are in fact undermined by the continual insistence of physical irrelevancy. There is no connection between the places where the hearse—accidentally—stops and any places in the lives of the main characters. Nor is there any connection between the physical details so sharply reported in these scenes and any details in the main story line—and the contrast is enforced by the contrast in tone, pace, and diction. The continual insistence of irrelevancy in the present makes flight into the past—for either escape or meaning—futile. While Faulkner fractured his narrative and the objective continuum of time in *The Sound and the Fury* to discover meanings in the subjective time patterns of his characters, Styron fractures his narrative to destroy whatever connections of causality and meaning might be gained by his flights into the past.

It is at just this point that Styron begins to work away from Faulkner and the earlier generation of writers. Not completely, for there is still much in his perceptions and his style that ties him to them, especially to F. Scott Fitzgerald. Hence, Peyton laments to Dick Cartwright, "Those people back in the Lost Generation. Daddy, I guess. Anybody who thought about anything at all. They thought they were lost. They were crazy. They weren't lost. What they were doing was losing us." Daddy, in fact, did not think of anything, at least not in the way Peyton suggests. He drifted helplessly through life—through the university, where he became a sot, into marriage with the socially attractive Helen, through professional failures, and into an alliance with Dolly. If he thought of anything it was only of Peyton, to whom he was incestuously attracted. And the reader, like Peyton, is led to search for links between his incestuous desires, his drinking, his failures, his infidelity, Helen's neurotic connection with her crippled daughter, Maudie, her hatred of Peyton, of men, and even of women as sexual vessels.

One weakness of the novel may be attributed to Styron's ambivalence. Part of his mind was conditioned by the ideas and the sensibility of those writers who most influenced him. But, as his next two novels clearly show, he was working imaginatively away from such influences. If the novel's weakness is due to his ambivalence, its strength lies in its movement from the world of the twenties to the world of the fifties, in its independence, and even, considering when it was written, its prophetic qualities.

In 1954, three years after publishing *Lie Down in Darkness*, and having received the Prix de Rome, he was interviewed for the *Paris Review*. Perhaps feeling his oats, he told the interviewers that having Peyton commit suicide on the day the atomic bomb was dropped was "just gilding the lily. If I were writing the same thing now I'd leave that out and have her jump on the Fourth of July." But sixteen years later he insisted that his generation had been initiated by the atomic bomb and the destruction of Hiroshima, and the never-ending sense of impending or potential warfare. Moreover, the war and the bomb are not imposed on the experience of *Lie Down in Darkness*; we are made to feel the impending threat of irrational destruction beneath the polished surface of the suburban world and in the very texture of the novel.

When war is the condition of life, the experience is open ended, open at both ends. And this experience, epitomized in the explosion of the first atomic bomb, was quantitatively and qualitatively different from that of Styron's predecessors. In 1945 a quantum gap was opening, and Styron was among the first writers to respond to it imaginatively. The war which began as a "hard-boiled matter of stamping out a lot of very real and nasty totalitarianism" ended on a note of violent irrationality, which was fully realized some years later by many who experienced the Cold War and the Korean War. It was at that point when what is now called the post-modern sensibility was being shaped, out of a feeling that the old rational laws of cause and effect made little sense.

Lie Down in Darkness is structured to undermine causal connections between past, present, and future. Although Styron is often at his best, in all of his novels, when developing an engaging plot line, he was working toward what Earl Rovit, in reference to another group of writers, has described as an "apocalyptic structure"—which has no center, no organic connections, only energy and fragments of an exploding surface. With no causal connections, no organic nexus, there are no physical, emotional, psychological, or ethical directions. The biblical experience of apocalypse was eschatological; it derived from a sense of the final struggle between warring powers of good and evil. But the modern experience of apocalypse goes beyond this and expresses a total nihilism and chaos; there is neither a sense of ending nor a sense of beginning, nor can the warring powers be ethically designated.

The central struggle, or agon, in *Lie Down in Darkness* is between Peyton's father and her mother. But how are we to describe the agon? Not in terms of good and evil or right and wrong. We cannot describe it at all, because the source and even the field of the agon is out of sight. There are only a few memorable clashes—one when Dolly begins her flirtation with Milton and Peyton ties up Maudie, one at Peyton's birthday party, and one at her wedding. Rather, the agon between Milton and Helen is dramatized with great skill in their centrifugal reactions to one another, in the energy, that is, which drives them apart. This is primarily accomplished through the shifting points of view which focus now on Milton and his relation to Dolly, now on Helen and her relation to Carey Carr. All the while we sense that Milton is drawn toward Dolly, and Helen toward Carr, by forces which are driving Milton and Helen apart. But we never see the source of this energy, and we never see the agon itself. We only see the symptoms or the effects in Milton's drinking, drifting, sentimentality, and incestuous desires, in Helen's morbid love for the crippled Maudie, her neurotic revulsion from sex, her developing religiosity.

Peyton's story is not one of the loss of innocence, as so many critics conclude. There is nothing for her to lose. She is desperately striving for an emotional, psychological, and ethical center. On the day of her wedding to Harry she tries to make her father understand this. "Don't you see, don't you see, Bunny? I come back here all sweetness and light trying my best to play the good sweet role, the prodigal daughter. . . . I've got my own reasons for coming home. I've wanted to be normal . . . to be able to say, 'Well now my rebellion's over, home is where I want to be.' " Rebellion is the wrong word, although it is the only word in Peyton's vocabulary that can express the feel of her drive and movement. But rebellion must be against something, must have some fixed source. And in her world, torn by the forces driving her mother and father, there is no center that Peyton can reach toward or run away from. New York is not a rejection of her home;

the novel opens and closes with the train which joins New York and Port Warwick, making them part of the same fabric. Harry is no rejection of Milton; he is, rather, a substitute which must also be rejected. And the crude and brutal Tony is no rejection of Harry, for he serves the same ambivalent need, which is to strike outward and inward at the same time.

The powerful interior monologue which concludes the story of Peyton Loftis works in a way that is diametrically opposed to its prototype in *Ulysses*, and serves to distinguish Styron's and Joyce's worlds. It does not give us a sense of formal or psychological unity, but is fully expressive of Peyton's apocalyptic experience. While Molly Bloom is almost continuously inert, Peyton is continually in motion. The frantic emotional and physical pace of this section contrasts dramatically with that of all the other narrative lines in the novel, especially the one carrying the hearse to the cemetery. Peyton is driven from Tony's to the bar to Lennie's to Berger's to Harry's, and finally to Harlem, where she jumps out of a bathroom window; the violence of her energy is reinforced by the repeated references to the atomic bombs which have just been dropped on Hiroshima and Nagasaki. And her irrational physical movement is complicated by her stream of consciousness, which is not really a stream, for the recollections do not seem to flow from one association to the next; they seem to explode out of her wild unconscious—disconnected moments of the past driven irrationally into the present. The violent energy is also expressed in the images that surface, especially the flying birds and the sense of drowning. The birds symbolize innocence, purity, freedom, and also the avenging furies of her conscious and unconscious guilt. Drowning is a symbol of orgiastic forgetfulness and of renewal. But, more important, together the images of flying and drowning evoke the contradictory and centrifugal movement that dominates the novel, the force that drives Milton and Helen apart and denies Peyton a stable center of emotional and moral reference.

Peyton's suicide ends with a note of resurrection: "Myself all shattered, this lovely shell? Perhaps I shall rise at another time, though I lie down in darkness and have my light in ashes." This is not in character for Peyton, despite the religious influence of her mother. And Styron must have sensed this, for he ends the novel with an entirely different kind of religious experience. At the Negro baptism, entirely irrelevant to the story line, the crowd looks out at the raft to see embroidered on the damask curtain "dragons and crosses and crowns, Masonic emblems, shields, bizarre and unheard-of animals . . . all these glowed against the curtain in green and red phosphorescent fabrics, literally hurting the eyes." Finally the majordomo appears, "Gabriel, chief lieutenant: a personage with a stern, muscular face . . . without modesty, almost contemptuously." When he speaks of the King of Glory, he stands "stern and erect and unperturbed, his robe a blue splash against the red shields and green prophetic talismans and crawling dragons." And he is followed by a shriek "like the first firecracker on a string, and it set off an explosion of yells."

This scene has an immediacy only matched by that of Peyton's monologue and the realistic descriptions of the hearse—three facets of the immediate present. The hearse serves to bring us back from the past to the present, to make the past part of the present in a volatile and unintelligible pattern. The baptism scene is also part of this present, and is grounded in realistic asides. "La Ruth belched. 'Stonewall,' she said, 'come on in here outa dat water! Put on dem sandals, boy. You gonna snag yo' feet on a oyshter.' " The experience of the baptism recalls the Book of Revelation, and the mili-

tant Gabriel connects it with the experience of irrational warfare that boils just beneath the surface of the novel. When Daddy Faith finally appears to the sound of a trumpet, he is a ridiculous figure, "a round tub of a man, as black as black ever could get. . . . He stood at the edge of the raft, smiling, benign, avuncular." And beneath the lamp which flickered LOVE, he announces that "de people of Isr'el done gone off to war . . . and dey sent down de atom bomb on de Land of de Risin' Sun and de sojers come home wid glory in dey th'oats and wid timbrels and de clashin' of bells." The realistic detail and the comic irrelevancy of this scene make it a parody of the religious resolution of *The Sound and the Fury*. The baptism does not wash away the sins of the world, as Ella Swan believes, nor does the religious experience offer any hope of resurrection or even of endurance. Instead it exposes the reality existing beneath the polished suburban surfaces and southern manners, and gives ultimate expression to the forces tearing apart the world of Peyton Loftis.

In his neglected novella, *The Long March*, first published in 1953 in *discovery No. 1*, Styron sacrificed range to find a form which expressed the human situation with conciseness and clarity, and in which he could affirm the values of Christian humanism in a way that was consistent with his vision.

At one point the protagonist describes the most frightening experience in his life:

"We were drunk, you see, polluted, all of us. I think there were five of us, all of us boots just out of Dago. Kids. We were on the tenth floor of this hotel and in this room and I believe we were about as drunk as anyone could get. I remember going in to take a shower in the bathroom. It was late at night, past midnight, and after I took this shower, you see, I came out into the room buck naked. Two of those drunk guys were waiting for me. They grabbed me and pushed me toward the window. I was so loaded I couldn't battle. Then they pushed me out the window and held me by the heels while I dangled upside-down buck naked in space, ten floors above the street." He paused and sucked at a beer can. "Can you imagine that?" he went on slowly. "How I felt? I got stone-sober in a second. Imagine being that high upside-down in space with two drunks holding onto your heels. I was heavy, man, just like now, you see. All I can remember is those teeny-weeny lights below and the tiny little people like ants down there and those two crazy drunk guys holding onto my wet slippery ankles, laughing like hell and trying to decide whether to let go or not. I just remember the cold wind blowing on my body and that dark, man, infinite darkness all around me, and my ankles beginning to slip out of their hands. I really saw Death then, and I think that all I could think of was that I was going to fall and smash myself on that hard, hard street below. That those crazy bastards were going to let me fall. I was praying, I guess. I remember the blood rushing to my brain and my ankles slipping, and that awful strange noise. And I was reaching out, man, clutching at thin air. Then I wondered what that noise was, that high loud noise, and then I realized it was me, screaming at the top of my voice, all over San Francisco."

Here Styron found a metaphor of the human situation toward which he had been reaching in *Lie Down in Darkness*, which he was to express more diffusely in *Set This House on Fire*, and which would even inform *The Confessions of Nat Turner*; it recalls his experience as a marine recruit "shanghaied into the 'clap shack.'" In an environment that is urban, military, and dark, man is surprised, ambushed, senselessly assaulted—not to the end of defeat or destruction, not to any end at all. He is suddenly and capriciously turned upside down, turned from a man with potentials of dignity and heroism into a helpless clown acutely aware of life's terror. This terror is caused not by a hostile power or even by an indifferent universe, but by a wanton sporting with individual life—"Imagine being that high upside-down in space with two drunks holding onto your heels."

The Long March is similar in many ways to Melville's *Billy Budd*. In both works the thematic conflict is between the innocent individual and the representative of social necessity. In both works social law is made manifest in a military order. In both works the hero's instinctive reaction to human injustice has immediate destructive consequences for his associates and for himself. Both works end in a martyrdom that is in fact socially just. But the difference between *The Long March* and *Billy Budd* is signal; the view of life after World War II is sharply differentiated from that of earlier periods. Melville dramatizes the tragic price of human preservation and social harmony; Captain Vere, as he condemns Billy, is deeply aware of this price. Colonel Templeton knows that military order and soldierly discipline are necessary on the battlefield, but despite his sensitivity, integrity, and realistic logic, the end he serves is not a human harmony, as it was with Vere. In fact the end is obsured from the sightlines of the novella.

The kind of war depicted in *The Long March* is just the kind of purposeless and pervasive war we have come to know so well in the second half of the twentieth century. For this is not World War II, the justice of which could guarantee some meaning to death and destruction. It is not even the battleground of the Korean War, where, despite the senselessness, there was still an identifiable enemy. This is a marine training maneuver. The enemy "was labeled Aggressor, on maps brightly spattered with arrows and symbolic tanks and guns, but although there was no sign of his aggression he fled them nonetheless and they pushed the sinister chase, sending up shells and flares as they went."

Captain Mannix, a Brooklyn Jew, and Lieutenant Culver, from whose viewpoint the story is told, are veterans of World War II who, having adjusted to the postwar prosperity, and being now too old and flabby for effective service, have been called back to train for the Korean War by the unreasonable and impractical mechanism of the reserve system. The book opens with an accident. Two mortar shells have misfired and exploded among a group of lunching recruits: "One noon, in the blaze of a cloudless Carolina summer, what was left of eight dead boys lay strewn about the landscape, among the poison ivy and the pine needles and loblolly saplings." In the first sentence Styron pictures the irrational violence exploding from beneath the placid surface of life, expressing explicitly and with sharper clarity a view that he had begun to conceive in his story of Peyton Loftis, and which would dominate the world of Cass Kinsolving.

Styron drew on his own experiences in 1950, when he was recalled to marine duty during the Korean War and compelled to participate in a forced training march. Within a realistic framework he develops the contradictory irrational potential—the destructive irrationality and an irrational affirmation—with the aid of comic devices. The central conflict is caused not by a direct and clearly embodied hostility, as it is in *Billy Budd*, but by Colonel Templeton's impersonal and apparently irrational order for a thirty-six-mile forced march. Mannix's determination to assert the human value of his own person and of his men in the featureless face of the Marine Corps is also irra-

tional; and Lieutenant Culver finds himself in a situation similar to Peyton's, caught between warring powers which cannot be ethically distinguished. Captain Mannix tries to achieve his end in an action that is doubly irrational: he will defy the colonel by driving his men to achieve the impossible, which is to complete the march. And his defeat is accomplished far less in the prospective court-martial than it is in the picture of the heroic captain turned into a clown, gratuitously wounded by a nail in his shoe, "toiling down the road with hobbled leg and furious flailing arms." And even more by the irony of his being turned into Templeton's accomplice: "You're goddamn right, Jack. . . . My company's going to make it if I have to *drag in their bodies.*"

The world is surely upside down when we see Mannix, with his compassion and sense of justice, fulfilling the role of Satan and Templeton assuming the role of priest. This is indeed the kind of hell Mannix saw as he dangled high up in space with two drunks holding onto his slippery heels. And in the confrontation between Mannix and Templeton Styron creates a modern version—or inversion—of the confrontation in Dostoevski's "Grand Inquisitor."

Still, we come to realize that this has all been a preparation for a final inversion. *The Long March* ends with a comic recognition. Back in their quarters Mannix, coming out of the showers, encounters the Negro maid, who looks at him and says, "Oh my, you poor man. What you been doin'? Do it hurt? . . . Oh, I bet it does. Deed it does." Mannix looks at her silently, blinking, as she repeats, "Deed it does." And "almost at precisely the same instant, the towel slipped away slowly from Mannix's waist and fell with a soft plop to the floor; Mannix then, standing there, weaving dizzily and clutching for support at the wall, a mass of scars and naked as the day he emerged from his mother's womb, save for the soap

WILLIAM STYRON / 107

which he held feebly in one hand. He seemed to have neither the strength nor the ability to lean down and retrieve the towel and so he merely stood there huge and naked in the slanting dusty light and blinked and sent toward the woman, finally, a sour, apologetic smile, his words uttered, it seemed to Culver, not with self-pity but only with the tone of a man who, having endured and lasted, was too weary to tell her anything but what was true. 'Deed it does,' he said."

As the story progressed Mannix had become more and more ridiculous, and more destructive and fanatic than even Colonel Templeton. But with the shift in tone, tempo, and perspective in the final scene, he is re-established as humane and heroic. We end the book with contradictory views of Mannix, and with the nonrational experience of having come to a deep understanding of the very values which were abrogated by Templeton and the facts of reality. Styron achieved this effect by a double inversion. First he turned the world upside down to convey the full terror of a world governed by capricious forces, and to show man senselessly surprised, ambushed, reduced, and humiliated. Here Styron was following in the long tradition, revived in the 1950's, of writers who evoked the incongruous terror and the gratuitous surprises of an absurd universe through comic means. Then, again, he turned the world upside down to illuminate old values in a new light. Here the comedy works to surprise us, through inversions of accepted views, into a fresh awareness: "Christ on a crutch" turns out to be a kind of Christ after all.

In *The Long March* Styron was able to clarify his vision and develop its ironies through an effort of concentration. Now he needed to expand, to find a form with space and scope commensurate with his vision's range and intensity. The background of *Set This House on Fire* (1960) resembles the civilian world out of which Mannix and Culver were called. There is the middle-class world of Peter Leverett, who functions as a kind of Nick Carraway, sensitive, innocent, firmly rooted in the social system and drawn first to the demonic Mason Flagg and then to the rebellious Cass Kinsolving. There is also the lower-class world of Cass, whose experience of the South was remote from Peter's. And there is the upper-class world of Mason Flagg—the splendid estate where he tells "Wendy-dear," his mother, that he was expelled from prep school again, this time for being caught in the chapel basement "stark naked with the weak-minded daughter of a local oysterman, both of them clutching bottles of sacramental wine." But in the foreground of the novel is Sambuco, Italy, inhabited by an American movie company, Mason Flagg, who is ostensibly writing a novel, and Cass Kinsolving, who, at the end of a long European debauch, is ostensibly trying to paint.

Italy was a good choice for the central action. It has traditionally been a kind of Arcadia for American writers and artists and functions ironically in the pattern of Cass's development. It was a major battleground for World War II and one seat of totalitarianism, and the experiences of war and totalitarianism are seminal in the novel. It was becoming a caricature of America and allowed Styron to gain some distance on his main subject.

Sambuco is situated high up on a mountain, overlooking a "magnificent sea" and a "barbaric valley" and slopes upon which "some wretched poor sheep were grazing." When Leverett arrives at the Gothic piazza, he finds himself "exposed to a battery of cameras and arc lights and reflectors, and now to the pop-eyed rage of a roly-poly little man in Bermuda shorts bearing down upon me, his lips curled around the butt of a cigar." The aggressive incongruity between the movie set with its glitter of American affluence and the stark Italian countryside with its implacable poverty recalls an incongruity of American life to which we are only now beginning to give full recognition. Leverett's father, a southern liberal, sees his fellow Americans as a "bunch of smug contented hogs rooting at the trough. Ciphers without mind or soul or heart. Soap peddlers!" And he tells his son that "what this great land of ours needs is something to happen to it. Something ferocious and tragic, like what happened to Jericho." This is the experience—the setting of his house on fire—that Leverett goes through vicariously as he listens to the story of Cass Kinsolving.

The novel continuously penetrates the meretricious physical, social, and psychological façade of American life. Moreover, it dramatically contrasts the façade with the senselessly violent irrationality it covers. The form of the novel has two major elements. First there is the narrative dialogue between Peter and Cass at Cass's home in South Carolina two years after the main action; this element is dominated by Peter's quest for knowledge. The second element is the plot, which is the subject of Peter and Cass's dialogue, and which is dominated by Cass's quest for salvation. Peter knew Mason Flagg long before Cass met him, they were at prep school together; but all he knew of Cass was that he was a masochistic alcoholic playing the obscene buffoon to Mason at Sambuco. And all he knew of the main story was that Mason raped the beautiful Francesca and possibly killed her, and that Mason himself was dead. He feels in some way responsible for Mason's death, and, as Cass reveals the true story, he undergoes a vicarious purgation.

A weakness of *Set This House on Fire* may derive from Styron's faith in the traditional forms of novel writing and in the redemptive possibilities of Christianity. Both the narrative dialogue and the plot are strongly linear, and in both there is a promise of fulfillment. But the powerful experience Styron evokes is not linear; it denies the possibility of epistemological, theological, and psychological progress. The total effect of the novel, however, accommodates its weakness, and reinforces its main theme, which is the contrast between meretricious and worn-out forms and the irrational and destructive energies which will not be contained by them.

This contrast is also dramatized in a dialectic of styles. Robert Gorham Davis, the most sensitive critic of Styron's style, criticizes the "worked-up unbelievable quality" of the action, and compares the "day dream quality" of Cass's romance with Francesca with that of Mason's wartime romance—which, like Gatsby's tale of Oxford, he fabricates. Davis sees Mason's fabrication as a model for the novel, which is a rich and elaborate fiction referring to nothing at all. Still, he honestly confesses to being dissatisfied with his evaluation, for there is too much life in the novel. What Davis fails to recognize is that the surface, worked-up, daydream quality—especially as it contrasts with the violent current of Cass's action and the turbulent undercurrent of his nightmares—creates the texture and meaning of the novel. The action of the novel does not work like Hemingway's, as an "objective correlative" to the protagonist's emotions. Like Peyton's monologue, it is driven by unfathomable energies expanding in all directions at once and exploding fragments from the surface. It conveys the nightmare world of which Cass, in his rebellion against it, is a manifest part.

Peter Leverett's Italian experience begins with a senseless surprise, ambush, and accident. Driving through the suburbs of Naples, he hears a noise from behind, "abrupt and thunderous, a shocking din which partook both of a salvo of rockets, and an airplane in take-off." He escapes a rear-end collision, the driver passing him perilously "with a noise like a string of firecrackers, and with the central finger of one fist raised in ripe phallic tribute." Peter chases him unsuccessfully; then, falling "into aching oppressive woolgathering," he smashes broadside into a motorscooter. The driver, Luciano di Lieto, has a history of accidents: he cut off two fingers at the age of twelve poking around in an automobile engine; he broke both legs and permanently injured an elbow when he wandered in front of a Neapolitan streetcar; and, "only months after this, barely out of his casts, experimenting with fireworks at a seaside *festa*, he bent his dark, crazy regard down upon the muzzle of a Roman candle, and blew out his right eye." At the very end of the novel, Leverett, having assuaged his guilt like a good American by paying the monthly hospital bills, learns that Luciano has recovered, has risen, ostensibly like Cass, from his own ashes. But he also learns that right after his release from the hospital Luciano suffered another accident by falling down a flight of stairs and broke his collarbone. The nurse writes Leverett in lines that close the novel, "The durability of this young man is truly remarkable! I have just now come from seeing him, where he is sitting up in bed, cheerfully smiling and eating like a pig. He sends his felicitations to you, and tells me that he has become affianced. I do somewhat pity the girl but I do not doubt that, if she is at all like Luciano, it will be a match of long duration. He will live to bury us all."

The Luciano story is a comic frame for the serious plot of the main story; regeneration, as in traditional comedy, is expressed in a marriage which parallels the blissful reconciliation of Cass to his family. But the comic Luciano has a tragic double, the idiot Saverio, whose murder of Francesca is another surprise, ambush, and accident. And we recall that in our last view of Saverio "he was babbling happily and didn't seem to have any knowledge or recollection of what he had done." Moreover, the picture of Luciano "cheerfully smiling and eating like a pig" reminds us of the caricature of Americans given by Peter's father—"a bunch of smug contented hogs rooting at the trough." Luciano is a comic reminder of the wanton and gratuitous power that Americans in their affluent contentment refuse to recognize. We are led to feel that the condition of life evoked seriously in the Cass-Mason line and comically in the Leverett-Luciano line will continue. And perhaps that Cass, rather than finding himself as an artist and as a man, merely finds a way to escape the reality of modern life as he draws cartoons, teaches amateurs, and fishes in the idyllic backwaters of South Carolina.

The implacable dark and turbulent undercurrent, which will not accommodate itself to either the redemptive promises of Christianity or the formal container of the traditional novel, is evoked in the excesses of style, which express the disproportion between dramatic activity and suppressed reality, in the long and powerful descriptions of Cass running and drinking and sinking into degradation, and also in the dream visions and memories that pervade the novel. Peter is troubled by dreams of treachery and betrayal even before he discovers Cass's cartoon in the Sunday *Times*. His dreams suggest that he never faced, or that he suppressed, the reality of his Italian experience, and also that he was an accomplice to some vague crime. His long dialogue with Cass is one of gradual discovery, but the nature of the crime is more than what is encompassed in Mason's raping of Francesca, Saverio's brutal murder, and Cass's misguided revenge on Mason. For the crime lies buried even in the mind of Cass, who mistakenly feels that he has come to terms with it, and it is expressed in his dreams and memories.

Cass's first important dream is a kind of extension of Peter's and suggests that Styron was developing his two characters as doubles. It begins in Raleigh, with his uncle driving him to the state prison, its high stone walls and guard towers foreshadowing the villa of Sambuco. Cass does not know the nature of his crime "other than that I had done something unspeakably wicked." When the steel gate clangs behind him he knows that his uncle has betrayed him or forgotten him, and his next thought, filling him with almost as much despair, is that the prison will be at least half full of Negroes. "I'd be spending the rest of my life among niggers"—this despite his belief that he had been long emancipated from such prejudice. Then the dream shifts and the real horror commences: "The prisoners had all gathered around me and were pointing at me, and sneering, and looking at me with hate and loathing and disgust, and calling me filthy names; and I heard one of them say: 'Any man that'd do that should be gassed!' Then I heard the others start to hoot and holler and shout: 'Gas him! Gas the dirty sonofabitch!' "

The next important dream, a Dostoevskian nightmare, comes after he has watched with helpless compassion an ageless peasant woman, "pop-eyed with toil, sweating, bent over like a broken limb beneath the everlasting load of fagots." She makes a "final desperate humping motion with her back but the enormous hummock of wood, badly balanced and off-kilter, came tumbling off her shoulders and fell to the cobblestones." In his dream he is riding in a bus along the mountain roads, and the bus driver, speeding through a village, runs over a dog. "All of its hinder parts right on up to its chest had been smashed flat—flat as those cutlets that the butcher down the street makes out of those thick slices of beef after pounding on them for half an hour." But the dog is still living, whimpering, its eyes rolling, trying to lift itself from the earth with its forepaws. The bus driver fetches a big stick and beats the dog on the head furiously, trying desperately to put the dog out of its misery. But the dog refuses to die and suffers miserably, "still trying to rise, while all the time the fellow kept thrashing away at his skull, hoping to free the beast from his torture." Then Cass sees that it is no longer the dog's head but that of the peasant woman with the fagots. "Lying there crushed and mangled, with her poor tormented body pressed against the dust, she let out piteous cries, shrieking, 'God! God! . . . Release me from this misery!' And each time she called out, *down* would come the flailing stick."

Accustomed to the associative connections of dreams, we are tempted to fit the elements of Cass's nightmares into a neat symbolic pattern. There is the vague, enormous crime, the betrayal by his family, the expressions of guilt, the alienation. There are the specific social evils: the treatment of blacks, prisoners being gassed, like Jews, the inexorable peasant poverty. Symbolic connections can no doubt be found by the careful reader, but such an exercise could obscure, indeed contradict, the primary fictional experience, which is one of disconnection. It would be more fitting to see Styron using the dreams to reinforce our feeling of unreasonable disconnectedness. It is not the links, then, but the gaps that are meaningful—between the clanging of the steel gate and the betrayal by his uncle, between his despair at being abandoned and his surge of prejudice, between his prejudice and his shame and his identification with gassed prisoners. Just as there is no linking reason for the peasant woman's unspeakable misery, and for torture to be the only form of humane charity. This disconnection is reinforced by the unreasonable resemblance of the peasant woman bearing her load of fagots to Saverio bearing his mountain of Peter's tourist baggage, and also between the accident with the speeding bus and Peter's accident with the motorscooter. Saverio and Luciano are the tragic and comic embodiments of wanton irresponsibility, the power which governs the world of the novel. And Cass is as wrong as the reader who sees the enormous crime in terms of social injustice. And wrong in thinking that he can redeem himself by bringing medicine to the dying peasant, or by reconciling himself to his family in the back country of South Carolina.

He is also wrong in placing his faith in art. This is shown in his unreasonable and sentimental reaction to his Paris vision. After forcing Poppy and the children to leave the apartment, he gazes out the window at the shabby street. The window is framed with huge elephant vines, swarming with ladybugs. He gazes at the web of a golden spider in the crotch of one of the vines. And he smells the baking of bread, listens to the music, and finds all his hatred and poison lost or forgotten. "I don't know quite how to describe it—this *bone-breaking* moment of loveliness. . . . It was as if I had been given for an instant the capacity to understand not just beauty itself by its outward signs, but the other—the *else*ness in beauty, this continuity of beauty in the scheme of all life which triumphs even to the point of taking in sordidness and shabbiness and ugliness." Many critics conclude that Cass is finding himself as an artist in the end, but it is important to remember that he is escaping from the modern world and from his complex responsibilities to it. Nor does Styron bring his own turbulent vision into an affirmative harmony.

Cass is wrong in thinking that he can turn his rejection of life into an affirmation. In the end he tells Peter that "as for being and noth-

ingness, the one thing I did know was that to choose between them was simply to choose being, not for the sake of being, or even the love of being, much less the desire to be forever—but in the hope of being what I could be for a time." The world of this novel is finally no different from that of *Lie Down in Darkness* or *The Long March.* Peyton could not choose being because it was dominated by the agon between her mother and her father, because there was no center, because there was nothing to choose. Mannix could not choose being because being was served and expressed by Templeton. Cass cannot choose being because being is dominated by the power of wanton irresponsibility, and because it will yield no harmony or connection.

The experience of disconnection is also reinforced by two important memories in the novel. The first is unfocused. As in his earlier novels war is the condition of life, and World War II rumbles beneath the surface as a powerful undercurrent. Cass fought in the war and ended in the psychiatric ward. He recalls his conversations with the psychiatrist and although, or perhaps because, there are no recollections of what led him to the psychiatric ward, these conversations seem to be the beginning of his search. Moreover, the novel is set in postwar Italy, Mason buys his supplies at the PX, and Cass's most meaningful conversations are with the fascist policeman, Luigi. America, as Cass's father suggested, has never suffered sufficiently to come to terms with reality, and Cass must confront reality in a war-torn land where totalitarianism and defeat were experienced and remain visible.

The second memory is focused. It is of Cass when he was a boy working in a Western Auto store deep in the back country of Virginia—far removed in time and space from the present time in Sambuco. Cass and Lonnie, the redneck clerk, drove out to "dispossess" a radio from a Negro farmer who had failed to keep up with his payments. They entered the empty shack to search. "Lonnie, stabbing his toe against a sprung floorboard, finally reached down behind the planking and, triumphant, fished up the pathetic radio—white, plastic, already cracked, not much larger than a box of salt or rice, which had brought witchery in the night and tinny bright sounds of singing and laughter. 'Hid it!' said Lonnie. 'The *wise* sonofabitch.' " And spying the crack in the plastic, he cried, " 'We'll see about who breaks what!' And then pivoted on his toes, and with the other leg outthrust like a fullback punting a football shot a cowboy-boot-shod foot out against the flimsy kitchen table, hard, and brought the whole clutter of china cups and plates and saucers, sugar in cans, flour and meal and bacon fat, down to the floor in one monstrous and godawful detonation." And Cass remembers how a "tremendous warm excitement came over me, a feeling that—well, it was almost a feeling of anger, too, as if I'd picked up some of this young lout of a maniac's fury and was set on teaching the niggers, too. By God, this feeling, you know, I remember it —it was in my loins, hot, flowing, sexual. I knew it was wrong, I knew it, I knew it— bestial, horrible, abominable . . . but it was as if once I'd lost my courage anyway, once I'd given in—like some virgin, you see, who's finally stopped struggling and said to hell with it—then I could actually do what I was doing almost even with a sense of righteousness."

The whole incident is narrated with a finer sense of detail, character, and feeling than anything else in the novel. It is a memory which has been exercising strong unconscious pressures on Cass, for he has been dreaming of Negroes. But it is the most unconnected incident in the book. It could be said that Styron was not able to fully develop 'or imagine the wellsprings of Cass's character. But the novel

has a powerful effect, and the effect results from the disconnections. Cass is haunted by expressions of violence that are not congruent with mental and physical surfaces. He insists to Peter that the genteel southerners and the northern liberals were ignorant or blind to the kind of experience into which Lonnie initiated him. And beneath the surface that Americans have created to disguise life also lie the violence of possessiveness, expressed in Mason's manipulation of Cass, the violence of arrogance, expressed by the movie company taking over Sambuco, the violence of class division, expressed in the life of the peasant woman with her mountain of fagots, the violence of laissez-faire individualism, expressed in the rape of Francesca, the violence of carelessness expressed by the bus driver running over the dog.

It is absolutely consistent with the nature of the novel for Cass's undirected striving to culminate in a sequence of actions out of a grade B movie—the rape, the murder, the chase to the cliff top—in a meretricious form that gives a false sense of excitement, resolution, and meaning. But the real culmination is the recognition that the murder of Francesca was an accident—Francesca happening to' pass Saverio, responding hysterically not because of his innocent touch but because she had just been raped by Mason, and enflaming a lustful violence—and that Cass's revenge was a mistake. The real culmination, then, is an experience of accident, mistake, or random violence, which is totally incongruent with the logic of the melodramatic scene enacted by Mason, Francesca, and Cass. And the recognition should remind us of the incongruity between the disconnected violations in Cass's dreams, recollections, and his life as an expatriate, on the one hand, and on the other, his pattern of quest and redemption.

Opposed to and lying beneath the forms

which offer a false sense of meaning and hope lies a violence that has a capricious life of its own, and which is expressed in violations that are absolutely unreasonable. This is the violation—of senseless surprise, absurd humiliation, and the recognition that it was all a mistake—which young Styron experienced as a marine recruit, and which he imaginatively transformed into the image of Mannix hanging high up in space with two drunks holding onto his slippery heels. This ultimate form of violence and violation derives from a power that has total control. In *The Long March* this power is served by Colonel Templeton. In *Set This House on Fire* it is manifested by allusions to totalitarianism in the references to World War II, the setting in Italy, the relation of Mason to Cass, the vengeance of Lonnie, the conversations with Luigi. That totalitarianism is only alluded to, that it escapes clear articulation, makes it all the more frightening. For the most terrifying form of total violation is when the power is unseen, unseeable, unknown, and unknowable. Frederick Hoffman, in *The Mortal No*, traces the history of violence from the period when assailant and victim could physically contend to the modern period, where the assailant is "impersonal, unreasonable, unreal, and unseen," where the assailant, in fact, has become the landscape. Kafka has made this experience most palpable in *The Trial*; therefore it is no wonder that Cass's dream of being imprisoned, abandoned, and threatened with gassing comes so close to the experience in Kafka's novel.

What makes the assailant or the power unseeable and unknowable is that it is literally formless and totally contradictory. Cass strives for the pure form of artistic harmony and of the God of love and salvation, but the power that energizes his world is an anti-form, like the Beast of Revelation. Most critics see Cass as having found salvation—love and harmony—in the reconciliation with his family, in the pastoral retreat, in the acceptance of his own limitations as an artist. But it seems to me that Styron was working intellectually at odds with his imaginative discoveries. He shows Cass's house set on fire. And what he exposes in the images, energies, and conflicting patterns of the novel is the perpetual conflagration, the eternal apocalypse suppressed beneath the meretricious surface of American life and the false hopefulness of Christianity. Luciano will thrive in this world. New Saverios will emerge. And Cass, like Styron, will not fully accept the lessons of hell, or learn from Luigi, the Italian who has stoically accommodated to modern reality. Cass, like Styron, intellectually simplifies the apocalyptic conflict and sees it in terms of melodrama, retaining his American optimism, and retreating to a primal Eden, which is as unrealistic and inconsistent with the novel's experience as Cass's vision from the Paris window.

In *The Confessions of Nat Turner* (1967) Styron worked out the pattern of redemption more fully, and the simplification leads to new social and aesthetic problems. Both Cass and Nat are redeemed by kinds of divine intercession, or *deus ex machina*. Cass is apparently redeemed by the miraculous appearance and the gratuitous murder of Francesca. First she leads him to change his life and selflessly serve her dying father, then she leads him to become her avenging hero, and finally she leads him away from the Old World where reality is inescapable, and back to the New World where, from the very beginning, reality has been suppressed by restorations of the Garden of Eden.

Nat Turner is inspired by two gods. A Negro slave educated by a benevolent white master and enjoying the relative ease of a house servant, he is turned into a fanatic by the God of Ezekiel, who comes to him in a vision, and inspires him to lead a vengeful and slaughterous revolt against the slavemasters of Southampton County, Virginia. And he is redeemed by the voice of the murdered Margaret Whitehead, coming to him in his prison cell and speaking to him in words of love from the New Testament. Both the Old Testament God of vengeance and the New Testament God of love turn Nat Turner away from the social reality of slavery in the American South. As in *Set This House on Fire*, the *deus ex machina* serves as an ethical, psychological, and artistic evasion.

Not that Styron was looking for an easy way out. Quite the contrary. What makes Styron's development as a writer so exhilarating to follow is just the difficulty and the magnitude of the challenges he seeks out, somewhat in the manner of Captain Mannix and Cass Kinsolving. In an interview with Robert Canzoneri and Page Stegner he claims that "one of the central mystiques of the writer of novels is that . . . you take the hardest way in order to see if you can surmount the problems. And I know that imposing upon myself this kind of tension has, to my mind, produced whatever good stuff I've ever produced." The challenge which Styron set for himself in this novel was one that no white southern writer had ever accepted, to "enter into the consciousness of a Negro in the early decades of the 19th century," in fact to become the unique individual of Nat Turner by narrating the story of his rebellion from his point of view.

Very little is known about Nat Turner. The closest thing to firsthand evidence is a twenty-page confession dictated to Thomas Gray, the white lawyer who served both the defense and the prosecution and who edited what he heard for the white jury and the white press. This compounded the challenge to Styron and led ten black writers to publish a critical attack on this volume, initiating a debate of great sociological and political importance. Styron's Nat Turner, then, is the product of a creative imagination, which the white southern historian C. Vann Woodward claims is "informed by a respect for history, a sure feeling for the period, and a deep and precise sense of place and time," but which most black writers claim is racist in its selection of data and distortion of black psychology.

In order to enter Nat's consciousness most fully, Styron chose the point in time after the abortive rebellion, after Nat committed his one act of violence and murdered Margaret Whitehead, just when, as Styron imagines it, Turner felt bereft of God. "The relationship with God seemed to be the central thing in my own conception of the man. The book ends on the day of his execution, and part of it is the story of his redemption." Part of Nat Turner's story may have been of redemption, although in the original confessions, Turner seemed to deny the need for redemption when he responded to Gray: "*Ques.* Do you not find yourself mistaken now? *Ans.* Was not Christ crucified?" But Styron made this part dominant when he shaped the story of Nat Turner's life into the pattern of fall and return to grace. And, more important, the redemptive pattern conflicts with and obscures the patterns of social and psychological insights.

Katherine Ellis, in an essay which analyzed the "true confession story," illuminates a pattern that can be found in *The Confessions of Nat Turner*. The "true confession" heroine whether she leaves her suburban home to become a streetwalker, or dances naked at her high school prom, is dissatisfied with her life, renounces the security and propriety of the middle class, and follows a path of self-destructive excess. Salvation appears unexpectedly and is usually unmotivated—the husband goes through a change of character, the boyfriend, who did not really renounce her but was detained by some irrelevant circumstance, returns—and the heroine suddenly sees the light. What she sees is that *she* has been wrong. The "true confession" always locates the fault within the heroine and never within the society that produced the conditions for her fall. And the reader finishes the story with a vicarious purgation and the happy feeling that in America everything turns out for the best.

In Styron's first two works there is no *deus ex machina* and no redemption. In *Set This House on Fire* there is enough in the novel to counteract the pattern of redemption; the pattern can be seen as part of the larger conflicting structure. Moreover Cass's rebellion is, in Ihab Hassan's terms, a "metaphysical rebellion" in the tradition of Ivan Karamazov and Captain Ahab, which is against the perpetual injustice of God's world. But in *The Confessions of Nat Turner*, while the rebellion is social, the redemptive pattern is dominant. And the movement toward redemption undermines the basis for rebellion. The outspoken criticism in *Ten Black Writers Respond* may be misguided in taking Styron to task for distorting history; a writer is under no obligation to be true to the facts, especially when the facts are so few and uncertain. But they are right in seeing Styron's Nat Turner as being oblivious to the social reality which he claims to respond to. And they are also right in seeing that Styron shows the flaw to be not within the system of slavery but within the mind of the rebel.

In an interview for the *New York Times* Styron describes the major conflict as one between the values and morality of the Old and the New Testament: "savagery and revenge" versus "charity and brotherhood." And the novel ends with Nat's realization that Margaret Whitehead, or perhaps his murdering this gentle white girl, " '*showed me Him whose presence I had not fathomed or maybe never even known.*' " So while Styron describes the system of slavery which not only violated the black man but completely traumatized him, "dehumanized the slave and divested him of his honor, moral responsibility, and manhood," he shifts his attention to what he describes as the "fateful impulse" which "brought Nat to disaster." The novel is ultimately confused because Styron shifts the disaster and the blame from without to within; the fault lies not in the social structure but within Nat's mind. It is this judgment that the black critics define as racist.

The issue of racism has been fully explored by the ten black writers and in Styron's replies. What I am pointing to here is a weakness in the novel that derives from Styron's ambivalence, which kept him from fully realizing either the social or the psychological possibilities. As Richard Gilman shows, the "whole physical construction, this thick detail, this 'sensitivity' to nature and lyric evocation of place, is all irrelevant to Nat Turner as a fictional creation, has nothing to do with his conflicts or hopes or fears, with his position within the field of fictional energies . . . with the moral or existential meanings which presumably Styron is pursuing." One of Styron's outstanding strengths as a novelist is in his descriptions, his evocations of place, which worked so well either to reinforce or to counterpoint the dramatic scenes in his earlier works, but in this novel they betray his uncertainty. Another of his strengths is in his handling of action, but here it leads to a simplification of his psychological insights.

Margaret Whitehead served Styron as a psychological springboard. The story of Nat Turner had been working in his mind since he read the original confessions in the late forties, and he had planned to make Turner the subject of his second novel. Years later, having finally started to write *The Confessions*, he traveled back to the scene of the rebellion, and as he approached the house of Mrs. Catherine Whitehead, he "tried to recollect its particular role in Nat's destiny." Then he remembered:

There was something baffling, secret, irrational about Nat's own participation in the uprising. He was unable to kill. Time and time again in his confession one discovers him saying (in an offhand tone; one must dig for the implications): "I could not give the death blow, the hatchet glanced from his head," or, "I struck her several blows over the head, but I was unable to kill her as the sword was dull . . ." It is too much to believe, over and over again: the glancing hatchet, the dull sword. It smacks rather, as in *Hamlet*, of rationalization, ghastly fear, an access of guilt, a shrinking from violence, and fatal irresolution. Alone here at this house, turned now into a huge corncrib around which pigs rooted and snorted in the silence of a spring afternoon, here alone was Nat finally able—or was he forced?—to commit a murder, and this upon a girl of eighteen named Margaret Whitehead, described by Drewry . . . as "the belle of the country." The scene is apocalyptic—afternoon bedlam in the wild harsh sunlight and August heat.

Styron shows Nat Turner to be motivated by the sublimation of his desire for the white woman of his dreams, who finally takes the form of Margaret Whitehead. In the interview with Canzoneri and Stegner, Styron points to the complexity of such sublimation when he explains the "love-hate relationship" between Nat, the puritanic but virile young man, and the "unconsciously flirtatious" eighteen-year-old white girl "who's the only nubile girl, so far as I can find out, killed during the insurrection": "The barrier is incredible, but it's tissue paper thin, and for just that reason it's all the more impermeable. And so the way that you break it down is in the most apocalyptic way that is possible to a human being. You break through it by killing." Louis Rubin makes an even better case for Styron when he interprets Nat Turner's real rebellion to derive not so much from his bondage or his exploitation but from society's depriving him of his right to love and be loved. "The world he inhabits is such that at best he can expect from whites only pity, and at worst outright hatred, while from his fellow slaves he can expect only inarticulate admiration at best, and at worst envy and contempt. Thus he cannot *give* himself to anyone. No one wants him for what he is. For everyone, white and black, friend and foe, he must play a role. . . . Denied, therefore, the right to give himself, to love, Nat can only hate, and the result is destruction."

Both Styron's observation and Rubin's interpretation tell us much about the potential of Nat's characterization, but unfortunately the novel is not developed to realize these complex insights or to make us feel their emotional impact. Margaret Whitehead is a paper character, cut from the pattern of southern romance. And her relation with Nat is too transparent a device, designed to reveal impulses which Styron in his interview for the *New York Times* defines as, "historically speaking, those of the traditional revolutionary—that is to say puritanical, repressive and sublimated." Nat Turner is a weak character not because of Styron's "racism," nor because it is impossible for a white man to create a successful black revolutionary. It is because Turner, billed as a unique and complex character, is diminished or explained away by such simplified psychology. This is not to say that Styron was wrong in seeing the traditional revolutionary as puritanical, repressive, and sublimated, just that he did not go far enough in developing this potential. We need only look for an example to Peter Weiss's characterization of Marat, whose sublimations are convincing and interesting, and who still emerges as heroic—and as a revolutionary.

The challenge that exercised Styron's imagination was to enter the consciousness of Nat Turner, to tell the story from his point of view. We are led to wonder whether Styron might have developed Nat Turner more convincingly and more interestingly, whether he might indeed have grappled more strenuously with the enigma of Nat's character, by choosing a different vantage—by learning from his experience in *The Long March* and *Set This House on Fire* to gain some distance on a man of heroic proportions. A secondary character—black or white, historical or contemporary, trying to comprehend the meager facts of the original confession necessarily distorted by the lawyer who transcribed it for the white jury—might develop the ironies and the clashes of perspective, might deepen and expand the scope of the novel, might leave Nat Turner an engaging enigma.

The failure of *The Confessions* may well be due to Styron's integrity and daring. For if in his early works he was bridging the experiences of the twenties and fifties, here he is building a bridge to a generation not content to view life as an accident, to see man as a clown suffering violation and indignity, or to accept injustice as irremediable. It may be that this view caused him to fall back on a pattern that obscures the realities of Nat Turner's world and of our own. But what makes Styron's development so exhilarating to follow is that like Mannix and Cass he takes "the hardest way," seeks out the existential challenge, and embodies the conflict between Christian humanism and

a world that denies such values. He believes in the traditional novel form, with its faith in character, plot, and ultimate knowledge. Yet at his best he evokes a world where irrational warfare is the condition of life, a world that undermines psychological connections, temporal causation, and any kind of certainty. If Styron is ambivalent, he makes us suffer the ambivalence—suffer the loss of humane values while remaining engaged in a struggle to preserve them.

Selected Bibliography

WORKS OF WILLIAM STYRON

BOOKS

Lie Down in Darkness. New York: Bobbs-Merrill, 1951.

The Long March. New York: Random House, 1956.

Set This House on Fire. New York: Random House, 1960.

The Confessions of Nat Turner. New York: Random House, 1967.

Published since the writing of this essay

Sophie's Choice. New York: Random House, 1980.

SHORT STORIES

"Autumn," *One and Twenty: Duke Narrative and Verse, 1924–1945,* edited by W. Blackburn. Durham, N.C.: Duke University Press, 1945.

"The Long Dark Road," *One and Twenty: Duke Narrative and Verse, 1924–1945,* edited by W. Blackburn. Durham, N.C.: Duke University Press, 1945.

"A Moment in Trieste," *American Vanguard, 1948,* edited by Don M. Wolfe. Ithaca, N.Y.: Cornell University Press, 1948.

"The Enormous Window," *American Vanguard, 1950,* edited by Charles I. Glicksberg. New York: New School for Social Research, 1950.

"[The] Long March," *discovery No. 1,* edited by

John W. Aldridge and Vance Bourjaily. New York: Pocket Books, 1953.

"The McCabes," *Paris Review*, 6:12–28 (Autumn-Winter 1960). (Part of Chapter VI of *Set This House on Fire*.)

ARTICLES AND REVIEWS

"Letter to an Editor," *Paris Review*, 1:9–13 (Spring 1953).

"The Prevalence of Wonders," *Nation*, 76:370–71 (May 2, 1953).

"The Paris Review," *Harper's Bazaar*, 87:122, 173 (August 1953).

"What's Wrong with the American Novel?" *American Scholar*, 24:464–503 (Autumn 1955).

"If You Write for Television . . ." *New Republic*, 140:16 (April 6, 1959). (On the television adaptation of *The Long March*.)

"Introduction," *Best Short Stories from the Paris Review*. New York: Dutton, 1959.

"Mrs. Aadland's Little Girl, Beverly," *Esquire*, 56:142, 189–91 (November 1961).

"The Death-in-Life of Benjamin Reid," *Esquire*, 57:114, 141–45 (February 1962).

"As He Lay Dead, a Bitter Grief," *Life*, 53:39–42 (July 20, 1962). (On Faulkner's funeral.)

"The Aftermath of Benjamin Reid," *Esquire*, 58:79, 81, 158, 160, 164 (November 1962).

"Two Writers Talk It Over," *Esquire*, 60:57–59 (July 1963). (Styron and James Jones.)

"Overcome," *New York Review of Books*, 1:18–19 (September 26, 1963). (Review of Herbert Aptheker's *American Slave Revolts*.)

"An Elegy for F. Scott Fitzgerald," *New York Review of Books*, 1:1–3 (November 28, 1963).

"The Habit," *New York Review of Books*, 1:13–14 (December 26, 1963).

"A Southern Conscience," *New York Review of Books*, 2:3 (April 2, 1964).

"Tootsie Rolls," *New York Review of Books*, 2:8 (May 14, 1964).

"MacArthur's Reminiscences," *New York Review of Books*, 3:3–5 (October 8, 1964).

"This Quiet Dust," *Harper's*, 230:134–46 (April 1965).

"Vice That Has No Name," *Harper's*, 236:97–100 (February 1966).

"William Styron Replies," *Nation*, 544–47 (April 22, 1968). (Reply to Herbert Aptheker's review of *Nat Turner*.)

"The Shade of Thomas Wolfe," *Harper's*, 236:96–104 (April 1968).

"Oldest America," *McCall's*, 95:94, 123 (July 1968).

"My Generation," *Esquire*, 70:123–24 (October 1968).

CRITICAL AND BIOGRAPHICAL STUDIES

Baumbach, Jonathan. *The Landscape of Nightmare*. New York: New York University Press, 1965.

Brandriff, Welles T. "The Rule of Order and Disorder in *The Long March*," *English Journal*, 56:54–59 (January 1967).

Canzoneri, Robert, and Page Stegner. "An Interview with William Styron," *Per/Se*, 1:37–44 (Summer 1966).

Clarke, John H., editor. *William Styron's Nat Turner: Ten Black Writers Respond*. Boston: Beacon, 1968. (Includes Turner's *Confessions*.)

Davis, Robert Gorham. "The American Individualist Tradition: Bellow and Styron," *The Creative Present*, edited by Nona Balakian and Charles Simmons. New York: Doubleday, 1963.

————. "Styron and the Students," *Critique*, 3:37–46 (Summer 1960).

Dempsey, David. "Talk with William Styron," *New York Times Book Review*, September 9, 1951, p. 27.

Fossum, Robert H. *William Styron: A Critical Essay*. Grand Rapids, Mich.: William B. Eerdmans, 1968.

Friedman, Melvin J. "William Styron: An Interim Appraisal," *English Journal*, 50:149–58, 192 (March 1961).

Galloway, David D. *The Absurd Hero in American Fiction*. Austin, Texas: University of Texas Press, 1966.

Geismar, Maxwell. *American Moderns*. New York: Hill and Wang, 1958.

Gilman, Richard. "Nat Turner Revisited," *New Republic*, 158:23–32 (April 27, 1968).

Gossett, Louise Y. *Violence in Recent Southern Fiction*. Durham, N.C.: Duke University Press, 1965.

Hassan, Ihab. "The Novel of Outrage: A Minority Voice in Postwar American Fiction," *American Scholar*, 34:239–53 (Spring 1965).

———. *Radical Innocence*. Princeton, N.J.: Princeton University Press, 1961.

Hoffman, Frederick J. "The Cure of 'Nothing!': The Fiction of William Styron," *Frontiers of American Culture*, edited by Ray B. Browne *et al.* Indianapolis, Ind.: Purdue University Press, 1968.

Kauffmann, Stanley. "Styron's Unwritten Novel," *Hudson Review*, 20:675–80 (Winter 1967–68).

Klotz, Marvin. "The Triumph over Time: Narrative Form in William Faulkner and William Styron," *Mississippi Quarterly*, 17:9–20 (Winter 1963–64).

Matthiessen, Peter, and George Plimpton. "The Art of Fiction," *Paris Review*, 2:42–57 (Spring 1954). Reprinted in *Writers at Work: The Paris Review Interviews*, edited by Malcolm Cowley. New York: Viking, 1958.

Monaghan, Charles. "Portrait of a Man Reading," *Book World*, 2:8 (October 27, 1968). (Interview with Styron.)

Nigro, August. *"The Long March*: The Expansive Hero in a Closed World," *Critique*, 9:103–12 (No. 3, 1967).

O'Connell, Shaun. "The Expense of Spirit: The Vision of William Styron," *Critique*, 8:20–33 (Winter 1966).

Plimpton, George. "William Styron: A Shared Ordeal," *New York Times Book Review*, October 8, 1967, pp. 2, 3, 30, 32, 34. (Interview with Styron.)

Roth, Philip. "Writing American Fiction," *Commentary*, 31:222–33 (March 1961).

Rubin, Louis D., Jr. *The Faraway Country*. Seattle: University of Washington Press, 1963.

———. "Notes on the Literary Scene: Their Own Language," *Harper's*, 230:173–75 (April 1965).

———. "The South and the Faraway Country," *Virginia Quarterly Review*, 38:444–59 (Summer 1962).

———. "William Styron and Human Bondage: *The Confessions of Nat Turner*," *Hollins Critic*, 4:1–12 (December 1967).

Sokolov, Raymond. "Into the Mind of Nat Turner," *Newsweek*, 70:65–69 (October 16, 1967).

Stevenson, David L. "Styron and the Fiction of the Fifties," *Critique*, 3:47–58 (Summer 1960).

Thelwell, Mike. "Back with the Wind: Mr. Styron and the Reverend Turner," in *William Styron's Nat Turner: Ten Black Writers Respond*, edited by John H. Clarke.

Urang, Gunnar. "The Broader Vision: William Styron's *Set This House on Fire*," *Critique*, 8:47–69 (Winter 1966).

Waldmeir, Joseph. "Quest without Faith," *Nation*, 193:390–96 (November 18, 1961).

Winner, Arthur. "Adjustment, Tragic Humanism and Italy," *Studi Americani*, 7:311–61 (1961).

—RICHARD PEARCE

Allen Tate

1899-1979

ONE OF Allen Tate's essays, "A Southern Mode of the Imagination," mentions an amiable old calumny against Kentucky: that it seceded from the Union after the fighting was over. Lincoln had promised not to disturb the institution of slavery in Kentucky if Kentucky stayed in the Union, and the promise was kept. Loyal to the Union throughout the Civil War, Kentucky was only nominally in the Union from December 1865, when the Thirteenth Amendment abolished slavery, until about the time of World War I, when the South generally began to look outside itself and see, Tate says, "for the first time since about 1830 that the Yankees were not to blame for everything." John Orley Allen Tate (to give him his full name), born in Winchester, Clark County, Kentucky, on November 19, 1899, is thus by origin an American for whom the ordinary doubleness of loyalty to region and nation is intensified. There is, indeed, another view of Tate, Tate as professional southerner, born too late to be a Confederate soldier and regretting it all his life, continuously refighting the Civil War in his imagination, and employing his talents to glorify a way of life that scarcely existed. This view is of value because it asks to be corrected, and that is what I propose to do: first by bringing together the biographical data, and looking at the early work and

some of the poems of the period 1922-38; then by turning to the fiction, particularly *The Fathers* (1938, 1960), and the essays; and finally by looking at some of the poems written since 1938.

True to the geography of his birth, Tate is a Borderer, a man who seems torn between conflicting loyalties but who has managed to find a coherent set of values. His ancestry is the not uncommon mixture of Scotch-Irish and English, with an additional strain of Roman Catholics on his mother's Maryland side of the family. Like William Faulkner and Robert Lowell he writes about his family, but not with literal exactness. Much is transformed by the imagination. Thus, for example, Tate's actual maternal great-grandfather, Major Benjamin Lewis Bogan, took it upon himself to "correct" Wordsworth's grammar in the *Lyrical Ballads,* while a character Tate invented, Major Lewis Buchan in *The Fathers,* speaks in the easy-going way of a man who "would not have understood our conception of 'correct English.'"

Tate's early education was, as Louise Cowan has said, "haphazard . . . a patchwork . . . irregular." He went twelve years to school altogether, including college. Any reader of Mrs. Cowan's valuable book, *The Fugitive Group* (1959), will be aware how much I am in her debt for the biographical part of this essay.

The twelve years included a single year at the Tarbox School, Nashville; three years at the Cross School, Louisville; and a half year each at two public high schools. He spent a final single year at the Georgetown University Preparatory School before entering Vanderbilt University, where, like many literary students, he was not at home in the study of mathematics and science. He liked languages, particularly Latin, and he liked metaphysics, but he had to hire a tutor in mathematics (in the witty way of the world it was Dorothy Bethurum, the medievalist) to prepare him for entrance. Close to graduation, in May 1922, a threat of tuberculosis sent him to a mountain resort in North Carolina. He returned to Vanderbilt to receive the bachelor's degree in 1923, as of the class of 1922.

Tate's formal education ended at Vanderbilt, but his lifelong friendship with John Crowe Ransom began there. In his sophomore year he was enrolled as a student of Ransom's in Advanced Composition, Ransom at that time being a thirty-one-year-old assistant professor of English, just back from wartime service in France, and the author of *Poems about God*. Tate got an A— in the course, with the comment that he did not display his best sentences to their best advantage. On the occasion of Tate's sixtieth birthday Ransom wrote that Tate as a student "had a native sense, or at least a very early sense, of being called to the vocation of literature, and he had decided to start his writing at the top. . . . He wrote essays about the literary imagination, with corollary excursions into linguistics and metaphysics; they were slightly bewildering to me in more ways than one. But I would not have stopped him if I could; he was a step beyond my experience." Ransom's ironic tone is evident, but there is no sarcasm in it.

Tate remembers taking another course from Ransom the next year, 1920. This one included the nineteenth-century Samuel Butler and the early Yeats, but it is possible that the more recent poems of Yeats reached the student before they reached the teacher; Ransom tells how Tate as an undergraduate wrote "in the consciousness of a body of literature which was unknown to his fellow students, and to my faculty associates and myself, unless it was by the purest hearsay. A new literature had made its brilliant beginnings, and there were advanced journals and books which were full of it if we had looked." At this early stage we see Tate looking for models outside the South and indeed outside the whole country.

Tate was the first undergraduate at Vanderbilt to be invited to join the Fugitives, a Nashville group of devotees of poetry and philosophy. Ransom was more or less the acknowledged leading spirit of the group, which included the poet Donald Davidson, who invited Tate to come to the meetings. Robert Penn Warren, with whom Tate shared a dormitory room, joined later. In the Fugitives' magazine (which originally came out between 1922 and 1925; it was reprinted in a single bound volume in 1966) Ransom's contributions—constituting the main burst of poetic activity in his career—perhaps overshadow the work of his friends, but nine of the two score or so poems that Tate contributed to *The Fugitive* were good enough to survive in his *Poems* (1960). One of the best of these, "Homily," first appeared in *The Fugitive* for March 1925. Its quality is good evidence for Ransom's claim that Tate "came unerringly into his poetic identity." It carries the motto "If thine eye offend thee, pluck it out," and it reached its present form several years after first publication:

> If your tired unspeaking head
> Rivet the dark with linear sight,
> Crazed by a warlock with his curse

Dreamed up in some loquacious bed,
And if the stage-dark head rehearse
The fifth act of the closing night,

Why, cut it off, piece after piece,
And throw the tough cortex away,
And when you've marveled on the wars
That wove their interior smoke its way,
Tear out the close vermiculate crease
Where death crawled angrily at bay.

A latter-day Thomas Rymer might paraphrase "Homily" as follows: "A drastic but effective cure for insomnia is decapitation." Seen in this light the poem has the flat-footed violence of a story of Hemingway's, "God Rest Ye Merry, Gentlemen," which is about a boy who tries to castrate himself but doesn't know what castration really is anatomically. The differences between poem and story are of course more to the point. Hemingway's boy is pitiable, and no real representative of modern man; he is closer to St. Paul. But Tate's insomniac is both representative and heroic. The head is tired, unspeaking, intensely active but with no object for its activity, driven mad by some perennial curse as from a magician or a parent. The light tone of "Why, cut it off" suggests that decapitation is not really meant; the cure for a sense of nada is not anti-rationalism. One can, however, imagine a kind of autopsy, in which it is discovered that gray matter didn't cause the trouble but the idea of death, which we all share.

Even at this early stage Tate was not content to write poems for *The Fugitive* only. "Euthanasia," a poem even earlier than "Homily" (it later became an elegy for Jefferson Davis), appeared in *The Double-Dealer* for March 1922. Hart Crane, a contributor to the same issue of the magazine, introduced himself to Tate by writing him a letter which said that he saw in "Euthanasia" the mark of T. S. Eliot. What Crane saw was not an echoing of anything specifically Eliot's (Tate had not in fact read Eliot at the time) but rather an early mastery or comprehension of a period style—the dry bones, burnt-out cinder style deriving from Hulme and Bergson. Crane's letter sent Tate to Eliot (he read the 1920 *Poems* that spring), and later when Tate passed through New York it was through Crane that he had the chance to meet writers from outside the South.

The Fugitives, though not as avant-garde as their contemporaries in New York, were at least committed to a new poetry, and one would have expected them to receive *The Waste Land* cordially; but roughly speaking only the younger Fugitives, led by Tate, were enthusiastic. Ransom actively disliked the poem. Donald Davidson and Robert Penn Warren read it in the *Dial* as soon as it came out, and discussed it with Professors W. C. Curry and Ransom. The room in a university dormitory that Tate shared with Warren and with Ridley Wills was decorated with scenes from *The Waste Land* which Warren drew by erasing lines of soot from the dirty plaster; Tate remembers "particularly the rat creeping through the vegetation, and the typist putting a record on the gramophone."

Two pieces by Tate appeared in the December 1922 issue of *The Fugitive*: a pro-Eliot editorial and a poem, "Nuptials," written in the Laforgue-Eliot manner. Ransom seems to have been not altogether happy about them. One night in the spring of 1923 Tate and Wills made fun of the burning issue of modernism versus traditionalism by writing *The Golden Mean and Other Poems*. The book consists of rival versions of poems on the same subject, Tate giving the subject a modernist treatment and Wills a traditionalist treatment. Tate's version of one of the poems, "The Chaste Land," ends with the words "Shanty, Shanty, Shanty," grotesquely annotated.

In July 1923 Ransom reviewed *The Waste Land* in the book review section of the *New York Evening Post*. This was not so much a review as a caveat to all poets of the future. Tate rose to Eliot's defense three weeks later; unfortunately, Ransom's essay must have brought him close to apoplexy or inarticulate dismay. He did not defend Eliot well. It was a little as if Poe had gone out after Quintilian; Quintilian had the last word. Ransom took Tate's outburst to be "but a proper token of emancipation, composed upon the occasion of his accession to the ripe age of twenty-three" —one of the few times, surely, that Ransom's onion-like irony turned to sarcasm (maybe not even then, if you think of "How Soon Hath Time"), though Tate had provoked it. He had said that Eliot wouldn't care what Ransom thought, and he has wondered since how Ransom ever managed to forgive him. The episode was but one moment of unpleasantness in a lifetime of friendship.

Nineteen twenty-four was the year of Tate's setting forth into the great world. He taught high school briefly in Lumberport, West Virginia, hoping to save enough money to accumulate a grubstake for New York. He got to New York for a visit in June, and Hart Crane introduced him to Malcolm Cowley, Kenneth Burke, Slater Brown, and other literary young men. Cowley and Tate remember the circumstances. Tate appeared at the apartment of a director of the Provincetown Playhouse "neatly dressed in a dark suit, carrying a preposterous walking stick and wearing a Phi Beta Kappa key." Cowley said to him: "We no longer wear our Phi Beta Kappa keys." He struck Cowley as having the best manners of any young man he had ever met: "He used politeness not only as a defense but sometimes as an aggressive weapon against strangers."

During the summer of 1924, as a guest of Warren in Guthrie, Kentucky, Tate met his first wife, the novelist Caroline Gordon. They married that fall on the strength of a job that Susan Jenkins (later the wife of Slater Brown) got him. The job was as assistant editor of a magazine that was a competitor of *Snappy Stories*; it was called *Telling Tales*, and it was put out by the ineffably named Climax Publishing Company. He stuck it out at this job until November 1925, when the Tates decided to try to live and write away from New York City. For ten dollars a month they rented eight rooms of a house near Patterson, New York. The landlady was a Mrs. Addie Turner.

As if it wasn't enough for Tate to be supporting his wife and himself on what he could earn by writing poems and book reviews, he concerned himself with the welfare of Hart Crane, who had been living off small loans from friends in New York. He offered Crane the use of two of the eight rooms to live in and write *The Bridge*. When Crane arrived in Patterson, however, he had just received two thousand dollars from the philanthropist Otto Kahn, and he was already spending it at a great rate. Many years later, Tate told an interviewer, Michael Millgate, about the southerner's "consciousness of superiority in poverty." The Tates were willing to be penniless patrons of a writer as poor as themselves, but from the beginning Crane seems to have enjoyed playing the role of dispenser of Otto Kahn's money.

There is no record of any agreement among the three as to the sharing of household jobs, but for a while Tate cooked breakfast, Mrs. Tate cooked lunch and dinner, and Crane did the dishes. The arrangement didn't last, and some time during the winter Crane began taking his meals with Mrs. Turner. He stopped helping Tate cut wood for the Tates' two stoves, his own room being heated by a kerosene stove. After some celebrating at Christmas and a period when Tate spent a lot of time hunting, all three writers settled down to work. Unfortunately, Crane's inspiration gave out in March, and not being able to work much himself he often interrupted the Tates in their work. It is amazing that the household in Patterson held together as long as it did; Crane left Patterson at the end of April. The Tates stayed on through the summer, raising a vegetable garden, but they were not up to a second winter in Patterson, and in the fall of 1926 they moved to a basement flat on Perry Street, in Greenwich Village.

The beginnings of the "Ode to the Confederate Dead" belong to this period. The very success of this poem in later years, the number of times it has been reprinted in anthologies, the notoriety Tate himself lent it with his essay "Narcissus as Narcissus" (1938)—these things have distorted the casual reader's notion of Tate. The title alone—and some readers recall little but titles—is cause of offense to many. Why "Ode"? Doesn't that mean public celebration? Let the dead bury their dead; no use picking old sores. That Tate would agree is not much help to those who won't bother to find out that he agrees.

The poem started out as an elegy and did not reach its final form until 1936. Early in 1927 Tate sent copies of the first version to Ransom, Davidson, and Crane. The Princeton Library owns the earliest typescript, with Ransom's marginal comments. Davidson did not like the poetic direction his friend seemed to be taking: "Your 'Elegy,'" he said, "is not for the Confederate dead but for your own dead emotion." Crane made some extremely perceptive criticisms, and understood immediately what the poem was about: "Chivalry, a tradition of excess, active faith . . . *'should be yours tomorrow'* but . . . will not persist nor find any way into action."

That is, the "Ode to the Confederate Dead" has a lot in common with *The Great Gatsby.*

The man at the gate of the Confederate graveyard has "knowledge carried to the heart" and Jay Gatsby has "some heightened sensitivity to the promises of life"; they come to the same thing. The man at the gate allows himself to imagine, if only for a moment, that the leaves he sees blown by the wind are charging infantry; Gatsby, when Nick Carraway tells him he can't repeat the past, says: "Can't repeat the past? Why of course you can." The man at the gate has "waited for the angry resolution/Of those desires that should be [his] tomorrow"; Gatsby "believed in the green light." Both men are accounted failures, or rather they fail and are memorialized in their failure. Neither is an international *Waste Land* character. The man at the gate is philosophical, like Hamlet, but he is not a prince; he is ineffectual, like Prufrock, but he is not ridiculous; he is as American as Jay Gatsby but he is not a vulgarian "in the service of a vast, vulgar, meretricious beauty." Poor Gatsby really did go to Oxford, but talks about it in such a way as to convince Nick Carraway he is lying; somewhere along the line the man at the gate has learned about Zeno and Parmenides, so that he understands the wider reference of his problem. I can't help thinking of the inventors of the two characters: Tate got a serviceable education at Vanderbilt, Fitzgerald an indifferent one at Princeton.

The beginnings of the Agrarian movement —led by four of the Fugitives (Davidson, Ransom, Tate, and Warren) and eight other southerners—belong to the same period as the first draft of the "Ode to the Confederate Dead." A Tennessee law signed on March 18, 1925, prohibited the teaching of evolution in the tax-supported schools of the state. That summer old William Jennings Bryan's advocacy of the law in Dayton, Tennessee, made the state and the South the butt of easy ridicule throughout the country. Practically at the moment of the Fugitives' success at doing their bit for American letters in the South, the Dayton trials were making it a laughingstock and worse— a place of ignoramuses and bigots. It was much as if, in 1963, a Birmingham, Alabama, poet were to be awakened by dynamite. What could he do but get out? At the time of the Dayton trials Tate had already, as he thought, escaped the South, and was rationalizing his course of action as the only one possible for a writer of southern birth. But in March 1926 he wrote Davidson that he had an idea for an essay on fundamentalism. In it he would "define the rights of both parties, science and religion," and he added that he was afraid "that science has very little to say for itself." He never wrote the essay though he did review *The Decline of the West* for the *Nation* under the title "Fundamentalism." In any case, Mrs. Cowan is surely right when she says that northern ridicule of the Dayton trials moved Tate in the direction of a defense of the South, when before he was on the side of its critics.

On March 1, 1927, Tate wrote Davidson that he had "attacked the South for the last time, except in so far as it may be necessary to point out that the chief defect the Old South had was that in it which produced, through whatever cause, the New South." Some of the Fugitives were about to discover the serpent in the garden disguised as science and industrialism. Later in the same month Tate was proposing to Ransom an idea for a Southern Symposium—a collection of poems and stories which would show the world what the South really stood for. But Ransom, doubting that he and Tate could find many such poems and stories ("In the Old South the life aesthetic was actually realized, and there are the fewer object-lessons in its specific art"), proposed instead a collection of essays celebrating an agrarian as against an industrial society. Tate

must have agreed to this; the result, three years later, was *I'll Take My Stand; The South and the Agrarian Tradition*, by Twelve Southerners —"an escapade," Ransom called it in 1959, "the last fling of our intellectual youth."

In 1925 Tate had set for himself a program of reading in southern history, and the fruits of this are his biographies of Stonewall Jackson (1928) and Jefferson Davis (1929). He also helped negotiate a contract between Robert Penn Warren and the publishers Payson and Clark for the writing of a biography of John Brown. An understanding of what was going on here is crucial to an understanding of Tate's later development.

As Tate saw the matter, the religion of the self-sufficiency of political man, the notion that man can fulfill his destiny solely through his political institutions, went into action during the American Civil War and won decisively. It has been winning all over the world ever since, though (I say this on my own) the greatly increased power of a barbarian version of it has tempered and gentled the American version. Among the Twelve Southerners, Andrew Lytle, Tate, and Warren had wanted to call the Agrarian manifesto "A Tract against Communism," but they were a minority; Yankeedom was enough of a Goliath for these Davids to take on without throwing the Bolsheviks into the bargain.

The religion of the self-sufficiency of political man was not a Yankee or even an American invention; but, according to Tate, the North really believed in it, and the South did not. The South was defeated, Tate said, because it did not possess "a sufficient faith in its own kind of God." This is an almost hopelessly old-fashioned way to write history, and some students of Tate's work have been quick to apologize for it, pointing out, for example, that both his biographies are labeled "narratives." But I would question the need of apologies. Couldn't he believe his thesis all the more for its unprovability by statistical methods? Tate's way of writing history is the same as Gibbon's, the same as Milton's in the last two books of *Paradise Lost,* and the same as St. Augustine's in *The City of God.* Civilizations rise and fall as they hold fast to or lose an active faith.

In Tate's version it is a little as if the Civil War had been a conflict between Yeats's men of passionate intensity and men who lack all conviction. It is of course more complicated than that and more interesting. For one thing, the division was not strictly North and South; there was that midwesterner who is reported to have said to a southerner: "We should have fit them easterners with their little paper collars." There were also men of passionate intensity on both sides. Representatives of these were John Brown and Stonewall Jackson: both martyrs, witnesses to their beliefs. In Tate's two biographies Jackson is shown to be as fanatical as Brown but he was a "good soldier," subordinate to Lee, and Lee in turn subordinated himself to President Jefferson Davis, who represents for Tate everything wrong with the South. His rise was without adversity, he complained constantly of "dyspepsia," he was obsessed to the end with his phantom Army Departments, even a "trans-Mississippi" one, and he treated Jackson and Lee as if they were secret weapons too terrible to use. He conducted the war as if he wanted to lose it, or if not lose it at least keep it going until the Old World came to his aid. As if Europe cared a straw about the society which Tate described fairly as "feudal, but without a feudal religion, and hence only semi-feudal." Europe, even Catholic Europe, had been busy for some time defeudalizing itself. Why should not the South do the same? The Agrarians could not stop this process, nor did they want

to restore anything unrestorable. "I never thought of Agrarianism as a restoration of anything in the Old South," Tate has said. "I saw it as something to be created . . . not only in the South . . . but in the moral and religious outlook of Western man."

Meanwhile Tate's poems had found a champion in the person of Ford Madox Ford, and Ford's recommendation was decisive in securing for Tate a Guggenheim Fellowship—an award, Tate has said, "that made all the difference to me." The Guggenheim allowed him to go to Paris, where he had a chance to get to know writers from a larger circle than that which New York attracted at the time. Every Sunday in the fall of 1929 he went with Hemingway to the bicycle races, almost every Sunday he went to the Bœuf sur le Toit, where the Fitzgeralds held court, and almost every night he sat with Ford at the Café des Deux Magots.

Tate was thirty-five years old and the author of five books when he got his first college teaching job. He took Robert Penn Warren's place at Southwestern at Memphis. He later taught at Princeton, New York University, the Kenyon School of English, the University of Chicago, and other universities. He taught at the University of Minnesota from 1951 until his retirement in 1968. He edited the *Sewanee Review* between 1944 and 1946. He has received many awards for his work, including the Bollingen Prize in Poetry in 1956, the Brandeis Award in 1961, the gold medal of the Dante Society of Florence in 1962, and the $5,000 award of the Academy of American Poets in 1963. He was elected president of the National Institute of Arts and Letters in 1964 and has been a member of the Board of Chancellors, the Academy of American Poets, since 1965.

Tate has married three times. Caroline Gordon obtained a divorce in the summer of 1959, and in August of the same year Tate married the poet Isabella Gardner, who was granted a divorce on March 28, 1966. Tate married Helen Heinz on July 30, 1966. Three sons have been born of this marriage—twins John Allen and Michael Paul, born August 30, 1967; and Benjamin Lewis Bogan on December 18, 1969. One of the twins, Michael Paul, died tragically in July 1968.

The present study cannot pretend to be definitive on biographical matters regarding Tate. Radcliffe Squires provides many additional details, and Tate himself has been engaged in writing a literary memoir, the first part of which was delivered as the Joseph Warren Beach Lecture at the University of Minnesota, April 16, 1970. For further details see the Bibliography appended to this essay.

In Tate's poems alone one can discover his distinctive set of mind, the extraordinary combination of insights and attitudes that sets him off from his contemporaries. The poems he wrote between 1922, when *The Fugitive* began, and 1938, when, with the publication of *The Fathers*, the first phase of his career was complete, are not a special version or combination of Ransom, Eliot, and Hart Crane, the poets Tate resembles most, but something separate and equally valuable.

Let me say first that there is little sweetness in Tate's poems of this first period; I mean the sweetness that Shakespeare's contemporaries noticed in him. There is sweetness everywhere in Ransom, there is some in Eliot, too ("The notion of some infinitely gentle/Infinitely suffering thing"), there is even some in Crane (as in "Black Tambourine"), but nothing quite like this in the earlier Tate. Or rather, there is little warmth as a quality perceived apart from an object, little warmth of "personality"

or "participation." Tate in this respect is a little like Dr. Cartwright of *The Fathers*: "just a voice, in the *ore rotundo* of impersonality, no feeling but in the words themselves." There are plenty of objects of the poet's affection, but that is something distinct or distinguishable:

Maryland, Virginia, Caroline
Pent images in sleep
Clay valleys rocky hills old fields of pine
Unspeakable and deep

Out of that source of time my farthest blood
Runs strangely to this day

The poet is related to his objects only by ties of blood; he lets the ties of affection speak for themselves. He enters later in the poem to inhabit an alien house: "There some time to abide / Took wife and child with me," where again the warmth is almost completely in the objects. The poet is provider, husband, father, but in his poems he suppresses almost to the disappearing point the warmth one is sure he feels.

"The Oath" is practically a statement of how it feels to suppress warmth:

It was near evening, the room was cold
Half dark; Uncle Ben's brass bullet-mould
And powder-horn and Major Bogan's face
Above the fire in the half-light plainly said:
There's naught to kill but the animated dead.
Horn nor mould nor major follows the chase.
Being cold I urged Lytle to the fire
In the blank twilight with not much left untold
By two old friends when neither's a great liar.
We sat down evenly in the smoky chill.

The objects of affection—the bullet-mould and powder-horn, the portrait, the fire itself—do not warm the room or the old friends, who are so cold that presently they are convinced that *they* are "the animated dead." Tate returns to twilight again and again. In "The Ancestors," another twilit poem, he asks the crucial question: "What masterful delay commands the blood / Breaking its access to the living heart?" Twilight should be "the pleasant hour" without the irony of that phrase in "The Meaning of Death, An After-Dinner Speech," but it cannot be this for modern man in his disbelief; he does not see fulfillment in twilight but the coming of dissolution:

> Punctilious abyss, the yawn of space
> Come once a day to suffocate the sight.
> There is no man on earth who can be free
> Of this, the eldest in the latest crime.

In a *Partisan Review* symposium on religion Tate said that all of his poems were about the suffering that comes from disbelief. The Morgenmensch of *Pippa Passes* can live through twilight and ignore it, or a Dostoevski can gloat and lick his chops over the imminence of night, but Tate lingers—arguing, to borrow his words in one of the "Sonnets at Christmas," that time of day's "difficult case."

The suffering of lovers is inevitable in such a world. In "Shadow and Shade" the lovers are as insubstantial as their world; they are, as Delmore Schwartz said, "merely shades within the universal shadow which is night and nature." And Tate cannot say "Ah, love, let us be true to one another":

> Companion of this lust, we fall,
> I said, lest we should die alone.

Love demands the surrender of one kind of integrity in the service of a higher integrity; lust does not. One kind of integrity is personal; the other is like a little white lie. In "Mother and Son" the mother "leans for the son's replies / At last to her importunate womanhood"; she waits for the answer to "her harsh command / That he should say the time is beautiful." The answer is not in the poem, or rather it stays in the son's mind and in the scene:

> The dreary flies, lazy and casual,
> Stick to the ceiling, buzz along the wall.
> O heart, the spider shuffles from the mould
> Weaving, between the pinks and grapes, his
>   pall.
> The bright wallpaper, imperishably old,
> Uncurls and flutters, it will never fall.

Poetic integrity is and is not a yea-saying to the universe; that is one reason, the other being talent, for the great beauty of the passage.

The fame of Tate's essay "Tension in Poetry" (1938) has partly obscured the physical and psychological fact of tension in many of his poems. By psychological tension I mean a resistance to surrendering, developing out of an inclination to surrender, some kind of integrity. Physical tension is simply a quality of Tate's usual poetic language: "a certain unique harshness of diction and meter," as Delmore Schwartz said, "and an equally curious violence of imagery and sentiment." In the poems you find the very words *strain, tense, tension, taut, tight, systaltic,* and the meter is not so much crabbed as tightly wound. Hold Tate's earlier poems across the room, as it were, and the aggregate seems as taut and tense as the long elastic cord under tension that you find under the outer covering of a golf ball. "Elegy," "The Paradigm," "Ode to Fear," "Ignis Fatuus," "The Eagle," and "The Subway" all have this quality, and perhaps come under the censure of a remarkable sentence in a letter that Hart Crane wrote to Tate in 1930: "So many true things have a way of coming out all the better without the strain to sum up the universe in one impressive little pellet." Crane is criticizing a whole movement toward pure poetry. Where are the relaxed, the diastolic poems? Knowledge cannot be carried to the heart unless blood is carried there first, and the heart gets its blood by relaxing.

I do not want to compound the error of James Russell Lowell's view of Poe ("the heart somehow all squeezed out by the mind") by applying it to Tate; I am saying that this is an across-the-room view. Come closer and you find things like this, from "A Dream":

The man walked on and as if it were yesterday
Came easily to a two-barred gate
And stopped, and peering over a little way
He saw a dog-run country store fallen-in,
Deserted, but he said, "Who's there?"

Or this stanza from "Last Days of Alice":

Bright Alice! always pondering to gloze
The spoiled cruelty she had meant to say
Gazes learnedly down her airy nose
At nothing, nothing thinking all the day.

Or these lines from "The Meaning of Death":

When I was a small boy living at home
The dark came on in summer at eight o'clock
For Little Lord Fauntleroy in a perfect frock
By the alley: mother took him by the ear
To teach of the mixed modes an ancient fear.

The modes of Tate's earlier poetry are tautness and relaxation; one is glad to have both, or one for the sake of the other.

Father Hopkins said: "Nothing is so beautiful as spring." His line could never make the grade among Tate's touchstones in "Tension in Poetry"; taken by itself, the line is almost pure extension or denotation. It is a statement; but such a statement coming from a poet like Hopkins, whose native inclination is to celebrate thinginess, proves chiefly his sheer barefaced honesty, his willingness to be taken for a fool. Though Tate himself warns us in "Tension in Poetry" that "no critical insight may impute an exclusive validity to any one kind" of poetry, that essay is not as good a guide

to Tate's poetry as Delmore Schwartz's essay of 1940. Schwartz showed how closely Eliot's tribute to Blake's honesty applies to Tate: "One of the essential facts about Tate's writing is the tireless effort and strained labor to be honest as a writer." His taut mode is a result of the effort to avoid the dishonest relaxation of a Stephen Vincent Benét. "It was not possible," Tate said in 1955, "that I should think Stephen Benét, an amiable and patriotic rhymester, as important as Hart Crane, an imperfect genius whose profound honesty drove him to suicide after years of debauchery had stultified his mind." In his relaxed mode, Tate follows the advice Crane himself gave him, that he should not "strain" to sum up the universe.

The bitter social criticism of the essays in verse ("Aeneas at Washington," "Retroduction to American History," "Causerie," and "Fragment of a Meditation") lies in the balance with the almost perfect ease of the final lines of "The Mediterranean":

We've cracked the hemispheres with careless
    hand!
Now, from the Gates of Hercules we flood

Westward, westward till the barbarous brine
Whelms us to the tired land where tasseling
    corn,
Fat beans, grapes sweeter than muscadine
Rot on the vine: in that land were we born.

This is almost personal, engaging, warm, but not quite; for once again the warmth is in the objects, not separable from them. After his fantastic voyage the American returns to his native country, and he can't say he loves it. But at least he understands it, and understanding may be the beginning of love. Tate's American has made the round trip, as Europeans are only beginning to do. The day of the one-way trip westward is over, and so is the day of no trip westward, the day of the mere European, who would say no doubt that we had a wasteful economy, to let such good grapes rot on the vine.

Several years ago Tate told Michael Millgate that he wrote *The Fathers* more or less by accident: "I was going to do a book concerning two different kinds of American families—pioneer families and colonial families—coming down about a hundred and fifty years and finally coming together; that is, two strains in my own family. I couldn't write it as history, so I decided to do just one side of the book that I'd originally planned."

The unwritten part of the book is represented in print by a short story, published in 1934, called "The Migration," the reminiscence of an old man named Rhodam Elwin, whose family migrated from Virginia to North Carolina and thence to Tennessee. Elwin represents the good Scotch-Irish pioneer in Tate's ancestry, the man who cleared the land and planted it to corn and wheat, not to tobacco. "Chew tobacco if you will," he says, "but never grow it." Growing tobacco in Tennessee is left to the English of Virginia, who buy up the land the Scotch-Irish cleared. "The Migration" is a complete story but too short and, as John Bradbury says in *The Fugitives: A Critical Account* (1958), is limited by being all pictorial, never scenic. It whets one's appetite for a fuller treatment.

Two years before "The Migration," Tate wrote his only other short story to date, "The Immortal Woman," which he has described as a dress rehearsal for *The Fathers*. The narrator of "The Immortal Woman" is a man named John Hermann, a native of Greencastle, Pennsylvania, who came to Georgetown with his family when he was a boy. He went directly from high school to service in the A.E.F. (not the Union Army, as Bradbury mistakenly says)

and came back from overseas paralyzed. "Something will hit you," he says, "the will of God, and you're no good for the rest of your life." He lives in poverty with his Aunt Charlotte, a seamstress. Confined to his wheelchair, he can do little but look out his window, listen to what his aunt's customers say, and pass the time in reflection. The great event of his narrative is the kiss he sees a young man with thick glasses bestow on an old lady. John Hermann has watched the old lady come into his view every fall of the ten years he has been paralyzed. During those years and, according to his aunt, for five years before, the old lady has come regularly, usually the last of October, to sit day after day on a green bench by the college gate and stare at an old house. A man Hermann takes to be her husband comes for her all but two times; one of those times a very old physician-looking man comes for her, and the other time the young man with the glasses takes her away for good. The young man kisses her, Hermann sees she is in tears, the young man leads her away, and that is the end of the story. Who is the young man?

And for that matter, who is the old lady and what is her interest in the house? We get hints of the answers from a Mrs. Dulany, a customer of Aunt Charlotte's. The old lady is the grandniece of the man who owned the house before the Civil War. He left it to his sister, the old lady's grandmother, who lived there with her husband and four children during the Reconstruction years. When she was a child, the old lady was a favorite of her mad Aunt Jane, the only one of the four children who did not move West. The old lady's father, George Posey, Junior, sent money back East to keep the household going, but during a visit of the old lady and her mother to Georgetown something happened ("Not, my dear," Mrs. Dulany says, "that anything really happened") to cause George Posey to stop sending money. That is all. Both John Hermann's story and Mrs. Dulany's story are full of portent but incomplete. How about Tate's story?

The best answer is that Tate felt it necessary to re-form and enlarge his materials for a novel. The factual detail that I have sketched out calls for allegorical interpretation, but *The Fathers* is not allegorical in the same way. Tate's problem in "The Immortal Woman" is the problem of all modern allegorists as he describes it in "Three Types of Poetry" (1934): "A modern poet, attempting allegory, undoes the history. We accept his figures and images as amiable make-believe, knowing that historical fact and poetic figure have no real connection." Does Tate undo the history in "The Immortal Woman"? Is it all idea, an Agrarian tract?

It is, very nearly. The old lady is the Southerner Obsessed, returning to a dead past year after year "in the elegy season." She returns compulsively or naturally, like a migratory bird. The physician, Dr. Lacy Beckitt, tries unsuccessfully to cure her. The house is the Old South—older than the United States, handed over to the violent and the mad and the fugitive, "too elegant for poor people, and too large; too shabby . . . for the rich." The George Posey of this story is a little like the actual Fugitives, supporting the Old South for a while, but, after some access of knowledge, moving on to new concerns. The young man, "who looked like a tower of new brick," is the New South; 1927 or 1928, the year of John Hermann's narration, is the time of its first triumph. The kiss is New in an almost obscene relationship with Old; the kiss reduces the old lady to tears because the alternative, to be left staring at the nada of the house, is worse. The kiss is like the series of centenary celebrations of the Civil War, where commercial interests agreed to exploit the old, nearly dead, emotions.

If "The Immortal Woman" were purer allegory it would be an inferior story; if Tate had been satisfied with adding factual details that would fill an allegorical scheme more completely, he would not have needed to write *The Fathers*. In going from the story to the novel he represented much more literally his mother's family, he filled in characters only sketched in the story, he created places for them to move around in, and he invented a plot (or adapted one—it is much like the plot of *The Duchess of Malfi*) to bring his characters to their destinies.

The Fathers can be described briefly as two hundred pages of enveloping situation followed by a rapid sequence of events and an extreme instance of *progression d'effet* in the final paragraph. A summary statement of what happens —the narrator calls it "the violence"—is a good introduction to the book: When Susan Posey, born Buchan, discovers what her in-laws are really like, she acts to prevent further intermarriage between the two families. She prevents the marriage of her brother Semmes Buchan and her sister-in-law Jane Posey by encouraging her husband's Negro half-brother Yellow Jim to enter the bedroom of his half-sister Jane. Jane's scream kills her mother, Jane enters a convent, Semmes shoots Yellow Jim, George Posey shoots Semmes, and Susan goes mad.

William Archer's objection to *The Duchess of Malfi*, that there are too many corpses at the end as compared with *Hamlet*, could also be made to *The Fathers*; this is a lot of violence, but two characters who survive it—George Posey and the narrator, Dr. Lacy Buchan—meet more ingenious fates.

So much of the violence depends on Susan Posey that as we read or reread (*The Fathers* is one of those novels like Faulkner's *The Hamlet* that seems almost designed to frustrate first reading and reward second and third and fourth readings), we ought to look at her closely. Who is she? She is "not beautiful" but "lovely"; she got her looks and character from her ancestors named Washburn, early settlers in Virginia and presumably Anglican; her mother, Sarah Semmes Gore, whose funeral is the opening scene of the book, is a Presbyterian married to an Episcopalian. Susan's marriage to George Posey in 1859 seems to have been the ordinary result of propinquity and sexual attraction; she is particularly attracted by his strange and romantic impulses. When the war begins, George Posey absents himself from Susan, not for open and honorable military service, but to be a smuggler; he buys arms in the North for the use of the National Rifles, formed by his grandfather Jeremaiah Gibson and now about to fight on the Confederate side. As far as we know, George Posey is only smuggling, but Susan feels he is being unfaithful to her. She says to her brother: "Lacy, I might have done better to marry some plain man. Like Jim Higgins. He would have been so grateful, and I should have known every minute where he was." Higgins is her father's overseer.

The culmination of Susan's feelings against the Poseys (a family "more refined than the Buchans, but less civilized") is her encouragement of Yellow Jim. Victimized himself by his parents and his half-brother George, Yellow Jim's victim is Jane. "A docility of nature that made her a joy to her family" also made her a perfect object of her sister-in-law's high-minded or Satanic malice. Jane is a "girl wholly without imagination who, in order to create excitement that she could not find in herself, imagined that because Jim was a runaway there was something sinister about him."

The fathers of the title are specifically Rozier Posey, George's father, a man of "secrecy of action and brutality of character"; and Major Lewis Buchan, surely one of the sweetest products of the American imagination. His military rank came from service in the county militia in the War of 1812. He does not write his address Pleasant Hill, the family name of the place, but Burke's Station. "Ain't that where we get our mail?" he says. He is a great reader and a unionist; he does not call those of the other persuasion "secesh" but "disunionist." His great friend and spiritual adviser Dr. Cartwright, the local Episcopal minister, "a pleasant worldling," he praises as "the kind of pastor a gentleman can talk to." When northern troops are about to burn Pleasant Hill, Major Buchan has too much pride to save the place by telling them he is unionist. He hangs himself, and his body would have been eaten by hogs except for Jim Higgins.

An important part of the novel is the relationship between George Posey and his brother-in-law Lacy Buchan, Major Buchan's youngest son, born in 1845 and the teller of the story in 1911. He is a retired physician and a bachelor. Tate told Michael Millgate that Lacy Buchan was perhaps a projection of himself and that George Posey was "a rather romantic projection" of one of his older brothers. In the last chapter of *The Sense of Life in the Modern Novel*, Arthur Mizener says that *Tate* is Posey, and he may be right. The relationship between narrator and hero is hard to pin down and yet it must be understood. Much of the enveloping situation of the novel is young Lacy's hero worship of George and the mature narrator's awareness of George's inadequacy. George is no Major Buchan. He cannot bear ceremony; he runs away from the funeral of Lacy's mother. The mating of animals embarrasses him; older members of the family excuse him by saying that he grew up in town. Young Lacy thinks George "could never have anything to do with death," but George has a great deal to do with death; though he says fighting is nonsense he shoots two men dead and provides weapons for the National Rifles. He thinks he cannot choose sides in the war but he does; he makes all the possible choices. After "the violence" he has what is probably the briefest career of private soldier, C.S.A., on record. He spends one night as a private, but the next day is made acting executive officer of the company he has armed. An old quarrel, the fact of his Catholicism, and his rapid rise in rank lead an old enemy of his to insult him, and he kills his enemy. He is given a safe-conduct pass and lives through the war as a noncombatant.

Above all, George Posey has a wholesome but too clear-eyed contempt for the impression Lacy had, "until manhood and education effaced it, that God was a Virginian who had created the world in his own image." He has too much clever contempt for the southernness and simpleness of Semmes Buchan. He tells "Cousin" John Semmes: "Your people are about to fight a war. They remind me of a passel of young 'uns playing prisoners' base."

Young Lacy is a hero worshipper of George, and this pleases George.

He stood looking at the long gallery, two storeys, on slender square posts, across the whole front of the house; and his lips moved. I thought he had spoken to me. I ran nearer.

"Brother George!" I cried.

He motioned me to him, put his hand on my head, and smiled down at me.

"You're my friend, Lacy boy."

Not much more than a year later, Lacy walks toward the battlefield of Bull Run and has a vision of his paternal grandfather telling him the truth about George Posey. He says George is Jason and Susan is Medea, but with the proud contempt of youth Lacy rejects the analogy. "You know everything," he says, "[and you're] dead—dead as a herring."

The *progression d'effet* in *The Fathers,* the tremendous acceleration of meaning in its final paragraph, has been admired and half understood about equally. "I'll go back and finish [the war]," Lacy says. "I'll have to finish it because [George] could not finish it. It won't make any difference if I am killed. If I am killed it will be because I love him more than I love any man." Frank Kermode has the briefest and best account. At the end of the novel "we learn of the last Buchan victim: Lacy. We know what to make of Posey, but there is always more to be made; as when Lacy, in his last sentence, declares his allegiance." The fact is, old Dr. Buchan, the narrator, has slipped his cable. How, in 1911, can he say "if I am killed"? The war is long over. Dr. Buchan is so carried away by the conclusion of his narrative that he thinks it is July 1861 again. He is the man at the gate in the "Ode to the Confederate Dead" really believing that the leaves are charging infantry. If young Lacy had been killed (and he wasn't), he would have been a witness to what George believed, not to what his father believed. The Confederate dead are not, or ought not to be considered, martyrs to the Lost Cause, but martyrs to the mixed-up, arms-procuring, murderous cause of George Posey, still very much alive in 1911.

Tate's *Collected Essays* (1959) looms large among the other books and I cannot pretend to do it justice in a few pages. In any case it is the part of Tate's work a student should study last, not first. The essays can be classified under three heads—criticism of society, literary theory, and judgment of particular authors and works. The three sorts of essay cohere. They cohere because they proceed from a single recognition: the imperfectibility of man. Tate's perfectibilists—he calls them positivists and social engineers, and included in their number are Descartes, Jefferson, and Poe—are fallen without knowing it; their angelic and diabolic activity is evidence of this. George Posey is their equivalent in *The Fathers*. Among Tate's imperfectibilists are Dante, Shakespeare, Flaubert, Dostoevski, Henry James, and Emily Dickinson. Major Buchan is their equivalent in *The Fathers*.

Frank Kermode demonstrates very well the relationship between Tate's literary criticism and his criticism of society: "It is an ancient and productive literary habit to compare things as they are with things as they used to be. 'We are scarce our fathers' shadows cast at noon.' Decisive historical events, types of the aboriginal catastrophe, acquire the character of images upon which too much cannot be said, since they sum up our separation from joy or civility. So, in Imperial Rome, men looked back to the Republic; so to this day they look back past the Reformation or the Renaissance or the Civil War, the points at which our characteristic disorders began. The practice has its dangers; the prelapsarian can become merely a moral and intellectual deep shelter, and there is some difficulty in drawing the line between the good old days of the vulgar myth and the intellectual's nostalgia for some 'organic society.' . . . [But] the myth of a valuable and archaic Southern civilization is not without basis. . . . An image of civility so distinctive, and so decisively destroyed by war, can stand quite as well as that of England before its Civil War for the vanquished homogeneous culture that preceded some great dissociation, the effects of which we now suffer. It had all the gifts save art; and that, as Henry James said, is a symptom of the unhappy society. What the English Civil War meant to Mr. Eliot the American means to Mr. Tate; the moment when the modern chaos began, though it cast its shadow before."

The argument can be carried a step further. "All are born Yankees," Tate says in "To the Lacedemonians," "All are born Yankees of the race of men." Yankeedom is universal, like Snopesism; both are images of the human condition. At about the time of World War I, as Tate says in the essay already quoted at the beginning of this essay, southerners began to look around, and they "saw for the first time since about 1830 that the Yankees were not to blame for everything." It was a belated recognition but better than none at all, and what Tate claims for southerners generally around 1917–19 can be claimed for individuals and whole nations at other times.

Tate's social criticism is loosely described as a "refusal to accept the modern world," and this is accurate if by the modern world we mean a place where the perfectibility of man in the ordinary secular sense is taken for granted. Tate's social criticism is always saying something like this: "If the social engineers get everything they want for us we shall not have the society I like." The society he likes Ransom describes as "the ordered and individual way of life which obtained in the Western economy before the industrial revolution developed into mass production. . . . And ever after the Agrarian movement I believe that Tate and I conducted our lives in much the same fashion; in a free society we assumed the right to live simply and to keep company with friends of our own taste, and with increasingly unpopular books in the library. We lived in an old-fashioned minority pocket of the culture, so to speak." It will never be a majority culture, and Tate would probably not like it if it became one.

Tate proceeds to specific literary judgments with an absolute minimum of critical theory. "Poetry," he says, "is neither religion nor social engineering"; it is all the possibilities occupying the space between. Poets have no gift to set a statesman right, but neither should they invent parables that try to compete with the New Testament ones that describe the kingdom of heaven. Both temptations are there, and they are most successfully resisted if the polar nature of the extremes is understood. "Tension in Poetry" finds an analogy in language itself, in the scale between extensive and intensive meaning. The rationalist poet, whose chief temptation is to set a statesman right, "begins at or near the extensive or denoting end of the line"; the romantic or Symbolist poet, whose chief temptation is to write new parables, begins "at the other, intensive end; and each by a straining feat of the imagination tries to push his meanings as far as he can towards the opposite end, so as to occupy the entire scale." Tate does not show us the system working for whole poems, but only for passages—touchstones.

It probably will not work for whole poems, much less for a whole body of work. When Tate examines a whole body of work he proceeds in a different but related way. He tends to place an author somewhere on the scale; placing is not judgment but a condition of judgment. Thus Drieser is way over on the denotative side; he is a propagandist, but in a good cause. And Emily Dickinson "could not in the proper sense think at all," but "her intellectual deficiency contributed at least negatively to her great distinction." The ideas she was incapable of entertaining were not worth entertaining, but her intuitions were of great value; her sensibility exceeded the dimensions, Tate says, of the puritan system. Tate's judgment of Hart Crane is similar; Crane "never acquired an objective mastery of any literature, or even of the history of his country —a defect of considerable interest in a poet whose most ambitious work is an American epic." In Tate's view, Thomas Hardy is a near-miss of the opposite kind. The mind of Emily Dickinson was never violated by puritan ideas, and Crane did not get his mind into his poetry, but Hardy at his worst is a propagandist for the ideas of Herbert Spencer. When in 1915 he found out that the brightest young men were no longer taking Herbert Spencer seriously he was hurt and dumbfounded; Hardy's "philosophy," Tate says, "tends to be a little beyond the range of his feeling." But this is the placing, not the judgment; the judgment is one of affection. If Hardy had been "better educated," Tate says, "he might have been like Browning or Swinburne—both men his inferiors."

Tate is not immune to the curse which has fallen on a majority of American writers after their first full measure of success; but a distinction has to be made between reputation and achievement. John Bradbury may have been right when he said that Tate's literary stock was higher in the early 1930's than it was at the time Bradbury wrote, in the late 1950's, but this is to say nothing of Tate's later achievement and his future reputation. The poetry after 1938 is not steady in its development, but Tate did write a number of poems during the war years and after that go beyond anything he had written earlier. The "Ode to Our Young Pro-Consuls of the Air," for example, is a felicitous rebirth of the subject matter of the early verse essays; the public subject is cast this time in strict stanzas. Tate's borrowing of the stanzas of Drayton's "Ode to the Virginian Voyage" is part of the meaning of his poem; the same of course can be said of Marvell's borrowing in his "Horatian Ode."

All of the "Sonnets at Christmas" (1934 and 1942) are good enough to invite comparison with the devotional sonnets of Donne and Hopkins, and the second in the 1942 group is Tate at his best:

The day's at end and there's nowhere to go,
Draw to the fire, even this fire is dying;
Get up and once again politely lying
Invite the ladies toward the mistletoe
With greedy eyes that stare like an old crow.

How pleasantly the holly wreaths did hang
And how stuffed Santa did his reindeer clang
Above the golden oaken mantel, years ago!

Then hang this picture for a calendar,
As sheep for goat, and pray most fixedly
For the cold martial progress of your star,
With thoughts of commerce and society,
Well-milked Chinese, Negroes who cannot sing,
The Huns gelded and feeding in a ring.

Most of Tate's themes are here—the inescapability of twilight, the *ignis fatuus* of the good old days, the commercial direction of the American dream, and the undesirability of the accomplishment of the fondest hopes of the social engineer: the Chinese people efficiently exploited and well fed, the Negroes no longer an outcast people and therefore bereft of their great gift for music, and the Germans turned into sexless consumers. The formal qualities of this sonnet, its diction, and its meter are what a poet knows of immortality in his own lifetime.

The real capstone of Tate's poetic career may very well be his "Seasons of the Soul" (1943–45), if it is not the projected nine-part autobiographical poem in terza rima of which only three parts—"The Maimed Man," "The Swimmers," and "The Buried Lake"— have been completed. "Seasons of the Soul" has attracted considerable critical attention—from, among others, Vivienne Koch, Lillian Feder, and R. K. Meiners. Miss Koch at her most perceptive mentions the descent of the poet into his own hell in this poem, and she approaches its theme when she says that it chronicles "the four ages of man in relation to the four aspects of the universe he inhabits"; each section is "placed" in one of the four elements of the ancients. Since Miss Feder's chief concern is to demonstrate Tate's classicism, her account of the poem corrects Miss Koch only at those points where Miss Koch is too eager

to show that Tate is a romantic. Meiners goes beyond Miss Koch when he suggests that the four ages of man are not so much a simple sequence as they are recurrent. As in so much modern criticism one wishes that all involved had talked over their readings together before committing them to print.

Seasons of the soul are recurrent obsessions. In the same way that season follows season, man turns over in his mind, year after year, the terms and conditions of his existence. Part One of the poem, "Summer," is the record of the obsessions of Active or Political Man; Part Two, "Autumn," of Solipsistic Man; Part Three, "Winter," of Sexual Man; and Part Four, "Spring," of Religious Man. I am paraphrasing crudely, well aware of the truth of Tate's observation that after all the readings are made a residue remains, the residue being what the poet was thinking as he wrote. He may have been thinking of the Four Last Things: Judgment (Summer), Death (Autumn), Hell (Winter), Heaven (Spring).

But taking the other tack, all four men can be seen to be the same man as all the seasons are part of a single cycle. Miss Koch is right in suggesting a kind of progress from part to part; it is an orderly sequence. This can be demonstrated if the reader of the poem imagines himself beginning at "Autumn," "Winter," or "Spring" instead of "Summer." The resulting sequences do not correspond to any man's development; the actual sequence is logical, restrained, "classical," in Miss Feder's sense. In our century of uneasy peace, war, disarmed and re-armed armistice, war resumed, turning hot and cold in turn (and maybe turning, finally, apocalyptically hot), a man is not a man until he is political, until he says his lines on that particular great stage of fools.

Part One, "Summer," is a poem about political responsibility; Hardy, Yeats, Auden, Empson, and Dylan Thomas have written similar ones. If we throw ourselves into political activity, especially the ultimate political activity of violence against fellow human beings, what happens to our hearts and heads? Intellect destroys charity (we are persuaded that the enemy within is the enemy without, that the Old Adam is the External Enemy) and perhaps even destroys itself:

> Shall mind itself still live
> If like a hunting king
> It falls to the lion's jaws?

Howard Nemerov has shown that a broader version of this theme is a central concern of Tate's, as in "The Meaning of Life": "There is that / Which is the commentary; there's that other, / Which may be called the immaculate / Conception of its essence in itself." This is metaphysical realism or nominalism according as warmth is accorded essence or commentary, idea or action, blueprint or building.

The image of pure engagement is not for Tate the image of the just man in the just war:

> It was a gentle sun
> When, at the June solstice
> Green France was overrun
> With caterpillar feet.

Tate has no Just Man, like Milton's Enoch, Noah, Abraham, Moses, Samson, and Christ; in Part One he is still showing an industrialized society destroying a relatively agrarian one. Or looked at another way, the Nazis really believed their propaganda, the French did not. We ought to prefer the demoralized French to the dehumanized Nazis if for no reason other than the prudential one. A dehumanized view of man is always a loser in the long run.

Similarly, the view of man as innocent is only a recollection, as of a First Summer:

> When was it that the summer
> (Daylong a liquid light)

> And a child, the new-comer,
> Bathed in the same green spray,
> Could neither guess the night?
> The summer had no reason;
> Then, like a primal cause
> It had its timeless day
> Before it kept the season
> Of time's engaging jaws.

The only adequate view of man is the Christian one; at the end of Part One we see Dante and Virgil—"Two men of our summer world" —meeting Chiron in the seventh circle of hell. This concluding seems to me forced.

But Part Two, "Autumn," is completely successful. The actual season is the season of the poet's birth (and the Gettysburg Address), the season of the "Ode" and "The Immortal Woman," the season that corresponds to twilight. The poet dreams of falling down a well into a strange house:

> I counted along the wall
> Door after closed door
> Through which a shade might slide
> To the cold and empty hall.

Presently he finds his "father in a gray shawl," and then his "downcast mother / Clad in her street-clothes, / Her blue eyes long and small," and neither recognizes him.

Meiners says that in the movement from Part One to Part Two "the private hell has shrunk to the dimensions of a well." There is indeed a shrinking or diminution, but not a qualitative one. The point is that the private hell is a microcosm of the public one. The private man who dreams that his parents don't recognize him is identical with the man who can't falsify himself by becoming *engagé*, if doing that involves the killing of charity and intelligence. The mother of "Mother and Son" who asks her son to say that the time is beautiful is rather like the political spirit of the

1930's and the 1940's which tried with some success to enlist the poets on the side of right-eousness. The responsibility of the poet, Tate said in 1950, is "to write poems, and not to gad about using the rumor of his verse . . . as the excuse to appear on platforms and to view with alarm." Since Tate was not of an age to be in combat in either world war that part of the question is academic; but he could well be proud of the wartime records of two of the poets—Robert Lowell and Anthony Hecht—who apprenticed themselves to him. (Not that these were the only ones; their number includes Theodore Roethke and John Berryman.) During World War II, Lowell was thrown into jail as a conscientious objector and Hecht served in the infantry.

Meiners says that after Part Two "there is no place to go," that Part Two breaks off with no lead into Part Three. But of course there is a place to go. Part Three, "Winter," is about sex, which is precisely where the alienated man goes, if not to drugs, drunkenness, beatness, and physical violence. And "sex" I think is the right word; here as with Eliot's carbuncular young man and Auden's Herod (who hasn't "had sex for a month") desire is hardly involved:

> Goddess sea-born and bright,
> Return into the sea
> Where eddying twilight
> Gathers upon your people—
> Cold goddess, hear our plea!

Venus came from the sea, but to ask her to return to it is rather like asking God the Father to undo the Incarnation. A return of Venus to the element of her prenativity is, nevertheless, better than a desiccated religion:

> Leave the burnt earth, Venus,
> For the drying God above,
> Hanged in his windy steeple,

> No longer bears for us
> The living wound of love.

God is killed nowadays by abstraction, by reduction to a Principle, by hanging by the neck until dead in a windy steeple, where there should be a bell. God no longer bears the wounds of Christ on the cross, but is dead in the way the sea gods of the next stanza—Neptune, Nereus, Poseidon, and Proteus—are dead. No one can say Venus is dead (it is like Katherine Anne Porter's *Ship of Fools,* where people worried about sex are not worried about storms or shipwreck)—she still provides

> Shade for lovers, where
> A shark swift as [her] dove
> Shall pace our company
> All night to nudge and tear
> The livid wound of love.

The stigmata of the first stanza become like gonads in all the stanzas of Part Three except the final one; the stigmata of a modern saint, Lawrence's or Hemingway's or Henry Miller's, are sexual organs.

> And now the winter sea:
> Within her hollow rind
> What sleek facility
> Of sea-conceited scop
> To plumb the nether mind!
> Eternal winters blow
> Shivering flakes, and shove
> Bodies that wheel and drop—
> Cold soot upon the snow
> Their livid wound of love.

The winter sea is the element of twentieth-century sexually oriented man; he has Freud, and Art too—the "sea-conceited scop / To plumb the nether mind"—but they do not seem to do much good; he is in Dante's seventh circle of hell, and procreation is "cold soot upon the snow."

The final three stanzas of Part Three are Tate at his most violent.

> Beyond the undertow
> The gray sea-foliage
> Transpires a phosphor glow
> Into the circular miles:
> In the centre of his cage
> The pacing animal
> Surveys the jungle cove
> And slicks his slithering wiles
> To turn the venereal awl
> In the livid wound of love.

The reader is asked to plunge beneath the water and observe what the shark of the earlier stanza would see. He—we—see Shelley's underwater foliage in winter dress. The shark finds his victim.

"The venereal awl" is very odd; none of the critics of the poem has been patient enough with it. It cannot be a periphrastic expression for penis, nor can it be a weapon (though it is turned in a wound as a weapon might be), for this is a shark, not a swordfish. It must be a mouth; awl-like because the shark twists as it attacks, like a bomber peeling off. The shark does seem to eat whoever is in the "jungle cove" unless all that slicking of slithering wiles is frustrated. And the eating if it does take place is like a sexual act; this shark is a real monster. It is the aggressor, and male in so far as it turns the venereal awl or kills, but it is also female—its part is the hollow part. The passage calls for moral interpretation. The masculine principle in the modern world is perverted to acquisitiveness and destruction, and the female principle is perverted to mindless and genderless gorging. And this is only to speak of the shark, and not the victim.

The image owes a lot to (it might even have its source in) the story of the death of Hart Crane as Tate tells it in one of his magnanimous tributes to that poet: "Toward the end of April, 1934, he embarked on the S.S. *Orizaba* bound from Vera Cruz to New York. On the night of April 26 he got into a brawl with some sailors; he was severely beaten and robbed. At noon the next day, the ship being in the Caribbean a few hours out of Havana, he rushed from his stateroom clad in pajamas and overcoat, walked through the smoking-room out onto the deck, and then the length of the ship to the stern. There without hesitation he made a perfect dive into the sea. It is said that a life-preserver was thrown to him; he either did not see it or did not want it. By the time the ship had turned back he had disappeared. Whether he forced himself down—for a moment he was seen swimming—or was seized by a shark, as the captain believed, cannot be known." Caroline Gordon's novel *The Malefactors* (1956), in which the names are fictitious but in which there is masterful representation of Tate's speech inflections, has the following bit of dialogue near the end; Tom Claiborne is speaking to Catherine Pollard:

> "Tell me, do you pray for Horne Watts?"
> "Yes."
> "How long have you?"
> "From the day I heard he had committed suicide."

Part Three like Part One ends with a translation of Dante. A passage from the thirteenth canto of the *Inferno*, which is also the epigraph to the whole poem, is translated as follows:

> I seized a branch, which broke;
> I heard the speaking blood
> (From the livid wound of love)
>
> Drip down upon my toe.

Only the blood of suicides can speak; the blood says:

> "We are the men who died
> Of self-inflicted woe,

Lovers whose stratagem
Led to their suicide."

"Seasons of the Soul" is not dedicated to the memory of Hart Crane, the literal suicide, but to the memory of John Peale Bishop, a man much closer to the common lot. The implication is that every man is more or less suicidal. We are all, like Scott Fitzgerald, the subject of Bishop's best poem, mediocre caretakers of our talents.

Meiners compares the beginning of Part Four with the opening lines of *The Waste Land*:

Irritable spring, infuse
Into the burning breast
Your combustible juice
That as a liquid soul
Shall be the body's guest
Who lights, but cannot stay
To comfort this unease
Which, like a dying coal,
Hastens the cooler day
Of the mother of silences.

Spring is irritable because it cannot stay, cannot settle down; it is much closer to Frost's "nothing gold can stay" than to Eliot's "cruelest month." Spring is the life principle associated in Tate's mind, as Howard Nemerov has shown, with liquid and fluid states and Becoming, as solid and rigid states are associated in his mind with Being and death. "The cooler day / Of the mother of silences" is like Ransom's "kinder saeculum" in "The Equilibrists" that begins with death. Death is the mother of silences (compare Wallace Stevens' death, who is the mother of beauty in "Sunday Morning"—a Yeatsian idea) in the sense that she hushes us all, but lovingly, as a mother hushes her children.

In the second stanza of Part Four we have a picture of innocence to place beside the other picture in Part One. Here Tate accuses himself of interpreting history in spatial terms—a history without time or death in it, as if he were George Posey running away from Sarah Buchan's funeral.

It was a pleasant land
Where even death could please
Us with an ancient pun—
All dying for the hand
Of the mother of silences.

The "us" is everybody who wrote or thought about death as orgasm. The tone of the next to last line rejects the "ancient pun" as frivolous or, one might say, a young man's substitute for orthodox eschatology; the remaining stanzas of Part Four are as orthodox as the poem gets. In wartime death is everywhere, thoughts of the moment of death occupy everyone, "It burns us each alone," but man in Plato's cave of Becoming, man who is enslaved to his body as Sisyphus is to his rock, can rest when he accepts the idea of death easily.

The last two stanzas introduce two specific mothers of silences; one, St. Monica, Miss Koch has identified, and the other is very like the mother of "Mother and Son":

Speak, that we may hear;
Listen, while we confess
That we conceal our fear;
Regard us, while the eye
Discerns by sight or guess
Whether, as sheep foregather
Upon their crooked knees,
We have begun to die;
Whether your kindness, mother,
Is mother of silences.

The kindness in the earlier poem was "her harsh command / That he should say the time is beautiful"; the kindness here I take to be the gift of life. Is death also a gift? Tate raises the question, but does not answer it.

With respect to Christianity, Tate can be

compared first with Eliot, and then with Ransom and Stevens. I intend no disrespect to Eliot when I say that his work shows a rather easy acceptance of orthodox values—no disrespect because I would say the same of Herbert, though not of Donne or Hopkins. Like Donne and Hopkins, Tate is not at ease in any orthodoxy; his work shows the strain of a man trying to work out his own salvation, like Yeats, but lacking the great style of Yeats. Where Yeats's language is a proud, seamless garment, Tate's language, just as proud, is tattered and patched.

Ransom's language is another seamless garment, but it is not instructive to compare his preternaturally high standard with Tate's uneven one; the instructive point of comparison is with respect to Christianity. "Almost thou persuadest me to be a Christian," Ransom once wrote Tate, "but I am a tough heathen." The date is early (1923), the language is jocular, and the occasion is dim (Ransom is referring to an unpublished poem of Tate's called "Yellow River"), but even so a real state of affairs is being represented, and Ransom came back to it at the end of his essay "In Amicitia." Tate's work shows that he has always been an uneasy Christian; the pull toward paganism is seen only in his translations and, best of all and in its true light, in the Jason and Medea episode in *The Fathers*. Ransom, on the other hand, has always been an uneasy heathen, one of those who have taken Christianity underground, as Eliot said would be necessary for some time. When Tate, before his conversion to Roman Catholicism, told Philip Blair Rice, Ransom's colleague on the *Kenyon Review*, that "something he had observed led him to think Ransom was about to have a conversion," Tate must have been confusing his own thoughts with Ransom's. Tate is far from being a writer of Christian apologetics, like Eliot; he is equally remote from the aestheticism of

Ransom and Stevens. Tate also gets into his work considerably more of the torment of the spirit than is to be found in these three.

But his work does not show the ultimate torment of a lost or condemned soul like Poe or Hart Crane. Crane stands mostly as an object lesson to Tate. When Tate said of Crane that "he had an abnormally acute response to the physical world, an exacerbation of the nerve-ends, along with an incapacity to live within the limitations of the human condition," he easily could have been speaking of George Posey, his brother of fiction.

Selected Bibliography

WORKS OF ALLEN TATE

POETRY

Mr. Pope and Other Poems. New York: Minton, Balch, 1928.

Three Poems: Ode to the Confederate Dead, Message from Abroad, and The Cross. New York: Minton, Balch, 1930.

Poems: 1928–1931. New York: Scribners, 1932.

The Mediterranean and Other Poems. New York: Alcestis Press, 1936.

Selected Poems. New York: Scribners, 1937.

Sonnets at Christmas. Cummington, Mass.: Cummington Press, 1941.

The Vigil of Venus. Cummington, Mass.: Cummington Press, 1943.

The Winter Sea. Cummington, Mass.: Cummington Press, 1944.

Poems: 1922–1947. New York: Scribners, 1948.

Poems. New York: Scribners, 1960.

The Swimmers and Other Selected Poems. London: Oxford University Press, 1970; New York: Scribners, 1971.

Published since the writing of this essay

Collected Poems, 1919–1976. Baton Rouge: Louisiana State Univ. Press, 1989.

FICTION

"The Immortal Woman," *Hound and Horn*, 6:592–609 (July-September 1933). Reprinted in Edward J. O'Brien, ed., *The Best Short Stories 1934* (Boston: Houghton Mifflin, 1934), and in Robert Penn Warren, ed., *A Southern Harvest* (Boston: Houghton Mifflin, 1937).

"The Migration," *Yale Review*, 24:83–111 (September 1934).

The Fathers. New York: Putnam, 1938. New edition, London: Eyre and Spottiswoode; Denver: Swallow Press, 1960.

BIOGRAPHIES

Stonewall Jackson: The Good Soldier. New York: Minton, Balch, 1928.

Jefferson Davis: His Rise and Fall. New York: Minton, Balch, 1929.

ESSAYS AND OTHER NONFICTION

"Correspondence: 'Waste Lands,'" *Literary Review*, August 4, 1923, p. 886.

"Last Days of a Charming Lady," *Nation*, 121:485 (October 28, 1925).

"Fundamentalism," *Nation*, 122:532 (May 12, 1926).

Reactionary Essays on Poetry and Ideas. New York: Scribners, 1936.

Reason in Madness: Critical Essays. New York: Putnam, 1941.

"The Fugitive 1922–1925," *Princeton University Library Chronicle*, 3:75–84 (April 1942).

The Hovering Fly. Cummington, Mass.: Cummington Press, 1948.

On the Limits of Poetry. New York: Swallow Press and Morrow, 1948.

"Religion and the Intellectuals," *Partisan Review*, 17:250–53 (March 1950).

"Self-Made Angel," *New Republic*, 129:17–18 (August 31, 1953).

The Forlorn Demon. Chicago: Regnery, 1953.

The Man of Letters in the Modern World. New York: Meridian, 1955.

"Reflections on American Poetry, 1900–1950," *Sewanee Review*, 64:59–70 (Winter 1956).

Collected Essays. Denver, Colo.: Swallow Press, 1959.

"Random Thoughts on the 1920's," *Minnesota Review*, 1:46–56 (Fall 1960).

"For John Ransom at Seventy-Five," *Shenandoah*, 14:5–8 (Spring 1963).

Essays of Four Decades. Chicago: Swallow Press, 1968; Oxford: Oxford University Press, 1970; New York: Apollo Editions, 1970.

"Miss Toklas' American Cake," *Prose*, 3:137–161 (Fall 1971).

Published since the writing of this essay

Memoirs and Opinions: 1926–1974. Athens, Ohio: Ohio Univ. Press, 1975.

The Poetry Reviews of Allen Tate, 1924–1944. Baton Rouge: Louisiana State Univ. Press, 1983.

BIBLIOGRAPHIES

Squires, Radcliffe. *Allen Tate and his Work*. Minneapolis: University of Minnesota Press, 1972. Pp. 309–55.

Thorp, Willard. "Allen Tate: A Checklist," *Princeton University Library Chronicle*, 3:85–98 (April 1942).

CRITICAL AND BIOGRAPHICAL STUDIES

Current studies of Tate's work are listed in the annual bibliographical issue of *Publications of the Modern Language Association*.

Allen, Walter. *The Modern Novel in Britain and the United States*. New York: Dutton, 1964. Pp. 124–28.

Berland, Alwyn. "Violence in the Poetry of Allen Tate," *Accent*, 11:161–71 (Summer 1951).

Bradbury, John M. *The Fugitives: A Critical Account*. Chapel Hill: University of North Carolina Press, 1958.

Burnham, James. "The Unreconstructed Allen Tate," *Partisan Review*, 16:198–202 (February 1949).

Cowan, Louise. *The Fugitive Group: A Literary History*. Baton Rouge: Louisiana State University Press, 1959.

Davidson, Donald. " 'I'll Take My Stand': A History," *American Review*, 5:301–21 (Summer 1935).

Feder, Lillian. "Allen Tate's Use of Classical Literature," *Centennial Review*, 4:89–114 (Winter 1960).

Fitzgerald, Robert. "Poetry and Perfection," *Sewanee Review*, 56:685–97 (Autumn 1948).

Flint, F. Cudworth. "Five Poets," *Southern Review*, 1:650–74 (Winter 1936).

Foster, Richard. "Narcissus as Pilgrim," *Accent*, 17:158–71 (Summer 1957).

Gordon, Caroline. *The Malefactors*. New York: Harcourt, Brace, 1956.

"Homage to Allen Tate" Issue, *Sewanee Review*, 67:528–631 (Autumn 1959). (Contains tributes from R. P. Blackmur, Malcolm Cowley, Donald Davidson, T. S. Eliot, Francis Fergusson, Anthony Hecht, Robert Lowell, Andrew Lytle, Jacques and Raïssa Maritain, Arthur Mizener, Howard Nemerov, Katherine Anne Porter, John Crowe Ransom, Herbert Read, Mark Van Doren, Eliseo Vivas, John Hall Wheelock, and Reed Whittemore.)

Kermode, Frank. "Old Orders Changing," *Encounter*, 15:72–76 (August 1960). (A critique of *The Fathers*, reprinted in *Puzzles and Epiphanies*. London: Routledge, 1962. Pp. 131–39.)

Koch, Vivienne. "The Poetry of Allen Tate," *Kenyon Review*, 11:357–78 (Summer 1949). (Reprinted in John Crowe Ransom, ed., *The Kenyon Critics*. Cleveland, Ohio: World, 1951. Pp. 169–81.)

Meiners, R. K. *The Last Alternatives: A Study of the Works of Allen Tate*. Denver, Colo.: Swallow Press, 1963.

Millgate, Michael. "An Interview with Allen Tate," *Shenandoah*, 12:27–34 (Spring 1961).

Mizener, Arthur. *The Sense of Life in the Modern Novel*. Boston: Houghton Mifflin, 1964.

Purdy, Rob Roy, ed. *Fugitives' Reunion, Conversations at Vanderbilt May 3–5, 1956*. Nashville, Tenn.: Vanderbilt University Press, 1959.

Schwartz, Delmore. "The Poetry of Allen Tate," *Southern Review*, 5:419–38 (Winter 1940).

"Southern Style," *Times Literary Supplement* (London), August 5, 1960, p. 496.

Squires, J. Radcliffe. "The Temperate Manichee," *Voices: A Quarterly of Poetry*, No. 134, pp. 49–51 (1948).

Squires, Radcliffe. *Allen Tate*. New York: Bobbs-Merrill, 1971.

Weber, Brom, ed. *The Letters of Hart Crane*. New York: Hermitage House, 1952.

— *GEORGE HEMPHILL*

Edward Taylor

1642-1729

*I*N THE winter of 1688-89 the minister of the Congregational church of the small frontier town of Westfield in the Massachusetts Bay Colony was composing, while alone in his study, a "Preparatory Meditation" addressed to Christ:

> I'm but a Flesh and Blood bag: Oh! do thou
>   Sill, Plate, Ridge, Rib, and Rafter me
>   with Grace.

He completed the poem sometime before the Communion Sunday of January 6, entitled it "30. Meditation. 2. Cor. 5.17.—He is a New Creature," which was the text of the sermon he was to preach on that Sunday, made a fair copy of the poem in a careful, precise hand, and eventually bound it along with scores of similar poems into a quarto volume of over four hundred pages. The crude binding, stuffed with the discarded rough drafts of poems, was in all probability done by the minister himself and the leather cover may have been cut from the tanned hide of one of his own farm animals. The volume, carefully preserved by his grandson Ezra Stiles, president of Yale College, passed to the poet's great-grandson, Henry W. Taylor, who deposited it in the library of Yale University in 1883 where it still remains.

Why did Edward Taylor write this poem?

Not, certainly, for contemporary fame. He never published his verses or, as far as we know, attempted to publish them although Cotton Mather quoted two stanzas from his "Upon Wedlock, and Death of Children" at the conclusion of his sermon *Right Thoughts in Sad Hours* printed in London in 1689. Taylor may even have forbidden his heirs to publish his work, although this supposed restriction rests on mere family tradition and is nowhere mentioned in extant manuscripts of Taylor's time. Rather, Taylor was composing his poetic meditations as periodic exercises (one poem about every two months) designed to put him in the correct spiritual posture for his communion with Christ at the administration of the Lord's Supper. Primarily, they were addressed to God or to Christ alone and not to any reader public or private. Yet, as Cotton Mather did with his diary, Taylor took good care to see that his manuscript was preserved—perhaps for the edification of his descendants. And thus, without consciously planning it, he achieved for himself a unique place in literary history. With the discovery of the Yale manuscript and publication of poems selected from it by Thomas H. Johnson beginning in 1937, it became clear that Edward Taylor was both last and first— the last important poet of the metaphysical school founded by John Donne and the first major poet to compose his work on what is now American soil.

Taylor is an anomaly. He wrote his best poems, the *Preparatory Meditations,* from 1682 to 1725 in the age of Dryden and Pope, the period of the heroic couplet, of superficial wit, elegance, and neo-classical formalism. If he had remained in England where he was born, it is difficult to believe that he would have completely escaped the influence of the Augustans. But his removal to the Bay Colony in 1668, when he was a young man, enabled him to turn his attention almost exclusively to the poetic modes of two generations previous to his—perhaps to Donne's *Holy Sonnets* and Crashaw's *Steps to the Temple,* certainly to George Herbert's *The Temple.* Although a progressive in politics (he welcomed the Revolution of 1688) he was retrogressive in his literary tastes and even by Massachusetts standards conservative in his Congregational faith and practice. He found the style of the deeply religious Anglican priest George Herbert, born fifty years before himself, congenial to his own profound piety, and indeed there is no evidence in the extant manuscripts that he ever bothered to read the major English poetry of his own time. In his religious beliefs he was, like most of his Bay Colony contemporaries, a Calvinist in all fundamental matters, but he was noted even among them for his very strict observance of the Sabbath and his hatred of innovation with respect to the administration of the Lord's Supper. He was a lifelong opponent of Solomon Stoddard's practice of inviting unregenerate as well as regenerate worshippers to the communion table and he attacked his Northampton neighbor in his poems, sermons, and in at least one unpublished theological tract.

Records of Edward Taylor's birth have not been found; the baptismal entries of the Taylor family in the parish church of Burbage, England, are incomplete, possibly because during the unsettled times of the Civil War period church records were neglected or destroyed. But the evidence of his diary and the extant wills of his father and eldest brother strongly support the long-held tradition that he was born in the hamlet of Sketchley, near Hinckley, Leicestershire, about 1642, the year of the Civil War battle of Edgehill which occurred a few miles from his birthplace. The first twenty-six years of his life were passed in England in the midst of the stirring events of the Puritan victory over the Cavaliers, the rise to power of Oliver Cromwell, the execution of Charles I, the establishment of the Commonwealth and the Protectorate, the death of Cromwell, and the restoration of Charles II. Eight years after Charles assumed power, Taylor found himself in Massachusetts, and for the rest of his life he viewed from a distance the major events of the parent country which were to have a profound effect on the destinies of the English-speaking peoples—the Glorious Revolution of 1688 which deposed the Roman Catholic James II and put into power the Protestant William and Mary, the era of Queen Anne and the great campaigns of Marlborough against France, the first years of the reign of the House of Hanover and the rise of Robert Walpole. We know from his correspondence with his lifelong friend the witchcraft judge Samuel Sewall that he took an interest in these historical events, but they are not reflected in his poetry, which was almost entirely religious and unaffected by occurrences of world-wide importance. He used such trivial incidents as a spider catching a fly or an unexpectedly heavy shower of rain to point a moral in some of his topical verses. The battle of the Boyne, the victories of Blenheim and Malplaquet are not mentioned.

The poet's father, William Taylor, was a successful midland yeoman farmer who taught his family of at least one daughter and five sons how to brew their own ale, shear and spin their own wool, produce their own honey, poultry, meat, vegetables. Consequently, when the young minister years later settled in the farming community of Westfield, he was already well versed in the matter of earning a living from the soil. At Westfield, he raised bees, kept cattle and horses, cultivated vegetables. But the farm and rural imagery of poems composed in his Massachusetts study probably derives as much from nostalgic childhood memories of the fertile flowering fields and orchards of his native Leicestershire as from the more rugged terrain of his new colonial home. The village streets of Sketchley with their blacksmith shop and bakehouse and creaking carts also afforded the farmer-poet appropriate, homely imagery for poems and sermons. So did the weavers' shops of nearby Hinckley. Indeed, Taylor's frequent use of weaving terms suggests that as a boy he may have been employed in this new industry.

William Taylor died in 1658 leaving the bulk of his estate to his eldest son, Richard. Edward had been educated under a nonconformist schoolmaster and was planning to earn his living by teaching. He had a good foundation in the learned languages—Greek, Hebrew, and Latin. It was as a schoolboy that he had probably studied the poetry of George Herbert, who was to have a lasting influence on him. Herbert's work was frequently used by Puritan schoolmasters as a model of poetic composition in English. If the regime of Cromwell had endured, Taylor would probably have remained in England as a schoolteacher—a career which he had begun at Bagworth. But the Restoration and the Act of Uniformity of 1662 put an end to these plans. The oaths required were against his religious convictions, he was evicted as schoolmaster, he was unable to attend Cambridge or Oxford without subscribing to the act, he was not permitted to preach, and he and his fellow believers were liable to fine and imprisonment if they attended nonconformist religious services. Hence in April of 1668 he embarked for the Bay Colony.

His diary tells of the seventy-day journey from Wapping on the Thames to Boston harbor, becalmed for days, then buffeted by contrary and severe winds until the "waves flashed over the ship" and the forecastle was filled ankle deep with water. During the difficult voyage, the future minister read the New Testament in Greek, "exercised" from Scripture for the edification of his fellow passengers, and made strange and eccentric notes on his observations of fish and birds. For, as Ezra Stiles recorded years later in a character sketch of his grandfather which he wrote in the blank pages of one of Taylor's manuscript books, he was "Very curious in Natural History." He wrote of "a pair of sunfish flapping on the water that cannot sink while the sun shines" and of a whale which made "a rough, hoarse noise, blothering in the water," and he saw "a flying creature like a spark of red fire (about the bigness of an humble-bee) fly by the ship."

Taylor's age and his previous education in England enabled him to obtain advance standing at Harvard College so that he was graduated in three years with the class of 1671 along with his friend and famous classmate Samuel Sewall. Taylor was appointed college butler during his stay at Harvard; he was responsible for keeping an account of kitchen and dining room utensils and for collecting weekly payments for food and drink. His diary records some of his college experiences. He was, for example, asked by his tutor—a certain Mr. Graves—to spy on his fellow students who "used to" imprison their unpopular tutor in his classroom by nailing the door shut. He was discovered and prevented from ascertaining the guilty parties, and he then had the problem of clearing himself with students and tutor. On another occasion he aroused the malice of some "whispering, back-biting tongues" by comforting the wife of Goodman Steadman who was "a woman of a troubled spirit." Indeed, the gossip became so malicious that Taylor offered to "lay down my place at Commencement" but was prevented from doing so by President Charles Chauncy.

Shortly after his graduation, Taylor was made scholar of the house at Harvard and evidently planned to settle there. But when the call for a minister came from the small town of Westfield, one hundred miles through the snow-covered wilderness to the west of Boston, Taylor, after considerable hesitation and after consulting with Increase Mather, President Chauncy, and others, decided to make the ministry his lifelong vocation. After an arduous trip on horseback in the dead of winter, Taylor arrived in Westfield early in December of 1671. He was to remain there until his death fifty-eight years later.

He had occasional doubts about his decision. He found himself in a primitive frontier community among men of no learning who had little in common with him except their religious faith. Years later in a letter to Judge Sewall he refers to his living in "these remotest swamps where little save Rusticity is." And just two years after his arrival he refused to organize his church on a permanent basis unless one of neighboring Northampton's leading citizens, David Wilton, came to live with him and help him. Northampton refused the request. Two years later Taylor and his congregation were threatened by King Philip's War, and in all probability both his house and church were fortified against Indian attack.

By 1674 he had met and fallen in love with Elizabeth Fitch, daughter of the distinguished Connecticut minister James Fitch of Norwich. He courted her in elaborate acrostic verse and in a curious love letter which in involuted prose reminiscent of the days of Sir Thomas Browne says that although Christ has most of his heart, there is still some space left for her. Piety if not passion won the lady who, incidentally, knew Wigglesworth's *Day of Doom* by heart and loved to recite it to her husband. They were married November 5, 1674. During their fifteen years of wedded life, she bore him eight children. Since Taylor had studied the crude medical lore of his time—among his manuscripts is a book on herbs and cordials—he acted as the town's physician, and in his capacity as doctor, minister, and father he had the heartbreaking experience of watching five of his own children die in infancy. He recorded his anguish in one of his most moving poems, "Upon Wedlock, and Death of Children," and in Meditation 40 (second series) written upon the occasion of his son James's death at the age of twenty-three in Barbados:

Under thy Rod, my God, thy smarting Rod,
    That hath off broke my James, that Primrose,
      Why?
Is't for my sin? Or Triall?

Elizabeth died July 7, 1689. Taylor wrote her elegy which, though full of the stereotyped language of that much-abused form, is expressive of his sincere grief and provides a memorable sketch of her person: "She was a neate good Huswife every inch."

During King Philip's War (1675-76) the Bay Colony suffered widespread devastation. Scores of villages were burned by Philip's Indian warriors; prisoners were frequently tortured and killed or held for ransom. For two years a man could not plow his fields or go to church without danger of ambush. Westfield with the unbroken wilderness stretching for miles to the east and west was in a particularly hazardous position. Had it not been for the obstinacy of Taylor and a few other leading citizens, the town would have been abandoned and the inhabitants moved to nearby Springfield. As it turned out, Taylor was right and Westfield was lucky. There were a few skirmishes, but never a major attack. During the entire war Westfield did not suffer more than a dozen casualties.

With Philip's war at an end, the new minister, now happily settled with wife and children, could lay his plans for the permanent organization of his church. According to Congregational custom, seven "foundation men" were chosen as senior members. At the ceremony of August 27, 1679, with representatives from neighboring churches in attendance, Taylor and his foundation men gave their long "Relations" of spiritual experience which entitled them to be senior members of the church, and the new minister gave his profession of faith and delivered a long sermon. Solomon Stoddard from Northampton, representing all of the neighboring churches, extended the right hand of fellowship. The new minister was ordained by imposition of hands, and the ceremony was concluded with a psalm and a blessing. With the church now regularly organized and with the threat of Indian attack greatly mitigated, Taylor could turn his attention more and more to the writing of poetry. He began his major work, the *Preparatory Meditations*, three years later.

In June of 1692, three years after the death of his first wife, Taylor married Ruth Wyllys of Hartford, Connecticut, a descendant (so it was claimed) of William the Conqueror and of two governors of Connecticut. She survived her husband by one year, and during their long life together she cared for the three surviving children of her husband's first marriage

as well as for her own six children by Taylor —five daughters and one son. Her fifth daughter, Kezia, became the mother of Ezra Stiles.

Until his retirement in 1725, Taylor carried on the duties of minister, preaching once or twice a week, of physician, of father to a large family, of farmer, and of leading citizen of a New England village. The Congregationalists of his time referred to themselves as saints of the visible church who attempted to manifest in their outward lives the evidence of saving grace which they experienced within. However, the administration of a community of saints was not without its difficulties. Taylor's church record contains accounts of drunkenness, fornication, and brawling. His church on at least three occasions was torn by schism and faction. A long-standing feud with one Benjamin Smith who, Taylor thought, was trying to deprive an elderly man of his property came to a head in 1712 when Taylor threatened Smith and his supporters with exclusion from the Lord's Supper unless Smith made a satisfactory public confession of his sins and profession of his repentance. Again in 1722 there was an obscure quarrel involving a constable which, according to pastor Stephen Williams of the neighboring town of Longmeadow, threatened the ruin of town and church. "Old Mr. Taylor is very fond of his own thoughts" wrote Williams in his journal. Finally, there was a long-drawn-out argument over the location of the new meetinghouse. Taylor wished it to be built on the same spot as the old building, but a new site on a hill overlooking the river was chosen. The aging pastor was persuaded to preach in it only with considerable difficulty, and shortly after its completion he retired from his ministerial duties.

Accounts of the poet's last years stress his extreme age. He died "greatly superannuated," recorded his grandson John Taylor. Samuel Sewall wrote that his classmate could not "walk to his Bed without support. He is longing and waiting for his dismission," and in a letter to Taylor he said, "May we industriously help one another along to the Regions of Light and Love, where there will be no Sleeping, no Sinning, no Sorrowing." He died June 24, 1729. The *Boston News Letter* carried his obituary: "He was eminently holy in his Life, and very painful and laborious in his Work till the Infirmities of a great old Age disabled him."

The more than two hundred *Preparatory Meditations* (1682-1725) written approximately one every two months as spiritual exercises preparatory to the administration of the sacrament of the Lord's Supper are entirely religious in subject matter and were motivated by the poet's sincere and intense religious beliefs. What are the cardinal principles of Taylor's faith? Seventeenth-century New England Puritans were Calvinists, and Taylor was no exception. He believed in the doctrine formulated in the Westminster Confession. An all-powerful God, before the foundations of the world were laid, decided to save and glorify certain souls (the elect) from the just punishment of original sin. The rest of mankind were doomed to eternal damnation. Christ, God's only begotten son, purchased by his active and passive obedience salvation for the elect. In the relationship with man, God operated under two covenants—the covenant of works and the covenant of grace. Under the covenant of works man was to be saved if he obeyed the law of God. This covenant was broken by the disobedience of Adam and Eve, but God out of his mercy instituted a new covenant, the covenant of grace, which became operative immediately after the Fall. The Puritans considered themselves to be under the covenant of grace by means of which salvation was achieved by faith in Christ, and not by works, this faith being made possible by God's free gift of saving grace. On the day of judgment, the soul of the elect would be united to their bodies and they would live forever in heaven. The souls and bodies of the damned would go to hell. It is evident from Taylor's sermons, his manuscript commentary "Harmony of the Gospels," theological notes, and confession of faith, as well as from his poetry, that he had very literal, factual conceptions of the Fall, heaven, hell, and the day of judgment. There is no liberalizing tendency in his thinking—no tendency, that is, to treat these matters figuratively or symbolically.

Although he lived in the age of Newton and Locke, he believed in the God of Calvin, a personal God, a God of Wrath and of Mercy. Terror of divine wrath and the "comfortable effects" of divine grace were real experiences to the colonial poet, and the reality of the experience is demonstrated by the quality of the poetry. The paramount question in the mind of every New England Puritan was "Am I one of the elect?" The decision to lead a life of outward holiness was taken to be evidence of election; but genuine assurance could only come from within. The emphasis on saving faith was particularly strong in New England as Edmund S. Morgan has pointed out in his *Visible Saints: The History of a Puritan Idea.* After 1640 a Congregationalist was not admitted to full church membership until he was able to satisfy the brethren that he had had a genuine experience of the operation of saving grace in his heart. Usually, he was required to make a public statement in a church meeting similar to the "Relation" that Taylor himself gave on the day of his ordination. The experience of the "comfortable" working of grace was supposed to be recurrent, as it obviously was in Taylor's spiritual life, for some of the most moving passages in his poetry express the feeling of assurance and exaltation, as in Meditation 2.102:

What Grace is here? Looke ery way and see
  How Grace's Splendor like the bright Sun,
    shines
Out on my head, and I encentred bee
  Within the Center of its radien lines.

The Puritans recognized two sacraments—baptism and the Lord's Supper—and defined them as "seals of the Covenant of Grace and means whereby the benefits of Redemption by outward signs be sealingly applied to believers." In his poetry, Taylor was concerned with only one of these sacraments, the Lord's Supper, which he believed united the partaker with Christ in a real, spiritual sense. The Puritans were careful to reject the Roman Catholic doctrine of transubstantiation (that the bread and wine were in fact the actual literal blood and body of Christ) but they insisted that the rite was more than mere ceremony. Taylor's contemporary Samuel Willard wrote, "What! nothing but a Ceremony? Oh no! It is a Sacrament that I am come to the Celebration of; this Bread is Christ; this Wine is Christ; here is a precious Redeemer, set up on this Table before me." This is the language not of a Catholic priest but of a New England Congregationalist whose sacramental beliefs were the same as Taylor's. There are frequent references in diaries and sermons of the period to the ecstatic union between Christ and the believer at the time of communion; it is the subject of a number of tracts and books. Taylor's work is in a recognized tradition, its chief distinction being that the *Preparatory Meditations* are in poetry rather than prose. Indeed, much of Taylor's diction is in the common Protestant tradition of the mystical marriage of Christ and the elect, which was frequently expressed in language derived from the Song of Solomon (or Canticles as Taylor called it)—thus Taylor speaks of his "wedding banquet" with Christ and of putting on a "wedding garment," phrases which are stereotypes of sacramental writing.

An occasion as solemn as the Lord's Supper required spiritual preparation. *"No preparation, no participation,"* wrote Thomas Doolittle in his *Treatise Concerning the Lord's Supper.* "It is not then putting on our finer cloaths on a Sacrament day, but the trimming of our hearts, that God expecteth at our hands." And Taylor preached in one of his 1693 sermons: "Not to prepare is a Contempt of the Invitation; and of the Wedden . . . It is to abide in a Sordid, and filthy, wicked and Sinfull State." The unprepared or unregenerate partaker of the Lord's Supper ate and drank his own damnation, according to orthodox opinion of the period. The *matter* of the Lord's Supper was "spiritual dainties"—a phrase common in the *Preparatory Meditations* and in the prose literature of the subject. The *partaker,* man, was born unfit for the Lord's table, and even after conversion, he still needed preparation through holy meditation. Doolittle urges the believer to reflect on four subjects: (1) on the love of God in man's redemption; (2) on the sufferings of Christ; (3) on the benefits purchased by the death of Christ; (4) on Sin—"And here it would not be unuseful nor unseasonable, to produce the Catalogue of thy sins." Three of these topics are common in the *Preparatory Meditations.* The love of God contrasted to the unworthiness of man corrupted by original sin is the principal subject of the first forty-nine meditations, and the benefits of Christ's redemption motivate the feeling of ecstatic joy with which many of the poems close. The sufferings of Christ, however, are not emphasized as frequently as in the work of a Catholic poet like Crashaw.

Meditation on the love of God, the benefits of redemption, and the sinfulness of man was a spiritual exercise which had its origin in the Roman Catholic Church and which followed an established procedure lasting on through Taylor's time and influencing Protestant religious poetry more, perhaps, than the poets themselves would admit. The subject has been thoroughly explored in Louis L. Martz's *The Poetry of Meditation*. A summary is all that is possible here.

Puritan meditative practice developed from an antecedent Catholic tradition, described (for example) in Ignatius Loyola's *Spiritual Exercises*. This meditative method had its first important poetic expression in Robert Southwell and was continued through Catholic and Protestant poetry in the works of Donne, Herbert, Crashaw, Vaughan, Marvell, Traherne, and Taylor. The method is explicated by the English underground Jesuit priest Edward Dawson in his "The Practical Methode of Meditation" (1614—reprinted in Martz's *The Meditative Poem)* which begins: "Meditation which we treate of, is nothing els but a diligent and forcible application of the understanding, to seeke, and knowe, and as it were to tast some divine matter; from whence doth arise in our affectionate powers good motions, inclinations, and purposes which stirre us up to the love and exercise of vertue, and the hatred and avoiding of sinne: it is the shortest and almost the only way to attaine to Christian perfection."

It is doubtful that Taylor was familiar with the work of this Jesuit. However, a similar method was followed by Puritan divines. One of the most important treatises on Puritan meditation is the fourth part of Richard Baxter's *The Saints' Everlasting Rest*, and it is this treatise which probably suggested to Taylor an orderly method of meditation which involved three faculties of the soul: Memory, Understanding, and Will. The subject matter, heavenly doctrine, is supplied by the Memory; it is analyzed and understood by the Reason or Understanding, and once understood, the Affections of the Will (the emotions) are aroused. Baxter even lists the emotions and the order in which they should be aroused, an order which is sometimes followed in a Taylor poem. They are Love, Desire, Hope, Courage, and Joy. *Joy* is the feeling frequently expressed in the last lines of a Taylor meditation.

Taylor, then, from Baxter or from writers influenced by Baxter, had a good theoretical basis for logical order in his poetry. Nevertheless, his meditations are less orderly, less closely knit logically than the poems of Donne and Herbert. From Crashaw to Vaughan to Taylor we find an increasing looseness of structure and an increasing irrationality which suggest the decadence of the great meditative tradition

In the act of meditation (according to Baxter) truth (heavenly doctrine) is brought from the head to the heart "by comparing the unseen delights of Heaven, with those smaller which you have seen, and felt in the flesh." Many of Taylor's poems are in the form of a "dramatic" soliloquy, an exhortation of the self in which the poet moves his own emotions and those of his reader by means of sensory language. There are two primary sources for Taylor's style—the metaphysical poets and the Bible.

The metaphysical poets frequently achieved their effects by the bizarre juxtaposition of images drawn from widely disparate fields of experience. Donne's famous stiff twin compasses, which illustrate the parted yet united lovers, are the classic example. They were fond of paradox and irony and their diction ranged from the cosmic to the colloquial. In all these respects Taylor is in the metaphysical tradition. His figures of speech and his diction are drawn from now forgotten abstruse theological tracts as well as from his life on Leicestershire and New England farms. The glossary in the Yale edition of the poems lists the dialect words of the Leicestershire and Massachusetts farmer as well as those of a tract against the heresy of Sherlock. The unseen world of the spirit is made visible in images of daily life—the book-lined study, the kitchen and parlor, the fields and woods, the streets of the village. Taylor's fondness for colloquial diction and homely imagery, derived from the metaphysical poets, was probably reinforced by the necessity of preaching to a semiliterate farmer congregation.

Taylor's interest in simile and metaphor is closely linked with an obsession with typology which he shared with many other seventeenth-century writers. Typology is the result of reading the entire Bible as a continuous history of God's chosen people; it had its origin in the Middle Ages, and it was emphasized and elaborated by the Puritans who based their whole religious position on the Bible, and who constantly looked for events in the Old Testament which foreshadowed events in the New Testament. Thus the ram which was sacrificed in place of Isaac foreshadowed Jesus who was sacrificed for man. The ram was the type; Jesus was the anti-type. Similarly, the Jewish passover was a type of the Lord's Supper. The comparison between the type and the anti-type was often carried to fantastic lengths. The first thirty poems of the second series of *Preparatory Meditations* are devoted to this subject.

An interest in typology led to elaborate analogizing with figures derived from the Bible. Thus in the *Preparatory Meditations,* Christ is gold or a restorative medicine made from gold, a cordial, the Rose of Sharon, a rose, medicine made of the rose, a pearl, a jewel of any kind (usually in a cabinet). The notion that Mary was a cabinet enclosing a jewel

was common in Christian typology. Taylor uses the cabinet-jewel combination, but usually in the sense of himself being the cabinet and Christ the jewel therein. The wicker cage and bird figure is similarly used, and also ointment or perfume in a box. Enclosing images derive ultimately from the Jewish tabernacle which housed God and from the ark which enclosed the tablets of God's law. Christ is also the Brazen Serpent, grapes (the bunch of grapes found by the scouts in Canaan was considered a type of Christ), and the wine pressed from the grapes. The red robes of Bozrah foreshadowed the robe of blood Christ wore at the Passion; Joseph's coat represented Christ's flesh as did the priestly garments of Aaron. Joseph's pit represented hell or the grave of Jesus. The whale which swallowed Jonah was the tomb of Jesus. Noah and Jacob were also types of Christ.

Grace in Taylor's poetry is often represented by water, wine, olive oil, aqua vitae, and beer—all except the beer being conventional figures. These liquids are conveyed to man by buckets, casks, channels, and golden pipes. The golden pipe imagery probably derives from Zechariah 4:11–14 where the Apostles are called golden pipes. Baptism is represented in the Old Testament by circumcision.

Taylor frequently refers to himself as God's music or as playing music in praise of God. The notion of man as God's music or musical instrument derives from medieval times when Christ was depicted as being stretched on the cross like the strings of a harp.

This practice of finding meaning in Old Testament events by reading into them analogies with the New Testament was similar to the Puritan habit of finding supernatural meanings in events, from the greatest to the most trivial, which occurred in the natural or everyday world. Thus in Cotton Mather's diary a comet was a message from God, and a dog urinating on a wall was not without significance. Mather could not carve a roast at the table without attaching theological or moral significance to the act. The result was what Yvor Winters has called a kind of punning piety, and puns in abundance can be found in Taylor's verse: "Your bark shall to a happy bay be brought." Now the seventeenth-century religious mind, brought up on a typological interpretation of the Scriptures, was by training an allegorical mind—whether the mind was Anglican, Catholic, Lutheran, or Puritan. But the Puritan mind, with its uncompromising insistence on predestination and God's Decrees, with its belief that every event however small had its meaning, developed this allegorical tendency to an unprecedented extent.

"You can open your Bibles, and read there of God and of Glory: O learn to open the creatures, and to open the several passages of providence, to reade of God and glory there. Certainly by such a skilful industrious improvement, we might have a fuller taste of Christ and heaven, in every bit of bread that we eat, and in every draught of Beer that we drink, then most men have in the use of the Sacrament." So wrote Baxter in *The Saints Everlasting Rest*. This Puritan tendency to invest all aspects of life with religious meaning had a profound and often unfortunate effect on Taylor's choice of images. Taylor saw nothing incongruous in using an image from everyday life (such as beer) to illustrate a serious theological idea (such as grace). Taylor had no regard for incongruous connotations. He saw resemblances rather than differences.

An interest in typology, the frequent use of "mixed" figures, a devout piety, and scores of verbal echoes and parallels suggest the influence of George Herbert on Edward Taylor. Herbert, in spite of his Anglicanism, was a favorite with English and Bay Colony Puritans. A copy of *The Temple* was in the library of Harvard's President Chauncy. The stanza form of the introductory poem to *The Temple*, "The Church Porch," probably was the model for the *Preparatory Meditations*. There are, nevertheless, important differences of style as well as of doctrine between the Puritan parson and the Anglican divine explained, in part, by the difference in family background and environment. Herbert came from an established family and was educated in the life of the court. Taylor was raised on a farm and spent most of his life in a frontier village. It is not surprising, then, that Herbert's poetry is quiet, subdued, subtly modulated and Taylor's verse is sometimes strident, crude, and harsh. Herbert rarely overwrites and Taylor frequently does. Yet at his best Taylor is the more powerful of the two poets.

The influence of the Bible is pervasive throughout all of Taylor's verse with the Song of Songs (Canticles) and Revelation the dominant books. Taylor's "erotic" and sensuous "baroque" style has been frequently discussed. Much of the "baroque glory" is repetition of imagery and phrase from the love poetry of Canticles which furnished the text for many of the *Meditations* and which, of course, Taylor interpreted allegorically as the foreshadowing of the mystical wedding between Christ (the groom) and the elect (the bride). The Puritan allegorical interpretation which derives ultimately from Origen explicated all of the sensuous details of the Song of Songs. For example, in Taylor's library was Thomas Wilson's *A Christian Dictionary* (1616) which explicates "lips like lilies" as the doctrine of the Word, "two breasts" as the two testaments of the Bible, "navel" as an instrument of spiritual nourishment, i.e., belief in the Word. Even when understood allegorically, however, the language is still sensuous and the Song of Songs gave the Puritan divine opportunity to indulge in a good deal of erotic imagery.

The Revelation of St. John the Divine was also of especial interest to the poet. Four volumes on the interpretation of this book were in his library. In 1696 he engaged in a debate by letter with Judge Sewall over the interpretation of the "sixth vial." Sewall thought that this vial referred to the kingdom of Antichrist in America, that is, the Spanish Catholics in the New World. Taylor argued that it referred to the destruction of the Pagan Turks. Only nine of the *Meditations* were composed upon a text from Revelation; however, Taylor's reference to the morning star and his other star, sun, moon, thunder, lightning, and earthquake imagery, his frequent use of vials, and his description of the celestial city with its walls and streets of gold and jasper usually come from Revelation.

With a structure derived from a centuries-old tradition of meditative practice, with a style imitative of the metaphysical poets one and two generations before his time, with images taken from the daily life of farm and study, and with frequent recourse to the Bible, Taylor for forty-three years wrote his bimonthly meditations. Let us examine a typical one, number 20 of the first series.

The text from St. Paul's letter to the Philippians 2:9, "God hath exalted him," provides the "heavenly doctrine"—the glorification of the man-God Christ and through Christ of the elect and of the poet himself. The theme is stated in the paradox of the fifth line: "A Mortall Clod immortalizde." As an aid to understanding this paradoxical doctrine, the poet visualizes the ascent of the man-God from earth to heaven:

A Turffe of Clay, and yet bright Glories King
    From dust to Glory Angell-like to fly.

The image of ascension is varied in the second, third, and fourth stanzas with scriptural references, Biblical language, and an odd use of a word Taylor was fond of, a word which he used both as a noun and a verb—"sedan" —referring to the sedan chair just becoming popular in the latter part of the seventeenth century. In stanza two Christ rides in "His Bright Sedan, through all the Silver Skies." At the end of the stanza the sedan becomes a chariot. In the third stanza the chariot figure is rejected and we see Christ climbing a golden and jasper ladder to heaven. In stanza four Christ is back in his chariot again (such inconsistency is typical of Taylor):

Methinks I see Heavens sparkling Courtiers fly,
    In flakes of Glory down him to attend:
And heare Heart Cramping notes of Melody,
    Surround his Charriot as it did ascend.

The emotional climax comes in the next stanza where the Affections are raised to their highest pitch in a burst of ecstatic joy:

God is Gone up with a triumphant Shout
    The Lord with sounding Trumpets melodies.
Sing Praise, sing Praise, sing Praise, sing Praises
        out,
    Unto our King sing praise seraphickwise.
    Lift up your Heads ye lasting Doore they
        sing
And let the King of Glory Enter in.

The language is mainly scriptural, but the intensity of Taylor's own feeling is real. The truth of heavenly doctrine has been brought home to the heart. The poem ends with a plea that the poet, like Christ, will be lifted to heaven, not by his own strength which is insufficient, but by Faith, Saving Grace, and the Word. Or as Taylor figuratively puts it:

Lend mee thy Wings, my Lord, I'st fly apace.
    My Soules Arms stud with thy strong Quills,
        true Faith,

My Quills then Feather with thy Saving Grace,
   My Wings will take the Winde thy Word
      displai'th.
Then I shall fly up to thy glorious Throne
With my strong Wings whose Feathers are
      thine own.

Two cardinal Puritan doctrines are predestination and the union of the elect with Christ. In the *Meditations* we see expressed again and again Taylor's belief in the spiritual union of the believer with Christ at the partaking of the Lord's Supper. In his other major work we see (as the title suggests) the operation of predestination, of God's immutable decrees as he brings the faithful through their earthly trials to heaven.

The date of *Gods Determinations* has not been established, but the precise, firm handwriting of the poem in the manuscript suggests an early date, probably between 1680 and 1700. The full title states the theme: *Gods Determinations touching his Elect: and The Elects Combat in their Conversion, and Coming up to God in Christ together with the Comfortable Effects thereof.* Like the earlier *Paradise Lost,* this poem is the author's attempt to justify God's ways to men but, unlike Milton's epic, the justification is made in Calvinistic terms, with the use of allegory, dialogue and debate, descriptive and narrative interludes, and a variety of verse forms. Taylor's dramatic allegory is a series of short poems of various kinds without unity of tone and loosely related by its major theme—the destiny of man. Like Wigglesworth's famous *Day of Doom* (1662) it depicts the damnation of the majority of mankind and the salvation of the few. It is chiefly concerned with the struggle between good and evil, between Satan and Christ for the soul of man, the struggle being depicted as a series of temptations and of battles, both physical and spiritual. Some of the elect are won to Christ with ease, others with varying degrees of difficulty, but in the end all of the predestined saved are rolled to glory in "Christ's coach."

A number of influences were at work on Taylor as he composed his dramatic allegory. In grammar school he had studied and perhaps acted in the Latin comedies of Terence and Plautus, and he had probably read various dialogues in Latin based on Bible stories. Then he began writing dialogues in English. The manuscript of his earliest extant verse contains "A Dialogue between the Writer and a Maypole Dresser." He copied a "play" by Robert Wild, "The Recantation of a Penitent Proteus" (1663), into the same manuscript— a monologue spoken by Proteus who had changed his religion to suit the times. Satirical verse debates such as Wild's "A Friendly Debate between a Conformist and a Non-Conformist" were common in the pamphleteering wars of the period among Anglican, Puritan, and Catholic. These were probably the sources of Taylor's dramatic dialogues and debates in *Gods Determinations* rather than (as some have supposed) the Elizabethan and Jacobean drama which the Puritan Taylor would have disliked if he had read it. There is no evidence that he did.

However, he may have been familiar with a few medieval plays. As Nathalia Wright has pointed out, he may, as a youth, have seen the Corpus Christi procession near Coventry. Or he may have been influenced by the morality plays through intermediary sources in the work of Spenser, Milton, and other poets. The debate of the heavenly graces in these plays may have suggested the dialogue between Justice and Mercy of Taylor's poem, and the conflict of vices and virtues in the morality drama may have had some influence on Taylor's depiction of the struggle between Christ and Satan.

The *Day of Doom* was certainly in the poet's mind as he composed his own poem on the destiny of man. Taylor's description of Christ, the Devil, and hell may have been influenced by Wigglesworth, but the verse of *Gods Determinations* is far superior to Wigglesworth's bouncing fourteeners. Taylor may also have been familiar with Lorenzo Scupoli's *The Spiritual Conflict*, first published in Italian in 1589 and translated into English as early as 1613, and, as Professor Martz has demonstrated, influential directly or indirectly on the poetry of Donne, Herbert, and Marvell. Scupoli defines the conflict as the conquest of the self; the conflict is between the higher will which he associates with reason and the lower will signified by the names of sense, appetite, flesh, passion. "Hereupon all our spiritual Battell principally consisteth in this, that this superior will being placed as in the midst between the divine wil, which stands above, and the inferior, which is that of the sence, continually assaulted by the one and the other, whilst either of these assaieth to draw it and to make it subject, and obedient unto them." The central idea of *The Spiritual Conflict* is the necessity of overcoming the passions. The passions darken the understanding, and the understanding then presents the objects in false colors to the will which is brought to love it more ardently than it should. In Shakespeare's phrase "Reason panders will." The same notions are evident in Taylor's lines from "The Accusation of the Inward Man":

The Understandings dark, and therefore Will
Account of Ill for Good, and Good for ill.
As to a Purblinde man men oft appeare
Like Walking Trees within the Hemisphere.
So in the judgment Carnall things Excell:
Pleasures and Profits beare away the Bell.
The Will is hereupon perverted so,
It laquyes after ill, doth good foregoe.

The Reasonable Soule doth much delight
A Pickpack t'ride o'th'Sensuall Appitite.

There is some similarity between Taylor's poem and John Bunyan's *The Holy War* (1682). Both works are concerned with the combat between God and the Devil for the soul of man, both are Calvinistic, and both are allegorical. In *The Holy War* the City of Mansoul, built by Shaddai (God) is attacked and captured by Diabolus (the Devil). The son of Shaddai, Emmanuel (Christ), goes to the rescue, conquers the city, and pardons the guilty and unfaithful inhabitants. Allies of Diabolus within the city continue to plot its overthrow, but means are eventually found by Shaddai to save the city and glorify its inhabitants. Virtues, vices, faculties of the soul, and the five senses are personified. The central conflict and the allegorical personifications bear some similarity to Taylor's poem, but there the resemblance ends. Bunyan's prose is simple, clear, and (for the most part) dull. Taylor's verse is colorful, colloquial, and complex, and Taylor's concept of the struggle between good and evil in the soul of man is more intricate and interesting than Bunyan's simple analysis.

Some of the most vivid writing in Taylor's poem depicts the "Elects Combat," that is, their battle against the temptations of the Devil. Battle imagery came naturally to the colonial poet. His infancy, we have seen, was passed in the midst of the turmoil of the English Civil War, and as he grew older, he must have heard many stories of armed conflict. He came to maturity during the militant Puritanism of Cromwell's regime, and the foundation of his church in Westfield was interrupted by the turmoil of King Philip's War. Furthermore, the church embattled, the Church Militant, was central to all Puritan thinking. "To hew Agag in pieces before the Lord is to his mind not the least attractive of religious duties" has been said of Edward Johnson, the author of *Wonder-Working Providence*. A chapter of this book bears the title "How the People of Christ ought to behave themselves in Warlike Discipline": "See then," says Johnson, "you store your selves with all sorts of weapons for war, furbish up your Swords, Rapiers, and all other piercing weapons. As for great Artillery, seeing present meanes falls short, waite on the Lord Christ, and hee will stir up friends to provide for you: and in the meane time spare not to lay out your coyne for Powder, Bullets, Match, Armes of all sorts, and all kinde of Instruments for War." Johnson frequently compares the Puritans of New England to that other embattled and chosen people, the Israelites, and the zest for battle is one aspect of the Hebraism of our New England ancestors. In describing the "Elects Combat," Taylor is not only writing from experiences close to him in England and New England, but also out of that Puritan obsession with the notion of the battle between the chosen people of God and the Devil, a notion which was fostered in the Bay Colony by the Mathers and others to whom it seemed that the climax of the drama of salvation was being enacted between the dark forces of the Devil and the wilderness on the one hand and small body of Saints on the other—with the final scene, the Judgment Day, only a few years in the future.

The most widely admired writing in all of Taylor occurs in "The Preface" to *Gods Determinations*:

Infinity, when all things it beheld
In Nothing, and of Nothing all did build,
Upon what Base was fixt the Lath, wherein
He turn'd this Globe, and riggalld it so trim?
Who blew the Bellows of his Furnace Vast?
Or held the Mould wherein the world was
    Cast?

Who Laid its Corner Stone? Or whose
    Command?
Where stand the Pillars upon which it stands?
Who Lac'de and Fillitted the earth so fine,
With Rivers like green Ribbons Smaragdine?
Who made the Sea's its Selvedge, and it locks
Like a Quilt Ball within a Silver Box?
Who Spread its Canopy? Or Curtains Spun?
Who in this Bowling Alley bowld the Sun?
Who made it always when it rises set
To go at once both down, and up to get?
Who th' Curtain rods made for this Tapistry?
Who hung the twinckling Lanthorns in the
    Sky?
Who? who did this? or who is he? Why, know
Its Onely Might Almighty this did doe. . . .
Whose Might Almighty can by half a looks
Root up the rocks and rock the hills by
    th'roots.
Can take this mighty World up in his hande,
And shake it like a Squitchen or a Wand.
Whose single Frown will make the Heavens
    shake
Like as an aspen leafe the Winde makes quake.
Oh! what a might is this Whose single frown
Doth shake the world as it would shake it
    down?
Which All from Nothing fet, from Nothing,
    All:
Hath All on Nothing set, lets Nothing fall.

Here an interesting complex of influences may be at work. One is reminded first of all of the beginning of Du Bartas' *Divine Weeks* as translated by Joshua Sylvester, a poem popular with seventeenth-century Protestant poets including Milton. It was almost certainly known by Taylor, and the opening lines describing the Creation may have been in his mind as he composed his "Preface":

Thou glorious Guide of Heav'ns star-glistring
    motion,

Thou, thou (true Neptune) Tamer of the
    Ocean,
Thou Earth's drad Shaker (at whose only
    Word,
Th'Eolian Scouts are quickly still'd and
    stirr'd) . . .

    And also grant (great Architect of wonders,
Whose mighty Voyce speakes in the midst of
    Thunders,
Causing the Rocks to rock, and Hils to teare;
Calling the things that Are not, as they were;
Confounding Mighty things by meanes of
    Weak;
Teaching dum Infants thy drad Praise to
    speak [)] . . .
Grant me such Judgement, Grace, and
    Eloquence,
So correspondent to that Excellence,
That in some measure, I may seeme t'inherit
(Elisha-like) my deare Elias spirit.

    CLEARE FIRE for ever hath not Aire
        imbrac't,
Nor Aire for-ay inviron'd Waters vast,
Nor Waters alwaies wrapt the Earth therein;
But all this *All* did once (of nought) begin . . .

There is a similar passage on the Creation in
Abraham Cowley's *Davideis* (1656). These poetic accounts have, of course, their origin in
the Bible. The series of rhetorical questions in
"The Preface" which include Taylor's most
famous line "Who in this Bowling Alley bowld
the Sun?" were probably inspired by Job 38:4–
8: ". . . who laid the corner stone thereof;
When the morning stars sang together, and all
the sons of God shouted for joy? Or who shut
up the sea with doors . . .?" And, as Thomas
H. Johnson has pointed out, there may be
echoes of the opening passage of Thomas
Shepard's *The Sincere Convert* (1652), "Who
set those candles, those torches of heaven on

the table? Who hung out those Lanthorns in
heaven to enlighten a dark world?" And Samuel Lee's *Eleothriambos* (1677), which was in
Taylor's library, contains a series of similar
rhetorical questions: "Who can solve the flux
of the Sea, either by the Moon or the Earth's
Motion? Who is so hardy as to dive to the tops
of the under-wave Mountains, or set their foot
on the ridge of those hidden Ararats? . . . What
Telescopes . . . ever pierced into that Sapphire
pavement . . . the Place of the Blessed?"

Finally, there is the ever-present influence
of the Calvinistic theology as set forth in the
Institutes, and in the other tracts in Taylor's
library. Taylor's concept of God's Justice and
Mercy, the notion of the special call and the
general call, the inefficacy of good works
in winning salvation, the methods used by
Satan in his temptation of the elect, the perseverance of the saints, the worthlessness of
natural man, and the complete sovereignty of
God are all derived from Calvin directly or
indirectly. For example, Taylor was well acquainted with the Calvinist William Ames,
whose book *Conscience with the Power and
Cases thereof* was in his library, and he probably took from it some of Ames's observations
on temptation. Ames says that temptations
should be considered a battle between the
Devil and the castle of man's soul. This battle
is, as we have seen, the subject of *Gods Determinations.* According to Ames, the Devil
attempts to make the Christian believe that he
is not one of the elect (just as Satan does in
Taylor's poem), and he may under the pretense of virtue draw men to danger and vice
(as Satan attempts to do in "The Effect of
the Reply" when he puts on an Angel's disguise). In this battle, says Ames, "Christ is
our Captaine and Generall . . . he is every
where present and beholds the combate with
his eye. This must needs be a strong incite-
ment to provoke us to do valiantly. For he

doth exhort us to fight, helpes us to overcome, aids us when we faint, and crownes those that conquer." There are marked verbal similarities between this passage and "Christs Reply"— "I am a Captain to your Will."

The religious ideas of *Gods Determinations*, then, are commonplaces of Calvinistic theology. Let us summarize the main action of the poem and comment on the poetic expression of these ideas. After the magnificent "Preface" which describes the Creation and the Creator with emphasis on God's majesty and terror, the worthlessness of sinful, natural man as a result of the Fall is depicted in vivid, idiomatic language:

He lookes within, and sad amazement's there,
Without, and all things fly about his Eares.
Above, and sees Heaven falling on his pate,
Below and spies th'Infernall burning lake,
Before and sees God storming in his Face,
Behinde, and spies Vengeance persues his
     trace. . . .
Thus over Stretcht upon the Wrack of Woe,
Bereav'd of Reason, he proceeds now so,
Betakes himself unto his Heels in hast,
Runs like a Madman till his Spirits wast,
Then like a Child that fears the Poker Clapp
Him on his face doth on his Mothers lap
Doth hold his breath, lies still for fear least hee
Should by his breathing lowd discover'd bee.

This is followed by "A Dialogue between Justice and Mercy" (the personified attributes of God) which presents the doctrine of the Atonement and Redemption—disobedient man merits eternal punishment to satisfy Justice, but Christ (here identified with Mercy) will suffer in place of man and thus purchase salvation for the elect. In bringing the elect to salvation, Justice will frighten him with threats of hellfire and humble his pride. Mercy, on the other hand, will offer him hope and con-

solation. Thus both Justice and Mercy act together to save the elect. In the next two poems men, in their fallen estate, are called by God. A few answer the call and are put into God's coach and ride in it to glory.

Taylor now drops the coach figure (although he returns to it later) and gets into the real subject of *Gods Determinations*, the various methods by which God brings the predestined elect to heaven, that is, the mysterious workings of grace in the heart of man. Some receive grace easily in infancy—perhaps Taylor intended these to be those placed in God's coach in the preceding poem. The others are divided into three ranks and their adventures make up the rest of *Gods Determinations*. They are pursued and tempted by Satan (who at times seems to be Justice personified). They are consoled by Christ (or Mercy personified). Satan throughout is depicted as an instrument of God's will. He is used (like a sheep dog, says Taylor in one poem) to drive the faithful into the fold. Satan's temptations are powerful and devious; yet, this being a Calvinistic poem based on predestination, the issue is never in doubt. Nevertheless, the various temptations employed by Satan are of some psychological interest. His method is to suit the temptation to the person. He threatens some with violence; others he calls cowards who have become slaves to Christ. At one point he puts on the disguise of an angel and tempts some with pride. His most powerful psychological attack is to tempt the soul to doubt the reality of its conversion because the conversion occurred too easily. If the soul's sin had really been forgiven (says Satan) the soul would have gone through more of a struggle than it did. When the soul replies that it is sure of having received grace, Satan proceeds to anatomize sin to show how completely man has become corrupted and how hopeless is the chance of salvation. As Calvin wrote in the

Institute, "Satan never attacks believers with a more grievous or dangerous temptation than when he disquiets them with doubts of their election."

Through several more poems Satan now directs his attacks on the souls and bodies of "those that first Came up to Mercys terms" or, as he elsewhere designates them, the first rank, until "The Souls Groan to Christ for Succour." In "Christs Reply," Christ answers in the style of a child's lullaby, assuring them that the "inward man" and the "outward man" will be purified of the sins imputed by Satan. Christ demands only faith, repentance, and the will to fight the Devil. The first rank, now reassured, express themselves in a hymn of praise, and Satan is forced to turn his attention to the second and third ranks—that is, those who held out against Mercy but were captured by Justice. He tries to convince the second rank that Grace cannot be effective in their case—they have scorned God's Mercy, and now, captured by Justice, they will be condemned to hell. The third rank is accused of being so worldly that they cannot possibly receive saving grace. Satan even suggests that hell does not exist:

Nay; what? or where is Hell Can any show?
This Bugbare in the Darke, 's a mere
    Scar-Crow.

He also insinuates that heaven and God are delusions. But even granting that heaven, hell, and God exist, the case is so much the worse for them, for they are moved by fear of hell and God rather than by love. Their secret love is for Satan (the world) and therefore they are doomed:

Set Heaven, and Hell aside its clearly shown,
Thou lov'st mee more than God thou seem'st
    to own.

Hence was it not for these, it plainly 'pears
Thy God for servants might go shake his ears.

The two ranks in despair turn to God for mercy and to the "saints" (the elect who have assurance of salvation) for advice. In a dialogue consisting of several poems, the saint assures the sinner (who represents the second and third ranks) that he, the saint, was once in the same predicament. He satisfies the doubts raised by Satan as to the possibility of the sinner's salvation. The members of the second and third rank are now convinced of their election, and after another hymn of praise and several poems describing the beauties of Christ's garden and the city of God, the predestined elect are packed into Christ's coach and ride off to glory:

In Heaven soaring up, I dropt an Eare
    On Earth: and oh! sweet Melody:
And listening, found it was the Saints who were
    Encoacht for Heaven that sang for Joy.
    For in Christs Coach they sweetly sing;
    As they to Glory ride therein.

A series of eight numbered poems written upon what Taylor called "occurrants," that is, a rainstorm, a fly caught in a spider's web, a wasp numbed with cold, his wife spinning (two poems), the death of two children, the act of lighting a fire by flint and steel, and a flood, illustrate the poet's habit of investing daily events, from the most trivial to the most important, with religious significance. The first of these, "[When] Let by rain," is the most obscure. In the first two stanzas the decision of whether or not to make a journey during a rainstorm suggests the difficulties of a more important religious decision:

Wager thyselfe against thy surplice, see,
And win thy Coate: or let thy Coate Win thee.

The theme of the poem may have been suggested by the decision Taylor had to make in 1671 of whether to stay on at Harvard as a fellow or accept the call of the ministry in Westfield. According to his diary, Taylor had difficulty in making up his mind. Furthermore, his decision was associated with a severe snowstorm which almost prevented his journey to Westfield and a fire which burned down Thomas Dewey's house soon after his arrival. A fire and a storm are mentioned in the poem although it is a rainstorm rather than snow.

"Upon a Spider Catching a Fly" presents a picture of a wasp falling into a spider's web. The spider treats it with caution, in fear of its sting and its strength, whereas the fly which next comes into his power is immediately killed. In the final stanzas, the meaning of the poem is stated—the spider is the Devil, and the insects in danger of his web are men who may be saved if by the grace of the Lord the web is broken. The faithful will then find themselves singing in "Glories Cage," instead of struggling in a spider's web. "Upon a Wasp Child with Cold" describes in rather charming language a wasp numbed by cold struggling back to life in the sun. The poem concludes with a prayer that God will have as much care for the poet as he showed for the wasp. In the next two poems, "Huswifery" and "Another upon the Same," the arts of spinning and weaving provide the basic images for a prayer to God who is requested to make the poet his spinning wheel and his loom, the resulting cloth to be used to adorn him and glorify God. "Upon Wedlock, and Death of Children" is a very moving lament for the deaths of two children by his first wife, a lament modified to subdued triumph by the firm conviction that they have gone to heaven to the glory of themselves, himself, and God:

I piecemeal pass to Glory bright in them.
I joy, may I sweet Flowers for Glory breed,

Whether thou getst them green, or lets them
    seed.

"The Ebb and Flow" deals with one of Taylor's recurrent themes—the fear that his heart has grown cold toward God, and the hope that, through God's grace, his affections will be warmed. In "Upon the Sweeping Flood" Taylor indulges in a kind of speculation habitual with himself and his Puritan friends, the possible relationship between a personal event and a natural event, here, as usual, in the heavens. The poet suggests that his sin, which seems to be that of carnal love, had acted as a "physick" on the heavens so that they "vomited," that is, poured out a cloudburst.

Most of these "occurrant" poems are either allegorical or symbolical. I do not wish to labor the difference between these terms here, but I would like to point out that the allegory or symbolism is only partially successful. There is not that close connection between idea, image or symbol, and appropriate feeling that we find in completely realized symbolic poetry. For example, in "Huswifery" the poet asks God to make his distaff the holy word, his affections the flyers, his soul the spool, his conversation the reel. The choice of terms is completely arbitrary. The flyers might just as well be identified with conversation, the holy word might be the reel. In "Upon a Wasp Child with Cold" the details of the wasp combing her velvet capital and hoisting up her petticoat are charming and striking, but they are not necessary to the meaning which Taylor tacks on at the conclusion. Perception is beginning to outrun meaning, as it does in the famous bird image in Marvell's "Garden." The complete divorce between perception and meaning did not occur in poetry until the second half of the nineteenth century, but in Marvell and Taylor we find the beginning of the cleavage.

Taylor's eight elegies follow the standard

pattern of this form in seventeenth-century Massachusetts—expression of grief for the deceased, reference to the dead's ancestors and descendants, praise for his accomplishments and Christian piety, consolation to the relatives, a triumphant vision of the soul of the deceased in heaven, and a reference to the body in the grave awaiting the day of judgment. These poems contain a good deal of stereotyped language, but genuine grief is apparent in the elegy on his first wife. In spite of the conventional style the poem is sincere and moving:

> Five Babes thou tookst from me before
>   this Stroake.
> Thine arrows then into my bowells broake,
> But now they pierce into my bosom smart,
> Do strike and stob me in the very heart.

The best elegy is on the death of Samuel Hooker, minister at Farmington, Connecticut, son of the famous Thomas Hooker who helped to found Hartford. The poem has two related subjects—the death of a great preacher and the religious decline of New England, a decline hastened by the death of Hooker for whom there is no adequate substitute. In his address to New England, to Connecticut, and to Hooker's family, Taylor laments the falling away from the true Congregational faith of so many inhabitants of the Bay Colony and deplores the rise of Presbyterianism, "Which is refined Prelacy at best." The poem is a part of the vast Jeremiad literature of the latter part of the seventeenth century when the preachers were thundering against New England's religious apathy. Taylor addresses New England in terms which, as a doctor as well as a poet and preacher, came naturally to him:

> Mourn, mourn, New England, alas! alas!
> To see thy Freckled Face in Gospell Glass:
> To feele thy Pulse, and finde thy Spleen's not
>   well:

> Whose Vapors cause thy Pericordium t'swell:
> Do suffocat, and Cramp thee, and grow worse
> By Hypochondrik Passions of the purse,
> Affect thy Brains toucht with the Turn, till
>   thou
> Halfe sick of Preachers false, and Gospell
>   Plow.
> Such Symptoms say, if nothing else will ease,
> Thy Sickness soon will cure thy sad Disease.

He then speaks to the children of Hooker, warning them to keep the faith of their father and grandfather:

> Be n't like such babes as parents brains out
>   pull
> To make a Wassill Bowle then of the Skull.
> That Pick their Parents eyes out, and the holes
> Stuff up with folly, as if no braind Souls.

The vivid reference to brains, skull, and eyes of the dead is typical of seventeenth-century unflinching contemplation of physical death and corruption.

Taylor copied a number of early poems by himself and by other authors into his diary manuscript. Of these, five are probably by Taylor, and of these five, "The Lay-mans Lamentation" is by far the best. After an invocation of twenty-six lines in which he praises the nonconforming ministers who were silenced by the Act of Uniformity, a dialogue takes place between a "proud prelate" and a "poor professour." The prelate defends the Act of Uniformity and attacks the characters and abilities of the silenced preachers. The "professour" defends the nonconforming ministers and in turn attacks the conforming priests and ends with a plea to the Lord to save the pious from the Anglican prelates. The Act of Uniformity was the direct cause, as we have seen, of Taylor's emigration to the Bay Colony, and this poem is written not only out of the bitterness of seeing the careers of men he admired cut short but also out of the knowledge that a career for himself, either as a preacher or a teacher, was now impossible in his native land.

About one half of Taylor's entire poetic output is to be found in an untitled manuscript of over four hundred pages bound by himself, probably in the year 1710, and containing approximately 21,500 lines of verse, chiefly in decasyllabic couplets. Because of its subject, I have supplied a title—*The Metrical History of Christianity*. The poem in its present state is in two parts, although such a division may not have been Taylor's original intention. The first part describes the history of the Christian church from the beginnings until the twelfth century, with particular emphasis on martyrdoms and sufferings of Christians under persecution or as a result of war and natural calamities such as fire, flood, and earthquake —these calamities being interpreted as manifestations of the wrath of God's Justice. The second part of the poem deals with the martyrdoms suffered under Queen Mary's reign in England. The entire work, with such a wide range of time and place, is unified by one theme: the alternate manifestations of God's Justice and God's Mercy in the history and destiny of man from the time of Christ. The work appears to be unfinished. It is likely that Taylor had intended to bring it down to his own period, with perhaps the New England experiment as a triumphant demonstration of the power of divine Grace.

In writing the *Metrical History,* Taylor employed, as his principal source, the *Ecclesiastica Historia Integram Ecclesiae,* commonly known as the *Magdeburg Centuries,* by Matthias Flacius and others. The *Centuries,* compiled in or near Magdeburg beginning in the year 1553, the first attempt to write a history of the church from the evangelical point of view, defended the Protestant interpretation of church history and attacked Roman Catholicism. Similarly, Taylor vents his bitter hatred of Popes, priests, worship of saints, the Mass, miracles caused by the worship of saints, visions, and the monastic life in vitriolic verses which are at times extremely vulgar and even obscene. The language is reminiscent of and perhaps inspired by the religious pamphlet warfare of seventeenth-century England between various Protestant sects as well as between Protestant and Catholic. We are reminded by this coarse humor in the *Metrical History* that even the best Puritan minds sometimes had more zeal than taste.

Taylor, like his contemporary Cotton Mather and other Puritans, was interested in "remarkable providences," that is, abnormal occurrences such as monsters, sudden death, signs in the sky which were taken as proofs of supernatural intervention in the natural world. His commonplace books record many of these events, some from his own experience, some from hearsay and from history. The discovery of huge bones in New York in 1705 and again in 1706 on the banks of the Hudson River created a sensation. Cotton Mather published an account of them in the *Transactions of the Royal Society* and mentioned them in his sermons. Specimens were sent to England to be housed in the museum of Gresham College. Taylor, who was shown two of the huge teeth, was stirred to write one of the most remarkable poems in the history of American literature, "The Description of the great Bones dug up at Clavarack on the Banks of Hudsons River A.D. 1705." Like his contemporaries, he considered these remains to be those of a giant whose thigh bone was seventeen feet long, whose knee pan was a foot in diameter, and whose teeth weighed several pounds apiece. These bones were proof of the Biblical statement "There were giants in the earth in those days." One hundred and ninety lines were devoted to the subject, of which the following are a fair sample:

This Gyants bulk propounded to our Eyes
Reason lays down nigh t'seventy foot did
    rise . . .
His nose like an Hanging Pillar wide
And Eyes like shining Suns, Each on Each side,
His Arms like limbs of trees twenty foot long,
Fingers with bones like horse shanks and as
    strong,
His Thighs do stand like two Vast Millposts
    stout,
Each seventeen foot in length or thereabout.

According to Samuel Sewall, Taylor was an eloquent preacher: "I have heard him preach a Sermon at the Old South upon short warning which as the phrase in England is, might have been preached at Paul's Cross." The evidence of Taylor's pulpit eloquence is in the sermon he preached on the day of his ordination, August 27, 1679, for the foundation services of the Westfield church, in the series of eight sermons on the Lord's Supper from Matthew 22:12 delivered at Westfield in 1694 in which he attacks Stoddardeanism; in two sermons on church discipline from Matthew 17:17-18 preached at Westfield in 1713-14, and in a series of fourteen sermons on the union of the divine and human natures in Christ entitled *Christographia,* preached at Westfield from 1701 to 1703. *Christographia* contains his best sermons. In addition to the theme of the mystical union of the human and divine in the person of Christ, they frequently deal with the mystical union of Christ with his bride, the church, the predestined elect saints of God, which is also the central motivating subject of the *Preparatory Meditations.* As a general rule a meditation was composed on the same Biblical text as the sermon preached on a Communion Sunday.

In structure and in style Taylor's sermons are in the tradition of the Puritan preaching of his time. Each sermon, as Taylor states on the title page of *Christographia,* is "opened, Confirmed, and Practically improoved." It is organized by means of the threefold division: Doctrine, Reason, and Use—that is, Declaration, Explanation, and Application. The purpose of the Puritan sermon was to explain the Scripture and to instruct the congregation in the practical application of scriptural doctrine. To this end, the style of Puritan preaching was plain and straightforward. Taylor's sermons, although containing learned allusions that must have impressed if not enlightened his Westfield congregation of farmers, are for the most part written in the traditional plain style with frequent employment of simple, homely figures of speech. There are, however, a few flights of rhetorical eloquence, usually on the comforts of God's grace, which remind us that Taylor was primarily a poet.

In his homely style Taylor describes the Quakers: ". . . . those Subverters of the Gospell of Salvation hatched in the Nest of Diabolicall Errours under the harbring feathers of the Old Clucking hen of Antichrist, in the last age, viz. those Strange and reason deserted rout of Quakers."

Typical of his rhetorical passages is the following: "What can all the Powers of Hell and Darkness do or Effect, think you, against God? . . . If the Influence of God in the outlets of his providence, makes a Pinke, A Rose, a Violet so sweet to us, if a touch of such influences make the liquour of the Grape, the fertility of the Field, the Cookery of our food, the Labour of the Bee, the satisfaction of the Cane juyce, yea and the Influences of a sorry mortall acting gratefully, leave such a Delightsomeness upon our spirit and senses and are so Edulcorated for us, What then are the sweet heart enravishments of the Consolations that are Contained in the Godhead itselfe from a little vent of whose influences these things are made so sweet unto the hearts of saints in Christ?"

Taylor's claim to greatness rests on his poems and not on his sermons, and chiefly on his major effort, the *Preparatory Meditations*. Because they are written in the metaphysical style and because of the obvious influence of George Herbert, they invite comparison with the work of Donne, Herbert, Crashaw, and Vaughan. Taken as a whole, the *Meditations* must be ranked below the achievements of these English poets. There are too many lapses in taste, there is too much repetition of theme and phrase, too much dependence on Biblical language, and not enough classical and humanistic refinement in the verse of the Puritan parson to claim equal rank with the British metaphysical school. But after the weaknesses of Taylor's verse are admitted, there still remains an impressive body of poetry when it is considered as a whole. As for individual poems, the quiet Herbertian piety of Meditation 1.6, the spiritual exaltation of 1.20, the imagery of light and dark in 2.68A, the powerful statements of the atonement and of victory over death in 2.112, and the ringing rhetoric of "The Preface" to *Gods Determinations* will remain permanent contributions to our American heritage of devotional poetry.

Selected Bibliography

WORKS OF EDWARD TAYLOR

SELECTED AND COLLECTED EDITIONS

Johnson, Thomas H., editor. *The Poetical Works of Edward Taylor*. Princeton, N.J.: Princeton University Press, 1943. (The first selected edition. Contains *Gods Determinations*, 31 "Sacramental" Meditations, and 5 miscellaneous poems.)

Stanford, Donald E., editor. *The Poems of Edward Taylor*. New Haven, Conn.: Yale University Press, 1960. (The first comprehensive edition, containing all of the *Preparatory Meditations, Gods Determinations*, 12 miscellaneous poems, a Foreword by Louis L. Martz, a glossary, and a census of manuscripts.)

Grabo, Norman S., editor. *Christographia*. New Haven, Conn.: Yale University Press, 1962. (First publication of the fourteen sermons preached at Westfield, 1701–03. Fully documented and with an Introduction.)

———. *Edward Taylor's Treatise Concerning the Lord's Supper*. East Lansing: Michigan State University Press, 1966. (First publication of eight sermons by Taylor.)

Murphy, Francis, editor. *The Diary of Edward Taylor*. Springfield, Mass.: Connecticut Valley Historical Museum, 1964. (With an Introduction. This is the second publication of the diary, which was first published in the *Proceedings of the Massachusetts Historical Society*, XVIII (1880), 5–18.)

Stanford, Donald E., editor. *Edward Taylor's Metrical History of Christianity*. Wooster, Ohio: Micro Photo, 1962. (A complete transcript of this 21,500-line poem.)

POEMS IN MAGAZINES

Johnson, Thomas H. "Edward Taylor: A Puritan 'Sacred Poet,'" *New England Quarterly*, 10:290–322 (1937). (First publication of selected poems from the Yale manuscript.)

———. "The Topical Verses of Edward Taylor," *Publications of the Colonial Society of Massachusetts*, 34:513–54 (1943). (First publication of Taylor's eight elegies, an acrostic love poem to Elizabeth Fitch, a declamation delivered at commencement, satirical verses on Pope Joan. The elegies on Elizabeth Fitch and Samuel Hooker have been reprinted in Stanford, *Poems of Edward Taylor*.)

Stanford, Donald E. "The Giant Bones of Claverack, New York, 1705," *New York History*, 40:47–61 (January 1959). (The only publication of this poem.)

———. "The Earliest Poems of Edward Taylor," *American Literature*, 32:136–51 (May 1960). (The only publication of five poems from Taylor's diary manuscript.)

BIBLIOGRAPHY

Gefvert, Constance J. *Edward Taylor: An Annotated Bibliography, 1668–1970.* Kent, Ohio: Kent State University Press, 1971. (The Serif Series, Bibliographies and Checklists: Number 19.)

CRITICAL AND
BIOGRAPHICAL STUDIES

Brown, W. C. "Edward Taylor: American 'Metaphysical,'" *American Literature*, 16:186–97 (November 1944).

Grabo, Norman S. *Edward Taylor.* New York: Twayne, 1961.

———. "Edward Taylor's Spiritual Huswifery," *PMLA*, 74:554-60 (December 1964).

Martz, Louis L. "Foreword," *The Poems of Edward Taylor*, edited by Donald E. Stanford. New Haven, Conn.: Yale University Press, 1960. Pp. xiii–xxxvii.

Stanford, Donald E. "Edward Taylor and the Lord's Supper," *American Literature*, 27:172–78 (May 1955).

———. "The Parentage of Edward Taylor," *American Literature*, 33:215–21 (May 1961).

———. "Edward Taylor's Spiritual Relation," *American Literature*, 35:467–75 (January 1964).

———. "Edward Taylor," *Beginnings of American Literature*, edited by Everett Emerson. Madison: University of Wisconsin Press, 1972.

Warren, Austin. "Edward Taylor's Poetry: Colonial Baroque," *Kenyon Review*, 3:355–71 (Summer 1941).

———. "Edward Taylor," *Major Writers of America*, edited by Perry Miller. New York: Harcourt, Brace, and World, 1962. I, 51–62.

Wright, Nathalia. "The Morality Tradition in the Poetry of Edward Taylor," *American Literature*, 18:1–18 (March 1946).

—DONALD E. STANFORD

Henry David Thoreau

1817-1862

Of the creative spirits that flourished in Concord, Massachusetts, during the middle of the nineteenth century, it might be said that Hawthorne loved men but felt estranged from them, Emerson loved ideas even more than men, and Thoreau loved himself. Less of an artist than Hawthorne, less of a thinker than Emerson, Thoreau made of his life a sylvan legend, that of man alone, in communion with nature. He was a strange presence in American letters—we have so few of them—an eccentric. The English tend to tolerate their eccentrics to the enrichment of their national life. In America, where democracy and conformity are often confused, the nonconforming Thoreau was frowned upon, and for good reason. He had a disagreeable and often bellicose nature. He lacked geniality. And then he had once set fire to the Concord woods—a curious episode, too lightly dismissed in the Thoreau biographies. He was, in the fullest sense of the word, a "curmudgeon," and literary history has never sufficiently studied the difficulties his neighbors had in adjusting themselves to certain of his childish ways. But in other ways he was a man of genius—even if it was a "crooked genius" as he himself acknowledged.

A memorable picture has been left by Hawthorne's daughter of the three famous men of Concord skating one winter's afternoon on the river. Hawthorne, wrapped in his cloak, "moved like a self-impelled Greek statue, stately and grave," as one might expect of the future author of *The Marble Faun*. Emerson, stoop-shouldered, "evidently too weary to hold himself erect," pitched forward, "half lying on the air." Thoreau, genuinely skillful on his skates, performed "dithyrambic dances and Bacchic leaps," enchanted with himself. Their manner of skating was in accord with their personalities and temperaments.

Behind a mask of self-exaltation Thoreau performed as before a mirror—and first of all for his own edification. He was a fragile Narcissus embodied in a homely New Englander. His life was brief. He was born in 1817, in Concord; he lived in Concord, and he died in Concord in 1862 shortly after the guns had spoken at Fort Sumter. A child of the romantic era, he tried a number of times to venture forth into the world. He went to Maine, to Staten Island, to Cape Cod, and ultimately to Minnesota, in search of health, but he always circled back to the Thoreau family house in Concord and to the presence of a domineering and loquacious mother. No other man with such wide-ranging thoughts and a soaring mind —it reached to ancient Greece, to the Ganges, to the deepest roots of England and the Continent—bound himself to so small a strip of ground. "He was worse than provincial," the cosmopolitan Henry James remarked, "he was parochial."

All of Thoreau's writings represent a continuous and carefully documented projection of the self. *Walden* announces itself autobiography—"I should not talk so much about myself if there were anybody else whom I knew so well." The book is an idealized and romantic account of Thoreau's sojourn in the woods. Even its beautiful digressions are a series of masks. In both of his works, *Walden* and *A Week on the Concord and Merrimack Rivers,* as in his miscellaneous essays, we find an ideal self rather than the Thoreau Concord knew. The artist in Thoreau improved on nature in the interest of defending himself against some of nature's more painful truths. However, the facts of literary history offer us sufficient clues to the study of the character and personality of the child christened David Henry Thoreau. (Later he chose to be called Henry David— a slight rearrangement, perhaps in the interest of euphony, yet symptom of the many rearrangements of the Thoreau self.)

It may be a small matter, but Thoreau, who abjured vanities and called on men to simplify their lives, listed among the meager belongings he took to Walden Pond a three-by-three-inch mirror—he who had all of Walden in which to look at himself. He kept, moreover, a mirror for his soul as well, in the most consistently written and religiously preserved journal of American letters. His life was indeed a life of constant self-contemplation and self-observation. Walden was "my own sun and moon and stars, and a little world to myself." If he looked often into his little mirror and the mirror of the Pond, he listened also, as Narcissus did, to the nymph Echo. He found the echoes of his own voice—so he said—almost the only "kindred voices" that he heard.

His inner quest, which he often made elo-quent, was to be both Spartan and Athenian. Men can be one or the other at different times. Thoreau tried to be both at once, and he worked hard to reconcile these irreconcilables. He was the sort of man who needs the constant vision of his countenance to assure himself that he is not dissolving altogether into the elements. The mirror he brought to his hut, the hut itself which he purchased from a shanty dweller and rebuilt, the manner in which he extolled Concord even while scolding it, reveal a different Thoreau from the self-portrait, and from the Thoreau image sentimentalized by generations of nature lovers who have never read him. He shrugged his shoulders at the tools of society, but used them constantly. He had enormous practical gifts; he could use his hands, knew much of the lore of nature, had considerable Yankee shrewdness and what we term colloquially "know-how." But in his moments of insight he recognized, as he did in one of his poems, that he was "a parcel of vain strivings tied/ By a chance bond together,/ Dangling this way and that." What attracts our attention in particular is not so much the "vain strivings," which might be attributed to many men, but the poet's imagining himself to be loosely strung together. Poetry, Thoreau once said, "is a piece of very private history, which unostentatiously lets us into the secret of a man's life." Behind the mask of nature lover, philosopher, man of craft and lore, Thoreau struggled to keep the parcel of himself from becoming unwrapped and scattered. He speaks in the same poem of having "no root in the land," and of drinking up his own "juices." His friends observed this in him; his was an inner rage that consumes. Beneath his outward euphoria lay always a deep melancholy.

Perhaps Thoreau's best known remark, made in *Walden,* was that "the mass of men lead lives of quiet desperation." This is often quoted with the assumption that Thoreau himself was

never desperate: that he at least achieved a tranquil and philosophic existence. The Concord farmers, however, who saw Thoreau's zeal and compulsions—the tenacities of this self-appointed "inspector of snow storms and rain storms"—would have regarded his assiduous journal-keeping as a life of greater desperation than their own rude lives of daily work. There is in all of Thoreau's writings an enforced calm; strange tensions run below the surface, deep obsessions. He is so preoccupied with self-assertion as to suggest that this was a profound necessity rather than an experience of serenity.

His struggle for identity gave him great powers of concentration and diligence. He was not a born writer, but he taught himself by imitation to carpenter solid verbal structures and give them rhythm and proportion. He went to school to Emerson, to Carlyle, to the Greeks, to the philosophers of India. He was first and foremost a reader of books—and only after them of nature. He read like a bee clinging to a flower, for all that he could extract from the printed page. He wrote poems, many of them banal; yet he poured a great deal of poetry into the more relaxed passages of his prose. This prose is seldom spontaneous; behind its emulation of the measure and moderation of the ancients one feels strain and subterranean violence. The violence often is converted into contempt and condescension for Thoreau's neighbors and the hardworking farmers of Concord.

Two acts established Thoreau's fame and his myth. The first was his building of a comfortable, heated, plastered cabin beside Walden Pond; this he did out of a "prefabricated" hut purchased for a few dollars from an impecunious shanty dweller. He set it well within the range of the railroad and of his fellowmen and pretended that he lived self-sufficiently in the wilderness. Here he dwelt for about two years.

He himself tallied exactly twenty-six months, but he did not deduct the month he lived under his mother's roof while waiting for the plaster to dry; nor the fortnight of a trip to the Maine woods. During his stay at Walden he worked hard hoeing his beans and determining the rude economy possible to him in simplifying his life. That he had access to his mother's cookie jar in town and enjoyed sundry dinners elsewhere, as we shall see, made no difference to his calculations. In his cabin he wrote *A Week on the Concord and Merrimack Rivers;* he extolled solitude and nature and spoke of "the unquestionable ability of man to elevate his life by a conscious endeavor." How he lived as America's first conscientious public "dropout" he would describe later in the memorable *Walden,* originally subtitled "Life in the Woods."

The second source of his fame and myth was his act of "civil disobedience." He gave us that valuable formulation of the privilege of dissent. He refused to pay his poll tax and went to jail—for one night. Someone else paid it—"interfered" said Thoreau—and the jailer ousted him from his cell. In truth, Thoreau did not fancy martyrdom. He was always willing to allow others—society—to do for him what he would not do himself. He was willing to use existing tools so long as these enabled him to pursue his private course and in his own distinctive way. "I quietly declare war with the State, after my fashion," he wrote in his celebrated essay and his own fashion seems to have been partly explained when he added, "I will still make what use and get what advantage of her I can, as is usual in such cases." The man of high principle here shed his principles. And he behaved also as if no other individuals existed in society. Whitman discerned in him "a morbid dislike of humanity."

From this it may be seen that the image

of Thoreau which has reached us is larger than the figure Thoreau's contemporaries knew. His myth of a lonely life in the woods, of man against society, has provided modern men with thoughts about their place in a tree-impoverished world, whose air is polluted—a world alienated from nature. Thoreau gave permanent form to the dream of men in great anonymous urban communities who want to "get away from it all." He also influenced individuals like Tolstoi and Gandhi who had in them a similar rage of reform; these men, however, possessed a larger sense of their fellowmen than did Thoreau.

In a society of diminishing liberties, Thoreau freed himself personally of some of society's tyrannies without offering any ultimate solution for the problems he so fervently discussed. Kamo-No Chōmei, the Japanese sage, in his *Hojoki,* written almost seven centuries before *Walden,* described his life in a ten-foot-square hut; but he lived in it for thirty years and, in the timeless ways of the East, found his answers within himself. Thoreau, who read the books of the East—though he could hardly have known those of a Japan as yet unopened to the West—did not regard his Walden cabin as a permanent home. He left it as abruptly as he built it, saying he had gone there only "to transact some private business." The *Hojoki* describes a way of life, *Walden* represented largely a gesture.

By the standards of his fellow citizens in Concord Thoreau seemed lazy and shiftless. They judged him with severity, but also with indulgence, for they knew his talents. He was a skillful artisan, a fine surveyor, an active amateur naturalist; and he was highly inventive. His resourcefulness extricated his parents from poverty. But he ran away from his accomplishments in a kind of morbid fear they might enslave him. Emerson, in his truth-seeking eulogy at Thoreau's grave, said that he counted it a fault in him that he had no ambition. And he went on to say that "wanting this, instead of engineering for all America, he was the captain of a huckleberry party." Emerson added, in his characteristic fashion, "Pounding beans is good to the end of pounding empires one of these days; but not if, at the end of years it is still only beans!" The observation was severe. Emerson expected perhaps too much from his temperamental disciple. Thoreau wanted to be a writer rather than an empire builder. Nevertheless Emerson discerned in Thoreau's daily life—despite its egocentric form—a drive to power and one can understand the philosopher's disappointment.

His allusion to the huckleberry party has some significance. Thoreau, when very young, had been taken by his mother to Fair Haven Hill, where the huckleberries were abundant; and she took him also at a tender age to the shores of Walden Pond. Small wonder that he clung to "the fabulous landscape of my infant dreams." These were memorable little journeys and Thoreau's personal geography became identified with the powerful, talkative parent who loomed large in all the years of his life. His father counted for much less; he is described as a "mousey" man, ineffectual in business, who apparently abdicated early to the houseful of women—his wife, her sisters, his daughters—a nest of femininity in which his younger son was cradled. We can understand therefore why huckleberry picking on Fair Haven Hill, to which he led the children of the town like some latter-day Pied Piper, was one of Thoreau's fondest pastimes. It was a repeated return to a landscape glamorized for him long before by his mother's love and attention. Walden and Fair Haven became symbolic transformations in the innermost world of Thoreau of the one great attachment of his life. The umbilical cord might be said to have never been cut. Nature, he once remarked, "is my mother at the same time that she is my sister. I cannot imagine a woman no older than I."

It is recorded that when he was about to graduate from Harvard he asked his mother what career he might follow. She replied: "You can buckle on your knapsack and roam abroad to seek your fortune." In early America, with the frontier near at hand, the remark seems natural enough. Yet Thoreau had a sudden fit of weeping. He read his mother's remark as if she were sending him away from her. His older sister came to his rescue. "No, Henry, you shall not go, you shall stay at home and live with us." Sometime later he said, "Methinks I should be content to sit at the back door in Concord, under the poplar tree henceforth, forever." And this was, in effect, what he did—for life. In his writings he would make a virtue of this embeddedness. He read the great legends and adventures of man into Concord, as James Joyce later read the Odyssey into Dublin. One could, with the aid of books, possess an imaginary world in a cabin by a New England pond. "My cottage becomes the universe," said the Japanese Chomei.

This quality of dependence, this clinging to his mother, and all that represented her, Concord, Fair Haven, Walden, caused Thoreau to seek—in his quest for a place in the world— models he could emulate, and his first and natural choice fell on his elder brother, John. But the brother died young of tetanus. Thoreau, it is recorded, promptly developed the same symptoms, as if he too had to die. Of the two sons, Henry David Thoreau had been designated, by family decision, to go to a university, although there had been some thought at first of making him a carpenter. Money was found and he went to Harvard. Here he acquired the habit of reading; and here he heard Emerson speak. It was a momentous experience to find so much inspiration in a fellow townsman.

Their friendship was to be at the very center of Thoreau's life, for his pliant nature imitated Emerson as he had imitated his brother. Lowell, visiting Concord in 1838, a year after Thoreau's graduation, wrote, "I met Thoreau last night and it is exquisitely amusing to see how he imitates Emerson's tone and manner. With my eyes shut, I shouldn't know them apart." And seventeen years later, F. B. Sanborn, one of Thoreau's biographers, still could notice that "in his tones and gestures he seemed to me to imitate Emerson." Thoreau's prose would always be filled with echoes of Emerson and he adopted certain essential qualities of his style while being addicted at the same time— as Emerson was not—to exaggeration and paradox.

For a while, after graduation, he taught school, but early abandoned this. He then sought the lecture platform, also in imitation of Emerson. From 1841 to 1843 he lived as a general handyman in the Emerson household. He attached himself to Mrs. Emerson; she must be seen as still another in the line of female figures—the sisters, aunts, mother— who had surrounded him from his earliest years. Emerson, in his qualified eulogy, described his handyman's aptitudes: "his senses were acute, his frame well-knit and hardy, his hands skillful in the use of tools." He worked neatly and with precision; he took care of the garden, instructed Emerson in husbandry—he brought the lore of the woods to the author of *Nature*. And his mentor, on his side, encouraged him to write, to keep a journal, to contribute to the *Dial* where Thoreau helped with editorial chores. Thus he came to know the transcendentalists.

No literary or social historian has yet written the full story of the years of Emerson and Thoreau in Concord although a large literature exists on the subject. We have a charming evocation in Van Wyck Brooks's *The*

Flowering of New England: but the painting is too much in the tones of the subjects themselves and while the book abounds in color and local substance it does not convey to us the limitations of this community in which so many high-minded people came and went. It is necessary to read ourselves back into a sparse and hardworking society possessed of a parochial yet strong sense of civic responsibility and Christian duty. At one end of the town there lived for some years an imaginative artist in the Old Manse, Nathaniel Hawthorne, and at the other, with rows of elms between, Mr. Emerson daily communicated his thoughts to his journal, wrote his lectures, and walked in his orchard. There was a great scratching of pens in various parts of the town. Thoreau kept his journal; the Alcotts, father and daughter—that is, Bronson Alcott and Louisa May—wrote regularly in their diaries; William Ellery Channing, the poet, and F. B. Sanborn, the teacher, kept records and later wrote the first biographies of Thoreau. Margaret Fuller came and went. There were other salty characters, not least the much-described Mary Moody Emerson, who used her shroud as a garment of daily wear; and the scholarly Mrs. Ripley, Emerson's long-time friend. On another social scale we must mention Mrs. Thoreau, one of the town's socially ambitious women who was described as having a "regal" presence. The place had some two thousand inhabitants counting farmers beyond the town's radius; and in an age of steadfast labor and isolation from the wider world (it took two hours by coach to cover the fourteen miles to Boston) there was sufficient time and energy to expend on the reforms dear to the heart of New England. Concord had its active Temperance Society; and the Middlesex Anti-Slavery Society dedicated itself unremittingly to the abolitionist cause. Thoreau himself was host to runaways and we know of his conducting one slave to a contact point on the underground railway to Canada. There was also the Concord Social Library, and town meetings were regularly held. The town bell summoned citizens and literary history tells us that the bell ringer refused to do his job when Thoreau called a meeting on behalf of John Brown; Thoreau on this occasion rang the bell himself.

We must remind ourselves of these multiple forces at work in this environment: the liberal causes were espoused passionately in a life of solid if rough creature comfort. We can measure the scale of life by visiting the Old Manse, and walking through its low-ceilinged rooms, and seeing the straight-backed chairs, the black horsehair seats, the frugal adornments, and all that is implied when we speak of plain living and high thinking. In such a society, with men of vigorous talent like Hawthorne and Emerson, and idiosyncratic individuals like Thoreau and Channing, thoughts tended to run to transcendental things. The long cold winters, with the deep snows of that era, were conducive to reading and to writing. Henry James, the novelist, who knew the later Concord, would characterize the town and environs as a kind of "American Weimar." Concord had had, long before, its single moment of history: the shot heard round the world had been fired within hearing and sight of the Old Manse and the battle between the farmers and the British had been watched by the Reverend Mr. Ripley from its windows. Touched thus by primary history, the town's very name gave a lofty tone to the place; and the tones of its discourse would echo through later decades and reflect the civilized American mind in close communion with nature and its own sense of secular and Divine order.

It might be said that Thoreau was a born transcendentalist and that Emerson's *Nature* might have been written for him. Going beyond affirmation of a romantic idealism, a faith in the self, in one's feelings and senses as distinct from the prescribing faiths, Emerson urged men to put trust in their "involuntary perceptions"—a highly modern view: today we would say that he urged men to try to be more in tune with their unconscious promptings. Octavius B. Frothingham, the historian of transcendentalism, spoke of the movement as "a wave of sentiment"; and Emerson's biographer, J. E. Cabot, phrased this more vividly when he said it was a stirring "of Puritan thought with a hint of smothered fires." Emerson wrote: "Build your own world. As fast as you conform your life to the pure idea in your mind, that will unfold its grand proportions." No deeper chord in Thoreau could have been touched. Ever after he studied the grandeur of the Self; for Emerson's teaching endowed human consciousness with supremacy in life and severed the bonds that tied man's will to religious dictates. V. L. Parrington would characterize this more harshly as "a mystical egocentric universe wherein the children of God might luxuriate in their divinity." Within these ideas one could find echoes of Rousseau, of Coleridge, of Goethe. The full tide of European romanticism had reached the western shores of the Atlantic. Cabot remarks that Emerson, in *Nature,* did not preach reliance on intuition as a self-conceit or "an exaggerated regard for one's own spiritual experiences," but to some extent this was the form of Thoreau's response. He had come upon a philosophy that would suffice for a lifetime. He was "Emerson's moral man made flesh." He could live for the universe as for Concord; he could sing the sense of the infinite in his own being. "I am a poet, a mystic and a transcendentalist," Thoreau announced. "I came into this world not chiefly to make this a

good place to live in, but to live in it, be it good or bad." Nevertheless he preached; and what he preached was "self-improvement." Cabot further tells us that "there was much talk in those days of spontaneity—the right and duty of acting oneself out, and following one's genius, whithersoever it might lead." This Thoreau did. There were complaints that transcendentalism unfitted the young men for business and the young women for society— "without making them fit for anything else." The idealism nevertheless was genuine. Emerson's thoughts were wide and humane, but as often happens, not everyone accurately interpreted the inspired message.

No one has ever examined the "interpersonal" relations between Emerson and his disciples and the manner in which this large-minded man attracted eccentricity to himself —as exemplified notably in Alcott, Thoreau, and Channing. One wonders what needs these acolytes fulfilled in Emerson's life and what sense of power he derived from their pronounced discipleship. We may speculate, however, that there came a moment when Emerson asked himelf whether he had acquired a handyman for life. Thoreau embedded himself in his household as completely as in his maternal home; indeed Emerson may have represented for Thoreau both his brother and his mother, in his example and his acceptance. The sage of Concord was alert enough not to accept passively so much ambivalence. His eulogy pronounced over Thoreau's grave is filled with significant asperities, some perhaps unintended. It is also frankly critical, as some of Emerson's journal entries also show. He sought to define Thoreau for himself, writing that the younger man's conversation consisted of "a continual twining of the present moment into a sentence and offering it to me." Thoreau's behavior in this household was as quixotic as when he lived at home. "Why is he never frank?" Emerson asked himself once. And he added, "I have no social pleasure with Henry, though more than once the best conversation." At the end of two years, Emerson urged the young man to launch himself in the world of letters. He obtained employment for him in New York, as tutor to the children of a relative on Staten Island. His motive was generous; he believed that Thoreau, as a poet and a sentient being, would contribute to the literature of the new America. But he was also tactfully elbowing the omnipresent handyman out of his household.

Thoreau went to New York. That he found the life in the city less congenial than the familiar woods and fields of Concord is understandable. Given his difficulties in relating to his human—as distinct from animal—environment, he could discover no comfortable friends in an urban community, even though New York in the early 1840's swarmed with writers and publishers, and Thoreau had helpful letters of introduction. The elder Henry James, whom Thoreau went to see with a letter from Emerson, found him to be "the most child-like, unconscious and unblushing egotist it has ever been my fortune to encounter in the ranks of mankind." The father of the future novelist saw in Thoreau "a sheer and mountainous inward self-esteem." He received him, however, with warmth and friendliness. Thoreau found helpful individuals in Manhattan, but he remained homesick, moody, despondent. Within a matter of months he returned from his exile, but not to the Emerson household. He went back to his family, back to his own room, his books, his papers, his botanical specimens. Shortly after this he built his hut beside Walden. He would re-enter the Emerson household two years later, but only for a well-defined term, to take care of the place while Emerson lectured abroad. The history of this friendship was one of gradual estrangement. "His virtues," Emerson said, "sometimes ran into extremes."

Literary history has never asked itself why Henry David Thoreau, aged twenty-eight, in the midsummer of 1845—on Independence Day—moved into the Walden cabin and embarked on what he called his "experiment" in simplifying the acts of life. It has accepted Thoreau's own explanation for this limited withdrawal from his family home. He wished, he said, to test the things by which society around him lived. He struck for a kind of personal freedom. The men in Concord, the neighboring farmers, led in his view unsimple lives. They were mortgaged to their encumbered properties and their daily labor. Thoreau would practice a rude economy and avoid enslavement: he would free himself for higher things, mainly reading and writing, and his observation of nature. The historical facts suggest, however, that Thoreau was led to his act by a crisis for which a cabin in the woods offered a radical solution. His life with the Emersons had been an extension of his life at home; he had left home, but had gone only as far as the home of a neighbor. He had then attempted to leave Concord and found not only that he was unable to launch himself in the wider world but that life without Concord was impossible to him. Returned from Staten Island, under the family roof, he at first took up his father's trade of pencil making. With his usual resourcefulness, he at this time studied the composition of the graphite in German pencils; he refined the materials used by his father and this led to an improved pencil and ultimately placed the Thoreaus in a position to sell graphite wholesale. Henry remained, however, at loose ends. He had no intention of pursuing the family business; and he seemed to have nowhere to go.

At this time there occurred a small incident

which seemed to shake him to his very roots. The woodsman and naturalist accidentally set fire to the fields and woods of Concord while cooking a catch of fish on the shore of Fair Haven Bay where he had gone with a friend. He summoned help after a two-mile dash through the woods; and returning he found a half-mile of flame before him. While help was coming, Thoreau climbed the highest rock of Fair Haven Cliff. "It was a glorious spectacle," he later wrote in his journal, "and I was the only one there to enjoy it." When sufficient help arrived, Thoreau descended from his perch and joined in the fire fighting. "The fire, we understand," said the Concord newspaper, "was communicated to the woods through the thoughtlessness of two of our citizens, who kindled it in a *pine stump*, near the Pond, for the purpose of making a chowder. As every thing around them was as combustible almost as a fire-ship, the flames spread with rapidity, and hours elapsed before it could be subdued." The newspaper spoke of the "sheer carelessness" of those who had started the fire. The whole town knew who these individuals were.

If this occurrence had in it an acting out of Thoreau's disdain for his fellowmen in the community, the flames that destroyed three hundred acres of woodland also expressed Thoreau's inner rage and his malaise. To treat the fire as a mere accident, as have most of those who have described it, is to overlook the fact that of all men in Concord Thoreau was the one who best knew that fires may not be lit out-of-doors without serious hazard. There was, however, a singular streak of blindness to certain details in Thoreau—he who prided himself on his practical knowledge and could be, when he was interested, all alertness and observation. Lowell spoke of this some years later when he wrote that "till he built his Walden shanty he did not know that the hickory grew in Concord. Till he went to Maine, he had never seen phosphorescent wood, a phenomenon familiar to most country boys. At forty he speaks of the seeding of the pine as a new discovery, though one should have thought that its gold dust of blowing pollen might have earlier drawn his eye. Neither his attention nor his genius was of the spontaneous kind." And in our time Joseph Wood Krutch has remarked that "reading the *Journal*, it is almost disconcerting to discover that at thirty-four he was not sure of the identity of the common thalictrum of the fields and that a year later he had to have help in naming a Luna moth!" The failure in alertness which led to the fire was but one of various such failures, those of a man in whom reverie could pre-empt immediate reality. The fire permanently established Thoreau in the minds of his fellows at Concord as a "woods-burner." The town could shrug its shoulders at his eccentricities. It could not, however, forgive so strange and serious a lapse which threatened life and its homes.

Thus less than a year before the retreat to Walden, Thoreau's reputation in Concord reached its lowest point. No one accused him of "sloth," for it was known how well he could work when he wanted to. The fire, however, caused some to speak of him as a "damned rascal." His journal of the time tells us nothing. Certain later entries show nevertheless that the incident rankled: he was enraged by its consequences: "Who are these men who are said to be the owners of these woods, and how am I related to them? I have set fire to the forest, but I have done no wrong therein, and now it is as if the lightning had done it. These flames are but consuming their natural food." This was written six years after the event. And he also wrote, "it has never troubled me from that day to this more than if the lightning had done it. The trivial fishing was all that disturbed me and disturbs me still." Only a man deeply troubled would write in this way so long afterward and deceive himself that he wasn't troubled. "I at once ceased to regard the owners and my fault—if fault there was in the matter—and attended to the phenomenon before me, determined to make the most of it. To be sure I felt a little ashamed when I reflected on what a trivial occasion this had happened, that at the time I was no better employed than my townsmen."

Thoreau's decision to move to Walden Pond seems to have been, on one level, a way of withdrawing from a town he experienced as hostile to him while at the same time remaining very close to it; a way also of asserting himself as an active "employed" man by embracing the career of writer and philosopher; an act of defiance which would demonstrate that his was a better way of life than that practiced by his fellows. Deeper still may have been the petulance of the child saying, in effect, to the town and to Emerson "see how homeless I am, you have forced me to live in a shanty away from all of you." He would arouse pity; he would also arouse interest. Some such jumble of motives lay behind his complex decision to give an impression of "hermiting" while not being a hermit. The epigraph he chose for *Walden* directly addresses the townspeople. It is a quotation from the book itself: "I do not propose to write an ode to dejection, but to brag as lustily as chanticleer in the morning, standing on his roost, if only to wake my neighbors up." On a subjective level, *Walden* reflects Thoreau's dejection: in the depths of the epigraph one hears the cry of a man who must vent his rage—and be heard by the entire town! That he was full of spleen during the spring of 1845 just before he built his cabin may be discerned in a letter written to him from New York by the younger William Ellery Channing. Channing seems to have provided the impulse for Thoreau's principal act:

"I see nothing for you in this earth but that field which I once christened 'Briars'; go out upon that, build yourself a hut, and there begin the grand process of devouring yourself alive. I see no alternative, no other hope for you. Eat yourself up; you will eat nobody else, nor anything else." There is a fund of psychological truth in Channing's answer to Thoreau's rage. Thoreau had long been devouring himself; he had said as much in the poem already quoted, "here I bloom for a short hour unseen,/ Drinking my juices up."

Whatever the deeper motivation, Thoreau's conscious feelings on his taking up his Walden residence are clearly expressed in his book: "I went to the woods because I wished to live deliberately, to front only the essential facts of life, and see if I could not learn what it had to teach, and not, when I came to die, discover that I had not lived. I did not wish to live what was not life, living is so dear; nor did I wish to practise resignation, unless it was quite necessary. I wanted to live deep and suck out all the marrow of life, to live so sturdily and Spartan-like as to put to rout all that was not life, to cut a broad swath and shave close, to drive life into a corner, and reduce it to its lowest terms, and, if it proved to be mean, why then to get the whole and genuine meanness of it, and publish its meanness to the world; or if it were sublime, to know it by experience, and be able to give a true account of it in my next excursion."

"Briars" consisted of a dozen acres beside Walden. The land belonged to Emerson. With his friend's permission, Thoreau began in March 1845, after receiving Channing's letter, to clear a spot and plan his cabin. Thus was inaugurated what would become the great Thoreauvian myth; yet it was in its own time little more than a rural comedy. Concord's idlest citizen, the woods-burning "rascal," a year after making himself notorious, builds himself a small home on the town's outskirts. He will be a hermit. But he walks to town almost daily; he chats with the townsfolk; he joins the idlers around the grocery stove; he visits his home. He dines in the homes of his friends. The diary of Mrs. J. T. Fields tells us much when it records Thoreau's filial piety. Thoreau was "an excellent son," she noted, "and even when living in his retirement at Walden Pond, would come home every day." At the same time he is thinking of a chapter in his book called "Where I Lived and What I Lived For."

Literary criticism, if it wished to treat *Walden* (1854) as a work of the imagination, might say that every poet lives in fancy rather than in fact. But literary history, unlike literary criticism, is in bondage to truth, and the truth is that Thoreau lived one kind of life and transformed it in his work into another—and then scolded his fellows for not following his ideals. Like his mother, who often put on grand airs in the town, Chanticleer crowed out of a world of make-believe. His first sentence in *Walden* announces: "When I wrote the following pages, or rather the bulk of them, I lived alone, in the woods, a mile from any neighbor, in a house which I had built myself, on the shore of Walden Pond, in Concord, Massachusetts, and earned my living by the labor of my hands only." History records, let us note in passing, that he did not write the bulk of these pages in the cabin; he took several years to complete the book, and what he wrote in the hut was *A Week on the Concord and Merrimack Rivers* —*Walden* was written largely in the family home; moreover much material was incorporated into it which belonged to other years than those of his Walden residence. He ends his first paragraph by saying "at present I am a sojourner in civilized life again." The words imply that he had been outside civilization when he lived in his cabin. Let us look at Tho-reau's sojourn beyond "civilized life" as it is documented by his latest and most careful biographer, Walter Harding.

"It was not a lonely spot. The well-traveled Concord-Lincoln road was within sight across the field. The Fitchburg Railroad steamed regularly past the opposite end of the pond. Concord village was less than two miles away, and the Texas house [the Thoreau family house] was less than that along the railroad right-of-way. . . . Ellery Channing . . . visited the cabin often. . . . It is true that his mother and sisters made a special trip out to the pond every Saturday, carrying with them each time some delicacy of cookery which he gladly accepted. And it is equally true that he raided the family cookie jar on his *frequent* [my italics] visits home. . . . The Emersons, too, frequently invited him to dinner as did the Alcotts and the Hosmers. They had all done so before he went to Walden Pond and continued the custom after he left. Rumor had it that every time Mrs. Emerson rang her dinner bell, Thoreau came bounding through the woods and over the fences to be first in line."

Thoreau's biographer points out that it was doubtful whether he could hear the dinner bell at such a distance, but the joke can be taken as symptomatic of something the town knew— that at Walden Thoreau's ear was cocked to the sounds of Concord: that he led neither the solitary nor the Spartan life his book later described. His mention in *Walden* of his dinings out suggests that he did not allow his "experiment" to change his customary social habits. "To meet the objections of some inveterate cavillers," he writes, "I may as well state, that if I dined out occasionally, as I always had done, and I trust shall have opportunities to do again, it was frequently to the detriment of my domestic arrangements. But the dining out, being, as I have stated, a constant element, does not in the least affect a comparative statement like this." The "comparative statement" included the sentence "It was fit that I should live on rice, mainly, who loved so well the philosophy of India."

"Hardly a day went by," Harding comments, "that Thoreau did not visit the village or was not visited at the Pond. . . . Emerson was, of course, a frequent visitor at the cabin. . . . On pleasant summer days Thoreau would often join the Emerson family on a picnic or a blueberrying party. . . . The Alcotts often took their friends out to the pond to see Thoreau. . . . The children of Concord were always happy to go out to Walden Pond and Thoreau was equally happy to have them."

Harding goes on: "Occasionally whole groups of Thoreau's friends came out together to the pond and swarmed into his little cabin. It became quite the fashion to hold picnics on his front doorstep. When it rained, his visitors took refuge inside. He had as many as twenty-five or thirty people inside the tiny cabin at one time. On August 1, 1846, the anti-slavery women of Concord held their annual commemoration of the freeing of the West Indian slaves on his doorstep and Emerson, W. H. Channing, and Rev. Caleb Stetson spoke to the assembled group. Afterward a picnic lunch was served to all the guests." There was also a "Walden Pond Society." This "consisted of those who spent their Sunday mornings out walking around Walden Pond enjoying the beauties of nature. Thoreau was unquestionably the high priest of that sect."

"Despite all the visitors," Thoreau's biographer concludes, "despite all his visits to Concord village and to his parents' home, despite his surveying and fence-building and carpentry, and despite the hours devoted to writing, it must not be forgotten that the experiment at Walden was primarily a period of solitude and of communion with nature for Thoreau." We can only ask, What kind of "experiment" was this—and what kind of "solitude"? By no definition of the word—and certainly not in terms of the traditional isolation and contemplation practiced by philosophers and visionaries throughout history—can Thoreau be said to have lived a solitary or even contemplative life at Walden. He "bivouacked there," wrote F. B. Sanborn, adding that he "really lived at home, where he went every day." He was thus a sojourner in civilized life; he was an observant "suburbanite"; he was simply a man who had at last acquired a room of his own, and accomplished this in a way which attracted the town's attention to himself. Young girls found excuses for knocking on his door and asking him for a drink of water; and if he pretended to be indifferent and handed them a dipper to drink from the pond, nothing could have been more satisfying. From being the town's idler, he was now the center of attention.

Thoreau is distinctly ambivalent in the chapter he writes on solitude. "I find it wholesome to be alone the greater part of the time. To be in company, even with the best, is soon wearisome and dissipating. I love to be alone." Yet he begins the very next chapter in *Walden*—which is called "Visitors"—by saying: "I think that I love society as much as most, and am ready enough to fasten myself like a bloodsucker for the time to any full-blooded man that comes in my way." By invoking his solitude at Walden, Thoreau was cultivating an illusion. He spent many hours alone, to be sure, and wandered far afield on lonely rambles: but no more alone than many an individual in his daily life. The real solitude of Thoreau's time was that of the men and women who traveled to America's heartland and who were totally cut off from society and thrown wholly upon their own resources. They faced danger; they learned the meaning of fear. Thoreau's experiment at no time posed for him any question of true aloneness, or of the terrors of the wilderness. Any momentary anxieties could be overcome by a swift walk to the homes of neighbors and kinfolk. Lewis and Clark, or Francis Parkman, might have laid much greater claim to genuine solitude, and the entire generation that ventured forth in the covered wagons. It may be of some significance that the subtitle "Life in the Woods" included in Thoreau's first edition of *Walden* was later dropped, perhaps in recognition that such a life had not been his true subject. Nor is it altogether clear that Thoreau was capable of facing the solitude of the prairies. In his struggle to keep his bundle of "vain strivings" together, in his deeply embedded state, he would have found the primeval forest terrifying and he would have fled the plains, to recover the protecting and embracing arm of the society he verbally repudiated. Sherman Paul has rightly observed that Thoreau's "stance as a philosopher made it clear that his demands on life were not simple or primitive."

To say this is to suggest that *Walden* is a book about a romanticized solitude Thoreau could not permit himself genuinely to experience. Thoreau's Concord life, in the midst of his eking out of his "scanty fare of vegetables" with fish; his curious account books of his frugality and economy; his proclamation of a style of life he approved of intellectually—but did not truly live—make for a paradoxical book. What are we to say of the passage in *Walden* in which Thoreau's fellowmen are scolded for not being as simple in their ways as he believed himself to be?

The pages he devotes to John Field, a shanty dweller and fishing companion, who struggles to provide for the simplest needs of his family, are an extraordinary piece of egotism written by a self-preoccupied and self-indulgent man. In arguing how simple life could be for Field—were he not misguided by social habits—Thoreau forgets that he speaks as a bachelor, living in a reasonably arrangeable world and squatting on Emerson's land. He closes his eyes altogether to Field's poverty. The passage is as cruel as it is sanctimonious: "I tried to help him with my experience, telling him that he was one of my nearest neighbors, and that I too, who came a-fishing here, and looked like a loafer, was getting my living like himself; that I lived in a tight, light, and clean house, which hardly cost more than the annual rent of such a ruin as his commonly amounts to; and how, if he chose, he might in a month or two build himself a palace of his own; that I did not use tea, nor coffee, nor butter, nor milk, nor fresh meat, and so did not have to work to get them; again, as I did not work hard, I did not have to eat hard, and it cost me but a trifle for my food; but as he began with tea, and coffee, and butter, and milk, and beef, he had to work hard to pay for them, and when he had worked hard he had to eat hard again to repair the waste of his system." This seems to have been delivered without a thought for Field's children, who needed the milk, butter, beef—all the nourishment Thoreau had had when he was a growing child and probably was now having in the hospitable homes of Concord. Hawthorne apparently had listened to this kind of homily, for he once noted that in Thoreau's presence "one feels ashamed of having any money, or a house to live in, or so much as two coats to wear."

"None of the brute creation requires more than Food and Shelter," Thoreau wrote in *Walden*, and when he amplified this he could add only clothing and fuel. Doubtless "brute creation" propagates without thought for the survival of the race; but what we see is that Thoreau left no place in his myth for the simple human affections. He discourses nobly on friendship and in a high intellectual way speaks of the nourishment men may derive from the meeting of their minds. Yet of the impulse to love, this lover of nature and worshipper of the simple life writes in *Walden* that "nature is hard to overcome, but she must be suppressed." By this he meant specifically that man must conquer the urge of sex. Thoreau's historians have strained to provide him with a history of love. There is obscure mention in his annals of a proposal of marriage; but the story is as strange as other episodes in his life. His poems show that he loved the young woman's younger brother; and he seems to have proposed only after his own brother was rejected by the girl. His constituted character had no room for love for anyone save the ubiquitous "I" of his journal.

Walden is not a document, nor even the record of a calculated experiment. It is a work of art pretending to be a documentary. Thoreau talked as if he lived in the wilderness but he lived in the suburbs. He furnished his home with pieces retrieved from Concord attics. We have seen that he plastered and shingled the cabin when cold weather came. We know that he took his shoes to the Concord cobbler; that he baked bread using purchased rye and Indian meal; that he slept not in rough blankets but between sheets. He gave himself the creature comforts few Americans in the log cabins of the West could enjoy. James Russell Lowell, in his celebrated essay, mercilessly denounces Thoreau's pretensions. The "experiment" presupposes, he wrote, "all that complicated civilization which it theoretically abjured. He squatted on another man's land; he borrows an ax; his boards, his nails, his bricks, his mortar, his books, his lamp, his fishhooks, his plough, his hoe, all turn state's evidence against him as an accomplice in the sin of that artificial civilization which rendered it possible that such a person as Henry D. Thoreau should exist at all." But the author of *Walden* discovered that his whim of living in the woods

caught the fancy of audiences. Men and women were willing to listen to the fiction of his rude economy as if he were Robinson Crusoe. It is perhaps to Daniel Defoe that we many turn for a significant literary predecessor. The writer who had pretended he was keeping a journal of the plague year in London, long after the plague, who could invent a story of a man confronting the loneliness of life on a desert island, may be regarded as the forefather of Thoreau's book. The narrative of *Walden* is a composite of Thoreau's experiences in and around Concord. The little facts are so assembled as to constitute a lively fable. Thoreau blended his wide reading and his purposeful observations to the need of a thesis: and in his mind he had proved his "experiment" long before he began it. In the process of ordering, assembling, imagining, and interpreting, the artist often took possession of his data in a robust, humorous, whimsical, paradoxical, hammered style.

Walden has moments of exquisite beauty when the disciplined verbal power finds a tone and a mood expressing Thoreau's deepest artistry: "This is a delicious evening, when the whole body is one sense, and imbibes delight through every pore. I go and come with a strange liberty in Nature, a part of herself. As I walk along the stony shore of the pond in my shirt-sleeves, though it is cool as well as cloudy and windy, and I see nothing special to attract me, all the elements are unusually congenial to me. The bullfrogs trump to usher in the night, and the note of the whippoorwill is borne on the rippling wind from over the water. Sympathy with the fluttering alder and poplar leaves almost takes away my breath; yet, like the lake, my serenity is rippled but not ruffled. These small waves raised by the evening wind are as remote from storm as the smooth reflecting surface. Though it is now dark, the wind still blows and roars in the wood, the waves still dash, and some creatures lull the rest with their notes. The repose is never complete. The wildest animals do not repose, but seek their prey now; the fox, and skunk, and rabbit, now roam the fields and woods without fear. They are Nature's watchmen,—links which connect the days of animated life." The lyrical absorption of the scene into the self and the communication of the senses is eloquent. The prose creates a mood of tranquillity.

So too Thoreau can endow his narrative with the cadence of a child's storybook: "Sometimes I rambled to pine groves, standing like temples, or like fleets at sea, full-rigged, with wavy boughs, and rippling with light, so soft and green and shady that the Druids would have forsaken their oaks to worship in them; or to the cedar wood beyond Flint's Pond, where the trees, covered with hoary blue berries, spiring higher and higher, are fit to stand before Valhalla, and the creeping juniper covers the ground with wreaths full of fruit; or to swamps where the usnea lichen hangs in festoons from the white-spruce trees, and toadstools, round tables of the swamp gods, cover the ground, and more beautiful fungi adorn the stumps, like butterflies or shells, vegetable winkles; where the swamp-pink and dogwood grow, the red alder-berry glows like eyes of imps, the waxwork grooves and crushes the hardest woods in its folds, and the wild-holly berries make the beholder forget his home with their beauty, and he is dazzled and tempted by nameless other wild forbidden fruits, too fair for mortal taste."

Walden belongs with the literature of imaginary voyages which yet possess, within the imagined, a great reality of their own. It contains a rustic charm, a tender lyricism in the pages devoted to the seasons and to animal life around the pond and in the neighboring woods. The book is composed of eighteen essays loosely strung together. They acquire their unity in the central themes of the work. Although Thoreau's residence lasted two years he telescoped it into a single year and drew upon materials out of more distant years. He begins in the early summer, and then goes through the autumn and the winter and the coming of spring, the eternal cycle of the seasons. If anything the winter sequence is the best written and the one most deeply felt. The embedded man is never happier than when the landscape is embedded in snow and the pond frozen over to its depths. Each chapter begins with poetic descriptions in which nature and the self merge; each chapter has its hortatory passages; and one suspects that generations of readers—when they have read Thoreau at all and not simply accepted his myth—have skipped the scoldings and the rooster-crowings and listened only to the poet of nature. F. O. Matthiessen long ago showed us the structure within the seeming discursiveness of *Walden*. Thoreau moves into his cabin after building it, and describes his manner of living, since reading is fundamental to it, his essay on this subject is placed early in the book; after that the sounds of nature and then the threnody of his fancied solitude. The life beside Walden is minutely described in the first six chapters. We then leave the cabin for the beanfield (the land was plowed with another's plow) and the nearby village. There is a long and striking passage on the railroad: Thoreau both likes and dislikes that symbol of power which has cut across the land. Then we come to his neighbors, the animal life, the pond in winter. If he records the cycles of nature and of animal life, he does not altogether record the human cycles from which he has removed himself— the fertilities of nature are scanted; the spring in which *Walden* ends is rather a spring of *re*birth.

Thoreau likes his paradoxes. He puns; he

fondles placenames and the origin of words. And he is always the self-absorbed Narcissus at his pool: "A lake is the landscape's most beautiful and expressive feature. It is earth's eye; looking into which the beholder measures the depth of his own nature. . . . Walden is a perfect forest mirror, set round with stones as precious to my eye as if fewer or rarer. . . . It is a mirror which no stone can crack, whose quicksilver will never wear off, whose gilding Nature continually repairs." In his delight in his great natural mirror he is also the minute observer; and the pages devoted to the pond itself move from personal image to word pictures of light on water-surface, underwater currents, dances of the water bugs, the poetry of the ripples, the great depths, the leaping of fish—a kind of nature ballet written in a prose closer to poetry than most of Thoreau's poems. He cast, as Henry James observed, a kind of "spiritual interest" over all that he observed.

He is at his most imaginative—that is, his ear is perhaps truest to poetry—in the playful chapter in which he tells of his "brute neighbors," beginning with a sylvan dialogue between a Hermit and a Poet. One feels in the writing of these pages echoes of the playfulness of Carlyle; but in terms of posthumous influence this passage may have importance in its striking resemblance to the recurrent rhythms of James Joyce's *Finnegans Wake*. It was inevitable that Joyce, early in his "Anna Livia Plurabelle" section, should pun on "Concord and the Merrimake," for that chapter is compounded of river names and water imagery and associations. Thoreau's "Was that a farmer's noon horn which sounded from beyond the woods just now?" and Joyce's "Is that the Poolbeg flasher beyant, pharphar, or a fireboat coasting nyar the Kishna?" seem to have common stylistic origins and the entire Thoreauvian passage finds strong echoes—in an Irish accent—in passages in *Finnegans Wake*.

Thoreau writes: "Hark! I hear a rustling of the leaves. Is it some ill-fed village hound yielding to the instinct of the chase? or the lost pig which is said to be in these woods, whose tracks I saw after the rain? It comes on apace; my sumachs and sweetbriers tremble." This has a singular rhythmic charm and one can find its parallel in Joyce. Did Thoreau and Joyce (who had much in common in their alienated temperaments) derive the rhythms and cadences from some common source? or did the Irish writer, in his exploration of rivers and water music, latch onto the peculiar Thoreauvian trouvaille of this chapter? In the strange world of letters in which songs sung in one country become new songs in another, the words of Thoreau by the Concord River have a powerful kinship with those of Joyce by the Liffey.

The "private business" which Thoreau wished to transact at Walden included the writing of a long-planned book, a record of a journey he had made with his brother John when he was twenty-two. John had died three years later and *A Week on the Concord and Merrimack Rivers* (1849) was both a record and a memorial. It is divided into the days of the week, where *Walden* would be shaped according to the changing seasons—as if Thoreau were saying that youth can count but in hours and days while maturity knows the cycles of eternity. *A Week* contains much that is illustrative of Thoreau's philosophy; yet criticism has rightly called it overwritten and self-conscious; it is a mixture of description and homily, of gathered facts and sensitivity, with Thoreau's own poems interlarded between passages. One might call it a mental scrapbook; only in part is it travel narrative, so that anthologists are often prompted to winnow out the contemplative digressions. "We were bid to a river party—not to be preached at," Lowell remarked. But he praised the language as having "an antique purity like wine grown colorless with age." The book contains the lore of the fisherman and nature lover, a personal sense of scene and landscape and a number of little insets culled from history, as for example, the story of an early settler, a pioneer woman who, taken prisoner by the Indians after they had killed her newborn infant, avenged herself by scalping her captors while they slept and collected a bounty for the scalps. Thoreau tells this bloody tale with historical art. But to reach such passages we wade through the tedium of private sermons set down without feeling for the book's essential unity. In *A Week* Thoreau is learning how to write *Walden.*

If *A Week* remembers, in part, the ecstasy of youth, it is a book written with a sense of lost childhood and adolescence. A significant link between it and *Walden* may be found in a quotation (in *A Week*) from the Chinese writer Mencius (Meng-tzu): "If one loses a fowl or a dog, he knows well how to seek them again; if one loses the sentiments of his heart, he does not know how to seek them again. . . . The duties of practical philosophy consist only in seeking after those sentiments of the heart which we have lost; that is all." It seems clear that between the writing of *A Week* and of *Walden* Thoreau came to feel that the sentiments of his heart were irrecoverable, for in *Walden* we read his celebrated parable which harks back to this quotation. It is set down almost irrelevantly with a remark that readers would pardon some "obscurities, for there are more secrets in my trade than in most men's." "I long ago lost a hound, a bay horse, and a turtledove, and am still on their trail. Many are the travellers I have spoken concerning them, describing their tracks and what calls they answered to. I have met one or two who had heard the hound, and the tramp of the horse, and even seen the dove disappear be-

hind a cloud, and they seemed as anxious to recover them as if they had lost them themselves." The obscurity of the parable disappears when it is placed beside the quotation from Mencius. What is more we can read a deeper secret than the loss of youth's first ecstasies. The symbols Thoreau uses represent the most faithful animals in man's life—his dog, guide, companion, devoted beyond the devotion of humans to his master, and his horse, a bay, a handsome animal, which embodies man's thrust, his drive, his animal instincts. A horse carries man and gives him a sense of support and direction. And finally the loss of the turtledove admits to a loss of love and tenderness, symbol of delicacy and affection. A man so bereft had indeed to seek comfort in cold thought. The parable speaks for an eternal quest for the ideal. It also tells us that Thoreau felt he had lost touch with the deepest part of himself—his instincts, his animal nature, with which all men must make some kind of truce. And so like the Eastern philosophers whom he read, he transcends this part of himself. He sits by a pond and meditates but only partly in serenity and humility. His thoughts often express petulance and anger, of a deeply irrational kind. Behind his mask of peace, Thoreau was not at peace with himself.

No discussion of Thoreau's writing can overlook his debt to the East, and particularly to India. Through Emerson he came to the *Bhagavad Gita;* he read the *Vedas* and the *Upanishads* and in these writings, filled with permissive religiosity and an exaltation of the quest for the self, showing the discipline of renunciation and contemplation, he discovered a body of belief highly congenial to his own anarchist nature. He understood the East, however, as a Westerner possessing a philosophy of action as well as of meditation. Robert Louis Stevenson recognized this when he wrote, "It was his ambition to be an Oriental philosopher; but he was always a very Yankee sort of Oriental."

Thoreau's stance was of a Buddha in Concord; that he called himself an "inspector of snow storms" in itself underlines the essential difference between him and the Eastern writers he read. They did not think of themselves as "inspectors" of anything, unless of their own state of being. Thoreau sought in them confirmation of his own feelings and solace for his own needs. His inner restlessness was too great, he was too troubled to arrive at their kind of peace. He was eclectic, empirical, bent on self-improvement; and it might suggest the difference between him and the Eastern philosophers if we remind ourselves that Chōmei lived for thirty years in his hut and made of it a continuous way of life where Thoreau, after two years, "left the woods for as good a reason as I went there." He added, "Perhaps it seemed to me that I had several more lives to live, and could not spare any more time for that one." The idea of having no time to spare for what he had first asserted as a transcendent way of existence, and of seeking instead a pluralistic existence—here the American distinctly parted with the Oriental. But where he was at one with them was often in his address to the immediate, in his attempt—not always successful —to see the object unadorned by subjective distortion. That he often failed we must write down to his inner disorganization. In his moments of serenity he arrived, a poetic fancy aiding, at insight; and he sometimes told these insights in the Eastern manner as we have seen, in enigmatic parables which force realization and awaken thought.

The "private business" Thoreau transacted at Walden represented one side of his mind and art; the public business he embraced thereafter has left its mark on mankind. Thoreau was that well-known figure, a man who can accept no authority but himself and who can become, in his moments of eloquence, the voice of the multitude against abuse of authority. Such individuals often waver between utopia and reality; in dismissing authority they offer no viable solution to man's constant need for order. That man has never achieved such order—as witness the barbaric wars of the twentieth century and the ensuing chaos—only certifies the dilemma. And because the dilemma has been constant in all history, man must reiterate in every age a need for fundamental freedom. Such a reiteration leads to action, nearly always violent, and violent even when it calls itself non-violent. Coercion in any form, even in passive resistance, is violent. These are the ambiguities and the cruel alternatives fate has offered man, making him an eternal seeker of rationality in an ever-irrational world.

Thoreau was sufficiently rational when in 1846 he came into Concord from Walden to take his shoes to the cobbler and was arrested by the town jailer for failure to pay the poll tax. He had refused to pay because he would have no truck with government and in particular a government which waged the Mexican war and condoned slavery. That the government on its side would simply collect the tax from the jailer if he in turn could not collect it from Thoreau did not concern him. This was of course a cycle of coercion, and Thoreau's action did not alter the iniquity, indeed it compounded it. As we have seen, an unknown person paid Thoreau's debt, and was also freed on the morning after his arrest. Bronson Alcott earlier had acted similarly and also been freed by a tax-paying friend. Mrs. Alcott wrote that "we were spared the affliction of his absence and he the triumph of suffering for his principles." Thoreau was distinctly deprived of such a triumph. But his indignation persisted. Two years later he expressed it in his lecture on "Civil Disobedience."

It is his most celebrated essay. He tells the story of his night's imprisonment with considerable charm and a certain whimsicality; the story is set into his simple argument calling upon men to offer noncompliance when their conscience dictates it—what came to be called "passive resistance," Gandhi's *Satyagraha*. In practice it has proved to be a passive way of making revolution; that it also can lead to violence does not alter its effectiveness in certain conditions. It cannot be effective in all conditions: one knows that had humans placed themselves on roadways to stop Nazi tanks, the Nazis would have ridden over them. Thoreau's civil disobedience presupposes a high state of conscience; and it presupposes also a form of principle tolerable only in a society which has moved beyond barbarism. "The only obligation which I have a right to assume is to do at any time what I think right," Thoreau said, and implicit in this is the grandeur of great libertarians but also the violence of John Brown.

"Civil Disobedience" is an unusually cogent statement for Thoreau, who was a man of sentiment rather than of profound thought and who tended often to contradict himself. It remains a remarkable statement on behalf of individualism, as well as man's right to oppose and dissent. In the frame of Thoreau's life, however, it reveals the arbitrary nature of his philosophy. His defense of John Brown, with his espousal of violence in that instance, is hardly the voice of the same man. In both lectures, to be sure, Thoreau condemns government; but the preacher of nonviolence suddenly forgets his preachings. Brown had been wantonly destructive; he had staged a brutal massacre in Kansas and killed innocents. He was a man

whose fanaticism might have made him in other circumstances a brutal Inquisitor. Thoreau's involvement in his cause has in it strong elements of hysteria. The passive countenance closes its eyes to truth; it sees only Brown's cause and Brown's hatred of authority. It does not see his cruelty or his counter-imposition of authority. The world has wisely chosen to remember "Civil Disobedience" rather than the three John Brown lectures—"A Plea for Captain Brown," "The Last Days of John Brown," and "After the Death of John Brown." Whether the personal anarchism Thoreau preached is possible in every age remains to be seen. In his philosophy Thoreau saw only his own dissent; he seems not to have thought of the dangers of tyranny by a minority, as of a majority.

As we survey the volumes of Thoreau's writings, the two completed books, the miscellaneous essays published posthumously, the poems and letters, what looms largest are the fourteen volumes of Thoreau's journals (1906) to which another volume was added in recent times on discovery of a lost notebook (1958). The journal was the mirror of his days; but it is not an autobiographical record in the usual sense. It is one of the more impersonal journals of literary history. Thoreau made it the account book of his days. There are notes on his readings, his observations of nature, his record of walks, scraps of talk, observations of neighbors; on occasion the journal becomes a log, a statistical record. He began to keep it when he was twenty and he kept it until his death a quarter of a century later. It tends to be discursive, sprawling, discontinuous. One finds in it much matter-of-factness and little feeling. "The poet must weep himself unstained and aloof," said Thoreau and his journal is distinctly "aloof." One discerns in it a continuing note of melancholy; there is little humor; the vein is always one of high seriousness. Mankind is regarded in the mass; the generalizations are large; there is not much leaning toward the precisions of science. Nor can one find any record of growth in these pages, some of them turgid and dull, others lucid and fascinating. From 1837 to 1861 we see the same man writing; he has learned little. If one notes a difference it is that he begins by being philosophical and in the end is more committed to observation.

The journal suggests that Thoreau was incapable of a large effort as a writer. He learned to be a master of the short, the familiar essay; he made it lively and humanized it with his whimsicalities. The method of the journal was carried over into his principal works, the journal providing the raw data, filed always for later use. Perry Miller admirably showed how Thoreau labored to convert these data into literary material. The assiduity with which he applied himself to his writing ultimately bore fruit. If Thoreau never forged a style and filled his work with the echoes of other styles, he nevertheless in the end learned his trade. Possessing no marked ego at the beginning of his adult life, he created a composite ego; and he learned to write by using a series of rhetorical tricks. Emerson recognized Thoreau's exaggerated mannerisms when he noted in his journal that "the trick of his rhetoric is soon learned; it consists in substituting for the obvious word and thought its diametrical antagonist. He praises wild mountains and winter forests for their domestic air; snow and ice for their warmth; villagers and woodchoppers for their urbanity, and the wilderness for resembling Rome and Paris." There were times, as in the description of the battle of the ants as if it were the Trojan war, when this trick of exaggeration is markedly successful. But after a while it tends to become tedious and seems

like a tic, as Perry Miller remarked. Lowell aptly characterized the style when he said Thoreau turns "commonplaces end for end, and fancies it makes something new of them." He added that Thoreau "had none of the artistic mastery which controls great work to the serene balance of completeness, but exquisite mechanical skill in shaping of sentences and paragraphs."

Lowell, Emerson, and of all writers, Robert Louis Stevenson wrote essays on Thoreau which characterized him more carefully and perceptively than most of his worshippers have since done. But because these were essays which were measured and critical of the man as reflected in his work, they have been dismissed as ungenerous and irrelevant. Indeed Lowell's brilliant essay has been called "infamous," perhaps because its criticism was uncompromising and lacked the urbanity and delicacy of Stevenson's. Lowell was a gregarious man; he met the world as he found it; he could therefore recognize the alienated side of Thoreau and see the profound narcissism of his nature—although he called it by another name. He said of Thoreau that he made "his own whim the law, his own range the horizon of the universe," and noted that he "confounded physical with spiritual remoteness from men." Emerson's judgments were contained in his funeral oration and they are stated with considerable subtlety. We have but to ponder a remark such as that Thoreau "chose wisely, no doubt, for himself, to be the bachelor of thought and nature" to recognize that Emerson is defining what was most absent from Thoreau's life—human love, and the give and take an individual must learn in his human relatedness. Stevenson noted the absence of "geniality" in Thoreau, "the smile was not broad enough," and like Emerson he spoke of Thoreau's failure to allow himself "the rubs and trials of human society." In a sentence of considerable point for our time, Stevenson equated drug taking with this kind of alienation. "A man who must separate himself from his neighbor's habits in order to be happy, is in much the same case with one who requires to take opium for the same purpose." Perhaps the best known part of Stevenson's essay was his characterization of Thoreau's views of friendship. He "does not give way to love any more than to hatred," wrote Stevenson, "but preserves them both with care, like valuable curiosities. A more bald-headed picture of life, if I may so express myself, or a more selfish, has seldom been presented . . . Thoreau is dry, priggish and selfish. It is profit he is after in these intimacies; moral profit, certainly, but still profit to himself. If you will be the sort of friend I want, he remarks naively, 'my education cannot dispense with your society.' His education! as though a friend were a dictionary. And with all this, not a word about pleasure, or laughter, or kisses, or any quality of the flesh and blood. It was not inappropriate, surely, that he had such close relations with the fish."

Emerson spoke with great candor of Thoreau's aggressiveness. "There was something military in his nature not to be subdued, always manly and able, but rarely tender, as if he did not feel himself except in opposition. He wanted a fallacy to expose, a blunder to pillory. I may say he required a little sense of victory, a roll of the drum, to call his powers into full exercise. It cost him nothing to say No; indeed he found it much easier than to say Yes. It seemed as if his first instinct on hearing a proposition was to controvert it, so impatient was he of the limitations of our daily thought. This habit, of course, is a little chilling to the social affections; and though the companion would in the end acquit him of any malice or untruth, yet it mars conversation. Hence, no equal companion stood in affec-

tionate relations with one so pure and guileless. 'I love Henry,' said one of his friends, 'but I cannot like him; and as for taking his arm, I should as soon think of taking the arm of an elmtree.' "

Men will continue to discover these strange ambiguities in the author of *Walden*. If we are to dress a literary portrait of him, we must place him among those writers in whom the human will is organized to a fine pitch in the interest of mental and emotional survival. We must rank him with the "disinherited" and the alienated, with the writers who find themselves possessed of unconquerable demons and who then harness them in the service of self-preservation. Out of this quest sometimes mere eccentricity emerges; at other times art. There are distinct pathological traits in Thoreau, a constant sense—a few have discerned it—of inner disintegration which leads Thoreau in his *Walden* imagery to a terrible vision of human decay. One may venture a guess that this little observed Poesque streak in Thoreau testified to a crisis of identity so fundamental that Thoreau rescued himself only by an almost superhuman self-organization to keep himself, as it were, from falling apart. In doing this he clung obsessively to nature. A much deeper history of Thoreau's psyche may have to be written to explain his tenuous hold on existence in spite of the vigor of his outdoor life: his own quiet desperation, his endless need to keep a journal ("as if he had no moment to waste," said his friend Channing), and his early death of tuberculosis at forty-five in Concord during the spring of 1862. His works were the anchor of his days. He overcame dissolution during his abbreviated life by a constant struggle to assert himself in words. Some such strivings shaped his own recognition of his "crooked genius."

His brief journeys and his writings about them enabled others after his death to put together the volumes published as *Excursions* (1863), *The Maine Woods* (1864), *Cape Cod* (1865), and *A Yankee in Canada* (1866). He had, as he said, "travelled a good deal in Concord"; and it is in that setting that his myth is best recognized and best understood.

Selected Bibliography

WORKS OF HENRY DAVID THOREAU

WORKS PUBLISHED DURING THOREAU'S LIFETIME
A Week on the Concord and Merrimack Rivers. Boston and Cambridge: James Munroe, 1849.
Walden; or, Life in the Woods. Boston: Ticknor and Fields, 1854.

POSTHUMOUS SELECTED PROSE COLLECTIONS
Excursions. Boston: Ticknor and Fields, 1863.
The Maine Woods. Boston: Ticknor and Fields, 1864.
Cape Cod. Boston: Ticknor and Fields, 1865.
A Yankee in Canada, with Anti-Slavery and Reform Papers. Boston: Ticknor and Fields, 1866.
Early Spring in Massachusetts. Boston: Houghton Mifflin, 1881.
Summer: From the Journal of Henry D. Thoreau. Boston: Houghton Mifflin, 1884.
Winter: From the Journal of Henry D. Thoreau. Boston: Houghton Mifflin, 1888.
Autumn: From the Journal of Henry D. Thoreau. Boston: Houghton Mifflin, 1892.
Miscellanies. Boston: Houghton Mifflin, 1894.
The Service. Boston: Charles E. Goodspeed, 1902.
Sir Walter Raleigh. Boston: Bibliophile Society, 1905.

POETRY
Poems of Nature, edited by Henry S. Salt. Boston: Houghton Mifflin, 1895.
Collected Poems, edited by Carl Bode. Baltimore: Johns Hopkins Press, 1964.

JOURNAL
Journal, edited by Bradford Torrey. 14 vols. Boston: Houghton Mifflin, 1906.
Journal, edited by Bradford Torrey and Francis H. Allen. 14 vols. Boston: Houghton Mifflin, 1949.
Consciousness in Concord (lost volume of the *Journal*), edited by Perry Miller. Boston: Houghton Mifflin, 1958.

COLLECTED EDITIONS
The Writings of Henry David Thoreau. Riverside Edition. 10 vols. Boston: Houghton Mifflin, 1894 [1893].
The Writings of Henry David Thoreau. Manuscript and Walden editions. 20 volumes. Boston: Houghton Mifflin, 1906.

LETTERS
Letters to Various Persons. Boston: Ticknor and Fields, 1865.
Familiar Letters of Henry David Thoreau, edited by F. B. Sanborn. Boston: Houghton Mifflin, 1894.
Correspondence, edited by Walter Harding and Carl Bode. New York: New York University Press, 1958.

BIBLIOGRAPHIES
Since 1941 there has been a continuing bibliography in the quarterly of the Thoreau Society, *Thoreau Society Bulletin* (Geneseo, New York).

Allen, Francis H. *A Bibliography of Henry David Thoreau.* Boston: Houghton Mifflin, 1908.
Burnham, Philip E., and Carvel Collins. "Contributions to a Bibliography of Thoreau, 1938–1945," *Bulletin of Bibliography*, 19:16–18, 37–40 (1946).
Harding, Walter. *A Centennial Check-List of the Editions of Henry David Thoreau's "Walden."* Charlottesville: University of Virginia Press, 1954.
Spiller, Robert E., *et al. Literary History of the United States*, vol. 3. New York: Macmillan, 1948.
Stovall, Floyd, ed. *Eight American Authors: A Review of Research and Criticism.* New York: Modern Language Association, 1956.
Wade, J. S. "A Contribution to a Bibliography

from 1909 to 1936," *Journal of the New York Entomological Society,* 47:163–203 (1939).

White, William. *A Henry David Thoreau Bibliography, 1908–1937.* Boston: F. W. Faxon, 1939.

BIOGRAPHICAL STUDIES

Atkinson, Brooks. *Henry Thoreau: The Cosmic Yankee.* New York: Knopf, 1927.

Bazalgette, Léon. *Henry Thoreau: Bachelor of Nature,* translated by Van Wyck Brooks. New York: Harcourt, Brace, 1924.

Brooks, Van Wyck. *The Flowering of New England.* Rev. ed. New York: Dutton, 1940. Pp. 286–302, 359–73.

Canby, Henry S. *Thoreau.* Boston: Houghton Mifflin, 1939.

Channing, William Ellery. *Thoreau, the Poet-Naturalist.* Boston: Roberts Brothers, 1873.

Emerson, E. W., and W. E. Forbes, editors. *Journals of Ralph Waldo Emerson.* 10 vols. Boston: Houghton Mifflin, 1900–14.

Harding, Walter. *The Days of Henry Thoreau.* New York: Knopf, 1966.

Krutch, Joseph Wood. *Thoreau.* New York: William Sloane Associates, 1948.

Rusk, Ralph L. *The Letters of Ralph Waldo Emerson.* 6 vols. New York: Columbia University Press, 1939.

Salt, Henry S. *The Life of Henry David Thoreau.* London: R. Bentley, 1890; revised, London: W. Scott, 1896.

Sanborn, F. B. *The Life of Henry David Thoreau.* Boston: Houghton Mifflin, 1882.

Seybold, Ethel. *Thoreau: The Quest and the Classics.* New Haven, Conn.: Yale University Press, 1951.

Shanley, James Lyndon. *The Making of Walden.* Chicago: University of Chicago Press, 1957.

Whicher, George F. *Walden Revisited.* Chicago: Packard, 1945.

CRITICAL STUDIES

Anderson, Charles R. *The Magic Circle of Walden.* New York: Holt, Rinehart and Winston, 1968.

Cook, Reginald L. *Passage to Walden.* Boston: Houghton Mifflin, 1949.

Harding, Walter. *A Thoreau Handbook.* New York: New York University Press, 1959.

———, editor. *Thoreau: A Century of Criticism.* Dallas: Southern Methodist University Press, 1954. (Contains among other essays Emerson's tribute and the essays by Lowell and Stevenson.)

Matthiessen, F. O. *American Renaissance.* New York: Oxford University Press, 1941.

Meltzer, Milton, and Walter Harding. *A Thoreau Profile.* New York: Crowell, 1962.

Paul, Sherman. *The Shores of America: Thoreau's Inward Exploration.* Urbana: University of Illinois Press, 1958.

Stroller, Leo. *After Walden: Thoreau's Changing Views on Economic Man.* Stanford, Calif.: Stanford University Press, 1957.

Torrey, Bradford. *Friends on the Shelf.* Boston: Houghton Mifflin, 1906.

—*LEON EDEL*

Mark Twain

1835-1910

MOST AMERICANS regard Mark Twain with special affection. They know him as a shaggy man who told stories of boyhood adventures so like their own or those they would like to have had that they become intimately a part of personal experience. His cheerful irreverence and unhurried pace seem antidotes for attitudes to which they necessarily but unwillingly surrender. His is the image of what they like to think Americans have been or can be: humorously perceptive, undeceived by sham, successful in spite of circumstance because of distinctive personal characteristics.

More often than not they smile approvingly at his portrayal of man as "a museum of diseases, a home of impurities," who "begins as dirt and departs as stench," created for no apparent purpose except the nourishment and entertainment of microbes. The words seem bold and appropriately bitter, iconoclastically vulgar but, for all of that, funny. Evolution failed when man appeared, for his is the only bad heart in all the animal kingdom; only he is capable of malice, vindictiveness, drunkenness; when he is not cruel, he is stupid, like a sheep. It does seem such a pity, commented Mark Twain, that Noah and his companions did not miss their boat. And he tempts readers toward the compulsive nightmare of our time by wondering if a device might not be invented

which could exterminate man by withdrawing all oxygen from the air for two minutes.

They admire Mark Twain's hardheaded exposures of human venality, but respond also to his unembarrassed sentiment, his compassion and simple humility. What any man sees in the human race, he once admitted, "is merely himself in the deep and private honesty of his own heart." Everything human is pathetic: "The secret source of Humor itself is not joy but sorrow. There is no humor in heaven." He would have agreed with Robert Frost that earth is the right place for love, but would have added that it is inevitably also the place for stumbling and then forgetting the hurt by recalling or inventing other, older, and less disreputable times.

No wonder then that Ernest Hemingway found all American literature to begin with Mark Twain. His escape to adventure, to the past, to humor which moves through and beyond reality, is not unlike Hemingway's escape from thinking through the simpler pleasures of wine, women, and manly exercise. Not only is Mark Twain's simple declarative style a parent of Hemingway's style; not only is his boy's-eye view of the world like Hemingway's view, like Willa Cather's, Sherwood Anderson's, even J. D. Salinger's; the publication of *The Mysterious Stranger* in 1916 reveals him mastered by the same cluster of opinions which produced the retreat to older times of Henry Adams, as well as the despair of the "lost generation" of Hemingway and Scott Fitzgerald, and the wasted land of T. S. Eliot.

It was as difficult to convince people of his time as it is to convince people of ours that Mark Twain never really existed except as a character, costumed and carefully rehearsed, cannily a crowd-pleaser. For in both a literary and psychological sense the shambling but perceptive humorist remembered as Mark Twain is a mask, a controlled, drawling, and whimsical voice, a posturing and flamboyant figure, behind which exists the man, Samuel Langhorne Clemens, who with the help of circumstance and receptive wit created him. Some would explain them, the image and the man, as twins, and Clemens as a man divided, but this is not in any real sense true. The image is partly self-portrait and, indeed, partly self-defense, but shrewdly retouched until the character who is Mark Twain becomes Clemens' most successful achievement, and the voice of Mark Twain speaks in a special literary relation to its creator.

It is probably true that the two became as confused in Clemens' mind as they have in the minds of people who have talked about Mark Twain, but the distinction is radical. Which is which or who did what to whom remains an important critical puzzle. To simplify more than is appropriate, it can be suggested that Mark Twain was a character who inserted himself, sometimes with joyous abandon, into almost everything which Samuel Clemens wrote. He was irrepressible but self-conscious, alert to his responsibilities as diagnostic spokesman for his time and as representative of much which wove itself into the pattern of contemporary notions of success. But failure to remember that Mark Twain was a medium

through whom stories were told, and that he was only in an indirect sense their author, is to fall into the attractively baited trap which opens even more invitingly before commentators on such other American writers as Whitman, Thoreau, and Hemingway, whose masks are more subtle and less clearly designated.

Which spoke when cannot always be determined, nor is the distinction in every case important, except that in some of the writings, and many of them the best, the burden of being Mark Twain is discarded and a voice speaks directly, undistorted by comic pose or anger. Either could have admitted, as one of them did, that his books were like water and the books of great geniuses like wine, but it was surely Mark Twain who supplied the twister to remind us that "everyone drinks water." Part of his character was that of a man among litterateurs, a journalist who detested, he said, novels and poetry, but who liked history, biography, curious facts, and strange happenings.

But it has not been necessary for Americans to read Mark Twain in order to remember him with affection. Probably more people know of Tom Sawyer's slick method of getting a fence whitewashed than have read the book in which it appears. Hollywood versions of Tom and Huck, of the prince who became a pauper, or of the Yankee from Connecticut who brought American knowhow to King Arthur's court have reached millions of viewers, as originally filmed or as adapted for television. A popular comedian has danced and sung his way through a celluloid Camelot. A spectacular Negro boxer has played the runaway slave whose simple loyalty confuses, then converts, Huck Finn. Tom Sawyer has tripped barefooted through a musical comedy, and plans have been considered for a musical adaptation of *Innocents Abroad*. More than one actor has found it profitable to dress and drawl as Mark Twain did, and to hold an audience laughter-bound by retelling some of the tales he told.

Mark Twain's laconic, soft speech, whimsical understatements, and outrageous exaggerations made him a platform favorite and pampered after-dinner speaker for more than forty years, and his witticisms were passed by word of mouth and faithfully recorded in newspapers. He saw to that, for he was in every best sense a showman who kept himself and his books effectively before the public. His heavy shock of hair, once red, but soon an eye-catching white, made him seem larger than he was, an illusion which it pleased him later in life to reinforce by dressing summer and winter in white serge or flannel. He learned early how to attract and hold attention, and he used the knowledge well. One way or another, he was the best known and most successfully published author of his generation.

He saw to that also, for—within limits—he was the canny businessman he liked to think himself. His lectures sold his books, and his books helped pack his lectures. As a publisher, he took pride in gauging public taste so well that each book supplied a popular demand. Many were not issued until subscription agents throughout the country had sold in advance enough copies to make them surely profitable. And subscription books in the late nineteenth century were gaudily attractive books, usually handsomely bound and illustrated—the kind almost anyone would be proud to have on his table, particularly when the author had just been or would soon be in town for a lecture.

For these reasons, though not only for these, Mark Twain's books found themselves in a preferred position in thousands of American homes. At the end of the century, he offered a twenty-two-volume Autograph Edition of his works, which found its way into thousands more, and into libraries, even small town and county libraries which could not afford to buy it but received it as a gift when house shelves became crowded or when it was replaced by the new, twenty-five-volume Underwood Edition a few years later. Shortly before Mark Twain's death in 1910 the Author's National Edition began to appear, and then, in the 1920's, the "definitive edition" in thirty-seven volumes. Few authors, perhaps not even Balzac or Dickens, achieved greater shelf space during their lifetime.

Such success has seemed appropriate, for it fit precisely to patterns which Americans have thought peculiarly their own. Mark Twain was a poor boy who by reason of native skill rose to wealth and fame. He was kin to Daniel Boone or Andrew Jackson because he had known the rigors of our frontier. Abraham Lincoln's rise from log cabin to President created a norm of which his career was a verifying variation—indeed, Howells called him the Lincoln of our literature. He had worked with his hands, like Andrew Carnegie, and then had a large house and servants. These things testified to the validity of what Emerson had said of the divine sufficiency of the individual. Here in truth was the powerful, uneducated democratic personality for whom Whitman had called. Mark Twain walked with kings and capitalists, but never lost the common touch. In his mansion at Hartford, his residence on Fifth Avenue, or his country place at Stormfield, he still remembered old times and old friends.

This poular image was never completely an accurate likeness, but is sufficiently well drawn to remain attractive. Samuel Langhorne Clemens was born on November 30, 1835, on the Missouri frontier, in a straggling log village called Florida, to which his parents had come from their former home among the hills of

Tennessee. His father was a local magistrate and small merchant, originally from Virginia, who had studied law in Kentucky and there met and married auburn-haired Jane Lampton, descended from settlers who had followed Daniel Boone across the mountains. One among thousands of Americans who in the early decades of the nineteenth century moved westward to seek opportunities in newly opened lands, John Marshall Clemens did not prosper in the hamlet in which his third son was born, and so, when Samuel was four years old, moved to Hannibal, a larger town with a population of almost five hundred, on the banks of the Mississippi River.

There, beside this river, Samuel Clemens grew through boyhood much as Tom Sawyer did, fascinated by the life which swarmed over its mile-wide surface or which sought refuge or sustenance on its shores. Through this frontier region passed the picturesque, sometimes mendacious or menacing, pilgrims of restlessly expanding America, up or down the river or across it toward the western plains. Young Samuel must have watched, as any boy might, admiringly, but fearfully also. He saw men maimed or killed in waterfront brawls, Negroes chained like animals for transportation to richer slave markets to the south. He had nightmares and walked in his sleep, and always remembered these things, the rude ways and tremendous talk, and the terror.

Better things were remembered also, like giant rafts and trading scows piled with produce or sweet-smelling timber, coming from or going where a boy could only guess. Gallant river steamers left wake behind in which small boys swimming or in boats could ride excitedly. Below the village lay wooded Holliday Hill, unrivaled for play at Robin Hood or pirate, and near its summit a cave tempted to exploration. Away from its boisterous riverfront, the village was "a heavenly place for a boy," he said, providing immunities and graces which he never forgot: hunting and fishing, a swimming hole, an inevitable graveyard, truant days at Glasscock's Island, and yearnings toward the better freedom of Tom Blankenship, the town drunkard's son, to whom truancy brought no penalties of conscience or recrimination.

But these days were soon over, for when Samuel was twelve years old, his father died, and the boy was apprenticed to local printers, and then—partaking of a tradition which Benjamin Franklin had established a century before—worked as compositor and pressman for his older brother Orion, who managed a not completely successful newspaper in Hannibal. There was room in its pages for humorous features which young Samuel composed, set in type, and printed over the flamboyant signature of "W. Spaminodas Adrastas Blab" and for miscellaneous items which he collected for "Our Assistant's Column." He even ventured verse, addressing one poem over the signature of "Rambler" ambiguously to "Miss Kate in II—l." The appropriation of so timeworn a pseudonym seems less indicative of literary consciousness than descriptive of desire. Samuel Clemens was not yet a rambler, though he wanted to be, for—again like Franklin—he chaffed under the discipline of a brother, or anyone else.

By the time he was seventeen he was able to think of himself as something more than a local writer. In May 1852 "The Dandy Frightening the Squatter" appeared in the *Carpet-Bag*, a sportsman's magazine in Boston, signed "S.L.C." Done in the slapstick tradition of native humor such as was being written or was soon to be written by pseudonymous favorites like Sam Slick, Orpheus C. Kerr, and Artemus Ward, it anticipates much of the later manner of Mark Twain: it celebrates the laconic shrewdness of the frontiersman; is told with some of the exaggerated flourishes of the western tall tale, seasoned with caricaturing strokes which may have been learned, even indirectly, from Dickens; and is laid in Hannibal on the Mississippi River. Comparison of its tone and language with Nathaniel Hawthorne's *The Blithedale Romance* or Herman Melville's *Pierre*, which also appeared in that year, suggests some of the things which, for better or worse, were happening or about to happen to writing in the United States.

But wanderlust soon hit young Samuel Clemens, so that he became in fact a rambler. At eighteen he left little Hannibal for St. Louis, the largest town in Missouri, where he saved his wages carefully until he could strike out beyond the limits of his western state, to discover whether a young man's fortune might not be more quickly made in larger cities to the east. He traveled first, by steamboat and rail, through Chicago and Buffalo, to New York, where he worked briefly as a job printer, until he moved southward to become a compositor in Philadelphia and later Washington, then again to Philadelphia, then west to Muscatine, Iowa, to set type for his almost equally peripatetic brother. Soon he was back in St. Louis, and then once more, for two years this time, joined his brother, now in Keokuk, Iowa.

Two years, however, was a long time for a rambler to remain in one place, and his fortune certainly was not being made. He spent the winter of 1856–57 in Cincinnati, but this was a way stop, for he had hit on the notion that a young man almost twenty-two might do well and have fun besides exploring opportunities for riches in South America, along the lush banks of the Amazon. So it was that in April 1857—the date is a turning point—he started down the Mississippi toward New Orleans, on his first step toward fame. What happened then—his meeting with the veteran steamboat pilot Horace Bixby, his own apprentice pilot days, his four years of life on the Mississippi—has often been told, and never better than by Clemens himself as he later remembered these years and threw about them the color of romance which only made more persuasive the realism of his detail.

But the abortive trip to South America is remembered for other reasons also, for to make it Samuel Clemens entered into a professional engagement of a kind which later would bring him world-wide acclaim. At Keokuk he shaped the first piece of the pattern which would make continued wanderings possible, even profitable, by arranging with the editor of the *Evening Post* that Samuel Clemens, rambler, would supply reports as regularly as possible on what he saw and did on his ramblings. Only three now appeared, probably because Clemens was deep in the more exciting business of learning to pilot a steamboat. Signed "Thomas Jefferson Snodgrass," they were desperately, self-consciously humorous, hardly distinguishable in language or tone from the work of any other journeyman journalist.

Snodgrass was a name always infinitely funny to Clemens. He used it again in writings in California; more than thirty years later in *The American Claimant* he presented two characters, "Zylobalsamum Snodgrass" and "Spinal Meningitis Snodgrass"; and in *Tom Sawyer Abroad* he spoke of the "celebrated author . . . Snodgrass." While steamboating on the Mississippi from 1857 to 1861, a licensed pilot by the spring of 1859, he is said to have contributed letters signed "Quintius Curtius Snodgrass" to the New Orleans *Daily Crescent*, and is said also to have written a burlesque of the pontifical river lore which a retired captain named Isaiah Sellers printed in a New Orleans paper over the signature of "Mark Twain." A favorite but unverifiable tradition insists that

Captain Sellers was so hurt by the ridicule and Samuel Clemens so conscience-stricken at the wound he had given that a few years later the younger man adopted the old captain's pseudonym—which, as everyone knows, is the leadsman's cry to the pilot when water which is safe, but barely safe, lies ahead.

When in 1861 the Civil War cut across the Mississippi so that river traffic from north to south or south to north was no longer possible, steamboating ceased to be a profitable occupation, and Samuel Clemens was without work. He took only a minor part in the war between the states: one not very dependable account suggests that he was detailed for river duty; the New Orleans Snodgrass letters suggest that he had some connection with militia drill in that city; and Mark Twain later delighted readers of the *Atlantic Monthly* with a humorous "Private History of a Campaign That Failed," which tells how he and a few companions formed themselves into an irregular company which searched vainly for a unit of the Confederate Army to which it might become attached. Whatever his service, it was brief and with the rebellious southern forces— a circumstance which is supposed to have made the later northernized Mark Twain extraordinarily circumspect in speaking of it.

In the summer of 1861 Clemens went farther west, with his brother Orion who had been rewarded for activity in Abraham Lincoln's campaign for the presidency by appointment as secretary of the newly opened Nevada Territory. Orion Clemens, never greatly successful, had little money, but brother Samuel, after profitable years as a river pilot, apparently had his pockets full and provided stage fare for both, traveling himself as unpaid secretary to the new secretary of the territory. The story of their journey across the plains and experiences in Carson City is later recounted in *Roughing It*, in which, as Huck Finn said

of him on another occasion, "Mr. Mark Twain . . . he told the truth, mainly." Here we learn of his adventures in staking out timber claims near Lake Tahoe, only carelessly to leave his campfire unattended so that much of the forest went up in flames. He tells of money invested in silver mines, as he and Orion were caught up in a wild seeking for wealth. Once he was a millionaire for ten days when he found a rich mine, but lost it through carelessness again. Stories of Samuel Clemens in Nevada, variously told by himself or by people who knew him, make up a large share of the public image of Mark Twain. A loose, shambling man, with unruly hair, who lounged about the frontier town in corduroys and shirt sleeves, swapping stories and listening to the way men spoke, he was ready, we are told, to take his chance with the best or worst at poker or in wildcat speculation.

Before he had been in Nevada a year, however, he was back at his old trade as a writer for newspapers, contributing burlesque sketches over the signature of "Josh" to the *Territorial Enterprise* in Virginia City. There he lived freely among friends like fiery Steve Gillis, a printer whose escapades were to keep them both in trouble. The unrestraint of that remarkable frontier paper stimulated Clemens to such journalistic hoaxes as "The Petrified Man" and "The Dutch Nick Massacre," which to his joy were copied as true in eastern papers. Here he first met Artemus Ward and spent convivial evenings with the popular humorist, who advised him how Mark Twain—for Clemens was now using that name—might extend his reputation. Already known as the Washoe Giant, the wild humorist of the Sage Brush Hills, famed as far as California, Samuel Clemens was ambitious for something more.

But then he ran foul of an anti-dueling statute when he challenged a rival newspaperman, and he and loyal Steve Gillis beat their way in the spring of 1864 to California, where a range of hills stood between them and Nevada jails. Clemens worked briefly as a reporter on the *San Francisco Call*, but it was "fearful drudgery," he said, "an awful slavery for a lazy man," so he left regular employment to free-lance for the *Golden Era* and Bret Harte's *Californian*. Then he became San Francisco correspondent for his former paper in Virginia City, until he ran headlong against the law again when Steve Gillis was arrested for barroom brawling and released on bail which Clemens supplied. Then when dapper Steve skipped over the mountains back to Nevada, his protector thought it appropriate to leave also.

This time he took flight to the Sierras, where he stayed on Jackass Hill with Steve Gillis' brother Jim, a teller of tales who was to receive later renown as Bret Harte's "Truthful James." Here, at Angel's Camp, he heard old Ross Coon tell of "The Celebrated Jumping Frog of Calaveras County." Clemens wrote it down, this "villainous, backwoods sketch," in just the rhythm of dialect in which Ross Coon told it, and he sent it east for place in a book of yarns to which Artemus Ward had asked him to contribute. By fortunate mischance it arrived too late for burial in Ward's collection. Instead, it was pirated by the *New York Evening Post* and became an immediate favorite, copied in newspapers all across the country, even in California to give its author prestige there as an eastern writer. For all the good it did him —he made nothing from it.

At just this time, in 1865, the Pacific Steamboat Company began regular passenger service between San Francisco and Honolulu, and Clemens took the trip, paying for it with letters to the *Sacramento Union,* thus setting to final form the pattern which four years later was to establish Mark Twain's reputation with *Innocents Abroad*. These Sandwich Island let-ters are exuberant, and sometimes vulgar. With him traveled an imaginary, completely irrepressible companion named Mr. Brown, whose sweetheart, he boasted, was so elegant that she picked her nose with a fork. When passengers became seasick, "Brown was there, ever kind and thoughtful, passing from one to the other and saying, 'That's all right—that's all right you know—it'll clean you out like a jog, and then you won't feel so awful and smell so ridiculous.' " It was good for Mark Twain to have someone to hide behind, and good especially for Samuel Clemens who could disguise timidities doubly removed.

Mark Twain liked these lovely Pacific islands: "I would rather smell Honolulu at sunset," he wrote, "than the old Police courtroom in San Francisco." And he liked the islanders who "always squat on their hams and who knows but they may be the original 'ham sandwiches.' " He liked their customs, especially the "demoralizing *hula hula*" which was forbidden "save at night, with closed doors . . . by permission of the authorities and the payment of ten dollars for the same." Sometimes he became almost lyrical about the beauties of the islands, but when he did, Mr. Brown pulled him up short to remind him that there were also in Honolulu "more 'sentipedes' and scorpions and spiders and mosquitoes and missionaries" than anywhere else in the world.

Clemens had now found the work which suited him best: he could ramble as he pleased and pay his way by being informative and funny, and donning masks which might excuse irresponsibility. In December 1866 he signed with the *Alta California,* the West's most prominent paper, as its "travelling correspondent . . . not stinted as to place, time or direction," who would circle the globe and write letters as he went. The first step in the journey was to New York, the long way around, by boat, and with the ebullient Mr.

Brown beside him. The letters written then are more lively than any he had done before, and without the restraints in concession to taste of his later travel accounts. Here he presents the jovial Captain Wakeman, whose tall tales, profanity, and Biblical lore were to live again in Captain Blakely in *Roughing It* and in Captain Stormfield who made a voyage to heaven. There is sentimentality in the account of a runaway couple married at sea, and slapstick aplenty in Mr. Brown's further inelegant concern with seasick passengers, but there is compassion also as Mark Twain writes of the misery of cholera in Nicaragua, and anger as he snarls at gouging Floridians.

When he arrives in New York, the letters take on fresh vigor, and reveal much which is sometimes said to be characteristic of an older Mark Twain. The "overgrown metropolis" had changed mightily since he had seen it thirteen years before when he was a "pure and sinless sprout." He looked with indignation now on the squalor of her slums where the "criminally, sinfully, wickedly poor" lived amid filth and refuse, victims of their "good, kind-hearted, fat, benevolent" neighbors. His social investigations came to climax when he was arrested for disorderly conduct and spent the night in jail, enraged as he talked with tramps, prostitutes, and former soldiers, pawns at the mercy of society's whim. It is not necessary to turn to a later Mark Twain for records of pessimism which damns the whole human race. It is solidly a part of him at thirty. Sin bothered him, even when he was being funny about it.

In New York he saw to the publication of his first book, *The Celebrated Jumping Frog of Calaveras County and Other Sketches*, just as he set out again to continue his wanderings, not around the world, but on an excursion to the Mediterranean and Near East on the steamship *Quaker City*. The letters which he sent back then, to the California paper and also to Horace Greeley's *Tribune* in New York, reached a public ripe for appreciation of his confident assumption that many hallowed shrines of the Old World did not measure to American standards. And such was public response to what he wrote that, when he returned to New York a few months later, the wild mustang of the western plains discovered himself a literary lion, sought by magazines, newspapers, lecture audiences, and publishers.

Caught up by currents of popularity, Samuel Clemens from this time forward was swept from one success to another. He had struck his bonanza, not in silver as he had once dreamed, but in selling his jocund alter ego in print and from the platform. He met and, after dogged courtship, married Olivia Langdon, daughter of a wealthy New York industrialist. With money advanced by his future father-in-law, he bought a share in a newspaper in Buffalo. The rambler finally would settle down, not permanently as an editor, for that occupation soon palled, but in a magnificent house which royalties and lecture fees would allow him to build in Hartford. He was through, he said, "with literature and all that bosh."

But when *The Innocents Abroad; or, The New Pilgrim's Progress* appeared in 1869, revised from the *Quaker City* letters (with Mr. Brown's offensive commentary, for example, deleted), reviewers found it "fresh, racy, and sparkling as a glass of champagne." The satire was alert, informed, sophisticated, and sidesplittingly funny. The accent was of western humor, but the subject, a favorite among men of good will since the Enlightenment of the century before, spoke of the decay of transatlantic institutions and their shoddiness beside the energetic freshness of the New World. Traveling American innocents haggled through native bazaars, delightedly conscious that every language but their own was ridiculous, and unconscious completely of their own outlandishness. Venice was magnificent, though her boatmen were picturesquely absurd, but the Arno at Florence was darkened by blood shed by the Medici on its shores. The Holy Land was hot and dirty, filled with beggars and larcenous dragomans—when confronted by a boatman at Galilee who demanded exorbitant fare, one of the pilgrims remarked, "No wonder Jesus walked." Because he was clever or because he was by nurture one of them, Clemens touched attitudes shared by many of his countrymen, even to admitting preference for copies of masterpieces because they were brighter than the originals.

To many readers *The Innocents Abroad* remains Clemens' second-best book, finding place in their affection behind *The Adventures of Huckleberry Finn* and just ahead of, or side by side with, *Life on the Mississippi.* As if anticipating Henry James, it takes a fresh look at the transatlantic world and the stature of Americans when measured against its requirements. Without James's subtlety, conscious art, or depth of penetration, it discovers faults on both sides so that it becomes a book which cosmopolites and chauvinists can equally admire. The hearty and headlong inelegance of the earlier, more carelessly devised travel letters has been pruned from it, and not only because Mark Twain was surrendering to prudish and Victorian notions of propriety. In submitting to the demands of public taste, Clemens was also learning something of the possibilities of converting a casual colloquialism to art.

Roughing It, in 1871, was also greatly successful, suited, said one commentator, "to the wants of the rich, the poor, the sad, the gay," and a sure recipe for laughter. Again it was a book of traveling, the kind that Mark Twain was always to write best, in which one story after another was strung along a journey overland or on water. Every ingredient was here—the tall tale, the straight-faced shocker, melodrama in adventure, insight into raw life among men unrestrained by convention, folklore and animal lore. The effect was of improvisation, for narrative must flow, Clemens later said, as a stream flows, diverted by every boulder, but proceeding briskly, interestingly, on its course.

Such motion did not characterize *The Gilded Age,* published in 1873, which he wrote in collaboration with his Hartford neighbor, Charles Dudley Warner. For the opening chapters Clemens drew on recollections of frontier life to produce situations not unlike those we associate with *Tobacco Road* or *Li'l Abner,* where back-country people dream expansively of fortunes they have neither energy nor ability to acquire. Colonel Beriah Sellers is a hill-town Mr. Micawber, but drawn from memory of people, even relatives, whom Samuel Clemens had known. Some of the river scenes are beautifully realized. And as the locale shifts to Washington and New York, the novel touches with satirical humor on political corruption, the American jury system, and the mania for speculation, so that it became a best seller and gave title to the age which it reviewed. But artistically it was not a success, for the narrative finally collapses under the weight of plot and counterplot, and is not remembered as one of Mark Twain's best.

Given a story to tell, Clemens was almost always able to tell it well. As raconteur he had come to maturity in *Innocents Abroad.* But the invention of stories did not come easily to him. As he approached forty, he felt written out. He collected miscellaneous writings in *Sketches Old and New* and, with an eye on the market, tried to fit further adventures of the popular Colonel Sellers into a new book which failed to go well but which he published many years later, in 1891, as *The American Claimant*. He labored over a boy's story based on his early life in Hannibal, but that did not go well either.

Finally, at the suggestion of a friend, he recalled his years of steamboating and wrote, with hardly any posturing at all, of "Old Times on the Mississippi" in seven installments for the *Atlantic Monthly* in 1875. Eight years later he was to add thirty-nine chapters to make the book called *Life on the Mississippi,* but the added material, arduously compiled, recaptures little of the charm of these earlier portions. In them the viewpoint is consistently that of a boy bound by the spell of the Mississippi who becomes a pilot and learns her secrets. It is a story of initiation. Seen from the pilothouse, the river loses much of her glamour; beneath her beauty, painted by sun and shaded by clouds, lurked an implacable menace of snags, hidden reefs, and treacherously changing shores. The face of the water was a wonderful book, he said, which he was never to forget, and piloting was a profession Clemens loved more than any he followed again: "a pilot in those days was the only unfettered and entirely independent human being that lived on the earth."

On the river he became "personally and familiarly acquainted with about all the different types of human nature to be found in fiction, biography, or history." He never read of or met anyone again without "warm personal interest in him, for the reason that I had known him before—met him on the river." But for all its attention to remembered detail, "Old Times on the Mississippi" was not in strictest sense realistic. Its narrator seldom looked aside to notice people not admitted to the pilothouse, like the sharpers, gamblers, and painted women who plied a profitable trade on Mississippi steamers, but kept his eyes on the river and his mind on the discipline she demanded from men who knew her charm but

also her mystery and menace, who were skilled, not only in finding their own way among her dangers, but in guiding others safely through. Thus a reminiscent account becomes more than re-creation of times that are gone and will not return because steamboating, like the whaling of which Melville wrote in *Moby Dick,* was the product of a way of life which was past. It speaks of appearance as opposed to reality, of innocence and experience, of man's duty in a world of perils, and also of a conception of the function of literature.

The Mississippi River appeared triumphantly again in *The Adventures of Tom Sawyer* which in 1876 placed Mark Twain once more at the head of best-seller lists. Probably no more continuingly popular book has ever appeared in the United States. On first reading it seems loose and shambling—as Mark Twain was loose and shambling. Episodes designed "to pleasantly remind adults of what they once were themselves" often remain longer in memory than the plot of murder and pursuit which must have been intended to hold younger readers. But there is artistry in it also, beyond the artistry of the raconteur who engraved minor realisms about provincial society for all time. Perhaps because he worked long over it, this first independent novel, published when its author was forty, is better constructed than any he was to write again. And its structure reveals levels of meaning which Mark Twain may not have known were there.

The story is divided into three almost exactly equal parts. There are ten chapters in the first part, ten in the second, and thirteen in the climactic third. The first part is separated from the second and the second from the third, each by an interchapter. Within each of the three parts events are detailed carefully, time moves slowly, incident by incident, day by day. In the interchapters time is accelerated, and weeks go by within a few pages. Each of the parts is different from the others in tone, in the kind of adventures in which Tom involves himself, and in the relationship of these adventures to the unifying theme of the whole.

The first ten chapters reveal boys engaged in characteristic play, stealing jam, playing hookey, swapping treasured belongings, until finally they visit a graveyard at midnight and there inadvertently witness a murder. Time has been chronicled exactly, from Friday afternoon to Monday night, then in the first interchapter, Muff Potter is arrested for the crime which the boys know he did not commit, and two weeks pass. The second part, Chapters 12 through 21, is divided into two major episodes, the Jackson Island adventure and the last day at school. Again time slows down, the boys are again at play, but no longer at simple play of boys among themselves for their own ends: it is directed now against adults, as if in revolt against what the world holds for boys who grow, as Tom has grown, beyond simple innocence to knowledge and, indirectly, participation in evil. After the second interchapter in which summer days are quickened by the boys' guilty knowledge of Muff's innocence, the plot moves to a cluttered climax.

In the last thirteen chapters the boys begin to act tentatively as adults act. Tom gives evidence in court, he and Huck stalk Injun Joe in a serious, common-sense manner, and they search for treasure which is real and not an imagined product of boyish play. But then Tom shucks off responsibility and goes to a picnic, leaving matter-of-fact Huck to watch for the murderer. And Huck does discover him but only to frighten him into hiding from which he may emerge to strike again. No adult or even adult-like action succeeds in *The Adventures of Tom Sawyer*. In the first part, Aunt Polly is foiled in efforts to have Tom whitewash a fence. In the second part, grownups arrange a funeral for boys who are not dead and the schoolmaster loses his toupee. Now, as the story draws to an end, bumbling adult planning goes astray, and Tom and Becky are lost in the cave for hours before search for them begins. But adult search does not find them, any more than adult efforts do away with the evil which is Injun Joe. Tom's imaginative exploration at the end of a string brings them to safety. Even when adults seal the mouth of the cave, it is not to capture the murderer, but to prevent a recurrence of Tom's kind of adventuring. This notion of the excellence of simple innocence, imaginative and irrepressible, and superior to adult methods of confronting the world, was one to which Mark Twain would often return.

After several years of miscellaneous publication, which included the popular, now forgotten, *Punch, Brothers, Punch and Other Sketches* in 1878 and a second account of European travel, *A Tramp Abroad*, in 1880, Clemens turned to the theme again in *The Prince and the Pauper,* in 1882, but with less success. The account of Tom Canty's adventures in the court of Edward VI was again addressed to boys and girls, tested by readings of the manuscript to the Clemens children and the children of friends, but it was addressed also to adults as an expression of its author's continuing assurance that, for all its shortcomings, democracy as practiced in the United States was superior to any other manner of living anywhere. It is the kind of melodramatic story which Tom Sawyer might have told, of a poor boy who became heir to a king and of a prince who learned humility through mixing with common men.

"My idea," Clemens told one of his friends, "is to afford a realistic sense of the severity of the laws of that day by inflicting some of their penalties upon the king himself." Poverty which brutalizes and restrictive statutes which force men to thievery are ridiculed, as well as superstition and meaningless ritual. The language of old England, with which Mark Twain had experimented in the surreptitiously printed, mildly ribald *1601, or Conversation as It Was by the Fireside in the Time of the Tudors,* two years before, comes in for a full share of burlesque. When Tom's nose "itcheth cruelly," he asks, "What is the custom and usage of this emergence?" He fills his pockets with nuts and uses the Royal Seal to crack them. When Henry VIII dies and his funeral is delayed to an appropriate ceremonial time in the future, the boy observes, " 'Tis strange folly. Will he keep?" Hardly any of the kind of humor which the public had come to expect from Mark Twain, or of sagacious insight into the frailties of man, is left out of *The Prince and the Pauper.*

In spite of this and largely, Clemens thought, because he had changed to a new publisher, unexperienced in selling copies in great number by subscription, *The Prince and the Pauper* did not do as well commercially as Mark Twain's previous books. So Clemens established his own publishing house and launched it in 1885 with another boy's book which he was careful to link in the public mind to his earlier, encouragingly popular account of young life by the Mississippi by identifying its hero in a subtitle as "Tom Sawyer's comrade." But *The Adventures of Huckleberry Finn* made no such immediate impression as its predecessor. At Concord in Massachusetts, still the mecca of genteel New England cultural aspiration, it was banished from the local library as presenting a bad example for youth. Years later, it was blacklisted in Denver, Omaha, and even Brooklyn. When chapters from it appeared in the *Century Magazine,* some readers found it indefensibly coarse, "destitute of a single redeeming quality."

But *The Adventures of Huckleberry Finn* has outlived almost every criticism of those who have spoken against it to become a native classic thrust forward exultantly in the face of any who still dare inquire, "Who reads an American book?"—its health endangered only by a smothering swarm of commentators who threaten to maim it with excessive kind attention. Except perhaps for *Moby Dick,* no American book has recently been opened with more tender explicatory care or by critics to whom we are better prepared to listen. The river on which or beside which the action develops is a great brown god to T. S. Eliot; and Lionel Trilling reminds us of the "subtle, implicit moral meaning of the great river" as he translates Emerson to contemporary idiom by explaining that "Against the money-god stands the river-god, whose comments are silent," that Huck is "the servant of the river-god," and that Mr. Eliot is right in saying "The river is within us."

Other commentators call attention to the social criticism, the satire, the savagery in this book of boy adventures; to its language so cleanly direct and simply natural that reasons for Hemingway's admiration for it come to mind; to its structure which is at one time or to one critic great art, at another fumbling improvisation; to the recurrent imagery, so like what E. M. Forster pointed to in writings of Marcel Proust and called repetition by variation. Its mythic quality is explained as reinforced by elements of popular lore and superstition or by parallels with primitive initiation rites. The once familiar three-part division of the blackface minstrel show, a genuinely indigenous art form, has been superimposed on *The Adventures of Huckleberry Finn* to reveal instructive similarities. Various interpretations of its theme, some inevitably religious, have been patiently explored. Its endlessness, as if the adventures might have gone on forever, has been persuasively held forth as similar to other distinctively American contrivances which emphasize process rather than product, like the skyscraper, jazz, the comic strip, chewing gum, and *Moby Dick*.

These things are all probably true, if only because attentive readers have discovered them. An encompassing and synthesizing rightness reveals itself now in the casual career of Samuel Clemens who drifted from one occupation to another, managing by accident of birth and qualities which moralists cannot always hold up for emulation to have been at many right places at exactly the right time. His was indeed a pioneer talent, and sometimes so unused to itself that it postured boisterously, almost always ready to break into laughter if response to what was said proved it ridiculous. Its melancholy, even when invaded by the mockery of burlesque, was related to that of home-starved men who sang sad songs on lonesome prairies or rivers, in forests or mountain camps. Its sentimentality was like theirs, ready to retreat to guffaw when detected. The aggressive playfulness which delighted in hoaxes and practical joking changed in almost classic pattern to anger like that of gods—or of simple men—when the joke is turned against them.

Clemens had known backcountry America and the overland push toward great fortunes in the gold-filled, silver-lined West. He had known, better than he learned to know anything else, her great arterial river through which the lifeblood of middle America had once flowed. And he had known men in these places, of all kinds, and then known riches and the company of well-fed, respectable people whom he also recognized as types known before. He had listened to men talk, boastfully or in anger, had heard their tales and their blandishments, and had learned to speak as they spoke. For his ultimate discovery was linguistic, the creation of a language which was simple, supple, and sustained, in what Richard Chase has called "a joyous exorcism of traditional literary English." No one had ever written like him before. What is more difficult to remember is that no one ever effectively will again because, to say it very simply, his models were not in literature but in life. Even he, when he tried to write something like something he had written before, succeeded only in producing books which were amusing because written in Mark Twain's manner.

The Adventures of Huckleberry Finn is the story of a boy who will not accept the kinds of freedom the world is able to offer, and so flees from them, one after another, to become to many readers a symbol of man's inevitable, restless flight. It is instructive to recall that it appeared in the same year that Clemens' friend William Dean Howells presented in *The Rise of Silas Lapham* another simple protagonist who retreated when confronted by perplexities, and a year before Henry James, who approached maturity through avenues almost completely different from those which Clemens followed, revealed both in *The Princess Casamassima* and *The Bostonians* the struggle of honest young provincials forced to reject promises offered by society. Each played variations on a familiar American theme, which Emerson had expressed, which Whitman approached, and Melville also, and which has reappeared often again. It poses what has been called the inescapable dilemma of democracy—to what degree may each single and separate person live as an unencumbered individual and to what extent must he submit to distortions of personality required by society? If Clemens presented it better than most, by endowing it with qualities of myth interwoven with fantasy, realism, satire, and superstition, it was not because his convictions were different. It was because he had mastered a language supple enough to reveal the honest observations of an attractive boy and the ambiguous aspirations of many kinds of men whom he came upon, and also the subtly ominous but compelling spirit which in this book is a river.

Huckleberry Finn's solution of the problem of freedom is direct and unworldly: having tested society, he will have none of it, for civilization finally makes culprits of all men. Huck is a simple boy, with little education and great confidence in omens. One measure of his character is its proneness to deceit which, though not always successful, is instinctive, as if it were a trait shared with other wild things, relating him to nature, in opposition to the tradition-grounded, book-learned imaginative deceptions of Tom Sawyer. The dilatory adventures of Huck and his Negro companion, both natural men enslaved, have even reminded some readers of the more consciously directed explorations in Faulkner's "The Bear" of Ike McCaslin and his part-Negro, part-Indian guide, if only because they suggest more than can easily be explained. American fictions, we are told, are filled with white boys who are influenced by darker companions.

Young Huck had become something of a hero to the inhabitants of the little river village because of his help to Tom Sawyer in tracking down Injun Joe. He had been adopted by the Widow Douglas, washed, dressed in clean clothes, and sent to school. With Tom he shared the incredible wealth of one dollar a day for each of them derived as income from the treasure they had discovered in *The Adventures of Tom Sawyer*. But Huck is not happy. Tom's make-believe is incomprehensible to him. The religion of retribution which Miss Watson, the widow's sister, teaches makes no sense at all. The religion of love which the widow suggests is better, but he will not commit himself. When his scapegrace father returns and carries Huck across the river to a desolate log house, the boy accepts the abduction with relief because, though he fears

his father's beatings and drunken rages, he is freed from restraints of tight clothing, school, and regular hours, and from the preaching and the puzzling tangle of ideas which confuse village life. But the bondage of life with his father chaffs also, so he steals down the river at night to Jackson Island, where he meets the Negro Jim, Miss Watson's slave, who had run away because his Christian owner was going to sell him.

Thus the first eleven chapters of *The Adventures of Huckleberry Finn* tell of adventures on land, with Huck bewildered or miserable or in flight. The next twenty chapters detail adventures on the river or beside the river, in a pattern of withdrawal and return, as Huck and Jim float with their raft toward what they hope will be freedom for both. On the river or its shores many kinds of men are encountered, most of them evil or stupid or mean: cutthroats, murderers, cheats, liars, swindlers, cowards, slave hunters, dupes and hypocrites of every variety. Even the isolation from society which life on a raft might be thought to afford is violated, for malevolence also intrudes there in grotesque guises. Nor is the movement of the great brown river to be trusted. It carries Jim beyond freedom to capture again by respectable, benevolent people whose conscience is untroubled by human slavery.

The final twelve chapters take place again on land. Tom Sawyer once more appears, filled with romance-bred notions of how Jim might be freed. And Huck joins in the laborious nonsense, for he admires Tom, if he does not understand him—often on the river when confronted with crisis or cleverly, he thought, surmounting difficulties, he wished Tom had been there to aid or commend him. But the boys' make-believe at rescue becomes a travesty, for Miss Watson had granted Jim his freedom— he was no longer a slave. The narrative ends hurriedly, as if embarrassed to linger while loose ends were tied. Huck's father is dead—Jim had known that since the first stage of their journey but in kindness had withheld the knowledge. One threat to Huck's freedom is gone, but another remains, for good people again pity the brave pariah boy and offer to adopt him. But Huck will not have it: "I can't stand it," he said. "I been there before."

Much has been made of these last chapters, in condemnation or approval. To some readers they certify Clemens' inability to control plot, to others they reveal a compulsive attraction toward elaborate inventions such as Tom Sawyer loved, but to still others they are exactly right, supplying an inevitable rounding out of tale and theme. And much has been made of the development of Huck's character, his initiation, or his disillusionment with the world and its ways, and especially the change in his attitude toward the Negro Jim whom he finally recognizes as a fellow being, more decent and honest than most of the white people who hold him and his kind in slavery. A few find special charm in the assumption that Huck does not develop in any fundamental sense at all, because as a child of nature he is changeless. But to all, it is Huck and his view of the world which secure for this book its high place among American writings.

For one of the things to notice about *The Adventures of Huckleberry Finn* is that Mark Twain is not the narrator. Huck makes that plain in the first paragraph: Mr. Mark Twain had written of him in *The Adventures of Tom Sawyer,* he said, but this would be his own story. And the first-person narrative which follows allows Huck to misspell and mispronounce words in a manner which could delight admirers of Mark Twain, and to act sometimes in a manner which he thought would have delighted Tom Sawyer, but it is his voice which speaks, authentically and without posturing.

Sometimes Mark Twain's accents are heard, as compellingly humorous as ever, tempting attention away from the boy who, with no humor at all, struggles to make himself understood. But Huck is finally the better witness, infinitely better than Tom Sawyer whose vision is blurred by boyish trickery very different from Huck's protective deceit.

Boyish Tom, however, seems to have been Samuel Clemens' favorite. He wrote of him again in *Tom Sawyer Abroad* in 1894 and in *Tom Sawyer Detective* in 1896, contrived books, imitative of earlier successes, and crowded with imagined adventure rather than experience. Yet, with boyhood behind him, even Tom was not to be envied. Clemens once thought of writing of the two boys as adults who return to their river village. "Huck comes back sixty years old from nobody knows where —and crazy." He imagines himself a boy again and watches everyone who passes to find the face of one of his boyhood friends. Then Tom returns, from years of "wandering in the world," and they talk of old times. "Both are desolate, life has been a failure, all that was lovable, all that was beautiful was under the sod."

But if old times in backcountry America were idyllically best, older times in Europe certainly were not. Far too many of his countrymen, Clemens thought, were beguiled by romantic notions popularized by Sir Walter Scott, which made overgrown Tom Sawyers of them all. Scott was "so juvenile, so artificial, so shoddy," not once "recognizably sincere and in earnest." His characters were "bloodless shams," "milk-and-water humbugs," "squalid shadows." Nor were American romancers, bred under Scott's influence, appreciably better. Among the most persistently anthologized of Clemens' short pieces is the humorously perceptive dissection of "Fenimore Cooper's Literary Offenses" in which he finds that "in the restricted space of two-thirds of a page, Cooper has scored 114 offenses against literary art out of a possible 115." He speaks of Cooper's "crass stupidities," his lack of attention to detail, and his curious box of stage properties which contained such hackneyed devices as the broken twig: "It is a restful chapter in any book of his when somebody doesn't step on a twig and alarm all the reds and whites for two hundred yards around. . . . In fact, the Leather-Stocking Series ought to have been called the Broken Twig Series." Surely, Clemens reasoned, history could be presented without such twaddle.

So Clemens wrote of the adventures of a sturdy, practical nineteenth-century mechanic who is knocked unconscious by a blow on the head and awakes to find himself under a tree near Camelot, amid a landscape "as lovely as a dream and as lonesome as Sunday." But *A Connecticut Yankee in King Arthur's Court*, published in 1889, was double-edged in satirical intention. The Yankee proves himself a better man than the magician Merlin and he overcomes the best of knights in single or multiple combat. He provides what he called "a new deal" for downtrodden common people, transforming Arthur's England into a technically efficient going concern in which gunpowder and mechanical skills triumph over superstition, injustice, and oppression. But "this Yankee of mine," explained Clemens, "is a perfect ignoramus; he is boss of a machine shop, he can build a locomotive or a Colt's revolver, he can put up and run a telegraph line, but he's an ignoramus nevertheless."

A Connecticut Yankee has been called Mark Twain's finest possibility, combining satire, the tall tale, humor, democracy, religion, and the damned human race. Loosely picaresque and brightly anecdotal, it was an attempt, Clemens explained, "to imagine and after a fashion set forth, the hard condition of life for the labor-ing and defenseless poor in bygone times in England, and incidentally contrast those conditions with those under which civil and ecclesiastical pets of privilege and high fortune lived in those times." But what finally emerges from beneath the contrast between Yankee ingenuity and medieval superstition is the portrait of an American. He is unlearned, with "neither the refinement nor the weakness of a college education," but quick-witted and completely, even devastatingly successful. Consciously created or not, it is the image of Samuel Clemens and of many of his friends. And it explains something of the nature of the literature which he and his fellows produced.

Meanwhile Clemens had thought for years that he might write a comic story about Siamese twins, one of whom was good, the other a rake, imagining that sidesplitting situations could result when, for example, the rake drank to excess and the teetotaler twin became intoxicated. Perhaps no idea was more grotesquely unfavorable for fiction, and Clemens never developed it fully, partly because, as he said, "A man who is not born with the novel-writing gift has a troublesome time of it when he tries to write a novel. . . . He has no clear idea of his story; in fact he has no story. He has merely some people in his mind, and an incident or two, also a locality . . . and he trusts that he can plunge those people into those incidents with interesting results."

When he did put shreds of this tale together in *Those Extraordinary Twins*, he pretended jocosely to reveal something of his casual literary method, particularly in dealing with characters who became lost amid the intricacies of plot. One female character named Rowena, for example, began splendidly but failed to keep up: "I must simply give her the grand bounce," he said. "It grieved me to do it, for after associating with her so much I had come to kind of like her after a fashion, notwithstanding she was such an ass, and said such stupid, irritating things, and was so nauseatingly sentimental." So he sent her "out into the back yard after supper to see the fireworks," and "she fell down a well and got drowned." The method seemed perhaps abrupt, "but I thought maybe the reader wouldn't notice it, because I changed the subject right away to something else. Anyway it loosened Rowena up from where she was stuck and got her out of the way, and that was the main thing."

Successful once, he resolved to try the stratagem again with two boys who were no longer useful ("they went out one night to stone a cat and fell down the well and got drowned") and with two supernumerary old ladies ("they went out one night to visit the sick and fell down a well and got drowned"). "I was going to drown some of the others, but I gave up the idea, partly because I believed that if I kept it up I would attract attention, and perhaps sympathize with those people, and partly because it was not a large well and would not hold any more anyway."

This was pure Mark Twain, in mood and language which many people liked best. Part of the fun was that what he said was so true or seemed so true in revelation of the shambling way he really wrote or liked to have people think he wrote stories. And the laugh was on him, or seemed to be, at the same time that it mocked conventional or sentimental writers who had no convenient wells in their back yards. Almost everybody agreed that Mark Twain made most sense when he was funniest. He could double people over with laughter as he pointed to their shortcomings or his own or of those people not quite so clever as they. The laughter was cleansing, but quieting also, for surely such amusing peccadilloes needed no correction.

Those Extraordinary Twins appeared in 1894 as an appendix to *The Tragedy of Pudd'n-head Wilson,* a better story which unaccountably had grown from it. Using the same device of the changeling which had provided the plot for *The Prince and the Pauper,* he told now of two children born on the same day in the Driscoll home at Dawson's Landing, one the son of the white master of the house, the other of a mulatto slave named Roxana, who switched the babies in their cradles so that her tainted son was brought up as Thomas à Becket Driscoll, heir to estates, while Tom, the white boy, became a slave. The bogus Tom grew to be a wastrel, a thief, and finally a murderer. When his mother threatened to expose him if he did not change his ways, he sold her to a slave trader.

The mulatto Roxana dominates the book, sentimentally perhaps, but illustrating again qualities of nobility like those which Huck discovered in the Negro Jim. But her attitudes on race are ambiguous and have puzzled people who would relate them to Huck's attitude or Jim's. When her son proved himself in every respect bad, she told him, "It's de nigger in you, dat's what it is. Thirty-one parts o' you is white, en only one part nigger, en dat po' little one part is yo' soul. 'Taint wuth savin', 'taint wuth totin' out in a shovel en throwin' in de gutter." Perhaps it is a mistake to expect consistency in a writer like Clemens. Or perhaps the greater mistake is to think that any one book of his can be used as commentary on any other.

Potentially more significant is the title character, a lawyer fond of philosophical maxims, but considered queer, a Pudd'nhead, by the rest of the community because he fails to conform to village standards. Among his strange hobbies is that of taking fingerprints, and he had years before made prints of the baby boys before they were changed about. When the trial for the murder which the bogus Tom had committed is held and Italian twins (the remnant of the Siamese twin idea) are blamed for it because they have the misfortune of being foreigners and strangers in the village, Pudd'nhead defends them, dramatically revealing by means of his prints that the true murderer is Roxana's villainous son.

The Tragedy of Pudd'head Wilson is filled with familiar failings, false starts, and rambling excursions. The title makes us wonder why it is Pudd'nhead's tragedy. But it contains excellencies also, of a kind which Sherwood Anderson was to use in writing about village people, and which have earned for it a reputation as "the most extraordinary book in American literature," filled with intolerable insights into evil. Even distorted by drollery, it penetrates toward recognition of social ills not unlike those which William Faulkner was later to probe. Beneath the burlesque which peoples the sleepy village of Dawson's Landing with representatives of decayed gentry bearing such exuberant names as Percy Northumberland Driscoll and Cecil Burleigh Essex runs a vein of satire which allows recognition of these people as ancestors of the Sartorises and Compsons. Pudd'nhead himself might have sat as model for Faulkner's Gavin Stevens, who comments on tradition-ridden life in Yoknapatawpha County. The octoroon who masquerades as white can be thought of as a tentative foreshadowing of Joe Christmas in *Light in August* or Sutpen's half-caste son in *Absalom, Absalom!*

Its failure is literary, the failure of words, not of ideas. Mark Twain is telling a story according to a familiar pattern, incident strung on incident as if they might go on forever. Humor, pathos, sentiment, anger, and burlesque rub shoulders with intimacy bred of long acquaintance. *Pudd'nhead Wilson* is serious in intention, for all its belly-laughs and tears. It faces up to problems made by the venality of man. Seldom is it more plainly evident that

Mark Twain's eyes rarely twinkle when he laughs. A social conscience here is plainly showing. Scorn looks boldly out from behind the burlesque. But the words do not come true, as Huck's words did or as Clemens' did when he remembered apprentice days on the river. He is saying what he wants to say, but in accents which ring false because they speak now as people expected him to speak.

Perhaps it is even possible to suppose that Mark Twain, who was responsible for so much of Clemens' incomparable contemporary success, became finally an encumbrance. As Stephen Crane once said, two hundred pages is a very long stretch in which to be funny. And the stretch is more enervating when the humorist understands that what he writes about is not of itself funny, but only seems so because of the way he writes about it. Man was more likely than not to be mean and do wrong— this even Huck knew, who was not humorous at all. Clemens seems to have known it also, and for a long time.

But Clemens had never kept his observations on the venality of man completely in focus, not even in *The Adventures of Huckleberry Finn*. Whether his seasoning of humor and relaxed excursions into anecdote are uniformly successful or not, they do reveal a distinctively practical approach to literature. I can teach anyone to write a successful story, he once advised a literary friend. All that needs to be done is catch the reader's attention with the first sentence and hold it by whatever means possible to the end. The story flows, he said, as a stream flows, and the storyteller's responsibility is to pilot the reader in safety and comfort through its often meandering channel.

During the twenty years between 1875 and 1894 Samuel Clemens was happiest, and wealthiest, and he wrote his best books. He lived then in luxury among a group of well-to-do litterateurs in Hartford. He lectured, assumed an occasional editorial commitment, and sought attractive books for distribution by his publishing house. His income was breathtaking, probably mounting more than once to a hundred thousand dollars a year. But money went as fast as it came, especially in speculative enterprises like the typesetting machine into which he poured much of his earnings. He dreamed like Colonel Sellers of making millions, as many of his contemporaries did, but by the mid-1890's he was bankrupt. A world tour then brought him increased fame and respect, produced *Following the Equator* in 1897, paid his debts, and provided new financial security. But at sixty, his effective literary career could be considered finished.

While resident in Europe he completed the writing of *Personal Recollections of Joan of Arc*, an account so seriously intended as the expression of a lifelong admiration that it was published in 1896 without Clemen's familiar pseudonym for fear that readers might expect another comic book from Mark Twain and laugh. The innocent faith of the Maid of Orleans represented a quality pitiably absent from modern life. She seemed "easily and by far the most extraordinary person the human race has ever produced." Untrained and without experience, she had within herself a capacity for goodness so pure and successful that it was condemned as heresy by men whom the world named good. But, hampered perhaps by the necessity of keeping close to what he had learned through years of reading of Joan's history, Clemens did not tell her story well, and few readers have agreed with him that it made his best book.

Grief and increasing bitterness had begun to close in upon him, to darken the rest of his life. His daughter Susie died suddenly while her parents were abroad, Mrs. Clemens was distressingly ill for years and then died, and his youngest daughter died suddenly one Christmas Eve. During the fifteen years which preceded his own death in 1910, Clemens lashed out often in anger at a world which had wounded him or reminisced with increasing compulsion on a world which was gone. He could not bear to return to Hartford where he had been happily successful, but moved restlessly from place to place, from residence in New York, to Florence in Italy, to Bermuda for his health, and finally to Stormfield in rural Connecticut, writing furiously at more projects than he could ever complete.

Readers who found Tom Sawyer silly or Huck Finn finally a profitless model were moved to wry approval of *The Man That Corrupted Hadleyburg* which in 1900 presented Clemens' most trenchant testimony to the fundamental dishonesty of man. Piercing the shell of respectability which traditionally had made each small town seem inhabited by kindly hearts and gentle people, he demonstrated how easily even prominently moral citizens could be led beyond temptation when confronted with opportunity to acquire wealth dishonestly but undetected. None were exempt, for every contest was rigged. No more astringent or cynical condemnation of contemporary mores had been issued by an American; even Stephen Crane's *Maggie* eight years before and Theodore Dreiser's *Sister Carrie* of the same year seem tempered with sentiments which Clemens could no longer feel. A year later, in *A Person Sitting in Darkness*, he struck savagely at the militant morality of missionaries, and in *King Leopold's Soliloquy,* in 1905, scornfully denounced pious exploitation of underdeveloped countries. *Extracts from Adam's Diary* in 1904 and *Eve's Diary* in 1906 were whimsical accounts of the dependence of even the first man on the superior management of women, and spoke feelingly by indirection of the loneliness of life without connubial and familial affection.

In 1906 he began to dictate his autobiography, reviewing, often without any defense of humor, incidents and personalities remembered from his rambling career. Some parts were so forthright that he thought they should not be published for a century after his death, but other parts were sent off for immediate serialization in the *North American Review*. Selected portions have been put together for *Mark Twain's Autobiography* in 1924, *Mark Twain in Eruption* in 1940, and *The Autobiography of Mark Twain* in 1959, each adding its effective extension to the image of a favorite American, who grumbled and growled, who smoked too much and cadged Scotch whiskey from his wealthy friends, but who had been places and who was known and loved all over the world.

In 1906 he also issued privately and anonymously what he called his "wicked book," *What Is Man?* which contains his most astringent diagnosis of man as a mechanism, the plaything of chance, his brain "so constructed that it can originate nothing." Man is a chameleon who "by the law of his nature . . . takes on the color of the place of his resort. The influences about him create his preferences, his aversions, his politics, his taste, his morality, his religion." All that he knows, all that he does, is determined by one inexorable law: "From his cradle to his grave a man never does a single thing which has any first and foremost object but one—to secure peace of mind, spiritual comfort, for himself." He is what he is, and nothing will change him. Self-seeking, self-admiring, he babbles of free will and love and compassion, which are fictions made to ensure his satisfaction with himself. "When-

ever you read of a self-sacrificing act or hear of one, or of a duty done for duty's sake, take it to pieces and look for the real motive. It's always there."

The book is not wicked, but it is tired, like the posthumous *Letters from the Earth*. Its words speak forthrightly, despairingly, echoing the words of other men who testified to man's slavery to forces beyond himself. They are palliative as well as condemnatory, as if their writer were explaining to himself as much as to other men why it was necessary for all men to do what he and they perforce had done. Resolution is not lacking, nor is anger. On its level, the book argues well. It presents its case. What is no longer there is the power of the inevitable word which is in so intimate a relation to the thing of which it speaks that meaning spills over to intimations which ordinary words can never reach. Once Clemens' words had clung thus close to things, but now they gestured and had less to say.

Six months before his death Clemens released an *Extract from Captain Stormfield's Visit to Heaven*, a favorite tale over which he had been puttering for many years. In it almost every contrivance of humor, sentiment, or dissection of human frailty that Mark Twain had ever used was expended again on the adventures of a crusty, matter-of-fact mariner who went flashing through the air like a bird toward paradise, racing a comet on the way as steamboat pilots used to race on the Mississippi. He has difficulty in finding wings that fit or a harp that suits him. He seeks long before finding the proper resting place for people from a planet so little valued by angels that they call it the Wart. He has trouble conversing with people who speak ridiculous languages, tumbles terribly in learning to fly, is surprised to find Jews and Moslems in heaven, and pleased that Shakespeare is placed "away down there below shoe-makers and horse-dealers and knife-grinders" to make room for an unknown tailor from Tennessee who "wrote poetry that Homer and Shakespeare couldn't begin to come up to; but nobody would print it, nobody read it but his neighbors, and they laughed at it." Recognition of wisdom masked by such burlesque is usually considered a test of an admirer of Mark Twain.

As a philosophical humorist he spoke on two levels, now one, now the other, seldom blending them to unity of tone or consistency of insight. Henry Nash Smith is correct in describing Mark Twain's popularity as a result of his exploitation of the comic contrast between things as they might be and things as they are. But Louis Budd is also correct in discovering Clemens neither original nor objective as a social philosopher. Convictions he had in plenty, and courage also; but he had a place to preserve and boyhood visions to sustain. His miseries were subtly compounded and his sense of sin extended as young dreams exploded to recriminatory nightmares at last.

No subtlety of interpretation is required for recognition of the bleak despair of Clemens' posthumous *The Mysterious Stranger*. The scene is Austria in 1590, where in the village of Eseldorf, a paradise for play like that which Tom and Huck had known, three boys are joined by a visiting angel, namesake and nephew of the fallen Satan. He entertains them with miracles, making little creatures of clay, breathing life into them, and then mashing them down as if they were flies. It seems cruel to the boys, but Satan explains that it was not cruel, only capricious and, as far as man could understand, ordained. Crippled by moral sense, in bondage to circumstance, his vision distorted by illusion, man pampers himself with ideals which exist only when he imagines them. What an ass he is! How hysterically mad are his

expectations: "No sane man can be happy, for to him life is real, and he sees what a fearful thing it is," for "there is no God, no universe, no human race, no earthly life, no heaven, no hell. It is all a dream—a grotesque and foolish dream. Nothing exists," said the angel, "but you. And you are but a *thought*—a vagrant thought, a useless thought, a homeless thought, wandering forlorn among the empty eternities."

Nothing remains of the Widow Douglas' reliance on the religion of love or Huck's possibility of escape from the world through flight. Again Clemens speaks, as he had in 1885, of ideas which unsettled many people of his time, but now others voiced them better than he, for some magic of language has disappeared from these late sputtering insights of anger and despair. The angel Satan speaks, but the words are Clemens', in reprimand as much to himself as to those who read him: "You have a mongrel sense of humor, nothing more," he charged; "you see the comic side of a thousand low-grade and trivial things—broad incongruities, mainly; grotesqueries, absurdities, evokers of the horse-laugh." But the "ten thousand high-grade comicalities" made by the juvenilities of man are sealed from your dull visions. "Will a day come when the race will detect these juvenilities and laugh at them—and by laughing destroy them?" In a perfect world there is no room for laughter, but this world is not perfect, and man in his poverty "has unquestionably one really effective weapon—laughter. Power, money, persuasion, supplication, persecution—these can lift at a colossal humbug—push it a little—weaken it a little, century by century; but only laughter can blow it to rags and atoms at a blast."

"Humor," Mark Twain once wrote when in another mood, "is only a fragrance, a decoration." If it is really to succeed in survival, it must surreptitiously teach and preach. Perhaps that is why so sober an admirer as James T. Farrell sees in Huck and Tom "two accusing fingers pointing down the decades of America's history," relentlessly questioning why it is in America, or perhaps anywhere else, that a man so rarely becomes what the boy gave promise of becoming. Samuel Clemens did see the world as a boy sees it, in its infinitude of possibilities for freedom and fun and in its darkened depths of disillusionment. And, like a boy, when embarrassed he laughed; when tentatively serious he laughed first, so that the responding laugh could be with, not at, him; even in tantrum, he seemed somehow comic, an object which in brighter spirits he might have ridiculed. "From a boyhood idyll of the good life to a boy's criticism of that life," says Wright Morris in accusation, "is the natural range and habitat of the American mind." Mark Twain's charm of innocence did isolate him from maturity. What he achieved artlessly so well that he invented a theory of storytelling art to explain it was received with riotous applause by his countrymen. With so natural a talent why should he then not attempt more? Clemens' inability to respond to that question explains much of Mark Twain and the milieu which made him possible. But it fails to explain all, or even what is most important.

Samuel Clemens created or became Mark Twain who boundlessly created laughter, but he was more than a buffoon. As comic realist he applies for place beside Laurence Sterne, Dickens, Joyce, Faulkner, and Camus, for his eyes like theirs have seen beyond locality to qualities which men universally, sometimes shamefully, share. To remember him only as a creator of boyhood adventure or as a relic of an American frontier or the voice of native idiosyncrasy is to do him disservice. His accomplishment finally contradicts his think-

ing, thus certifying his literary achievement. Much that is excellent in American literature *did* begin with him, and Lionel Trilling is correct when he says "that almost every contemporary American writer who deals conscientiously with the problem and possibilities of prose must feel, directly or indirectly, the influence of . . . [his] style which escapes the fixity of the printed page, that sounds in our ears with the immediacy of the heard voice, the very voice of unpretentious truth."

But he was anticipated also, ten years before his first triumphant entry to public notice, by another native observer who admitted men "victims of illusion" and life "a succession of dreams." Samuel Clemens, Mississippi pilot, had not yet become Mark Twain but Emerson had someone much like him in mind when he described "a humorist who in a good deal of rattle had a grain or two of sense. He shocked the company by maintaining that the attributes of God were two,—power and risibility, and that it was the duty of every pious man to keep up the comedy."

Perhaps it was a basic lack of piety in the sense of dedication to the demands of literature ("and all that bosh") which deprived Samuel Clemens of an ability consistently to keep up the comedy. Laughter is not joy, funny fellows are notoriously prone to tears, and the comic view has never sustained man's highest vision of himself or his possibilities because, as Baudelaire once said, the comic is imitation, not creation. But his countrymen seldom chide Mark Twain for what he is not; what he was is good enough, and plenty. It is probably true that the sense of the comic, the ability to laugh, is in him who laughs, and not in the object which excites his laughter. If the thousand low-grade and trivial things which quickened mirth among his countrymen were more often displayed than Samuel Clemens' occasional genuine and high-grade comicalities, the fault was not his alone, and he is not to be blamed for his anger, except that it came too late, when his words were tired. He shocked his countrymen by explaining what they were, and they laughed. Their continuing laughter measures his genius and their own, and the limitations they have shared together.

Selected Bibliography

The most complete edition is *Mark Twain's Works*, 37 volumes (New York: Harper, 1929). See also Merle Johnson, *A Bibliography of Mark Twain* (New York: Harper, 1935), and E. H. Long, *Mark Twain Handbook* (New York: Hendricks House, 1957), which list important critical articles.

PRINCIPAL WORKS OF MARK TWAIN

The Innocents Abroad; or, The New Pilgrim's Progress. Hartford, Conn.: American Publishing Co., 1869.

Roughing It. Hartford, Conn.: American Publishing Co., 1872.

The Gilded Age (with C. D. Warner). Hartford, Conn.: American Publishing Co., 1874.

The Adventures of Tom Sawyer. Hartford, Conn.: American Publishing Co., 1876.

A Tramp Abroad. Hartford, Conn.: American Publishing Co., 1880.

The Prince and the Pauper. Boston: Osgood, 1882.

Life on the Mississippi. Boston: Osgood, 1883.

The Adventures of Huckleberry Finn. New York: Webster, 1885.

A Connecticut Yankee in King Arthur's Court. New York: Webster, 1889.

The Tragedy of Pudd'nhead Wilson. Hartford, Conn.: American Publishing Co., 1894.

Personal Recollections of Joan of Arc. New York: Harper, 1896.

Following the Equator. Hartford, Conn.: American Publishing Co., 1897.

The Man That Corrupted Hadleyburg and Other Stories and Essays. New York: Harper, 1900.

Extract from Captain Stormfield's Visit to Heaven. New York: Harper, 1909.

The Mysterious Stranger. New York: Harper, 1916.

Mark Twain's Autobiography, edited by A. B. Paine. New York: Harper, 1924.

Mark Twain's Letters from the Sandwich Islands, edited by G. Ezra Dane. Palo Alto, Calif.: Stanford University Press, 1938.

Mark Twain's Travels with Mr. Brown, edited by G. Ezra Dane. New York: Knopf, 1940.

Mark Twain in Eruption, edited by Bernard De Voto. New York: Harper, 1940.

The Autobiography of Mark Twain, edited by Charles Neider. New York: Harper, 1959.

Mark Twain–Howells Letters, edited by H. N. Smith and W. M. Gibson. Cambridge, Mass.: Belknap Press, 1960.

Mark Twain's Letters to Mary, edited with commentary by Lewis Leary. New York: Columbia University Press, 1961.

Mark Twain: Letters from Earth, edited by Bernard De Voto, with a preface by Henry Nash Smith. New York and Evanston: Harper and Row, 1962.

Mark Twain's Letters to His Publishers, 1867–1894, edited with an introduction by Hamlin Hill. Berkeley and Los Angeles: University of California Press, 1967.

Mark Twain's Correspondence with Henry Huttleston Rogers, 1893–1909, edited with an introduction by Lewis Leary. Berkeley and Los Angeles: University of California Press, 1964.

Mark Twain's Hannibal, Huck & Tom, edited with an introduction by Walter Blair. Berkeley and Los Angeles: University of California Press, 1969.

CRITICAL AND BIOGRAPHICAL STUDIES

Andrews, Kenneth R. *Nook Farm: Mark Twain's Hartford Circle.* Cambridge, Mass.: Harvard University Press, 1950.

Asselineau, Roger. *The Literary Reputation of Mark Twain.* Paris: Libraire Marcel Didier, 1954.

Bellamy, Gladys C. *Mark Twain as a Literary Artist*. Norman: University of Oklahoma Press, 1950.

Benson, Ivan. *Mark Twain's Western Years*. Palo Alto, Calif.: Stanford University Press, 1938.

Blair, Walter. *Mark Twain and Huck Finn*. Berkeley: University of California Press, 1960.

Branch, Edgar M. *The Literary Apprenticeship of Mark Twain*. Urbana: University of Illinois Press, 1950.

Brashear, M. M. *Mark Twain, Son of Missouri*. Chapel Hill: University of North Carolina Press, 1934.

Brooks, Van Wyck. *The Ordeal of Mark Twain*. Revised edition. New York: Dutton, 1933.

Budd, Louis J. *Mark Twain: Social Philosopher*. Bloomington: University of Indiana Press, 1962.

Clemens, Clara. *My Father, Mark Twain*. New York: Harper, 1931.

Cox, James M. *Mark Twain: The Fate of Humor*. Princeton, N.J.: Princeton University Press, 1966.

De Voto, Bernard. *Mark Twain at Work*. Cambridge, Mass.: Harvard University Press, 1942.

———. *Mark Twain's America*. Boston: Little, Brown, 1935.

Eliot, T. S. Introduction to *The Adventures of Huckleberry Finn*. New York: Chanticleer Press, 1950.

Ferguson, J. DeLancey. *Mark Twain: Man and Legend*. Indianapolis: Bobbs-Merrill, 1943.

Geismar, Maxwell. *Mark Twain: An American Prophet*. Boston: Houghton Mifflin, 1970.

Hill, Hamlin. *Mark Twain and Elisha Bliss*. Columbia: University of Missouri Press, 1964.

Howells, William Dean. *My Mark Twain*. New York: Harper, 1910.

Kaplan, Justin. *Mr. Clemens and Mark Twain*. New York: Simon and Schuster, 1966.

Krause, Sydney J. *Mark Twain as Critic*. Baltimore: Johns Hopkins Press, 1967.

Leary, Lewis. *Mark Twain's Wound*. New York: Crowell, 1962.

Liljegren, S. B. *The Revolt against Romanticism in American Literature as Evidenced in the Works of S. L. Clemens*. Upsala: Lundequistska Bokhandeln, 1945.

Lynn, Kenneth S. *Mark Twain and Southwestern Humor*. Boston: Atlantic-Little, Brown, 1960.

Paine, Albert Bigelow. *Mark Twain: A Biography*. Revised edition in 2 volumes. New York: Harper, 1935.

Schönemann, Friedrich. *Mark Twain als literarische Persönlichkeit*. Berlin: Verlag der Frommananschen Buchhandlung, Walter Biedermann, 1925.

Scott, Arthur L., ed. *Mark Twain: Selected Criticism*. Dallas: Southern Methodist University Press, 1955.

Smith, Henry Nash. *Mark Twain: The Development of a Writer*. Cambridge, Mass.: Belknap Press of Harvard University Press, 1962.

Trilling, Lionel. Introduction to *The Adventures of Huckleberry Finn*. New York: Rinehart, 1948.

Tuckey, John S. *Mark Twain and Little Satan: The Writing of The Mysterious Stranger*. West Lafayette, Ind.: Purdue University Studies, 1963.

Wagenknecht, Edward. *Mark Twain: The Man and His Work*. New Haven, Conn.: Yale University Press, 1935.

Wecter, Dixon. *Sam Clemens of Hannibal*. Boston: Houghton Mifflin, 1952.

—LEWIS LEARY

John Updike

1932-

BLESSED WITH multiple talents, prolific in their expression, John Updike is doubtless a prodigy. At a stage when most young writers have scarcely identified their strengths, Updike was already a seasoned professional. Soon after graduating from Harvard, at twenty-two, he sold his first story to the *New Yorker*, joining its staff for two years and remaining a steady contributor thereafter.

In 1971, when he published *Rabbit Redux*, Updike was the author of five other novels (*The Poorhouse Fair*, 1959; *Rabbit, Run*, 1960; *The Centaur*, 1963; *Of the Farm*, 1965; *Couples*, 1968). In addition, he had published over eighty stories, enough to fill four volumes (*The Same Door*, 1959; *Pigeon Feathers*, 1962; *The Music School*, 1966; *Bech: A Book*, 1970), as well as numerous reviews, essays, parodies, sketches (most of which are collected in *Assorted Prose*, 1965), and three volumes of verse (*The Carpentered Hen*, 1958; *Telephone Poles*, 1963; *Midpoint and Other Poems*, 1969). There are, moreover, several works for children, an opera libretto, and a pageant Updike wrote for Ipswich's 1968 celebration of its seventeenth-century day. In that year, the author was thirty-six.

Prodigious as are the bare facts of his output, his proficiency is more impressive. Whatever their ultimate critical verdict, few judges deny Updike's expertise. Though occasionally drawing attention to itself, his prose is always precise and supple, equally adapted to fine emotional nuance and the painterly objectivity with which he limns the external world. In large-scale narrative, Updike's craft sometimes falters, but it serves him unerringly in forms as different as the light-verse jingle and the critical essay, the dramatized meditation and that quick glimpse of character or way of life that constitutes a modern story.

Of this last form, he is a master. In one phrase, he can take us to the heart of a character, like the pathetic homosexual in "At a Bar in Charlotte Amalie" (*The Music School*), whose "lips . . . were too quick, snapping in and out with a grin as if he were trying to occupy both sides of his situation, being both the shameless clown and the aloof, if amused, onlooker." Or he can make a single event telling, as in "The Rescue" (*The Music School*), where a young wife, doubtful of her husband's fidelity, is convinced of his innocence by encountering an image of loneliness, spread-eagled on a ski slope. Simply lucid, wry in its implication, such a tale is also palpable, down to the grass widow's red fingernails and the blind self-concern, emblem of her condition, with which she appropriates the heroine's last cigarette.

At his best, Updike is the detailed realist, filling his stories with facts that guarantee belief. If he must prove that some characters in "The Bulgarian Poetess" (*The Music School*) are literary experts, he inserts the right information as easily as he supplies, in *Couples*, a disquisition on photosynthesis for Ken Whitman or an architectural restoration for Piet Hanema. Ours is a period dominated by apocalyptists destroying fabricated worlds and by symbolists who take off for nowhere from nothing; but Updike offers the novel's traditional pleasures: through his insight he brings freshness to the familiar, while through his concreteness he makes familiar what was previously unknown.

In his verse, however, he frequently exploits the familiar (animals, artifacts, mundane occupations) as an occasion to display his talent for comic rhyme, or toys with the unknown by ridiculous peculiar names or by spinning fantasies based on odd news clippings. Sometimes, Updike can be witty, as in the pedagogic use to which he puts an apple:

My child, take heart: the fruit that undid Man
Brought out as well the best in Paul Cézanne.

Too often, he is merely cute.

Lacking sufficient gaiety or antic imagination, Updike's verse affords few smiles. When, occasionally, he attempts serious poetry (particularly in *Telephone Poles),* it is scarcely more evocative. One exception is the passionate "Seven Stanzas at Easter." Sharply phrased, this poem argues against the metaphoric conception of religious ritual and helps to explain Updike's preference for literal believers, however destructive, over men who want to make dogma comfortable.

According to the author, if even his lightest verse goes well, it gives him "a pleasure and satisfaction not lower than in any other form of literary activity." However, readers may deplore his refusal to withhold from publication work that displays little besides this delight in his technique.

Yet even in the abyss of insignificance he may lodge a nugget of perception, like this fashion note in an otherwise negligible Christmas sketch: "this year's high heels do not jounce the face but wobble the ankles, so that women walking have the tremulous radiance of burning candles as, step by step, they quiver in and out of balance." Wary of missing such pleasures, we read on; but should we forgive Updike's distributing his genius rather than distilling it for the exclusive production of major works?

In a caustic review of James Agee's letters to Father Flye, Updike hints at an answer. According to friends, Agee was destroyed by mass-media seductions that caused him to bury his talent in the anonymous sands of *Time*. But, as Updike argues, "a culture is enhanced, rather than disgraced, when men of talent and passion undertake anonymous and secondary tasks. Excellence in the great things is built upon excellence in the small; Agee's undoing was not his professionalism but his blind, despairing belief in an ideal amateurism."

Disapproving of so austere an ideal ("I would write ads for deodorants or labels for catsup bottles if I had to"), Updike can argue that his trivial or popular work has cultural value precisely because he is skilled. Moreover, despite early poverty, his youthful marriage, and a growing family, Updike did not, like many of his colleagues, seek a buffer against insecurity through teaching, editing, or other permanent full-time jobs.

Some of his "secondary tasks" are included in *Assorted Prose*: slight parodies, like one purporting to satirize a golf manual by offering minute information on how to drink from a cup, or several of those "Talk of the Town" notes from the *New Yorker* that are the literary equivalent of marzipan. But the rest of the volume is more substantial, containing brilliant memoirs, book reviews, and a masterpiece of sports writing (on Ted Williams) that shows the flexibility Updike's professionalism makes possible.

Of particular interest are the reviews. In addition to proving Updike an erudite, discerning judge of other men's work, they frequently contain valuable reflections of his own. Thus, in a piece on Denis de Rougemont, Updike formulates the relationship between two of his favorite subjects ("Our fundamental anxiety is that we do not exist—or will cease to exist. Only in being loved do we find external corroboration of the supremely high valuation each ego secretly assigns itself"), while in defending Salinger, he explains his own preoccupation with those largely spiritual anxieties that afflict the middle class: ". . . Salinger's conviction that our inner lives greatly matter peculiarly qualifies him to sing of an America where, for most of us, there seems little to do but to feel. Introversion, perhaps, has been forced upon history; an age of nuance, of ambiguous gestures and psychological jockeying on a national and private scale, is upon us, and Salinger's intense attention to gesture and intonation help make him . . . a uniquely pertinent literary artist."

Besides depicting subjective experience through nuance in speech and gesture, Updike and Salinger share other characteristics. Both are obsessed with life's transiency and the power of love to act as antidote or counterforce; both are nostalgic about youth, with its honesty and illusions of permanence; and both deal with relationships that are fundamentally private.

Yet Salinger is more sentimental than Updike in presenting his subjects and themes. Though Salinger's characters may enter a never-never land, like that of the Glass family, where everyone loves everyone and not even death dissolves bonds, Updike's heroes often discover that intimacy involves disappointment, that love is itself transitory, and that the search for permanence may hinder life. In his review of *Franny and Zooey*, Updike criticizes Salinger for dividing the world into sheep (children or innocents) and goats (adults or worldlings); in Updike's fiction, contrasts are less morally stark.

Indeed, in the strict sense, Updike isn't a moralist. Though his characters may raise moral questions, Updike avoids unequivocal answers. One cannot extrapolate from his fiction a code of values, as one can, for example, derive the value of sensitivity from Salinger, sympathy from Malamud, courage from Hemingway. With the partial exception of George Caldwell in *The Centaur*, Updike's characters are likely to be true or false to themselves, more or less in touch with reality, rather than good or bad.

Nor is Updike primarily concerned to describe place or analyze culture. Much of his work is laid in a single Pennsylvania town, but Olinger could be any small community; and its mores, sparsely presented, have no crucial effect on the inhabitants. Though his work expresses hostility to modern America, his charges are much less specific than those of writers like Styron or Mailer. Even in *Couples*, which treats contemporary suburbia, Updike uses place and historical moment mostly as a backdrop against which his characters interact.

But though he presents all interaction as it is perceived by the participants, Updike is also not a psychologist. Seldom does he take us into a character's mind; if he does, it is never to explore the anatomy but only to establish the perception. Often, his characters have troubled souls, and Updike himself is deeply concerned with matters of religion; but his people don't experience breakdowns or conversions, as people do in Salinger, and Updike's religious ideas can't be easily labeled, as can those of Flannery O'Connor.

As Updike says in his *Paris Review* interview: "narratives should not be *primarily* packages for psychological insights, though they can contain them, like raisins in buns. But the substance is the dough, which feeds the story-telling appetite, the appetite for motion, for suspense, for resolution. . . . Insights of all kinds are welcome; but no wisdom will substitute for an instinct for action . . ." If this term is understood to include inner and outer territory, we can say that Updike does concentrate on action, rather than on judgment or analysis. Since he is a serious writer, his action always has a point; but establishing the point is usually less important to him than creating the action. More exactly, he trusts that action, if described truthfully enough, will establish its own point, make us aware of some possibility inherent in human behavior. And since he believes that human behavior is always ambiguous, Updike wants his stories to reflect this fact.

Because he treats ordinary people doing usual things and also avoids issuing injunctions or underlining his ideas, Updike is simultaneously palpable and elusive. Therefore, critics complain that he writes beautifully but has nothing to say, neglecting to recall that, in fiction, saying can be showing. In "The Sea's Green Sameness" (*New World Writing*, 1960), Updike openly declares his confidence that reality can come to us through language: "All I expect is that once into my blindly spun web of words the thing itself will break: make an entry and an account of itself."

Because of this aesthetic program, Updike's fiction is most usefully comprehended when grouped not according to theme, setting, or character, but according to subject: the thing itself. General notions about the past, love, and faith recur in all his work, as do settings and character types; with reference to subject, his fiction may be divided into relatively discrete halves. More self-contained is the group comprising two novels, *The Centaur* and *Of the Farm*, as well as several stories that concern his own family, despite a change of names. In the second group (including his first two novels and *Couples*), Updike treats more varied relationships (between husbands and wives, young and old, rebels and conformists).

Within each group there are successes and failures irrespective of the author's age at composition. Sometimes Updike selects an important situation, such as the family conflict in *Of the Farm*, and treats it fully, with precision. Sometimes, as in certain short stories, he selects an episode so trivial that his technique seems merely willful. On the other hand, he occasionally inflates his subjects with gimmicks seemingly forbidden by his general aesthetic mode—*The Centaur* is a good example of this defect.

Therefore, since Updike's career does not fall into phases—does not break into stylistic halves, like Bellow's, or into ideological halves like Hemingway's—the following survey is not chronological. Rather, the autobiographical novels and stories are discussed as a group, followed by the fiction of wider range. And since Updike's artistic development is also unsteady—unlike, say, that of Faulkner, with his "great years" and subsequent decline—the arrangement in each group is qualitative rather than temporal. Which also reminds us that Updike has only reached the midpoint of his career, a career, in competence and regularity of performance, that already promises to break the dominant pattern of American literature, whose writers peak early and then fall to feeble self-imitation.

In Updike's preface to the Vintage collection of his favorite Olinger stories, he warns his readers not to simply equate fact and fancy, but by comparing Updike's interviews with his tales, we learn that much of his fiction is thinly disguised autobiography. (In the case of "The Lucid Eye in Silver Town," a sketch first published as a story was subsequently included among the memoirs of *Assorted Prose*.) Whether we read them in *The Centaur* or in "The Dogwood Tree" (a boyhood reminiscence), whether the hero is called Allen Dow, Clyde Behn, or John Updike, the facts are always the same. The "genius" of his mother, Updike has written, "was to give people closest to her mythic immensity." Similarly, Updike uses his family to construct a myth of parents and children.

Here is the myth and its basis in fact:

John Updike was born in 1932 in a poor Pennsylvania Dutch community named Shillington, but rechristened in his fiction to mirror an attitude (O-linger). Well educated, driven by ambition, his mother apparently fails to share Updike's fondness for the town. Forced by poverty to move to the farm belonging to Updike's grandparents, Mrs. Updike seems to have welcomed the change because it kept her son from declining into Shillington mediocrity; but (in his fiction at any rate) Updike represents his father as deploring the shift. A high-school math teacher, still remembered for his unorthodox pedagogy and his devotion to students, Wesley Updike stands, in Updike's stories, for service to others as definitively as Linda Grace Hoyer (the mother's *nom de plume* for the stories she herself writes for the *New Yorker*) stands for vigorous self-expression.

Outwardly, the mother's influence seems predominant. "Consciousness of a special destiny made me both arrogant and shy," Updike's surrogate confesses at the beginning of "Flight"; and the author's early career did forecast a bright future. Elected both class president and editor of his high-school paper, Updike also distinguished himself at Harvard (which his mother recommended because of its alumni record of successful writers): he graduated *summa cum laude*, after having spent four years as the *Lampoon's* leading wit.

For both the author and his characters, however, achievement is only part of the story. In Updike's autobiographical fiction, the gifted, sensitive young men are usually isolated from their peers and deficient in health (Updike himself failed his army induction physical because of allergies, and one friend has testified to his compulsive need for attention). Moreover, because of their mothers' fierce ambition, Updike's heroes are often made to regard love of other women as a betrayal both of filial loyalty and of their own promise.

Nevertheless, they do marry (as Updike did after his junior year), but frequently lead discontented lives. However, their author's marriage, as he indicates in the *Paris Review*, is a working partnership; and after a brief fling at art school (the Ruskin School of Drawing and Fine Art in London, which he attended on a scholarship), he began a phenomenally successful career. Updike has said that his father's Depression-bred fear of poverty underlies his own workmanlike habits; we may conjecture that they are also supported by his mother's drive.

Of Updike's story collections, *Pigeon Feathers* is most completely devoted to recapturing this past. But though Updike employs an epigraph from Kafka on the gradual loss of the self's sense of history, many of his autobiographical tales belie Kafka's warning that we will "scrape the very skin from" our bodies in the act of recollection. Although stories like "The Alligators" (from this volume) or "The Happiest I've Been" (from *The Same Door*) are vivid and engaging, they are too like family snapshots, of which Updike is admittedly a devoted viewer.

In *The Music School*, Updike includes more of these valentines, but from a piece like "In Football Season" we infer that even he suspects them of being too slight. Thus, he forces significance. "Do you remember a fragrance girls acquire in autumn?" the story begins; but this is how it ends: "Girls walk by me carrying their invisible bouquets from fields still steeped in grace, and I look up in the manner of one who follows with his eyes the passage of a hearse, and remembers what pierces him." This terminal infusion of spiritual dread (shattering a light meditation on lost pleasure) is incongruous, like a crash of cymbals at the end of a ballad.

In other pieces Updike attempts meaning through accretion. Ostensibly experiments, "The Blessed Man of Boston, My Grandmother's Thimble, and Fanning Island" and "Packed Dirt, Churchgoing, a Dying Cat, a Traded Car" (both from *Pigeon Feathers*), show instead their author's laziness. Trying to bring illumination from anecdotal snippets merely by juxtaposing them, Updike makes all too pertinent his plaintive request for divine aid ("O Lord, bless these poor paragraphs, that would do in their vile ignorance Your work of resurrection").

The Centaur, Updike's third novel and his most ambitious exercise in personal nostalgia, is also an experimental work in which divinity is asked to accomplish what might better have been left to the author. Attempting to celebrate his father, Updike employs a mythological parallel to dignify the hero and unify the plot. Instead, the device proves pretentious and con-

fusing. Though no Updike novel has received a more discordant and evasive press, *The Centaur* won the National Book Award; and although its form contradicts Updike's normal procedure, this is the author's favorite work ("the one simultaneously most adventurous and authoritative, the one that, for all its antics, cheated least, and delivered its goods most squarely"). Both facts fit an anomalous production.

On its realistic level, however, *The Centaur* is plain enough in purpose and action, though neither is sufficient for a long novel, much less one so baroque. After a brilliant quasi-literal, quasi-mythical chapter (*The Centaur's* one successful experiment), we learn that the book is Peter Caldwell's recollection of dear dead days in Olinger. As we discover from a later chapter, Caldwell is currently a "second-rate abstract expressionist living in an East Twenty-third Street loft with a Negro mistress." Hoping to make peace with a present so much less brilliant than he had anticipated, Peter tries to use sex to assuage his disappointment. But his father's memory blocks this design, as he meditates, "I miss . . . in the late afternoons, the sudden white laughter that like heat lightning bursts in an atmosphere where souls are trying to serve the impossible." The purpose of the preceding chapters is to show that "for all his mourning" this was the atmosphere in which Peter's father moved.

Ludicrous and heroic, George Caldwell is the novel's principal triumph. Science instructor at Olinger High, Caldwell thinks himself a failure, though he is such a success that, years after they have studied with him, people still recall his crucial effect on their lives. Foolishly self-deprecating, his unorthodox methods yield brilliant results. Faced with an unruly bunch of dumb pupils, he unveils creation by turning geological epochs into hours on the clock. Needing to explain the decimal system, he scoops up a pile of snow (as did Wesley Updike himself), and hurls a frigid decimal point at the blackboard. Pretending to hate his students, Caldwell in effect gives them his life—suffering ingratitude, administrative interference, and his wife's dissatisfaction with a teacher's salary—so as to minister to the mind and heart of youth. To a dumb girl tormented by parental pressure, Caldwell gives advance information on a quiz. When a diver he has coached tries but fails in competition, Caldwell alone applauds. Similarly, though he insists he is useless as a father, George both protects Peter's body and nurtures his soul.

But with youth's harsh simplicity, Peter, who is embarrassed by the man's eccentricities, frequently ignores Caldwell's marvelous selflessness. Thus, when they pick up a hitchhiker on the way to school, Peter is furious that Caldwell allows the bum to steal the new pair of gloves he had purchased for his father but Caldwell had found too good to wear. Accosted by a drunk, when their car breaks down and they are forced to seek a night's lodging, the father reacts tolerantly when the drunk tries to extort money by pretending that Caldwell is a designing pederast, but Peter finds the hilarious episode entirely sordid. In fact, the son is jealous of all who receive his father's affection at the same time that he realizes his own stature is but a reflection of their gratitude toward the older man: "being Caldwell's son lifted me from the faceless mass of younger children and made me, on my father's strength alone, exist in the eyes of these Titans."

Caldwell's complexity and Peter's ambivalence toward him provide *The Centaur* with richly lifelike material. Though it doesn't quite make a plot (moving dizzily instead through illustrative tableaux), it nevertheless achieves a sort of climax. Toward the end of the book, when they are stalled in a snowstorm and

Caldwell marvels at another driver who passes without offering help, Peter pronounces a tribute to George: " '. . . there's nobody else like you, Daddy. There's nobody else like you in the world.' "

Unfortunately, this climax occurs without adequate preparation; so much of the novel deflects attention from the relationship between father and son that we don't fully comprehend or anticipate Peter's sudden inspiration. Rather too much is heard concerning Peter's feelings toward Mrs. Caldwell and of his emerging independence through a young girl's love. This too reaches a climax, but one that is embarrassingly sentimental: when Peter's sweetheart conquers his shame by accepting the sores that inspired it. Other material from Updike's Olinger stories, concerning mother and grandparents, also clutters the book, as does nostalgic recall of schooldays. Characters are introduced and dropped; relationships, like that between the Hummels, are fully established but never resolved. Characteristically well observed, these items confuse a novel already verging on obscurity.

The obscurity is caused by Updike's decision to wrap his childhood memories in the august mantel of myth. Thus Caldwell is also Chiron, noblest of the centaurs, mythological instructors of youth. Unfortunately, mythical and actual have only tenuous links. Whereas Chiron was wounded by an arrow during the centaurs' battle at a marriage feast, Caldwell is shot by a tangible form of his students' animosity. For the myth to work, Peter should be Prometheus, but he is surely no hero. Though his psoriasis is compared to birdmarks and he complains of being chained to a rock, the disease which "females transmitted . . . to their children" is too plausibly understood as a psychosomatic symptom of maternal domination, and the rock is apparently the maternal power that alienates Peter from his peers.

Most serious, it is difficult to equate the end of the myth with the end of the novel. Whereas Chiron atoned for Prometheus' theft of fire by sacrificing his own life, Caldwell does not die literally. Rather, he evidently accepts the idea of death because he "discover[s] that in giving his life to others he enter[s] a total freedom." But if this is so, in what sense does the discovery save Peter? As Updike has declared, we are to understand that Caldwell will now go on enduring mortal doubt and suffering, but in that case he is merely consenting to work for his family—a laudable decision, but scarcely mythmaking.

Intended, in large part, to vouch for his father's greatness, the myth seems like special pleading. More annoyingly, it neither aids comprehension nor establishes tone. Supplying an index at his "wife's suggestion," Updike coyly confesses that "not all characters have a stable referent." Some stable referents are rather sophomoric. Thus Medusa is a study-hall proctress with pencils in her hair, and Caldwell is always making feeble jokes about the mythological parallel (for example, to a janitor: " 'Don't think I don't appreciate what a job it is to keep this stockyard clean. It's the Augean stable every day of the week.' ").

Where, at last, does the mythology come from? Since we are told that the book is Peter's reminiscence, it might come from him; why then did Updike make him a painter rather than a writer? In the latter case, we could have agreed (with Updike's most generous critics) that the myth offers literary proof of Peter's final respect for his father. As things stand, Updike seems all too justified when, in the unedited copy for his *Paris Review* interview, he calls the novel a "gag."

Despite the first chapter, memorable scenes

throughout, and the engaging central character, *The Centaur* is not successful. Technically a sport, it must, I think, be considered Updike's most egregious example of inflation. Buried within its chinese boxes is a good short novel about the relationship between father and son and the ethics of selflessness, but that novel should not have been so difficult to find.

When Updike writes about his mother, he is more direct. In such stories, relationships are so complicated and feelings so profound that *The Centaur*'s prankishness seems to be out of the question. Coming from an obviously crucial preoccupation, these are among Updike's most subtle and powerful tales.

Like all the rest of them, "Should Wizard Hit Mommy?" (*Pigeon Feathers*) shows how little he need sacrifice actuality to explore truth. At night, by fabling their children to sleep, men confirm themselves as fathers. Protective though the gesture be, it can prove dangerous to the protector. Once in the world of make-believe, we may be attacked by buried memories from our own childhood. On this premise Updike's story is cleverly based.

"Each new story," the narrator tells us, "was a slight variation of a basic tale: a small creature, usually named Roger (Roger Fish, Roger Squirrel, Roger Chipmunk), had some problem" which he takes for solution to a wizard. One time, the narrator's daughter chooses a skunk as hero, and this initiates a revealing improvisation. The skunk's problem is his odor, which repels other small animals, so that he asks the wizard to grant him the smell of roses. But when his mother discovers the change, she returns him to the wizard and insists that he be made, once again, her son: a proper skunk. Although the other animals come to accept the skunk despite his reversion, the narrator's daughter asserts that the mother should be punished for her insistence; but the narrator, espousing filial loyalty, disagrees. Then when he completes his paternal ritual by rejoining his wife, he shows what the tale reveals about man's fate. For as he looks at his wife's body, pregnant with their third child, he feels a surge of resentment. Unlike the little skunk, who affirmed mother without losing his friends, the adult male renounces mother only to gain a wife who cannot love him so exclusively.

Perhaps the most brilliantly written of this group (all from *Pigeon Feathers*), "Flight" is an even clearer image of the conflict in Updike's heroes between love for the mother and love for others. First-person reminiscence, it is saved from formlessness by the controlling image of flight; though it reviews *The Centaur*'s family history, it approaches universality not through technical contrivance but through the depth of its description.

"Flight" is divided into three sections. First, Allen Dow introduces himself and recalls the moment when, standing on a hill overlooking Olinger, his mother suddenly announced: " 'There we all are, and there we'll all be forever. . . . Except you, Allen. You're going to fly.' " In the next section, he gives us a highly compressed and therefore particularly effective capsule version of the Olinger legend. There follows a precise depiction of young love. After losing a school debate, the boy tastes the delight of "bury[ing] a humiliation in the body of a woman." But he also experiences the rage of a woman whose dreams are being destroyed.

Though Mrs. Dow responds furiously to her son's first love, we cannot simply deplore her anger because Updike has previously established its sympathetic basis. Moreover, her rival, Molly, is manifestly no equal. However, what really saves this story from clichés inherent in its subject is Updike's development of Allen's response. Neither cleaving to Molly as a way of freeing himself nor submitting to

his mother, Allen begins to hate the girl for occasioning the woman's exposure. Thus, he starts to punish Molly with the skill of "an only child who had been surrounded all his life by adults ransacking each other for the truth." In truth, he was not yet ready to fly from Olinger, but by fighting to retain her hold on him, Mrs. Dow unwittingly forces Allen to perceive her in a new light; and this pushes him from the nest. " 'All right,' " he lets fly at her. " 'You'll win this one, Mother; but it'll be the last one you'll win.' "

Almost a sequel to "Flight," "The Persistence of Desire" presents the same young man, this time under the alias Clyde Behn, revisiting Olinger as an adult. During a trip to the oculist, where he seeks relief from a recurrent nervous tic, Clyde meets the girl, also differently named, whom he had rejected in the other story. Out of a conceited notion that he had deprived her of something special, Clyde determines, though both are married parents, to repair his past offense. What he ignores, however, is Janet's failure to participate in his self-assertive nostalgia; and Updike draws some wry humor from the distance between the male's sentimentality, so utterly self-referring, and the female's concern, so obviously sincere despite a politeness that offends Clyde.

Like "Should Wizard Hit Mommy?" this story is easy to identify with, and its meaning arises naturally from mundane details. For example, as Behn awaits the doctor, he reads, quite expectedly in this context, a medical journal that declares: ". . . the cells of the normal human body are replaced *in toto* every seven years." This is the key to his persistence in tracking Janet through the doctor's examining rooms, seeking some response to his desire. Like Jay Gatsby in F. Scott Fitzgerald's novel, Clyde covets not the girl "but some idea of himself that went into loving her." And like

Fitzgerald, whose nostalgia is similar to Updike's, the author finds the right formula to express so intense and futile a need. Nick Carraway comprehends Gatsby's fervor when the distraught man casually remarks that Daisy's love for Tom was "just personal." When Janet parries Clyde's invitation by asking him, " 'Aren't you happy?' " he responds with some of Gatsby's odd lucidity: " 'I am, I am; but . . . happiness isn't everything.' "

"The Persistence of Desire" seems the masterwork in its group because, without sacrificing verisimilitude, it offers Updike's deepest insight into the source of nostalgia. For Clyde, as for his creator, actual pleasure is less intense than remembered joy, because memory, with its power to stop time, returns to us an imperishable self. Thus, when Janet hands Clyde a note, perhaps fixing some assignation, though he cannot make out its message—because his eyes have been dilated in his examination—he can perceive the familiar shape of her handwriting. This suffices; he will not need to meet her. Placing the paper in his pocket, he feels he has donned "a shield for his heart. In this armor he stepped into the familiar street. The maples, macadam, shadows, houses, cement, were to his violated eyes as brilliant as a scene remembered; he became a child again in this town, where life was a distant adventure, a rumor, an always imminent joy."

In his fourth novel, *Of the Farm*, a tale even more limpid and natural, Updike offers a more complex consideration of nostalgia and of man's relationship to his family. Short, plotted simply enough to be classified a novella, *Of the Farm* is actually Updike's subtlest piece of autobiographical fiction. Though smaller in scope than his masterpiece, *Rabbit, Run*, it is artistically more polished, without taint of obviousness. For Updike's belief that ordinary relationships contain manifold complications,

this book provides impressive evidence. In general, Updike's mimetic emphasis makes his fiction peculiarly resistant to summary; *Of the Farm* is the most irreducible of his works.

Its surface seems irreducible by being so meager. When the book first appeared, most reviewers pronounced it uneventful, and its plot is certainly bare:

Since his mother is getting too old to care properly for her farm, Joey Robinson promises to leave Manhattan for a weekend of chores that include mowing the meadow. Returning home with his new, second wife and her adolescent son, he experiences a rivalry between Mrs. Robinson and Peggy so intense as to threaten his marriage. As the weekend wears on, quarrels break out, only to subside without warning. Melodramatically, the mother rages; suddenly "hysteria [falls] from her like a pose." The wife seems daunted, but soon she fights back. On Sunday, Joey takes the old woman to church. His mother had wanted him to retain the farm after she died; now she agrees that it be sold. Soon the city-dwellers will depart.

What does it all mean? The Sartrean epigraph offers a clue: "Consequently, when, in all honesty, I've recognized that man is a being in whom existence precedes essence, that he is a free being who, in various circumstances, can want only his freedom, I have at the same time recognized that I can want only the freedom of others." To Sartre, freedom means doing; to Updike seeing. To Sartre, we redefine our lives by changing our acts; to Updike, we change our attitudes. But for both writers, the past brings the threat of imprisonment in its potential for rigid definition.

"All misconceptions," Joey Robinson asserts, "are themselves data which have the minimal truth of existing in at least one mind. Truth, my work had taught me, is not something static, a mountain-top that statements approximate like successive assaults of frost-bitten climbers. Rather, truth is constantly being formed from the solidification of illusions." The truth of his mother's life had solidified into her shared illusion of their special fate. As the novel progresses, that illusion melts; at its conclusion, Joey is able to remount the stream of life.

Like Allen Dow in "Flight," Joey had been only partly liberated from his mother's influence. " 'I've always felt young for my age,' " he tells us by way of introduction; soon we learn why. Entering his house, he habitually "resent[s] how much of myself [is] already here. . . . I [am] so abundantly memorialized it seem[s] I must be dead." Since, like all Updike's sensitive heroes, Joey longs for a kind of ongoing immortality, in which no moment is ever wholly lost, for him, maturation means decay more than growth. Looking at Richard, standing next to Peggy, the boy's mother, Joey becomes jealous, even though Peggy is his wife, for he wishes to possess in her both wife and mother, going to her in Richard's "size."

Drawn to his mother's vision of his promise, Joey has made only frail gestures of self-assertion. He married, but his first marriage failed. He denied his mother's wish that he become a poet, but he lives in the grip of poetic nostalgia. Marrying Peggy was another bid for freedom, but this too is incomplete. That his mother can so challenge his choice shows how little he has made peace with it. That he so fears Peggy's past (both in her child and the husband he suspects she may still love) shows how fervently he seeks the support of total acceptance. Therefore, desiring a perfect corroboration of his own identity, he comes home. But, as Peggy says, it is cowardly to expect either his mother or his wife to give him self-direction.

Rather Joey can only stand on his own if he frees himself from the figure he cuts in both their myths. Mrs. Robinson neglected her husband to devote herself to Joey, for Joey was, so to speak, the objectification of her own self-image. When Peggy charges her with this neglect, and Mrs. Robinson counters by calling it liberation, Joey witnesses the clash of alien perspectives. "I saw," he thinks, "that my mother's describing as a gift her failure to possess my father . . . had touched the sore point within [Peggy] around which revolved her own mythology, of women giving themselves to men, of men in return giving women a reason to live."

For a time, Joey tries to simulate freedom through the most basic fact of manhood. Conceiving Peggy as a field, he sows the seed of his possession; but in so doing, he takes his wife on his mother's terms. Making of Peggy an ersatz farm, he turns to her for sex, not love, and thus confirms his mother's denigration.

As in "Flight," Updike's hero cannot be free until he accepts the truth about both of his women; for only then will he acknowledge the change that has taken place in himself. His mother is no longer "the swift young" woman of whom he has felt himself deprived. She has "entered, unconsciously, a far territory, the arctic of the old," where her vision of his life will also die. Peggy may be inferior to Mrs. Robinson, but she is Joey's choice and now deserves his loyalty. Time has indeed passed; Joey is a man. Now he must accept a man's responsibilities.

This he does in two scenes, both of which involve the process of revision. First, Joey tells Richard a fairy tale that recalls the similar device in "Should Wizard Hit Mommy?" But in that story the teller is drawn back to his mother's self-referring vision of his character, whereas in this novel Joey uses the fairy tale to express his freedom, his ability to break out of the past. The fairy tale concerns a frog-prince with a watertight skin. One day the prince's self-delight turns to boredom until he learns of a treasure in his guts. "So he went down a circular staircase out of his head . . . and the lower he went, the smaller he got, until finally, just when he was sure he had reached the dungeon where the treasure was, he disappeared!" But with the return of spring, the frog runs upstairs, throws open his lids, and looks out. After Joey finishes he goes downstairs expecting to perceive "some nostalgic treasure unlocked by the humidity within the stones, plaster, wood, and history of the house," but instead he smells the dampness of Peggy's hair.

This affirmation of present joy is approved by his mother after both she and Joey hear a Sunday sermon on Adam's obligation to the living Eve. "'In reaching out to her,'" the preacher says, "'Adam commits an act of faith.'" Woman, as Karl Barth says, is an invitation to man's kindness, and "'kindness needs no belief.'" Joey's love for Peggy will not bring him the self-confirmation of filial love, but it is nonetheless "'implicit in the nature of Creation, in the very curves and amplitude of God's fashioning.'"

A deeply religious woman, Mrs. Robinson apparently now sees that it would be a sin to try to maintain her hold on Joey. Therefore, she admits that Peggy suits him better than his first wife, Joan (later symbolizing the admission by asking Peggy to have a picture taken, which will probably replace Joan's). Then, after admitting Peggy's right to her son, she has a seizure, foretelling her death. But when, in her weakness, she pledges Joey to get a good price for her farm, he repays her respect for his freedom by affirming the reality of their bond: "'*Your* farm?'" he retorts. "'I've always thought of it as our farm.'"

The book's action is a record of those shifts, feints, self-dramatized assaults and stage-man-aged climaxes which are the universal components of family quarrels. Its power is an expression of thematic counterforce. Filled with the loveliness of primal pleasures—the farm, early mornings, one's youth—it also depicts the danger of fixation upon them. Definition requires that we keep faith with our past; freedom demands that we move beyond it. Grand though she is, Mrs. Robinson must yield to Peggy, just as Joey the boy must give way to Joey the man. But the three principal characters can only make their mutual adjustments after they have seen their situation from the individual perspectives that make it up. Subtly, naturally, *Of the Farm* performs this feat.

In Updike's less autobiographical fiction, themes from the Olinger stories recur in different form. Instead of personal nostalgia, we have nostalgia for pre-urban America. Thus the dominant characters in these stories are old men or young ones who feel at odds against the modern world. Instead of the effort to recapture one's past, we have a quest for permanence that involves religion. As in *Of the Farm*, love itself seems a religious obligation; sometimes, because Christianity has been polluted by institutionalism or diluted by a social gospel, love can seem the deepest expression of spiritual thirst. But at the same time, Updike notes the difficulty of satisfying this need. In his autobiographical stories, the hero can only recapture in fugitive moments that perfectly self-confirming love he once experienced. In these stories, the hero experiences similar difficulty through sex. Faced with woman's irrevocable otherness, he beats against the barrier between them or he pursues his ideal complement by attempting to love many women. No mortal, however, can provide the constancy and total acceptance that might hush the clock's tick. Lacking the support of faith, Updike's modern heroes can neither accept man's contingency nor find permanence through the world.

With varying success, this reality is portrayed in Updike's other novels and many of his stories. Some of the less autobiographical fiction, however, is much more casual. Most of Updike's famous marital anecdotes, for example, are usually no more complicated than his bittersweet little valentines. Trivial in situation, they are memorable only for catching a charming irony or for proving Updike's professionalism.

Typical of this group are stories about Richard and Joan Maple. In the first of them, "Snowing in Greenwich Village" (*The Same Door*), Updike lightly amuses. Two years after their marriage, happily installed in a Village apartment, the Maples are entertaining a female friend. Joan has a cold, but, secure in her new love, she urges Richard to walk their friend home. Though she "anticipat[es] how he would bring back with him, in the snow on his shoulders and the coldness of his face, all the sensations of the walk she was not well enough to risk," she neglects to realize that she is tempting him to be unfaithful. In "Giving Blood" (*The Music School*), one of the latest and best of the Maple stories, a rift in the marriage provides a more substantial subject. Exasperated with their mutual unhappiness, the Maples experience an unexpected rejuvenation of their love when forced to donate blood. The freshness of this experience, its external threat, brings them momentarily together; but when they deliberately attempt to prolong the novelty by lunching in town rather than at home, the old dissension revives.

Unfortunately, this story is too artful; coming to rest in a terminal pun, it reminds us obtrusively that wordplay and contrivance typify the whole. In stories whose only virtue is natural observation, Updike often spoils the effect by an ostentatious display of craft.

Far more amiable is the dramatic monologue "Wife-Wooing" (*Pigeon Feathers*). While they are both fussing with the children's dinner, the narrator woos his wife with memory; later, he tries wit. Nothing avails; she is too tired for love. The following morning, he looks gleefully at the ravages etched in her face by those duties which had made her deny him. That same night, however, although he has now forgotten his desire, she gives the cue: "the momentous moral of this story being, An expected gift is not worth giving."

Several of Updike's dramatic monologues are far more serious. Of these, the most important is "Lifeguard" (*Pigeon Feathers*). Spoken by a divinity student who is earning tuition at the beach, this tale is a sustained conceit that comes closer than usual to an expression of Updike's fundamental beliefs.

"That there is no discrepancy between my studies," the speaker announces in his initial buoyancy, "that the texts of the flesh complement those of the mind, is the easy burden of my sermon." Then, using sunbathers as symbols, he both demonstrates and develops this thesis. Acknowledging his lust for the women he sees, the lifeguard maintains that "to desire a woman is to desire to save her," since, though sex is tragically brief, it gives man an intimation of self-transcendence. But for the swimmer unsatisfied by intimations, who is borne out to sea by time's "treacherous undercurrents," the lifeguard stands ready with two means of rescue: his swimming ability and his faith. As he sadly confesses, however, he has yet to hear a cry for help; men are all too willing now to enjoy body, sun, and sand, forgetting what Tillich calls "ultimacy." Though it is Sunday morning, neither lifeguard nor bather is in church.

This latter fact is reflected in one of Updike's best tales. Like all his successes, "The Christian Roommates" (*The Music School*), almost documentary in detail, achieves its revelation without straining. Every year collegiate bureaucracy marries souls, in blithe disregard of their differences and vulnerability. Updike regards the effect of one such confrontation: between Orson Ziegler and Hub Palamountain.

Orson is characteristic of Updike's protagonists: bright, gangling, provincial, his inner doubts emblazoned on his face in the form of eczema. Fresh from a brilliant high-school career, he looks forward to a comfortable future when he will become the town's leading physician, like his father, and marry his childhood sweetheart. Hub is his antithesis: with his parents, who are divorced, he has little contact; arrogant and eccentric, Hub wishes to be a saint. Science he shuns because it is a modern form of *hubris*; meat he will not touch because it is produced through slaughter. Moreover, Hub has an annoying habit; at odd hours, he prays.

The freshman religious crisis is a stock situation. Equally familiar are the student types with whom Updike surrounds his principals. As usual, such material is transfigured by Updike's precise observation without losing the truthfulness that turned it into a cliché. For example, we might consider the moment when Hub disturbs Orson by describing two years of work in a plywood mill, as " 'a kind of excessive introspection—you've read *Hamlet?*' " In the time-honored manner of one dependent on knowing the answers, Orson feels threatened: " 'Just *Macbeth* and *The Merchant of Venice,*' " he admits, fully missing Hub's point.

What he cannot miss is the fervor of Hub's commitment. At first, he rather objects to the other students' smart-aleck derogation of Hub. But as soon as he begins to feel the lure of Hub's faith, he senses that he must either follow the example or make a total break. " 'I pray, too,' " he protests, " 'but I don't make

a show of myself.' " Years later, when Orson becomes exactly the man he had always anticipated, he doesn't pray at all.

Among Updike's short stories, "The Bulgarian Poetess" (*The Music School*) is to the subject of love what "The Christian Roommates" is to the subject of religion. Possibly the most moving of Updike's tales, it seems to owe its power to a carefully controlled degree of personal application.

Perhaps because American life is so actual in his pages, Updike is one of our most popular authors in the Soviet Union. As a result, in 1964 he was invited to make a tour of Russia, Rumania, and Bulgaria, and from that experience he has fashioned a number of stories about Henry Bech, a once-brilliant writer whose work has steadily declined both in quality and in sales. With obvious reference to his creator, Bech feels himself in danger of "eclectic sexuality and bravura narcissism." Like Updike in *Couples,* "his search for plain truth" carries him "further and further into treacherous realms of fantasy." This decline attains some dignity only because it is pursued with much of the fervor belonging to a quest and because it has cost Bech his audience (here Updike differs; *Couples,* an immediate best seller, was sold to the movies for half a million dollars).

Updike's essential romanticist, Bech equates the needs of soul and heart. "He had loved, briefly or long, with or without consummation, perhaps a dozen women; yet all of them, he now saw, shared the trait of approximation, of narrowly missing an undisclosed prototype." But although he has written an essay concerning "the orgasm as perfect memory," he finds love a mystery; the mystery being "what are we remembering?"

Ironically, we are remembering what we never had. "Actuality is a running impoverishment of possibility": therefore the only truly desirable woman is the one we don't get. Meeting a gentle, intelligent poetess in Bulgaria during the final days of his tour, Bech experiences perfect love, while Updike finds the perfect words to express it. As they part, Bech places in the woman's hands a copy of his latest book with the following inscription: "It is a matter of earnest regret for me that you and I must live on opposite sides of the world." Putting this story beside "The Persistence of Desire," one has Updike's basic notion about love: either it enshrines a lost past or projects an unattainable future; in the present, it withers.

So does faith. That is the theme of Updike's first novel, his only one concerned with religion entirely outside the context of love. Though set in the future, *The Poorhouse Fair* is only an exaggerated version of the present. If modern secularism continues unchecked, Updike implies, this is what it will come to.

Weaned from the Christian vision of irrevocable human limits, modern society confesses the unsoundness of its secularism through the institutions it has produced. Designed to succor and protect, the poorhouse irritates its inmates. Since they represent disease and death, they threaten modern optimism and are therefore hidden away, depersonalized, forgotten. But what they signify should never be ignored because it can never be altered; failing to communicate with their elderly, modern men lose their unique chance to comprehend the human condition.

Death does not simplify the oldsters. Though they turn gray in its shadows, they do not lose their humanity. Though about to face last things, they are not so detached from life as to welcome prefect Conner's vision of a glorious welfare state. Will it come " 'soon enough for us?' " Mrs. Mortis asks him.

"Not you personally perhaps. But for your children, and your grandchildren."

"But for us ouselves?"

"No." . . .

"Well, then," Mrs. Mortis spryly said, "to hell with it."

Emboldened by the approach of death, such honesty makes the old enlightening. What they reveal is the avid heart of man. Because it is something they can own, they even cherish their pain. Though cowardly in other ways, Lucas refuses aid for his abscessed ear. Like Hook, clinging to his knowledge of original sin, Lucas cleaves to suffering because it confirms his existence.

This is what Conner disapproves. Seeking to eliminate man's trials on earth, the prefect wants to alter creation. Unfortunately, he is totally self-deceived. Alienated from the oldsters, he also cannot comprehend himself. When he tags their chairs, thinking to give them pride of ownership, he is surprised not only by their fury but by his own unexpected regret at losing their approval. Ironically, though devoted to amelioration, he feels himself growing old under the burden of ease: "Conner was bored. He yearned for some chance to be proven; he envied the first rationalists their martyrdoms and the first reformers their dragons of reaction and selfishness. Two years remained before automatic promotion. The chief trouble with the job was the idleness. . . . He was infected with the repose that was only suitable to inmates waiting out their days."

Seeking to deprive men of suffering, secularism threatens to deprive them of all emotion. Even when Conner achieves a sort of martyrdom, he finds he lacks the belief that would lend it dignity. St. Stephen, to whom Updike compares him, was stoned for announcing the true messiah; Conner's apostleship is sterile.

Yet for all his hatred of imperfection, modern man is nostalgic about the past. This is the cause of the annual poorhouse fair, where "a keen subversive need" is demonstrated "for objects that showed the trace of a hand, whether in an irregular seam, the crescent cuts of a chisel, or the dents of a forge hammer." But while purchasing such artifacts, the younger people cheat the old artisans.

Hook, whom Updike claims to be a surrogate for his grandfather, formulates the result of modern malaise. Having lost religion, Hook asserts, the human family will ultimately decline: "As the Indian once served the elusive deer he hunted, men once served invisible goals, and grew hard in such service and pursuit, and lent their society an indispensable temper. Impotent to provide this tempering salt, men would sink lower than women, as indeed they had. Women are the heroes of dead lands."

Appropriately, Conner's mother was "excessively permissive," the non-parent of progressive education. At the end of the book, then, Hook compassionately desires to save Conner from spiritual orphanhood by placing in his hands some accommodation to the limits of mortality and the agonizing fact of death. But Hook cannot think what to tell the younger man. In this novel, the wisdom of the past has become incommunicable, and the link between generations has been permanently sundered.

Like a decaying apple, *The Poorhouse Fair* exudes a tangy odor of waste. Though toughly knowing, its oldsters are both repelling and selfish, while its young people, for all their outer sufficiency and conscientiousness, are foolish and soft. In portraying this combination of crusty old age and sterile modernism, Updike creates several effective vignettes, but the book lacks a plot. As a result, the argument seems to progress above rather than within the action. And although Updike clearly sympathizes with Conner's humane intentions,

the man is so self-deceived and foolish that Updike's anti-secularism is made to seem a bit pat. Individual scenes are lifelike and complex, but the book is too fragmented to be convincing.

Moreover, Updike's diagnosis of modern ills now appears imperceptive. Thirteen years after its publication, one can hardly believe that the welfare state threatens to eliminate all social evils; rather the reverse. Thus, *The Poorhouse Fair* helps to explain why Updike is well advised to eschew ideology; while, at the same time, it provides valuable clues to themes in his later, less emphatic work.

Particularly those in his novel, *Couples*. Updike has said in a *New York Times* interview that the behavior in both novels illustrates an answer to the same question: "After Christianity, what?" Providing this link is helpful. Otherwise, as one sees in the reviews, *Couples* can be judged unredeemed pornography.

For the most part, the novel seems to disapprove of what it displays by realizing Updike's prediction in *The Poorhouse Fair* of an America in which "the population soared . . . and the economy swelled, and iron became increasingly dilute, and houses more niggardly built, and everywhere was sufferance, good sense, wealth, irreligion, and peace. The nation became one of pleasure-seekers; the people continued to live as cells of a body do in the coffin, for the conception 'America' had died in their skulls." This describes Tarbox, Massachusetts, twenty of whose inhabitants are shown as parts of one incestuous organism. Lacking real purpose, they spend themselves in copulation; ignoring morality, they also shun the outside world. Not even death has much power over their hearts. On the night of President Kennedy's assassination, they give a party.

This picture of suburban life might have been harrowing; but, as Updike confessed in his interview, he was trying for a heightened verisimilitude, approaching fantasy. In combination with his characteristic refusal to moralize, this makes the novel simultaneously implausible and equivocal. What we get then is a repetitious charade in which cardboard grotesques are unexpectedly equipped with real genitals. In one of the novel's few positive notices, Wilfrid Sheed argues that people like this *would be* shallow and absurd. Why then must the point be reiterated through 458 pages?

Though principally a portrait of doomed characters, *Couples* contains one relative exception. Bearing unmistakable signs of Updike's approval, Piet Hanema is an antique-loving craftsman, who adores the physical universe, and assuages his fear of death in the act of love. But, given his orphaned status and oral-genital fixation, he often seems an unconsciously facetious version of Updike's symbolic desire to get back to the womb. Could an enemy have more cruelly parodied Updike's obsession with mother love than the author does in the moment when Piet, without a tinge of irony, risks neck and marriage to suckle his married, pregnant mistress's breast?

Piet also fails as a hero for being too like his confreres. Updike tries to remedy this by creating two foils. Thus, Ken Whitman, whose wife Piet appropriates, is soulless, sexless, and scientific, while Freddy Thorne, who helps abort the lady's child, is atheistic, death-worshiping, and sterile. But Ken is no more complicated than Albee's Nick in *Who's Afraid of Virginia Woolf?*—which might suffice for an evening's entertainment but is too meager for a long novel—and Freddy is so often the book's *raissonneur* that it is confusing to have him also act as Piet's counter-ego.

Couples is Updike at his most wastefully evidential (one whole book, concerning the Applesmiths, is superfluous documentation). The rest is clumsily symbolic. At the finale, for example, the town church is struck by lightning, leaving intact only one emblem of God: a colonial weathercock! Though it contains a great deal of talk about God and sin, this is as close as the talk comes to providing the novel's action.

Art could have reduced the grayness, but, as Updike says, he wished to chasten his style here with circumstantiality. Circumstance we get in full measure, described in prose that vacillates between Updike's fruitiest and most flatfooted. Committing himself to banal characters, his dialogue seldom rises above their level. Occasional deviations jar like sermons in a bordello. As for the plot—when Updike gets around to it, he concocts an improbable mixture of Boccaccio and Victorian melodrama. Only verisimilitude might have supplied pertinence to this fictional Kinsey report; but in *Couples* fiction is a lot stranger than truth.

Lacking sustained insight, Updike's observation here seems voyeuristic; so much suckling so lovingly described also makes one suspect advocacy—despite all the conceptual disclaimers. Lacking order, the exemplification becomes tedious. Unfailingly vivid, filled with occasional flashes of characteristic subtlety (particularly in the last scenes of marital dissolution), *Couples* is nevertheless a travesty of Updike's most impressive book.

The hero of which, Rabbit Angstrom, also affirms life through his virility. But whereas everyone in Tarbox apes Piet, the others in *Rabbit, Run* battle Angstrom. This gives Updike's second novel a dramatic tension so grievously absent from *Couples*. Less trivial in what it illustrates, the novel also embodies its implications in a tighter plot. Finally, it achieves Updike's most magnanimous blend of toughness and compassion.

Slightness, mute observation, inflation of theme: these flaws in Updike can be considered personal. When he goes soft, however, he rather reflects a common contemporary problem. "After such knowledge, what forgiveness?" For the modern writer, it seems impossible to embody value. Thus, when Updike molds characters who express an affirmation, he must either elevate them with myth or unwittingly expose them, when their pretensions are refused, as mundane fornicators. Only in Rabbit Angstrom does he present someone whose value is neither exaggerated nor unconvincing.

Carelessly read, the book seems to deny this. Many of its first reviews, with titles like "Desperate Weakling" or "Down with the Poor in Spirit," judged Angstrom an example of human depravity. Ambiguous he surely is; but this is what makes him persuasive. Initially, Rabbit seems only selfish. But we soon come to admire his refusal to accept compromise or corruption. As he tells the Reverend Mr. Eccles, " 'I once played a game real well. I really did. And after you're first-rate at something, no matter what, it kind of takes the kick out of being second-rate.' " Quickened by this glory buried in his past—like Piet, the architectural restorer, or Caldwell, the teacher—Rabbit has known the pleasure of meaningful work. (Updike once said that the search for proper work drives all his characters.) Now, however, Rabbit is reduced to selling kitchen gadgets in the five and dime; yet those around him accept the MagiPeel Peeler and reject basketball as kid's stuff.

To make matters worse, Rabbit must grub for money to support a woman he no longer loves. Trapped in the small apartment his wife never cleans, he longs for the orderly home in which, like any Updike hero, he was the center of attention. "Just yesterday, it seems to him, she [his wife, Janice] stopped being pretty." Now Janice spends her time watching television, swilling bourbon, swelling with the second child she will drag up no more intelligently than the first. No wonder Rabbit dreams of his lost innocent love for his sister and rages at the girl when he later encounters Mim on a "heavy date."

Unimpressed by the obligations of work and marriage, Rabbit would like to believe that value exists beyond this world. If he cannot, he fears he will feel "hung in the middle of nowhere, and the thought hollows him, makes his heart tremble." But throughout the novel, the local church stands "gray, somber, confident," challenging him to disperse its smug darkness with an inner light. This he cannot do; he has "no taste for the dark, tangled visceral aspect of Christianity, the *going through* quality of it, the passage *into* death and suffering that redeems and inverts these things, like an umbrella blowing inside out. He lacks the mindful will to walk the straight line of a paradox."

All he knows is self, proven on pulse and skin. Thus, like other Updike heroes, he can only seek transcendence through a woman's body. But, unlike the others, he convinces us that transcendence is what he seeks, that love infuses his sexuality. With Ruth, the prostitute he joins after abandoning his wife, "it is her heart he wants to grind into his own, to comfort her completely." When they first go to bed, Rabbit strips her makeup; as their affair progresses, he melts her protective layer of cynicism. Amidst the sordidness of Ruth's condition and Rabbit's selfishness Updike creates a real tenderness which is all the more notable for its absence in most of the author's pictures of erotic love.

This tenderness comes from Rabbit's self-assertion. Living in honest contact with his own desires, he has them to give to others. Moreover, they enable him to work his will. As he tells Ruth, " 'All I know is what's inside me. That's all I have.' " But " 'If you have the guts to be yourself . . . other people'll pay your price.' "

Ultimately Updike shows that the price is exorbitant; first he establishes the world's poverty. Throughout the book, respectable people deplore the hero, calling him a deserter and whoremaster; but what is their respectability? During his first escape, in which he drives half the night only to find he has followed a circle, Rabbit stops to get gas and is lectured on maturity by a man with whisky on his breath. Equally suspicious are the maxims of his wife's family. Though Mrs. Springer takes the tone of outraged virtue, she cares less for Janice's welfare than for the scandal. Rabbit's old coach espouses marital obligation, though he has been twisted into perversity by his own. When Rabbit repents, his father-in-law rewards him with a steady job selling used cars with set-back odometers. Every Sunday people dress for church, but their most influential preacher is the Mickey Mouse M.C. whom Janice watches religiously on television. Though society conspires to rout the Rabbit in Angstrom, it wishes merely to drive the beast underground. Instinctively clapping his hand on the soft bottom of Mrs. Eccles, Rabbit is later shocked when, at the very height of his repentance, she returns his pass. However, this hypocrisy merely explains why Rabbit cannot accept his world; it does not justify him.

A similar function is performed by the contrast between Rabbit's vital amoralism and the humanistic kindness of the Reverend Mr. Eccles. Though a churchman, Eccles is even less capable than Rabbit of accepting life or of finding comfort in orthodox Christianity. Like Conner in *The Poorhouse Fair*, he strives for amelioration, though he does so far more attractively than his prototype and his failure is therefore more pathetic.

Embodying the social gospel of modern Christianity, Eccles acts the role of frocked marriage counselor. Promulgating his congregation's values, he tries to draw Rabbit back to respectability. But because his beliefs are only a moralistic version of convention, he lacks the power to convert Rabbit's fervent soul. Instead, Eccles feels drawn to Rabbit's beliefs which, though animal, soar higher than his own. Preaching to Rabbit—appropriately, on a golf course—Eccles is offended by the arrogance of his faith. " 'There's something that wants me to find it,' " the sinner insists. And when Eccles taunts him to produce some confirmation, Rabbit simply hits a golf ball, sending it "along a line straight as a ruler-edge," crying out "with a smile of aggrandizement . . . 'That's it.' "

Mystical in his worship of the natural universe, Rabbit's faith is still more real than that of Eccles. This the latter realizes, so when he visits the elder Angstroms he finds himself siding not with the father, who mouths society's wrath, but with the mother, for whom Rabbit can do no evil. Confounded by his own apostasy, Eccles fears for his soul. Visiting an old Lutheran minister, he is told that he is in danger of losing it. " 'If Gott wants to end misery,' " Kuppenbach thunders, " 'He'll declare the Kingdom now. . . . .You say role. I say you don't know what your role is or you'd be home locked in prayer. *There* is your role: to make yourself an exemplar of faith. *There* is where comfort comes from: faith, not what little finagling a body can do here and there, stirring the bucket. In running back and forth you run from the duty given you by God, to make your faith powerful, so when the call comes you can go out and tell them, "Yes, he is dead, but you will see him again in Heaven. Yes, you suffer, but you must *love* your pain, because it is *Christ's* pain." ' " Eccles is disgusted by this rigid expression of piety, but we know how firmly Updike stands behind it not only from Hook's central utterance in *The Poorhouse Fair* (" 'There is no goodness, without belief. There is nothing but busy-ness' ") but from Eccles' final admission. " 'Harry,' " he confesses to the sinner he could not save, " 'you know I don't think that thing exists in the way you think it does.' " To his wife, Eccles admits that he believes nothing.

By immersing himself in worldliness and seeking humane improvement, man cannot enrich his life. For that, as Kruppenbach says, he must give himself to God. But if he is incapable of such a sacrifice, he can at least take the route of substitute belief, as Rabbit does. It may also fail, and it will surely offend the Pharisees, but it can at least escape the deadness of dishonesty. By running, Rabbit comes as close as possible to the sanctity of ultimate truth.

Having considered his sanctity, we must recall his sin. More than the Springers, his parents, or Eccles, Rabbit attains sentience, but his method—total self-communion—is necessarily destructive. In nothing else does Updike so display his comprehension of life's ambiguity. Wanting us to admire Rabbit's authentic energy, Updike does not forget its terrible cost. For all Rabbit's tenderness, he is also brutal; seeking to make Ruth into a mirror of his existence he literally brings her to her knees. And by the end of the novel he has plunged her into despair, just as he has helped Janice to become a murderess.

Nevertheless, Rabbit is only speaking the truth when, at his daughter's graveside, he insists that he did not kill her. Only through a community of guilt is he implicated, but he has spent the whole book trying to escape that community; it is the others who dragged him back. Therefore, as always, he can only run away, expressing through this pathetic and desperate act, his one great insight: "Funny, how what makes you move is so simple and the field you must move in is so crowded. Goodness lies inside, there is nothing outside . . ."

Such comprehension of selfhood is not moral; but without it, morality is irrelevant. Such retreat into the smallness of one's soul is not religious; but without it, there can be nothing for God to find. Rabbit runs over others; the others beat themselves down. Despite his animality and its tragic consequences, Rabbit admits the inarguable facts of life. He is a beginning, not an end; but in a dead-end culture even so poor a beginning has its value. Therefore, his creator, scrupulously neutral till the last words, permits himself a final cry of affirmation: "Ah: runs. Runs."

Appreciating even so gross a keeper of the sacred flame, Updike expresses his compassion. Even in his meanest character, he finds something sympathetic. Therefore, the book's most powerful writing is devoted not to Rabbit but to Janice, in the scene where she drunkenly drowns her child, and thus Ruth is given the book's best passages of experimental internal monologue. Eccles is pitiable for the thwarting of his good intentions. Something may even be said for his wife, because her militant, bitchy Freudianism is a defense against the humanitarian sentiment in her husband that has no place for individual love. Updike always seeks to avoid moral melodrama; in *Rabbit, Run,* he almost totally succeeds.

Formally, the book is also a success. Its present tense and short sentences perfectly convey Rabbit's physicality. Only the plot in *Of the Farm* is more galvanic. Even the book's repetition is functional, showing Rabbit running in ever widening circles until he realizes that escape is only a straight line out. Taut and precise, Updike's prose is here firmly at the service of object, character, and event.

Only in two ways does this novel disappoint. Powerfully felt, it is somehow less supple than *Of the Farm.* Thus we get such examples of insistence as the final appearance of Rabbit's coach, reduced to repentant mush by his high-handed wife; Updike might better have omitted so blatant a validation for his hero. More serious, the book's moral poise is occasionally threatened by unneeded testimonials. So, Ruth tells Rabbit, " 'In your stupid way you're still fighting,' " though this declaration is false to their love's marvelous tact, and old Mrs. Smith, whose garden Rabbit tends, too obviously blesses him for keeping her alive.

Still, this is a first-rate novel; for without sacrificing immediacy, its image of life stimulates reflection. But, with Updike, one hesitates to conclude on such a note. Criticism normally makes fiction sound too tendentious, since criticism is the discovery of pattern whereas fiction is the re-creation of life. To repeat, it is through his power of re-creation that Updike makes his greatest appeal. Therefore, what we have barely considered—language, dramaturgy, characterization—is what most repays exploration and analysis. What I have tried to do is outline major subjects and themes as well as indicate which of Updike's works deserve further reading. Because reading Updike brings us as close as current American fiction can to "the thing itself"—which criticism can never do more than point at.

Selected Bibliography

BOOKS BY JOHN UPDIKE

The Carpentered Hen and Other Tame Creatures. New York: Harper, 1958. (Poems.)
The Poorhouse Fair. New York: Knopf, 1959. (Novel.)
The Same Door: Short Stories. New York: Knopf, 1959.
Rabbit, Run. New York: Knopf, 1960. (Novel.)
Pigeon Feathers and Other Stories. New York: Knopf, 1962.
The Centaur. New York: Knopf, 1963. (Novel.)

Telephone Poles and Other Poems. New York: Knopf, 1963.
Assorted Prose. New York: Knopf, 1965.
Of the Farm. New York: Knopf, 1965. (Novel.)
The Music School: Short Stories. New York: Knopf, 1966.
Couples. New York: Knopf, 1968. (Novel.)
Midpoint and Other Poems. New York: Knopf, 1969.
Bech: A Book. New York: Knopf, 1970. (Stories.)
Rabbit Redux. New York: Knopf, 1971.
Museums and Woman and Other Stories. New York: Knopf, 1972.
Buchanan Dying. New York: Knopf, 1974. (Play.)
A Month of Sundays. New York: Knopf, 1975. (Novel.)
Picked-Up Pieces. New York: Knopf, 1975. (Assorted Prose.)
Marry Me. New York: Knopf, 1976. (Novel.)
Tossing and Turning. New York: Knopf, 1977. (Poems.)
The Coup. New York: Knopf, 1978. (Novel.)
Problems & Other Stories. New York: Knopf, 1979.
Too Far to Go. New York: Fawcett, 1979. (Stories.)
Rabbit Is Rich. New York: Knopf, 1981. (Novel.)
Beck is Back. New York: Knopf, 1982. (Novel.)
Hugging the Shore. New York: Knopf, 1983. (Essays.)
The Witches of Eastwick. New York: Knopf, 1984. (Novel.)
Facing Nature. New York: Knopf, 1985. (Poems.)
Roger's Version. New York: Knopf, 1986. (Novel.)
Trust Me. New York: Knopf, 1987. (Stories.)
Just Looking: Essays on Art. New York: Knopf, 1989.
Self-Consciousness: Memoirs. New York: Knopf, 1989.

BIBLIOGRAPHY

Gearhart, Elizabeth A. John Updike: A Comprehensive Bibliography with Selected Annotations. Norwood: Norwood Editions, 1978. Reprinted. Folcroft, Pa.: Folcroft Library Editions, 1980.
Olivas, Michael A. Annotated Bibliography of John Updike Criticism 1967-1973: & a Checklist of His Works. New York: Garland Publishing, 1975.
Taylor, C. Clarke. John Updike: A Bibliography. Kent: Kent State University Press, 1968. (This contains errors and omissions, but, by default, it is indispensable.)

CRITICAL AND BIOGRAPHICAL STUDIES

Bell, Vereen. "A Study in Frustration," *Shenandoah*, 14:69–72 (Summer 1963).

Brenner, Gerry. *"Rabbit, Run*: John Updike's Criticism of the 'Return to Nature,' " *Twentieth Century Literature*, 12:3–14 (April 1966).

Burchard, Rachael C. *John Updike: Yea-sayings*. Carbondale: Southern Illinois University Press, 1971.

Burgess, Anthony. "Language, Myth and Mr. Updike," *Commonweal*, 83:557–89 (February 11, 1966).

Chester, Alfred. "Twitches and Embarrassments," *Commentary*, 34:77–80 (July 1962).

Detweiler, Robert. "John Updike and the Indictment of Culture-Protestantism," in *Four Spiritual Crises in Mid-Century American Fiction*. Gainesville: University of Florida Press, 1963. Pp. 14–24.

———. *John Updike*. U.S. Authors Ser. Boston: G.K. Hall, 1977; rev. ed., 1984.

Doner, Dean. "Rabbit Angstrom's Unseen World," *New World Writing*, 20:58–75 (1962).

Enright, D. J. "Updike's Ups and Downs," *Holiday*, 38:162, 164–66 (November 1965).

Galloway, David D. "The Absurd Man as Saint," in *The Absurd Hero in American Fiction*. Austin: University of Texas Press, 1966. Pp. 21–50.

Gilman, Richard. "A Distinguished Image of Precarious Life," *Commonweal*, 73:128–29 (October 28, 1960).

———. "The Youth of an Author," *New Republic*, 148:25–27 (April 13, 1963).

Greiner, Donald J. *The Other John Updike: Poems, Short Stories, Prose, Play*. Athens: Ohio University Press, 1981.

Hamilton, Alice and Kenneth. *The Elements of John Updike*. Grand Rapids, Mich.: Eerdmans, 1970.

Harper, Howard M., Jr. "John Updike—The Intrinsic Problems of Human Existence," in *Desperate Faith*. Chapel Hill: University of North Carolina Press, 1967. Pp. 162–90.

Howard, Jane. "Can a Nice Novelist Finish First?" *Life*, 61:74–82 (November 4, 1966).

Hyman, Stanley Edgar. "The Artist as a Young Man," *New Leader*, 45:22–23 (March 19, 1962).

———. "Chiron at Olinger High," *New Leader*, 46:20–21 (February 4, 1963).

Macnaughton, William R. *Critical Essays on John Updike*. Critical Essays on American Literature Ser. Boston: G.K. Hall, 1982.

Mizener, Arthur. "The American Hero as High-School Boy: Peter Caldwell," in *The Sense of Life in the Modern Novel*. Boston: Houghton Mifflin, 1964. Pp. 247–66.

Podhoretz, Norman. "A Dissent on Updike," in *Doings and Undoings*. New York: Farrar, Straus, 1964. Pp. 251–57.

Samuels, Charles Thomas. "The Art of Fiction XLII: John Updike," *Paris Review*, No. 45, pp. 84–117 (Winter 1968).

———. "Updike on the Present," *New Republic*, 165:29–30 (November 20, 1971).

Sheed, Wilfrid. "Play in Tarbox," *New York Times Book Review*, 73:1, 30–33 (April 7, 1968).

Spectorsky, A. C. "Spirit under Surgery," *Saturday Review*, 42:15, 31 (August 22, 1959).

Tallent, Elizabeth. *Married Men & Magic Tricks: John Updike's Erotic Heroes*. Berkeley: Creative Arts Book, 1982.

Taylor, Larry E. *Pastoral and Anti-Pastoral Patterns in John Updike's Fiction*. Carbondale: Southern Illinois University Press, 1971.

Uphaus, Suzanne H. *John Updike*. Modern Literature Ser. New York: Ungar Publishing, 1980.

"View from the Catacombs," *Time*, 91:66–68, 73–75 (April 26, 1968).

Ward, J. A. "John Updike's Fiction," *Critique*, 5:27–40 (Spring-Summer 1962).

Wyatt, Bryant N. "John Updike: The Psychological Novel in Search of Structure," *Twentieth Century Literature*, 13:89–96 (July 1967).

Yates, Norris W. "The Doubt and Faith of John Updike," *College English*, 26:469–74 (March 1965).

—*CHARLES THOMAS SAMUELS*

Robert Penn Warren

1905-1989

REVIEWING Robert Penn Warren's *The Legacy of the Civil War* (1961) Alfred Kazin suggested that the same title defines the whole of Warren's output, by now some twenty books in thirty-five years. It is a just suggestion, deceptive only in making Warren, who shares the existential preoccupations of such writers as Camus, Sartre, and Malraux, a more narrowly American, a more exclusively historical writer than he in fact is. Born a southerner, he has remained one spiritually, but his allegiance has been complex and tormented. His knowledge of and profound concern for the American South have taught him about the penalties and advantages of being not only American but also human. And this double lesson has flowered in extraordinary, widely differing ways in part at least because he has spent his life in intimate touch with the leaders of intellectual movements of various kinds, from the Vanderbilt Fugitives to the Agrarians and New Critics. He is very much a man of his time, and of history too.

Born in 1905 in Guthrie, Kentucky, Warren graduated in 1925 from Vanderbilt University and two years later took his M.A. at Berkeley, going on to Yale and, as a Rhodes scholar, to Oxford. At Vanderbilt he met Allen Tate (another Kentuckian), John Crowe Ransom, and Donald Davidson, and joined them in editing

The Fugitive (1922–25), a magazine dedicated to the idea of the poet as an outcast soothsayer. In 1929, a year before receiving the Oxford B.Litt. degree, Warren published his first book, *John Brown: The Making of a Martyr*. After returning to the United States he held various teaching posts in the South until in 1934 he went to Louisiana State University. A year later *Thirty-Six Poems* appeared and was well received. Warren the poet, like Warren the teacher, had arrived.

At Louisiana he again met Cleanth Brooks, whom he had been with at Vanderbilt and Oxford. Together they founded the *Southern Review* (1935–42) and then collaborated on a "New Critical" textbook, *Understanding Poetry* (1938), which in demanding minute and disciplined analysis revolutionized the teaching of poetry in American universities and colleges. In 1942 Warren took up a post at the University of Minnesota, leaving for Yale in 1950. He retired in 1956 to devote himself to writing, but subsequently resumed his connection with Yale.

Warren's early intellectual associations have determined many of his abiding concepts and might even be said to have formed the pattern of his career. His essays witness to his belief that a work of art creates its own terms and must be taken on them: its fullness, its mercuriality and complexity, its inclusion of "impure" figures such as irony and paradox, are its own form of power; and this power has nothing to do with the unequivocal, generally serviceable propositions and facts on which everyday life has to be based to work at all.

Yet Warren, a founding and surviving Fugitive, has always shared Ransom's anti-aestheticism. "I subordinate always Art to the aesthetic of life," Ransom wrote to Tate in 1927, "its function is to initiate us into the aesthetic life, it is not for us the final end." Warren's distaste for the remoteness of aestheticism extended into distaste for the man with the blueprint: the megalomaniac idealist such as John Brown. But Warren the empiricist held fast to the actualities of Tate's True Southern Spirit (*"Nous retardons"*) only to find the reformer in him objecting to that spirit and then denouncing, as the epitome of modern secularism and soulless stereotyping, its replacement, the "New" South.

Such are the conflicts and paradoxes of Warren's encounter with the "deep, twisting strain of life." In him the equilibrium for which the New Critics extol the Middle Ages has occurred only rarely and unstably. He has within him, but disordered, all the elements of an immaculate balance; and a nervously alert mind has done the rest, keeping those elements in constant disturbance. He belongs within his own defense of Proust, Eliot, Dreiser, and Faulkner who all, he says, "tried . . . to remain faithful to the complexities of the problems with which they were dealing," against "the mind which is hot for certainties." Always arguing for "the arduous obligation of the intellect in the face of conflicting dogmas," he is not the man to provide slogans or catchphrases—or not to provide them either. It all depends on the exigencies of his sense of irony and his respect for the grain of life. To him irony is not static but a tug-of-war.

Not surprisingly, then, his "aesthetic of life" is almost impossible to codify but fascinating in evolution. One of the four Fugitives who became Agrarians, he was also one of the three contributors to *I'll Take My Stand* (1930) who wanted that manifesto against mechanization called "A Tract against Communism." His own contribution, "The Briar Patch," subjects theory to an onslaught of data—a favorite procedure of his ever since. Unless, he argued, rural life in the South rearranged itself around agricultural nuclei, Negroes would keep on defecting to an illusory better life in northern industrial cities. In *Segregation* (1956), however, he was less Procrustean, conceding a less rigid image of the Negro and expressing more openly his belief in man's capacity to assess and announce his own potential.

This respect for individual dignity underlies all Warren's incursions into the privilege, responsibility, and pain of self-knowledge. Identity, for him, is a religious condition: one of the rites of passage through life. This is why in "Literature as a Symptom," contributed to the volume *Who Owns America?* (1936), he opts for regionalism, not socialism, as the galleon to which the modern artist should attach his canoe. Regionalism permits individuality; socialism, dealing in a class abstraction, cannot. Warren's is a simplifying view, of course, just as rigid in its stereotyping of socialism as some socialism is in its public propaganda. All the same, his devotion to the South, the region whose most cherished virtues ensured its defeat, embodies his common sense. That part of the land has known subjugation, acknowledges history, would define a charmed life as a life where charm and elegance count, whereas the North fancies itself and its industrial ingenuity as invulnerable. This is not just to work the Dixie past against an untested present; it is to set in focus what Warren in

Segregation calls "the philosophy of the ad-man, the morality of the Kinsey report, and the gospel of the bitch-goddess."

Like the other Agrarians, Warren finally relinquished social reform for the arena where he had some power and say: literature and criticism. Necessarily, then, the secluded critic impeded the experience-hungry novelist; but no writer has worked harder than Warren to substantiate narrative through close, doting observation of the physical, emotional world. He sees it, captures it, makes the page tremble with it. His homework is always done, and not by his mind alone: there is little of his writing that will not pass the test of empirical exactness, and few of his intellectual characters reach a conclusion without being sidetracked by a clamant sense of something rich in the memory or miraculously at hand. The writer in him has always welcomed the routine and discipline of teaching as a means of producing "truly profound and humanistic people." And what Warren the ex-Fugitive from southern penury has disseminated through northern colleges has its physical equivalent in the hectic counterpoint of his writings: no endeavor but he tries to work the opposite against it, searching always for wholeness and completeness.

On the one hand, he makes a special case for the South, speaking of a change of heart as even now a possible "treachery . . . to that City of the Soul which the historical Confederacy became," and specifying the Civil War as the South's "Great Alibi" by means of which "the Southerner makes his Big Medicine. He turns defeat into victory, defects into virtues." The war gave the South a mandate for incessant obsolescence and made nostalgia seem a forward-looking mood.

On the other hand, while noting how the South remains more obsessed about its identity than the North, he cuts through to wider perceptions. All men, not southerners only, are "trapped in history"; southerners, like Jews, *happen* to feel it more acutely than most and have at hand all the apparatus of paranoia. This is one of the incidents of history; things might have been otherwise, but were not. Civil war, Warren argues, is "the prototype of all war" and the most grievous proof of all war's pain. So too the studiedly severe argument which intelligent southerners conduct within themselves emerges as both futile and honorable: an earnest of compassionate, bewitched patriotism. Such a mind as Warren's is indeed trapped in history, is full of "bitter paradoxes," just as loyal to a defeated past and a convicted geography as to the tasks of conscience in the present and in the congenially liberal North.

No wonder Warren seems torn apart, dramatizing in his own head the thesis that "it's human to be split up" and, like the guilty lovers in his novels, risking discovery. No wonder he himself deals in the sad science of abstractions until human nature and his own identity disappear into a fog consisting of "the Great Twitch," "the Great Sleep," "Higher-Law Men" (Abolitionists), original sin, pragmatism, and "charismatic arithmetic." Against vast forces of nature he works his own vast-sounding concepts. But the quarrel with himself remains, a process of self-study conducted in public; and his paradoxes, large or small, sometimes stifle one another. Not finding answers, Warren proves the value of keeping alive a needed attitude and the discomfort of being a resolute participant rather than the spectator an ex-Fugitive and powerless Agrarian might have become. His "texture of relations"—to his past, to his work, to familiars and strangers—is something he fingers endlessly; and in the long run it is the feel, not the feel's meaning, that he communicates, although many meanings are tried on for size on the way.

His early poems in *The Fugitive* introduce his interest in the melodrama of history, in "The agony of gasping endless/columns,/Skulls glaring white on red deserts at noon." But only one of these poems appeared in his first book, *Thirty-Six Poems* (1935), and this, "To a Face in the Crowd," characteristically probes the immensity and blankness of the past, memorializing nameless progenitors in a racial elegiac: "We are the children of an ancient band/ Broken between the mountains and the sea." Such a vision, anticipating the ground bass of the novels, is that of human involvement: we are all, through blood and time, connected, even to those we cannot know about.

Many of the poems in this first collection are little cascades of worry: Warren muses on vicissitude and the seasons, deciding the only peace is to be as stone, but gaining no pleasure or comfort from his stylish affirmation. The question "Why live?" recurs, but the copperheads, rocks, harvests, cardinals, jays, and the dead from the Civil War, have no answer. Mute life-forces compel man onward according to no ascertainable syllabus. In "Watershed" the poet yearns for the hawk's high, synoptic view: life on the hard surface of this planet is too fragmented, too teeming, and the variety of created things in all their phases defeats attempts at résumé. *Tout passe* is the leitmotiv, and Warren senses terrors in the earth's very familiarity. One choice—that between being someone and being at peace—is unavoidable: to be someone demands sacrifice and should instill responsibility; to try to efface oneself for the sake of peace is to ape the rocks vainly.

Already Warren is the master of literate paradox, the split man willing himself into unity. In "The Return: An Elegy" the son anticipates finding his mother dying like a fox in the hills and, in a startling identification of himself and her with the early pioneers, submits to remorse that varies from the portentous to the austere. Another poem, "Eidolon," sketches the insomnia of a runaway boy miserably returned. He lies "in the black room" with his father and grandfather, dreaming of the white eidolon that reveals how to meet a future he did not will upon himself.

It is not surprising that Warren incorporates a great deal of landscape into these poems: the land holds all ancestors; it is the compost that lies down whereas the society of men, ever changing, is the compost that moves about. What grows is the sense of an ancestrally determined obligation to be a definite someone: "The act/Alone is pure," so a completed act is no longer pure. All that is pure is the instant of movement. Man has a choice, especially a young man; the seasons have not. Man can, if he wishes, identify with his environment ("I am as the tree and with it have like season") but he remains distinct from it. Life twists and turns, coiling like the copperhead, and men express their bewilderment in lazy, self-deceiving metaphors: "The stiff trees rear not up in strength and pride/But lift unto the gradual dark in prayer." But who knows *what* the trees are doing? This is a poetry of conundrums, hard-edged in phrase but sometimes flatulent ("arrogant chastity of our desire"). Warren would write just as vividly without being as melodramatic, just as poignantly without the verbal diluteness, but the antitheses—idea and fact, word and flesh, inorganic and human, process and identity—survived to be the polarities of all his work to come.

In *Eleven Poems on the Same Theme* (1942) he no longer vacillates but states his problems in a manner compressed and impersonal. The poems say more and replace distraught obsession with a reconciled stare. The result is a fugue on the most fundamental problem of all: human fraternity versus, but also sustaining, sin.

The tone and manner of "End of Season," one of the most striking and spectacular poems, are something new. The poem opens with a bland imperative: "Leave now the beach, and even that perfect friendship" and the almost blasé attitude extends to include a mannered iteration: "Leave beach, *spiagga, playa, plage,* or *spa.*" But such sallies are only fool's gold to attract the reader into cruder, less idyllic territory: "The Springs where your grandpa went in Arkansas/To purge the rheumatic guilt of beef and bourbon." The speaker is bemused by effects and his idea only just straggles through. Purity, desiderated, is "wordless," so the only way to salvation of any kind is through a submarine solitude: "the glaucous glimmer where no voice can visit." But, in the mailbox at home, letters wait; there is no escape, terrestrial or spiritual. All that is left is "Hope, whose eye is round and does not wink."

In another poem, "Bearded Oaks," the lovers lie together, "Twin atolls on a shelf of shade," hoping in vain for exemption from identity. Their hope, being futile, is hopeless, like the innocence and purity evoked in "Picnic Remembered" and again bathed in the amber marine light that connotes illusory safety.

There is no way back; and resolute attempts to forget ensure only that we remember. *Eleven Poems* describes a progress toward self-knowledge. First there is a fall from some blithe, cushioned state; then a traumatic first taste of separateness; and finally a resolve to trust vaguely in the larger hope of "love's grace" in a world that sees American volunteers killing now on one side, in Spain, now on another, in Finland. Aspiring man (Alexis Carrel with his test-tube heart) only discovers his limitations and is then tempted to abandon hope. Warren's principal method in these poems itself reflects his theme. He sets sharp, Auden-like vignettes of individuals against or amid a vague malaise that recalls the romantic discontent of all times ("What has availed/Or failed?/*Or will avail?*/Hawk's poise,/The boxer's stance,/The sail"). As if proving the shock of separateness, certain images leap out from their context: "And seek that face which, greasy, frost-breathed, in furs./Bends to the bomb-sight over bitter Helsing-

fors." So too, certain facile injunctions ("Go to the clinic") bark vainly against the pull of spiritual desolation. There are no bright and brisk correctives to the growing sense of guilt.

These poems reconnoiter until they bump against life where it will not yield. But not all the collisions determine, as they well might, the structure of the poems. Warren, always fond of long lines and willing to let adjectives crowd nouns, works regularly into transitional passages in which, under the appearance of motivic accumulation, he marks time while shuffling ideas, one of which eventually gains purpose and urges the poem to its next goal. Most of Warren's poems oscillate in this way at some point or other, and only his over-all strength of purpose brings them to a conclusion rather than merely stopping them. As a result, litter lies by the way, colorful but otiose:

The peacock screamed and his feathered
  fury made
Legend shake, all day, while the sky ran pale
  as milk;
That night, all night, the buck rabbit stamped in
  the moonlit glade,
And the owl's brain glowed like a coal in the
  grove's combustible dark.

This fondness for minor pageantry sometimes impedes the novels too while the idea behind it all, like a snubbed survivor, waits at a distance. Hence Warren's strength and weakness: he never neglects the surfaces of life and he sometimes fails to retrieve his interpretation or his point before it vanishes beneath a clutter of instances.

Thirty-Six Poems presents man's share in the world's evil through images of decay, sequestered animals, and the division of son from parents. The vision is not profound, but ecological and domestic. *Eleven Poems*, a subtler collection by far, registers evil in ways more massive, more sustained. The advance is from desultory studies to a polyptych of man bearing darkness within him wherever he goes. An inclusive certainty of grasp succeeds the previous grasshopper techniques, and a gathering sense of mystery informs and unites the eleven poems included. Gravid, slow-moving, and enameled, they introduce religious terms only to clinch an argument or, more often, to transfigure retrospectively a succession of images.

Selected Poems, 1923–1943 (1944) gathers together most of the poems from these preceding volumes and includes some new pieces too. "Variation: Ode to Fear" with its refrain, *"Timor mortis conturbat me,"* and its list of cumulative banal occasions ("When Focke-Wulf mounts, or Zero,/And my knees say I'm no hero") is a mock-ode, intendedly brittle and grotesquely poignant. The speaker, nauseated by cant, routine, slogans, hypocrisy minor and major, skimped or flip comments on Jesus, Saint Joan, and Milton, by silly discord and jejune pursuits—in short by the ephemera that engross diurnal man—relates all to the fear of death. This underestimated poem exposes a world too complex for any romantic, homogeneous mood or any sublime posture.

So too "Mexico Is a Foreign Country: Five Studies in Naturalism" includes a much wider array of emotions than the earlier poems. Gritty, facetious, sly, and willfully vulgar, the five parts introduce a Warren less resolutely grandiloquent, who now imports undignified objects and unprofound views into his lines:

If only Ernest now were here
To praise the bull, deride the steer,
And anatomize for chillier chumps
The local beauties' grinds and bumps . . .

It is not satire but a pert way of documenting the near-Dadaistic side of intelligent distress: ". . . here even the bladder achieves Nirvana,/And so I sit and think, 'mañana.' "

If such verse is destructive it also instructs.

The poet's jaundiced review of the trivialities that survive all great ideas and noble motives attends a deeper, unshifting perception. All passes: "Viene galopando," says the old Mexican, "el mundo." This time round, the poet is willing to notice anything; nothing is excluded or lost, and the gain is a more complex view, all antinomies and incongruity:

I do not know the mango's crime
In its far place and different time,
Nor does it know mine committed in a
    frontier clime . . .

It is God, the archetypal parent, who has now to be forgiven; and not only for the guilt man feels but also for making the world as harsh in meaningless contrasts as it is, and for conferring such delusive ideas as those of peace and innocence. Man and mango have to work out their respective salvations alone: "In separateness only does love learn definition." And the disquiet that pervades Warren's poems must finally, to any sensitive reader, seem a form of anger at causation. It is one thing to note that "Because he had spoken harshly to his mother,/The day became astonishingly bright," but quite another thing to confront the guilt consequent on having been born at all. Warren often degrades intermediate causes, relegating love ("Fellow, you tupped her years ago/That tonight my boots might crunch the snow") to animal level, man's nature to happenstance, and human intimacy to frantic parasitism.

These themes and motifs reappear full-scale in "The Ballad of Billie Potts." The prodigal son returns home and is murdered by parents who fail to recognize him. Warren handles this folktale from western Kentucky through alternating narrative and commentary, the one rich and awkward with doggerel sounds and Kentucky speech mannerisms, the other lofty, meditative, and often diffuse. A bizarre poem, it approaches caricature and cartoon, yet the moral—the wasted chance of trust—comes through unspoiled and, if anything, sharpened and straitened through contrast. Such a moral could hardly be exaggerated; it gains strength through being given such a hard time technically. Billie's father is an innkeeper who ambushes solitary travelers, each time doing violence to the recurring possibility of man's being a brother to man. Each time he attacks he destroys a chance of human community which, merely by doing nothing, he could preserve. He has free choice in this, but interferes with an established and maintainable peace until he causes the death of his own son. The point is that when Billie returns, rich and looking it, Billie too is a stranger who fits a stereotype, innocently counting on the absence of ill-will as all men must if they are not to become either paralyzed with fear or brutish through distrust. But his father "set the hatchet in his head," wrecking both the occasion for charity and the paternal-filial bond.

The father works by a defective ethic, regretting not the act of murder but his choice of victim. He regrets for immoral reasons, and Warren thus proves that an impersonal reflex of charity is superior to emotions that are merely partial. The world is full of strangers: therefore man must devise and uphold a code that gives each new relationship a chance to flourish. Whatever Billie's delusions about himself, he is entitled to human rights; but he loses more as a human than he could gain as a known son. And life's grand design is poorer far for his death than his parents are in bereavement. Special criteria, such as Billie's birthmark which the parents find when they dig up his body, are beside the point; it is the commonplace that counts in the arithmetic of goodwill.

If "Billie Potts" is blasphemous, it blasphemes as only the poem of a believer can. If Billie's father is God, striking categorically down irrespective of identity or age, then Warren has fixed on the harshness of mortality to make one point: trust in the long run is inevitable, whether it amounts to ignorance of fatalism. The only virtue in learning from experience is that life goes on, perpetually offering new chances against the old, depressing background:

(There is always another country and always
    another place.
There is always another name and another face.
And the name and the face are you, and you
The name and the face . . .)

Innocence cannot be retrieved, but it can be created out of evil: a man's children always start clean, and all the father can do is be humble before life's incessant renewals and seek to know himself, and his kind, better. For knowledge can sometimes improve man or help him to adjust, even if it can never perfect or redeem the defective, coiling human heritage: ". . . water is water and it flows,/Under the image on the water the water coils and goes/ And its own beginning and its end only the water knows."

It is this concern that shapes Warren's outlook: the effort toward self-knowledge and responsible identity amidst the inscrutable flux. This is why, for ten years, away in a sense like Billie Potts, he deserted poetry for fiction. He could best express his main obsessions in narrative. He required space, sheer length, and mere succession to demonstrate his views on time's "brumal deeps" and "the great unsolsticed coil" of human destiny. Poems, distilling and compressing, present conclusions but not the dullness, the tedium, the *longueurs* of life. Proof sooner or later has to be made through accumulation, through a mass of "circumstantial texture" presented in full. The poems are points of light above the hubbub of the novels, but always related to that hubbub—its violence and eventfulness—through deploying the same view of history and guilt.

Already he had published *Night Rider* and *At Heaven's Gate*, experimenting in both novels with forms of commentary. The hand of the novelist shows intermittently in "Billie Potts," and it is no surprise to learn that, around 1944, when *Selected Poems* came out, Warren toyed with the idea of a novel about another ax-murder, this of a Negro slave by the nephews of Thomas Jefferson. But eventually, because the narrative required too much commentary, Warren decided against a novel and instead drafted a stage version with Jefferson as a chorus, along the lines of "Proud Flesh," an unpublished play he wrote in 1939, which later became the novel *All the King's Men*. What finally evolved was not a play but a dramatic poem enabling Warren to "get out of the box of mere chronology, and of incidental circumstantiality."

Between *Selected Poems* and this dramatic poem, *Brother to Dragons: A Tale in Verse and Voices* (1953), came the Pulitzer Prizewinning *All the King's Men* (1946), the long story *Blackberry Winter* (1946), a collection of short stories titled *Circus in the Attic* (1948), and "A Romantic Novel," *World Enough and Time* (1950). It was this period which fixed Warren's literary stance, claimed him for the novel, and settled in his own mind the criteria by which, ever the reticent moralist, he would select the matter to build his fiction from. It is only fair to trace his poetry and dramatic verse across this gap in time, for *Brother to Dragons* follows naturally from "Billie Potts" and the first two novels contain much that the poetry, seen whole, helps to clarify at once, the tropes and anagoges of the one genre helping to unite

in the mind the more pedestrian and enumerative figures diffused through the other.

Brother to Dragons, meticulously and fluently written, has little of the stilted, air-beating rhetoric ("But I do not cuddle the hope that even your words could revoke the seminal assurance of time") that disfigures "Proud Flesh." The ax-slaying of a Negro by the sons of Jefferson's sister in 1811 generates a vivid, lavish parable in which the poet, as "R. P. W.," is a twentieth-century "interlocutor" desperately involved in the problem of evil versus aspiration. There is no direct action; the poem consists of events recapitulated during lunges of wideranging commentary, and traces Jefferson's advance from the ashamed bitterness of the disillusioned idealist to an attitude of skeptical pragmatism. Other characters—including Lilburn Lewis, the mother-fixated murderer, Meriwether Lewis, falsely accused of embezzlement, and Lucy, Lilburn's mother, who returns to win justice for her son—join as vocal and disputatious revenants in R. P. W.'s historic interview.

As Warren explains in his foreword, "historical sense and poetic sense" complement each other, the one a reminder of "the big myth we live," the other of "the little myth we make." History dwarfs and baffles; poetry augments and illumines. In a sense, the characters, far from antagonistic to one another, are dispersed segments of a compound ghost all sociably pursuing an identical comfort. They are less themselves than they are epitomes of prevalent human attitudes engaged in what Warren, in an address at Columbia University, called "continual and intimate interpenetration, an inevitable osmosis of being." R. P. W. puts it this way: "the Victim is Victor . . . because the Victim is lover of injustice." And one's reluctance to give intellectual attention to such wordplay is essential to Warren's success. We suspect paradox because it offers an unpalatable or preposterous dogma and shocks us with the long view from an opposite, complementary position such as history's. The result is to increase our sense of contiguity and of life's indivisibility.

Warren proves that only a synthesis of perspectives can teach us to live responsibly, while the verse itself—now a bemused liturgy of country detail, now a terse report of bloodletting, now a pattern of abstract nouns that reads like a denouement—embodies this diversity, increasing the centrifugal pull but motioning at the center. One of Warren's most powerful works, this colloquial catechism is as far as he could go without imposing the methods of the novelist on the poet's habitual shorthand. It ends with R. P. W. leaving "that perfect friendship" on the headland to rejoin his father who is dozing in the car. He takes with him something "Sweeter than hope," a prelude to a peace which nevertheless cannot come easily.

In *Promises: Poems 1954–1956*, which won Warren his second Pulitzer Prize when it appeared in 1957, he specifies his something "Sweeter than hope" in genealogies and modest proposals for his son and daughter. (He had married writer Eleanor Clark in 1950.) The father has given them the past and a future; he knows who they are historically, what they will be if they allow themselves only the right illusions. A neighbor's lovely child dismays him because, whatever parents think, beauty itself is only a promise, not an amulet. Rosanna, Warren's daughter, is safe in the sunlight of her laughter, but only while a child; and already much has happened to her that she still cannot know about. The son, Gabriel, gets sterner treatment as Warren sifts the past and separates the possibilities that died from the facts that are. Accident, he says, is relentlessly successful. The idea of family predominates, and even families are accidental stabilities based on an ineluctable past. Warren states the details with tender, unstraining empathy:

What was the promise when, after the last
   light had died,
Children gravely, down walks, in spring dark,
   under maples, drew
Trains of shoe boxes, empty, with windows,
   with candles inside,
Going *chuck-chuck*, and blowing for crossings,
   lonely, *oo-oo*?

He sees through the paraphernalia of these ingenuous rehearsals; sees through the ground itself to where "Side by side, Ruth and Robert," his own parents, lie forever. Their repose seems to guarantee the children's future, and he tells Gabriel about his own boyhood, similarly guaranteed by a vision or hallucination of one "old, rough-grizzled, and spent" who asked "Caint you let a man lay!" and then moves on "in joy past contumely of stars or insolent indifference of the dark air."

These lovely poems show Warren at his most relaxed, addressing the children on a storytelling, game-playing level while, in his mind's eye, he sets them against vast landscapes and exigent inheritances. Musing on forefathers, he realizes where his power ends and invokes "the light of humanness . . . under the shadow of God's closing hand." The hand *will* close; the thing to worry about is when. Of all the poems, perhaps "Infant Boy at Midcentury" says most for all three, the father and his two, through admitting so much of the world, and so much of his world-nurtured apprehension, into the presence of an almost overwhelming tenderness: on the one hand there are ticking clocks, "stew and stink," "the barracks bath," and "Praetorian brutes"; on the other, the time when

. . . on a strange shore, an old man, toothless
   and through,

Groped hand from the lattice of personal
    disaster, to touch you.
He sat on the sand for an hour; said *ciao, bello,*
    as evening fell.

Warren's basic wish in these poems begins
with a tough-minded aphorism that sums up
all his work: "the heart most mourns its own
infidelity," and in a series of fervent impera-
tives makes Browning points: "Enfranchise the
human possibility"; "Grace undreamed is grace
forgone." How fitting that the clearest account
of his religious sense should entail this paternal
assembly of generations tapering down into the
irrevocable existence of two children.

The next book, *You, Emperors, and Others:
Poems 1957–1960* (1961), was disappointing.
A few poems apart, the tone is captious and
weary, the mockery is routine ("In the age of
denture and reduced alcoholic intake"), and
the lyrical gestures are vapid ("Sleep, my dear,
whatever your name is"). There is something
acerb here that detests but obsessively records
the modern scene. The best poems, such as
"The Letter about Money, Love, or Other
Comfort, If Any," "Prognosis," and "Ballad:
Between the Box Cars," are narrative parables
which, like the long-winded titles, the long
lines, the showy epigraphs, and the Byronic
rhymes ("Jantzen" and "pants on"), betray the
presence of a novelist who resembles a rogue
elephant in shoving aside or trampling the
finicking perfectionism of the poem-maker.

The book has a prelude in "Original Sin,"
a poem whose meticulous, rhyming stanzas lur-
idly relate an impersonal "you" to the omnipresence of horror: "The nightmare stumbles
past, and you have heard / It fumble your door
before it whimpers and is gone." This poem—
like *Brother to Dragons* a key to the whole
of Warren—illuminates the jumpiness which
dominates *You, Emperors, and Others*. A profound dislike of human nature is what finally

relates the poems to the fiction and gives dimension to Warren's equally profound dismay
with himself. The "you"-figure is not so much
a mask as a mirror that won't answer back
when something "sweeter than hope" is betrayed. As Tobias Sears says in *Band of Angels*, "it's so hard right in the middle of things
to remember that the power of soul must work
through matter, that even the filthiness of things
is part of what Mr. Emerson calls the perennial miracle the soul worketh, that matter often
retains something of its original tarnishment."
Much of Warren's restlessness comes from his
discovering that hard truths, even when swallowed repeatedly, do not soften. Hence too
some of his almost gloating fascination with
"the filthiness of things," even things we are
used to.

In his introduction to the Modern Library
edition of Conrad's *Nostromo* Warren takes
pains to define "the philosophical novelist" as
one "for whom the documentation of the world
is constantly striving to rise to the level of
generalization about values, for whom the images always fall into a dialectical configura-
tion, for whom the urgency of experience, no
matter how vividly and strongly experience
may enchant, is the urgency to know the meaning of experience." In its voluminous and emphatic way this sheds light on Warren himself.

We have only to read a random page of
Warren's prose to see that experience "en-
chants" him in the same measure as his desire
to find meanings is urgent. Warren the sophisticated, highly educated teacher and penetrating critic has had to compete with Warren
the pageant-loving southerner whose gift for
exact lyrical abandon shows on every page. His
progress and his upsets are the natural out-
come of that conflict—not just because philosophy curtails angels' wings or because sensual

delight saps analytical intellect, but because Warren has always been intellectually ambitious as well as a natural respecter of natural forces. Take the definition quoted above: it is clever, persuasive denial of the creative artist's willpower. The "documentation," notice, does its own striving; so does the "image." It is as if Warren, reluctant to announce the passion to interpret as a feat of the mind, disguises it as a natural process that goes on independently of, perhaps even in spite of, the writer himself. Hence his vision:

. . . every act is Janus-faced and double,
And every act to become an act must resolve
The essential polarity of possibility.
Thus though the act is life and without action
There is no life, yet action is a constant
     withering
Of possibility, and hence of life.
So by the act we live, and in action die.

Put like this, in *Brother to Dragons*, Warren's existential perplexity seems ambiguous. Compelled to engage in acts of will, men almost always find compensation in the pleasures of the senses: "I have a romantic kind of interest," he admitted in a *Paris Review* interview, "in the objects of American history: saddles, shoes, figures of speech, rifles, etc. They're worth a lot. Help you focus." And, for him, the complications of living and writing come about through "the anguish of option"—that between taking phenomena for their own sake and trying to interpret them.

The option is national. American society, as Warren says, came into being suddenly, and intelligent Americans are still grappling with the suddenness, the improvised nature, of it all. Warren pores over the nation's history, trying to decide how free and how determined the individual is. The War between the States was a second, hurried attempt at clarity; and the southerner, as he points out

in *Segregation*, has a unique knowledge of what moral identity means on both the national and personal levels. In fact man's ability to analyze relates him even more subtly to history: to think about life is to become even more intimately enmeshed in it. Reflection proves that we carry the burden for much we are not responsible for and that, all the same, we have no genuine identity until we assume responsibilities unique to ourselves.

To attempt such a theme is no minor undertaking, and Warren's own attempts have not always been successful. The technical problems alone are immense; they involve him in his own theme. For example, writing on Katherine Anne Porter, he says that "the thematic considerations must, as it were, be validated in terms of circumstance and experience, and never be resolved in the poverty of statement." The truly philosophical novelist finds the work beginning to do itself, whereas another kind of novelist (Warren's type) has to keep making the thinker in him be a novelist.

His first published novel, *Night Rider* (1939), deals with the Kentucky tobacco wars of 1905–08 in which the growers organized themselves against the big buyers. But the literally benighted development of Perse Munn, the central character, has an allegorical force transcending the regional interest. (Warren printed an introductory note warning that *Night Rider* was not intended as a historical novel.) Munn travels erratically backwards through a self-imposed dark night of the soul, and the narrative is less documentary in impact than metaphorical. Munn covets power, espouses the cause of the Association of Growers of Dark Fired Tobacco, and gradually comes to enjoy his involvement with mobs: they give him a sense of dynamic immersion as well as the identity of a firm role. Demagoguery is both his narcotic and his undoing; he not only takes more than he gives but loses private tenacity of spirit the more his public power grows. He worries how to define "the true and unmoved center of his being" and becomes involved in violence, but involved like a sleepwalker, losing through self-destruction all he gains through being self-assertive.

Things move too fast for him. His marriage degenerates, the Association splits, illegal night-riding becomes a common terror, defection and dissension increase, and he yearns for a boyhood world where, as in the stereopticon, things stand still when you want them to. Imponderables multiply beyond his capacity to control and order them. He cannot, like Ianthe Sprague, the only relative he could turn to in Philadelphia while studying law, adapt himself: Ianthe liked to have the newspaper read to her at disjunctive random. To her neither order nor, therefore, chaos mattered. Brutalities and burnings, losses and accusations pile up until Munn has to escape to the rural retreat of Willie Proudfit, a man who has come through and who tells Munn about his own share of the American dream—open spaces, buffalo, gunfights, and eventual return to Kentucky. By now Munn has lost everything except the passion to vindicate his emptiness; he decides to kill Senator Tolliver, the father-figure who deserted the growers' cause and whom he hates for involving him (as he thinks) in the whole mess. Yet, as he tells Tolliver, his motive is not "because you are filthy, but for myself. To know what I am." Munn's last act embodies the only wisdom left to him: for so long one of the living dead, he eliminates paradox by attracting the fire of state troops who have been following him.

Night Rider is full of violent events counterpointed by Munn's self-probings. It is an exciting, thought-compelling book, but somehow lacks a dimension. All Warren's favorite concepts—will, identity, time, power, violence, escapism, guilt, and responsibility—get their turn

in a vivid demonstration; but Willie Proudfit, as an instance of self-rehabilitation, seems ancillary and rudely imported. His self-communing pales beside the spectacular action, depriving the reader of the full meditative torment which brought such a character as Munn into being. Here Warren fights shy of "poverty of statement" and one misses what one gets from Malraux's *Man's Hope*, another novel about the mishaps of collective endeavor; and that is a sense of the novelist's undivided involvement in the theme he picks.

The next novel, *At Heaven's Gate* (1943), takes the theme further, once again offering characters who define themselves at the expense of natural order (just as Munn callously exploits everything, everyone, to hand), but also diagnosing their spiritual emptiness exhaustively. Again, too, there is an interpolated backwoods character who, like Willie Proudfit, has redeemed himself through homage to the source of his being: nature, family, tradition. Ashby Wyndham has sinned against his brother but atones in some degree through honest self-appraisal. And where Proudfit seems perfunctorily hauled in, Ashby Wyndham is there from the start, in jail, and he occupies alternate chapters as a grumbling integer in a novel conceived on lines both Dante-like and contrapuntal. Warren had already advanced a long way in ability to manipulate and interweave large, contrasting masses of experience.

Sue Murdock, defying the suave tyranny of her financier father, vents Warren's usual question: "Oh, what am I?" She deserts the man she loves, Jerry Calhoun, for being a mere carbon copy of her father, joins the retinue of bohemians run by Slim Sarrett, a homosexual poet-boxer, and becomes his mistress. Sue in the lower depths ("that dim, subaqueous world") is like Munn at Proudfit's home ("a submarine depth"). She too is capable of cruel outbursts. Munn works cruelty into his matrimonial lovemaking and she forces Jerry to take her physically in the room beneath her father's. They both rage against the outrage they think done to them, but impotently so.

Sue, moving from man to man, reveals the futility of defining oneself through others: if the effort succeeds, the self-definer only exhausts his host; if it fails, he uses the intimacy for a self-asserting revenge. The benighted and baffled despoil the best—those who in Slim's words "manage to maintain some shreds of reality and humanity." The agonizing thing is that the unstable person such as Sue cannot let those she clings to be anything but impervious: she requires a monolith and construes all tenderness as weakness, all confessed diffidence as failure. She punishes her own faults in others at the same time as she repudiates her father, the one man who meets her needs, for his tyranny.

Bogan Murdock, ruthlessly foreclosing homesteads, is the public's creature as well as his own man. He associates himself with the dashing audacity of such as Andrew Jackson, but his panache is grounded in insensitivity. He is a born survivor, "a great big wonderful dream" (as one character describes him) sanctioned by those he exploits. His is the image of the utter stranger, the man too weak deep down to know what part weakness plays in being truly human. If his daughter is asking for the moon (for a relationship that does not modify the other person) then he is a creature of lunar coldness, grandly asking nothing but power.

Yet both, simple in their wrongness, create enormous complexities in the lives of others; Warren uses them to compound further the complexity he finds here, as always, readymade in history (Murdock has much in him of Luke Lea, the sometime United States senator and convicted swindler from Tennessee). Warren's overall view is of the incalculable,

unpredictable repercussions our least endeavors provoke. Identity, in particular, is not a fixity but a studiously maintained transaction with other people. The means of self-establishment is also the prime agency of confusion, especially for those who want perfection and utter consistency.

This is what Jack Burden discovers in *All the King's Men* (1946) when he becomes involved with Governor Willie Stark's political party machine. To him Stark is not so much a tyrant as a divinely appointed savior; not an idealist but a practical, misunderstood redeemer of Louisiana. And it is from this opinion that Burden, with his Ph.D. thesis in history following him around in a parcel, advances to learn about the corruption that binds all men together. He digs up facts that Stark can use against people in his campaigns and thus brings about the suicide of Judge Irwin, who he then discovers is his own father, rather than Ellis Burden, "the Scholarly Attorney," who had been his mother's husband at the time of his birth. History's cupboards sometimes ought to be left closed. He now has to reappraise the past in the light and horror of this knowledge. Burden's Landing, his birthplace, is not simply a backwater where his mother and former friends have obviously sustained an outmoded, questionable way of life; it is a symbol of the incompleteness of modern man's knowledge. Where, previously, visiting the Landing he felt "sad and embarrassed and, somehow, defrauded," he learns to say "I could now accept the past which I had before felt was tainted and horrible." The Landing, although embarrassing Jack with its obsolescence and phony consistency, possesses part of him forever, and he has to accept this fact in order to live.

A double standard emerges. Stark, ruthlessly pursuing the public good, succeeds by using the past to smear members of the present, but only until a modern idealist, Adam Stanton, shoots him for treating people as things. Stark knows that man is indivisible from history (though he denies it publicly); Burden tries to persuade himself of the contrary. Stark is right but uses his knowledge perniciously, dehumanizing both history and the living. Burden, wrong but tentative and therefore impressionable, acquiesces because he cannot respect history or its share in what individual people are. He learns the truth only when Stark's dispassionate policy and his own misapplied expertise bring ruin to Judge Irwin and, in so doing, expose the true ancestry of Jack Burden. The past endures.

So, through an example of personal shock demolishing inhuman abtractness, Warren condemns unspiritual secularism. Stark, like Bogan Murdock, wields power that derives from the fact that he can "vicariously fulfill certain secret needs of people about him"; but the people, whatever the demagogue says, cannot be separated from their own history any more than the demagogue can from his. The blandishments made possble through a booming technology may fool the people some of the time, but not all of them all of the time. Adam Stanton denounces Stark's six-million-dollar hospital as political window dressing and then, trapped in his own geometry, eventually accepts the directorship. Even the rampant idealist must finally admit the power and insidiousness of context, the glutinous hold of the social fabric. Stark tries to unravel the corrupt web of his life until, by interfering, he dooms his own son to an early death; Stanton, idealist too frequent, is killed in assassinating Willie. The repercussions of their conduct have already proliferated in countless, irrevocable ways; and Jack Burden, man of ideas, has to ponder the remnants, conscious always of how

the idealists (Stanton, John Brown, Jefferson) match the pragmatists in callousness. What defeats them all is mere contingency: "I eat a persimmon," Burden thinks, "and the teeth of a tinker in Tibet are put on edge."

Part of the meaning of *All the King's Men* is that none of the evils totalitarianism claims to remedy is worse than totalitarianism itself. The same point occurs in "Proud Flesh" (in which the central character is called Talos instead of Stark). Later versions are the two stage adaptations of the novel and the motion-picture script. Understandably, Warren has been unable to leave the theme alone, not only assisting in adaptations but footnoting it in various essays.

Most of all, he has been careful to separate Willie Stark and his "state" from their matrices, Huey Long and Louisiana. The novel, he explains, grew from an experience of two worlds: factual and mythical. In the first a debilitated craving for elegance matched "drool-jawed grab and arrogant criminality"—a world that reminded him of "the airs and aspirations" attributed to Von Ribbentrop the ex-champagne salesman and to the clique around Edda Ciano. "For," as he says, "in Louisiana, in the 1930's, you felt somehow that you were living in the great world, or at least in a microcosm with all the forces and fatalities faithfully, if sometimes comically, drawn to scale." The other world, that of folklore and fabliau violence, included the glamour that gathered about Long's name and doings, refracting and inflating his image until it seemed a monstrous, sly outcrop from the Louisiana magma itself, mocking and outdoing the cypress swamps, the hovels of the moss-pickers, the arsenical green of water the sun never touches, cottonmouth moccasins, and clicking, buzzing insects.

It is significant that Warren's first attempt to draw the "iron-groom" figure of Talos-Stark-

Long was the verse drama begun in 1938 "in the shade of an olive tree by a wheat field near Perugia." He began with the myth: popular imagination improvised because it did not know, any more than Warren did, what the private Huey Long was like. And his continuing preoccupation with this demagogue-figure is as much mythological as reportorial; for all his profuse, complicated circumstantial evidence, his accounts have the impact of a folk ritual prepared by a poet who responds intensely to the organic power of "the dark and bloody ground" (the Indian name for Kentucky). His own summation is worth noting: denying he "was" Jack Burden, or Jack Burden only, he says he was all the characters and remains inextricably absorbed in them. "However important for my novel was the protracted dialectic between 'Huey' on the one side, and me on the other, it was far less important, in the end, than that deeper and darker dialectic for which the images and actions of a novel are the only language."

The theme is man, earthbound, earth-held, not one with nature but licensed by nature and obliged, always, to subject his aspirations to his religious sense: that is, to his sense of being indivisible from an organic whole he has not himself created. This essential derivedness and rootedness of man appears in Warren's note on the hitchhiker he picked up while driving to North Louisiana in 1934: he was "a country man, the kind you call a red-neck or a wool-hat, aging, aimless, nondescript, beat up by life and hard times and bad luck." Warren goes on to build a vision that tells us much about his way of apprehending a world in which people, as well as vegetation, provide the humus in which initiative grows and sometimes runs wild: "He was the god on the battlement, dimly perceived above the darkling tumult and the steaming carnage of the political struggle.

He was a voice, a portent, and a natural force like the Mississippi River getting set to bust a levee. . . . it is certain that the rutted back roads and slab-side shacks that had spawned my nameless old hitchhiker . . . had, by that fall of 1934, made possible the rise of 'Huey.' My nameless hitchhiker was, mythologically speaking, Long's *sine qua non*."

For each of his tawdry Olympians Warren provides this kind of underworld; it remains when the Olympian has gone. Perse Munn, Bogan Murdock, and Willie Stark are consumed by the element that spawned them, and that element includes the retreated and revulsed characters such as Willie Proudfit, Ashby Wyndham, and Jack Burden. In the long run, Warren's contrasts and probings must be read as examples only and not imputed back to him. As he told Ralph Ellison in the interview for the *Paris Review*, the writer's business is "not to illustrate virtue but to show how a fellow may move toward it—or away from it." In short, a field study, not a sermon.

At its most complex and cogent the field study amounts to Coleridge's inexhaustible repercussion. In shooting the albatross the Ancient Mariner tries to cancel the soul's relationship to the universe; but he is finally convinced by his imagination that such canceling is impossible and must yield to what Warren, writing on Melville, calls a "solution achieved in terms of . . . exercise of will." Violence rarely solves anything, although it seems to abolish a physical hindrance.

Imagination has two uses: popular and private. The first can produce and sanction monsters; the second can induce private nightmare. Bogan Murdock, like Willie Stark, is something the people thought up; Perse Munn is his own monster, spawned in his own whirling head at night. But there are virtuous uses too: rare for the popular imagination because massive numbers entail simplification and formulas, but fairly common for such as Coleridge's mariner and, in, say, *At Heaven's Gate* alone, Uncle Lew with the clubfoot, Duckfoot Blake, the maladroit Mr. Calhoun, Aunt Ursula the paralyzed, Private Porsum, and even Ashby Wyndham.

They all avoid abstraction: it stunts the reality of other people and warps the abstractor. Willie Stark, on the other hand, can be just as abstract-minded as Cass Mastern, Burden's Civil War ancestor. Man, says Willie, "is conceived in sin and born in corruption and he passeth from the stink of the didie to the stench of the shroud." It is a blank and bland formulation, just as jejune as Mastern's weird assertion that "It is human defect—to try to know oneself by the self of another. One can only know oneself in God and in His great eye." Cass is the well-meaning man who releases his Mississippi slaves but only to even worse hardship in the North. He feels strongly that he cannot control the consequences of his actions, but dies believing that "It may be that only by the suffering of the innocent does God affirm that men are brothers." Thus, both Stark and Mastern, in the end, learn truth when it is too late to reform things but not to accept them.

Jack Burden, reflecting on persimmon and the Tibetan tinker, comes to a similar conclusion in the end. His Great Sleep and Great Twitch were mere behaviorism. Yet the casuistries that kept him deludedly serene were hardly more specious than the Scholarly Attorney's unscholarly formulations about the cosmos: "Separateness is identity and the only way for God to create, truly create, man was to make him separate from God himself, and to be separate from God is sinful." Humanity is a congeries of clinging separate entities, and the only truth is in an independent, imaginative response to the knowable. Such is Warren's advice, and such his main fictional concealment of himself.

A single volume, *The Circus in the Attic* (1948), contains all of Warren's short stories, of which *Blackberry Winter,* published separately in 1946, is outstanding in the history of the genre as well as the most compact epitome of Warren's output. A man in his early forties recalls his initiation into manhood and the ways of nature. When a city-clad stranger comes to work on the farm during a time of storm and flood (like December 1811 in *Brother to Dragons*) the boy, little apprehending the devastation and stoicism evident everywhere, fastens to him and thus vicariously "goes away." This symbolic infidelity the adult narrator has come to regret; like the speaker in several of Warren's early poems he is saddened that as a boy he responded poorly to the beleaguered devotion of his parents. Guilt, ever-present in Warren's writings, dogs him until like old Jebb in the story he realizes the past is as unalterable as a ruined crop. Moreover, as if perfidy were not enough, it was perfidy at the wrong time: "blackberry winter" is when the genial spring unnaturally regresses and turns its back, reneging, just like the boy.

Once again Warren explores man and his relationship to the land. Neither is wholly predictable: the Negro maid uncharacteristically strikes her child; the river floods. There are no absolutes, but only risky combinations of transient circumstances. And the boy responds to the disorder of the time by holding to what is newest. "I did follow him, all the years," the narrator says remorsefully, stressing "did" to evoke the ghost of a foregone alternative.

Nothing of Warren's more convincingly demonstrates how complex his traditionalism is. The inevitability of change is a southern fact too, even though, as he is always saying, the supposed and usually mythical stability of the past is succeeded only by the instability of an unknown future. Man makes uneasy truces with nature which is reliable only because, in the mass, it never dies.

Predictably, then, Warren's favorite images express both an entranced horror with nature and horrified relief at man's power to control. Submerged in nature, man can know a vegetable peace; against it he can achieve a sterile safety. But he cannot safely ally himself with it, for it is inscrutable. Images of flood depict the odds. In "History among the Rocks" it is "a creek in flood" which will tumble and turn "a body, naked and lean." In *Brother to Dragons* R.P.W. speaks of "that deep flood that is our history," exemplifying "the drowned cow, swollen," while *Blackberry Winter* presents another cow "rolling and roiling down the creek." A poem in *Promises* tells how "A drowned cow bobbled down the creek" and Warren's most recent novel is itself called *Flood*. Man cannot flood out the flood of history and time. On the other hand he can create roads, imaging the direct-mindedness of efficient modernity and facilitating the hectic placelessness to which the nation turns in escape. Only history has unlimited accommodations and Warren's vision of America, a land cut cleanly across by numbered highways, is ironical: man applies Mercator to things fluid, aiding navigators but dominating nothing. *All the King's Men* opens with Jack Burden going on Highway 58 "northeast out of the city"; it is a straight, white-shimmering highway with a water-mirage forever ahead—"that bright, flooded place." *Flood* opens with a highway and stays on it for several pages; and nothing could be clearer than this from *Brother to Dragons*:

Up Highway 109 from Hopkinsville,
To Dawson Springs, then west on 62,
Across Kentucky at the narrow neck,

Two hours now, not more, for the road's fair.
We ripped the July dazzle on the slab . . .

"Mexico Is a Foreign Country" makes its point with sinister levity: "The highways are scenic, like destiny marked in red"; and *Segregation* commemorates Highway 61 cutting south from Memphis, "straight as a knife edge through the sad and baleful beauty of the Delta country." *Flood* ends with "the chrome and safety glass of cars passing on the new highway, yonder across the lake." New mastodons for old.

Such images, recurring, evoke one another and crystallize Warren's feeling that man can best nature only by cutting across, by disregarding and dividing, never by eliciting secrets from within. The highway, symbol of initiative, speed, and control, is sterile, plagued by fatigue, mirages, boredom, advertising, and death. The flood, symbol of revenge, impersonality, and accident, is the element that contains the highways. And, just as no road ever conquers what it cuts through, so no neat network of ideas can open up history; such is the gist of Warren's treatment of his intellectual characters. But men who live close to nature achieve understanding, inchoate as it is. They accept earth as their element and source, privilege and torment.

Most of Warren's best stories are painful, guilt-ridden commemorations of some young person's rites of passage. Grandfather Barden in "When the Light Gets Green" waits four years for death and love. But his grandson, prey to familiar Warren incapacities, cannot love: he lies, feels guilty, and, grown adult, feels even guiltier for still being unable to comprehend his deficiency. It is, probably, an unexpressed resolve to submit as little as necessary to the processes of mortality. Another boy, in "Christmas Gift," is similarly confounded by premature difficulties; but he copes by exchanging tokens with the doctor: candy for the chance to roll a cigarette. The boy in "Testament of Flood" does all his growing up in one instant of recognition. And, just as the young take their stand, gropingly or with unpracticed severity, so do those who have no future at all. Like Grandfather Barden, Viola the Negro cook in "Her Own People" lies in bed; discharged, she has nowhere to go, only death to look forward to. So she creates guilt all around her, exposing the spiritual debility of those who, like her employers, dare not love or live.

These are the problems of home, of growth within the tribe: having home, leaving it, aching to return, and being unable to dismiss intervening years. Home is also to be defined unsentimentally as any available intimate basis. For young and old alike, there must be a rock to build on even if it is only being unloved or unloving. The professor in "The Unvexed Isles" discovers how much of an unsophisticated, homesick midwesterner he is, but in re-establishing his marriage on this admitted truth cannot be wrong. Home is where candor sites it. So too the gelid marriage in "The Love of Elsie Barton: A Chronicle" stabilizes itself on bleak habit. Warren presents a choice: return to the source of one's being, like Billie Potts, or found a new home in maturity. All men crave the place where they are not naked or totally vulnerable. Bolton, the muted hero of "Circus in the Attic," is a case in point. He has repudiated his ancestors and must therefore find something to cleave to: his soft-pine circuses carved in secret, his draftee stepson, or writing his desultory, halfhearted history of the county.

Yet the longed-for world of home remains a terra incognita, less welcoming than present adversity. The reason is that childhood identity begins with the search for freely chosen, as distinct from inherited, attachments—and the guilt of cutting free. Warren's best stories prove

the search a new imprisonment; his least successful posit odd, fey ironies on situations not evaluated by characters who are themselves inscrutable.

Warren, like Bolton's father, has become increasingly "aware of the powerful, vibrating, multitudinous web of life which binds the woman and child together, victor and victim." The search for new complicities returns man to old paradoxes. Life's patterns vary little; only private, poetic truth is abundantly various; historical and cosmic truth is infinitely monotonous—something to hold to but also something aloof.

Such acknowledgments and bafflements underlie the complications of *World Enough and Time* (1950), Warren's most mandarin performance. Based initially on a pamphlet. *The Confession of Jereboam O. Beauchamp* (1826), it has an epigraph from Spenser's *Faerie Queen* and takes its title from Marvell. Jerry Beaumont, self-appointed knight-errant of the night, is a latter-day Artegall who ingenuously becomes his own victim, and Warren himself, for all the elaborate counterpoint of his narrative method and his intense preoccupation with identity ("Myself, oh, what am I?" asks Beaumont), lapses into the amenities of costume romance, a genre he condemns but likes to write in. The novel has a dazzling, intricate surface pitted with masterfully distanced dialogue; and nothing could be more to Warren's point. Surfaces can be recaptured but motives and inspirations cannot. "Their lips move but you do not hear the words . . . Nor hear the rustle of the heart," as he says in "Billie Potts."

Beaumont, trained as a lawyer, is drawn into state politics and, like most of Warren's idea-men, yearns to "define" himself through spectacular action. The yearning is Byronic as well as Spenserian. Beaumont, romantically assuming the cause of the supposedly dishonored Rachel Jordan, sets out to kill Cassius

Fort, her former lover and his own mentor and backer. The rationale, or excuse, for this is dangerously abstract: "Could a man," he asks, "not come to some moment when, all dross and meanness of life consumed, he could live in the pure idea? If only for a moment?" Like Willie Stark he wants to force glory from "the filth we strew"; but it is the same longing as the disillusioned Jefferson describes in *Brother to Dragons*:

. . . the sad child's play
And old charade where man puts down the bad
    and then feels good.
It is the sadistic farce by which the world is
    cleansed.
And is not cleansed, for in the deep
Hovel of the heart that Thing lies
That will never unkennel himself to the
    contemptible steel. . .

No man effaces nature. A yearning for purity is laudable but belongs to adolescence, to the world of Warren's early poems. Human glory has to flourish in the daily world somewhere between purity and filth; and romanticized violence, like the murderous sadism of Lilburn Lewis, condemns itself. So at first sight does Beaumont, terrified of drowning in history; but he is trapped. His aspiration is too great for the conditions of man's life, yet where else can he pursue it? His crime and penance, "being a man and living in the world of men," coincide exactly, as for Jack Burden. Small wonder that frustration so often in Warren's writings erupts into violence, out of which a little comes—of catharsis or satiety, but little enough when pitted against the world and time.

Beaumont, an Adam Stanton brought to judgment, is hard to decipher: is he coy martyr or glorious fake? The double narrative—an impersonal historian documenting without passion and Jerry himself venting his untidy soul—clouds everything. He is, basically, as unknowable as John Brown. Between the historian's confessed inadequacy and Beaumont's love of melodrama there is no choosing. There is no adding the two together either: massed data are useless when some areas remain blank. And Beaumont's escape with Rachel into the fetid Eden of the swamp is another of Warren's submarine-uterine removals. Beaumont deserts ideas for the Great Sleep and thus, unlike Beauchamp in the original document, has time to brood. Warren postpones his death until he has had time to admit things to himself about the impossibility of identity in isolation (to be unborn again), the impossibility of self-cleansing through condemning others (like Perse Munn), the superiority of truth to innocence and peace, the self-indictment that transcends codified justice, and the spectrum between law as a public absolute and law as a private appointment.

The novel is overwhelming. A galaxy of theatrically casuistical quandaries, it seems more complicated and less assimilable than life itself. Nothing becomes clear without generating tangential problems that are then added to what is central. The narrative merges into its theme, not so much defining complexity as increasing it through irrelevance. In such a context even the commonplace abruptness of death seems more enigmatic than usual. Warren never reduces the pressure and yet, wasting nothing, gains nothing he could not have gained less voluminously. It is as if, despairing of making sense out of so much complexity, he piled up data to overwhelm the reader too. Bewilderment is the novel's theme and, oddly enough, in view of all the oratorical intelligence on show, the only experience of which it ultimately extends our knowledge.

The same problem reappears in *Band of Angels* (1955). Continually drawn to questions of identity and motive Warren has Amantha Starr open the novel with "Oh, who am I?"

Brought up on a Kentucky plantation and then sent north to school, she discovers on her father's death that she is half Negro. After being sold into slavery she is bought by Hamish Bond who becomes her lover and brings her momentary peace, or surcease, at any rate. But Bond is an imposter; his real name is Alec Hinks, and this revelation sets Amantha questioning everything, especially names, signs, appearances, tokens—in short, all the means of communication and identification. Warren's divided account of Beaumont has a parallel in this divided girl. Product of miscegenation, she is also the articulate, self-pitying victim of such as Bond (who profits through her confusing freedom with not being a slave), Seth Parton, the self-apotheosized rustic from Oberlin (she and he expect too much pain from piety), Tobias Sears the Transcendentalist she marries, and Rau-Ru, Bond's colored henchman who eventually acquires an alias of his own—"Lt. Oliver Cromwell Jones." After much social and political upset in which individual rights and concerns disintegrate, Amantha and Tobias move to St. Louis and thence to Kansas where Tobias, who used to think (like Beaumont the knight-errant) of "dying into the undefiled whiteness of some self-image," begins to accept life and himself. Amantha, inspirited by his example, undertakes a similar self-revision and sheds the self-pity that made her more the victim of herself than of anyone else. She comes through, learning at last that identity depends on accepting one's separateness: "Don't ever call me poor little Manty again!" she tells Tobias, and the novel ends with her overwhelmed by the "awfulness of joy" and "all the old shadows" of their lives, as she says, "canceled in joy" too.

Amantha donnishly voices one of Warren's principal worries. "You do not live your life," she says, "but somehow, your life lives you, and you are, therefore, only what History does

to you." Finally, however, she repudiates such self-excusing and realizes she cannot honestly attribute her rape to events at Harpers Ferry. And Warren himself insists that self-definition to counter incessant "osmosis of being" is as much a Christian duty as a Christian privilege. He will not countenance organized security or any imposed direction for the soul. But surely there is a point at which legislated security, especially in the South, gives the soul what it needs to work in: freedom from persecution, a civil right less fascinating than self-definition and for that reason often ignored in favor of metaphysical and religious bagatelles.

In *The Cave* (1959) Jasper Harrick, a Korean veteran who has failed to find himself even in combat, returns home to Tennessee and takes to exploring caves, reassuring his mother that "in the ground at least a fellow has a chance of knowing who he is." When Jasper is trapped underground his supposed friend, Isaac Sumpter, delays the rescue in order to turn it into a publicity stunt. And after Jasper dies the gathered crowd embark on a crazed orgy: "Thousands of people, he didn't know how many, had come here because a poor boy had got caught in the ground, and had lain there dying. They had wept, and prayed, and boozed, and sung and fought, and fornicated, and in all ways possible had striven to break through to the heart of the mystery which was themselves." Major and minor characters alike find Jasper's entombment catalytic in resolving their own lives. They explore and rediscover themselves and one another, seeking the temporary oblivions of violence or love, but seeking also, through such self-venting and self-exposure, to make themselves firm.

The novel depicts a hillbilly auto-da-fé in which the loudspeakers, television cameras, prayers, spotlights, songs, chants, and slogans travestying the subterranean doom of Jasper yet constitute the only means of making it meaningful to others and making those others articulate to themselves. The story advances through a series of colliding, related dilemmas, and Warren for once leaves the irony to reveal itself. Isaac Sumpter, deep in the spiritual dark of being technically a murderer, goes off to a career in the dud Samarkand of "Big Media"; but he reaches his point of departure only after a long, comprehensive, and wholly convincing elenchus of a kind unusual in Warren. And those other "strange prisoners"—Jack Harrick, the life-devouring brawler and womanizer, now dying; Nick the mis-married restaurant-owner haunted by a corrupting image of Jean Harlow; Timothy Bingham the bank manager living by rote, not by the heart—come to developing, palpable life in a prose which, stopping just short of caricature, is as earthy, dynamic, and viscid as anything Warren has written. Those who gather at the cave find a meaning for their lives and not, like Amantha Starr invoking Harpers Ferry, an excuse.

Logically the next stage in Warren's demonstration—after Amantha's excuses and the crowd's voluptuous empathy in *The Cave*—should have been a homage to communal piety; and this is roughly what *Wilderness* (1961), in its perfunctory, mannered way, supplies. Adam Rosenzweig, clubfooted son of a Jewish Bavarian poet and liberal, comes to America during the Civil War in search of justice and freedom. In various ways, through bloodshed, mob violence, and commonplace compassion, he enters into a new community whose least aggressive impulse is stated by Mose the illiterate ex-slave after he has watched someone dying: "I would'nt keer, not if 'twas me. Layen thar bleeden." Also with Adam and Mose is a brutal planter, Jed Hawksworth, who has been run out of his native North Carolina. The three of them, becoming themselves in the "wilderness" of carnage and verminous mistrust

created by the war, might have come out of Stephen Crane. The badge of *their* courage is that of a harshly tested identity. Adam kills a man and, after accounting to himself, undertakes a laconic dialectic that finally reconciles him to being involved, however grievously, with other men. "*We always do what we intend*," he begins, at first impressed and awed by what he has done; but suddenly a sense of guilt desolates him. Then "*What I have done . . . I did for freedom*" yields to "*I did nothing I did not have to do*." After a recrudescence of his "if only" mood of remorse, he decides that every man is "a sacrifice for every other man." Everyone has betrayed him, including even his own father. But in this moment of clear sight he realizes too something like joy: "*Ah, he thought, this is it!* He felt the exaltation of one who discovers the great secret." And, dizzy with new power—even more elated than when, caught up in a mob, he almost stabbed a captured Negro—he steals a boot from the dead man and puts it on. Another rite has been staged.

A novel of short sentences and long meditations, *Wilderness* is terse, bleak, and disturbing not least because the three men, traveling as sutlers to the Federal Army, distract us little from the relentless simplicity of the plot and Adam's inevitable apocalypse. In *Flood* (1964), however, Warren resumes and raises to a beautiful symphonic level the same allegorical method, this time combining his profound concern for the past with the problems of durable identity. Two men, Brad Tolliver, native son who has been too long away, and Yasha Jones, guilt-haunted movie director, arrive in Fiddlersburg, Tennessee, to make a film about the town before it is evacuated for the building of a new dam. They stay with Brad's sister, whose husband is serving a life sentence in the jail nearby, and gradually come to know

Fiddlersburg, past and present, with an intimacy they find both useful and upsetting.

The whole book is rich with interacting, wholly functional patterns that complement one another: history's flood with flood man-made; Brad's involvement with Fiddlersburg through memory and suffering, Jones's involvement through response to novelty and his search for integrity within himself; the flood that ends one era but begins another; the preternatural vigor of the town's last days contrasted with the inertia of the past and of the unknown future. Brother Potts, dying, tries to hang on long enough to conduct a memorial service, and Frog Eye, the swamp rat, endures as a walking elegy of the almost forgotten past's survival.

Much intelligence and compassion underlie this assured novel. Warren seems to have got himself more evenly, more complicatedly distributed among the characters than before. So the "argument" proceeds in concert (as in *Brother to Dragons*) and not through one mind alone. Brad, like Jack Burden, goes home, learns, but cannot stay; Jones, homesick but for nowhere in particular, goes off to happiness with Brad's sister, having asked Brad, "How can one really define an accident . . . Unless . . . we have already defined it?" Will and choice are resurgent, and Brad reconciles himself to searching out—creating if necessary— "the human necessity," a choice that enfranchises to the full "the human possibility." Something like hope obstinately perpetuates itself.

No sharp-edged dogma emerges from these learned lessons. That is not Warren's way. He remains true to his dictum that "the poet wishes to indicate his vision has been earned" and that it "can survive reference to the complexities and contradictions of experience." He often tangles his notions on ancestry, history, childhood, identity, will, violence, and grace into an opaque conceptual thicket. But he does make us think and he does undertake all the intellectual formulations that Hemingway avoids and Faulkner turns into verbal skywriting. That is enough because he also gives us action and the same stoical sense of doom as they do. He knows life, is agonizedly involved in it, and his versatile searchings must strike a chord in every thoughtful reader. His dives into the dirt are more than an eccentric penance; they remind him, against all his hoping, of what is there: grief, wrath, injustice, blood, and evil. But, as he says in "Late Subterfuge," "Our grief can be endured" and "we have faith from evil bloometh good."

"There is no *you*," runs one sentence in *Flood*, "except in relation to all that unthinkableness that the world is." Warren shows what mind and heart can do with the unthinkable and, without pretending to understand, makes it thinkable-about, daring and exhorting others to approach it. That is the self-expending generosity of his achievement, the grandeur of its indignant impersonality, and also, in two senses, its only hope.

[*Publisher's note:* Robert Penn Warren was named poet laureate of the United States on 26 February 1986. He died of cancer in his Vermont home on 15 September 1989.]

Selected Bibliography

WORKS OF
ROBERT PENN WARREN

POETRY
Thirty-Six Poems. New York: Alcestis Press, 1935.
Eleven Poems on the Same Theme. Norfolk, Conn.: New Directions, 1942.
Selected Poems, 1923–1943. New York: Harcourt, Brace, 1944.

Brother to Dragons: A Tale in Verse and Voices. New York: Random House, 1953.

Promises: Poems 1954–1956. New York: Random House, 1957.

You, Emperors, and Others: Poems 1957–1960. New York: Random House, 1960.

Published after the writing of this essay

Selected Poems: New and Old (1923-1966). New York: Random House, 1966.

Incarnations: Poems 1966–1968. New York: Random House, 1968.

Audobon: A Vision. New York: Random House, 1969.

Or Else. Poems 1968-1973. New York: Random House, 1974.

Chief Joseph of the Nez Perce. New York: Random House, 1983.

NOVELS AND SHORT STORIES

Night Rider. Boston: Houghton Mifflin, 1939.

At Heaven's Gate. New York: Harcourt, Brace, 1943.

All the King's Men. New York: Harcourt, Brace, 1946.

Blackberry Winter. Cummington, Mass.: Cummington Press, 1946.

The Circus in the Attic and Other Stories. New York: Harcourt, Brace, 1948.

World Enough and Time: A Romantic Novel. New York: Random House, 1950.

Band of Angels. New York: Random House, 1955.

The Cave. New York: Random House, 1959.

Wilderness. New York: Random House, 1961.

Flood. New York: Random House, 1964.

Published after the writing of this essay

Meet Me in the Green Glen. New York: Random House, 1971.

A Place to Come to. New York: Random House, 1977.

PLAYS

"Proud Flesh." Unpublished, 1939. (First performed, 1946.)

"All the King's Men." Unpublished, 1947.

All the King's Men. New York: Random House, 1960.

NONFICTION

John Brown: The Making of a Martyr. New York: Payson and Clarke, 1929.

"The Briar Patch," in *I'll Take My Stand,* by Twelve Southerners. New York: Harper, 1930.

Understanding Poetry, edited by Cleanth Brooks and R. P. Warren. 1st ed., New York: Holt, 1938; 2nd ed., 1951.

Understanding Fiction, edited by Cleanth Brooks and R. P. Warren, 1st ed., New York: Appleton-Century-Crofts, 1943; 2nd ed., 1959; 3rd ed., 1960.

Segregation: The Inner Conflict in the South. New York: Random House, 1956.

Selected Essays. New York: Random House, 1958.

Remember the Alamo! (Landmark children's book.) New York: Random House, 1958.

The Gods of Mount Olympus. (Legacy children's book.) New York: Random House, 1959.

The Legacy of the Civil War: Meditations on the Centennial. New York: Random House, 1961.

Published after the writing of this essay

Who Speaks for the Negro? New York: Random House, 1965.

Jefferson Davis Gets His Citizenship Back. Lexington: University Press of Kentucky, 1980.

Portrait of a Father. Lexington: University Press of Kentucky, 1988.

BIBLIOGRAPHY

Casper, Leonard. "The Works of Robert Penn Warren: A Chronological Checklist," in *Robert Penn Warren: The Dark and Bloody Ground.* Seattle: University of Washington Press, 1960.

CRITICAL AND BIOGRAPHICAL STUDIES

"*All the King's Men:* A Symposium," *Folio,* vol. 15 (May 1950).

Bentley, Eric. "The Meaning of Robert Penn Warren's Novels," *Kenyon Review,* 10:407–24 (Summer 1948).

Bradbury, John M. *The Fugitives: A Critical Account.* Chapel Hill: University of North Carolina Press, 1958.

Brooks, Cleanth. *The Hidden God.* New Haven, Conn.: Yale University Press, 1963.

Casper, Leonard. *Robert Penn Warren: The Dark and Bloody Ground.* Seattle: University of Washington Press, 1960.

Cowan, Louise. *The Fugitive Group: A Literary History.* Baton Rouge: Louisiana State University Press, 1959.

Cowley, Malcolm, ed. *Writers at Work: The Paris Review Interviews.* New York: Viking Press, 1958.

Fiedler, Leslie A. "On Two Frontiers," *Partisan Review,* 17:739–43 (September-October 1950).

Flint, F. Cudworth. "Mr. Warren and the Reviewers," *Sewanee Review,* 64:632–45 (Autumn 1956).

Ford, Newell F. "Kenneth Burke and Robert Penn Warren: Criticism by Obsessive Metaphor," *Journal of English and Germanic Philology,* 53:172–77 (April 1954).

Frank, Joseph. "Romanticism and Reality in Robert Penn Warren," *Hudson Review,* 4:248–58 (Summer 1951).

Frohock, W. M. "Mr. Warren's Albatross," *Southwest Review,* 36:48–59 (Winter 1951)

Heseltine, H. P. "The Deep, Twisting Strain of Life: The Novels of Robert Penn Warren," *Melbourne Critical Review,* 5:76–89 (1962).

Hynes, Sam. "Robert Penn Warren: The Symbolic Journey," *University of Kansas City Review,* 17:279–85 (Summer 1951).

Isherwood, Christopher. "Tragic Liberal," *New Republic,* 99:108 (May 31, 1939).

Kazin, Alfred. *Contemporaries.* Boston: Little, Brown, 1962. Pp. 178–83.

Létargeez, J. "Robert Penn Warren's Views of History," *Revue des langues vivantes,* 22:533–43 (1956).

Lowell, Robert. "Prose Genius in Verse," *Kenyon Review,* 15:619–25 (Autumn 1953).

Matthiessen, F. O. "American Poetry Now," *Kenyon Review,* 6:683–96 (Autumn 1944).

Mizener, Arthur. "Amphibium in Old Kentucky," *Kenyon Review,* 12:697–701 (Autumn 1950).

Mohrt, Michel. *Le nouveau roman américain.* Paris: Gallimard, 1955.

O'Connor, William Van. "Robert Penn Warren's Short Fiction," *Western Review,* 12:251–53 (Summer 1948).

Rubin, Louis D., Jr. "All the King's Meanings," *Georgia Review,* 8:422–34 (Winter 1954).

Sochatoff, Fred, ed. *All the King's Men: A Symposium.* Pittsburgh: Carnegie Press, 1957.

Strugnell, John R. "Robert Penn Warren and the Uses of the Past," *Review of English Literature,* 4:93–102 (October 1963).

Tate, Allen. *"The Fugitive, 1922–1925,"* *Princeton University Library Chronicle,* 3:75–84 (April 1942).

Tyler, Parker. "Novel into Film: *All the King's Men,*" *Kenyon Review,* 12:369–76 (Spring 1950).

Virtanen, Reino. "Camus' *Le Malentendu* and Some Analogues," *Comparative Literature,* 10:232–40 (Summer 1958).

Warren, Robert Penn. *"All the King's Men:* The Matrix of Experience," *Yale Review,* 53:161–67 (Winter 1964).

Wilson, Angus. "The Fires of Violence," *Encounter,* 4:75–78 (May 1955).

—*PAUL WEST*

Eudora Welty

1909-

EUDORA WELTY was born in 1909 in Jackson, Mississippi. She went to school there; and there, after making excursions to Wisconsin (for an A.B. degree) and to New York (for courses in advertising at Columbia), she returned to live and do her work. Some people in the South might not think of her as being entirely southern. Her father came from Ohio, never a part of the South; and her mother was a native of West Virginia, which is only geographically southern. Once when she was just beginning to be known, she complained playfully to a young reporter that the only thing that had made her suffer as a child was the stigma of having a Yankee for a father. She was probably recognizing that the reporter was himself no southerner and would be amused to hear a person from Mississippi say something like that, but she was probably also describing a sting that once had been real. Now by repeated choice Eudora Welty has confirmed the mode of life that accident of birth bestowed; and if choice of residence has anything to do with what one is, she is, by virtue of a place chosen many times, as southern as Mississippi soil itself.

Her conspicuous attachment to a region does not, however, mean that she accepts the label "regionalist." "Place," she has written in her essay "Place in Fiction" (1956), "is one of the lesser angels that watch over the racing hand of fiction." It is an angel like character, plot, and the rest, but a small angel, subservient to feeling, who wears the crown, "soars highest of them all and rightly relegates place into the shade." The importance of place is that an author's feelings tend to be associated with it; thus place serves naturally as a repository for feelings that must eventually inhabit the novel taking shape in his head. Respect for place, moreover, makes an author pay attention to detail, makes him work harder to portray things with clarity, and finally prepares him to see through things as well. Of Faulkner's "Spotted Horses" Miss Welty has written: ". . . in all that shining fidelity to place lies the heart and secret of this tale's comic glory." In such faithfulness lies at least part, certainly, of the secret of her own wonderfully effective stories. Yet Eudora Welty's master is always fiction itself, never Missssippi.

For a full account of Eudora Welty's life down to 1962 the reader may consult Ruth M. Vande Kieft's book-length essay. Even a brief sketch, however, should mention that she spent two years as a student at Mississippi State College for Women (Columbus) before going north to take her degree and that her early interests were painting and photography. Miss Welty's career as a writer began formally in June of

1936 with the publication of "Death of a Traveling Salesman" in a little magazine called *Manuscript,* edited by John Rood. Since then her stories have appeared in a variety of magazines, from the *Southern Review* to the *New Yorker.* They have been anthologized, commented upon, translated into numerous languages including Burmese and Japanese, and collected into four volumes, *A Curtain of Green* (1941), *The Wide Net* (1943), *The Golden Apples* (1949), and *The Bride of the Innisfallen* (1955). She has also published, in addition to several uncollected pieces, five novels, *The Robber Bridegroom* (1942), *Delta Wedding* (1946), *The Ponder Heart* (1954), *Losing Battles* (1970), and *The Optimist's Daughter* (1972), a small collection of critical essays, *Three Papers on Fiction* (1962), and a children's story, *The Shoe Bird* (1964). Many honors have come to her, among them two first prizes in the O. Henry Memorial Contest, a Guggenheim Fellowship, election to the National Institute of Arts and Letters, the William Dean Howells Medal of the Academy of Arts and Letters, appointment as Honorary Consultant of the Library of Congress, and several honorary degrees. She has taught or lectured at many institutions in this country and at Cambridge University in England.

From the first her stories attracted the attention of discriminating readers. Among her earliest admirers was Ford Madox Ford, who tried diligently during the last year of his life to find a publisher for her collected stories. Her most effective champions, however, were the people associated with the *Southern Review* in nearby Baton Rouge: Albert Erskine, who had discovered her for the *Review*; Robert Penn Warren, who became one of her first real critics; and Katherine Anne Porter, who encouraged her and wrote an introduction to the volume when it finally appeared. The wide range of the stories in *A Curtain of Green*

strongly suggested that the author had been conducting a series of experiments in fiction. The setting for most of the stories was small-town or rural Mississippi, but the characters included murderers, psychotics, suicides, deaf-mutes, the mentally retarded, the senile, and a host of people whom southern gentility used to refer to as "common." There were enough such characters, in fact, to prompt metropolitan reviewers to use terms like "Gothic," "grotesque," and "caricature" and to make superficial comparisons with Faulkner and Poe. As Miss Porter has observed, however, Eudora Welty's caricatures are "but individuals exactly and clearly presented." If some characters in her stories are unsavory, they are nevertheless real; and like other forms of truth, they properly evoke a mixed response.

One of the stories, "A Memory," both illustrates and produces that response. The narrator is a young girl, sensitive and naively austere, who tells how her daydreams on a city beach were interrupted by the appearance of a disquieting group of bathers—a man, two women, and two boys, "brown and roughened, but not foreigners." The sight of these well-meaning but ugly people cavorting on a public beach erases from the girl's mind all thoughts of the boy she loves, the subject of her morning reverie; and the disorder the people leave behind makes her feel keenly both the beauty and the insubstantiality of most youthful dreams. Anyone who has visited such a beach will recognize these bathers and possibly deplore them, but the story does not ask us either to laugh or to condemn. It does not ask us to side with the girl. Neither does it try to persuade us that the girl has achieved a real understanding of her experience or even that we ourselves have. As the memory of the young boy rushes back, compounded now with the morning's unpleasantness, she weeps inexplicably for "the small worn white pavilion" that uselessly ornaments the discredited beach. We too see it, feel with the girl, and are inexplicably disturbed.

The postmistress at China Grove, Mississippi, in "Why I Live at the P.O." is as disturbed as the girl in "A Memory" and as vulgar as the rednecked bathers there; she is also funny. Miss Porter has called her "a terrifying case of dementia praecox," but this diagnosis is probably an exaggeration. As her monologue progresses (such names as Stella-Rondo, Shirley-T., and Papa-Daddy are enough to indicate the tone of it), we look back at a recent disruptive sequence of events in the family circle which has so outraged her sense of fair play that she has gathered up everything she can lay claim to and carried the lot down to the post office, her post office ("the next to smallest P.O. in the entire state of Mississippi"), where for five days she has reigned unchallenged and happy, or so she says. If there is anything terrifying about all this, it is not the questionable psychosis or even the speaker's alienation, but the exposure of human pettiness, unwittingly burlesqued in the language and gestures of an ethically insensitive narrator. Undoubtedly the postmistress of China Grove has been grievously abused by people quite as insensitive as she is, but one feels no inclination either to support her quarrel or to side with her excommunicated victims.

A similar hesitation perplexes us at the end of "Lily Daw and the Three Ladies," in which a young mentally retarded girl frustrates the good intentions of three female pillars of society by making a marriage just as they are about to send her to the Ellisville Institute for the Feeble-Minded of Mississippi. The story does not suggest whether we are to rejoice at Lily's triumph, which will surely be brief, or at the discomfiture of the three absurd ladies. Nor does "Petrified Man," a longer story, reveal its secret. No reader is likely to sympathize with Leota, the beauty operator whose narrative dominates it, or with Mrs. Fletcher, the customer who provides a willing ear, or with Mrs. Pike, who accepts Leota's friendship, imposes upon her hospitality, and uses her copy of *Startling G-Man Tales* to identify the petrified man in a visiting carnival as a rapist wanted for assaulting four women in California. The rapist provides no outlet for our feelings, and all the others are as distasteful as they are funny so that we find little relish in any laughter that the story may provide. Again we have been presented with a spectacle of petty barbarism that we feel is authentic and suspect may be universal. It can best be characterized as a trap for those who would cast stones.

Robert Penn Warren has remarked on the theme of isolation that appears in most of these early stories. Lily Daw, for example, is isolated by her childlike mind from the adult community she is determined to join; and all the unpleasant people in "Why I Live at the P.O." are isolated from one another as well as from the rest of Mississippi. Then there are the pair of newlywed deaf-mutes in "The Key," the old couple who struggle against the frost in "The Whistle," Old Mister Marblehall with his two lonely lives, the young people in "Flowers for Marjorie," the frightening pair of old women in "A Visit of Charity," and the heroic isolation of Phoenix Jackson in "A Worn Path." Most memorable of all perhaps are the two traveling salesmen. First, there is Tom Harris of "The Hitch-Hikers," in whose car, stopped at a small Delta town, one hitchhiker has fatally wounded another. In the fate of these three lonely people, in the town's inadequate response to the event that they bring to it, and in Harris' unexpected encounter with a lonely stranger, we come—and maybe Harris does also—to a sharper awareness of universal human loneliness and of the universal urge to find some kind of relief for it. Then there is the dying salesman R. J. Bowman, stumbling along the moonlit hill road in the back country, terrified by the explosions of a heart gone berserk but needlessly embarrassed by something no one else hears or cares about. The one clear example of psychotic isolation in *A Curtain of Green* is Clytie, a demented young woman of a decadent family who in her story runs about town staring into faces until at last she finds in the surface of a barrel of rain water the face she has been looking for and plunges beneath that surface to her death.

Now and then, however, one of these lonely characters will challenge his isolation in some way, usually by resorting to an act of poetry. Even for simpleminded Lily Daw the means of escape is to imagine a wedding and a normal life until something of both are suddenly and fantastically within her grasp; and for Ruby Fisher in "A Piece of News" it is the more nearly normal but still childlike capacity for daydreaming that makes her seize upon the chance appearance of a name like hers in a scrap of newspaper from another state and build from that a delicious fantasy in which she plays the role of a glamorous backwoods Camille. For Powerhouse, a Negro jazz pianist reminiscent of the late Fats Waller, it is the off-duty activity of the improvisational genius that moves his fingers in public performances. Condemned by his race and his circumstances to play as long as he lives the monotonous role of court jester to a middle-class population, Powerhouse is reduced to creating his own private world of variety and excitement. He has a telegram, he declares, which says "Your wife is dead" and is signed "Uranus Knockwood." This improbable fiction provides creative release for Powerhouse and most of his musicians as they drink beer in a Negro restaurant during the break for intermission. When an unimaginative member of the group suggests that Powerhouse step over to the pay telephone and find out the "truth," he seethes inwardly, "That is one crazy drummer that's going to get his neck broken some day."

By contrast, for the loneliness of young Steve in "Keela, the Outcast Indian Maiden" no solution, imaginative or otherwise, is practicable. Steve's sense of isolation results from guilt acquired when, as a barker in a carnival, he drummed up trade for a small clubfooted Negro man who was dressed up as an Indian woman and forced several times a day to eat a live chicken. Fortunately the show was raided and the Negro sent home to Cane Springs, Mississippi; but the young man, though legally exonerated, has ever since led an Ancient-Mariner-like existence, wandering from place to place, confessing. We see him at his moment of ultimate confrontation; having come at last to Cane Springs, he has found a restaurant operator, named Max, who can take him to the club-footed Negro's home, and there he hopes to receive forgiveness. What he finds instead is a grinning little man, virtually mindless and without sense of injury and thus incapable of forgiving anything. Steve's real tragedy, however, is his inability to recognize that the restaurant operator has been moved by the incident and would offer sympathy. His conclusion is a despairing, "I got to catch a ride some place." We feel that this character will probably take his isolation with him.

A very different kind of story but one that anticipates in theme Miss Welty's second collection is the title story, "A Curtain of Green." This tells of a young widow, Mrs. Larkin, whose husband has died the summer before when a great chinaberry tree by the driveway suddenly tilted forward, "dark and slow like a cloud," upon his car and crushed him to death. Mrs. Larkin's response to nature's blow has been to challenge the ambiguous curtain of green that stands between man's pretense at maintaining order and whatever it is that continually creates man's world and controls its destiny. Instead of commanding a naughty nature to return to its place or at least to make a show of respecting its betters, Mrs. Larkin chooses to subvert her enemy by participating in its luxuriant wildness (particularly evident in a place like Mississippi) and discovering its mysterious purpose, whatever that may be. Her neighbors, of course, do not know what to make of her. She plants whole catalogues of things; she plans not at all for neatness and makes no gesture of sharing any bounty that comes to her. At the end of her story, however, the purpose of the nonhuman world remains as mysterious as ever; for Mrs. Larkin succeeds only in finding herself one afternoon identified with the daemon of the chinaberry tree—or at any rate a similar daemon—as inexplicably she stands behind her kneeling Negro helper and threatens him with an upraised hoe. She is prevented from senseless murder by a "human" impulse, or by a moment of faintness, or perhaps by the equally senseless intrusion of a summer rain, which makes her hesitate. Anyhow she lowers her hoe and soon afterwards falls on her back amidst the rank growth and lies there quietly, as a silent nature assumes again its beneficent mask and showers her face with raindrops.

In her second collection, *The Wide Net and Other Stories,* Eudora Welty extended her range somewhat. At one extreme is "First Love," a touching story in which young Joel Mayes, deaf-mute, bootblack, and orphan in the Natchez of 1807, finds his first opportunity to know and communicate love in an encounter with Aaron Burr. During the time preceding Burr's preliminary trial for treason Burr stays at the inn where Joel was deposited as an orphan and where he has since lived as a servant. The boy shares his humble room with Burr, penetrates the older man's reserve, sees his anxieties, observes his last desperate conferences with Blennerhassett, and comforts him

in his nightmares. Protected by his own physical infirmities from perceiving too clearly the disturbing things about Burr's personality, Joel notices the man's capacity for greatness and his need for love, which love Joel gives in the only way he can, with the clasp of his hand. The story does not invoke our sympathy for Burr, however; it asks us only to see Burr's part in Joel's awakening to a fuller participation in humanity. At the other end of the range is a "Gothic" tale, "The Purple Hat," in which a fat and aging armed guard at a New Orleans gambling casino tells how over the years he has fed his insatiable curiosity on a mysterious, perennially middle-aged woman with a purple hat. Peering down from his place on the catwalk beneath the dome of the casino, the guard has seen countless young men ensnared by their fascination for the woman's hat and for the mysterious vial with plunger that serves as one of its ornaments. As this unpleasant story nears an end, we realize that the woman is about to ensnare the young alcoholic who has been listening with us to the guard's recital.

These two stories are at the virtuosic limits of Miss Welty's performance in the short story and command our attention much as stories or paintings produced on a dare. Nevertheless, they also exhibit many of the solid virtues that distinguish her other work: her respect for the visual impression, which abides even when she is most concerned to insist on the existence of something beyond the immediately visible; her ability to make language suggest several dimensions of reality simultaneously, by use of allusion, by selection of detail, and by free (and sometimes licentious) use of metaphor; and above all her almost infallible ear for idiomatic diction and rhythm and her unembarrassed use of both.

The other six stories of *The Wide Net* are more naturalistically presented, and each shows humanity in some way addressing itself to the mysteries beyond that curtain of green which Miss Welty's authentic reporting establishes. For example, at the climax of "A Still Moment" Lorenzo Dow, evangelist, Audubon, painter and ornithologist, and Murrell, outlaw of the Natchez Trace, confront a heron in the forest. The three men are one in the intensity of their vision: "It was as if three whirlwinds had drawn together at some center, to find there feeding in peace a snowy heron." Yet it is Audubon who challenges the bird and the natural world that it represents. To paint the bird, he must know it intimately; so fixing the creature as best he can with his memory, he pulls the trigger and kills it. The shot is their signal for dispersal. Lorenzo Dow, bent on saving souls, rides away, thanking Heaven for an escape from the temptation to love nature. Murrell lets the shot stand for the one with which he would have given Lorenzo his death. Audubon, signifying by his concatenation of gestures the mystery and the ruthlessness of art, puts the dead bird in his bag, later to draw and paint and learn again the futility of trying to fathom the even more mysterious loveliness that surrounds him in the Mississippi forest.

Two stories in the book court trouble by what might be called spurious penetrations of the curtain. In one of these, "The Winds," the violence of an equinoctial storm is made to symbolize the transition of a young girl to adolescence and thence to maturity. Miss Welty's technique is misplaced here, for the correspondence is too obvious and worn to be redeemed by any but the most extraordinary of strategies. Even less successful is "Asphodel," in which three maiden ladies celebrate their liberation from a community tyrant and mad woman, Miss Sabina, by picnicking on the abandoned lawn of what once was Miss Sabina's home, now a pasture for goats. There as they spread their banquet and recount the dead woman's story, they suddenly see a naked man standing by the columns of the vanished mansion. "That was Mr. Don McInnis," says one of them, thinking it is Miss Sabina's unfaithful husband, presumably long dead. "It was not," says another. "It was a vine in the wind." "He was buck-naked," says the first. "He was as naked as an old goat. He must be as old as the hills." Clearly we are to think of a reincarnation of Dionysus as the ladies flee in a mixture of anger, indignation, and suppressed pleasure. Unfortunately there is too much telling here and too little presentation; we have had a ghost story, and we are not convinced.

The remaining three stories in the book are among Miss Welty's best, both as demonstrations of technique and as transparent re-creations of the natural world in which we see clearly enough what is before us but also perceive more than meets our eyes. "Livvie" has received more attention than the other two. This is the tale of a young woman who, at the death of her ancient husband, Solomon, transfers her devotion to the brash young fieldhand Cash, who has tried to claim it in advance. The story is thus one of temptations. At the climax the gaudily dressed young buck and his skittish woman end their Easter chase at Solomon's bedside, perhaps with murder in mind, only to discover there that the wise old man is prepared to surrender his authority with dignity and forgiveness and to die virtually of his own free will. Seldom in fiction has January given way to May with such grace and avoidance of pain. Nature wins effortlessly here, and the peach tree is blooming as the young couple burst out of the house into the sunlight. In "At the Landing" nature is less gracious. There the girl of the story, Jenny, also escapes when an aged guardian (this time a grandfather) dies; but Jenny's Dionysus arrives in the form of a river man, "Floyd . . . with his wrist hung with a great long catfish," who rescues her from the river flood, takes her to a secret place on the top of a hill, violates her, feeds her, and leaves her without specifically making her his own. Thus before achieving a second union with her god, Jenny must patiently and shamelessly follow him from one mud flat to another and finally submit to a succession of painful rapes by the primitive river men who casually take her in an abandoned houseboat. This is Jenny's initiation, the price she must pay for a chance at the life she would seek with those who live on the far side of the curtain of green. Yet payment gives Jenny no guarantee of achievement. As the story ends Billy Floyd has not come to claim her, and she continues to wait.

The most successful story in *The Wide Net* is the one from which the book takes its title. The net itself is a seine that young William Wallace Jamieson borrows from Old Doc on the hill when his wife Hazel, pregnant and depressed by a sense of neglect, has left a note saying she is going to drown herself. Hazel, of course, is going to do nothing of the sort, but her threat provides an occasion for a river dragging in which William Wallace, like Mrs. Larkin of the earlier collection, confronts the mysterious curtain of green: "The willow trees leaned overhead under muscadine vines, and their trailing leaves hung like waterfalls in the morning air. The thing that seemed like silence must have been the endless cry of all the crickets and locusts in the world, rising and falling." As the stream fills their net with fish, eels, and even alligators, the initial apprehensiveness for Hazel's life vanishes. They become wanderers, explorers, in a world mysterious, inviting, and endless. Once William Wallace in a perfunctory dive for the body of his wife senses in the watery depth that he has somehow fathomed the cause of her unhappiness, which is simply that strange insatiable longing that characterizes all sentient humanity; but he does not long reflect on the matter. With the others he

eats fish, sleeps in the sunshine, thrills to the electric charge of a summer thunderstorm, and eventually returns to town to discover the impracticality of his expeditions. Hazel is alive and well, yet no one regrets the effort. "The excursion is the same when you go looking for your sorrow as when you go looking for your joy," says Doc. Hazel is happy with the reassurance that her husband loves her, but William Wallace is happier.

In between these two successful collections of short stories Miss Welty published her first novel, called *The Robber Bridegroom* after one of Grimm's fairy tales. In addition to the general shape of Grimm's story, suggestions and reminiscences of a number of other tales are discoverable there, among them "The Little Goose Girl," "Rumpelstiltskin," "Little Snow White," "The Fisherman and His Wife." "Beauty and the Beast," Charles Perrault's "Cinderella," and the Hellenic myth of Cupid and Psyche. Moreover, a great deal of American folklore and near-folklore gets worked into the narrative, the stories of Davy Crockett and Mike Fink, the atrocities of Big Harpe and Little Harpe, and tall tales about Indians, frontiersmen, and bandits of the Natchez Trace. So much of this sort of thing appears, in fact, that one critic has been moved to credit the author with recovering "the fabulous innocence of our departed frontier."

Such an observation about *The Robber Bridegroom* gets additional justification from the pose Miss Welty assumes in telling her story. It is something like the one assumed by a canny maiden aunt, whose diction, asides, and silly puns are all devices of a naturally gifted teller of tales who knows how to make children giggle, shiver, and sit still. Children in the South are familiar with such performances, and it is to be assumed that children elsewhere know something like them. Almost any passage will illustrate: "Now Rosamond was a great liar, and nobody could believe a word she said. . . . she did not mean to tell anything but the truth, but when she opened her mouth in answer to a question, the lies would simply fall out like diamonds and pearls. Her father had tried scolding her, and threatening to send her away to the Female Academy, and then marching her off without her supper . . . Salome, on the other hand, said she should be given a dose of Dr. Peachtree." Part of our delight in this sort of thing undoubtedly is nostalgic, but that pleasure would pale here if it did not serve as a doorway to something else.

Miss Welty gives us all that Grimm gives and considerably more. The latter tells how a young maiden was bestowed by her father unknowingly upon a murderous bandit and how she eventually succeeded in capturing that bandit by her courage and her wits. This is clearly the basic plot of the novel; but Miss Welty has fattened it on the fruit of the Natchez Trace and allowed it to mature in the light of her own sophisticated reflection, and she does not expect us to take much of it simply at face value. A clue to what she would have us see comes two thirds of the way through the book when Clement Musgrove, father to the girl Rosamond, says of Jamie Lockhart, "If being a bandit were his breadth and scope, I should find him and kill him for sure. . . . But since in addition he loves my daughter, he must be not the one man, but two, and I should be afraid of killing the second. For all things are double, and this should keep us from taking liberties with the outside world, and acting too quickly to finish things off." Sophisticated fairy tales sometimes suggest that things in life may be double (for example, Perrault's "Cinderella"), but even in these tales characters are not given to reflecting on the matter or working out enunciations of principle. Moreover, in genuinely primitive stories we do not get beyond the limited "breadth and scope." Grimm's story gave the girl two suitors, a bad one to outwit and a good one to live with happily ever after. Putting the two together, as Miss Welty has done, would have spoiled all the "fabulous innocence" and made a solution impossible.

Each of the three principals in the story is double in some way. For example, Clement Musgrove is both a wanderer and a planter. Rosamond, his daughter, is as beautiful as truth itself, but she is a congenital liar; and Jamie Lockhart, we know, is bandit as well as bridegroom. Clement's ambiguity may be explained as restlessness: he is the man who lost his youth with the death of a first wife and now perfunctorily spins out his days with an efficient shrew. Only in the presence of Rosamond, who preserves the image of her youthful mother, does he find happiness. Soon after the story begins he meets Jamie at an inn and learns of his heroic qualities in an encounter the two have with Mike Fink; thereafter his dream is to find happiness for the young man, who would make a fine heir, in a union with the lovely Rosamond. But the young people are really people and not pawns, and they must make their own arrangements. This means a period of adventuring, testing, exposing, rejecting and accepting, and finally coming to understand and respect that doubleness which is the occasion for conflicts between them and the condition of their continuing interest and happiness in one another.

The ability to perceive and appreciate doubleness is not a common gift; but Clement possesses naturally, as we have seen, a high degree of it. His meditation continues: "All things are divided in half—night and day, the soul and body, and sorrow and joy and youth and age, and sometimes I wonder if even my own wife has not been the one person all the time, and I loved her beauty so well at the beginning that it is only now that the ugliness has struck through to beset me like a madness." He is being too generous here. Salome, his shrewish second wife, is not double at all; neither are the savage Goat, son of a neighboring widow, Mike Fink, the two Harps (to use Miss Welty's spelling), or the marauding Indians. Perhaps that is why such characters in this book strike us as evil instead of merely wicked or naughty as they would in a fairy tale where the rest of the characters are equally one-sided. Still Clement's perceptions are good enough to enable him to single out Jamie, who knew in his heart "that he was a hero and had always been one, only with the power to look both ways and to see a thing from all sides." And it is Jamie's perceptivity that enables him in turn to see Rosamond's saving "duplicity"; for Rosamond's fibbing apparently is another instance of that creative kind of fabrication that enables Ruby Fisher and Powerhouse of *A Curtain of Green* to redeem their unsatisfying lives. Thus poetry of a kind rewards all three: Jamie and Rosamond with a fine mansion, a hundred slaves, and rich merchants to go boating with, and Clement with the knowledge that his children have such things. Miss Welty has him return to the Trace, of his own will, alone: "For he was an innocent of the wilderness, and a planter of Rodney's Landing, and this was his good." We suspect that his was the greatest good, after all.

Eudora Welty's second novel, *Delta Wedding*, appeared in 1945. It was well received on the whole, though certain New York critics chided her for failing to recognize the moral and sociological shortcomings of life in the Mississippi Delta. The story is built around the visit of a little nine-year-old girl, Laura McRaven, of Jackson, to the country place Shellmound, where her uncle, Battle Fairchild, and his wife, Ellen, preside over a household of eight children and a ninth expected, associated aunts and great-aunts, and numerous Negro servants. The occasion for her visit is the forthcoming marriage of Battle's seventeen-year-old daughter, Dabney, to Troy Flavin, Shellmound's overseer, aged thirty-four. For Battle and Ellen Fairchild the event seems to threaten a first break in the integrity of their immediate family. To young Laura the thought of having a vacation with all her cousins is almost more exciting than the prospect of seeing a wedding, especially since her mother has died earlier in the year and she cannot therefore take her rightful role in it as flower girl. As the story proceeds, however, the substitute comes down with chickenpox, and Laura does indeed participate in the wedding. Afterwards, on a late summer picnic, held in honor of the returning honeymooners, her heart overflows with happiness as her sense of finding acceptance in her mother's family matures within her.

Even so, Laura McRaven is not at the center of *Delta Wedding*, and we do not see Shellmound through her eyes. The author guides our attention freely over the whole collection of people who at this point in time constitute "the Fairchilds." Seldom has a family been portrayed so effectively. We see it and sympathize with it, gladly or perhaps reluctantly, as our predisposition requires; and as our experience permits, we see the universality of it as well. A plantation family in the Mississippi Delta does not differ essentially from large families that have developed elsewhere in other agrarian economies—in the American Middle West, in rural England, in France, or in Russia. The mystery celebrated in *Delta Wedding* is the love that can bind such a family together even after the frontier, sociological or geographic, which has required it to stand together in a particular place has passed on. She might easily have written about some decaying family, for there are many such in Mississippi and in other parts of the South. She has chosen instead to write of a rarer kind.

The principal characters may be divided into two groups, one large and one small. First, there are the blooded Fairchilds headed by Battle, master of Shellmound. These include Battle's four sons, Orrin, Roy, Little Battle, and Ranny; and his four daughters, Shelley, Dabney, India, and Bluet. In addition there are two brothers, George, who lives in Memphis with his wife, Robbie; and Denis, dead in World War I, whose demented widow lives in the town and whose retarded child, Maureen, lives at Shellmound. Two great-aunts, Aunt Mac and Aunt Shannon, live in the house; two maiden sisters, Primrose and Jim Allen, live not far away in a smaller house which really belongs to George. Still another sister, Tempe, has married an alcoholic and lives at Inverness. Laura McRaven is also a blooded Fairchild, but her mother, Annie Laurie Fairchild, decided to marry a young lawyer and move to Jackson. The second group consists of characters who are Fairchilds by association. There are three of these: Ellen, who for all her eight children is still regarded as a Virginian and an outsider; Robbie, who has married George but who at the beginning of the novel has run away from him; and Troy Flavin, a man from the hills of northeastern Mississippi, unaware of the cultural gulf that separates him from his bride-to-be.

It is possible to think of the main action of the novel as the merging of these two groups in the marriage of Troy and Dabney. All the activity that confronts us as we read has to do with preparation for the wedding, the events surrounding it, or the picnic given in the couple's honor as they return from their honeymoon. Troy's intrusion into this established family is certainly symbolic of the main action even if it is not identifiable with it; and the family's acceptance of him is symptomatic of the complex of attitudes that will make possible a resolution of conflicts at the end. But Troy's conflict is no more at the true center of this novel than Ellen's, which is deeper and more painful. After spending years in the circle of Fairchilds, Ellen is still something of an alien. Her role has been to endure things, not to precipitate them. Hence she will not herself resolve conflicts, but her reservoir of sympathy and strength will help to ensure that resolutions last. Like Troy Flavin she contributes to the action and illuminates it, but she works at the periphery of the storm.

At dead center is Ellen's brother-in-law George, blooded Fairchild, abandoned by his wife just as he was about to return to Shellmound for Dabney's wedding. This storm threatens disaster for the whole clan. The event that precipitated it took place two weeks before the time of the narrative. All the family except Battle and Ellen had gone on a fishing excursion to a place called Drowning Lake. Afterwards they were coming home by the shortest path, the railway track, and had all reached the trestle just as the local passenger train, popularly called the Yellow Dog, suddenly threatened to overtake them. No real crisis would have arisen, however, had not Maureen, dancing on the crossties, caught her foot and George, ignoring all danger, knelt and worked patiently to free the child before the train should catch them both. The engineer saw them in time and stopped the train, and all the others jumped or fell into the dry creek bed below; but Robbie was furious that her husband should have elected to stay with an idiot child and thus run the risk of leaving her a widow. We do not see Robbie face to face until halfway through the novel when she decides to return and make a public display of her vexation. Her reunion with George is the true Delta wedding of the piece. At the end she is reconciled with the Fairchilds—as much as one can ever be with a whole family—and she and George have decided to leave Memphis, return to the little house near Shellmound, and be Fairchilds for the rest of their lives. Thus the end of the action is the vindication of that family bond—mysterious, compelling, and in the final reckoning good, as Robbie's behavior testifies. The three characters for whom vindication seems most important, however, are George, Laura, and Ellen; and these are the characters who help us most to participate in that sense of family which few readers in a restless age are lucky enough to experience directly.

Delta Wedding, the embodiment of that sense, is too rich to be summed up in a few pages, but one or two details which serve as clarifying symbols should be mentioned. Obviously significant in this way is the little night lamp that Aunts Primrose and Jim Allen give to Dabney as a wedding present. When the candle inside is lighted, the clay-colored chimney reddens and reveals a picture of a city—London, the aunts say—engulfed by flames, which seem frighteningly real as the candle gives them motion. The lamp is supposed to suggest the transformation that can come to people and families when some great spiritual happiness—or perhaps a crisis—warms them from within. The image that enables Laura to grasp the mystery of the Fairchilds is more revealing. All the laughing, kissing relatives make her think of the birdhouse in a zoo that her father has taken her to: ". . . the sparkle of motion was like a rainbow, while it was the very thing that broke your heart, for the birds that flew were caged all the time and could not fly out." Shellmound is the cage which Laura is compelled to try to enter; her need for love will not let her hold back indefinitely, and yet she knows that, once inside, she may not ever again be able to break free. We recall this when we see her double triumph at the end of the novel, signalized by her simultaneous acceptance into the family and her decision to return to her father in Jackson.

Another detail unites Laura and Ellen in a significant way. In the first part of the book we hear Ellen refer to a lost garnet pin that Battle has given her. As the novel proceeds, she continues to look for it, even to the point of sending Shelley, India, and Laura on a visit to Partheny, an old Negro woman who has mindless moments, experiences trances, and may perhaps return the article if she has stolen it or discover its whereabouts in a vision if she has not. The pin is a badge of acceptance which Ellen once needed desperately but which she now seeks for the sake of sentiment. Laura eventually finds the pin in the grass at an old abandoned house, Marmion, rightfully hers but in the years immediately ahead destined to serve as a home for Dabney and Troy. Returning across the Yazoo to Shellmound, however, she is tumbled into the river by her companion Roy, who fishes her out and apologizes. In the scramble she loses the rosy pin. At the end of the novel she has decided not to tell Ellen either of finding the pin or of the unfortunate accident by which it was lost a second time; for she knows deep inside that the pin itself does not particularly matter. Now, lost forever, it is a treasure that secretly belongs to them both and unites them.

In the end what makes this family a living, continuing thing is the capacity of a sufficient number of the people in it to participate with compassion, selflessness, and intensity in the daily lives of all the others, whether linked by blood or by simple affection. As George says at one point, "I don't think it matters what *happens* to a person, or what comes." There is always something going on in a family like this one: people marry, die, run away, play games, join armies, or fight duels. But family living is participation moment by moment in whatever comes or happens; and George's unusual capacity for that is the door by which Robbie returns and the window by which Laura comes to see. Near the end of the story it also enables him to offer the embrace in which Ellen finds, without loss of her love for Battle, the supreme consolation of friendship and the fulfillment of a life.

The Golden Apples consists of seven separable pieces, all with titles of their own and all previously published. Yet this collection, if it may be called that, stands together as a recognizable whole just as clearly as *Delta Wedding* with its formally inseparable parts. It also makes much of the authentic contemporary setting which distinguished *Delta Wedding*, but it reintroduces that element of the fabulous which had all but dominated *The Robber Bridegroom* seven years earlier. The pattern for this combination had been displayed in "Asphodel," one of the stories in *The Wide Net;* but there the shape of Greek myth had resisted fusion with its Mississippi setting, and an improbable "Gothic" tale resulted. In *The Golden Apples* fusion does occur, and for the space of seven stories a credible Mississippi becomes a mirror with a range stretching geographically east, west, north, and south and temporally from the Mississippi of the 1920's at least as far back as primitive Greece. Also somewhere within this broad sweep is the region of Celtic folklore as preserved in the poems of William Butler Yeats and particularly in "The Song of the Wandering Aengus," which tells of an elusive Ondine and of the quests she inspires for, among other things, the golden apples of the sun. Thus the golden apples of classical mythology, which Atlas stole for Hercules, symbolize also the quest of a Mississippi Irishman, King MacLain, who fished for trout in many streams, dreamed of gold till his life wore out, and passed his restlessness on to others without ever quite realizing what it was he had been looking for. So that we may know, Miss Welty has another of the principal characters, Virgie Rainey, contemplate with melancholy the futility of her own wandering, past and to come. In her mind's eye she sees a picture that once hung on the wall of her music teacher's studio, a picture of Perseus holding the head of the Medusa. Her teacher had explained that it was the same thing as Siegfried and the dragon, but now Virgie knows that there is really no end to what the picture stands for: "Endless the Medusa, and Perseus endless." At the end of the book, as she sits staring into the rain that happens to be falling at that moment, she thinks suddenly that even such a familiar occurrence as rainfall is never confined simply to Mississippi. It is "the rain of fall, maybe on the whole South, for all she knew on the everywhere." And as she continues to stare, she hears through the rain's percussive music "the running of the horse and bear, the stroke of the leopard, the dragon's crusty slither, and the glimmer and the trumpet of the swan," and she senses her participation in the perennial vibrations of earthly life.

The title of the first chapter, "Shower of Gold," specifically invites us to think of the Danaë story. In the monologue of Virgie Rainey's mother, Miss Kate Rainey of Morgana, Mississippi, we learn how King MacLain, a tea and spice salesman long given to unexplained absences (he is the story's Zeus figure), on one brief return home met his albino wife, Snowdie, in the woods and got her with twins. When Zeus visited Danaë in her cell, of course, he begot Perseus; but Snowdie's twins are a Castor and Pollux, destined to disturb their father's peace of mind as Perseus did, though less seriously. This, in fact, is the main business of the amusing story that Katie Rainey tells, how King MacLain returned home on one of his visits and got as far as the front steps only to be put to flight by the spectacle of two little boys masked with Halloween false faces, decorated with scraps from their mother's sewing basket, and roaring on roller skates around the MacLains' wooden porch like a Mississippi tornado.

Like Castor and Pollux the twins eventually go forth to seek gold of their own. One of them, named Lucius Randall but called Ran, goes only a few blocks. He courts and marries Jinny Love Stark, an attractive and sensual but uninspired young woman of a locally prominent family. Jinny Love is soon unfaithful to Ran in her casual, unfeeling way; then he to her, though not unfeelingly. He leaves their home, returns to the house where he grew up (now a boardinghouse), and engages desperately in an affair with a country girl named Maideen Sumrall. That Jinny Love may represent false gold and Maideen the true never occurs to him, even after Maideen has committed suicide. At the end of this story, "The Whole World Knows," he is crying out to his father and to his brother in anguish, "What you went and found, was it better than this?" But Ran is destined only to desire the gold, never actually to see it. In a later story we find him again, adjusted to small-town life, wived once more and more or less comfortably blind.

His brother Eugene fares little better. In "Music from Spain" we find that he has wandered westward, all the way to San Francisco, where he is married to a woman of Latin extraction by whom he has had one golden child. The child has recently died. At breakfast one morning Eugene suddenly reaches across the table, slaps his wife, and walks out of the apartment. For the first hour or so his quest, unexpectedly resumed, is as aimless as it is fantastic; but it achieves some point when quite by chance he rescues from the noonday traffic rush a Spanish guitarist whom he and Emma had heard in a recital the previous evening. Eugene knows no Spanish, and the Spaniard knows no English; but the two eat lunch together, walk up and down the hill streets of San Francisco, and make their way finally to "Land's End," where, misunderstanding one another's gestures, they grapple furiously in a mutual release of tensions. Afterwards as a token of reconciliation Eugene uses his last penny to buy coffee for the Spaniard and then makes his way home again. Back at the apartment he finds nothing changed. Emma has neither understood the slap nor remembered it, all the day's wandering has come to nothing, and the glitter of Eugene's dream has now vanished forever. Later we learn that he returned to Morgana and died there.

The Perseus of *The Golden Apples* is Loch Morrison, whom we first encounter as a small boy in the long story "June Recital." The Morrison home is next door to the now abandoned MacLain house; and Loch, confined to his bed with malaria, is amusing himself by inspecting it through his father's telescope. The telescope enables him to spy upon Virgie Rainey and her sailor friend, whom she entertains on a bare mattress in an upstairs room. Downstairs the lovemaking is counterpointed by the frantic activity of old Miss Eckhart, retired piano teacher, who once lived in the Rainey home and rejoiced in Virgie as the only pupil in Morgana with any talent. Now Virgie has prostituted that talent by playing "professionally" at the local movie theater; and Miss Eckhart with the madness of frustration and senility absurdly tries to set the house on fire. King MacLain, temporarily in town, with two of his friends puts out the fire and saves the building. Virgie escapes, as does the sailor, and the town turns the whole business into gossip.

This story is the crossroads of the book. Virgie Rainey and King MacLain, the two principal wanderers in it, pass here and almost meet, while a third wanderer, younger than either, watches, appropriately from a distance and through a glass. It precedes the dispiriting chapters that deal with the fruitless wandering of Ran and Eugene, MacLain's acknowledged offspring and his legitimate successors; and it prepares the reader for one more story apiece about Loch and Virgie, who wait until the Zeus of Morgana is too old for escapades and then steal his dream away.

Loch Morrison's second story comes close to tragedy, but it marks his discovery of strength to escape the trap that made King MacLain, for all his canny ways, more like a small-town philanderer than a god. Loch, as Boy Scout and lifesaver, is spending a week at Moon Lake with a group of girl campers, whom he despises. The girls adore him, of course, but he declares his indifference by spending much of his time in his tent and the rest crashing through the treetops like Tarzan of the Apes. His testing comes when Easter, a young girl from the local orphanage and quite possibly another offspring of King MacLain's, makes a bad dive and embeds her head in the soft mud of the lake bottom. Easter's attractive power is similar to Loch's. She is independent and daring, and she has breasts coming. Jinny Love Stark, who later will capture Ran MacLain, taunts her for not having a family or a decent name; but Easter maintains her dignity. She intends to become a singer, she says. Loch's success in rescuing and reviving the girl lifts him over the imperceptible line that separates childish Boy Scout from genuine protector. The arduous process of artificial respiration provokes a variety of responses. Some of the girls are frightened, some are contemptuous, a fellow orphan bids for Easter's winter coat in case she dies, and Jinny Love Stark's mother is appalled by the suggestiveness of the business. Loch, however, shares none of these feelings. Rejecting praise, he simply does his

work and then returns to the privacy of his tent, where he briefly resumes his silly chest beating and then abandons gestures to stare thoughtfully into the night. We learn later that he has abandoned Morgana for New York and done well there.

The last story, originally called "The Hummingbirds" but retitled "The Wanderers" for the book, tells how Virgie Rainey, having tried repeatedly to break with Morgana, returns during her mother's last days, watches over the old woman, and buries her when she dies. In describing the funeral Miss Welty has left out nothing proper to such an event: the cakes, ham, and deviled eggs, the profusion of cut flowers, the sitting up with the body, the continual murmur of clichés, the relatives from remote corners of the state, the stray preacher who knew the deceased in her childhood, the meeting of friends, the condoling, the old people arriving, the trip to the cemetery, the farewells, and the loneliness after. In this vast ceremonial occasion most of Morgana and the nearby hamlet of MacLain pass before us. Prominent are those who have attracted our attention before: Miss Snowdie, who now supervises the "laying out" of her friend; King MacLain, weary, senile, too old to gather golden apples; Ran MacLain and Jinny Love, unfeeling as ever but wedded again and reunited with the community; the memory of Eugene (dead) and of Loch (transferred to New York) and of Loch's mother (a suicide) and of Miss Eckhart (also dead), who tried vainly to give them her Beethoven.

Miss Welty's control here shows an advance over that of *Delta Wedding*, where a tendency to diffuseness was sometimes evident in such passages. In this last chapter of *The Golden Apples* she lets everything filter through the consciousness of Virgie Rainey, whose review of the details we see is steadily bringing her to an awareness of her own action, which is the action of the book: that is, her seizure of "kingship" from King MacLain. MacLain's wandering, we learn, has finally been stopped by Miss Snowdie (she used a detective agency), who now makes a home for him, watches his diet, and dictates all his movements. Virgie, younger but aware of youth's brevity, has returned home at least partly out of kindness; she has dutifully outlived the dying and now enjoys the freedom that selflessness and time have conferred upon her. She is also ready for understanding.

The crisis comes during the funeral service proper. While a child in a peach-colored dress is singing "O Love That Will Not Let Me Go," MacLain sneaks into the hall and tiptoes down to the table where the ham has been set out, there to nibble at forbidden flesh and steal a little marrow bone to suck on. As he returns to the room, he catches Virgie's glance and makes a face at her ". . . like a silent yell. It was a yell at everything—including death, not leaving it out—and he did not mind taking his present animosity out on Virgie Rainey; indeed, he chose her. Then he cracked the little bone in his teeth." Virgie is not fully aware of what is happening at this point, but she knows enough to refute the mindless old lady who keeps repeating, "Child, you just don't know yet what you've lost." She does not bother. Neither does she bother to respond to King MacLain's grimace. She knows both the pain of her wound and the joy of her freedom, and in the richness of that strangely compounded knowledge she senses her kinship with all the MacLains, especially with Mr. King, her spiritual father. Where his sons Ran and Eugene have failed him, she of no blood kin at all has succeeded.

Virgie Rainey visits two graveyards in "The Wanderers," one at Morgana to bury her mother and another seven miles down the road to see again where the MacLains are buried. She makes her pilgrimage to the latter the day after her mother's funeral, after she has decided on the spur of the moment to leave town immediately and thereby shocked and offended some. Once at the village of MacLain, Virgie climbs up on the old stile in front of the courthouse and sits in the rain thinking of the MacLains buried and living and of Miss Eckhart, there by Miss Snowdie's wish, and of Perseus and Beethoven, all wanderers, all hummingbirds. On her perch she reminds us more of Yeats's golden nightingale, reluctantly transcending time, cognizant of what is past, passing, and to come. And as she sits there listening to the magical percussion of the rain, she sees as on a screen before her the "hideous and delectable face" Mr. King MacLain has made, smiles, and hears the world beating in her ears.

After *The Golden Apples* no book-length work of Miss Welty's appeared for more than four years. Then in December of 1953 the *New Yorker* published her short novel called *The Ponder Heart*. Separate publication followed in 1954 and a dramatization for Broadway, by Jerome Chodorov and Joseph Fields, in 1956. In this book the narrative voice of *The Robber Bridegroom* found an appropriate visible embodiment in the dominating person of Miss Edna Earle Ponder, spinster and manager of the Beulah Hotel in Clay, Mississippi. Otherwise *The Ponder Heart* seemed more like an expanded short story than a successor to the other novels, and it depended more heavily than the rest of Miss Welty's work on local color for its effectiveness. Miss Ponder's listener is a young girl, old enough to drive a car (which has broken down—the reason for her being at the Beulah) but not too old to be imposed on with a story the length of a long Mississippi summer "evening," or afternoon. We see her only briefly, however, as she sits there on the porch vainly trying to read; and we never learn her name. Throughout the afternoon the only voice we hear directly is the narrator's, unsophisticated, recognizably provincial, and inexhaustible, relieved only by the "transcribed" conversation of others who come and go in her story of Uncle Daniel Ponder and the heart that brought him much joy in life and now near the end much sadness as well.

Uncle Daniel is an amiable old gentleman, mentally retarded, who lives with his niece at the Beulah, where he vainly waits for guests to stop or old friends from the town to drop in for a visit. His life, as Miss Edna Earle tells it, was uneventful until he reached his forties; and then his father, Grandpa Ponder, managed to marry him off to a local widow named Teacake Magee. This marriage soon fell through, however; and Grandpa, by now thoroughly exasperated by his son's habit of giving everything away, had him committed to the asylum in Jackson. The asylum proved to be no solution either, for Daniel was neither mad nor neurotic, just innocent; he quickly escaped and married a poor-white seventeen-year-old named Bonnie Dee Peacock. Grandpa's death soon after made Daniel rich, and the Ponder wealth became a matter of great interest to Bonnie Dee and her family.

For the rest of the novel Edna Earle's voice ripples along with no significant shift in attitude. We continue to get digressions about life in Clay, the importance of knowing one's place and having a family connection, her never-to-be-realized hope of marriage with Mr. Springer, a traveling salesman. The story of Uncle Daniel, however, becomes less consistently amusing. Bonnie Dee runs away, returns, shortly afterwards sends Daniel back to the Beulah, abuses the Ponder credit until stopped, then recalls her husband abruptly early one afternoon and just as abruptly dies before supper during a violent thunderstorm. The Peacocks bury her after what is surely one of the funniest funerals in literature, as Edna Earle reports it; but throughout we are kept ignorant about what really happened during that fateful thunderstorm, and we do not learn until the Peacocks have charged Daniel with murder and brought him to trial. There in the courtroom scene Edna Earle gets around to telling us, though not the court, how Daniel found his young wife terrified at the mounting storm, tickled her playfully to divert her attention to himself, and was still tickling her neck when she died of fright. Daniel himself brings the trial to an end, literally by giving away most of his fortune, drawn out of the bank when an inexperienced teller was on duty. Thus with a profligate gesture of love he alienates most of the citizens of Clay, who take the gift but in the embarrassment of their spiritual poverty cannot give in return.

The loneliness to which the two surviving Ponders thus inadvertently condemn themselves, however, is graced with its own kind of triumph. Apparently by losing her hope of marriage and children and giving her life to the "nitwit" in her house, Edna Earle has discovered her own capability for love and the capability that seems to be within all those who discover the power of the Ponder heart. Her occasional moralizing prepares us for a concluding demonstration of her own charity as Uncle Daniel makes his way down to greet the visitor. "I'd like to warn you again," she says, "he may try to give you something—may think he's got something to give. If he does, do me a favor. Make out like you accept it. Tell him thank you." With this small gesture love blossoms visibly on the porch of the Beulah, and moralizing and narrative are both vindicated.

Miss Welty's third collection of short stories appeared on the tide of public interest that surrounded *The Ponder Heart*; but *The Bride of the Innisfallen*, as it was called, did not become a popular book. Nevertheless, the seven stories there constituted a technical advance over anything she had done up to this time. In three of these she continued her custom of using the contemporary deep South as the scene, in one she used for the first and only time a Civil War setting, and in two others she drew upon her European travels. In the remaining story she moved the reader directly to a mythical island in the Mediterranean and there had the sorceress Circe give her own version of Odysseus' visit. In none did plot, or external activity sequentially and logically ordered, have the importance that it had had in much of her other work. Journalistic critics understandably resented this aspect of the new stories and wrote with some asperity about it, but vindication of her method has come with repeated readings. What the characters in the stories learn is based upon their own observations, collected by them and then evaluated without strict reference to space and time. We, even as careful readers, can never know more data than these poetically gifted characters know; but the author guides us beyond the frame of the story to a level of understanding that with the characters themselves remains principally a level of feeling. In all the stories the path to understanding is self-evident but not marked; the reader must pay strict attention. In only one of them is the main character given no hope of eventually catching up with the reader; and that is Circe's story, which ends with the semi-goddess's cry of frustration at being unable to penetrate the clay-bound mystery that mortals with their "strange felicity" seem to know. The other six stories in *The Bride of the Innisfallen* communicate with varying capability that "strange felicity" peculiar to mortals. Their success is due in large part to the author's respect for the clay of the region, wherever she has happened to be working.

"Ladies in Spring" is a story about a Mississippi spring and a young boy's initiation in it. The most important of the ladies is Miss Hattie Purcell, mistress of the post office at Royals, Mississippi, and rainmaker for that community. The narration focuses on the consciousness of the boy Dewey, as he goes fishing with his father (nicknamed Blackie), passes the postmistress in the woods, catches a six-inch goggle-eye, and sees a mysterious second lady calling to his father from the trees. This lady, we suspect, is Opal Purcell, Miss Hattie's niece, who joins them as they walk home in the pouring rain. Opal says she has been out looking for poke salad, and Dewey gives no sign that he disbelieves her. Back at the post office he remains with Miss Hattie until the rain stops and then goes home to scare his mother with the fish he has caught. Shortly thereafter he idly returns to the river bank, where he sees a small black stray dog and thinks for the moment that it looks like Miss Hattie. Fifteen years later it occurs to him that Opal Purcell was probably the one who called to his father that afternoon from the willow trees.

The beauty of the author's technique in elaborating this bare story is that it scarcely seems to be a technique at all. It is almost as if the season itself had taken young Dewey in hand, sowing data like seeds for the awakening to come later. Take, for example, the wetness that appears everywhere in the story as soon as the drought breaks—in the trees, on the grass, on the flowers that pop out as the water begins to fall, and on the faces of the country people in the little town. Wetness also seems to bring out details of color, particularly blue and pink, as they turn up in the flowers, in the clothes hung out to dry, and in the patchwork quilt that Opal throws over her head to run from one house to another. The movie house is "magnesia-bottle blue," and three red hens wait on its porch. When Opal declares that her excursion in the woods has been innocent, she has wet cheeks and a blue violet hanging in her dress; later these details are transformed in Dewey's observation that the "big sky-blue violets his mother loved were blooming, wet as cheeks." His father's nickname is Blackie, and black is the color of his face when the secrets of his life momentarily weigh heavily upon him; black is also the color of the mysterious little dog that Dewey sees on his return to the scene of the fishing, and the little black dog looks like the mysterious rainmaking postmistress. But all this connectedness is left in the story just as it comes to Dewey, a collection of hints, rich and strange, and scarcely more conclusive in its immediacy than such things can ever be at the moment of perception in real life. To comprehend a story of this kind, one must be willing to live with it a bit, as one lives with Turgenev's *Sportsman's Sketches,* which it resembles.

Another initiation story is "Kin," told by a young woman, Dicey Hastings, who has returned to her former home, a little courthouse town, "several hours by inconvenient train ride from Jackson," for a visit with her Mississippi relatives. Into the delicious and interminable round of talk that can go on among leisurely southern women whose complex blood connections give them topics comes an unexpected letter which prompts Dicey's Aunt Ethel to insist that she and her cousin Kate spend an afternoon at Mingo, home of Uncle Felix and once a favorite objective for Sunday excursions. The two girls accede reluctantly. Uncle Felix is an incredibly ancient widower, barely hanging on to life and enduring his last days under the watchful eye of an unlovely spinster, related on both sides of the house, whom they call Sister Anne. They arrive at the country place to find it overrun with strangers and learn that Sister Anne has turned the parlor over for the day to an itinerant photographer, who is making portraits of all the country folk there and

will also make one of Sister Anne, free. Uncle Felix has been moved temporarily to the storeroom. There the girls visit with him and are touched by his pathetic attempts to identify himself and them and make out what place he is in. Dicey recalls painfully the happy moments that Uncle Felix once gave her with his stereoptican, which lies now unused on a barrel there in the storeroom; and she receives a "message" that he gives her written on the flyleaf of a hymnal. It speaks of a Daisy long forgotten and of some midnight meeting long past. The pity that all this moves them to and the shock that Sister Anne's commonness gives them are both parts of the awakening of these young women to the evanescence of their own youth and the inevitability of their mortality.

"The Burning," frequently criticized for being enigmatic, brings its characters to the same points of awareness but does so with finality. The story is not enigmatic about anything that matters. It tells how a band of Sherman's soldiers forced their way into a plantation home near Jackson, raped one of the two ladies they found there, forced these ladies, Miss Myra and Miss Theo, out of the house along with their maid, Delilah, looted the place (with the help of a number of dispossessed Negro slaves), and burned it to the ground. The fire reveals the presence of a fourth person in the establishment, a youth named Phinny, the sequestered bastard of one of the persons in the household, possibly Miss Myra, when he bellows like a bull until the flames consume him. Afterwards the ladies and Delilah wander across the fields until they find a deserted hammock. There with the hammock rope Miss Theo murders Miss Myra and makes a fumbling but ultimately successful attempt to hang herself. Delilah returns to the ruins of the house and gathers up the bones of the unfortunate Phinny. Then she makes her way into oblivion.

The point of the story begins to clarify as

references are made to a large Venetian mirror into which the ladies stare when the soldiers invade their parlor. The mirror, blackened but still usable, lies there among the ruins as Delilah stops to gather her bones. In it she sees, however, not the ruin about her but something she herself has never seen before, the image of a vanished Venetian civilization, lords and ladies, gorgeous red birds, and monkeys in velvet—all symbolic of the society that until recently flourished at that very spot and also seemed immortal. Frightened at the thought of approaching night with its tangible army of hostile creatures, live birds, bats, and serpents, Delilah gathers up her bones, seizes a Jubilee cup and a black locust stick, and follows the smell of horses, fire, and men until she finds safety from all three at the river's edge. The moment she enters the water to wade across, her old knowledge of when it will rain next, once laughed at by her betters as superstition, rises to the surface of her mind as the only certainty remaining in a now discredited world.

"Going to Naples," "The Bride of the Innisfallen," and "No Place for You, My Love," are alike in that they carry Eudora Welty out of her own private region. That they are all successful indicates that though she writes best about what she knows, she generally knows whatever she sees. The least impressive of the three, "Going to Naples," suffers only by comparison with the company it keeps. The first part of the story takes place on the *Pomona,* a slow ship sailing from New York to Naples in a warm September of a Holy Year. Most of the passengers are Italian-American pilgrims and old people going home to Italy to die. An American spinster provides a slight focus for some of the things we see, but she does not figure significantly in the action. Our attention is directed mainly to the relationship of Mrs. C. Serto and her daughter Gabriella, who is eighteen, marriageable, but still fat and a bit hysterical even for a late adolescent. Mrs. Serto's unspoken objective for the journey is to find a husband for Gabriella, but the arrival at Naples undoes her. Everything changes as suddenly the author bombards us with what are for us, and for Gabriella, exotic details of the Italian scene. For Mrs. Serto, whose ancient mother meets her on the pier, however, it is all one complex, glorious, and unexpected invitation to resume once more her own role of daughter; and resume it she does, leaving Gabriella slightly bewildered but wiser in her temporary displacement.

Tangible clay makes no such dramatic entry in "The Bride of the Innisfallen." It is there from the beginning. The consciousness at the center of this story is that of a young American girl in London who is running away from her husband. Through her senses we get the details of the murky, rain-dreary Paddington Station and the collection of characters she encounters on her long ride through southern England and Wales into the night. Then there is the tedious crossing of the choppy Irish Sea, the smoky lounge of the *Innisfallen,* and finally the arrival at Cork, with the sights and sounds of the awakening city in the bright light of morning as the boat glides up the river Lee. Like the American girl making her escape, we grope for meaning in this tantalizing succession of data and almost pass by the one bit that seems to have power to bring much of it into focus.

Just as the *Innisfallen* is about to dock, someone on the pier shouts, "There's a bride on board!" And "Sure enough, a girl who had not yet showed herself in public now appeared by the rail in a white spring hat and, over her hands, a little old-fashioned white bunny muff." The bride we suddenly see, however, is the sad young wife, who has seemed lost in the aimlessness symbolized by the plethora of precise detail that has marked her progress westward during the preceding hours. The girl lets the incident pass without special notice, until she stares at the chalk marks that the customs officer leaves on her suitcase, "like a gypsy's sign found on her own front door." "A rabbit ran over my grave," she thinks, and, leaving her suitcase in the parcel room, she walks forthwith into the streets of Cork.

There Easter and suggestions of new life are all about her: rhododendrons swimming in light, boughs bursting with leaves, little girls in confirmation dresses racing up and down the streets like "animated paper snowflakes." She tries unsuccessfully to compose a message to send to her abandoned husband but decides to let the past go. The image of the bride has done its work. This is her Easter, her confirmation, and her new land. Hearing animated talk in a nearby pub, she turns and walks "into the lovely room full of strangers."

The ending of "No Place for You, My Love" is less happy. This is the first story in the collection; it is also probably the best. The title suggests the theme of it, and the text reads like a descent into hell. Two strangers figure in the story: a married man from Syracuse and a young woman from Toledo who is having an affair with another married man. The place is New Orleans on a Sunday in summer—"those hours of afternoon that seem Time Out in New Orleans." The two meet by accident in a restaurant, go for a ride southward from the city, all the way to the Gulf, through a section that is unlike anything else in the southern United States. There they find Cajuns, mosquitoes, crawfish, snakes, and at the end a shack where they can buy beer and sandwiches. Above all there is heat—heat everywhere, with the road running through it like a quivering nerve—but no love do they find, and their abortive relationship expires with a shriek as they return to the city.

The drive back to New Orleans is the re-

vealing part of the story. Above them are the stars of the southern sky, and about them in all directions the red glows of smudge fires. It is on this half of the excursion that he makes the one attempt to come to terms with her, but the kissing is futile and it is not repeated. Finally he sees where they are—riding across "a face, a head, far down here in the South—south of South, below it. A whole giant body sprawled downward then, on and on, always, constant as a constellation or an angel. Flaming and perhaps falling, he thought." Only Milton has described it better. What it all amounts to for the woman we never know. For the man from Syracuse it marks the end forever of his youthful expectations of romantic love.

This story found a conspicuous place for display in the second edition of Brooks and Warren's popular *Understanding Fiction,* and that may help keep attention turned in the direction of *The Bride of the Innisfallen* until the other stories, too, receive some of the critical attention they deserve. The essay "How I Write," reprinted with the story, may also remind readers that Eudora Welty has produced a small but respectable body of criticism along with her fiction. Three more essays, "Place in Fiction," "Words into Fiction," and "The Short Story," have been collected in a Smith College pamphlet, and the first and last of these three have been published separately. Most readers, however, will find it easiest to look for the critical studies in the periodicals in which they first appeared. In addition, she has done reviews of fiction by other writers: Henry Green, William Faulkner, Isak Dinesen, and William Sansom; and she has written a fine essay in praise of Katherine Anne Porter, "The Eye of the Story," which, as might be expected, contains some of her own more important observations about fiction.

Most of Eudora Welty's criticism belongs in the category of apology. Fiction is a mystery like any other kind of human creativity, she maintains, and it cannot be explained. For her, writing means beginning with something definitely known and disentangling the significance from it. This process necessarily involves selection and alteration; but if the writer is gifted and his activity is part of a general concern for human beings, the end of it all will be a truth, human understanding, and another act of communication between people. As for critical analysis, she prefers that that be considered a different kind of thing: "Criticism can be an art too," she says in "How I Write"; but she adds, "It's a mistake to think you can stalk back a story by analysis's footprints and even dream that's the original coming through the woods." Like Faulkner she refuses to write extended theoretical discussions of her art or confer upon it a spurious dignity by playing the role of artist in public. She remarked to Miss Porter many years ago that she was "underfoot locally"; and if reports may be believed, she is still very much that way, underfoot and involved in whatever concerns the lives of those who share soil, air, and water with her. This is her distinction and strength.

In her own way she has also been involved in Mississippi's troubles of the 1960's. Clearly the murder of Medgar Evars outraged her, as it outraged honest people everywhere; and it prompted her to write a short sketch for the *New Yorker*—"Where Is the Voice Coming From?"—which represented an unnamed redneck explaining how he shot from ambush a defenseless Negro. Two years later she replied to criticism by friends from outside the state, some of whom had expected a more forthright commitment of her talents, in an essay "Must the Novelist Crusade?" Briefly her answer was that a crusading novelist is a contradiction in terms. Like any other human being a novelist must love his fellow man and seek justice; but his way of doing that is to show rather than to argue—to let us see our feelings and face our actions rather than to beat drums and deliver judgments. The novelist writes out of concern, and he writes with passion; but he does not distort a work of passion for the sake of a cause. "To write honestly and with all our powers," she says, "is the least we can do, and the most."

A fictional complement to this answer was "The Demonstrators," published in the *New Yorker* late in 1966. This is not one of Miss Welty's best stories, but it is certainly one of her most interesting. A young physician, whose politically liberal wife has recently left him, on a single evening ministers to an old schoolteacher and to a young Negro couple who have given one another fatal wounds with an ice pick. The mode of the young doctor's existence is symbolized by the persistence that keeps the dying teacher alive; and his dilemma, by his recognition of a cup of fine china in the hand of the Negro who brings him water at the deathbed of the girl. Afterwards he broods in the morning sunlight and reads a vulgar and condescending account of the affair in a local paper; but he cannot bring himself to leave the community. A sentimentalist might suggest that the author has here projected her own frustration. This could be so. Nevertheless, Miss Welty's artistic conscience is probably clear, and she seems not to have despaired yet either for Mississippi or for the human race.

A more ambitious piece, "The Optimist's Daughter," appeared in the *New Yorker* for March 15, 1969.* The title of this long short story, or novelette, is ironic; for the optimist is a retired Mississippi judge, Clinton McKelva, who has deliberately chosen optimism as the only attitude that can enable him to face such things as the helpless and angry fatal decline of his first wife, Becky, the disappointing in-

* Miss Welty has since published a revised and slightly longer version of *The Optimist's Daughter* in book form (Random House, 1972).

eptitude and vulgarity of a second and much younger spouse, Wanda Fay, and finally his own fatal illness. The story comes to us through the consciousness of Judge McKelva's widowed daughter, Laurel, who has flown down from Chicago to comfort her father during what turns out to be a futile attempt to repair a detached retina and then, after his death, stays on to see that the funeral is conducted with full respect to him and to the expectations of his contemporaries. Unlike her father, Laurel is not an optimist; and her responses reflect the agonizing pressure of some of the realities that her father's pose had enabled him to endure.

The story has four movements. First, there is the long vigil in the New Orleans hospital, which ends abruptly when Wanda Fay in an act of childish desperation precipitates prematurely the old man's death. Then there is the Mississippi home funeral, reminiscent in its predictable proprieties and anecdotes of the one in *The Golden Apples* of twenty years before and, in the appearance of Wanda Fay's relatives from Texas, of the bizarre Peacock funeral in *The Ponder Heart*. After that there is an interval during which Wanda Fay returns to Texas for a visit with her parents and Laurel stays on temporarily in the house, preparing to surrender it to Wanda Fay, who is now "the last of the McKelvas." It is during this period that the optimist's daughter's renewed association with the house enables her to recall the Becky Clinton who fiercely resented the removal from West Virginia that her "good" marriage had forced upon her. Laurel now understands the hostility with which her mother in the last years of life expressed her frustration at the irreconcilable contradictions of her attachments to house, artifacts, husband, and childhood memories; and as the story nears an end, Laurel too experiences a similar surge of anger when she comes suddenly upon her mother's breadboard,

now ruined by Wanda Fay's cracking walnuts on it with a hammer. She even comes close to striking Wanda Fay as the stupid girl arrogantly returns from Texas to claim her rights as a McKelva, but she forbears. After this unpleasantness Laurel returns to Chicago, carrying with her a painful sense of emptiness and loss, knowing something about human love that she did not know before, and perhaps sensing that her father's optimism may have had its uses.

The novel that Miss Welty published in 1970 was even more impressive than this novelette of 1969. In *Delta Wedding* of 1948 she had presented a brief glimpse, and that at second hand, of a Mississippi beyond the rich delta land. In this later novel, *Losing Battles,* she focuses her attention on the hill country in the northeastern part of the state, with its hills, gullies, undeveloped roads, and second-growth timber. The time is summer, in the 1930's; and the place, the community of Banner, Mississippi. Here as in *Delta Wedding* we get a detailed and loving look at one of those ceremonial occasions by which stable families and communities everywhere routinely affirm and renew their identity. The occasion in *Losing Battles* is ninety-year-old Granny Vaughn's birthday, an event regularly observed by great numbers of relatives, mostly Beechams (though Granny now lives with the Renfro family of her granddaughter Beulah), who live within driving distance. The special thing about this particular reunion is that it marks the return of young Jack Renfro from serving a sentence at the state penitentiary at Parchman and his reunion with his wife, Gloria, and their infant daughter, Lady May. For Jack Renfro, thus, there are two reunions; and the purpose of the action of the novel is to weld them into one.

As Granny Vaughn's clan gathers in the hill home to make its affirmation of unity, another powerful force is leaving the Banner scene. This is Miss Julia Mortimer, retired schoolmistress, who gave her life in an effort to make the sons and daughters of Banner look beyond their Mississippi microcosm. Much of the tension in the story is a consequence of Miss Julia's unremitting efforts to improve the natives of Banner and what she considers to be the primitive mode of life they cling to. For the most part her efforts have miscarried and simply caused the more promising young people to seek their fortunes elsewhere. This is why her last thoughts have been on Gloria, an orphan and prize pupil who did stay in Banner and even succeeded her mentor as local teacher but who married, to Miss Julia's dying dismay, Jack Renfro. Gloria genuinely loves her young husband, but she cannot comprehend at first what it means to belong to a family, any more than Miss Julia could. Thus she resists full adoption into the clan until the vexed Beechams initiate her with a bath and force-feeding of fresh watermelon that seems to have disturbed, quite unnecessarily, even some of Miss Welty's more sympathetic reviewers. Understandably after such boisterous treatment, however, Gloria continues to feel alienated for a time; but slowly the fact of her acceptance begins to sink in, and eventually the fund of charity in Jack Renfro tips the balance to make her consent to be one of them.

Taken singly, the members of the Banner clan are like any other group of human beings —varied in talent and temperament, and for the most part neither saintly nor very bad. Taken together they are far more admirable than they are individually—probably because in their roles as members of a group they lose some of that selfishness that lies at the root of human ugliness. This is what the intellectually proud but lonely Miss Julia has never fully understood: individually the Renfros and the Beechams may be stupid, petty, or mean;

as a group they can be amazingly generous, capable of loving their enemies on occasion, and almost always capable of reaching out to take in the lonely, the estranged, and if necessary even the willfully eccentric. Thus the battles that the characters in this novel wage and lose are battles they wage in the hope of being able to remain alone, as isolated individuals. For example, Miss Julia, who wanted to be buried in solitary dignity under the steps of the schoolhouse, loses her last battle in death when the Banner people claim her for their own and honor her with burial in the community graveyard. Gloria surrenders the dream that Miss Julia has tried to give her, accepts the childlike Jack fully, as he accepts her, and returns to live with him in the house with Granny Vaughn and the other Renfros. The paradox is that, whether they know it or not, all these people are infinitely richer for having submitted to the ties that bind; and the strength they find is a direct consequence of the concession they have made. It is altogether appropriate that the novel should end with a rejoicing Jack Renfro, who has lost most of his battles since well before the novel began, bursting into the old evangelical hymn of victory "Bringing in the Sheaves."

Comparisons of Eudora Welty with other writers in the southern United States have been fairly frequent. In choice of subject, of course, she resembles all those who have written accurately about Mississippi, and she also has demonstrable affinities with those modern authors who have written of other states in the deep South. Being a southern woman, she is also often compared with Katherine Anne Porter, Caroline Gordon, Carson McCullers, and Flannery O'Connor. Being southern, however, is at once the most important and the least important thing about Eudora Welty. Mississippi has been her sustenance for so long that one can scarcely conceive what she would have become had she fed elsewhere. Whatever her place, she would have been a maker of something, for that is her nature. She has, as she herself confessed, a visual imagination and a penchant for seeing things in their connectedness; and the simultaneous unraveling and compounding of the networks she finds in life about her produces those complex pieces that more often than not seem to have grown like crystals from simple sketches into the strange new entities that are her stories. Occasionally her tendency to see things in terms of other things has got her into trouble. Some of the descriptions in *A Curtain of Green,* especially, invite the term "baroque" because of uncontrolled and nonfunctional metaphors. The stories there have a few warts on them. In recent years these lapses have not occurred. As for structure, that has been present in Eudora Welty's work from the beginning.

Miss Welty is not without the southern writer's sense of the past or feeling for the metaphysical, but she has never allowed her writing to play a partisan role in either of these areas. Her one story about the Civil War could have been told with the same truth about almost any war, and her tales of the Natchez Trace would have much the same validity if told about the Wilderness Road or the path westward left by Lewis and Clark. That is, she is historically minded without being antiquarian. Her sense of the metaphysical is frequently but unobtrusively displayed for readers who may be tuned in to it. We can see it at work in Mrs. Larkin's strange perversity, in the intimations that come to William Wallace during the river dragging, in the roles that Livvie and Jenny Lockhart and several of the characters in *The Golden Apples* unknowingly assume, and in the pathetic frustration of the semi-divine′ Circe with her realization that silly mortals have a divinity all their own, though they themselves may be unaware of it. Some readers may regard these intimations of transcendence as aspects of an outdated provincialism; but they are pervasive enough to make one suspect that for this writer such things represent the ground of her being. And, at any rate, the tangible is always there, too, and very much in focus.

Selected Bibliography

WORKS OF EUDORA WELTY

A Curtain of Green and Other Stories. New York: Doubleday, Doran, 1941.

The Robber Bridegroom. New York: Doubleday, Doran, 1942.

The Wide Net and Other Stories. New York: Harcourt, Brace, 1943.

Delta Wedding. New York: Harcourt, Brace, 1946.

The Golden Apples. New York: Harcourt, Brace, 1949.

The Ponder Heart. New York: Harcourt, Brace, 1954. Originally published in the *New Yorker,* 29:47–138 (December 5, 1953).

The Bride of the Innisfallen. New York: Harcourt, Brace, 1955.

Three Papers on Fiction. Northampton, Mass.: Smith College, 1962. (Contains "Place in Fiction," originally in *South Atlantic Quarterly,* 55:57–72 (January 1956), and later published in a limited edition, New York: House of Books, 1957; "Words into Fiction"; and "The Short Story," originally in *Atlantic Monthly* (as "The Reading and Writing of Short Stories"), 183:54–58 (February 1949) and 46–49 (March 1949), and separately by Harcourt, Brace, 1950).

The Shoe Bird. New York: Harcourt, Brace and World, 1964.

Losing Battles. New York: Random House, 1970.

The Optimist's Daughter. New York: Random House, 1972.
Published since the writing of this essay
One Writer's Beginnings. Cambridge, Mass.: Harvard University Press, 1984.
The Hitch-Hikers. New York: Dramatists Play Service, Inc., 1986.

SELECTED UNCOLLECTED ITEMS

"Ida M'Toy," *Accent,* 2:214–22 (Summer 1942). (Sketch.)

"Pageant of Birds," *New Republic,* 109:565–67 (October 5, 1943). (Sketch.)

"A Sketching Trip," *Atlantic Monthly,* 175:62–70 (June 1945). (Story.)

"Hello and Goodbye," *Atlantic Monthly,* 180:37–40 (July 1947). (Story.)

"In Yoknapatawpha," *Hudson Review,* 1:596–98 (Winter 1949). (Review, William Faulkner.)

"How I Write," *Virginia Quarterly Review,* 31:240–51 (Spring 1955). Reprinted in Cleanth Brooks and R. P. Warren, *Understanding Fiction,* 2nd ed. New York: Appleton-Century-Crofts, 1959. Pp. 545–53. (Essay.)

"A Flock of Guinea Hens Seen from a Car," *New Yorker,* 33:35 (April 20, 1957). (Poem.)

"A Touch That's Magic," *New York Times Book Review,* November 3, 1957, p. 5. (Review, Isak Dinesen.)

"Henry Green: A Novelist of the Imagination," *Texas Quarterly,* 4:246–56 (Autumn 1961). (Essay.)

"Time and Place—and Suspense," *New York Times Book Review,* June 30, 1963, pp. 5, 27. (Review, William Sansom.)

"Where Is the Voice Coming From?" *New Yorker,* 39:24–25 (July 6, 1963). (Sketch.)

"The Eye of the Story," *Yale Review,* 55:265–74 (Winter 1965). (Essay.)

"Must the Novelist Crusade?" *Atlantic Monthly,* 216:104–08 (October 1965). (Essay.)

"The Demonstrators," *New Yorker,* 42:56–63 (November 26, 1966). (Story.)

BIBLIOGRAPHY

Gross, Seymour L. "Eudora Welty: A Bibliography of Criticism and Comment." *Secretary's News Sheet* (Bibliographical Society, University of Virginia), 45:1–32 (April 1960).

CRITICAL AND BIOGRAPHICAL STUDIES

Appel, Alfred, Jr. *A Season of Dreams.* Baton Rouge: Louisiana State University Press, 1965.

Glenn, Eunice. "Fantasy in the Fiction of Eudora Welty," *A Southern Vanguard,* edited by Allen Tate. New York: Prentice-Hall, 1947. Pp. 78–91. Reprinted in *Critiques and Essays in Modern Fiction, 1920–1951,* edited by John Aldridge. New York: Ronald Press, 1952. Pp. 506–17.

Hardy, John E. "*Delta Wedding* as Region and Symbol," *Sewanee Review,* 60:397–417 (Summer 1952).

Morris, Harry C. "Eudora Welty's Use of Mythology," *Shenandoah,* 6:34–40 (Spring 1955).

Ransom, John Crowe. "Delta Fiction," *Kenyon Review,* 8:503–07 (Summer 1946).

Rubin, Louis D., Jr. "The Golden Apples of the Sun," in *The Faraway Country: Writers of the Modern South.* Seattle: University of Washington Press, 1963. Pp. 131–54.

Vande Kieft, Ruth M. *Eudora Welty.* New York: Twayne, 1962.

Warren, Robert Penn. "The Love and the Separateness in Miss Welty," *Kenyon Review,* 6:246–59 (Spring 1944). Reprinted in R. P. Warren, *Selected Essays.* New York: Random House, 1958. Pp. 156–69.

—*J. A. BRYANT, JR.*

Nathanael West

1903-1940

NATHANAEL WEST was born Nathan Weinstein in New York City on October 17, 1903, the child of Jewish immigrants from Russia. His mother, Anna Wallenstein Weinstein, came of a cultivated family, and had been a beautiful girl, courted in Europe by the painter Maurice Stern. As a housewife she turned stout and bossy. West's father, Max Weinstein, a building contractor, was slight, kind, and shy. Of West's two sisters, the elder, Hinda, somewhat resembled the mother, and the younger, Lorraine (called Laura), was more like the father. West was particularly devoted to his father, and so close to his younger sister that in later life he repeatedly said he could never marry less fine a woman than his sister Laura.

The boy West attended P.S. 81 and P.S. 10, both in Manhattan, where he showed no academic distinction. He was a thin, awkward, and ungainly child. Summers he went to Camp Paradox in the Adirondacks, and a former counselor remembers him as "a quiet chap and not much of a mixer." Baseball was his passion, although he tended to daydream in the outfield. When a fly ball hit him on the head and bounced off for a home run, he got the nickname, "Pep," that stayed with him all his life.

Otherwise West seems to have spent most of his time reading. If his sisters' recollection can be trusted, he read Tolstoi at ten, and by thirteen he was familiar with Dostoevski and other Russian literature, Flaubert, and Henry James. He trained his bull terrier to bite anyone who came into his room when he was reading. After his graduation from P.S. 10, West enrolled at De Witt Clinton High School, where he soon distinguished himself as one of the weakest students in the school. He took no part in any extracurricular activity. In June 1920, West left Clinton without graduating.

In September 1921, West was admitted to Tufts University, on the strength of what now seems to have been a forged transcript from De Witt Clinton. Two months later, as a result of academic difficulties, he withdrew. In February 1922, he was admitted to Brown University as a transfer student from Tufts, this time on the basis of the transcript of the record of another Nathan Weinstein at Tufts. Once enrolled at Brown, West got serious, and managed not only to pass his courses but to graduate in two and a half years.

At Brown, West developed another personality, or showed another side of his personality than the solitary dreamer. He became an Ivy League fashion plate, wearing Brooks Brothers suits and shirts, and a homburg. A college friend, Jeremiah Mahoney, recalls that West looked like a "well-heeled mortuary assistant." Although his manner was reserved, he was friendly and gregarious, generous with his large allowance from his father, and a fairly good banjo player. With girls, he tended to be either too shy or too brash. One summer, West and another college friend, Quentin Reynolds, worked as hod carriers for West's father, and West not only built muscles on his thin frame but got on surprisingly well with the workmen.

West received little or no education in the Jewish religion, and although he was probably ritually circumcised, he was never confirmed in a Bar Mitzvah ceremony. During his years at Brown, West threw off what he could of his Jewishness, and suffered from the rest. "More than anyone I ever knew," his friend John Sanford later reported, "Pep writhed under the accidental curse of his religion." West had nothing to do with any organized Jewish activity on campus, hung around the snobbish Gentile fraternities, and was intensely anxious to be pledged and intensely bitter that he never was. "Nobody ever thought of Pep as being Jewish," a college friend has said, but apparently the Brown fraternities did.

West's great success at Brown was as an aesthete. He dabbled in mysticism, ritual magic, and medieval Catholicism, quoted from obscure saints, discovered Joyce, and for a while was a Nietzschean. S. J. Perelman, a college friend who later married West's sister Laura, recalls that West was the first man on campus to read *Jurgen*. He was equally devoted to Baudelaire, Verlaine, and Rimbaud, Huysmans and Arthur Machen. His personal library was the largest any Brown man had at the time, and he loaned books liberally. Relying on the other Nathan Weinstein's credits in science and economics, West was able to confine himself almost entirely to courses in literature, philosophy, and history. His principal extracurricular activity was working as an editor of *Casements*, the Brown literary magazine. He drew its first cover design, naturally of casements, and contributed a poem, "Death," and an article, "Euripides—a Playwright." The 1924 *Liber Brunensis,* the yearbook, identified West as a genius with an unpredictable future.

After his graduation in 1924, West persuaded his father to send him to Paris, where he spent two happy years and grew a red beard. He returned to New York early in 1926, worked for his father for a while, and then in 1927, through a family connection, got a job as assistant manager at the Kenmore Hotel on East 23rd Street. Put on night duty, he was able to spend the nights reading. He gave rooms to his Brown friends and *their* homeless friends, among them Dashiell Hammett, who finished *The Maltese Falcon* as West's bootleg guest at the Kenmore. In 1928 he progressed to the same job at a fancier hotel, the Sutton on East 56th Street, where he put up other indigent writers, at reduced rates or no charge at all, among them Erskine Caldwell and James T. Farrell. After the stock market crash, which ruined West's father, the Sutton's sun deck became a favored spot for suicides, and West took to calling it "Suicide Leap."

West's first novel, *The Dream Life of Balso Snell,* seems to have been first written in college, but he rewrote it at the Sutton, and in 1931 he managed to get it privately printed in a limited edition of 500 copies. One review appeared, in *Contempo,* but otherwise *Balso Snell* caused no stir whatsoever. The book listed "Nathanael West" as author and thus marked West's official change of name. He had spent much of his class time at Brown doodling "Nathan von Wallenstein Weinstein," which was the name signed to his *Casements* contributions, but even that had turned out to be not Gentile enough. West explained to William Carlos Williams how he got the name: "Horace

Greeley said, 'Go West, young man.' So I did." West's anti-Semitism was now considerable. He referred to Jewish girls as "bagels," and avoided them.

In 1931, West took a leave from the Sutton and he and Sanford, another aspiring novelist, rented a shack in the Adirondacks near Warrensburg, New York. Here they wrote in the mornings and fished and hunted in the afternoons. West was working on *Miss Lonelyhearts,* reading each sentence back aloud, producing about a hundred words a day. He rewrote the manuscript five or six times, in the Adirondacks, then back at the Sutton; finally, having quit the Sutton, in a hotel in Frenchtown, New Jersey.

Late in 1932 West and the Perelmans bought a farmhouse in Bucks County, Pennsylvania, and Mrs. Weinstein soon moved in to take over the cooking and try to persuade West to return to the hotel business. In 1933 *Miss Lonelyhearts* was published, and it was reviewed enthusiastically. Unfortunately, the publisher, Horace Liveright, chose that moment to go bankrupt, the printer refused to deliver most of the edition, and by the time West got another publisher to take it over, the reviews were forgotten. Altogether *Miss Lonelyhearts* sold fewer than 800 copies, and West's total income from his first two books and three years of writing came to $780.

In 1932 West had become co-editor with Dr. Williams of a little magazine, *Contact,* and he published articles and chapters of *Miss Lonelyhearts* in it and in *Contempo* in 1933. In August 1933, he became associate editor of a magazine, *Americana,* edited by Alexander King. Before *Americana* expired in November, West managed to publish a Hollywood story, "Business Deal," and some excerpts from *Balso Snell* in it. West then wrote some stories for the slick magazines, but did not succeed

in selling any. He applied for a Guggenheim fellowship, with F. Scott Fitzgerald as one of his sponsors, but failed to get it.

West next wrote *A Cool Million* in a hurry, hoping to profit from the reviews of *Miss Lonelyhearts* and make some money. It appeared in 1934, was unfavorably reviewed, sold poorly, and was soon remaindered.

West's personal life in the East was no more successful than his literary career. *Balso Snell* was dedicated to Alice Shepard, a Roman Catholic girl who had gone to Pembroke College with West's sister Laura. He was secretly engaged to her from 1929 to 1932, then publicly engaged, but they never married, although West had bought a marriage license and carried it around with him for several years. His poverty was the explanation given out, but in Sanford's opinion the engagement foundered on the religious difference.

West had been to Hollywood for a few months in 1933, when *Miss Lonelyhearts* was sold to Twentieth Century-Fox and West received a writing contract at $350 a week. He was given little to do, saw his novel made into a Lee Tracy murder thriller, and came back to New York in July disillusioned and bitter. Nevertheless, in 1935, when every other possibility seemed closed to him, West returned to Hollywood and went to work for Republic Studios as a script writer. He switched to RKO Radio in 1938, and also worked for Universal-International Pictures. In the remaining few years of his life, West turned out a number of trivial screenplays, alone or in collaboration, among them *Five Came Back, I Stole a Million,* and *Spirit of Culver.* As a result of his facility as a script writer, West was able to live in comfort and security for the first time since the 1929 crash. He worked a few hours a week dictating to a secretary, and spent most of his weekends on hunting trips, following the season down from Oregon through California into Mexico each year. He acquired two hunting dogs, which slept on his bed, and he explained to people that he needed a house and servants for the dogs.

West made it clear that he despised the "pants pressers" of Hollywood, and he tried to escape in a number of fashions. He collaborated on two plays for Broadway, but the first never got there and the second only lasted two performances, winning from Brooks Atkinson the accolade "nitwit theatre." He became a fellow traveler of the Communist party, signing the call for the American Writers Congress in 1935, joining the Screen Writers Guild, and working strenuously on behalf of Loyalist Spain and other causes. (Earlier, in 1933, he had published a Marxist poem in *Contempo*. Before leaving for California in 1935 he had picketed Orbach's with other Communist sympathizers and was jailed for a few hours "for obstructing traffic.") He was, luckily, unable to get his political orientation explicitly into his fiction.

West published *The Day of the Locust* in 1939, hoping its success would get him out of Hollywood, but despite some good reviews it was a commercial failure, selling fewer than 1,500 copies. (West's publisher, Bennett Cerf, explained to him that it failed because women readers didn't like it.)

West's isolation ended suddenly and surprisingly in 1940, when he fell in love with Eileen McKenney, the protagonist of Ruth McKenney's *My Sister Eileen*. They were married in April, and spent a three-month honeymoon in Oregon, hunting and fishing. On West's return he got a higher paid job at Columbia Pictures; later Columbia bought *A Cool Million* and a screen treatment of it on which West had collaborated. The great happy period of West's life, begun in the spring, did not last out the year. On December 22, the Wests were returning from a hunting trip in Mexico, when West, a poor driver, went through a stop sign near El Centro, California. Their station wagon crashed into an automobile. Eileen died instantly, West an hour later on the way to the hospital. He was thirty-seven. His body was shipped to New York and buried in a Jewish cemetery.

Since his death West's reputation has risen continuously. *Miss Lonelyhearts* has sold 190,-000 copies in paperback, and *The Day of the Locust* 250,000. Scholarly articles about West, here and abroad, multiply cancerously. *Miss Lonelyhearts* has been made into a play, a more faithful film than the Lee Tracy one, and an opera. In 1946 it was translated into French by Marcelle Sibon as *Mademoiselle Cœur-Brisé,* with an introduction by Philippe Soupault, and it has had a visible effect on later French fiction. Since 1949, all West's books but the first have been published in England. When the four novels were reissued in this country in one volume in 1957, all the reviews were favorable, and there was general agreement that West was one of the most important writers of the thirties, as American as apple pie. West's picture appeared on the cover of the *Saturday Review*, looking very Jewish.

The Dream Life of Balso Snell (1931) is almost impossible to synopsize. A poet named Balso Snell finds the wooden Trojan Horse and has a picaresque journey up its alimentary canal. In the course of his travels he encounters: a Jewish guide; Maloney the Areopagite, a Catholic mystic; John Gilson, a precocious schoolboy; and Miss McGeeney, John's eighth-grade teacher. Each has a story, sometimes several stories, to tell, and their stories merge with their dreams and with Balso's dreams in a thoroughly confusing, and deliberately confusing, fashion. The book ends with Balso's orgasm, still in the bowels of the horse, during a dream of rapturous sexual intercourse with Miss McGeeney. Balso is dreaming the schoolboy's dream, and may have become the schoolboy.

The overwhelming impression the reader gets is of the corruption and repulsiveness of the flesh. In one of John Gilson's fantasies of beating a mistress, he explains his action: "I have a sty on my eye, a cold sore on my lip, a pimple where the edge of my collar touches my neck, another pimple in the corner of my mouth, and a drop of salt snot on the end of my nose." Furthermore, "It seems to me as though all the materials of life—wood, glass, wool, skin—are rubbing against my sty, my cold sore and my pimples." When Balso encounters Miss McGeeney, a middle-aged tweedy woman disguised for the moment as a beautiful naked girl, she offers him her poetic vision: "Houses that are protuberances on the skin of streets—warts, tumors, pimples, corns, nipples, sebaceous cysts, hard and soft chancres."

In a dream within his dream, Balso is attracted to girl cripples: "He likened their disarranged hips, their short legs, their humps, their splay feet, their wall-eyes, to ornament." He cries tenderly to one of them, Janey the hunchback: "For me, your sores are like flowers: the new, pink, budlike sores, the full, rose-ripe sores, the sweet, seed-bearing sores. I shall cherish them all." One of Balso's beautiful memories in the book is of a girl he once loved who did nothing all day but put bits of meat and gravy, butter and cheese, on the petals of roses so that they would attract flies instead of butterflies and bees.

As the human body is seen as a running sore, Christianity is seen entirely in terms of Christ's wounded and bleeding body. Maloney the Areopagite is writing a hagiography of Saint Puce, a flea who was born, lived, and died in the armpit of Jesus Christ. Maloney's blasphemous idea that Saint Puce was born of the

Holy Ghost enables West to mock the mysteries of Incarnation, as the flea's feasting on the divine flesh and blood enables West to mock Eucharist. The Passion is burlesqued by Maloney, who is encountered naked except for a derby stuck full of thorns, trying to crucify himself with thumbtacks, and Beagle Darwin, a fictional invention of Miss McGeeney's, who does a juggling act, keeping in the air "the Nails, the Scourge, the Thorns, and a piece of the True Cross."

Nor is West's bitterness in the book reserved for Christianity. Judaism comes in for its share. The song in praise of obscene roundness that Balso makes when he starts his journey concludes:

> Round and Ringing Full
> As the Mouth of a Brimming Goblet
> The Rust-Laden Holes
> In Our Lord's Feet
> Entertain the Jew-Driven Nails.

The guide turns out to be not only a Jew, but a Jew who at the mention of such melodious Jewish names as Hernia Hornstein and Paresis Pearlberg finds it necessary to affirm: "I am a Jew. I'm a Jew! A Jew!" Balso answers politely that some of his best friends are Jews, and adds Doughty's epigram: "The semites are like to a man sitting in a cloaca to the eyes, and whose brows touch heaven."

The strength of *Balso Snell* lies in its garish comic imagination. Maloney's crucifixion with thumbtacks is not only a serious theme that West's later work develops, it is also funny, and as a parody of the stance of Roman Catholic mysticism, devastating. The account in John Gilson's journal of his Gidean and Dostoevskian murder of an idiot dishwasher is repulsive but genuinely imagined, and its unconscious sexual motivation is boldly dramatized: stripping for the crime, John notices his genitals tight and hard; afterwards he feels like a happy young girl, "kittenish, cuney-cutey, darlingey, springtimey"; when he sees sailors on the street, he flirts and camps and feels "as though I were melting—all silk and perfumed, pink lace." The hunchback Janey is a nightmarish vision of the female body as terrifying, transformed into comedy: she has a hundred and forty-four exquisite teeth, and is pregnant in the hump.

Some of West's language in the book foreshadows his later triumphs. Janey imagines death to be "like putting on a wet [bathing] suit—shivery." John describes his dual nature to his fantasy-mistress, Saniette: "Think of two men—myself and the chauffeur within me. This chauffeur is very large and dressed in ugly ready-made clothing. His shoes, soiled from walking about the streets of a great city, are covered with animal ordure and chewing gum. His hands are covered with coarse woollen gloves. On his head is a derby hat." Sometimes John speaks in a voice we can hear as the youthful West's. He tells Balso: "I need women and because I can't buy or force them, I have to make poems for them. God knows how tired I am of using the insanity of Van Gogh and the adventures of Gauguin as can-openers." John explains his position in a pamphlet, which he sells to Balso for a dollar. In it he confesses: "If it had been possible for me to attract by exhibiting a series of physical charms, my hatred would have been less. But I found it necessary to substitute strange conceits, wise and witty sayings, peculiar conduct, Art, for the muscles, teeth, hair, of my rivals."

The weaknesses of *Balso Snell* are all characteristically juvenile. The principal one is the obsessive scatology, which soon becomes boring. "O Anus Mirabilis!" Balso cries of his rectal entrance to the Trojan Horse, and his roundness song takes off from that anal image. "Art is a sublime excrement," he is told by the Jewish guide (who seems to justify only the first half of Doughty's aphorism). John sees

journal-keepers in excremental imagery: "They come to the paper with a constipation of ideas —eager, impatient. The white paper acts as a laxative. A diarrhoea of words is the result." When the idiot dishwasher swallows, John compares it to "a miniature toilet being flushed." As John beats Saniette, he cries: "O constipation of desire! O diarrhoea of love!" He has visions of writing a play that will conclude when "the ceiling of the theatre will be made to open and cover the occupants with tons of loose excrement." Balso speaks "with lips torn angry in laying duck's eggs from a chicken's rectum." James F. Light reports that West was fond of quoting Odo of Cluny's reference to the female as *"saccus stercoris,"* but the book's scatological obsession is clearly not restricted to the female. It is no less than a vision of the whole world as one vast dungheap.

Balso Snell is complex and stratified, so much so that at one point we get Janey's thinking as Beagle imagines it in a letter actually written by Miss McGeeney and read by Balso in his dream within a dream. But the book has no form, and consists merely of a series of encounters and complications, terminated rather than resolved by the orgasm. We can sense West's dissatisfaction with it as not fully realized in his re-use of some of its material in later works. Some of *Balso Snell* is extremely schoolboyish, like the guide's aphorism, "A hand in the Bush is worth two in the pocket," or Balso's comment on Maloney's story of the martyrdom and death of Saint Puce: "I think you're morbid. . . . Take cold showers."

When *Miss Lonelyhearts* was published two years later, in 1933, West told A. J. Liebling that is was entirely unlike *Balso Snell*, "of quite a different make, wholesome, clean, holy, slightly mystic and inane." He describes it in "Some Notes on Miss Lonelyhearts" as a "portrait of a priest of our time who has had a religious experience." In it, West explains, "violent images are used to illustrate commonplace events. Violent acts are left almost bald." He credits William James's *Varieties of Religious Experience* for its psychology. Some or all of this may be Westian leg-pull.

The plot of *Miss Lonelyhearts* is Sophoclean irony, as simple and inevitable as the plot of *Balso Snell* is random and whimsical. A young newspaperman who writes the agony column of his paper as "Miss Lonelyhearts" has reached the point where the joke has gone sour. He becomes obsessed with the real misery of his correspondents, illuminated for him by the cynicism of William Shrike, the feature editor. Miss Lonelyhearts pursues Shrike's wife Mary, unsuccessfully, and cannot content himself with the love and radiant goodness of Betty, his fiancée. Eventually he finds his fate in two of his correspondents, the crippled Peter Doyle and his wife Fay. Miss Lonelyhearts is not punished for his tumble with Fay, but when on his next encounter he fights her off, it leads to his being shot by Doyle.

The characters are allegorical figures who are at the same time convincing as people. Miss Lonelyhearts is a New England puritan, the son of a Baptist minister. He has a true religious vocation or calling, but no institutional church to embody it. When Betty suggests that he quit the column, he tells her: "I can't quit. And even if I were to quit, it wouldn't make any difference. I wouldn't be able to forget the letters, no matter what I did."

In one of the most brilliant strokes in the book, he is never named, always identified only by his role. (In an earlier draft, West had named him Thomas Matlock, which we could translate "Doubter Wrestler," but no name at all is infinitely more effective.) Even when he telephones Fay Doyle for an assignation, he identifies himself only as "Miss Lonelyhearts, the man who does the column." In his namelessness, in his vocation without a church, Miss Lonelyhearts is clearly the prophet in the reluctance stage, when he denies the call and tells God that he stammers, but Miss Lonelyhearts, the prophet of *our* time, is stuck there until death.

Miss Lonelyhearts identifies Betty as the principle of order: "She had often made him feel that when she straightened his tie, she straightened much more." The order that she represents is the innocent order of Nature, as opposed to the disorder of sinful Man. When Miss Lonelyhearts is sick, Betty comes to nourish him with hot soup, impose order on his room, and redeem him with a pastoral vision: "She told him about her childhood on a farm and of her love for animals, about country sounds and country smells and of how fresh and clean everything in the country is. She said that he ought to live there and that if he did, he would find that all his troubles were city troubles." When Miss Lonelyhearts is back on his feet, Betty takes him for a walk in the zoo, and he is "amused by her evident belief in the curative power of animals." Then she takes him to live in the country for a few days, in the book's great idyllic scene. Miss Lonelyhearts is beyond such help, but it is Betty's patient innocence—she is as soft and helpless as a kitten—that makes the book so heartbreaking. She is an innocent Eve to his fallen Adam, and he alone is driven out of Eden.

The book's four other principal characters are savage caricatures, in the root sense of "caricature" as the overloading of one attribute. Shrike is a dissociated half of Miss Lonelyhearts, his cynical intelligence, and it is interesting to learn that Shrike's rhetorical masterpiece, the great speech on the varieties of escape, was spoken by Miss Lonelyhearts in an earlier draft. Shrike's name is marvelously apt. The shrike or butcherbird impales its prey on thorns, and the name is a form of the word "shriek." Shrike is of course the mocker who hands Miss Lonelyhearts his crown of thorns, and throughout the book he is a shrieking bird of prey; when not a butcherbird, "a screaming, clumsy gull."

Shrike's wife Mary is one vast teasing mammary image. As Miss Lonelyhearts decides to telephone Mary in Delehanty's speakeasy, he sees a White Rock poster and observes that "the artist had taken a great deal of care in drawing her breasts and their nipples stuck out like tiny red hats." He then thinks of "the play Mary made with her breasts. She used them as the coquettes of long ago had used their fans. One of her tricks was to wear a medal low down on her chest. Whenever he asked to see it, instead of drawing it out she leaned over for him to look. Although he had often asked to see the medal, he had not yet found out what it represented." Miss Lonelyhearts and Mary go out for a gay evening, and Mary flaunts her breasts while talking of her mother's terrible death from cancer of the breast. He finally gets to see the medal, which reads "Awarded by the Boston Latin School for first place in the 100 yd. dash." When he takes her home he kisses her breasts, for the first time briefly slowing down her dash.

The Doyles are presented in inhuman or subhuman imagery. When, in answer to Fay's letter of sexual invitation, Miss Lonelyhearts decides to telephone her, he pictures her as "a tent, haircovered and veined," and himself as a skeleton: "When he made the skeleton enter the flesh tent, it flowered at every joint." Fay appears and is a giant: "legs like Indian clubs, breasts like balloons and a brow like a pigeon." When he takes her arm, "It felt like a thigh." Following her up the stairs to his apartment, "he watched the action of her massive hams; they were like two enormous grindstones." Undressing, "she made sea sounds; something flapped like a sail; there was the

creak of ropes; then he heard the wave-against-a-wharf smack of rubber on flesh. Her call for him to hurry was a sea-moan, and when he lay beside her, she heaved, tidal, moon-driven." Eventually Miss Lonelyhearts "crawled out of bed like an exhausted swimmer leaving the surf," and she soon drags him back.

If Fay is an oceanic monster, Peter Doyle is only a sinister puppy. In bringing Miss Lonelyhearts back to the apartment at Fay's order, he half-jokes, "Ain't I the pimp, to bring home a guy for my wife?" Fay reacts by hitting him in the mouth with a rolled-up newspaper, and his comic response is to growl like a dog and catch the paper with his teeth. When she lets go of her end, he drops to his hands and knees and continues to imitate a dog on the floor. As Miss Lonelyhearts leans over to help him up, "Doyle tore open Miss Lonelyhearts' fly, then rolled over on his back, laughing wildly." Fay, more properly, accepts him as a dog and kicks him.

The obsessive theme of *Miss Lonelyhearts* is human pain and suffering, but it is represented almost entirely as female suffering. This is first spelled out in the letters addressed to Miss Lonelyhearts: Sick-of-it-all is a Roman Catholic wife who has had seven children in twelve years, is pregnant again, and has kidney pains so excruciating that she cries all the time. Desperate is a sixteen-year-old born with a hole in her face instead of a nose, who wants to have dates like other girls. Harold S. writes about his thirteen-year-old deaf-and-dumb sister Gracie, who was raped by a man when she was playing on the roof, and who will be brutally punished if her parents find out about it. Broad Shoulders was hit by a car when she was first pregnant, and is alternately persecuted and deserted by an unbalanced husband, in five pages of ghastly detail. Miss Lonelyhearts gets only two letters about male suffering, one from a paralyzed boy who wants to play the violin, the other from Peter Doyle, who complains of the pain from his crippled leg and the general meaningless of life.

The theme of indignities committed on women comes up in another form in the stories Miss Lonelyhearts' friends tell in Delehanty's. They seem to be exclusively anecdotes of group rape, of one woman gang-raped by eight neighbors, of another kept in the back room of a speakeasy for three days until "on the last day they sold tickets to niggers." Miss Lonelyhearts identifies himself with "wife-torturers, rapers of small children." At one point he tries giving his readers the traditional Christian justification for suffering, that it is Christ's gift to mankind to bring them to Him, but he tears up the column.

Ultimately the novel cannot justify or even explain suffering, only proclaim its omnipresence. Lying sick in bed, Miss Lonelyhearts gets a vision of human life: "He found himself in the window of a pawnshop full of fur coats, diamond rings, watches, shotguns, fishing tackle, mandolins. All these things were the paraphernalia of suffering. A tortured high light twisted on the blade of a gift knife, a battered horn grunted with pain." Finally his mind forms everything into a gigantic cross, and he falls asleep exhausted.

The book's desperate cry of pain and suffering comes to a focus in what Miss Lonelyhearts calls his "Christ complex." He recognizes that Christ is the only answer to his readers' letters, but that "if he did not want to get sick, he had to stay away from the Christ business. Besides, Christ was Shrike's particular joke." As Miss Lonelyhearts leaves the office and walks through a little park, the shadow of a lamppost pierces his side like a spear. Since nothing grows in the park's battered earth, he decides to ask his correspon-

dents to come and water the soil with their tears. He imagines Shrike telling him to teach them to pray each morning, "Give us this day our daily stone," and thinks: "He had given his reader many stones; so many, in fact, that he had only one left—the stone that had formed in his gut."

Jesus Christ, Shrike says, is "the Miss Lonelyhearts of Miss Lonelyhearts." Miss Lonelyhearts has nailed an ivory Christ to the wall of his room with great spikes, but it disappoints him: "Instead of writhing, the Christ remained calmly decorative." Miss Lonelyhearts recalls: "As a boy in his father's church, he had discovered that something stirred in him when he shouted the name of Christ, something secret and enormously powerful." Unfortunately, he recognizes, it is not faith but hysteria: "For him, Christ was the most natural of excitements."

Miss Lonelyhearts tells Betty he is "a humanity lover," but Shrike more aptly identifies him a "leper licker." "If he could only believe in Christ," Miss Lonelyhearts thinks, "then everything would be simple and the letters extremely easy to answer." Later he recognizes that "Shrike had accelerated his sickness by teaching him to handle his one escape, Christ, with a thick glove of words." He decides that he has had a part in the general betrayal of suffering mankind: "The thing that made his share in it particularly bad was that he was capable of dreaming the Christ dream. He felt that he had failed at it, not so much because of Shrike's jokes or his own self-doubt, but because of his lack of humility." Miss Lonelyhearts concludes that "with him, even the word Christ was a vanity." When he gets drunk with Doyle, he calls on Christ joyously, and goes home with Doyle to bring the glad tidings to both Doyles, to heal their marriage. He preaches "love" to them and realizes that he is only writing another column, switches to preaching Christ Jesus, "the black fruit that hangs on the cross-tree . . . the bidden fruit," and realizes that he is only echoing Shrike's poisoned rhetoric.

What Miss Lonelyhearts eventually achieves, since he cannot believe in the real Christ, and refuses to become a spurious Christ, is Peter's condition. He becomes the rock on which the new church will be founded, but it is the church of catatonic withdrawal. After three days in bed Miss Lonelyhearts attains a state of perfect calm, and the stone in his gut expands until he becomes "an ancient rock, smooth with experience." The Shrikes come to take him to a party at their apartment, and against this rock the waves of Shrike dash in vain. When Mary wriggles on Miss Lonelyhearts' lap in the cab, "the rock remained perfect." At the party he withstands Shrike's newest mockery, the Miss Lonelyhearts Game, with indifference: "What goes on in the sea is of no interest to the rock." Miss Lonelyhearts leaves the party with Betty: "She too should see the rock he had become." He shamelessly promises her marriage and domesticity: "The rock was a solidification of his feeling, his conscience, his sense of reality, his self-knowledge." He then goes back to his sickbed content: "The rock had been thoroughly tested and had been found perfect."

The next day Miss Lonelyhearts is burning with fever, and "the rock became a furnace." The room fills with grace, the illusory grace of madness, and as Doyle comes up the stairs with a pistol Miss Lonelyhearts rushes downstairs to embrace him and heal his crippled leg, a miracle that will embody his succoring all suffering mankind with love. Unable to escape Miss Lonelyhearts' mad embrace, terrified by Betty coming up the stairs, Doyle tries to toss away the gun, and Miss Lonelyhearts

is accidentally shot. He falls dragging Doyle down the stairs in his arms.

It is of course a homosexual tableau—the men locked in embrace while the woman stands helplessly by—and behind his other miseries Miss Lonelyhearts has a powerful latent homosexuality. It is this that is ultimately the joke of his name and the book's title. It explains his acceptance of teasing dates with Mary and his coldness with Mary; he thinks of her excitement and notes: "No similar change ever took place in his own body, however. Like a dead man, only friction could make him warm or violence make him mobile." It explains his discontent with Betty. Most of all it explains his joy at being seduced by Fay—"He had always been the pursuer, but now found a strange pleasure in having the roles reversed" —and how quickly the pleasure turns to digust.

The communion Miss Lonelyhearts achieves with Doyle in Delehanty's consists in their sitting silently holding hands, Miss Lonelyhearts pressing "with all the love he could manage" to overcome the revulsion he feels at Doyle's touch. Back at the Doyles, after Doyle has ripped open Miss Lonelyhearts' fly and been kicked by his wife, they hold hands again, and when Fay comes back in the room she says "What a sweet pair of fairies you guys are." It is West's ultimate irony that the symbolic embrace they manage at the end is one penetrating the body of the other with a bullet.

We could, if we so chose, write Miss Lonelyhearts' case history before the novel begins. Terrified of his stern religious father, identifying with his soft loving mother, the boy renounces his phallicism out of castration anxiety —a classic Oedipus complex. In these terms the Shrikes are Miss Lonelyhearts' Oedipal parents, abstracted as the father's loud voice and the mother's tantalizing breast. The scene at the end of Miss Lonelyhearts' date with

Mary Shrike is horrifying and superb. Standing outside her apartment door, suddenly overcome with passion, he strips her naked under her fur coat while she keeps talking mindlessly of her mother's death, mumbling and repeating herself, so that Shrike will not hear their sudden silence and come out. Finally Mary agrees to let Miss Lonelyhearts in if Shrike is not home, goes inside, and soon Shrike peers out the door, wearing only the top of his pajamas. It is the child's Oedipal vision perfectly dramatized: he can clutch at his mother's body but loses her each time to his more potent rival.

It should be noted that if this is the pattern of Miss Lonelyhearts' Oedipus complex, it is not that of West, nor are the Shrikes the pattern of West's parents. How conscious was West of all or any of this? I would guess, from the book's title, that he was entirely conscious of at least Miss Lonelyhearts' latent homosexuality. As for the Oedipus complex, all one can do is note West's remarks in "Some Notes on Miss Lonelyhearts": "Psychology has nothing to do with reality nor should it be used as motivation. The novelist is no longer a psychologist. Psychology can become much more important. The great body of case histories can be used in the way the ancient writers use their myths. Freud is your Bullfinch; you can not learn from him."

The techniques West uses to express his themes are perfectly suited to them. The most important is a pervasive desperate and savage tone, not only in the imagery of violence and suffering, but everywhere. It is the tone of a world where unreason is triumphant. Telling Miss Lonelyhearts that he is awaiting a girl "of great intelligence," Shrike "illustrated the word *intelligence* by carving two enormous breasts in the air with his hands." When Miss Lonelyhearts is in the country with Betty, a gas station attendant tells him amiably that "it wasn't the hunters who drove out the deer, but the yids." When Miss Lonelyhearts accidentally collides with a man in Delehanty's and turns to apologize, he is punched in the mouth.

The flowering cactus that blooms in this wasteland is Shrike's rhetoric. The book begins with a mock prayer he has composed for Miss Lonelyhearts, and every time Shrike appears he makes a masterly speech: on religion, on escapes, on the gospel of Miss Lonelyhearts according to Shrike. He composes a mock letter to God, in which Miss Lonelyhearts confesses shyly: "I read your column and like it very much." He is a cruel and relentless punster and wit. In his sadistic game at the party, Shrike reads aloud letters to Miss Lonelyhearts. He reads one from a pathetic old woman who sells pencils for a living, and concludes: "She has rheum in her eyes. Have you room in your heart for her?" He reads another, from the paralyzed boy who wants to play the violin, and concludes: "How pathetic! However, one can learn much from this parable. Label the boy Labor, the violin Capital, and so on . . . ." Shrike's masterpiece, the brilliant evocation of the ultimate inadequacy of such escapes as the soil, the South Seas, Hedonism, and art, is a classic of modern rhetoric, as is his shorter speech on religion. Here are a few sentences from the latter: "Under the skin of man is a wondrous jungle where veins like lush tropical growths hang along overripe organs and weed-like entrails writhe in squirming tangles of red and yellow. In this jungle, flitting from rock-gray lungs to golden intestines, from liver to lights and back to liver again, lives a bird called the soul. The Catholic hunts this bird with bread and wine, the Hebrew with a golden ruler, the Protestant on leaden feet with leaden words, the Buddhist with gesture, the Negro with blood."

The other cactus that flowers in the wasteland is sadistic violence. The book's most harrowing chapter, "Miss Lonelyhearts and the Lamb," is a dream or recollection of a college escapade, in which Miss Lonelyhearts and two other boys, after drinking all night, buy a lamb to barbecue in the woods. Miss Lonelyhearts persuades his companions to sacrifice it to God before barbecuing it. They lay the lamb on a flower-covered altar and Miss Lonelyhearts tries to cut its throat, but succeeds only in maiming it and breaking the knife. The lamb escapes and crawls off into the underbrush, and the boys flee. Later Miss Lonelyhearts goes back and crushes the lamb's head with a stone. This nightmarish scene, with its unholy suggestions of the sacrifices of Isaac and Christ, embodies the book's bitter paradox: that sadism is the perversion of love.

Visiting Betty early in the novel, aware "that only violence could make him supple," Miss Lonelyhearts reaches inside her robe and tugs at her nipple unpleasantly. "Let me pluck this rose," he says, "I want to wear it in my buttonhole." In "Miss Lonelyhearts and the clean old man," he and a drunken friend find an old gentleman in a washroom, drag him to a speakeasy, and torment him with questions about his "homosexualistic tendencies." As they get nastier and nastier, Miss Lonelyhearts feels "as he had felt years before, when he had accidentally stepped on a small frog. Its spilled guts had filled him with pity, but when its suffering had become real to his senses, his pity had turned to rage and he had beaten it frantically until it was dead." He ends by twisting the old man's arm until the old man screams and someone hits Miss Lonelyhearts with a chair.

The book's only interval of decency, beauty, and peace is the pastoral idyll of the few days Miss Lonelyhearts spends with Betty in the country. They drive in a borrowed car to the deserted farmhouse in Connecticut where she was born. It is spring, and Miss Lonelyhearts "had to admit, even to himself, that the pale new leaves, shaped and colored like candle flames, were beautiful and that the air smelt clean and alive." They work at cleaning up the place, Betty cooks simple meals, and they go down to the pond to watch the deer. After they eat an apple that has ominous Biblical overtones, Betty reveals that she is a virgin and they go fraternally to bed. The next day they go for a naked swim; then, with "no wind to disturb the pull of the earth," Betty is ceremonially deflowered on the new grass. The reader is repeatedly warned that natural innocence cannot save Miss Lonelyhearts: the noise of birds and crickets is "a horrible racket" in his ears; in the woods, "in the deep shade there was nothing but death—rotten leaves, gray and white fungi, and over everything a funereal hush." When they get back to New York, "Miss Lonelyhearts knew that Betty had failed to cure him and that he had been right when he had said that he could never forget the letters." Later, when Miss Lonelyhearts is a rock and leaves Shrike's party with Betty, he tries to create a miniature idyll of innocence by taking her out for a strawberry soda, but it fails. Pregnant by him and intending to have an abortion, Betty remains nevertheless in Edenic innocence; Miss Lonelyhearts is irretrievably fallen, and there is no savior who can redeem.

The book's pace is frantic and its imagery is garish, ugly, and compelling. The letters to Miss Lonelyhearts are "stamped from the dough of suffering with a heart-shaped cookie knife." The sky looks "as if it had been rubbed with a soiled eraser." A bloodshot eye in the peephole of Delehanty's glows "like a ruby in an antique iron ring." Finishing his sermon to the "intelligent" girl, Shrike "buried his triangular face like the blade of a hatchet in her neck." Miss Lonelyhearts' tongue is "a fat thumb," his heart "a congealed lump of icy fat," and his only feeling "icy fatness." Goldsmith, a colleague at the paper, has cheeks "like twin rolls of smooth pink toilet paper." Only the imagery of the Connecticut interlude temporarily thaws the iciness and erases the unpleasant associations with fatness and thumb. As Miss Lonelyhearts watches Betty naked, "She looked a little fat, but when she lifted something to the line, all the fat disappeared. Her raised arms pulled her breasts up until they were like pink-tipped thumbs."

The unique greatness of *Miss Lonelyhearts* seems to have come into the world with hardly a predecessor, but it has itself influenced a great many American novelists since. *Miss Lonelyhearts* seems to me one of the three finest American novels of our century. The other two are F. Scott Fitzgerald's *The Great Gatsby* and Ernest Hemingway's *The Sun Also Rises.* It shares with them a lost and victimized hero, a bitter sense of our civilization's falsity, a pervasive melancholy atmosphere of failure and defeat. If the tone of *Miss Lonelyhearts* is more strident, its images more garish, its pace more rapid and hysterical, it is as fitting an epitome of the thirties as they are of the twenties. If nothing in the forties and fifties has similarly gone beyond *Miss Lonelyhearts* in violence and shock, it may be because it stands at the end of the line.

A Cool Million, subtitled "The Dismantling of Lemuel Pitkin," is a comic, even a parody, novel, to some extent a reversion to the world of *Balso Snell.* It tells the story of Lemuel Pitkin, a poor but honest Vermont boy, as he attempts to make his way in the world. As he confronts each experience with the old-fashioned virtues of honesty, sobriety, good sportsmanship, thrift, bravery, chivalry, and kindness, he is robbed, beaten up, mutilated, cheated, and victimized. In an interwoven subplot, Elizabeth Prail, a neighbor who similarly represents decent American girlhood, is sexually mistreated: raped, beaten by a sadist, kidnapped by white slavers and sold into prostitution, turned out to walk the streets, and so forth. Meanwhile their town banker, "Shagpoke" Whipple, a former President of the United States, creates an American fascist movement and takes over the country.

The total effect is that of a prolonged, perhaps overprolonged, jape. The stages of the action are the stages of Lem's dismantling: thrown into jail in a frame-up, he loses all his teeth because the warden believes teeth to be the source of moral infection; rescuing a banker and his daughter from a runaway horse, Lem loses an eye; kidnapped by agents of the Communist International, he is involved in an automobile collision and loses a thumb; trying to save Betty from rape, he is caught in a bear trap that the villain has planted, which costs him a leg, and while unconscious in the trap he is scalped by a Harvard-educated Indian. He is eventually hired as stooge for a vaudeville act and demolished during each performance; when he is hit with a mallet, "His toupee flew off, his eye and teeth popped out, and his wooden leg was knocked into the audience." Evenutally Lem is shot down onstage while making a speech for American fascism. As a result of his martyrdom Whipple's Leather Shirts triumph and Pitkin's Birthday becomes a national holiday, on which the youth of America parade singing "The Lemuel Pitkin Song."

What form the book has comes from these ritual stages of dismemberment, but in a truer sense *A Cool Million* is formless, an inorganic stringing together of comic set-pieces, with the preposterous incidents serving merely to raise the various topics West chooses to satirize. Thus Betty's residence in Wu Fong's brothel sets off pages of comic description, first of the brothel as a House of All Nations, then, when Wu Fong is converted by the "Buy American" campaign of the Hearst newspapers, into an all-American establishment. West joyously describes the regional costumes and decor of each girl at considerable length, concluding with the cuisine: "When a client visited Lena Haubengrauber, it was possible for him to eat roast groundhog and drink Sam Thompson rye. While with Alice Sweethorne, he was served sow belly with grits and bourbon. In Mary Judkins' rooms he received, if he so desired, fried squirrel and corn liquor. In the suite occupied by Patricia Van Riis, lobster and champagne wine were the rule. The patrons of Powder River Rose usually ordered mountain oysters and washed them down with forty-rod. And so on down the list: while with Dolores O'Riely, tortillas and prune brandy from the Imperial Valley; while with Princess Roan Fawn, baked dog and firewater; while with Betty Prail, fish chowder and Jamaica rum. Finally, those who sought the favors of the 'Modern Girl,' Miss Cobina Wiggs, were regaled with tomato and lettuce sandwiches and gin."

The introduction of a Pike County "ring-tail squealer" and "rip-tail roarer" gives West an opportunity to improvise tall talk and anecdotes concluding: "His bones are bleachin' in the canyon where he fell." The Indian chief who scalps Lem is a Spenglerian philosopher and critic of our gadget civilization, and his speech to the tribe to rouse them for the warpath is a long comic diatribe, culminating in: "But now all the secret places of the earth are full. Now even the Grand Canyon will no longer hold razor blades." Later Lem and Whipple join up with a traveling show exhibiting a Chamber of American Horrors, and West gives himself a chance to describe some of the horrors of American life. In one exhibit,

all the materials are disguised: "Paper had been made to look like wood, wood like rubber, rubber like steel, steel like cheese, cheese like glass, and, finally, glass like paper." In another, function is disguised: "The visitor saw flower pots that were really victrolas, revolvers that held candy, candy that held collar buttons and so forth." West here is entirely indiscriminate. The accompanying pageant of American history consists of sketches "in which Quakers were shown being branded, Indians brutalized and cheated, Negroes sold, children sweated to death," as though these acts were on the order of disguising paper to look like wood.

It is at once comic and depressing, the fitting work of a man Robert M. Coates has called "the most thoroughly pessimistic person I have ever known." If its indictment of American material civilization does not go very deep, its awareness of the precariousness of American freedom does, and the book is perhaps strongest as a political warning. Writing just after the accession of Hitler, West felt the vulnerability of America to totalitarianism disguised as superpatriotism, and he makes it disturbingly convincing. Whipple's bands of the mindless and disaffected, got up in fringed deerskin shirts, coonskin caps, and squirrel rifles, are the same joke as Lena Haubengrauber's clients washing down roast groundhog with Sam Thompson rye, but here it images our nightmare. Recruiting on street corners, Whipple alternates appeals to destroy the Jewish international bankers and the Bolshevik labor unions with shouts of "Remember the Alamo! Remember the Maine!" and "Back to the principles of Andy Jackson and Abe Lincoln!"

In his final tribute to the martyred Lemuel Pitkin at the end of the book, as his storm troops parade down Fifth Avenue, Whipple makes it clear that the true enemy from which his National Revolutionary party has delivered the country is "sophistication." Lem's life represented the expectations of American innocence, frustrated by "sophisticated aliens," and the revolution has been made by those who share Lem's expectations. As such it is the revolt of the frustrated and tormented lower middle class, a fantasy foreshadowing of the riot at the end of *The Day of the Locust*. To become the Horst Wessel of American fascism, in West's ugliest joke, Lem has stepped out of a Norman Rockwell cover for the *Saturday Evening Post*.

What makes this cautionary tale convincing in *A Cool Million* is West's sense of the pervasiveness of American violence. It is like the savagery of Russian life in Leskov or Gorki. We see Betty Prail at twelve, the night her family's house burns down and her parents are killed in the fire. When the firemen finally arrive, drunk, they do nothing to put out the fire. Instead they loot the house while the chief rapes Betty, leaving her naked and unconscious on the ground. She is then sent to an orphan asylum, and put out at fourteen to be a maid in the household of Deacon Slemp, where in addition to her other duties she is enthusiastically beaten twice a week on the bare behind by the Deacon, who gives her a quarter after each beating.

In this world where firemen are looters and rapists and church elders perverts and hypocrites, policemen appear only to beat up the victims of crimes. When Lem is first seized by the police, on his way to the big city to make his fortune, a patrolman clubs him on the head, one detective kicks him in the stomach, and a second kicks him behind the ear; all three actions unrelated to any of the remarks they make to Lem, but rather, natural reflexes. When Lem faints from the wound he received from stopping the runaway horse, he is found by a policeman, who establishes communication by kicking him in the groin. The brutal image of the police in the book is always the raised truncheon, the doubled fist, the foot drawn back.

The weaknesses of the book are perhaps the inevitable weaknesses of the form, jokes that do not come off and failures of tone. Sometimes the book is almost unbelievably corny and heavy-handed. When he is in this mood, West will even have someone address a Chinese in pidgin and be answered in flawless English.

The uncertainty of tone is mainly in regard to sex. When West is openly vulgar, he is fine, but on occasion he seems to smirk, and then he is less fine. A scene between Lem, captured by Wu Fong's men, dressed in a tight-fitting sailor suit, and set up as a homosexual prostitute in the brothel, and his client, a lisping Indian maharajah, is perhaps the most extreme failure. The first rape of Betty by the drunken fire chief is disturbing and effective, but her thousandth rape is boring and meaningless, as comedy, social comment, or even titillation. Betty is almost invariably unconscious when raped, an oddly necrophiliac touch, and sometimes the details lead us to expect a salacious illustration on the next page.

West's last book, *The Day of the Locust* (1939), is a novel about a young painter named Tod Hackett, working at a Hollywood movie studio as a set and costume designer, and some people he encounters. These are principally Faye Greener, a beautiful young girl whom he loves; her father Harry, an old vaudeville comic; Earle Shoop, Faye's cowboy beau; Miguel, Earle's Mexican friend who breeds fighting cocks; Abe Kusich, a dwarf racetrack tout; and Homer Simpson, an innocent from the Midwest also in love with Faye. In the course of the novel Harry dies, and Faye and her friends go to live with Homer. The action is climaxed by a wild party at Homer's, after which Faye and Miguel end up in bed. This results, the next day, in Homer's demented murder of a boy, which in turn precipitates a riot in the streets, on which the book ends. The title comes from the plague of locusts visited on Pharaoh in the Book of Exodus.

Like the characters in *Miss Lonelyhearts,* the characters in *The Day of the Locust* tend to be symbolic abstractions, but here with some loss of human reality. Tod, who never quite comes to life (mainly, I think, because of West's efforts to keep him from being autobiographical), represents The Painter's Eye. All through the book he is planning a great canvas, "The Burning of Los Angeles," which will sum up the whole violent and demented civilization. It is to show the city burning at high noon, set on fire by a gay holiday crowd, who appear carrying baseball bats and torches: "No longer bored, they sang and danced joyously in the red light of the flames." In the foreground, Tod and his friends flee the mob in various characteristic postures: Faye naked and running rather proudly, throwing her knees high; Homer half-asleep; Tod stopping to throw a stone at the crowd. Meanwhile the flames lick avidly "at a corinthian column that held up the palmleaf roof of a nutburger stand."

Faye is nothing like the Fay of *Miss Lonelyhearts* (as the Betty of *A Cool Million* is nothing like the Betty of *Miss Lonelyhearts*— West was overeconomical of names). Faye is seventeen, "a tall girl with wide, straight shoulders and long, swordlike legs." She has "a moon face, wide at the cheek bones and narrow at chin and brow," her hair is platinum-blonde, her breasts are "placed wide apart and their thrust" is "upward and outward," her buttocks look "like a heart upside down." She dresses like a child of twelve, eats an apple with her little finger curled, and has a brain the size of a walnut.

Like Betty in *Miss Lonelyhearts,* Faye represents Nature, but now Nature's appearance of innocence is seen as deceptive, and Faye is as far as can be from Betty. Tod looks at an inviting photograph of her, lying "with her arms and legs spread, as though welcoming a lover," and thinks: "Her invitation wasn't to pleasure, but to struggle, hard and sharp, closer to murder than to love. If you threw yourself on her, it would be like throwing yourself from the parapet of a skyscraper. You would do it with a scream. You couldn't expect to rise again. Your teeth would be driven into your skull like nails into a pine board and your back would be broken. You wouldn't even have time to sweat or close your eyes." What then is Tod's conclusion? "If she would only let him, he would be glad to throw himself, no matter what the cost." Luckily, she never lets him.

All experience rolls off Faye. She smells to Tod like "buckwheat in flower"; when she leans toward him, drooping slightly, "he had seen young birches droop like that at midday when they are over-heavy with sun." When she announces her intention of becoming a call girl, Tod decides that "her beauty was structural like a tree's, not a quality of her mind or heart. Perhaps even whoring wouldn't damage it for that reason." A spell of whoring does not in fact damage it, and when Tod sees her later: "She looked just born, everything moist and fresh, volatile and perfumed." In her natural acceptance of the world of sexuality, she is, as Homer tells Tod proudly, "a fine, wholesome child."

This vision of Nature emphasizes its infuriating invulnerability, and Tod not only wants to smash himself on it, but in other moods, to smash Faye. He thinks: "If he only had the courage to throw himself on her. Nothing less violent than rape would do. The sensation he felt was like that he got when holding an egg in his hand. Not that she was fragile or even seemed fragile. It wasn't that. It was her completeness, her egglike self-sufficiency, that made him want to crush her." Seeing her again, Tod feels: "Her self-sufficiency made him squirm and the desire to break its smooth surface with a blow, or at least a sudden obscene gesture, became irresistible." When Faye disappears at the end of the book, Tod cannot decide whether she has gone off with Miguel or gone back to being a call girl. "But either way she would come out all right," he thinks. "Nothing could hurt her. She was like a cork. No matter how rough the sea got, she would go dancing over the same waves that sank iron ships and tore away piers of reinforced concrete." Tod then produces an elaborate fantasy of waiting in a parking lot to knock Faye unconscious and rape her, and he steps from that into the riot of the book's last scene.

The men around Faye are in their different fashions as mindless as she. Her father, Harry Greener, after forty years in vaudeville and burlesque, no longer has any personality apart from his clowning role. "It was his sole method of defense," West explains. "Most people, he had discovered, won't go out of their way to punish a clown." West invents a superb clown act for him, presented in the form of an old clipping from the Sunday *Times,* but the clowning we see in the book is of a more poignant sort, his comic act peddling home-made silver polish.

Faye's cowboy, Earle Shoop, is an image of virile idiocy. "He had a two-dimensional face that a talented child might have drawn with a ruler and a compass. His chin was perfectly round and his eyes, which were wide apart, were also round. His thin mouth ran at right angles to his straight, perpendicular nose. His reddish tan complexion was the same color from hairline to throat, as though washed in by an expert, and it completed his resemblance to a mechanical drawing." His conversation consists of "Lo, thar," "Nope," and "I was only funning."

The Mexican, Miguel, is an image of pure sensuality: "He was toffee-colored with large Armenian eyes and pouting black lips. His head was a mass of tight, ordered curls." When Faye responds to him, "his skin glowed and the oil in his black curls sparkled." Early in the book we see him rhumba with Faye, until jealousy drives Earle to smash him over the head with a stick. Later he tangos with her, a tango that ends in bed. "Mexicans are very good with women," Tod decides, as the moral of the episode.

Homer is the most completely abstracted character in the book. As Mary Shrike in *Miss Lonelyhearts* is entirely reduced to Breasts, so Homer is entirely reduced to an image of Hands, enormous hands independent of his body. We see him waking in the morning: "Every part was awake but his hands. They still slept. He was not surprised. They demanded special attention, had always demanded it. When he had been a child, he used to stick pins into them and once had even thrust them into a fire. Now he used only cold water." We see him plunge his hands into the washbasin: "They lay quietly on the bottom like a pair of strange aquatic animals. When they were thoroughly chilled and began to crawl about, he lifted them out and hid them in a towel." In the bath: "He kept his enormous hands folded quietly on his belly. Although absolutely still, they seemed curbed rather than resting." When Homer cuts his hand opening a can, "The wounded hand writhed about on the kitchen table until it was carried to the sink by its mate and bathed tenderly in hot water."

When Faye cries at their first meeting, Homer makes "his big hands dance at the end of his arms," and "several times his hands moved forward to comfort her, but he succeeded in curbing them." As he and Faye sit and eat: "His hands began to bother him. He rubbed them against the edge of the table to relieve their itch, but it only stimulated them. When he clasped them behind his back, the strain became intolerable. They were hot and swollen. Using the dishes as an excuse, he held them under the cold water tap of the sink." When Faye leaves, Homer is too bashful to say anything affectionate, but: "His hands were braver. When Faye shook good-bye, they clutched and refused to let go." After she leaves, "His hands kept his thoughts busy. They trembled and jerked, as though troubled by dreams. To hold them still, he clasped them together. Their fingers twined like a tangle of thighs in miniature. He snatched them apart and sat on them."

This garish and remarkable image is built up throughout the book to embody all of Homer's repressed violence; the hands are strangler's hands, rapist's hands. For reasons impossible to imagine or justify, West let it all go to waste. When Homer's violence finally does break out, when Faye's leaving has driven him out of his mind, he kills a boy who has hit him in the face with a stone by stomping him to death, never touching him with his hands.

The most grotesque character in this gallery of grotesques is the dwarf, Abe Kusich. When Tod first meets him, he is wearing perfect dwarf headgear, a high green Tyrolean hat. Unfortunately, "the rest of his outfit didn't go well with the hat. Instead of shoes with long points and a leather apron, he wore a blue, double-breasted suit and a black shirt with a yellow tie. Instead of a crooked thorn stick, he carried a rolled copy of the *Daily Running Horse*." His tiny size is made pathetic in an image of his catching Tod's attention by tugging at the bottom of his jacket, but it is accompanied by an unbelievable pugnacity, verbal and physical. He is a small murderous animal like Homer's hands, and he too finally erupts into violence, responding to a kick in the stomach from Earle by squeezing Earle's testicles until he collapses.

West's earlier title for *The Day of the Locust* was *The Cheated,* and the latent violence of the cheated, the mob that fires Los Angeles in Tod's picture, and riots in the flesh at the end of the book, is its major theme. The cheated are recognizable by sight in Hollywood: "Their clothing was somber and badly cut, bought from mail-order houses." They stand on the streets staring at passers-by, and "when their stare was returned, their eyes filled with hatred." They are the people who come to California to die. Maybe they weren't really desperate enough to set a single city on fire, let alone the whole country." His ultimate discovery is that they are.

Some of the cheated come to Harry's funeral, "hoping for a dramatic incident of some sort, hoping at least for one of the mourners to be led weeping hysterically from the chapel." As he stares at them, "it seemed to Tod that they stared back at him with an expression of vicious, acrid boredom that trembled on the edge of violence." In the book's last scene, the cheated line up by the thousands outside Kahn's Persian Palace Theatre for the première of a new picture. The mob terrifies Tod, and he now recognizes it as a demonic collective entity, unstoppable once aroused except by machine guns. In one of West's rare Marxist slantings, the mob includes no workingmen, but is entirely "made up of the lower middle classes." Tod concludes:

"It was a mistake to think them harmless curiosity seekers. They were savage and bitter, especially the middle-aged and the old, and had been made so by boredom and disappointment.

"All their lives they had slaved at some kind of dull, heavy labor, behind desks and counters, in the fields and at tedious machines of all sorts, saving their pennies and dreaming of the leisure that would be theirs when they had enough. Finally that day came. They would draw a weekly income of ten or fifteen dollars. Where else should they go but California, the land of sunshine and oranges?

"Once there, they discovered that sunshine isn't enough. They get tired of oranges, even of avocado pears and passion fruit. Nothing happens. They don't know what to do with their time. They haven't the mental equipment for leisure, the money nor the physical equipment for pleasure. Did they slave so long just to go on an occasional Iowa picnic? What else is there? They watch the waves come in at Venice. There wasn't any ocean where most of them came from, but after you've seen one wave you've seen them all. The same is true of the airplanes at Glendale. If only a plane would crash once in a while so they could watch the passengers being consumed in a 'holocaust of flame,' as the newspapers put it. But the planes never crash.

"Their boredom becomes more and more terrible. They realize that they've been tricked and burn with resentment. Every day of their lives they read the newspapers and went to the movies. Both fed them on lynchings, murder, sex crimes, explosions, wrecks, love nests, fires, miracles, revolutions, wars. This daily diet made sophisticates of them. The sun is a joke. Oranges can't titillate their jaded palates. Nothing can ever be violent enough to make taut their slack minds and bodies. They have been cheated and betrayed. They have slaved and saved for nothing."

As the marching Leather Shirts were West's fantasy of American fascism, this vicious mob of the cheated lower middle class is his fantasy of American democracy, and it is overpowering and terrifying. The rest of Hollywood, the cheaters, have no more cultural identity than the "cheated," but their plight is comic or pathetic rather than menacing. They in-

habit the Chamber of American Horrors, come to life. They live in "Mexican ranch houses, Samoan huts, Mediterranean villas, Egyptian and Japanese temples, Swiss chalets, Tudor cottages, and every possible combination of these styles." Tod sees "a miniature Rhine castle with tarpaper turrets pierced for archers. Next to it was a little highly colored shack with domes and minarets out of the *Arabian Nights*." The house Homer rents is Irish peasant style: "It had an enormous and very crooked stone chimney, little dormer windows with big hoods and a thatched roof that came down very low on both sides of the front door. This door was of gumwood painted like fumed oak and it hung on enormous hinges. Although made by machine, the hinges had been carefully stamped to appear hand-forged. The same kind of care and skill had been used to make the roof thatching, which was not really straw but heavy fireproof paper colored and ribbed to look like straw." The living room is "Spanish," with red and gold silk armorial banners and a plaster galleon; the bedrooms "New England," with spool beds made of iron grained like wood.

The people are as spurious as the houses and things. An old Hollywood Indian called Chief Kiss-My-Towkus speaks a language of "Vas you dere, Sharley?" Human communication is impossible anywhere in Hollywood. At a party of movie people, the men go off to talk shop and at least one woman assumes that they are telling dirty jokes. Harry and Faye are unable to quarrel in words, but have bitter wordless battles in which he laughs insanely, she sings and dances. Even Faye's sensual gesture of wetting her lips with her tongue as she smiles is meaningless. At first Tod takes it to be an invitation, and dreams: "Her lips must taste of blood and salt." Eventually he discovers the truth: "It was one of her most characteristic gestures and very effective. It seemed to promise all sorts of undefined intimacies, yet it was really as simple and automatic as the word thanks. She used it to reward anyone for anything, no matter how unimportant."

One of the clues West gives to his conception of the nature and destiny of his characters is subtly dropped in a comic scene. Tod and Homer meet a neighbor of Homer's, Maybelle Loomis, and her eight-year-old son, Adore, whom she has trained as a performer. He is dressed as an adult, his eyebrows are plucked, and he sings a salacious song with a mechanical counterfeit of sexuality: "When he came to the final chorus, his buttocks writhed and his voice carried a top-heavy load of sexual pain." In a more personal display, Adore makes horrible faces at Homer, and Mrs. Loomis apologizes: "He thinks he's the Frankenstein monster." Adore *is* the Frankenstein monster, and it is he who is killed by Homer in the book's last scene. But Homer too is the Frankenstein monster, getting out of bed "in sections, like a poorly made automaton," and his hands are progeny monsters. Earle is a lesser monster, a wound-up cowboy toy, and Miguel is a phallic Jack-in-the-box. More than any of them, Faye is a Frankenstein monster, a mechanical woman self-created from bits of vanished film heroines, and her invulnerability is the invulnerability of the already dead. Here is the novel's deepest indictment of the American civilization it symbolizes in Hollywood: if the rubes are cheated by the image of an artificially colored orange, Tod is more deeply cheated by a zombie love; our dreams are fantasies of death.

In his article "Some Notes on Violence," published in *Contact* in 1932, West writes: "What is melodramatic in European writing is not necessarily so in American writing. For a European writer to make violence real, he has to do a great deal of careful psychology and

sociology. He often needs three hundred pages to motivate one little murder. But not so the American writer. His audience has been prepared and is neither surprised nor shocked if he omits artistic excuses for familiar events." The action of *The Day of the Locust* is the releasing of springs of violence that have been wound too tight: Abe's sexual maiming of Earle, Miguel smashing Abe against the wall in retaliation, Homer's brutal murder of Adore, the riot of the cheated. All of these are directly or indirectly inspired by Faye: Earle and Abe and Miguel are competing for Faye, Faye has made Homer insane, Homer's act triggers the mob's insanity.

The party scene consists of a progressive stripping of Faye. She receives her five male guests wearing a pair of green silk lounging pajamas with the top three buttons open. By the time she dances with Miguel all the buttons are open. In the succeeding fight her pajamas are badly torn, and she takes off the trousers, revealing tight black lace drawers. When Homer finds her in bed with Miguel, she is naked. It beautifully represents a metaphoric stripping of Faye in the course of the book. Darwin writes that we observe the face of Nature "bright with gladness," and forget the war to the death behind its innocent appearance. Faye is that bright glad face of Nature, and the stripping gradually reveals the violence and death her beauty conceals. The novel is a great unmasking of a death's head.

West's literary techniques in *The Day of the Locust* develop organically out of his themes. The imagery for Hollywood is wild and surrealist. Tod's friend Claude Estee, a successful screen writer, has a lifesize rubber dead horse, bloated and putrefying, in his swimming pool. The supermarket plays colored spotlights on the food: "The oranges were bathed in red, the lemons in yellow, the fish in pale green, the steaks in rose and the eggs in ivory." As

Tod walks through the movie lot looking for Faye, it becomes the nightmare of history: stepping through the swinging door of a Western saloon, he finds himself in a Paris street; crossing a bridge marked "To Kamp Komfit," he finds himself in a Greek temple; he walks on, "skirting the skeleton of a Zeppelin, a bamboo stockade, an adobe fort, the wooden horse of Troy, a flight of baroque palace stairs that started in a bed of weeds and ended against the branches of an oak, part of the Fourteenth Street elevated station, a Dutch windmill, the bones of a dinosaur, the upper half of the Merrimac, a corner of a Mayan temple." "A dream dump," he concludes. "A Sargasso of the imagination!"

"Having known something of the Hollywood West saw at the time he was seeing it," Allan Seager has written, "I am of the opinion that *Locust* was not fantasy imagined but fantasy seen." Although West probably invented the specific details of the dead horse and the pale green supermarket fish, the fireproof paper thatch and his old favorite the Trojan Horse, there is a sense in which Seager's remark is true: these things are no more garish than what West actually did see in Hollywood. West's technique in the book is often, as Seager suggests, what the artists call *objets trouvés*: he finds in reality the symbol he needs, rather than creating it. When *The Day of the Locust* appeared, I recall thinking how masterfully West had invented the bloody sex-drenched details of the cockfight that leads up to the book's final party. Having since been to cockfights, I now know that every symbolic detail was realistically observed, and the object of my admiration in connection with the scene is no longer West's brilliance of invention but his brilliance of selection.

The humor of the book arises out of its themes, the incongruities of Hollywood and its lack of a cultural identity. Standing on the porch of his plantation mansion, Claude Estee cries, "Here, you black rascal! A mint julep," and a Chinese servant promptly brings a Scotch and soda. What do the Gingos, an Eskimo family brought to Hollywood to make retakes of an Arctic film, eat? Naturally, smoked salmon, white fish, and marinated herring, bought at Jewish delicatessens. The spoken language in the book is a tribute to the delicacy of West's ear. It includes Harry Greener's vaudeville jargon: "Joe was laying up with a whisker in the old Fifth Avenue when the stove exploded. It was the broad's husband who blew the whistle." Along with it there is the very different belligerent idiom of Abe Kusich, shouting "No quiff can give Abe Kusich the fingeroo and get away with it," calling Earle a "pee-hole bandit," or boasting after he has incapacitated him, "I fixed that buckeroo." At the same time there is the witty and epigrammatic conversation of Claude and Tod. Typically, Claude describes Mrs. Jenning's brothel as "a triumph of industrial design," Tod answers that he nevertheless finds it depressing, "like all places for deposit, banks, mail boxes, tombs, vending machines," and Claude then improvises on that set theme. Claude is clearly West's ideal vision of himself: "He was master of an involved comic rhetoric that permitted him to express his moral indignation and still keep his reputation for worldliness and wit."

Some of the images in the book are as powerful as any in *Miss Lonelyhearts*. One is bird blood. We see it first as Earle plucks some quail: "Their feathers fell to the ground, point first, weighed down by the tiny drop of blood that trembled on the tips of their quills." It reappears magnified and horrible as the losing cock's beak breaks: "A large bubble of blood rose where the beak had been." Another powerful image is of Homer crying, at first making a sound "like that of a dog lapping gruel," then in his madness sobbing "like an ax chop-

ping pine, a heavy, hollow, chunking noise."
A third image is the scene of male communion
between Tod and Homer, resembling that between Miss Lonelyhearts and Doyle, and like
it a prelude to violence. Tod and Homer leave
the party to sit out on the curb, and Homer
sits inarticulate, with a "sweet grin on his
face," then takes Tod's hand and makes "trembling signals of affection."

The book's most vivid sustained image, perhaps more powerful than anything in *Miss
Lonelyhearts,* is the riot, which is nightmarishly
sexual as well as threatening. Swept along by
the mob, Tod is thrown against a young girl
whose clothes have been half torn off. With
her thigh between his legs, she clings to him,
and he discovers that she is being attacked
from behind by an old man who has a hand
inside her dress and is biting her neck. When
Tod frees her from the old man, she is seized
by another man, as Tod is swept impotently
by. In another part of the crowd, they are
talking with delight of a pervert who ripped
up a girl with a pair of scissors, as they hug
and pinch one another. Tod finally kicks off
a woman trying to hang on to him, and escapes
with no more than his leg broken, and a vision
of the mob for his painting as "a great united
front of screwballs and screwboxes."

Despite this and other very powerful scenes,
I think that *The Day of the Locust* ultimately
fails as a novel. Shifting from Tod to Homer
and back to Tod, it has no dramatic unity,
and in comparison with *Miss Lonelyhearts,* it
has no moral core. Where Miss Lonelyhearts'
inability to stay in Betty's Eden is heartbreaking, Tod's disillusion with Faye is only sober-
ing and where the end of the former is tragic,
the end of this, Tod in the police car screaming
along with the siren, is merely hysteric.

There is humor but little joy in West's novels, obsessive sexuality but few consummations
(except for that sit-up-and-lie-down doll Betty
Prail). The world West shows us is for the
most part repulsive and terrifying. It is his
genius to have found objective correlatives
for our sickness and fears: our maimed and
ambivalent sexuality, our terror of the idiot
mass, our helpless empathy with suffering, our
love perverted into sadism and masochism.
West did this in convincing present-day forms
of the great myths: the Quest, the Scapegoat,
the Holy Fool, the Dance of Death. His
strength lay in his vulgarity and bad taste, his
pessimism, his nastiness. West could never have
been the affirmative political writer he sometimes imagined, or written the novels that he
told his publisher, just before his death, he
had planned: "simple, warm and kindly
books." We must assume that if West had
lived, he would have continued to write the
sort of novels he had written before, perhaps
even finer ones.

In his short tormented life, West achieved
one authentically great novel, *Miss Lonelyhearts,* and three others less successful as
wholes but full of brilliant and wonderful
things. He was a true pioneer and culture hero,
making it possible for the younger symbolists
and fantasists who came after him, and who
include our best writers, to do with relative
ease what he did in defiance of the temper of
his time, for so little reward, in isolation and
in pain.

Selected Bibliography

The only book so far published on West is James
F. Light, *Nathanael West: An Interpretative
Study,* to which I am indebted for nearly all of
my biographical information. All four of West's
novels are available in the one-volume *The Complete Works of Nathanael West.* (New York:

Farrar, Strauss, and Cudahy, 1957.) A West library thus consists essentially of two books.

WORKS OF
NATHANAEL WEST

The Dream Life of Balso Snell. Paris and New York: Contact Editions, 1931.

Miss Lonelyhearts. New York: Liveright, 1933.

A Cool Million. New York: Covici-Friede, 1934.

The Day of the Locust. New York: Random House, 1939.

"Some Notes on Violence," *Contact,* 1:132–33 (October 1932).

"Some Notes on Miss Lonelyhearts," *Contempo,* 3:1–2 (May 15, 1933).

"Business Deal," *Americana,* 1:14–15 (October 1933).

"Soft Soap for the Barber," *New Republic,* 81:23 (November 1934).

BIBLIOGRAPHY

William White. "Nathanael West: A Bibliography," *Studies in Bibliography,* 11:207–24 (1958). (Papers of the Bibliographical Society of the University of Virginia, Charlottesville, Virginia.)

————. "Nathanael West: Bibliographical Addenda (1957–1964)," *Serif,* 2, 2:5–18 (1965).

CRITICAL AND
BIOGRAPHICAL STUDIES

Aaron, Daniel. "The Truly Monstrous: A Note on Nathanael West," *Partisan Review,* 14:98–106 (February 1947).

————. "Writing for Apocalypse," *Hudson Review,* 3:634–36 (Winter 1951).

Anderson, Carter A. "West's Revisions of *Miss Lonelyhearts,*" *Studies in Bibliography,* 16:232–43 (1963). (Papers of the Bibliographical Society of the University of Virginia, Charlottesville, Virginia.)

Coates, Robert M. "Messiah of the Lonely Hearts," *New Yorker,* 9:59 (April 15, 1933).

————. Introduction to *Miss Lonelyhearts.* New York: New Directions, 1946, 1950.

Cohen, Arthur. "Nathanael West's Holy Fool," *Commonweal,* 64:276–78 (June 15, 1956).

Comerchero, Victor. *Nathanael West, The Ironic Prophet.* Syracuse, N.Y.: Syracuse University Press, 1964.

Gehman, Richard B. Introduction to *The Day of the Locust.* New York: New Directions, 1950. (Reprinted in the Bantam edition.)

Liebling, A. J. "Shed a Tear for Mr. West," *New York World Telegram,* June 24, 1933, p. 14.

Light, James F. *Nathanael West: An Interpretative Study.* Evanston, Ill.: Northwestern University Press, 1961.

McKenney, Ruth. *Love Story.* New York: Harcourt, Brace and Company, 1950. Pp. 175–76, 195–97.

Martin, Jay. *Nathanael West: The Art of His Life.* New York: Farrar, Straus and Giroux, 1970.

Podhoretz, Norman. "A Particular Kind of Joking," *New Yorker,* 33:156–65 (May 18, 1957).

Reid, Randall. *The Fiction of Nathanael West: No Redeemer, No Promised Land.* Syracuse, N.Y.: Syracuse University Press, 1967.

Rosenfeld, Isaac. "Faulkner and Contemporaries," *Partisan Review,* 18:106–14 (January–February 1951).

Ross, Alan. Introduction to *The Complete Works of Nathanael West.* New York: Farrar, Strauss, and Cudahy, 1957.

Sanford, John. "Nathanael West," *Screen Writer,* 2:10–13 (December 1946).

Troy, William. "Four Newer Novelists," *Nation,* 136:672–73 (June 14, 1933).

Williams, William Carlos. "Sordid? Good God!" *Contempo,* 3:5, 8 (July 25, 1933).

————. Review of *The Day of the Locust, Tomorrow,* 10:58–59 (November 1950).

Wilson, Edmund. "Postscript," *The Boys in the Back Room.* San Francisco: Colt Press, 1951.

—STANLEY EDGAR HYMAN

Edith Wharton

1862-1937

IT WAS the fashion among Edith Wharton's
friends, initiated by Henry James, to describe
her in terms of glowing hyperbole, to see her
in the guise of a great golden eagle swooping
down from her high built palace of adventure
to stir up the poor old croaking barnyard
fowls. The woman is almost lost sight of in
their boasts of her activities and possessions:
the lovingly clipped and tended gardens, the
gleaming, perfectly appointed interiors, the
big, fast motor (purchased with the proceeds
of the current book) bearing its multilingual
owner and her faithful band over the roads
of Europe to seek out in every nook and
cranny the beauty that must redeem a modern wasteland. One imagines rooms refur-
bished and gardens relandscaped, all over
Europe and the American East Coast, to conform with the mandates which she laid down
in *The Decoration of Houses* and *Italian Villas
and Their Gardens*. Indeed, there are moments when the lady whom Percy Lubbock
describes in her Paris garden, fresh and trim,
basket on arm, clippers in hand, ready for
the daily task of shearing the heads of yesterday's roses, seems but the symbol of a
larger self dedicated to sprucing up our very
planet.

This is a long way from the picture in the
minds of some American critics of a precious
and snobbish old lady. Yet one can see how
both pictures came into being. Perfection irritates as well as it attracts, in fiction as in life.
As some of Mrs. Wharton's acquaintances
complained that her taste in furnishing was
too good, her French too precisely idiomatic,
so have some of her critics found her heroes
and heroines too exquisite, too apt to exclaim
in rapt unison over little known beauties in
art and literature with which the majority of
her readers may not be equally familiar. The
glittering structure of her cultivation sits on
her novels like a rather showy icing that de-
tracts from the cake beneath. That same majority may be put off by descriptions, however
vivid, of physical objects and backgrounds
that obtrude on the action, by being made
to notice, even in scenes of tensest drama, a
bit of red damask on a wall, a Jacqueminot
rose, a small, dark Italian primitive. As Edmund Wilson points out, Mrs. Wharton was
not only the pioneer but the poet of interior
decoration.

Such cultivation was certainly not typical
of her generation. Ladies of the New York
and Newport of her day, educated by tutors,
may have aquired a sound basis in German,
French, and Italian, but they used these languages, if at all, more for dinner parties than
for books. They did not spend their spare

time, like Edith Newbold Jones, in their fathers' libraries, nor did they publish, at the age of sixteen, privately printed volumes of poetry. In fact, the very rarity of such intellectual achievement in the family of George Frederic Jones has lent comfort to the bearers of an old legend, totally without foundation, that Edith was the daughter of her brothers' English tutor, a clever young man with a mild painter's talent who was killed in the West by Indians. The theory seems to spring from the same kind of thinking that cannot conceive a Shakespeare born in Stratford. But I find it easier to believe that Lucretia Stevens Rhinelander Jones, granddaughter of a Revolutionary patriot and a conventional society matron in a then small-town New York, should have had a brilliant rather than an illegitimate daughter, and the fact that Edith, being so much younger than her brothers, was brought up like an only child seems adequate explanation for the hours that she spent alone in her father's library in West 23rd Street.

In her memoirs she describes as her good fortune that she was forbidden, on moral grounds, to read the ephemeral rubbish of the day and so was not distracted from the classics on the paternal shelves. It was obvious, she tells us, though I am not sure how quickly we agree, that a little girl "to whom the Old Testament, the Apocalypse and the Elizabethan dramatists were open, could not long pine for Whyte Melville or even Rhoda Broughton." In the sternly impressive list of her early reading, with its heavy emphasis on history and poetry, the only American names are Prescott, Parkman, Longfellow, and Irving. The other Melville, Herman, "a cousin of the Van Rensselaers, and qualified by birth to figure in the best society," she never, as a girl, even heard mentioned. Culture and education, to the Joneses and to their group, still meant Europe.

Europe, however, was not only the fountain of arts; it was also good for one's health and pocketbook. The Joneses were badly hit by the inflation that followed the Civil War and took their little daughter for long, economizing visits to Italy and France. It was a life of hotels and watering places, seeing only fellow Americans and their servants, but there were compensations for a sensitive child in driving out to the Campagna and wandering among the tombs of the Appian Way, in collecting fragments of porphyry and lapis lazuli on the slopes of the Palatine, and in such Parisian sights as the Empress Eugénie in her *daumont*, with the little Prince Imperial at her side and a glittering escort of officers. At the same time the young Henry James was knocking about the continent, staying in pensions and picking up material for his first international tales. On both, the European experience was to have a lasting effect. But what was to have a much greater influence on Edith Jones as a writer, and to supply her with the subject material for her most important work, was neither her father's library nor her early impression of Europe, but her own clear, direct, comprehensive little girl's vision of the New York society in which her parents lived.

In 1862, the year of her birth, and for perhaps two decades thereafter, this was a small, sober, proper, tightly knit society, of Dutch and English descent, which lived in uniform streets of chocolate house fronts on income largely derived from municipal real estate. It was wary of the arts, beyond a dip into Longfellow or Bryant, or an evening of *Norma* at the Academy of Music, and disdainful of politics and any business that smacked of retail. The men practiced law in a listless sort of way and sat on charitable boards and had the leisure and taste to appreciate with their wives long meals of good food washed down by the "Jones Claret" or the

"Newbold Madeira." Young Edith, sharply aware of their indifference to beauty in the arts, found their society stifling and stultifying, but as an elderly woman, surrounded by a world that seemed to her to have lost its values, she decided ruefully that the merit of those "amiable persons" had been to uphold standards of education and good manners and of scrupulous probity in business and private affairs.

As a young girl and as a debutante, she was miserably shy, a quality that was to dog her all her life, and that she was later to encase behind the enamel of formality, but by the time of her marriage, at the age of twenty-three, she had become at least outwardly reconciled to the observances of social life. Edward Robbins Wharton was an easygoing, friendly Bostonian, of no intellectual pretensions, who adored his much younger wife and always kept a thousand dollar bill in his purse in case "Pussy" wanted anything. They lived in New York and Newport and went every year to Europe, and no children came to interrupt their social and sightseeing routine. Obviously, it was not an existence to satisfy indefinitely a mind rendered immune to Rhoda Broughton by the beauties of the Apocalypse, and gradually the young wife started to write, here and there a poem, then a sentimental short story with an uplifting conclusion, then a serious book on interior decoration, then travel pieces, at last a historical novel. In her memoirs she describes her writing as the natural sequence of a childhood habit of "making up" on bits of brown wrapping paper, but Edmund Wilson suggests that she took it up because of the tensions of an incompatible marriage and at the advice of Dr. S. Weir Mitchell, an early pioneer in female neuroses and himself a novelist. Fragments of her diary, recently published by Wayne Andrews, in which she notes that she could en-

dure the "moral solitude" of her marriage only by creating a world of her imagination, certainly seem to substantiate Wilson. At any rate, there was the gap of a generation between those brown paper scribblings and the publication of her first volume of fiction at the age of thirty-seven.

The tales in *The Greater Inclination* (1899) and in its successor, *Crucial Instances* (1901), have some of the flavor of James's stories of artists and writers of the same period. They are apt to be set against European backgrounds and to deal with such themes as the temptation to the serious artist of commercial success or the bewildering influence upon him of the art of an older, richer civilization. They are clever and readable, if a trifle thin, and in three of them, "The Pelican," "The Rembrandt," and "The Angel at the Grave," Mrs. Wharton shows herself already in full command of the style that was to make her prose as lucid and polished as any in American fiction. It is a firm, crisp, smooth, direct, easily flowing style, the perfect instrument of a clear, undazzled eye, an analytic mind, and a sense of humor alert to the least pretentiousness. We may later wonder if her style was adapted to all the uses to which she put it, but at this point it perfectly presents to us, in all their pathetic and confused dignity, the brave little lady who lectures with an ignorant boldness to women's groups on every aspect of arts and letters, first for the love of her baby and ultimately for the love of her own voice, the proud and splendid widow who is induced only by direst poverty to part with her false Rembrandt, and the dedicated spinster who devotes a lifetime to maintaining her grandfather's house as a shrine for a public that has forgotten him. The defect in Edith Wharton's poetry, of which she published three volumes, is that this same style, consciously ennobled and stripped of laughter, becomes as dull and over-ornamented as the privately printed verse of any number of aspiring ladies who sought refuge from the distraction of social life. But poetry is subjective, and Mrs. Wharton, like many persons of wide reading and disciplined exterior, was inclined to be mawkish in subjective mood.

Her first novel, *The Valley of Decision*, appeared in 1902, when she was forty, and its scene is laid in Italy, that charnel house of English and American historical fiction. It is Edith Wharton's *Romola*, except that it is a better book than George Eliot's, for the fruits of her research are strewn attractively through the pages and not spooned into the reader like medicine. But although she captures remarkably the spirit and color of the eighteenth century, nothing can save the novel from its pale and lifeless characters. It is like a play with perfect settings in which the actors stand stiffly in the middle of the stage, their eyes fixed on the prompter. Only when Odo as a boy visits his grandfather's castle in the mountains, and later in the grand ducal gallery when he faces the portraits of his interbred ancestors, is there any true linking of characters and sets. The theme, however, is of some interest to the student of Edith Wharton, for it presages the political and social conservatism that was later to enchain her. Odo brings reform to Pianura only to find himself the harbinger and later the prisoner of the Reign of Terror. His creator was always afraid that even a needed cleaning of sewers might cause the collapse of the civilization above them.

The next two years find Mrs. Wharton still experimenting. *Sanctuary* (1903) demonstrates, a bit comically, the combined influence of Paul Bourget and James. In the first part of this absurd but charming little tale Kate Peyton marries a cheat and a liar in order to become the mother of the moral defective whom he might otherwise sire upon a woman less

capable of raising such offspring—surely almost a parody of a Bourget theme—and in the second, twenty-five years later, she contrives to keep this offspring from committing an odious fraud by radiating sympathy to him in silent Jameslan waves. *The Descent of Man* (1904) is another volume of short stories, similar in tone to the earlier ones except for "The Dilettante," which marks an advance in the development of a male character who is to pervade all of Mrs. Wharton's fiction, the cold, cultivated, aristocratic egoist who feeds on the life and enthusiasm of simpler souls. The story has a clever twist at the end when the dilettante's betrothed jilts him on discovering that the lady who has been his intimate friend for years has *not* been his mistress. It is a theme that we shall meet again.

The House of Mirth (1905) marks her coming of age as a novelist. At last, and simultaneously, she had discovered both her medium and her subject matter. The first was the novel of manners and the latter the assault upon the old Knickerbocker society in which she had grown up of the new millionaires, the "invaders" as she called them, who had been so fabulously enriched by the business growth following the Civil War. New money had poured into New York in the 1880's and 1890's and turned the Joneses' quiet old Fifth Avenue into a dizzy parade of derivative façades from Azay-le-Rideau to the Porch of the Maidens. The Van Rensselaers and Rhinelanders might purse their lips at the ostentation of the Vanderbilts, but in a dollar world the biggest bank balance was bound to win out. A Livingston would marry a Mills, as in an earlier day a Schermerhorn had married an Astor. For what, really, did that older world have that was so special? It was all very well for James to describe the Newport of his childhood, surviving into this gilded age, as a little bare white open hand suddenly crammed with gold, but the fingers of that little hand closed firmly enough over the proffered bullion. The sober brown stucco of Upjohn's country villas concealed a materialism as rampant as any flaunted by the marble halls of Richard Morris Hunt. Mrs. Wharton saw clearly enough that the invaders and defenders were bound ultimately to bury their hatchet in a noisy, stamping dance, but she saw also the rich possibilities for satire in the contrasts afforded by the battle line in its last stages and the pathos of the individuals who were fated to be trampled under the feet of those boisterous truce makers.

Lily Bart, the heroine of *The House of Mirth*, stems from both worlds. Her father is related to the Penistons and the Stepneys, but is driven by her mother, a more ordinary creature, to make a fortune which, not being of invader blood, he is bound to lose. Lily, orphaned, is loosed on the social seas with only her beauty and charm for sails and no rudder but a ladylike disdain for shabby compromises and a vague sense that there must be somewhere a better life than the one into which she has drifted. Her rich friends, who use her as a social secretary to write notes and as a blind to shield them from importunate and suspicious husbands, cannot understand the squeamishness which keeps her, at the critical moment, from extracting a proposal from the rich bachelor whom she has not been too squeamish to pursue. Her respectable relatives, on the other hand, of an older society, cannot understand her smoking or gambling or being seen, however briefly, in the company of married men. Lily falls between two schools. She cannot bring herself to marry the vulgar Mr. Rosedale for all his millions, or the obscure Lawrence Selden, for all their affinity. She postpones decisions and hopes for the best and in the meanwhile seeks to distract herself. But we know from the start that she is

doomed. She has only her liveliness, and what is that in a world that puts its store in coin and hypocrisy? The other characters, of both new and old New York, seem strangely and vindictively united in a constant readiness to humiliate her: Grace Stepney to tell tales on her, Mrs. Peniston to disinherit her, Bertha Dorset to abandon her in a foreign port, Gus Trenor to try to seduce her, his wife to say he has. We watch with agonized apprehension as Lily turns and doubles back, as she keeps miraculously rehabilitating herself, each time on a slightly lower level. For no matter how hard she struggles, without money she is unarmed in that arena. And in the end when she finally compromises and is willing to marry Rosedale, it is too late. He will not have her, and she falls to the job at the milliner's and the ultimate overdose of sleeping tablets. But we finish the book with the conviction that in the whole brawling, terrible city Lily is the one and only lady.

The different levels of society in *The House of Mirth* are explored with a precision comparable to that of Proust whom Mrs. Wharton was later so greatly to admire. We follow Lily's gradual descent from "Bellomont" on the Hudson and the other great country houses of a world where the old and new societies had begun to merge, to the little court of the Gormers, who, although rich enough to be ultimately accepted, are still at the stage of having to fill their house with hangers-on, to the bogus intellectual world of Carry Fisher who pretends to like interesting people while she earns her living helping climbers up the social ladder, to the final drop into the gilded hotel of the demimondaine Norma Hatch. Lily learns that money is the common denominator of all these worlds and that the differences between them consist only in the degrees of scent with which its odor is from time to time concealed. Van Wyck Brooks accused Mrs. Wharton of knowing nothing of the American West, and perhaps she did not, but she had a firsthand knowledge of where the profits of the frontier had gone. Lily Bart, weary on foot, watching the carriages and motors of her former friends ply up and down Fifth Avenue, Mrs. Van Osburgh's C-spring barouche, Mrs. Hatch's electric victoria, is seeing the natural successors of the covered wagon.

I do not suppose that Mrs. Wharton intended Lawrence Selden to constitute the last and greatest of Lily's trials, but so he strikes me. He is a well-born, leisurely bachelor lawyer, with means just adequate for a life of elegant solitude, who spends his evenings, when not leafing through the pages of his first editions, dining out in a society that he loves to ridicule. Lily knows that he is a neutral in the battle of life and death in which she is so desperately engaged, and she asks only that he hold her hand briefly in moments of crisis or brush her lips with a light kiss. He does, in the end, decide to marry her, but as she had been too late for Rosedale, so is he too late for her, and he can only kneel by her bed and give to her lifeless lips the last of his airy kisses. Mrs. Wharton's attitude toward Selden's type of man is enigmatic. He may be a villain in "The Dilettante," or he may at least pose as a hero in *The House of Mirth*. She is careful in the latter to point out for his sake, whenever he condemns Lily Bart, that appearances have been against her. Perhaps she conceived him as an abused lover in the Shakespearean sense, as an Othello or a Posthumus. But Othello and Posthumum are quick to believe the worst because of the very violence of their passions. An eye as dry as Selden's should be slower to be deceived. I incline to the theory that Mrs. Wharton really intended us to accept this plaster-cast figure for a hero, but that she had a low

opinion of heroes in general. When Lily suddenly retorts to Selden that he spends a great deal of his time in a society that he professes to despise, it is as if the author had suddenly slipped into the book to express a contempt that the reader is not meant to share.

The enigma of Selden inevitably leads to a consideration of the deepest friendship of Edith Wharton's life. "The year before my marriage," she relates in her memoirs, "I had made friends with a young man named Walter Berry, the son of an old friend of my family's (and indeed a distant cousin)." Despite the note of kinship thus cautiously sounded, there is a legend that he proposed to her and was turned down as a not good enough match. This might, if true, explain in the light of revenge some of his acts of coldness to her in later years. At any rate, he became a friend of the young Whartons, and it was during one of his visits to their house in Newport that she showed him the "lumpy pages" of an early manuscript and had the mortification of hearing his "shout of laughter," a peal that was never quite to cease ringing in her ears. But a minute later he said good-naturedly: "Come, let's see what can be done," and settled down beside her to try to model the lump into a book. In that modeling process she claimed, decades later, that she had been taught whatever she knew about the writing of "clear concise English."

I do not believe it, though I am sure that she did. There seemed no limits to her admiration of Berry. "He found me when my mind and soul were hungry and thirsty, and he fed them till our last hour together." Evidently, he supplied her with the intellectual and spiritual companionship that she had never found with Edward Wharton. The latter, as her writing and fame developed, had shrunk to a kind of cipher in her life. Consuelo Balsan recalls him "as more of an equerry than an equal, walking behind her and carrying whatever paraphernalia she happened to discard." It was only to be expected, under the circumstances, that she should prefer Berry, though recently uncovered evidence makes it seem unlikely that theirs was a love affair.

What sort of man was he? James seems to have liked him and to have enjoyed their faintly catty old bachelors' correspondence in which Mrs. Wharton, because of her raids into the secluded retreats of friends, is described as "the angel of devastation." But to others of her circle Berry was less sympathetic, and to Percy Lubbock he was a dogmatic and snobbish egotist, the evil genius, indeed, of her life. "None of her friends," he put it bluntly, "thought she was the better for the surrender of her fine free spirit to the control of a man, I am ready to believe, of strong intelligence and ability—but also, I certainly know, of a dry and narrow and supercilious temper."

Mrs. Wharton's attitude toward evasion of the marriage vow was always ambiguous. Divorce (though she was to come to it herself) she considered crude and antisocial, and the facile forming of new marital ties unspeakably vulgar. On the other hand, the dishonesties and evasions of concealed adultery struck her as offensive and degrading, while any open disregard of the conventions led to a slow, sordid end in those shabby European watering places with which the minds of her contemporaries seemed always to identify extramarital passion. Perhaps, finally, the latter course seemed best to her. At least the spirit that was capable of facing it seemed the finest spirit. Paulina Trant in "The Long Run" (*Xingu*) has all her creator's sympathy when she offers to give up her husband and home for love, and Halston Merrick, who logically and sensibly tries to reason her out of it, appears as the shallowest of lovers. There must have been womanly moments, for all of Edith Wharton's admiration of Berry, when he struck her as a bit of Halston Merrick, when she saw him with eyes that made even Lubbock's seem charitable by comparison. It is perhaps to such moments that we owe the curious ambivalence in her treatment of heroes.

Despite the great critical and popular success of *The House of Mirth*, Mrs. Wharton did not return to her New York subject matter for another eight years. Perhaps she was afraid of exhausting it too quickly. *Madame de Treymes* and *The Fruit of the Tree*, so radically different from each other, both appeared in 1907. The first is a true Jamesian tale of innocents abroad, as subtle and fine as any of James's own but with more liveliness and humor. It portrays the duel between John Durham, an American hero in the tradition of James's Christopher Newman, and a wily, charming Parisian aristocrat, Madame de Treymes, over the latter's sister-in-law, poor little Fanny Frisbee of brownstone New York, who has found only misery in her French marriage. Principles and ideals, for the last time in Edith Wharton's fiction, are found on the side of the Stars and Stripes, and Madame de Treymes ruefully recognizes the moral superiority of the Yankees in her final sob: "Ah you poor, good man!" In later years, unhappily, Mrs. Wharton's Americans abroad were to become the corruptors and not the corrupted.

The Fruit of the Tree is an experiment in a totally new field, the novel of reform. Mrs. Wharton began her task of research conscientiously enough with a tour of a factory near her country home in Lenox, Massachusetts, but she soon lost interest in her theme and succumbed to an unworthy compromise. In order to be able to draw her factory manager and trained nurse from models in her own world, she endowed them both with old and distinguished families which had only recently lost their money, thus giving to these parts of her book a curious air of social masquerade. Even so, the reader's interest is caught when Amherst, the priggish manager, marries the widow owner of the factory, having misconstrueed her passion for himself as a zeal for the cause of the workers, and settles down in blithe ignorance to what he imagines will be their shared task of reform. But at this point Mrs. Wharton changes her theme altogether. Bessie Amherst, bored with the workers and interpreting, perhaps correctly (again the enigma of the Wharton hero), her husband's interest in reform as indifference to herself, goes galloping over icy roads until she falls from her horse and receives an incurable back injury, which condemns her to a long period of hideous and futile agony. The novel now turns abruptly into a problem novel about euthanasia in the manner of Bourget, for Bessie's sufferings are abbreviated by the needle of the trained nurse with the social background. Mrs. Wharton handles both themes competently, but the book simply collapses between them. The failure of *The Fruit of the Tree* is just the opposite of that of *The Valley of Decision*; the settings, and not the characters, fade away. It is, however, a less disastrous fault. Bessie Amherst, indolent, selfish, but quite ready to be led by any man who will take the trouble to understand her, is interesting enough to make the novel readable even today, when industrial reform of the type in question has long since been effected and when euthanasia, if still illegal, has ceased to be morally shocking.

The Hermit and the Wild Woman (1908) is another volume of slender, contrived Jamesian stories of artists and dilettantes, but *Tales of Men and Ghosts* (1910) contains some superb chillers. A tricky ending to a serious short story will sometimes detract from the total effect and make it seem superficial or

sentimental, or both, but in a ghost story it has a valid, even an indispensable, function. The egotism of Mrs. Wharton's constantly recurring bachelors is brought out more effectively in "The Eyes" than in any of her other short stories or novels. Culwin tells a listening group about a fire, which includes his young protégé, of the eyes, the old eyes with sunk orbits and thick, red-lined lids and look of vicious security, that haunt him at night whenever he has performed what he deems an unselfish act, which the reader, of course, knows to have been just the opposite. As he finishes his tale he marks the horror on the features of the protégé, with whose youth and bloom he has tried to water his own dry nature, and turning to look in the mirror behind him, he sees at last whose eyes they are.

Mrs. Wharton's other ghost stories may be considered out of chronology because their style and effectiveness does not vary, except to improve, with the years. This kind of tale requires a skill that never left her, the skill of telling a story reduced to its bare bones, without the aid of social problems or manners or mores or even of human nature, except in its most elemental sense. She always believed that the storytelling faculty was basic and indispensable in any writer. She was like a representational artist who looks askance at an abstract painting and wants to know if the man who executed it can really draw. At times she would try her hand, almost as one might try a puzzle, at a story that was nothing but technique, like "Roman Fever," where the interest is concentrated in the last line that gives the whole meaning to what has gone before. Her technique in ghost stories is to keep the supernatural to the minimum that will still irradiate the tale with horror. Character can be important as in "The Eyes," but it is by no means essential. As long as there is one plain human being, as in "All Souls," to register terror for the reader, there is an adequate cast.

Time, as we shall see, brought to Mrs. Wharton an attitude of disapproval toward the changing social scene which was to sour her later work, but the ghost stories, by their very nature, escaped this, and her grasp of the secret of chilling her reader continued to improve to the end. "The Lady's Maid's Bell," an early venture, suffers from a slight overdose of the eerie. There is not only the bell; there is the constantly reappearing ghost of Emma Saxon. "Pomegranate Seed," a later tale, corrects this. A second wife's happiness is destroyed and her life turned to nightmare by the appearance, at irregular intervals, on the hall table, addressed to her husband in a faint, female handwriting, of envelopes which unnerve him but which he refuses to discuss. The conviction that these missives come from the dead wife begins to dawn on the reader at the same time that it dawns on her successor, and in the mood of horror that we share with her we completely accept her husband's final disappearance. The ghost of the first wife never comes on the scene to derogate from her letters as Emma Saxon does from the bell.

In the compilation *Ghosts* (1937), published in the last year of Mrs. Wharton's life, two of the best of the eleven stories, "Miss Mary Pask" and "Bewitched," deal, not with the supernatural, but with the appearance of it. Here Mrs. Wharton sets herself the difficult task of scaring the reader in a ghost story without the aid of a ghost. The atmosphere has to be made correspondingly more ominous; Mary Pask must be whiter and more wraithlike on that foggy night in Brittany than if she were a true spirit, and the New Englanders of "Bewitched" must be gaunter and grimmer than the characters of *Ethan Frome* to make sufficiently terrible the ending that proves Venny Brand to have been masquerad-

ing. The last story of the collection, and its masterpiece, "A Bottle of Perrier," is not really a ghost story at all, but a tale of hatred and murder in the African desert where an eccentric Englishman lives in a lonely castle with his butler and a host of Arab servants. Mrs. Wharton's style is at its richest as she sets her African scene: "The afternoon hung over the place like a great velarium of cloth-of-gold stretched across the battlements and drooping down in ever slacker folds upon the heavy-headed palms. When at length the gold turned to violet, and the west to a bow of crystal clasping the dark sands, Medford shook off his sleep and wandered out." And the final sentence which reveals for the reader where the body of Almodham has all the time been rotting is like one of those screaming chords at the end of Strauss's *Salome*: "The moon, swinging high above the battlements, sent a searching spear of light down into the guilty darkness of the well."

In 1911 Mrs. Wharton published the short novel with which her name has ever since been linked and which sometimes threatens to preempt the whole of her niche in the history of American literature. She says in her memoirs that in writing *Ethan Frome*, she felt for the first time the artisan's full control of his implements. In later years its continuing success was to plague her, as the success of "Daisy Miller" plagued James, for she could never agree with the critics who claimed that it was her best work. Yet it is surely among her best. When I think if it, I visualize a small painting, perfectly executed to the last detail, of three silent figures in a small dark cottage kitchen, with snow glimpsed through a window, the terrible Zeena in the center, white and pasty and gaunt, and, scattered on the table, the pieces of a broken dish. But I could never put the story as fiction in the same class with *The House of Mirth* on the very ground that to me it *is* a picture and, as such, one dimensional. Lily Bart and the society in which she lives are turned around and around and studied from different angles. It is not fair, of course, to compare a long novel with a novelette, but the tremendous reputation of *Ethan Frome* evokes such a defense.

There has been some disposition in critics to view with distrust Mrs. Wharton's excursions into life among the needy, as evidenced by *Ethan Frome*, "The Bunner Sisters," and *Summer*, to see her as the great lady from "The Mount" in Lenox, peering at Ethan and his womenfolk from the back seat of her big motor. I doubt if these comments would have been made had the stories been published under another name, for the keenness of Mrs. Wharton's observation was not affected by the social status of her models. Only, in later years, when she attempted to describe persons and places that she had never seen did she fail in her job. I am totally persuaded of the reality of that notions shop kept by Ann Eliza Bunner and her sister and by the dank public library where Charity Royall dreams away her listless days. The reason why *Summer* and "The Bunner Sisters" are less convincing than *Ethan Frome* does not lie in any failure of observation or imagination on the part of the author, but in the fact that one feels her presence, which in *Ethan Frome* the device of a narrator has successfully eliminated. When Charity Royall sees her mother's kinsfolk on the mountain "herded together in a sort of passive promiscuity in which their common misery was the strongest link," and when Evalina Bunner, contrasted to the Hochmullers, is described as "a faintly washed sketch beside a brilliant chromo," we see clearly enough what is meant, but we are standing on that mountain and at Evalina's wedding with Mrs. Wharton herself, and we feel with a touch of constraint the incongruity of our presence.

The Reef (1912) was greeted with a burst of congratulation from all the Jamesian circle. "Racinian" was the adjective used by the master, and indeed a Racinian unity of mood is achieved by centering the action in an old, high-roofed chateau of brick and yellowish stone, bathed in the pale light of October afternoons. The rooms in which the characters tensely talk are like a series of paintings by Walter Gay. It is a quiet, controlled, beautiful novel, but its theme has always struck me as faintly ridiculous. Mrs. Leath, a widow, is at last about to marry George Darrow, her old bachelor admirer, and her stepson, Owen, is entertaining a similar plan with respect to the beautiful young family governess, Sophy Viner, when the discovery that Darrow and Sophy have once been lovers reduces all the characters to a state of quiet depression. Even conceding that in 1912 such an affair might have disqualified Sophy as a bride for Owen, would Mrs. Leath, a woman who had lived all her adult years in France, consider that her own happiness had to be sacrificed as well? Of course, Mrs. Wharton's answer would be that Mrs. Leath is a woman of the finest sensitivities and that the affair occurred at a time when she had every reason to believe Darrow attentive to herself, but I still cannot get away from the suspicion that at least part of the horror of the situation lies in the fact that Sophy is a governess. The final chapter, so jarringly out of tune with the rest of the book, tends to confirm this suspicion. When Mrs. Leath goes to Sophy's sister's hotel to tell Sophy that she has given Darrow up, she is received by the sister in a dim, untidy, scented room, complete with lover and masseur. Coarse and bloated as the sister is, Mrs. Leath can nonetheless see in her what the beautiful Sophy will one day become, and when she discovers that the latter has departed for India in the company of a disreputable woman, she takes her hasty leave, presumably to return to Darrow and happiness.

The only moral that I can make out of this is that Sophy Viner, a paid dependent who is an appendage rather than a true part of the social pattern, may be expected, under the first bad influence, to drop to a life of semi-prostitution. If the problem to which the book is addressed be justified as a problem common to the era, there remains to be justified the point of view of the author, which for once seems so narrowly prudish and class-conscious as her bitterest critics have ever accused it of being.

The Custom of the Country, happily, in the following year, 1913, is a return to the rich, sure ground of New York and the novel of manners, only this time the central character in the conflict of social groups is not a victim but an invader. Undine Spragg is a creature of alloy, as sentimental in her judgments of herself as she is ruthless in her judgments of others. A father is only a checkbook, a husband a means of social advancement, a baby a threat to the figure. No amount of association with cultivated persons or of exposure to the art of Europe can ripple the surface of her infinite vulgarity. She never knows the toll in human misery of her advance to the social heights, for it never occurs to her to look back. The story of how she hews her way through the old New York ranks of the Marvells and Dagonets, already weakened by prior compromises with the invaders, and even into the society of the Faubourg Saint-Germain from which James's "American" was barred, is vivid and fascinating. Undine gets into as many dangerous corners as Lily Bart, but by miscalculation rather than by inertia, and the same shrewd, restless cerebration that gets her in can be counted on to get her out. In *The House of Mirth* our compassion goes out to Lily; in *The Custom of the Country* it goes

out to the society which Undine is trying to crash.

The flaw in the novel that keeps it from ranking equally with its predecessor is that Mrs. Wharton hates Undine too much. She sees in her incarnate the devil of the modern world, that world where all fineness of soul and graciousness of living have been submerged in a great tide of insipid and meretricious uniformity whose origin seems to lie vaguely in the American Middle West. New York has been lost to the flood, and even Europe is no longer safe. The family of the Marquis de Chelles are not sufficiently humiliated by his marriage to Undine; they must also see their tapestries stripped from their walls by her next husband, Elmer Moffatt. What would the wiles of even Madame de Treymes have accomplished against Elmer? James complained to Mrs. Wharton that she had not sufficiently developed the theme of the relationship between the Chelleses and Undine. Surely, he was wrong. Surely, as the book indicates, no such relationship could have even existed. What Mrs. Wharton fails to prove is that Chelles would have married Undine at all. For she is really too awful to be quite so successful with quite so many men. Her vulgarity destroys the allure that such a woman would have been bound to have and that her creator was not to understand until her last, unfinished novel.

Lily Bart takes only one trip to Europe in the course of her saga, but Undine spends half of hers there. It was abroad, indeed, that Mrs. Wharton must have observed her prototypes, for in these years she had been spending less and less time in her own country. She had always been attracted by the order and grace of French living and by the assured social position of intellectuals in France, so different from what she had experienced in New York. She had a deep respect for traditions and ceremonials that gave her some assurance that the existing form of society had a basis in the past, and, by a like token, a hope for preservation in the future. The New York of her younger years had had traditions, but she had found them merely restricting. The dead hand of a Manhattan past had seemed to her simply dead. Her writings, for example, had never been recognized by her friends and relations as anything but a vaguely embarrassing habit that was better not mentioned. Her husband, it was true, took a rather childish pride in her growing fame, but in all intellectual matters he was as bad as the others. "Does that sort of thing really amuse you?" he asked when she showed him a striking passage in R. H. Lock's study of heredity and variation. "That is the answer to everything worth-while!" she moaned in her journal. "Oh, Gods of derision! And you've given me twenty years of it! *Je n'en peux plus.*"

This cry of the heart is dated 1908 when she was forty-six. Release was on its way. In 1910 the Whartons sold the house in Lenox and moved permanently to France. In the same year Edward Wharton had a nervous collapse and was placed in a sanatorium. In 1913 they were divorced. She had found at last a world where everything blended: beautiful surroundings, intellectual companionship, a society that combined a respect for the past with a vital concern for the present. London was within easy reach, and she could be in constant touch with writers whose conversation was as polished and civilized as their prose: James Bourget, Lubbock, Howard Sturgis. It is easy to comprehend the charm of such a life, but what did it have to do with the contemporary American scene that it was her profession to study? James in his later years built his characters into an exotic world of his own imagination. It was not necessary for the creator of Maggie Verver or Milly Theale to have an up-to-date

knowledge of life on the other side of the Atlantic. It was enough that he had been born American. But Edith Wharton was concerned with representing the life and manners of New York, and for this she needed more than the chatter of tourist friends.

In a surprisingly insipid little book, *French Ways and Their Meaning* (1919), made up of articles originally written to acquaint Americans coming to France during the war with the character of their allies and hosts, Mrs. Wharton descants on the Gallic qualities of taste, reverence, continuity, and intellectual honesty. The picture that emerges, quite unintentionally, is of a nation chained to ancient forms and observances which could hardly have survived four years of trench warfare with the first military power of Europe. Mrs. Wharton was paying France what she deemed the greatest compliment she knew in describing as national virtues the qualities that most attracted her in her own polite, intellectual circle. There is some of the self-justification of the expatriate in the attitude that her adopted country had to possess to the fullest degree, and her native land to the least, the civilized atmosphere which she found so indispensable in daily life. As a result, there was always a presumption in favor of France in her thinking, just as there was one against America, an injustice that is everywhere reflected in this misleading little book. When she speaks of French culture, Richelieu and the Academy are invoked, but when it is a question of American, she cites only the middle western college girl who "learnt art" in a year.

When crisis came, at any rate, she had proved a true, if not a legal, citizen of France. She scorned the expatriates who scuttled home at the first rumble of danger in the summer of 1914 and whom she later described in *The Marne*. She was passionately involved from the beginning with the land of her adoption and threw herself into work for the refugees and the wounded with a fervor and efficiency which resulted in her being decorated by Poincaré and named an officer of the Legion of Honor. She regarded the war from a simple but consistent point of view: France, virtually singlehanded, was fighting the battle of civilization against the powers of darkness. It was the spirit that made men fight and die, but it has never, unfortunately, been the spirit of fiction. Reading *The Marne* (1918) and *A Son at the Front* (1923) today gives one the feeling of taking an old enlistment poster out of an attic trunk. It may be a significant comment on the very nature of Armageddon that the only literature that survives it is literature of disillusionment and despair. Mrs. Wharton knew that the war was terrible; she had visited hospitals and even the front itself. But the exhilaration of the noncombatant, no matter how dedicated and useful her services, has a shrill sound to postwar ears.

The corrosive effect of war on a civilization already vulgarized by American money induced in Mrs. Wharton a mood of nostalgia for the old quiet New York world of her childhood that she had once found so confining. Much later she was to write: "When I was young it used to seem to me that the group in which I grew up was like an empty vessel into which no new wine would ever again be poured. Now I see that one of its uses lay in preserving a few drops of an old vintage too rare to be savoured by a youthful palate."

There was no rose color, however, in the glasses through which she viewed the past. She did not flinch at sight of the old prejudices; she simply reinterpreted them. Mrs. Lidcote, in "Autre Temps" (*Xingu*, 1916) has been ostracized for leaving her husband for a lover, but when she returns to New York, a generation later, to take her stand by her daughter who has done the same thing, she discovers that times have changed and that her daughter can now marry her lover and be received by the very people who have cut Mrs. Lidcote. The times, however, have changed only for the daughter's generation. Society will not revise its judgments of individuals, and Mrs. Lidcote must dine upstairs on a tray in order not to embarass a dinner party gathered to beam on the young lovers. But there is another, subtler moral in the story, and that is in the suggestion that Mrs. Lidcote, with all her suffering, has had a richer life than her daughter with her easy divorce and remarriage. She may feel like a lonely anachronism as she returns to her exile in Europe, but there is no envy in her reflections: "Where indeed in this crowded, topsy-turvy world, with its headlong changes and helter-skelter readjustments, its new tolerances and indifferences and accommodations, was there room for a character fashioned by slower sterner processes and a life broken under their inexorable pressure?"

But this is nostalgia for the very brand that did the burning! Ten years later, in *Twilight Sleep*, Mrs. Wharton was to go even further in her stand against the vapid painlessness of the postwar world by ridiculing the heavy doping of mothers in childbirth. The past came to have a certain validity to her simply by being the past. The New York of her childhood, that "cramped horizontal gridiron of a town without towers, porticoes, fountains or perspectives, hide-bound in its deadly uniformity of mean ugliness," having vanished, became as fascinating as Atlantis or Troy. It is to this attitude of apology toward her parents' generation that we owe her finest novel.

The title, *The Age of Innocence*, refers to the New York of the 1870's in the girlhood of Edith Jones and gives to the book the flavor of a historical novel, as is often pointed out by critics. The fact not always recognized by critics is that it was a habit of

Victorian novelists to set their stories in the era of their childhood. The novelist of manners has since shown a tendency to revert to a usually recent past where social distinctions, which make up so much of his subject matter, were more sharply defined, or at least where he thinks they were. *The Age of Innocence* (1920) is written in a Proustian mood of remembered things that evokes the airless atmosphere of an old, ordered, small-town New York as vividly as a conversation piece by Eastman Johnson. Here the dilettante bachelor, Newland Archer, as usual a lawyer, is at last placed in a story adapted to bring out the best and the worst in him. For he must have enough passion and imagination to aspire to break through the barriers of convention that surround him and yet be weak enough so that he cannot finally escape the steely embrace of an aroused tribe. Newland knows that he never really has a chance from the beginning; that is his pathos. He is engaged to May Welland, and he will marry May Welland and spend a lifetime with May Welland, and that is that, and both he and May's beautiful, Europeanized, disenchanted cousin, Ellen Olenska, realize it and accept it.

We have a suffocating sense of a creature trapped and doomed as poor Newland comes to the awareness, from the exchanged glances, coughs, and silences that surround him, that all of his vast family and family-in-law, including his own wife, are convinced that he is enjoying the very affair that he has failed to achieve and are united in irresistible tact to cut it short. But Mrs. Wharton is not suggesting that Newland and Ellen, in their renunciation of each other, have condemned themselves to a life of unrewarding frustration. Rules and regulations have now their validity to her, no matter what passions they crush. "It was you," Ellen tells Archer, "who made me understand that under the dullness there are things so fine and sensitive and delicate that even those I most cared for in my other life look cheap in comparison." And a generation later Archer sees no cause to repine in thinking back over his married life with May: "Their long years together had shown him that it did not so much matter if marriage was a dull duty, as long as it kept the dignity of a duty: lapsing from that, it became a mere battle of ugly appetites. Looking about him, he honored his own past, and mourned for it. After all, there was good in the old ways."

It is Edith Wharton's tribute to her own background, this affirmation that under the thick, smoky glass of convention bloom the fine, fragile flowers of patient suffering and self-sacrifice. To run away from society may be as vulgar in the end as to crash it. Newland Archer builds a shrine in his heart around the image of Ellen from which he derives strength to endure his uneventful and moderately useful life, a life where civic and social duties are judiciously balanced and where the impetus of Theodore Roosevelt even gets him into the state legislature, if only for a single term. We see him more completely than any other of Mrs. Wharton's heroes, and the reader who doubts that such a type existed has only to turn the pages of the voluminous diary of George Templeton Strong, published long after Edith Wharton's death.

The comparison with Strong's diary is also relevant in that *The Age of Innocence* is the first of Mrs. Wharton's novels to have all the action seen through the eyes of one character. The interest is thus centered in Newland Archer, as the interest in the two later books where she used the same method, *The Mother's Recompense* and *The Children*, is centered in Kate Clephane and Martin Boyne. Unlike James, however, she refused to be limited in her own comments to her central character's point of view. Archer's conventional way of looking at life, at least in the first half of the book, is too dull a lens for the reader, and his creator never hesitates to peer over his shoulder and point out all kinds of interesting things on the New York scene that we would otherwise miss. James would have objected to this. He would have argued that the spiritual growth of Archer, like that of Lambert Strether in *The Ambassadors*, would have a richer significance if viewed entirely through Archer's mind. It was one of their principal points of division. Mrs. Wharton refused to subordinate to any rule of design the "irregular and irrelevant movements of life" that to her made up the background of her stories.

It is interesting that her name should be so constantly linked with James's, considering how different were their approaches to their art. His influence is visible, superficially, in her early work, and, of course, they were both interested in Americans in Europe, but there the resemblance ceases. James was subtle, speculative, and indirect; Edith Wharton was always clear and to the point. Percy Lubbock speaks of her aversion to the abstract, to any discussion of the conundrum of life's meaning. She dealt with definite psychological and social problems and handled them in her own definite way. Her sentences never have to be read and reread, like James's, for richer and deeper disclosures. Furthermore, she and James, although good friends, never appreciated the best in each other's work. He found her most successful when most under his influence, as, for example, in *The Reef*, while she distrusted the whole artistic bent of his later years, feeling that he was severing himself more and more from "that thick nourishing human air in which we all live and move." If she must be regarded as anyone's disciple, it would be more accurate to note her relation to George Eliot, whose clear, strong style,

broad canvas, and obsession with moral questions always fascinated her.

As long as Mrs. Wharton had elected, after the war, to continue writing about the social life of a city that she had given up even visiting, she would have done better to restrict herself to the eras of its history with which she was acquainted. The four stories that make up *Old New York* (1924) evoke the atmosphere of the last century as successfully as anything in *The Age of Innocence*. But she was too concerned with the world around her to write only of the past. She wanted nothing less than to interpret the age in which she lived and to seek out the origin and cause of the increasing number of things in it that angered her. Also, her way of life had become expensive—a house north of Paris, another on the Riviera, twenty-two servants—and she needed a wider audience. To take advantage of the big pay of the American women's magazines, it was necessary to write about Americans of the moment.

The Glimpses of the Moon (1922) was first serialized in the *Pictorial Review*, which may give the clue to its author's remarkable lapse of style and taste. The jacket of the book depicts an Italian villa on Lake Como by moonlight to evoke the mawkish, gushing mood of an opening chapter which makes the reader rub his eyes and look again to be sure that he is dealing with Edith Wharton. Nick and Susy Lansing, two bright young penniless hangers-on of the international set, have married on the understanding that their bond may be dissolved at the option of the first to find a richer spouse. Nick is again the dilettante hero, writing a novel about Alexander the Great in Asia because it takes less research than an essay, but now, for the first time, reader and author see him from radically different points of view. To the reader he is, quite simply, an unmitigated cad, perfectly content to live in the borrowed houses of rich friends so long as his wife agrees not to steal the cigars or to take any overt part in the blindfolding of their hostesses' deceived husbands. On these two commandments hang all his law and his prophets, and when Susy has violated both (in each case, for his sake), he abruptly abandons her to pursue an heiress. It is impossible to imagine how Mrs. Wharton could have picked such a man as the hero of a romance unless she seriously believed that he represented what a gentleman had sunk to in the seventeen years which had elapsed since the publication of *The House of Mirth*. But could even Lawrence Selden have degenerated to a Nick Lansing? And could Lily Bart ever have stolen cigars? Surely the world had not been entirely taken over by the Lansings and their dismal set of international drifters who blur together in a maze of furs and jewels and yachts. Mrs. Wharton's preoccupation with vulgarity had for the moment vulgarized her perceptions.

The lapse in her style can be illustrated by contrasting three descriptions of ladies of fashion. The first is from *The House of Mirth*. Lawrence Selden is taking his shrewd, leisurely note of the person of Lily Bart, and his speculations provide our first insight into the central problem of her chracter: "Everything about her was at once vigorous and exquisite, at once strong and fine. He had a confused sense that she must have cost a great deal to make, that a great many dull and ugly people must, in some mysterious way, have been sacrificed to produce her. He was aware that the qualities distinguishing her from the herd of her sex were chiefly external: as though a fine glaze of beauty and fastidiousness had been applied to vulgar clay."

The second is from the scene in *Madame de Treymes*, published two years later, where John Durham contemplates Fanny de Malrive after her call upon his mother and sister at their hotel and discerns in her fluster a ground for hope as to his future. The passage, with a faint Jamesian ring, is finely conceived: "The mere fact of her having forgotten to draw on her gloves as they were descending in the hotel lift from his mother's drawing-room was, in this connection, charged with significance to Durham. She was the kind of woman who always presents herself to the mind's eye as completely equipped, as made of exquisitely cared for and finely-related details; and that the heat of her parting with his family should have left her unconscious that she was emerging gloveless into Paris, seemed, on the whole, to speak hopefully for Durham's future opinion of the city."

Turning to *The Glimpses of the Moon*, we see one of Susy Lansing's friends, not only through Susy's eyes, but through the angrily disapproving eyes of Mrs. Wharton. The idea to be conveyed is that the lady described is as banal as her motor and her motor as banal as a magazine advertisement, but as the style is literally the style of a magazine advertisement, we can only wonder what reason the author has to sneer: "But on the threshold a still more familiar figure met her: that of a lady in exaggerated pearls and sables, descending from an exaggerated motor, like the motors in magazine advertisements, the huge arks in which jeweled beauties and slender youths pause to gaze at snow-peaks from an Alpine summit."

Fortunately the novels that followed *The Glimpses of the Moon* are not all quite as slick. If they are not good novels, neither are they potboilers. But it seems a pity that Mrs. Wharton should have chosen to lay all the blame for the shapelessness of the postwar world on her native land. In book after book her complaints grow shriller and shriller until at last everything across the Atlantic is tainted with the same grotesque absurdity. She gives to her American towns such names as Delos, Aeschylus, Lohengrin, and Halleluja, and to their inhabitants, in their brief hours away from money-making, a total gullibility in dealing with religious and medical charlatans. Their fuzzy zeal for good causes envelops their hideous skyscrapers in a stifling cloud of euphoria. And the American face! How it haunts her! It is as "unexpressive as a football." It might have been made by "a manufacturer of sporting goods." Its sameness encompasses her "with its innocent uniformity." How many of such faces would it take "to make up a single individuality"? Years before, she had written to an English friend about James: "America can't be quite so summarily treated and so lightly dismissed as our great Henry thinks." Yet, reading her later novels, we can only wish that she had dismissed America altogether.

Kate Clephane in *The Mother's Recompense* (1925) returns to a society in New York which has ostracized her, as it ostracized Mrs. Lidcote in "Autre Temps," to find, unlike Mrs. Lidcote, that it *can* revise its judgments. She is completely accepted by the people who once cut her and thinks the less of them for their tolerance. She finds only one person in New York who seems to have any real moral fiber, and that is her daughter who, perhaps for the same reason, strikes the reader as a rather wooden girl. When Kate discovers that Anne is ignorantly about to marry her own former lover, she tries desperately to break up the match without telling the girl why and finally surrenders to the situation in order to avoid "sterile pain." But having renounced sterile pain for her daughter, she elects it for herself by refusing the offer of marriage from a devoted old admirer who has been shocked, but only momentarily, by her confession.

Mrs. Wharton resented the critics who deplored the ending of the book and spoke of the "densities of incomprehension" with which she now felt herself surrounded. The clue to Kate's sacrifice, she hinted, lies in the quotation from Shelley on the flyleaf: "Desolation is a delicate thing." My own interpretation is that Kate, imbued with the sensitivity of one who, like Mrs. Lidcote, has been broken on the wheel of a sterner age, feels more keenly than anyone else the horror of Anne's marriage. What she hates in the modern world is not so much that things can happen as that people no longer really care that they do. Anne is caught in the situation of marrying her mother's lover because her mother has *had* a lover, and for that there must be expiation on the mother's part, alone in her shabby Riviera village, without the comfort of her old admirer. For Kate to go from the litter of fallen rose petals and grains of rice of her daughter's wedding to her own would be joining forces with the noisy, thoughtless world of vacuous toasts in which all delicacy of feeling has vanished. Those who believe in the old, harder standards must be willing to suffer alone, without sympathy or even comprehension. But this, evidently, is not sterile pain. Kate Clephane is intended to inhale a finer aroma from the bouquet of her loneliness than her daughter will ever know.

So far Mrs. Wharton had only skirmished with America. The story of the Lansings takes place in Europe, and Kate Clephane's drama is too much of the heart to have the locality of first importance. But she was preparing herself for a closer study of what had happened to America, and she had now spotted a type that she considered a representative victim of the disease of modern vulgarity, if, indeed, it was not the virus itself. Pauline Manford in *Twilight Sleep* (1927) is the daughter of an invader from "Exploit" who has first been married to a son of the age of innocence, Arthur Wyant. But time has profoundly altered both types. The invader's daughter is no longer prehensile or even crude; she has become bland and colorless and pointlessly efficient, building a life of public speeches and dinner parties around causes that she does not even try to understand, while Wyant, no longer the cool, well-dressed New York gentleman with a collector's eye for painting and porcelain, has degenerated to a foolish gossiping creature whom his wife has understandably divorced for a sneaky affair with his mother's old-maid companion. That is what has come of the merger of the old and new societies; it has cost each its true character. Pauline Manford, with invader's blood, has survived better than has Wyant, but hers is a lonely and precarious survival in a rosy cloud floating on an ether of fatuity from which she views with frightened eyes the moral collapse of her family. The invaders and their daughters have in common the faculty of immense preoccupation, the former with their businesses, the latter with their causes. But both are blinded to all that is beautiful or significant in the world around them by the dust stirred up by their febrile activities.

In Mrs. Manford Edith Wharton was groping at the outline of a well-known American phenomenon, the committeewoman who, married to a man who cares only for his business, seeks refuge in bogus Utopias where beauty is expected to spring like a phoenix from the ashes of pain. If Mrs. Wharton had only stayed in America, how quickly she would have comprehended such a woman! But Mrs. Manford is nothing but a caricature, mixing up her speeches to the birth control league and the society for unlimited families, going to the "Busy Man's Christ" for "uplift" treatments and seeing her children only by secretarial appointment. Mrs. Wharton seems to have no sense of the violent resentment that may underlie such a woman's placid stare or of the hatred of spouse and possessive passion for offspring that her false air of good sportsmanship may conceal. The American committeewoman is not apt, like Mrs. Manford, to be surrounded by a family who regard her goings-on merely with a cheerful, amused tolerance. *Twilight Sleep* is a formidable battering ram used on a straw woman.

There was to be one more last grim sketch of the final decadence resulting from the now ancient merger between old New York and the invaders. In the short story "After Holbein," a senile Mrs. Jaspar sits down alone every night at the end of her great dining room table, imagining that she is still the hostess at a dinner party, while her smirking servants go through a pantomime of serving guests. Anson Warley, a veteran bachelor, dilettante, and diner out, who has scorned her parties in the days of her greatness, suffering now himself from loss of memory, goes to her house by mistake, and the two old broken-down creatures squeak and gibber together, drinking the soda water which they take for Perrier-Jouet and admiring flower vases stuffed with old newspapers. It has been said that there is no compassion in this story, but how much compassion does a short story need? It is a chilling, cleverly executed little piece, a sort of dance of death, pointing a grim moral in the ultimate inanity of two lives dedicated to the ceremonial of the dinner party.

American mothers she had now done, together with their husbands, both of the invader and dilettante variety, but what about children? They had never played much of a role in her books, as, indeed, they had played little in her life. Mrs. Winthrop Chanler has written that she was actually afraid of them. But if she was ignorant of the American nurseries and schools, she was very much aware of those pathetic little waifs, the products of multiple marriages, who were dragged about Europe in the wake of rich, pleasure-seeking parents and finally abandoned with governesses in seaside hotels. The various Wheater offspring in *The Children* (1928) have sworn to remain together under the lead of Judith, the eldest, in spite of what other custody arrangements their various parents and "steps" may make. The children are sometimes amusingly, sometimes touchingly drawn, but the sketches are still superficial and "cute," and the background of rich expatriate life in European resorts is filled in with the now heavy hand of her satire.

The more interesting though secondary topic of the book is the relationship between Rose Sellars, the quiet, gentle widow of exquisite tact, with whom I suspect Mrs. Wharton may have a bit identified herself, and Martin Boyne, again the tasteful middle-aged bachelor, who has made a fortune, like other Wharton heroes, offstage and has now plenty of time to idle abroad. Rose Sellars immediately understands and accepts the fact that Boyne's preoccupation with the Wheater children is, unknown to himself, a manifestation of his hopeless passion for little Judith. The novel was published in the year that followed Walter Berry's death, and the relationship between the two characters seems analogous to what may have existed between their creator and Berry: she, loving and eager, but restrained by the fear of embarrassing them both by a scene that might expose the small beer of his feeling, and he, detached but admiring, half disappointed and half irritated at his own inability to respond to a gratifying if sometimes cloying affection. It is tempting to speculate that Martin Boyne's fate is the author's revenge on his deceased counterpart. We leave him in the end, old and desolate, staring through a ballroom window at the beautiful Judith who, dancing with young men, is no longer even aware of his existence.

After *The Children* Edith Wharton embarked, although then in her late sixties, on the most ambitious experiment of her literary career: the fictional biography of a young middle western American writer, Vance Weston, told in two novels: *Hudson River Bracketed* (1929) and *The Gods Arrive* (1932). She opens his story in a town which is, typically enough, called "Euphoria" and plunges fearlessly into details of middle western life, as if Sinclair Lewis by dedicating *Babbitt* to her had given her some special insight into an area of America that she had never even seen. The result is as bad as might be expected, but Vance Weston soon leaves his home town and comes to New York and an old house on the Hudson where his creator is on more familiar ground and where he meets a highly accomplished young lady, Halo Spear, who recites German poetry to him. "Just listen to the sound of the words," she says, when he protests his ignorance of the tongue.

It is easy to ridicule this long saga with its distorted picture of the New York publishing world, its uncouth young writers and artists ("Zola—who's he?" somebody yawned. "Oh, I dunno. The French Thackeray, I guess."), its irritatingly efficient heroine who can change travel accommodations and rent villas as easily as she can spout Goethe, its insensitive hero whose obsessive egotism becomes ultimately tedious, its ponderous satires of popular novelists and literary hostesses, but it nonetheless contains a strong picture of a young genius who educates himself and fights his way to literary success with a ruthlessness of which he is too preoccupied to be more than dimly aware. We sympathize when he is stifled in the ignorant, carping atmosphere of his invalid first wife's home and with his artist's need to rip away even at the most basic family ties. Here at last in Edith Wharton's fiction is a picture of a man. It may have all kinds of personal significance that he is neither a New Yorker nor a gentleman. As he develops cultivation in Europe, however, he develops some of the hardness of the older Wharton heroes, and when he leaves Halo at last for a round of parties in London, there is not much to choose between him and Martin Boyne. But that is in the second volume which, like so many sequels, should never have been written. Both reader and author have become bored with Vance. Yet one cannot but be impressed by the fund of creative energy that could produce such a book on such a subject in the author's seventieth year.

At the very end of her life Edith Wharton turned back once again to the rich field of her childhood memories, and immediately the shrill bitterness disappears, and the old, clear, forceful style is back to the aid of its mistress. If she had finished *The Buccaneers* (1938) it might well rank among the best of her work. The little band of social-climbing maidens who find New York too difficult and leave it to triumph in London are unique in her fiction as possessing both her approval and affection. Old New York seems merely petty and narrow now in the person of Mrs. Parmore, while the parvenu is actually given charm and vitality in that of Colonel St. George. The author's point of view is expressed by the English governess of the St. George girls, Laura Testvalley, an erudite but romantic spinster of Italian descent, a cousin of the Rossettis, who adores her covey of Daisy Millers and guides them up the slippery rungs of the London social ladder. Until the girls have achieved their titles the mood of the book is light and amusing; thereafter it becomes more serious. For they have, after all, missed happiness, and Nan, as the author's notebooks reveal, will find hers only by leaving the Duke of Tintagel for Guy Thwarte.

Mrs. Wharton had not only cast aside for once her disapproval of those who are discontented to remain in the social grade of their origin; she had even cast off four decades of classicism in taste and morals to plot an ending that was to celebrate the triumph of "deep and abiding love." Yet how many times in her stories and novels have we not been told that no love can survive the cold shoulder of society, the disintegrating shabbiness of a life in second-class watering places! And is Nan now to get away with it, to escape the fate of Anna Karenina?

But if Mrs. Wharton, at the end, permitted herself to indulge in the vision of a love that was to make up for everything, the love that Ellen Olenska and Newland Archer had renounced, she was still enough of a Yankee puritan to stipulate that such a love had to be paid for. If Nan and Guy are to have their happiness, Laura Testvalley must lose hers. Her engagement to Guy's father will not survive her role in his son's elopement. Laura, the author's representative and a bit her alter ego, must be sacrificed to the gods of order. One wonders if at the last those gods did not, to Laura's creator, show some of the lineaments of the gods of derision whom she had so bitterly apostrophized in her journal thirty years before.

With her posthumously published works, *The Buccaneers* and *Ghosts*, the total of Edith Wharton's fiction comes to thirty-two volumes. Obviously, her ultimate reputation in American letters will rest upon only a fraction of this list. *Ethan Frome*, I have no doubt, will always be read, but it is out of the main stream of her work. I believe that she will be remembered primarily for her two great novels of manners: *The House of Mirth* and *The Age of*

Innocence. In these she succeeded in re-creating an unadventurous and ceremonious society, appropriately sheltered behind New York brownstone, looking always to the east rather than to the west, and the impact upon it of the winds that blew from both directions. There were plenty of minor writers who attempted to delineate this society, but among those of the first rank Mrs. Wharton, at least in the first decade of our century, had it to herself. It is true, of course, that some of James's characters come from the same milieu, but they are rarely considered in relation to their native land or cities. The reason Mrs. Wharton succeeded where so many others have failed is that in addition to her gifts as an artist she had a firm grasp of what "society," in the smaller sense of the word, was actually made up of. She understood that it was arbitrary, capricious, and inconsistent; she was aware that it did not hesitate to abolish its standards while most loudly proclaiming them. She knew when money could open doors and when it couldn't, when lineage would serve and when it would be merely sneered at. She knew that compromises could be counted on, but that they were rarely made while still considered compromises. She knew her men and women of property, recently or anciently acquired, how they decorated their houses and where they spent their summers. She realized that the social game was without rules, and this realization made her one of the few novelists before Proust who could describe it with any profundity. In American fiction her nearest counterpart is Ellen Glasgow.

Edith Wharton died in her house near Paris of a stroke in 1937, at the age of seventy-five. A great deal has been written about her in articles and memoirs, but almost always about the great lady, rarely the writer. This is nobody's fault, for Mrs. Wharton took a certain pride in keeping her writing behind the scenes, in presenting herself to the world, so to speak, on her own. One short piece, however, by Iris Origo, describes a weekend on Long Island that Mrs. Wharton spent with old friends during a brief visit to America to receive a degree from Yale. It is one of the rare recorded occasions when the survivor from New York's age of innocence, the real figure behind the novelist, predominated over the brilliant and formidable lady of perfect houses and gardens. Iris Origo relates how Mrs. Wharton refused to be led into any discussion of persons or events in France, of Carlo Placi or Madame de Noailles, and how, at each such attempt, she gently and firmly steered the conversation back to old friends and old memories in New York. The W's house on 11th Street, had it really been pulled down? Did her hostess remember the night they had dined there before the Colony Club ball? The X's daughter, the fair one, had she married her young Bostonian? Had Z indeed lost all his money?

"For the whole evening, this mood continued. At one moment only—as, the last guest gone, she turned half-way up the stairs to wave good-night—I caught a glimpse of the other Edith: elegant, formidable, as hard and dry as porcelain. Then, as she looked down on her old friends, her face softened, even the erectness of her spine relaxed a little. She was no longer the trim, hard European hostess, but a nice old American lady. Edith had come home."

Selected Bibliography

**WORKS OF
EDITH WHARTON**

NOVELS AND COLLECTIONS OF SHORT STORIES
The Greater Inclination. New York: Scribners, 1899.

The Touchstone. New York: Scribners, 1900.

Crucial Instances. New York: Scribners, 1901.

The Valley of Decision. New York: Scribners, 1902.

Sanctuary. New York: Scribners, 1903.

The Descent of Man and Other Stories. New York: Scribners, 1904.

The House of Mirth. New York: Scribners, 1905.

Madame de Treymes. New York: Scribners, 1907.

The Fruit of the Tree. New York: Scribners, 1907.

The Hermit and the Wild Woman and Other Stories. New York: Scribners, 1908.

Tales of Men and Ghosts. New York: Scribners, 1910.

Ethan Frome. New York: Scribners, 1911.

The Reef. New York: Appleton, 1912.

The Custom of the Country. New York: Scribners, 1913.

Xingu and Other Stories. New York: Scribners, 1916.

Summer. New York: Appleton, 1917.

The Marne. New York: Appleton, 1918.

The Age of Innocence. New York: Appleton, 1920.

The Glimpses of the Moon. New York: Appleton, 1922.

A Son at the Front. New York: Scribners, 1923.

Old New York: False Dawn (The 'Forties); The Old Maid (The 'Fifties); The Spark (The 'Sixties); New Year's Day (The 'Seventies). New York: Appleton, 1924.

The Mother's Recompense. New York: Appleton, 1925.

Here and Beyond. New York: Appleton, 1926.

Twilight Sleep. New York: Appleton, 1927.

The Children. New York: Appleton, 1928.

Hudson River Bracketed. New York: Appleton, 1929.

Certain People. New York: Appleton, 1930.

The Gods Arrive. New York: Appleton, 1932.

Human Nature. New York: Appleton, 1933.

The World Over. New York: Appleton-Century, 1936.

Ghosts. New York: Appleton-Century, 1937.

The Buccaneers. New York: Appleton-Century, 1938.

Published since the writing of this essay

Roman Fever and Other Stories. New York: Scribners, 1978.

Ghost Stories of Edith Wharton. New York: Scribners, 1985.

POETRY

Verses. Newport, R.I.: C. E. Hammett, Jr., 1878.

Artemis to Actaeon and Other Verse. New York: Scribner's, 1909.

Twelve Poems. London: The Medici Society, 1926.

NONFICTION

The Decoration of Houses (with Ogden Codman, Jr.). New York: Scribners, 1897.

Italian Villas and Their Gardens. New York: Century, 1904.

Italian Backgrounds. New York: Scribners, 1905.

A Motor-Flight through France. New York: Scribners, 1908.

Fighting France, from Dunkerque to Belfort. New York: Scribners, 1915.

French Ways and Their Meaning. New York: Appleton, 1919.

In Morocco. New York: Scribners, 1920.

The Writing of Fiction. New York: Scribners, 1925.

A Backward Glance. New York: Appleton-Century, 1934.

TRANSLATIONS

The Joy of Living. By Hermann Sudermann. New York: Scribners, 1902.

COMPILATIONS

The Book of the Homeless. New York: Scribners, 1916.

Eternal Passion in English Poetry (with Robert Norton and Gaillard Lapsley). New York: Appleton-Century, 1939.

ANTHOLOGIES

Auchincloss, Louis. *The Edith Wharton Reader.* New York: Scribners, 1965.

CRITICAL AND BIOGRAPHICAL STUDIES

Andrews, Wayne. Introduction to *The Best Short Stories of Edith Wharton.* New York: Scribners, 1958.

Auchincloss, Louis. *Edith Wharton, A Woman in Her Time*. New York: Viking Press, 1971.

Bell, Millicent. *Edith Wharton and Henry James*. New York: Braziller, 1965.

Brooks, Van Wyck. *The Confident Years*. New York: Dutton, 1952.

Browne, E. K. *Edith Wharton, Etude Critique*. Paris: Librairie E. Droz, 1935.

Edel, Leon. "Edith Wharton," in *The Dictionary of American Biography*, Volume 22. New York: Scribners, 1958.

————. *The Master* (Volume V of a biography of Henry James). New York: Lippincott, 1972.

James, Henry. *Letters to Walter Berry*. Paris: Black Sun Press, 1928.

Kazin, Alfred. *On Native Grounds*. New York: Reynal and Hitchcock, 1942.

Lubbock, Percy. *Portrait of Edith Wharton*. New York: Appleton-Century-Crofts, 1947.

Nevius, Blake. *Edith Wharton, A Study of Her Fiction*. Berkeley and Los Angeles: University of California Press, 1953.

Origo, Iris. "The Homecoming." *New Statesman and Nation*, February 16, 1957.

Wilson, Edmund. *The Wound and the Bow*. Boston: Houghton Mifflin, 1941.

————. *Classics and Commercials*. New York: Farrar, Straus, 1950.

—LOUIS AUCHINCLOSS

Walt Whitman

1819-1892

NEARLY everyone agrees that Walt Whitman is America's greatest poet. But many Americans agree reluctantly or grudgingly and, perhaps because the influential contemporary critics of poetry—"the new critics"—have either scorned or ignored Whitman, they do not trouble to discern the true qualities of Whitman's poetry but content themselves with admitting that in some undefined way it is "powerful." Yet even those readers who hail Whitman's greatness with enthusiasm and read him with ever renewed pleasure do not always find it easy to say precisely what it is about the poems that they admire. The true qualities of Emily Dickinson's poetry, for example, or of Wordsworth's or T. S. Eliot's or Donne's, can be more readily defined than can the true qualities of Whitman's. And we can more readily state the quality of our pleasure in these poets than we can in the case of Whitman. He is elusive, both as man and poet.

Consider the first two lines of *Leaves of Grass* (here as elsewhere I quote from the later editions of *Leaves of Grass* without attention to the differences of detail which sometimes exist between these and the early editions):

One's-self I sing, a simple separate person,
Yet utter the word Democratic, the word En-
 Masse.

There is a disconcerting abstractness and generality about that "One's-self." We would expect the poet to say "Myself," but we discover that even when he does, in "Song of Myself," he still gives us very little concrete information about a man named Walt Whitman. The poet described *Leaves of Grass* as in effect an autobiography—"an attempt from first to last, to put a *Person*, a human being (myself, in the latter half of the nineteenth century in America) freely, fully and truly on record." But there is much less of direct, concrete autobiography in *Leaves of Grass* than, say, in Wordsworth's *Prelude*. In fact we discover, after reading *Leaves of Grass* carefully, that what Whitman has put on record is not "myself" but, as the above quotation suggests, a "Person"—or better, a persona or series of personae. In order to understand Whitman's enormous, sprawling, uneven book, we will have to understand something about the origin and nature of these self-projected images which are only equivocally the "real" Whitman. And of course Whitman projected images of himself in life as well as in his poetry (they are often the same ones). He was an inveterate poseur and he had more than a little vanity. His well-known, carefully cultivated poses include the worldly dandy we briefly glimpse in the early 1840's; the somewhat Christlike carpenter and radical of the early fifties; the bearded, well-bathed, burly, bluff "camerado" of later years; then the male nurse and good gray poet of his Washington years; and finally the venerable sage of Camden. Whitman was in his way an intellectual as well as a highly unorthodox poet. He had his neurotic side—covert, bisexual, quirky, elusive, power-seeking, bohemian, libidinous, indolent. Which is to say that Whitman's poses were not mere play-acting but arose from a deep maladjustment to the nineteenth-century America he lived in. One cannot always be sure whether he became the celebrant of this America in spite of or because of his maladjustment; both possibilities are involved.

Many modern readers are likely to be made uneasy by Whitman's announcement that he is going to "sing" one's-self. But we should not forget that traditionally poets, particularly if they were prophetic or epic poets, did "sing," rather than fabricate what a contemporary critic of poetry would probably call a "symbolic construct." Of course, Whitman often "sang" stridently and, in the bad sense, "rhetorically." Some American readers will connect with Whitman's singing what they consider his immoderate chauvinism, his spread-eagleism, his sometimes philistine celebration of America's material success. But by now our traditional sense of cultural inferiority, vis-à-vis Europe, has certainly gone by the board and we need no longer be embarrassed by Whitman's vaunting Americanism (the Europeans have always loved it). It is becoming increasingly easy to find his philistinism not only excusable but, on occasion, delightfully characteristic. For example, in "Song of the Exposition" we hear Whitman hailing the Muse of poetry as the "illustrious emigré" who has come to America to observe its advanced technology. She is

Bluff'd not a bit by drain-pipe, gasometers, artificial fertilizers,
Smiling and pleas'd with palpable intent to stay,
She's here, install'd amid the kitchen ware!

These pleasingly comical lines are certainly not among Whitman's greatest utterances, but neither are they likely to do any damage to culture.

Whitman promises to sing "a simple, separate person," yet before we have read very far in *Leaves of Grass* or very much about the poet by his biographers, we see that neither Whitman nor the images of himself that he projects can be described as "simple"—far from it. We see too that there is difficulty in that word "separate." We discover that the so-called "separate" person, or self, is always merging with other persons or with the "En-Masse" or becoming an abstraction. And sometimes the poems make us feel that the "person" is separate not only in the sense of being self-reliant or integral ("Me imperturbe, standing at ease in Nature"), and not only in the sense that he is citizen in a democracy with a vote as good as any other man's, but that this person's separateness becomes a radical alienation which seems to carry him almost to the point of loving death. For Whitman is indeed a poet who can think of death (in the memorable words of Wallace Stevens) as "the mother of beauty."

We note the paradox involved in one of Whitman's key words—"identity"—when we read that besides singing the individual, he is going to "utter the word Democratic." Naturally enough the democratic paradox is the central metaphor of *Leaves of Grass*, arising from the double allegiance of democratic man, on the one hand, to the inviolable integrity of the self and, on the other, to the united body of all men. In Whitman's poems the individual "identity" is always identifying itself and then, as it were, unidentifying itself with the "En-Masse." This often becomes disconcerting and is inevitably one of the origins of the diffuseness, vagueness, and lack of inner structure and dramatic tension which characterize much of Whitman's verse. For example, in "Starting from Paumanok" (the piece that serves as a kind of poetic table of contents for *Leaves of Grass*), we read:

Victory, union, faith, identity, time,
The indissoluble compacts, riches, mystery,
Eternal progress, the kosmos, and the modern
 reports.

Intriguing perhaps, but it is far from perfectly clear what is being talked about, except that in some way in modern America the individual becomes integral in his separateness to the extent that he is absorbed into the indissoluble union of all men. Out of this paradox arises all the strength and weakness of Whitman's poetry, and it is here that we must begin to look for the meaning of this poetry, rather than in his real or fancied relation to neo-Platonism, Hegelianism, mysticism, and all the other philosophical or religious isms that Whitman scholars have so much overemphasized.

Ever since D. H. Lawrence's *Studies in Classic American Literature*, critics have been elaborating on Lawrence's perception of the "doubleness" or "duplicity" of our best writers —Cooper, Hawthorne, Melville, Mark Twain, for example. We do not perhaps think of Whitman at first as being available to this kind of approach. We are likely to think of him as the uncomplicated, optimistic, basically unquestioning celebrant of democratic man and his untroubled progress in an open, pragmatic world. And of course Whitman *is* this celebrant. Yet, as I have pointed out, merely by

being the bard of democracy, Whitman involves himself in "doubleness" and contradiction. Then we recall the poems in which death figures so prominently; we recall the vituperative criticism of democracy in *Democratic Vistas*; we take note of his carefully maintained poses; and we cannot help thinking that there is complexity and contradiction in Walt Whitman, as well as in the other classic authors. "I cannot understand the mystery," Whitman wrote in a notebook perhaps as early as 1847, "but I am always conscious of myself as two." In the notebook he conjectures that the "two" are "my soul and I" and in his poetry he was later to discover many ways of expressing the "two." A central metaphor of the great poem "Crossing Brooklyn Ferry" is Whitman's statement that "I too knitted the old knot of contrariety." And when he gets off the famous (to some people notorious) lines in "Song of Myself,"

> Do I contradict myself?
> Very well then I contradict myself,
> (I am large, I contain multitudes),

he is not merely indulging in bravado or apologizing for contradictions of logic or fact. He is stating a basic truth about himself and his poetry. No doubt Whitman's mind is not so complex or his contradictions so drastic as, say, Melville's. And no doubt his poetry is totally unlike what we often think of as the poetry of paradox—that of Donne and the other metaphysical poets, for example. Nevertheless, the way to understand Whitman and his best poems is to learn what we can about how he knitted his knot of contrariety.

Whitman was in truth the "slow arriver" he called himself, for he was well into maturity when the first edition of *Leaves of Grass* was published in 1855. He had been born in 1819, at West Hills, Long Island, the second of nine children, several of whom turned out to be of unsound mental and physical constitution. His father was a not too successful carpenter, and Walt seems to have derived little from this apparently morose and inarticulate man except a belief in the more radical wing of Jeffersonian-Jacksonian politics. His mother was the mainstay of the family, as is suggested by the daguerreotype that shows her broad, firm, pensive face. Walt's lifelong attachment to his nearly illiterate mother is one of the remarkable and ennobling facts of his life. His mother was "the most perfect and magnetic character, the rarest combination of practical, moral, and spiritual, and the least selfish, of all and any I have ever known, and by me O so much the most deeply loved." But moving as this utterance is (made on the occasion of his mother's death), we must see in it the origin of Whitman's never successfully established sexuality, with its apparent bisexual quality tending toward the homosexual.

The move of the Whitmans to Brooklyn when Walt was four was only one of several that occurred during his childhood and youth and that contributed to the generally unsettled and anxious life the family lived. As he said in later years "the time of my boyhood was a very restless and unhappy one; I did not know what to do." After a certain amount of desultory schooling, Walt worked in various capacities for newspapers and printers. He even tried his hand at teaching school. But it was newspaper work that he was drawn to, and by 1846 the somewhat indolent young man had worked hard enough at it to become the editor, for two years, of the Brooklyn *Eagle*, a flourishing paper which expressed the opinions of the Democratic party and made Whitman something of a public figure in the rapidly growing town. His life continued to be unsettled, after the *Eagle* editorship, although we do hear of his sometimes assisting his father on carpentering jobs. During the years before 1855 doubtless his real empolyment was an inner one—the gradual evolution in his mind of the remarkable book he was to publish, setting the type himself, in that year.

There will always seem to be something miraculous about the first edition of *Leaves of Grass*, with its showpiece, the (then untitled) "Song of Myself." How did this editor, saunterer, loafer, schoolteacher, small-time politico, opera-goer, and (as we may guess) mediocre carpenter come to be one of the world's great poets? Of course, there can be no final answer to this question, even if we had many more materials to work with than we have. There is next to nothing in Whitman's newspaper writing to suggest a gradually emerging set of ideas or a style that in any specific sense forecasts *Leaves of Grass*. Whitman's early notebooks are sparse and hardly suggest, any more than do the few early poems that survive, the qualities of the poetry in the 1855 edition. Lacking these materials, we are tempted to conjecture whether some decisive event in Whitman's life may have at once freed and consolidated his powers of intellect, emotion, and imagination. Whitman worked in New Orleans on a newspaper called the *Crescent* in the spring of 1848, and the so-called "New Orleans episode" has always figured prominently in the speculations of his biographers. Can the not so young man (he was 29) have been awakened emotionally by the Paris of the South? Did he become involved with a woman for the first time—perhaps, as some shadowy evidence suggests, an octoroon? Is there any truth in Whitman's statements in a letter of 1890 to John Addington Symonds that he was the father of six illegitimate children, and that "My life, young manhood, midage, times South, etc., have been jolly bodily"? This famous letter, as it goes on, *sounds* like a patent fabrication (which could be beautifully read by W. C. Fields—"Though unmarried I have had six children—two dead—one living Southern grandchild, fine boy, writes to me occasionally"), but it is possible that there is truth in it. Yet Whitman's sexuality seems to have been diffuse, somewhat infantile, and except for periods of anxiety (of which his notebook jottings give evidence) not directed toward women. It is therefore most unlikely that a passionate love affair occurred in New Orleans, or that, even if it did, it could have had much to do with the awakening of emotional power which produced the poems of 1855, a full seven years after his New Orleans sojourn.

The conjecture has also been made that Whitman at some time before 1855, after various unhappy sexual attempts, came to realize that he was homosexual and that his acceptance of this freed him of inhibitions and gave power and form to his imagination. But he seems actually to have been bisexual rather than truly homosexual. The conjecture has also been advanced that Whitman may have had some overwhelming mystical experience which changed the whole course of his life—perhaps like the blinding light that struck down St. Paul on the road to Damascus. The objection to both of these speculations is, first, that there is no evidence for them and, second, that they both assume in Whitman a capacity for sudden and dramatic changes in his nature. Such changes are of course possible in some personalities and have been decisive in the emergence of many poets. But this does not seem possible in the life of Walt Whitman, whose emotional experience, except in his best poems, was diffuse and who, as I have said, accurately described himself as a "slow arriver."

What can be said, then, about the embryon-period (Whitman would like the expression) of *Leaves of Grass*? A full discussion, which of course cannot be launched here, might well begin with two quotations from the poet. First his statement that "I was simmering, simmering, simmering. Emerson brought me to a boil." Second there is his remark that his journalistic writing (he is talking about his contributions to the *Democratic Review*, but the words apply as well to nearly everything he wrote before *Leaves of Grass*) "came from the surface of the mind, and had no connection with what lay below—a great deal of which indeed was below consciousness. At last came the time when the concealed growth had to come to light."

In Emerson's essays Whitman read much about the self and its all but autonomous power, and the plight and destiny of the self was to become Whitman's real subject. Less serene and isolated from life than Emerson, more instinctively aware of the powers of the unconscious, he was gradually able to free the latent powers of his unconscious mind and through poetry endow the self with these powers, so that the self became for him not merely a moral or mystical entity as it tends to be in Emerson, not merely one term in the political paradox of the self vs. society, but the decisive part of a poetic metaphor—the other part of which is, variously, other selves, nature, or society. The characteristic quality of Whitman's best poetry arises either from the dramatic (often comic) tensions evoked when the self is shown to be in a state of contradiction or polarity to the not-self or from the lyric harmony, often meditative, retrospective, and "mystical," which is evoked when the self is felt to be identical with the not-self or some aspect of it. The poems which do not in some way involve the metaphor of the self are more likely than not to be inert catalogues, empty rhetoric, "cosmic," vague, or in other ways unsatisfactory.

We can trace the process by which the idea

of the self was endowed with emotional power in Whitman's highly significant though not entirely successful poem called "The Sleepers," with its hauntingly dreamlike (though at first apparently miscellaneous) images of the shipwreck, the "beautiful gigantic swimmer" who becomes a "brave corpse," George Washington bidding a fatherly farewell to his soldiers, and above all the mother, who is seen variously as having a shadowy lover, as a "sleepless widow" looking at the coffin of her husband, and as an Indian squaw who resembles a goddess. Doubtless it is all too easy to say that Whitman has performed the therapeutic act of becoming able symbolically to represent his unconscious desire to kill his father and possess his mother; but it is not irrelevant to say so. Whitman at any rate conceives of the poem as narrating the descent of the conscious mind into the perilous night and then emerging with new strength. Before the descent the poet describes himself as "wandering, confused, lost to myself, ill-assorted, contradictory." But his mood afterwards—aggressive, self-confident, creative—is suggested by the following:

I am a dance—play up there! the fit is
    whirling me fast! . . .
Onward we move, a gay gang of blackguards!
    with mirth-shouting music and
    wild-flapping pennants of joy!

This brief discussion will perhaps suggest that there was nothing mysterious about Whitman's emergence as a poet, except the general mystery of the emergence of genius. We do not, in any case, require an octoroon or an influx of cosmic light to account for it.

When *Leaves of Grass* appeared in 1855 readers (of whom there were very few indeed) discovered therein twelve untitled poems and a preface explaining the poet's view of poetry and its purpose. The poet, Whitman says, must not content himself with making beautifully contrived verses. He must be a prophet, a seer, a bard, a teacher, and a moralist. Not that, as a moralist, the poet teaches improving lessons or preaches uprightness. He is a moralist in the sense that he speaks for—"promulges," Whitman likes to say—the future and for democracy. His aim is "to cheer up slaves and horrify despots." But he is a spiritual leader, too; for the age of religion is past and the poet must assume the role of the priest. He must make himself the most perfect of men, the archetype of the spiritually and organically normal. "Of all mankind the great poet is the equable man. Not in him but off from him things are grotesque or eccentric or fail of their sanity. . . . He is the arbiter of the diverse and he is the key." Also the poet is a kind of spokesman for his people. His is not only an individual voice but also the voice of his nation. "He incarnates its geography and natural life and rivers and lakes." But more than that; the poet, seeing "the beauty and sacredness of the demonstrable," abandons the conventional myths of traditional poetry and shapes "solid and beautiful forms of the future," providing his countrymen (as Whitman was to argue more at length in *Democratic Vistas*) with native archetypes of the imagination and modes of instinctive response and feeling which will give coherence to a new and still unformed civilization. He rejects no fact of life from his poems; yet he is not a "realist": his poetry "is to be transcendent and new; it is to be indirect and not direct or descriptive or epic." As for the form of poems, they are to be "organic," evolving free metrical patterns "as unerringly and loosely as lilacs or roses on a bush." And it is significant that Whitman uses the phrase "poems or music or oration or recitation," because his poems often have a musical structure—so much so that sometimes we can follow the patterns of aria and recitative in his poetry as Whitman had learned them from the Italian operas he loved so well. And he thinks too that the poem is in a sense an oration, meant to be "sung" or declaimed; Whitman was in fact a would-be orator and made several attemps to become a public speaker or lecturer.

It is clear that the Bible had a deep influence on Whitman's style. The opening lines of "Song of Myself" are:

I celebrate myself, and sing myself,
And what I assume you shall assume,
For every atom belonging to me as good
    belongs to you.

I loafe and invite my soul,
I lean and loafe at my ease observing a spear
    of summer grass.

If we compare this with any of the innumerable passages from the Bible—say Psalm 8—we see one of the main origins of Whitman's mode of versification.

What is man, that thou art mindful of him?
    And the son of man, that thou visitest
    him?

For thou hast made him a little lower than
    the angels, and hast crowned him with
    glory and honor.

Thou madest him to have dominion over the
    works of thy hands; thou hast put all
    things under his feet.

Characteristically, Whitman's "organic" style, like that of Hebrew poetry, is based on the device of "parallelism." His rhythms are those of repetition—of word, image, or idea—and counterbalance of phrases and lines. His poems proceed through cycles of statement and restatement, the restatement providing the poem with momentum because it not only restates but at the same time amplifies, modulates, or qualifies what has been said and prepares us, it may be, for the next rhythmic cycle.

There is no tightly knit overall structure to "Song of Myself." But in general the "plot" of the poem can be called the gradual universalization of the self. The first four sections present the leading themes and motifs of the piece, make a personal statement about the age and health of the poet (although this was not in the first edition), proclaim the poet's freedom from all "creeds and schools," affirm the elusiveness and yet the autonomy of the self, which is "a mystery" not to be discovered by mere "trippers and askers" and yet is

Sure as the most certain sure, plumb in the
    uprights, well entretied, braced in the
    beams,
Stout as a horse, affectionate, haughty,
    electrical.

From the very beginning the poem assumes a dialogue form, as is suitable for a prophet-poet, by addressing "you"—that is, any man or woman in a perfectly equalitarian life (of which the leaves of grass are the general symbol). The tone is both that of the potential lover and that of the teacher.

In section 5, the "plot" of the poem begins. Here the self is imagined to be engaged in a dialogue with itself, as the soul might be imagined to be in dialogue with the body. The emotion evoked is quite frankly autoerotic and this emotion leads Whitman to one of his most beautiful statements of his feeling of being in harmony with all of nature:

. . . a kelson of the creation is love,
And limitless are leaves stiff or drooping in
    the fields,
And brown ants in the little wells beneath
    them,

And mossy scabs of the worm fence, heap'd
   stones, elder, mullein, and poke-weed.

From this point, though by no means in a straight or continuous line, all "goes onward and outward" (see the end of section 6) in the poem, until toward the end, the identification of the self not only with the nation and with all mankind but with the immortal and the divine—"the great Camerado"—is affirmed. The poem develops into a rhapsody celebrating the democratic life, the fecund creativity of the self, and a benign universe in which death is overcome by a kind of maternal process of reincarnation. This accords well with the Preface and its announced program for the poet as prophet and seer.

But if this were all the poem did, it would be merely one of the better of Whitman's many affirmative and optimistic poem-prophecies, instead of the truly great poem it is. For one thing it is in American literature the first truly *modern* poem. It repudiated the conventional genteel and romantic poetry of Whitman's day and in doing so (it is not too much to say) made modern poetry possible. For although the poem is not "realistic," its assumption is the modern one, that all of experience, and not just what which is innately "poetic" or "proper," is available to poetry. Whitman's other main contribution to modernism—that of bringing a persistent prose element into the lyric style—helped him to give to "Song of Myself" a sense of the immediacy of experience. For example, in lines like

The blab of the pave, tires of carts, sluff of
   boot-soles, talk of the promenaders,
The heavy omnibus, the driver with his
    interrogating thumb, the clank of the
    shod horses on the granite floor,

poetry discovered a hitherto little treated subject, the city. In lines like the following we find what later came to be called imagist poetry:

The little one sleeps in its cradle,
I lift the gauze and look a long time, and
    silently brush away flies with my hand.

The youngster and the red-faced girl turn
    aside up the bushy hill,
I peeringly view them from the top.

The suicide sprawls on the bloody floor of the
    bedroom,
I witness the corpse with its dabbled hair, I
    note where the pistol has fallen.

But it is not only its modernity that makes "Song of Myself" important. There is also the comic quality of the poem. For the happy fact is that Whitman was unable to maintain the high moralistic or "Emersonian" tone he sought to maintain. A purely lawless gaiety and upwelling wit find their way into "Song of Myself." Retrospectively reading Whitman's definition of prophecy which occurs in a tribute to Carlyle in *Specimen Days*, we are not surprised at this. "The word prophecy," he writes, "is much misused; it seems narrow'd to prediction merely. That is not the main sense of the Hebrew word translated 'prophet'; it means one whose mind bubbles and pours forth like a fountain, from inner divine spontaneities revealing God. . . . The great matter is to reveal and outpour the God-like suggestions pressing for birth in the soul." We are not surprised to find that in "Song of Myself" many such inner divine spontaneities have revealed themselves; nor are we surprised that such lawless impulses do not always accord with, and in fact often gaily or whimsically subvert, the moralizing poet who is supposed to be "the most equable of men." The comic tone of the poem, which in the end all but takes command, begins perhaps at section 20, where, after talking rather too long about "the clean-hair'd Yankee girl" who "works with her sewing machine" and what seems like half the rest of the population of the United States, Whitman suddenly asks,

Who goes there? hankering, gross, mystical, nude . . . ?

As I have said elsewhere in writing about Whitman, "Whoever he is, he is not in a position to utter morality." At this point the poem takes on a new vitality and richness. The poet seems liberated from a moral requirement and begins to reveal and outpour what is really pressing for expression. "Speech," which is the "twin of my vision," provokes him by saying *Walt, you contain enough, why don't you let it out then?*" Doubtless it will depend on one's own sense of what humor is how far one is prepared to respond to "Song of Myself" as a comic poem (although Constance Rourke long ago described it as such in her *American Humor*). But many readers are bound to be drawn to a poet who suddenly exclaims, "Hurrah for positive science! long live exact demonstration," who says with racy insouciance,

Unscrew the locks from the doors!
Unscrew the doors themselves from their
    jambs!

or who can with grave and whimsical astonishment observe, perhaps after reading an article on evolution,

I find I incorporate gneiss, coal, long-threaded
    moss, fruits, grains, esculent roots,
And am stucco'd with quadrupeds and birds
    all over.

Sometimes, to be sure, it is difficult to know whether one is laughing *at* Whitman or *with* him. What, for example, of a line like "Partaker of influx and efflux I"? At any rate, I think we are laughing (if we laugh at all) *with*

Whitman most of the time and certainly when he suddenly announces in section 44 (the seventh inning of the poem, as it were): "It is time to explain myself—let us stand up."

As in all comedy there is in "Song of Myself" an ever renewed sense of incongruity. For it is not true as D. H. Lawrence, Santayana, and many others have charged that Whitman has no sense of incongruity or paradox, that he is capable only of a mystic or pantheistic tendency to "merge" with all things. He does not in his best poems allow his identity to be absorbed into the mere chaotic flux of experience. He is a poet, as he tells us near the beginning of "Song of Myself," who is "both in and out of the game and watching and wondering at it." He is a poet whose words are "reminders" of "life untold, and of freedom and extrication." And indeed the recurring motif of "Song of Myself" is the identification of the self with other selves, often highly incongruous ones, followed by the extrication of the self from its momentarily assumed identity. This repeated dialectic act, or assumption and rejection of masks, accounts for much of the inner brilliance and wit—which as anyone can see is *not* simply boisterous humor—of "Song of Myself." In his inferior poetry Whitman loses his capacity to think of the self as being in a dialectic tension with the not-self, and he loses his comic muse. I do not of course mean that Whitman's greatness rests solely in his capacity for comic effects. But I think there is more truth and self-understanding than at first meets the eye in his remark to his Camden friends in 1889: "I pride myself in being a real humorist underneath everything else."

Before leaving the discussion of Whitman's comedy, one should at least note that according to Constance Rourke the native American humor has two sides to it. It is not only aggressively and uninhibitedly assertive; often it modulates into meditative or even elegiac solil-oquy. This tone is well woven into the great last lines of "Song of Myself" with their ex-quisite and more than a little artificial wit:

The spotted hawk swoops by and accuses me,
　　he complains of my gab and my loitering.

I too am not a bit tamed, I too am
　　untranslatable,
I sound my barbaric yawp over the roofs of
　　the world.

The last scud of day holds back for me,
It flings my likeness after the rest and true as
　　any on the shadow'd wilds,
It coaxes me to the vapor and the dusk.

I depart as air, I shake my white locks at the
　　runaway sun,
I effuse my flesh in eddies, and drift it in lacy
　　jags.

I bequeath myself to the dirt to grow from the
　　grass I love,
If you want me again look for me under your
　　boot-soles.

You will hardly know who I am or what I
　　mean,
But I shall be good health to you nevertheless,
And filter and fibre your blood.

Failing to fetch me at first keep encouraged,
Missing me one place search another,
I stop somewhere waiting for you.

　　The democratic en-masse whom Whitman addressed and celebrated failed spectacularly to purchase the first edition of *Leaves of Grass*. It went virtually unread except by a few lit-erary people to whom Whitman sent copies; it received few favorable reviews, among them one or two Whitman wrote himself. And it would be, in fact, several years and several editions later before Whitman began to acquire a reputation, here and abroad—it was in Eu-rope that Whitman found some of his earliest sympathetic readers and it is an open question whether to this day he has not always been better appreciated abroad than at home. And even in his Washington and Camden years, when he did begin to be widely known in his own country, he was known more as the public figure and the prophet than as the poet he ac-tually was. Time was required to dispel the early notoriety of Whitman's poetry, which was damned as incomprehensible and obscene, and bring real understanding. One important ex-ception among the readers of the 1855 edition was Emerson, and his enthusiastic letter, in which he wrote "I greet you at the beginning of a great career" and expressed a desire to meet the poet, must have given the disap-pointed Whitman much solace. At any rate, Whitman published, in what some of the new poems show to be a rather defiant mood, a second edition in 1856. The book was spon-sored by Fowler and Wells, publishers of books on phrenology, a "science" in which Whitman was much interested. There were thirty-two poems and an appendix containing favorable reviews of the first edition, Emerson's letter, and an open reply to Emerson.

　　Of some significance is the fact that in the two outstanding poems of the new edition—"Song of the Open Road" and "Crossing Brook-lyn Ferry"—the self is conceived, as in so much of Whitman's later poetry, as being in motion. In "Song of Myself" the self stood confident and "aplomb in the midst of irra-tional things." Whitman has begun to lose his sense of the perfect and arrogant autonomy of the self, and now sends it on pilgrimages and voyages whose destination, it must be ad-mitted, is not always clear. "Song of the Open Road" is a kind of American version of the medieval allegories of the itinerary of the soul to God and a forerunner of all those later American writers, from Dos Passos and Robert

Penn Warren to Saul Bellow, who have written of the American "on the road." The poem's main virtue is its exuberance and its bracing apostrophe to the free spirit and the free will. One does not even mind the dubious French:

Allons! with power, liberty, the earth, the
    elements,
Health, defiance, gayety, self-esteem, curiosity;
Allons! from all formules!
From your formules, O bat-eyed and materi-
    alistic priests.

The weakness of the poem is that it does not find an imagery adequate to the emotions invoked. Whitman hails "You objects that call from diffusion my meanings and give them shape" but he does not capture enough of these objects in a recognizable structure.

"Crossing Brooklyn Ferry" is one of Whitman's most successful poems, more of a unity, surely, though less ambitious than the most notable poem that derives from it, Hart Crane's "The Bridge." There is nothing of the comic spirit of "Song of Myself" in "Crossing Brooklyn Ferry," or of the excessive assertions of "Song of the Open Road." The mood is meditative and purely lyric. But Whitman's theme is his familiar one: the mystery of identity. Whitman muses on the paradox of individuality, which is at once different from and a part of the flux of nature ("I too have been struck from the float forever held in solution") and which is at once different from and a part of society, represented here by the small world of people momentarily gathered on the ferry. Whitman's assertions about the simple, separate person and the en-masse are here modulated into a quietly beautiful statement of faith in an ordered, harmonious, and benign universe. Union, harmony, and order are well symbolized by the repeated journeys of the ferry, by the ebb and flow of the tides, and by other "similitudes of the past and the fu-

ture," such as "the fine centrifugal spokes of light round the shape of my head in the sunlit water" and by "the slow-wheeling circles" the sea gulls make in the sky.

Any poem, and particularly one by a poet like Whitman, is likely to be given depth and authenticity if the poet is able to question or doubt himself, whether ironically or by candid admission. The self-doubting, self-proving quality is entirely missing from a poem like "Song of the Open Road," but in section 6 of "Crossing Brooklyn Ferry" Whitman admits that both he and his poems are a mixture of the good and the bad:

The best I had done seem'd to me blank and
    suspicious . . .
I am he who knew what it was to be evil,
I too knitted the old knot of contrariety.

But it is Whitman's success in finding related symbols for his subject that ensures the success of "Crossing Brooklyn Ferry." The "dumb, beautiful ministers," as he calls the images he sees, "furnish" their "parts" not only "toward eternity" and "toward the soul" but toward the completed form of the poem. One may readily agree with Thoreau that "Song of Myself" and "Crossing Brooklyn Ferry" are the best of Whitman's early poems.

The 1856 edition of *Leaves of Grass* had hardly more public success than the 1855, and Whitman returned to newspaper work, becoming the editor of the Brooklyn *Times*. But he was again able to respond to disappointment by making new plans for his poetry. In 1857 we find him jotting notes on "the great construction of the new Bible. Not to be diverted from the principle object—the main life. . . . It ought to be ready in 1859." This suggests not only that Whitman was determined to go on as a poet but that he had worked out in his mind at least a general plan for the poetical "Bible" *Leaves of Grass* eventually became. Outwardly Whitman would seem to have continued to be self-confident during the years immediately before the third edition of *Leaves of Grass*, which appeared in 1860. He had a respectable job, and he had taken up an apparently convivial social life with the more or less bohemian patrons of Pfaff's beer cellar. William Dean Howells remembered having seen him there on one occasion playing the lion to a group of young men. In shaking hands, Whitman had reached out his hand "to me," says Howells, "as if he were going to give it to me for good and all."

But was all as well with Whitman as it seemed to be? The 1860 edition of the poems contains "Out of the Cradle Endlessly Rocking" and "As I Ebb'd with the Ocean of Life" —two of his finest poems, to be sure, but reflecting a profound melancholy and self-doubt. The fact that the 1860 edition contained the "Calamus" poems and that parts, at least, of "Out of the Cradle" may be read as a dirge for a lost love leads to the supposition that Whitman had found and lost a male lover and that this loss had been a tragedy to him but had released the creative emotions, so different from those in "Song of Myself," which characterize his elegiac mood. This must remain a supposition, however, since the evidence to corroborate or refute it is lacking.

There can be no doubt, at least, that the homosexual overtones of the "Calamus" poems sound far more authentic emotionally than do the heterosexual expostulations of the "Children of Adam" poems which also appeared in this edition. Although the "Children of Adam" group apparently struck Emerson as being too sexual (for he spent an afternoon on Boston Common trying to argue Whitman out of publishing them), they are actually "sexual" only in intention. Whitman is utterly unable to speak of heterosexual love except as a remote abstraction—an inability which led D. H. Lawrence to exclaim "Oh, beautiful generalization! Oh, biological function! 'Athletic mothers of these States —' Muscles and wombs. They needn't have had faces at all."

But the "Calamus" poems, if not among Whitman's best, are at least emotionally convincing and, in the calamus leaves, the phallic calamus root, the dark waters of the pond, the "paths untrodden," Whitman finds images appropriate to the emotion. These are, we are told, the poet's most intimate utterances:

Here the frailest leaves of me and yet my
    strongest lasting,
Here I shade and hide my thoughts, I myself
    do not expose them,
And yet they expose me more than all my
    other poems.

The love spoken of in a poem like "Whoever You Are Holding Me Now in Hand" is not merely abstract. It is tender, yet arduous and dangerous.

I give you fair warning before you attempt
    me further,
I am not what you supposed but far
    different. . . .
The way is suspicious, the result uncertain,
    perhaps destructive.

It is furtive and timorous:

Or else by stealth in some wood for trial,
Or back of a rock in the open air. . . .
Here to put your lips upon mine I permit you,
With the comrade's long-dwelling kiss or the
    new husband's kiss,
For I am the new husband and I am the
    comrade.

Death, one of Whitman's essential themes, is strongly felt in a poem like "Scented Herbage of My Breast":

Yet you are beautiful to me you faint tinged
    roots, you make me think of death,

Death is beautiful from you (what indeed is
    finally beautiful except death and love?)
O I think it is not for life I am chanting here
    my chant of lovers, I think it must be for
    death.

The tenderness and yet the danger of comradely love, or "adhesiveness," as Whitman
calls it, using a phrenological word, are better
expressed and more convincing in the personal
and confessional "Calamus" poems than is the
"political" assertion of some of the others that
comradely love is the basis (apparently the
only basis as we would gather from "I Hear
It Was Charged against Me") of a new democratic society. A more than slightly false ring
emanates from lines like "I believe the main
purport of these States is to found a superb
friendship, exalté, previously unknown" and
so on.

    "Out of the Cradle" is one of Whitman's
most complex and beautiful poems. In form
it somewhat resembles an opera, beginning
with a rich overture in which the themes are
stated and the mood evoked.

Out of the cradle endlessly rocking,
Out of the mocking-bird's throat, the musical
    shuttle,
Out of the Ninth-month midnight,
Over the sterile sands and the fields beyond,
    where the child leaving his bed wander'd
    alone, bareheaded, barefoot,
Down from the shower'd halo,
Up from the mystic play of shadows twining
    and twisting as if they were alive
Out from the patches of briers and
    blackberries,
From the memories of the bird that chanted
    to me,
From your memories sad brother, from the
    fitful risings and fallings I heard,
From under that yellow half-moon late-risen
    and swollen as if with tears,

From those beginning notes of yearning and
    love there in the mist,
From the thousand responses of my heart
    never to cease,
From the myriad thence-arous'd words,
From the word stronger and more delicious
    than any,
From such as now they start the scene
    revisiting,
As a flock, twittering, rising, or overhead
    passing,
Borne hither, ere all eludes me, hurriedly,
A man, yet by these tears a little boy again,
Throwing myself on the sand, confronting the
    waves,
I, chanter of pains and joys, uniter of here and
    hereafter,
Taking all hints to use them, but swiftly
    leaping beyond them,
A reminiscence sing.

This is followed by passages of recitative and
aria. One may note, however, that the finale
by no means matches the overture in symphonic complexity, being comparatively muted
and, despite the suggestive images of the bird,
the sea, and the old crone rocking the cradle,
relatively downright and matter-of-fact in tone.
The conclusion is a short recessional rather
than a finale.

    The main theme of "Out of the Cradle,"
although it does not exhaust the meanings of
the poem, is the origin of the poet's genius.
Whitman asks for and receives from the sea
a "clew" or "word," and we are led to understand that his poetic genius originated in childhood and its first intuition of the alienation
and loss which are the lot of all beings and
which culminate in death. "Out of the Cradle,"
then, is a poem about the origin of poetry and
to this extent resembles certain books of Wordsworth's *Prelude*. If this is not clear from the
poem itself, we have as guideposts the two

earlier titles Whitman gave to it: "A Child's Reminiscence" and "A Word Out of the Sea." Is Whitman right in tracing the origin of his poetry as he does? Surely he is only half right, for the world of experience posited in "Out of the Cradle," whether in its origin or its expressed form, is not that of "Song of Myself."

But if the main theme of the poem is clear, it is not so clear what else, if anything, the poem means. Is it, as is often said, an "organic" poem, affirming a whole view of reality in which life and death or love and death are understood as compensatory parts of a living universal rhythm? One's objection to this opinion might be based on any number of perceptions about the poem. For example, is the "old crone" who rocks the cradle at the end of the poem a benign mother, ushering new life, spiritual or otherwise, into being? One might think so at first, but what of the rather obvious ambivalence the poet feels toward this "old crone" with her "sweet garments"? Shrouds can be sweet, and we are probably not engaging in a too ingenious mode of interpretation if we conjecture that at a different level of meaning that cradle is distinctly coffin-like. Many of Whitman's poems do assert an organic universe and an immortal and universal rhythm of life, but "Out of the Cradle" is not one of them. And in fact the quality of experience conveyed by this poem—the experience, we are told, out of which poetry is born —involves love without an object, it involves anxiety, alienation, insoluble contradiction, and ultimate despair, a despair not assuaged by the sentimental resignation with which it is embraced.

The illusion of a universe in which opposites and contradictions are reconciled is sustained only at the very beginning of the poem. There the "musical shuttle" out of "the mocking-bird's throat" draws into a unity that which is "down" and that which is "up":

Down from the shower'd halo,
Up from the mystic play of shadows twining
    and twisting as if they were alive. . . .

And at the beginning of the poem the poet can confidently speak of himself as the "chanter of pains and joys, uniter of here and hereafter." The feeling of reconciliation and harmony rises to an early pitch in the aria of the two birds:

> *Shine! shine shine!*
> *Pour down your warmth, great sun!*
> *While we bask, we two together.*

But the illusion of unity and continuity is not sustained, or is sustained only fitfully, after this aria. For now the she-bird has suddenly disappeared, and the he-bird sings his melancholy dirge, pouring out meanings, as Whitman says, "which I of all men know."

A reader mindful of Whitman's love of melodrama, of which he encountered plenty in his favorite Italian operas, will find the first ominous note in this ominous poem in the "surging of the sea," for this surging is described as "hoarse," and although we may see nothing necessarily frightening in this at first, the context of the poem forces us to remember that ghosts and other demonic creatures are often said to speak with a hoarse and sepulchral voice. Even the "white arms out in the breakers tirelessly tossing" which Whitman recalls seeing during the childhood experience he is recapturing or re-creating do not seem on reflection to be so attractive and winsome as they do at first. There is something threatening, something beyond human control, something suggestive of a universe indifferent to human destiny, in that tireless tossing. Or perhaps there is something merely suggestive of death, for the arms of a corpse in the sea might toss tirelessly.

The object of love is now unattainable,

though there is still the compulsion to pursue it in panic and madness, a pursuit now seen as an activity of nature itself:

> *O madly the sea pushes upon the land,*
> *With love, with love.*

And whereas the white and black were once held together in a unison,

> *Two together!*
> *Winds blow south, or winds blow north,*
> *Day come white, or night come black,*

they are now seen in opposition:

> *What is that little black thing I see there in*
>   *the white?*

The song of the he-bird rises to a pitch of desperate assertion:

> *Shake out carols!*
> *Solitary here, the night's carols!*
> *Carols of lonesome love! death's carols!*
> *Carols under that lagging, yellow, waning*
>   *moon!*
> *O under that moon where she droops almost*
>   *down into the sea!*
> *O reckless despairing carols.*

And finally the song recedes into a resigned reminiscence of what used to be: *"We two together no more."*

Although we hear "the aria sinking," "all else" continues; the stars shine, the winds blow, the notes of the bird echo. But "all else" does not continue in a compensatory or organic harmony. Instead the world has fallen apart. There is no object for "the love in the heart long pent" even though it is "now loose, now at last tumultuously bursting." This is a world characterized by loss and alienation—not presided over by a benign Great Mother, as Whitman of all poets might have wished, but haunted and agitated by the "angry moans" of the "fierce old mother incessantly moan-

ing." Through the fissures of a disjoined world there enter the demonic powers always drawn upon by the imagination of melodrama. Does the boy, the poet-to-be, receive comforting and joyous answers to his questions about his destiny? Far from it:

> The undertone, the savage old mother
>   incessantly crying,
> To the boy's soul's questions sullenly timing,
>   some drown'd secret hissing,
> To the outsetting bard.

At this point the bird is addressed as "demon or bird," and it seems impossible not to take "demon" in both of its usual meanings: the poetic genius and a sinister emanation from some unknown realm. The latter meaning is confirmed by the imagery that occurs a little later in the poem, where the bird is called a messenger, as if from some infernal place:

> The messenger there arous'd, the fire, the sweet
>   hell within,
> The unknown want, the destiny of me.

Perhaps it is also confirmed by the still later phrase "my dusky demon and brother."

The language and imagery in which "Out of the Cradle" culminates, whether we are thinking of the fivefold invocation to death, the dusky demon, or the old crone, do not, it must be clear, reflect a world of pain assuaged, contradictions reconciled, and disruptive powers placated. Nor does the poem assert that poetry originates in such a world—quite the contrary. "Out of the Cradle" is more unflinching, more uncompromising, more extreme in its perception of disorder and anxiety than its critics have seen, although these critics would readily perceive the same qualities in the works of other American writers of dark imagination, such as Poe, Hawthorne, and Melville.

"As I Ebb'd with the Ocean of Life" is a powerful dirge on the inability of man to understand the universe or to convince himself that finally the self has any more substance, stability, and form than the "chaff, straw, splinters of wood, weeds, and the sea-gluten" which the sea casts up and which the poet contemplates as he dejectedly walks along the beach. Here he is not even sure, as he was in "Out of the Cradle," that man can be a struggling, creative being; in this poem he seems to be a mere "castaway," a "little wash'd up drift/ A few sands and dead leaves." But like "Out of the Cradle," this poem derives its power both from the sheer lyric beauty of the lines and from an inner contradiction, this time furnished by an ironic self-regard:

O baffled, balk'd, bent to the very earth,
Oppress'd with myself that I have dared to
    open my mouth,
Aware now that amid all that blab whose
    echoes recoil up me I have not once had
    the least idea who or what I am,
But that before all my arrogant poems the real
    Me stands yet untouch'd, untold,
    altogether unreach'd,
Withdrawn far, mocking me with mock-
    congratulatory signs and bows,
With peals of distant ironical laughter at every
    word I have written,
Pointing in silence to these songs, and then to
    the sand beneath.

The nadir of despondency reflected in these lines seems not to have lasted very long, and by 1861 with the coming of the war and its accompanying excitement, Whitman gradually entered on his later years of at least partial public acceptance and even fame. He was destined to write only a few more first-rate poems, though he wrote many that were good and a great many that were bad. But he was able to find increasing satisfaction in his mode of life, his private and public activities, and in his

notoriety. The war came as a kind of tonic to Whitman, as we can see from the vigor and excitement of the *Drum-Taps* group of poems, which he began to write in 1861. He thought of the war as promising a spiritual regeneration to the country, for he had become increasingly disillusioned with the national political and moral condition in the years that followed his time of active politicking in Brooklyn. And he saw in the war a new challenge and opportunity for the poet who was also a patriot-phophet.

In 1862 Whitman embarked upon his Washington years. He went to Virginia in December of that year to be with his brother George, who had been wounded at Fredericksburg. He had already begun to make a sort of career out of his propensity for being a "wound dresser" and hospital visitor by paying calls to injured stage and horsecar drivers whom he knew in New York. Now he decided to settle in Washington in order to bring some cheer to the wounded soldiers in the improvised and ill-staffed hospitals there. During these years "Walt Whitman, a kosmos, of Manhattan the son" became more fatherly, and he was a familiar and welcome sight in the wards, where he brought gifts and comfort to the soldiers, after his day's work in one of several government offices where he found employment.

It was in Washington, too, that a Walt Whitman movement of sorts began to take shape at the instigation of a small group of admirers like John Burroughs, William O'Connor, and Eldridge, Whitman's onetime Boston publisher. Although this admiration, often amounting to the adoration of disciple for master, must have been comforting to a neglected poet and undoubtedly resulted finally in a wider acceptance of his poetry, the effects were not all good. It seems clear that many of Whitman's avid supporters and disciples in these and later years were interested in him as a kind of messiah, or at least as a prophet with a program for democracy, spirituality, "cosmic consciousness," and one thing and another. This perhaps tended to alienate Whitman from his own best genius and to confirm in him the self-publicist that from the beginning had never been bashful about proclaiming the greatness of Walt Whitman.

Whitman published *Drum-Taps* in 1865, and later a sequel that included "When Lilacs Last in the Dooryard Bloom'd." Yet with the exception of the lilacs poem it is hard to agree with the poet when he says that these poems are better than anything he had previously written. There is some truth in the review by the youthful Henry James (a most unfair review on the whole, as James later admitted), with its complaint that the *Drum-Taps* poems are the product of a "prolonged muscular strain." There is indeed more heat than light, more willfulness than beauty in the poet's martial and hortatory utterances. But a poem such as the well-known "Cavalry Crossing the Ford" is a highly successful piece of imagist picture-drawing. And elegiac pieces, like "Reconciliation" and "As I Lay with My Head in Your Lap, Camerado," have a fine lyric quality.

There is more than a little theatricality and a kind of muffled melodrama about "When Lilacs Last in the Dooryard Bloom'd," with its two mysterious "companions" whom the poet calls "the knowledge of death" and "the thought of death" and who accompany him in his ritual retreat

Down to the shores of the water, the path by
  the swamp in the dimness,
To the solemn shadowy cedars and ghostly
  pines so still.

The purpose of this withdrawal is to praise death, the ultimate democracy, which Whitman does in a mood of hushed consecration:

Come lovely and soothing death,
Undulate round the world, serenely
  arriving, arriving,
In the day, in the night, to all, to each,
Sooner or later delicate death.

And then, although death is called a "dark mother" it is presented more like a bride.

What saves the poem from mere mysticism is of course the symbols: the "powerful western fallen star" standing for the assassinated Lincoln, the lilac signifying rebirth or resurrection, and the hidden bird signifying as in "Out of the Cradle" the poet and the power of poetry. These symbols are brought into a unity which, if not perfect, is adequate to Whitman's purposes.

Reflecting on the mystical invocation to death and the poet's attention to his own emotions, we may well ask: why doesn't the poem say something about Lincoln, especially in view of the fact that Whitman had often seen the President and was later to complain, in *Specimen Days*, that none of the portraits he had seen truly caught Lincoln's real appearance and quality? Not that an elegist is necessarily bound to paint a portrait, but from one's reading of the traditional elegies of Europe, such as Milton's "Lycidas," one would expect to hear more about the fame, honor, and accomplishments of the dead man than the phrase "the sweetest, wisest soul of all my days and lands" that the poet puts in at the last possible moment. Nor, except for the passing vignettes, such as the people mourning at the depots as the coffin journeys westward, is there a coherent sense of the kind of society Lincoln lived in—and this again is at odds with the traditional elegy. The poet who comes to pay tribute to the dead President pays tribute instead to death itself. We have here what may be called (if with some hesitation) an American form of elegy—a kind of lyric melodrama in which everything personal, except the loneliness of the poet, is made abstract and impersonal and in which a mourning society is seen, not as any specific *kind* of society, but only on the one hand as fragmented groups of people and on the other as an abstraction. But this is perhaps to forget what is more important, the rare poetic qualities of Whitman's language:

When lilacs last in the dooryard bloom'd,
And the great star early droop'd in the western
   sky in the night,
I mourn'd, and yet shall mourn with
   ever-returning spring.

Ever-returning spring, trinity sure to me you
   bring,
Lilac blooming perennial and drooping star in
   the west,
And thought of him I love.

Although he would recapture it momentarily in brief lyrics, Whitman had made the last great utterance of his elegiac-meditative powers in "When Lilacs Last in the Dooryard Bloom'd." Nor would he again be able to use as successfully as he had in the years between 1855 and 1860 his sense of the tensions and contradictions involved in the drama of the self. These, rather than his "philosophy," are the true sources of his best genius. Readers who overemphasize Whitman's "philosophy" find in later poems like "Passage to India" (1868) an advance over "Song of Myself" because, so the argument goes, the poet has learned to free himself of preoccupation with the merely (merely!) private self and to write on universal philosophic, political, moral, and "cosmic" themes. But Whitman's weakness was not his penchant for writing about the private self and the realities it encounters. On the contrary, that is his source of strength, and his weakness is his penchant for "philosophy" (of

which he had none in any precise sense), as we understand when we perceive that it led his mind to become so increasingly prone to rhapsodies celebrating a vague, homogenized, "democratic" universe which could exist nowhere and contain no one.

This does not mean that there aren't many interesting poems in the later editions of *Leaves of Grass* in the sections that Whitman labeled "Whispers of Heavenly Death," "Songs of Parting," "Sands at Seventy," and "Good-Bye My Fancy," nor that there aren't many early poems, not discussed in the present essay, that repay study. Quite apart from the great poems there remain such fine things as "There Was a Child Went Forth," "To a Locomotive in Winter," "A Noiseless Patient Spider," "The Base of All Metaphysics," "Song of the Redwood Tree," "On the Beach, at Night," "Sparkles from the Wheel," "Prayer for Columbus," and "The Dalliance of Eagles."

In 1871, before Whitman left Washington, he published *Democratic Vistas*, in which, along with the 1855 Preface and parts of *Specimen Days* (1882), is to be found much of his best prose (although the thorough reader will want to go on to things like "A Backward Glance o'er Travel'd Roads," the letters, and, for those especially interested in Whitman's ideas about the nature and origins of poetic language, "Slang in America" and *An American Primer*). *Democratic Vistas* is Whitman's most considerable pronouncement on social and cultural issues. In this eloquent work we see a writer who still clings to his own spiritualized or transcendentalized version of the Jeffersonian-Jacksonian credo and applies it to the spectacle of the Grant administration days at the outset of the Gilded Age. Most of what he sees he does not like, and readers who suppose Whitman to be a mere mindless celebrant of democracy are always surprised at the vituperation and satire of some of the passages of *Democratic Vistas*. For example, we find Whitman attacking the "dry, flat Sahara" of American life. He thinks that "society, in these States, is canker'd, crude, superstitious, and rotten" and that there is "more hollowness of heart" in his countrymen than ever before. "The depravity of the business classes" is matched only by the decadence of "fashionable life," in which he sees only "flippancy, tepid amours, weak infidelism, small aims, or no aims at all." Like Howells, Mark Twain, and Henry Adams, Whitman believed that in the postwar period something heroic and aspiring, as well as a certain honesty, plainness, and purposefulness, had been lost from American life.

As was noted above Whitman had long before 1871 given up his active interest in politics, and in fact the *Vistas* is not, except indirectly, a political diatribe. It is not in the tradition of Marxism, but follows, in its highly characteristic way, the tradition of social prophecy that includes Coleridge, Ruskin, Arnold, and Morris. It seeks to get at political and social realities through observations on culture, on manners and morals, on spiritual qualities, and on literature and the place of the writer in society. Unlike Tocqueville, who saw forty years earlier that the real danger in a democracy is not too much disunity and rebellion but too much centralization and conformity, Whitman is worried by the chaos and fragmentation of American life (of course one must remember that this would be easy to feel at the time Whitman wrote) and urges that "the quality today most needed" is "more compaction and more moral identity." He does not tell us how this is to come about, except by his old formula according to which the freer and more individual the individual is the more identity he will feel with the en-masse. One is moved to ask Whitman precisely what kind of and what degree of institutional mediation is needed between the individual and society so that each may continue to exist but be protected from the other. On this score, we get no answer from Whitman.

We might well expect, however, that the author of "Song of Myself" would have something of value to say about the self in *Democratic Vistas*. And in fact his presentation of "personalism," as he calls it, is very striking. Whitman's intuition of the value of the self he expresses as follows: "There is, in sanest hours, a consciousness, a thought that rises, independent, lifted out from all else, calm, like the stars, shining eternal. This is the thought of identity—yours for you, whoever you are, as mine for me. Miracle of miracles, beyond statement, most spiritual and vaguest of earth's dreams, yet hardest basic fact, and only entrance to all facts." True, Whitman thinks of the self as a moral or perhaps metaphysical entity, without referring it to its own history or, in any concrete way, to its existence in society. And a basic weakness of *Democratic Vistas*, shared by many other nineteenth century writings of the sort, is its unquestioning belief in progress, its lack of an objective sense of history and of an understanding of society as the locus of evolving institutions. "Society," for Whitman, remains an abstraction or a feeling of "adhesive" love of comrades. History is apparently a benign and maternal process which, now that "feudalism" (that is, everything that happened before 1776) has been transcended, can be counted on not to confront man with tragic or insoluble dilemmas. But although Whitman's optimism and his fundamentally non-historical view of things do not accord very well with our twentieth-century realism, we must still agree that in any humane society "personalism" will always be the "hardest basic fact, and only entrance to all facts." To have asserted that this is so is doubtless the main glory of *Democratic Vistas*.

With some accuracy Whitman described *Specimen Days* as perhaps the "most wayward, spontaneous, fragmentary book ever printed." It is an uneven book, much devoted to reminiscence and to random thoughts on nature, men, and ideas. It has three main parts: a short introductory section devoted to memories of the writer's youth and family background; a section of notes and jottings descriptive of his activities during the war; and a third section of nature observation and *pensées* on things in general. The first section is disappointingly sketchy and one wonders anew why so professedly autobiographical a writer should say so little about himself, but there is interest in his memories of his family and in his notes on "My Passion for Ferries," "Broadway Sights," "Omnibus Jaunts and Drivers," "Plays and Operas Too," and one retains the picture of the young Whitman frolicking on the Long Island beaches (Coney Island!) and declaiming "Homer or Shakespeare to the surf and sea-gulls by the hour."

The section on the Civil War days, terse (for Whitman) notations and sketches of the battles and the soldiers he recalls, is perhaps the most valuable part of *Specimen Days* and constitutes one of the most distinguished contributions to the strangely small body of distinguished writing about the war. It takes its place with Stephen Crane's *The Red Badge of Courage*, J. W. De Forest's *Miss Ravenel's Conversion from Secession to Loyalty*, Ambrose Bierce's sketches and tales, and Melville's poems collected in *Battle-Pieces*. In the latter pages of the book the reflections upon Carlyle, Poe, and Emerson stand out vividly, as do some of the less artificial descriptions of nature—these last especially intended, as the author says, "to bring people back from their persistent straying and sickly abstractions, to the costless average, divine, original concrete."

The impulse to get back to nature which we notice in *Specimen Days* was incident to Whitman's gradually failing powers. He had been in uncertain health ever since February of 1873, when, after sitting at his office desk in the Treasury Building (reading a novel by Bulwer-Lytton), he had returned to his room at night and sustained his first paralytic shock. He made a slow recovery from this attack, but after resuming his work for a brief time, he left Washington for good and settled with his brother George in Camden, N.J. Here he lived as a semi-invalid until 1884, when he moved into a small house of his own on Mickle Street. He devoted himself as before to writing poems, to planning new revised editions of *Leaves of Grass*, to ferry and horsecar riding when he was able to make his lamed left leg function well enough so that he could get out. Occasionally he gave lectures (a favorite was one on Lincoln) and readings. During the summers he stayed at Timber Creek with a farming family. In his late years he had become world famous, and not only did he gather about him a new group of local admirers and disciples (notably Horace Traubel, a young socialist lawyer); he also received eminent visitors from abroad, including Sir Henry Irving, Edmund Gosse, and Oscar Wilde. He was visited by scores of unknown pilgrims, including a Mrs. Gilchrist, a widow with two children, who left the Pre-Raphaelite circles she frequented in England and came to America with the professed intention of marrying the poet whose writings had meant so much to her. But Whitman's main preoccupation as always was with *Leaves of Grass*. A characteristic utterance was (as Traubel quotes him): "There's the book—the dear book—forever waiting—and I seem to be more feeble than ever." Whitman lived on until March 26, 1892.

That Whitman should often have been misunderstood is partly his own fault. For with the zealous aid of his immediate disciples he all but convinced himself that he was the "caresser of life"—the intimate companion of all things and all people, indeed of experience itself. He all but convinced himself too that he was a philosopher and a religious thinker. And he all but convinced himself that he was the national bard of an optimistic, expansive America. To a certain extent all these images of Whitman are true, but we cannot be satisfied with these images, since they do not adequately account for the poet who wrote the poems we admire.

There is something wrong, then, with the following formulation by Whitman's definitive biographer, echoing, as it does, earlier attributions of "mysticism," "primitivism," and "barbarism" made by writers as different as Lawrence and Santayana: "this was the real Walt Whitman, undiscriminating, easily stimulated by noise, color, and movement, happy to lose himself in the ceaseless flux of people going and coming." Whitman himself did not necessarily think this was true, for he said, in an important passage of "Song of Myself," that he was "both in and out of the game and watching and wondering at it." It will not do to think of "the real Whitman" as the poet who merges with the flux of experience, because this ignores another Whitman who is just as important: the Whitman who showed a lifelong capacity for recalcitrance to experience and who opposed to the inchoate flow of life the finished form of his poems and who made of his personal and public life a series of significant gestures that culminate in the ideal. For he had the power of turning his famous poses into exemplary acts and indestructible ideals which belong to any American's cultural heritage.

Whitman's idea of himself as a philosopher, religious thinker, and national bard is to be found in his description of the destiny of the poet, or, as he is oddly called, the "literatus,"

in *Democratic Vistas*. In speaking of the need for a moral and spiritual regeneration in America, Whitman allots to the literatus a highly important place. His task is to create "archetypal poems" which will give unity of soul and imagination to his people and to exercise the offices of moral and spiritual leadership once exercised by organized religion. For, as Whitman writes, "the priest departs, the divine literatus comes." One is not surprised to learn that the ideal bards of the future will apparently resemble Walt Whitman. At least they will not be like the "genteel little creatures" whose "perpetual, pistareen, paste-pot work" is sometimes mistaken for genuine American poetry. The literatus must be moved by "autochthonic lights and shades"; he must be intensely aware of his place, race, and nationality; he will see that "America demands a poetry that is bold, modern, all-surrounding, and kosmical, as she is herself"; his poetry must be affirmative, forward-looking, and "ideal"; it must celebrate comradeship and nature; it will be free of "the idea of the covert, the lurid, the maleficent, the devil, the grim estimates inherited from the Puritans, hell, natural depravity, and the like." True, Whitman does say that "in the future of these States must arise poets immenser far, and make great poems of death." But we inevitably get the feeling from *Democratic Vistas*, though not from "Out of the Cradle Endlessly Rocking" or "When Lilacs Last in the Dooryard Bloom'd," that the thought of death is easy to entertain and is merely a part of the life process of a progressive universe.

The reader will see that even if we take this portrait of the literatus as a self-appraisal, it is a description of the poet as prophet and promulger of a program rather than of the poet as poet, and that some of Whitman's own best qualities go unmentioned: there is nothing here about Whitman the comic poet and delineator of the self. Also it is plain that the most characteristic and important American literature in modern times has not met Whitman's prescriptions. The "grim estimates" of the Puritans have survived in one form or another from Henry James to Faulkner. The American writer at his best has not been the affirmative public oracle Whitman envisioned. He has been a private, often an isolated writer; he has usually approached social questions, if at all, on the assumption that moral values do not derive from society or the nation but are innate in the individual; and he has often been most convincing when he has taken a dark, even a pessimistic and despairing view of our society. That some of the same things may be said of Whitman himself is a measure of the distance between the real Walt Whitman and the self-image of the prophet-poet he liked to project.

To be sure, there is much about the literatus to remind us of "the real Walt Whitman," whom everyone discusses but whom no one can quite discover. Whitman's poetry often apostrophizes an optimistic, "orbic," "kosmical" America, an America devoted to "a strong-fibred joyousness and faith, and the sense of health al fresco." But there is nothing to remind us of that essential Whitman—the divided, covert, musing, "double," furtive man who wrote the poems we have come in recent years especially to prize. The testimony of Leslie Fiedler is relevant here. "Our Whitman," writes Mr. Fiedler, "is the slyest of artificers . . . he is a player with illusion; his center is a pun on the self; his poetry is a continual shimmering on the surfaces of concealment and revelation that is at once pathetic and comical." Mr. Fiedler goes on to say that he was not, or not in essence, the tribal bard: "he was only a man, ridden by impotence and anxiety, by desire and guilt, furtive and stubborn and half-educated. That he became the world's looked-for ridiculous darling is astonishing enough; that he remained a poet through it all is scarcely credible." These words are from Mr. Fiedler's excellent essay called "Images of Walt Whitman." For a further description of the poet who is here being called "our Walt Whitman," one might look into the pages of the first book really to understand this poet, Constance Rourke's *American Humor*. But there is also Randall Jarrell's essay entitled "Some Lines from Whitman" (in his *Poetry and the Age*) and my own book of 1955, *Walt Whitman Reconsidered*.

To be sure, these writings were once thought by many academicians to be, in the word of one of them, "aberrant." Perhaps in some quarters they still are. But if so, "unorthodox" would be a better word than "aberrant." For there has indeed been an orthodoxy among most Whitman scholars. It is not the orthodoxy of the original disciples and of Edgar Lee Masters, which makes Whitman a messiah and tribal bard. It is the orthodoxy of the history-of-ideas approach to literature, which makes Whitman a philosopher or possibly a theologian of the mystic variety (not that vain Walt wouldn't have been pleased by the compliment). This purely intellectualist approach is to be found, for example, in James E. Miller's recent *A Critical Guide to Leaves of Grass* and in Gay Wilson Allen's useful but misleading *Walt Whitman Handbook*, with its talk of immanence and emanation, acosmism and cosmotheism, pantheism and panpsychism. The *Handbook* never gets around to a discussion of Whitman's real subject, which was the plight and destiny of the self. And it is impossible to sympathize with Mr. Allen's contention that "an exhaustive comparative study needs to be made of the relations of Whitman's thought to the [Great] Chain of Being." Whitman's leading conceptions are the self, equality, and contradiction—appropriate preoccupations for the poet of American democracy. What use had he, in a democratic culture, for the philosophic counterpart of European hierarchies?

Abroad Whitman has always been regarded as the national poet of America, a prophet-bard who spoke with the very voice of his native land. But in his own country his position remains somewhat anomalous. In his essay called "The Poetry of Barbarism" Santayana noticed (and exaggerated) this anomaly. Whitman, wrote Santayana, is "surely not the spokesman of the tendencies of his country, although he describes some aspects of its past and present condition: nor does he appeal to those whom he describes, but rather to the *dilettanti* he despises. He is regarded as representative chiefly by foreigners, who look for some grotesque expression of the genius of so young and prodigious a people." There is no doubt that many more Americans have read Longfellow than have read Whitman, and so far as one can tell, Whitman, though he wished to speak to all Americans, is not nowadays more widely read than the other difficult modern poets—for indeed his poetry is "difficult" compared with that of his contemporaries. But in an important sense Whitman really is "the spokesman for the tendencies of his country." Obviously he celebrates and "promulges" our material progress and our spiritual, moral, and political values (and, as I observed earlier, the feelings of cultural inferiority which used to make Americans apologize for his declamatory style and occasional stridency, bathos, or philistinism have largely been allayed). But more important, Whitman is the representative of his country because he and his poetry mirror in a radical if incomplete way the very contradictions of American civilization. For, as was suggested at the beginning of this essay, to begin to understand Whitman is to understand him in his contradictions. His inner op-

positions, his ambiguities, his wit, like his democratic faith, his optimism, and his belief in the self, are native to the man as they are to America. For these reasons one cherishes Walt Whitman—and takes him to be in a real sense "the spokesman for the tendencies of his country."

Selected Bibliography

WORKS OF WALT WHITMAN

Leaves of Grass. Brooklyn, 1855.
Leaves of Grass. Brooklyn, 1856.
Leaves of Grass. Boston: Thayer and Eldridge, 1860.
Drum-Taps. New York, 1865.
Leaves of Grass. New York, 1867.
Democratic Vistas. Washington, D.C., 1871.
Leaves of Grass. Boston: Osgood, 1882.
Specimen Days and Collect. Philadelphia: Rees Welsh, 1882.
Leaves of Grass. Philadelphia: David McKay, 1891.
Calamus, edited by R. M. Bucke. Boston: Laurens Maynard, 1897.
The Wound Dresser, edited by R. M. Bucke. Boston: Small, Maynard, 1898.
An American Primer, edited by Horace Traubel. Boston: Small, Maynard, 1904.
The Gathering of the Forces, edited by Cleveland Rodgers and John Black. New York: Putnam's, 1920.
Walt Whitman's Blue Book: The 1860–61 Leaves of Grass *Containing His Manuscript Additions and Revisions. Volume I: Facsimile of the Unique Copy in the Oscar Lion Collection of the New York Public Library; Volume II: Textual Analysis by Arthur Golden.* New York: New York Public Library, 1968.

SELECTED COLLECTED EDITIONS
Complete Poetry and Selected Prose and Letters, edited by Emory Holloway. New York: Random House, 1938.

The Complete Poetry and Prose of Walt Whitman, with an Introduction by Malcolm Cowley. New York: Pellegrini and Cudahy, 1948.

The Poetry and Prose of Walt Whitman, edited by Louis Untermeyer. New York: Simon and Schuster, 1949.

The Works of Walt Whitman: The Deathbed Edition in Two Volumes. Volume I: Collected Poetry; Volume II: Collected Prose. New York: Funk and Wagnalls, 1969. Foreword, Introduction, Prefatory Note by Malcolm Cowley.

Since the early 1960's New York University Press has been issuing well-edited volumes in a new complete *The Collected Writings of Walt Whitman.*

BIBLIOGRAPHIES

Tanner, James. "Walt Whitman Bibliographies: A Chronological Listing, 1902–1964," *Bulletin of Bibliography*, 25:131–32 (1967).

————. *Walt Whitman: A Supplementary Bibliography, 1961–1961.* Kent, Ohio: Kent University Press, 1968.

White, William. "A Current Bibliography," *Walt Whitman Review*, 8 (1962); 11 (1963).

————. *Walt Whitman's Journalism: A Bibliography.* Detroit: Wayne State University Press.

CRITICAL AND BIOGRAPHICAL STUDIES

Allen, Gay Wilson. *Walt Whitman Handbook.* Chicago: Packard, 1946.

————. *The Solitary Singer.* New York: Macmillan, 1955. Reissued with revisions, New York: New York University Press, 1967.

————. *Walt Whitman.* New York: Grove Press; London: Evergreen Books, 1961. Revised edition, Detroit: Wayne State University Press, 1969.

Asselineau, Roger. *L'Evolution de Walt Whitman après la première édition des Feuilles d'Herbes.*

Paris: Libraire Marcel Didier, 1954. In English, *The Evolution of Walt Whitman: The Creation of a Book.* Cambridge, Mass.: Harvard University Press (Belknap), 1962.

Canby, Henry Seidel. *Walt Whitman, An American.* Boston: Houghton Mifflin, 1943.

Chase, Richard. *Walt Whitman Reconsidered.* New York: William Sloane Associates, 1955.

Christman, Henry M., ed. *Walt Whitman's New York: From Manhattan to Montauk.* New York: Macmillan, 1963.

de Selincourt, Basil. *Walt Whitman: A Critical Study.* New York: Kennerly, 1914.

Fausset, Hugh I'Anson. *Walt Whitman: Poet of Democracy.* New Haven: Yale University Press, 1942.

Holloway, Emory. *Whitman: An Interpretation in Narrative.* New York: Knopf, 1926.

Lewis, R. W. B., ed. *The Presence of Walt Whitman. Selected Papers from the English Institute.* New York: Columbia University Press, 1962.

Miller, Edwin H. *Walt Whitman's Poetry: A Psychological Journey.* Boston: Houghton Mifflin, 1968.

Miller, James E., Jr. *A Critical Guide to Leaves of Grass.* Chicago: University of Chicago Press, 1957.

————. *Walt Whitman.* New York: Twayne, 1962.

Pearce, Roy Harvey, ed. *Whitman: A Collection of Critical Essays.* Englewood Cliffs, N.J.: Prentice-Hall, 1962.

Perry, Bliss. *Walt Whitman, His Life and Work.* Boston: Houghton Mifflin, 1906.

Schyberg, Frederik. *Walt Whitman*, translated by Evie Allison Allen. New York: Columbia University Press, 1951.

Waskow, Howard J. *Whitman: Explorations in Form.* Chicago: University of Chicago Press, 1966.

—*RICHARD CHASE*

Thornton Wilder

1897-1975

DESPITE the three Pulitzer prizes awarded him Thornton Wilder may very well turn out to be one of the few enduring writers of our time. That such is likely to be the case not enough of his contemporaries seem to be aware: his course, though extraordinarily successful, has been devoid of the sensational. There have been countless other authors (most of them already consigned to oblivion) who in his day have been far more "discussed." That was inevitable for a man who has neither hastened to follow nor troubled to oppose the current mode, who has gone his own way, and who has clearly never sought the popularity which has periodically been his. The key to his significance, perhaps, is the number of important paradoxes brilliantly reconciled in his writings.

A romanticist at heart—and what writer of imagination is not?—he has always shown an intellectual preference for the classic. In his works emotions run deep rather than wild, and are never permitted to outrage the form. On the other hand, the form is always a clear crystal within which the bright light never flickers.

His interest has been consistently in great themes and subjects, yet in practice his art is akin to that of the miniaturist. In the foreword to his earliest pieces he meditates on the fact that the history of literature would have been very different if writers had not permitted themselves "to be pretentious"; some authors "would rather fail with an oratorio than succeed with a ballad." Wilder himself has rarely given himself to less than the noblest of concepts, but had he ventured on the long stretches of the oratorio, we may be sure that he would have been less concerned with the grand architecture than with the charm and splendor of the individual arias—which, nevertheless, would be persuasively connected. He has always chosen to show much in little. This same early foreword concedes "his inability to sustain a long flight." The spacious air of his works is owing not to form but idea.

Like all good bookworms, he is in love with the past. But his re-creation of the past belongs very much to the present. He has never tried to write a museum piece.

No writer of his time has been more uniformly concerned with moral issues; none is less didactic. Didacticism he has branded as an attempt at "coercion." "Beauty is the only persuasion."

His experience and interests have made him cosmopolitan. Yet no storyteller has been more attentive to locale and setting.

He has always avoided the provincialism of modern American naturalists. Nevertheless, many of his dramatic compositions and one of his novels are, without loss to their universality, profoundly American. He is a man of the world, and he could have been born only in the United States.

When Thornton Niven Wilder was born at Madison, Wisconsin, on April 17, 1897, it was to parents whose own allegiances were destined to influence their son vitally. His father, Amos Parker Wilder, editor and publisher of a newspaper, was a very religious Congregationalist, and his mother, née Isabella Thornton Niven, was the daughter of a Presbyterian minister.

Amos Wilder was appointed to the post of American consul general to Hong Kong and for six months during 1906 Thornton attended a German school at Hong Kong. Later that same year he was sent to Berkeley, California, for his schooling. In 1911 when he returned to China he went as a boarding pupil to an English mission school at Chefoo for a year. He was again in the United States in 1912, going to school first at Ojai, California, and then at the Berkeley High School, from which he was graduated in 1915. From 1915 to 1917 he attended Oberlin College, where he lost no time appearing as a writer in the *Oberlin Literary Magazine*. In 1917 he transferred to Yale, his father's old college, and the family was reunited at New Haven. Having found his vocation, young Wilder kept the *Yale Literary Magazine* plentifully supplied with his works.

In 1918, after having been frustrated because of poor eyesight in several efforts to enlist in the armed services, he was at last accepted by the Coast Artillery. In 1919 he returned to Yale, and the next year took his B.A. degree. In 1920–21 he spent a year as a resident of the American Academy at Rome, where he began writing *The Cabala*. Back in the United States he taught French at Lawrenceville School in New Jersey (1921–28,

with two years off for study and writing), and presently began doing graduate work at Princeton, where he was awarded his M.A. degree in 1926. That same year his first volume was issued, but *The Cabala* was largely ignored or patronized by the critics. In 1927 the American Laboratory Theatre produced a play, *The Trumpet Shall Sound*, that he had published in the *Yale Literary Magazine*, but it attracted little attention.

It was *The Bridge of San Luis Rey* which made him famous overnight. A best seller, it won the Pulitzer Prize for 1928, and was converted into a popular movie. As a novel it was highly praised and elaborately condemned. It was followed by a crop of novels which imitated Wilder's device of bringing together a group of characters by some trick of circumstance at a moment pivotal to their lives.

Wilder's sudden and well-merited affluence enabled him to give up teaching and devote himself to his true calling. *The Cabala* was now being reread with new appreciation, and a volume culled from his very earliest works, a series of tiny plays, *The Angel That Troubled the Waters*, was published in 1928. He was also in a position to gratify an old wish of his mother's, to live in a home of their own. He built for her a large, roomy house a few miles from the Yale campus, and this is still his permanent residence.

After another trip to Europe, where he began writing *The Woman of Andros*, he came back to go on a lecture tour across the country. From 1930 to 1936 he taught one semester each year at the University of Chicago, and also did script writing for several Hollywood movies. During these years Wilder was a very busy man: he also adapted André Obey's *Le Viol de Lucrèce* for Katharine Cornell, wrote a new novel, *Heaven's My Destination*, taught at the University of Hawaii for a semester (in 1935), and began his adaptation of *A Doll's*

House, in which Ruth Gordon appeared in 1937.

But it was not until 1938 that he had his second success with the public, which, indeed, began as a failure. When *Our Town* was presented on the Boston stage, the reviews were so bad that the performances for the second week were canceled. When it opened in New York, however, it was an immediate hit and was awarded the Pulitzer Prize for that year.

In December of 1938 *The Merchant of Yonkers*, with Jane Cowl in the leading role, was a failure and closed in a few weeks. The ensuing years found Wilder lecturing for the State Department in South America, writing the Hollywood script for a Hitchcock movie, *The Shadow of a Doubt*, and enlisting (1942) in the Air Force, in which, despite his poor eyesight, he was commissioned a captain.

While in the service he had a third smashing hit when *The Skin of Our Teeth* was produced with Tallulah Bankhead, Frederic March, and Florence Eldridge in the stellar roles. In 1943 this play won Wilder his third Pulitzer Prize.

During World War II he was on duty in Africa, then Italy, and finally the United States, until his separation from military duty in September of 1945. His next major endeavor was the novel *The Ides of March*; after its publication in 1948 Wilder lectured at Harvard and elsewhere. *The Merchant of Yonkers*, revised under the new title of *The Matchmaker*, was shown in 1954 with much success in England, and later (1955) in New York, where Ruth Gordon assumed the title role. At the Edinburgh Festival *The Alcestiad* was produced in 1955. Hindemith converted one of Wilder's one-act plays, "The Long Christmas Dinner," into an opera, performed at Mannheim in German (1961), and Louise Talma did the same for the long play *The Alcestiad*, first heard at Frankfurt am Main (1962). In 1962 three

new one-act plays from two projected cycles, *The Seven Deadly Sins* and *The Seven Ages of Man*, were seen in New York. Early in 1964, still another version of *The Matchmaker*, the musical comedy *Hello Dolly!*, with Carol Channing in the leading role, opened in New York.

In the spring of 1962 Wilder retired to the Arizona desert, because of a need for uninterrupted time and quiet in order to lose himself in writing "long-delayed." His sister, Miss Isabel Wilder, a distinguished novelist in her own right, to whom he is very close, takes care of his affairs, and stands as a buffer between him and a world which is always eager to see to it that the creator has no time for his creations. He has confessed to me that when he is writing, he prefers to live where nobody knows him, but where he can have the refreshment of casual chats with strangers.

A mere glance at the titles of Thornton Wilder's writings is enough to establish the wide variety of his accomplishment. Variety there is—unlike the work of such contemporaries of his as Thomas Wolfe and certain of the naturalists who were content to write the same book over and over under a series of new titles—yet throughout his career there can be discerned the mind and temperament of the author. Whether Wilder takes us to modern or ancient Rome, to New Hampshire or Missouri in our time, or on a dizzying whirl through the centuries, his hand is everywhere manifest.

His collection of early pieces, *The Angel That Troubled the Waters* (published only after the success of *The Bridge of San Luis Rey*), affords little hint of his later auctorial triumphs. The volume consists of sixteen "three-minute plays." Plays they certainly are not, as even the stage directions make clear (e.g., in one of them we are informed that Judas' thirty pieces of silver are cast upward from his hand and "hurtle through the skies, flinging their enormous shadows across the stars and continue falling forever through the vast funnel of space"). More seriously, the pieces are all too brief to be capable of representation on the boards: they would be over before they seemed to begin.

Nevertheless, they not only reveal an imagination both poetical and moral but are already also symptomatic of two important facets of Wilder's genius: his attraction to the theater (where he was going to come into his own only after some years of experimentation with the one-act form and several ventures in the field of the novel), and his "passion for compression," as he himself has expressed it. While still a boy he was irritated by the "needless repetition," "the empty opening paragraphs, the deft but uninstructive transitions," and the superfluous summarizing conclusions of most writing (still being held up as models of excellence in our schools). If the pieces are too brief for any telling dramatic effect, they at least show the artist conscious of a principle which he feels he must perfect.

In the incidents he chose he was nothing if not ambitious, and of the sixteen playlets three are imposing because of their own merit: "And the Sea Shall Give up Its Dead," in which an empress, a theatrical producer, and a priest are stricken with terror on the Day of Judgment as they understand that they must lose their identities before falling "into the blaze of unicity"; "Now the Servant's Name Was Malchus," another flash of the cosmic, in which Malchus asks Our Lord that his name be expunged from the Holy Writ, and Our Lord reflects upon His life on earth ("My promises were so vast that I am either divine or ridiculous"); and "Mozart and the Gray Steward," Wilder's version of a celebrated legend, in which the ailing composer accepts the stipulation connected with a commission to write a requiem that it be given out anonymously,

since it must be the voice for "those millions sleeping, who have no one" but Mozart to speak for them.

Throughout there is a deeply earnest concern with moral values (without didacticism or unction), one of the most salient features of Wilder's finest writing. There are also various hints of the manner of the great play *The Skin of Our Teeth,* before it could have been conceived: of its amusing pretended flippancy, in "Proserpina and the Devil," and of its sweep in both "And the Sea Shall Give up Its Dead" and "Now the Servant's Name Was Malchus." Just as, despite the long distance to be traversed between the Haydnesque Opus 2 piano sonatas of Beethoven and his late sonatas, the growl of the mature lion can be heard in those early works, so in this volume of little pieces there are premonitions of things to come.

But the publication of *The Angel That Troubled the Waters* was justified, if by nothing else, by the brilliant foreword which Wilder wrote for it. Besides the various articles of his credo already quoted from this piece, there are other reflections worthy of attention. The artist, says Wilder, "knows how life should be lived at its best," and is aware of his falling short of that best—"knows he is failing in living and feeds his remorse by making something fair." The non-creator only suspects his own failure and consoles himself "in golf, or in love, or in business." Conscious that his era is one unsympathetic to writings of "religious" tendency, the author declares that it is precisely in this vein that he "would most like to do well." This is acute self-knowledge. Wilder is religious in the sense that Aeschylus is religious. He totally disclaims any didactic purpose.

The Cabala (1926) was praised for its beautiful prose, its "jewels of charming observation and felicitous expression," though the *New York Times* doubted that it contained enough substance to appeal "to the rank and file of the world." Granted that *The Cabala* is not equal to Wilder's best. While his skill in compression and eloquence of restraint in style are everywhere in evidence, he has not learned yet the subtleties of over-all unity of which his very next book will prove him a master. The one shortcoming of the book is its episodic character; it therefore, despite its many excellences, fails to qualify as a novel.

Some have seen the influence of Henry James in this book, others of Proust and Cabell; in Wilder's case this influence-hunting is fairly unprofitable. He has, like all writers of stature, thoroughly assimilated what he has read, and what he has written is his own. Certainly the most important force operating on him must have been his observations in Rome during his year there.

The air of the classic world breathes upon this delightful book from its first page. It is Virgil's country: from the fields a wind descends "in a long Virgilian sigh, for the land that has inspired sentiment in the poet ultimately receives its sentiment from him." (There has been some attempt by critics to identify the leading characters with the pagan deities: the Cardinal, Jupiter; Alix and Blair, Venus and Adonis; Marcantonio, Pan; Miss Grier, Demeter; Samuele, Mercury—a pretty idea, not particularly rewarding to follow.) What fascinates the young novelist is the apartness of a closed circle of men and women (the "Cabala" of the title), aristocratically adhering to long outmoded concepts, from the vulgar pragmatic life of their twentieth-century contemporaries. Like Chekhov of *The Cherry Orchard,* he sees the futility and charm of their ways, the debilitation and the grace, with sympathy, though with neither approval nor condemnation. In the background is the crassness of modern values, introduced on the second page, as a foil to the Virgilian evocation of the first, in the persons of three Italians returning

home after twenty years as shopkeepers in New York, "their savings in the diamonds on their fingers."

Of the three stories which *The Cabala* has to tell, the first concerns itself with the boy-prince Marcantonio, of ancient line, who is already so engulfed in sexual excesses that his mother fears the match she has arranged for him to be in jeopardy. She entreats the narrator, a young American whom the Cabala nickname "Samuele," to help reform the lad. Samuele is shocked that the aged Cardinal, spiritual leader of the circle, is less anxious to see Marcantonio saved than to keep him quiet until the marriage has taken place. It is a mystery to the old cleric "why this young fellow couldn't have had his five or six little affairs and gotten over it." On reflection, the American thinks he has learned something from the Cardinal: "Never try to do anything against the bent of human nature." Nevertheless, he undertakes with puritan zeal to lash the boy into a state of repentance. At first he is only too successful, but in the end the enforced abstinence drives Marcantonio into accepting the mocking challenge of his sister as a partner in incest, after which horrifying act there is nothing for him to do but commit suicide.

In the second story Samuele's American friend, James Blair, becomes the unconscious villain of the novel—so far as it has a villain (there are no villains in Wilder's work). Blair is a student of every sort of phenomenon connected with antiquity. Arid of soul, the typical dry-as-dust scholar, he fills notebooks with his discoveries; these will eventually be donated to Harvard's library, where their unintelligibility will confer upon them "an incomputable value." His pursuit of facts proceeds from "the will to escape something else." It is the misfortune of Alix, Princess d'Espoli, the lovely, witty, adorable center of the Cabala, to fall in love with Blair. She seems to be entrapped by his very saplessness. He is able neither to value nor to comprehend this creature the very breath of whose life is love. His rejection of her has the quality of a mortal blow upon her sensitive, exquisite nature.

The third story revolves about the relationship to the Cardinal of Astrée-Luce, a large-limbed, bony woman, a devoted French royalist who lives only to see the divine right of kings promulgated as a dogma of the Church. In her worship of the eighty-year-old Cardinal, simple-souled Astrée-Luce does not realize that his faith has been gradually undermined by the play of his rationalistic mind. He succeeds only in annihilating God for her. "Murder was child's play compared to what he had done." The very foundations of the world destroyed for her, and looking upon the Cardinal as a devil, she grasps a gun and shoots at him, but she misses. In the end she is more concerned with the harm she may have done him than with what he has done to her. They both come to understand that "no actions were too complicated but that love could understand, or dismiss them." With that understanding "they began their lives all over again." This chapter constitutes the most exciting and touching part of the novel.

Written with authentic sentiment, *The Cabala* is also diamonded with wit. ("She wrote a hymn and they made her a Dame of the British Empire." "She seemed to be forever surrounded by a ballet of curates and widows, who at her word, rose and swayed and passed the scones.") Most worthy of remark is the large gallery of vividly created personalities— even those who do not figure in the foreground, such as the wealthy Miss Grier, lonely and insomniac, who inveigles people into staying up with her till dawn by providing champagne and music; the Duchess d'Aquilanera, black-faced, fierce-eyed, whose yellow, dirty hands

are covered with paste emeralds; and Léry Bogard, of the French Academy, whose face is "delicately tinted by exquisite reading and expensive food." The book is altogether a work of remarkable urbanity. It contains but one passage without which it would be the better: the recounting of the familiar details connected with the death of Keats in Rome but attaching them to a modern poet—a juvenile touch in an otherwise thoroughly mature performance.

"A little masterpiece," "sensitive and pitiful," "a novel instinct with pure grace," a novel with a "deceptive clarity of style that masks pellucid depths" were some of the just judgments which greeted *The Bridge of San Luis Rey* (1927), and which time has ratified. In an era overrun by naturalistic novels, against which James Branch Cabell was almost the only challenger, Wilder calmly took his place as a leading storyteller who could not be satisfied with a documentation of the externalities of life, yet without adopting Cabell's deliberate escape from the realities of experience.

In his second volume Wilder's versatility was already plain—its setting, characters, stories, and tone are totally different from its predecessor; yet the same author is evident in the preoccupation with vital questions of moral dimension as well as in the unostentatious finish of the prose. Again he has a series of tales to tell, but this time he achieves unity appropriate to the novel, not only through the questions raised but by a skillful interlacing of the personalities of one story in the destinies of another.

Five human beings were on the osier-woven bridge, on the highway between Lima and Cuzco, Peru, on the noon of July 20, 1714, when they were hurled to their death in the gulf below. Why, the novel undertakes to explore, did the accident—if accident it was— occur to those particular five? Was it blind chance, was it the hand of God, or were these five in some way the authors of their own deaths? When he has told his tale Wilder makes us feel that it was not one of these forces but a combination of all three which must explain such an event—and in affording this answer he reminds us that the mystery of human experience must lie somewhat outside the definable borders of both science and dogma. The sense of the wonder of life is augmented by another brilliant device. Like the Greek oracles, if Wilder does not provide a direct answer to the questions asked, he does provide one to a question that has not, but should have been, asked: Is the expenditure of love, when frustrated of its object, wasted? In the investigation of the other questions this one is answered quietly, with profound humanity, and in a manner devoid of a trace of sentimentality.

The Marquesa de Montemayor loves her daughter Clara with a raging obsession; Clara, only repelled by the violence of her mother's affection, escapes from it by marrying a nobleman and going off to Spain. Despite her awareness of Clara's coldness, the Marquesa makes a religion out of maternal love. "The knowledge that she would never be loved in return acted upon her ideas as a tide acts upon cliffs. Her religious beliefs went first, for all she could ask of a god, or of immortality, was the gift of a place where daughters love their mothers." Above all things else she wants Clara to say, "You are the best of all possible mothers." Her letters to her daughter are later to become a classic of the language (Wilder had the letters of Madame de Sévigné in mind), for they are rich no less in "the notation of the heart" than in style. In exchange the letters from Clara are brilliant for their "sheer virtuosity of giving pain neatly." Unknown to her fellow townsmen are both the scope of the Marquesa's reading and her literary gift: they see in her only a crazy old woman who drinks too much,

who is fit to be put in jail and reported to the Inquisition.

From the Convent of Santa María and the protection of the Abbess there, a truly good, practical woman, whose days are consecrated to good works, the Marquesa takes little Pepita to be her companion. In her new environment Pepita pines for the Abbess, whom she loves with a completely unselfish devotion. She writes a letter to the Abbess pleading to be allowed to return to the convent, but does not mail it, for she feels the request to be selfish. The Marquesa reads this letter and from it comes to see how much egotism there was in her own love for Clara, how little of Pepita's brave humility. She understands that she has loved her daughter not for Clara's sake, but her own. She is now ready to "begin again." Two days later she and Pepita are on the bridge when it collapses.

The twin brothers Manuel and Esteban have been raised at the convent too. A telepathic closeness develops between the two, and "a need of one another so terrible that it produced miracles as naturally as the charged air of a sultry day produces lightning." Camila, a promiscuous but brilliant actress, who understands love only as an emotion to be projected from the stage, comes to Manuel to write letters for her while she is carrying on her sordid little affairs, unknown to the Viceroy, whose mistress she is. Manuel falls in love with her, and begins to suffer deeply because of the futility of that love; he does not confide in his brother, but he does not need to utter words to be understood by Esteban, and the latter, in whose heart there is room only for love of Manuel, makes the shocking discovery that "even in the most perfect love one person loves less profoundly than the other."

Manuel dies of blood poisoning, and Esteban is inconsolable. Even their great friend, the Abbess, cannot loose him from his grief.

Captain Alvarado, who travels about the world trying to forget the death of his beloved daughter, almost persuades Esteban to quit Peru. The young man half-agrees, tries to commit suicide—he cannot leave the city where his brother lies buried— is saved by the Captain, falls to the floor sobbing, "I am alone, alone, alone," and in the end agrees to sail with his rescuer. Esteban is on his way to the port the next day, when he is on the bridge at noon.

Uncle Pio is singing-master, coiffeur, masseur, reader, secretary, errand-boy, banker, and maid to Camila, the actress. From the time he was twenty he has had three aims in life: to be varied, secret, and omniscient; "to be always near beautiful women"; and to be near those who love the Spanish masterpieces in drama. He came from the Old World to Peru, and in Camila Perichole he discovered the means of satisfying all three passions at once. He found her when she was twelve, took her under his wing, and subjected her to the severest artistic discipline. They have a loyal friendship, though they have no need of each other physically, and between them they attempt to "establish in Peru the standards of the theatres in some Heaven whither Calderón had preceded them." Critical of her every nuance upon the stage, he is undisturbed by her cheap liaisons. There is nothing more wonderful in the world "than a beautiful woman doing justice to a Spanish masterpiece." Love he regards as a sickness proper to late youth; one emerges from it "pale and wrung, but ready for the business of living."

But Camila tires of the theater, and decides to become a lady. She gives up her career to build herself a villa at a fashionable watering place. Her son by the Viceroy, rachitic little Jaime, subject like his father to convulsions, has a wretched life of it in the midst of his mother's newfound respectability. Because of all he has stood for, Pio is banished from Camila's life, to his great anguish. He has lost all purpose in living.

Suddenly Camila's beauty is ravaged by smallpox. Familiar with passion but not with love (many who have lived a life of passion "can tell us less of love than the child that lost a dog yesterday"), she feels her life is over. Pio, still loyal to her, manages a final interview with her and begs her to allow him to take Jaime for a year and train him for the stage. When she refuses, he forces her, because of her financial indebtedness to him, to agree, provided the boy is willing. The next day Jaime joins Pio at the inn. Both are on the bridge when it gives way.

Accident, some undecipherable purpose of God, and personal passion seem all to figure in the conjunction of these five persons on that fatal noon. But in the aftermath of their catastrophe, as in Shakespearean tragedy, we find in the survivors a deepened wisdom. The Abbess perceives that in her preoccupation that her work be continued after she is gone, she was deficient in the kind of love Pepita had for her and Esteban for his brother. Camila now would give anything to tell Pio how she loved him or to solace the sufferings of little Jaime; hearing that the Abbess lost two persons whom she loved when the bridge fell, she offers herself to the sisterhood, and at last finds peace there in selfless service. Clara returns to Peru for a visit; to the Abbess she delivers a passionate defense of her mother, the Marquesa, and hears of Pepita and Esteban and Camila. The Abbess says, compassionately, "All of us have failed." Despite one's wish to do penance for that failure, however, "in love our very mistakes don't seem to be able to last long." At the close, the Abbess reflects that "soon we shall die and all memory of those five" will perish. Nevertheless the love they gave and which we had "will have been enough . . . There is a land of the living and a land of the dead and the bridge is love, the only survival, the only meaning." Each of the five persons on the Bridge of San Luis Rey when it fell was himself such a bridge.

Though the variety of Wilder's gifts was further manifested by the publication of *The Woman of Andros* (1930), a gem of a novel and (in my judgment) his most exquisite creation, the book failed of achieving popular success. Most astonishing of all, from our present perspective, was the attack on the novel by Michael Gold, an unfailingly vulgar high priest of the then-new cult of vulgarity, so-called "Marxist Literary Criticism" (as though by nature such a thing could exist)—perhaps the worst mania ever to seize control of the American literary scene. The Great Depression was in full swing; the Communists were quick to make their own capital of it and in the world of letters they were only too successful. This was no time to be an artist was the general cry, and one of the hideous lies which was in great danger of universal acceptance was that the best propaganda was the best art. It was one's duty to write about social injustice as it existed *today,* and sheer inhumanity to give a thought to aesthetic or philosophic values. Gold attacked Wilder as though by writing *The Woman of Andros* he had created the Depression—or, indeed, as though if he had written in the flourishing naturalistic mode he might have averted it. The controversy thus inaugurated, in which many took one side, many another, is not worth the study now. The heavily propagandist novels and plays which so delighted the public in the thirties are all now happily forgotten. In those days it was as open an invitation to social ostracism for a man to appear in public without his "social conscience" as without his trousers. In such a climate it was an act of sheer courage for Wilder to have published *The Woman of Andros.* H. S. Canby spoke with understated

truth when he said of this novel that, compared with *The Bridge of San Luis Rey,* "it will not be so popular, but it will be as much approved" —one gathers he meant: in the long run.

Taking the basis of his plot from Terence's *Andria,* but giving it a tragic turn, Wilder wrote here again a book quite unlike any of its antecedents. This brief novel is one of the most classic things—in the Greek, not the neoclassic, sense—in our language. Bathed in transparent light, like the light peculiar to Greece itself, it is caressed by the air of Platonism. And throughout one is aware of the sea! the sea!

As is proper to such a work, the plot is simple and single; the narrative is luminous with many unobtrusive observations on life which, unintentionally, reveal their author's deep humanity. ("He made a fool of himself, but in good hands one does not mind." "The loneliest associations are those that pretend to intimacy." "The mistakes we make through generosity are less terrible than the gains we acquire through caution.") These passages are aesthetically right for the novel, though critic Rex Burbank takes exception to them as intrusively subjective. They are no more so than the Choruses of Sophocles. This book could never have been written in the totally objective style of the Hemingway school: it would have lost all its quality.

Wilder, too, demonstrates a new taste for significant description—not description for its own sake, the worst kind of writing, but description which pushes the narrative forward. Indeed, the work opens with such a sentence, almost cosmic, setting the tone for the whole: "The earth sighed as it turned in its course; the shadow of night crept gradually along the Mediterranean, and Asia was left in darkness."

The story takes place on "one of the least famous of the islands," Brynos. Its two leading characters are Chrysis, the woman from Andros, thirty-five, a beautiful hetaera deeply versed in the classics and, like all good Platonists, a kind of pre-Christian; and the young man Pamphilus, who possesses the temperament which enables one to understand why the seeds of Christianity were to find such fertile soil in the Greek world.

Pamphilus, son of Simo, a wealthy merchant, spends much time at Chrysis' house, where some dozen young bachelors are invited once a week; they lie on couches, eat exotic foods, and talk; she recites whole tragedies, and teaches the lads how to speak and behave in the Athenian mode—all of which is highly unconventional to Brynos. She also keeps a houseful of the old and lame, picked up here and there, whom she supports. At her banquets she encourages debates on ideas; young men, she declares, are the best philosophers because, no matter how clumsy, "they rush upon ideas with their whole soul." Once she recounts a story (the basis of which Wilder was to employ again with great effect in *Our Town*) of how a dead hero was permitted to revisit the earth for one day, on condition he relive the most uneventful day of his life, this time as both participant and foreknowing observer. What he now saw filled his heart with pain: the living too are dead because they value so little their fleeting life. It is with just such eyes that Pamphilus sees those about him. "How does one live? Where does one begin?" are for him the great questions. Chrysis finds release from her aloneness in bright talk, but looks upon herself as one already dead. For this youth only she feels the tie of an unexpressed love.

Straying among the rocks one morning, Pamphilus meets a slip of a girl, Glycerium, Chrysis' sister, who is allowed out of the house only at night for a walk. The girl has broken her promise in order to know what the sea looks like by day. After that the two meet again. The third time they become lovers.

Some months later Chrysis, who has been bearing a great pain in her side, is now awaiting death with equanimity. Her concern is for those she must leave behind—most of all for Pamphilus, who suffers too much about the living, who does not know how to look the other way. This agonizing over the miseries of others is something new in the world: Pamphilus is a herald of the future.

Pamphilus, realizing that his chances for marrying the girl he loves seem more and more unlikely, goes to the dying hetaera to swear that no harm will come to her sister even if marriage proves impossible. But Chrysis feels that what happens to us is unimportant: only the life of the mind is real. She has known the worst the world can do, yet she can praise all of life. She urges him to accept, like her, whatever the gods offer, the bright and the dark.

At her sister's funeral Glycerium tries to throw herself on the pyre, but is saved by her lover, who enfolds her in his arms. His father tries to make him understand the fatality of the marriage the youth desires: the girl is not a Greek citizen and would never fit into the pattern of island life. But he dearly loves his son, and one night after all of Chrysis' household have been sold, Simo purchases the girl from her buyer. Pamphilus comes home to find Glycerium peacefully sleeping under his mother's care. But she and their child die in childbirth.

Pamphilus feels in all the joy and suffering he has witnessed some mysterious meaning. The stars are shining tranquilly over the land "soon to be called Holy,"and which even then is "preparing its precious burden." So ends the novel. Pamphilus has been seeking for the meaning that Christ is soon to enunciate.

In his attack Gold had asked: "Is Mr. Wilder . . . a Greek or is he an American?" It is impossible to say to what extent this may have influenced Wilder (though from what one can learn of his habits, it is altogether possible he never read Gold's article), but from this time forth he turned his attention more and more frequently to the American scene—a fact calling for neither regret nor congratulation: Wilder is at home in any locale. The important consideration is that when his setting is American he does not forfeit universality.

The Long Christmas Dinner and Other Plays (1931), a collection of six one-act plays, marks a return to his first love, the dramatic form. Of these, three are amusing in themselves and three are particularly interesting as studies in the techniques he was to employ in his later plays.

"Queens of France" is a sprightly piece, time 1869, showing an unscrupulous New Orleans lawyer milking a loose woman, a bourgeoise, and a spinster schoolteacher of their funds by persuading each that she is the true heir to the throne of France. In "Love and How to Cure It" a young man madly in love with a London music-hall ballerina of sixteen intends to commit suicide because of her dislike of him; he is dissuaded by an old comedian who, speaking tenderly of his dead wife, remarks that she loved him so much that she even spared him knowledge of her fatal illness; like the Marquesa of *The Bridge*, the boy sees that true love is selfless, and he promises to persecute the girl with his attentions no more. "Such Things Happen Only in Books" finds a novelist and his wife living in an old house in a New Hampshire village; he complains that life never offers any real plots—only in books do cooks feed outsiders secretly in the kitchen, wives take on young lovers, murderers return to the scene of the crime. As the play unfolds we learn that, unknown to the writer, all these things are occurring under his very roof.

"The Long Christmas Dinner," like the later full-length play *Our Town*, celebrates the miracles of birth and death, and of the continuity of human experience. Traversing ninety years without pause in a series of Christmas dinners shared by several successive generations of an American family, it reinforces the idea that what is fundamental to life does not vary with time. Few characters are individualized: girls and boys become mothers and fathers, and presently die. Only one girl becomes an old maid, and only one boy a rebel—their departures from the pattern only emphasize the extent to which the others cling to it. The play is a precursor to *Our Town* in both tone and technique. Births, deaths, and time are telescoped at the dramatist's will. Encroaching age is indicated in this play by the simple device of having the character, at the appropriate moment, put on a white wig. Birth and death are unaccompanied by the pain and anguish which would be the focus of attention of a naturalist. Newborn babies are simply wheeled in by the current nurse, and the mothers are as astonished and delighted as though a stork had brought them. When a character is about to die he has merely to walk slowly toward the "death" exit. ("Sad things aren't the same as depressing things.") Death brings gentle sorrow but no misery. There is a homely sweetness in all this. If there is a stab at the heart, it is in the recurrent phrase, after someone's death, "I never told her how wonderful she was"—a sentiment that will figure dramatically in *Our Town*, and was already implicit in Clara's relationship to the Marquesa.

"Pullman Car Hiawatha" is a further step toward *Our Town*. The only scenery is an elevated runway upstage and two flights of stairs descending from it. Here in advance of the later play we find a Stage Manager who is general factotum: he acts as Chorus and delivers lines of the minor characters. From him we learn that we are looking at Pullman car Hiawatha on December 21, 1930, en route from New York to Chicago. When he summons the actors ("Come on, everybody"), all enter carrying the chairs which are to represent the berths. We hear the conversation of various passengers and overhear their private thoughts. We listen as well to the speeches of certain personifications: Grover's Corners, Ohio; a field; Parkersburg, Ohio; the Hours—each is accorded a chance to deliver his or her sentiments. A Tramp, traveling under the car, appears and demands his right to be heard too. The only incident of the play concerns the death of the ill Harriet before a doctor can be summoned. She is reluctant to go with the angel who has come for her ("I haven't done anything with my life") and she wishes to be punished for a long time for her shortcomings; her chief desire is "to be all new." (This idea will be repeated in the last act of *Our Town*.) Reviewing her life, she understands that it was her husband's love which gave meaning to it (the concluding idea of *The Bridge of San Luis Rey*). Since she understands everything now, her death, as in Browning's *Prospice*, is a fulfillment of life. Time is telescoped again and the train reaches Chicago.

"The Happy Journey to Trenton and Camden" has been a favorite with acting groups. It is nearest *Our Town* in technique. A husband, wife, son, and daughter leave their house in Newark to visit a married daughter in Camden, New Jersey. The absence of a stage set enables the dramatist to achieve the fluidity of a movie. The family is first at home, then takes leave of neighbors, next gets into an auto, makes the journey to Camden, arrives there, is welcomed. Four chairs serve as the four seats of a car; these are arranged by the Stage Manager, who also delivers the speeches of various minor roles. All other props (such as the car's steering wheel) are created by pantomime of the actors. During the trip a funeral procession goes by; the mother sighs, remembering their son lost in the war. There is nothing resembling a plot in this little play, but it makes good theater by virtue of its simple humaneness.

If *The Woman of Andros* has been the least appreciated of Wilder's best work, *Heaven's My Destination* (1935) has been the most misunderstood. Nothing could be further from a true appraisal of the novel's hero, George Brush, than one critic's summation of him as a "nit-wit Babbitt, a religious fanatic and unholy nuisance." Harry Hansen hoped that Wilder himself would never have the misfortune to meet a George Brush in the flesh— yet Miss Isabel Wilder has encouraged me to believe that there is some autobiographical element in her brother's depiction of his hero!

To begin with, Sinclair Lewis largely resented his countrymen and concentrated fiercely upon their shortcomings; Wilder loves his fellow Americans and, not blind to their faults, sees them with the charity with which we view those we love. Moreover, nothing could be further fom Wilder's purposes or methods than Lewis' raw, heavy-handed, black-and-white satire. It is an irony that Lewis should have been the generalissimo of American letters in charge of the onslaught against our cultural vacuities. It is not by onslaught that such vacuities are filled, and there was more than a little of Babbitt in Lewis himself. Too often he makes us feel that his chief grievance is that in the United States writers and artists are not able to drive the Cadillacs of successful financiers. Wilder's on the other hand, is a richly cultivated intelligence.

As J. H. Raleigh implies, George Brush is a modern Quixote. This man is full of the noblest intentions, and everywhere he encounters hostility because of his sincere desire to help others and maintain his own moral integrity. To an extent his experiences illustrate the readiness of the world to give the truly unselfish man a black eye as the reward for his goodness. At the same time his experiences reinforce one's faith in goodness, no matter what the penalties innocence must suffer. (This is, perhaps, what is autobiographical in the portrait.) But the book, like Cervantes', is also a huge comedy, and Wilder does Brush's foes the justice of showing that his hero is much too ignorant for a crusader. He is a hilarious mixture of the best principles and the most ludicrous personal limitations. In an age where every respectable religious seminary, Catholic, Protestant, or Jewish, has accepted the findings of scholarship that the Bible is the work of many hands during many centuries, and therefore requires a careful detachment of later interpolations from original compositions, Brush insists upon the most rigorously fundamentalist interpretation of the Scriptures. He also looks upon women's smoking as the ultimate depravity. But such narrowness in so good a man is as pathetic as it is comic. He himself misses felicity because of his archaic views; but the opposition of the world to all he stands for is not because of his narrowness, but because of his stubborn selflessness. Under the influence of the Bible and of Gandhi, he has taken a voluntary oath of poverty, and is no more interested in financial success than he is in depravity. One might say that his chief trouble in life comes from his trying logically to live up to his principles—if one could say that he is ever really in trouble. For despite experiences which would destroy anyone else, George Brush has no pity for himself. To him all sickness is the product merely of discouragement, and no matter what happens to him he is never discouraged for more than a moment.

If his goodness makes him seem simpleminded, he is nevertheless compounded of divers forces. Of powerful physique and unfailing good health, he has the humbleness of a saint without knowing it. For the time in which this very young man lives—the depression years—his principles are no less sturdy than amazing. "I think," he says, "everybody ought to be hit by the depression equally." Successful as a book salesman, he is only upset when he has more money than he can spend on his simple needs. He disapproves of interest —and unintentionally aggravates the imminent ruin of a bank when, on closing a small account, he refuses to withdraw more than the original sum he deposited. He is tireless in his attempts to help others in distress, no matter to what moral depths they have sunk— and it is usually his fate to incur their hatred. His own goodness is only an irritant to those around him, and some are provoked into inventing mischief with which to undo him. But he cannot be undone. Whether he had (without knowing it) been made drunk, taken to a bawdy house, or thrown into jail, his own integrity protects him from destruction or corruption, and his ill-wishers are left only the more disgusted, confused, or amazed at his inviolability. The basic thing about the hero of this hilariously funny novel is not the stupidities born of his ignorance, but his dauntless, unpriggish, unsanctimonious will to be good in a world that finds goodness harder to tolerate than evil. The whole conception is an elaboration of a maxim from *The Woman of Andros*: "Of all the forms of genius, goodness has the longest awkward age." This novel is a comedy whose subject is the early steps of a man of just such genius.

What has not been noted is that whereas the debased, cynical, or lost persons in the book are people who might be found almost anywhere in the civilized world, this really good man comes near being exclusively American. His *kind* of innocence is unimaginable except among us.

It is interesting that George Brush's creation was in advance of Gertrude Stein's influence upon Wilder's thinking. He admits to being impressed, in talks with her after the publication of *Heaven's My Destination*, by her conviction that in the daily lives of Americans, a people who have identified themselves with the destiny of the world, will be found the elements of the universal and eternal. Such, at any rate, was his own conviction in the writing of *Our Town* (1938).

It was Wilder's search for the universal and eternal which made him turn again to the theater. "The novel," he has written, "is preeminently the vehicle of the unique occasion, the theatre of the generalized one." The theater, in the days of its greatness, has always been ritualistic, religious. "It is through the theatre's power to raise the exhibited individual action into the realm of idea and type and universal that it is able to evoke our belief." For this reason, as in his earlier experiments, Wilder dispenses with scenery and sets. "When you emphasize *place* in the theater, you drag down and limit and harness time to it." The soundness of this objection requires as proof no more than one's recollection of how free of place were the theaters of Aeschylus, Sophocles, Shakespeare, and Racine. And the dramatist states his aim quite clearly: "*Our Town* is not offered as a picture of life in a New Hampshire village. . . . It is an attempt to find a value above all price for the smallest events in our daily life. I have made the claim as preposterous as possible, for I have set the village against the largest dimensions of time and place. The recurrent words in this play . . . are 'hundreds,' 'thousands,' and 'millions.' "

The play is a hymn to everyday living and its potentialities. In the last act an idea related an an anecdote in *The Woman of Andros* is given full dramatic expression: Emily, who has just died, is allowed to relive an unimportant day in her life, and she chooses her twelfth birthday. As the day slips by, her anguish increases, and she cries: "We don't have time to look at one another. . . . I didn't realize. . . . Oh, earth, you're too wonderful for anybody to realize you." And another character, who has been long dead, comments: "Now you know! That's what it was to be alive. . . . To spend and waste time as though you had a million years. To be always at the mercy of one self-centered passion, or another." But there is no bitterness in Wilder's intention. The Stage Manager, who is godlike in his omniscience and compassion, stands above this merely personal perspective: "We all know that *something* is eternal." And what is eternal has nothing to do with places, names, earth, or even the stars; "that something has to do with human beings." For five thousand years the world's greatest minds "have been telling us that" and yet "people are always losing hold of it." At the very conclusion of the last act, the Stage Manager makes this comment upon our planet: It is "straining away all the time to make something of itself. The strain's so bad that every sixteen hours everybody lies down and gets a rest."

There you have the prevailing tone of the play. By some kind of magic it moves comfortably in an atmosphere that is largely homely and sometimes effortlessly sublime. Of plot there is almost nothing: against the background of fellow townsmen's friendliness and self-preoccupation, a boy and a girl fall in love, become engaged, marry; the wife dies in childbirth. That is all there is to the story as such. But somehow the playwright's deliberately chosen commonplace events are never humdrum, are rather suffused with a delicate poetry, and seem haunted by the shadow of the eternal. Like all masterpieces, the sum total of this beautiful work defies analysis. One could attribute some of its universality to its destruction of the formalities of the boxed-in stage, and the fluidity achieved by using the Stage Manager (as in earlier one-act plays) as Chorus, Property Man, and Actor Ready to Take On All Minor Roles—yet all these are only matters of technique. An even more cunning device is Wilder's deliberate confusion of time, allowing various scenes to go backward and forward over the years. Part of the magic of this unique play may come from the paradox that its persons are of the simplest; in this New England village, so far as "any culture or love of beauty" go, "there ain't much," as the Stage Manager concedes, beyond *Robinson Crusoe*, the Bible, Handel's *Largo*, and Whistler's *Mother*. Yet (it is a long distance Wilder has traveled since *The Cabala*) it is precisely through these run-of-the-mill folk that the dramatist's humanity restores what the tumult and the shouting of the day rob us of: the mystery and awesomeness of life itself.

The play which will hereafter be called *The Matchmaker* is an "only slightly modified" version (produced in 1954) of *The Merchant of Yonkers* (1938). This slapstick farce was a further attempt "to shake off the nonsense of nineteenth-century staging" by making fun of it. Though based to a certain extent upon a Viennese adaptation of an older English play, its concerns are Wilder's own: "the aspirations of the young (and not only the young) for a fuller, freer life." The plot centers around the sly game played by Dolly Levi, the matchmaker: she leads Horace Vandergelder, a merchant of Yonkers, to believe that she is arranging a union between him and a beautiful, rich young orphan (the product of her own imagination), while smoothing the way to marrying him herself. Laid in the early 1880's, the piece has the mad rush characteristic of the farce, as well as some of its time-honored furnishings: trapdoors; hiding under tables and

in cupboards; hats left betrayingly in evidence; overhearing behind a screen; young men escaping detection by donning women's clothes; mistaken identity; and so on. The pace is brisk and the lines are highly amusing.

But even in a farce, which need do no more than supply an evening's diversion, Wilder was bound to have something to say. Vandergelder lives only for accumulating money—until Dolly teaches him otherwise. "Money should circulate like rain water," she believes. She cannot bear the thought that his money lies idle, frozen. Despising those who cannot use others to pile up wealth, he feels the world is made up of fools. Perhaps he is right, Dolly says—yet everyone "must decide whether he'll live . . . a fool among fools or a fool alone." She chooses to live among human beings and even court danger, if necessary, rather than play safe. The best way to keep us fools out of harm's way is to allow us the few "human pleasures that are our right in the world." And that takes money—though not too much of it. The difference between poverty and a little money is enormous "and can shatter the world." The difference between a little money and a very great deal of money "is very slight —and that, also, can shatter the world." Money is like manure, worthless unless "spread about encouraging young things to grow." And that Dolly looks upon as her particular vocation. An artist in her own way, she is not satisfied with life as she finds it, and deems it necessary to alter a little here and there. By the time she is through, everyone is the better for it.

Not long after its cordial reception by the critics, *The Skin of Our Teeth* (1942) became the center of the second great controversy in Wilder's career when its author was accused by Joseph Campbell and H. M. Robinson of plagiarizing *Finnegans Wake*. The dramatist has since acknowledged that his play "is deeply indebted" to Joyce, but the charge makes as little sense as the dust stirred up a decade earlier by Michael Gold—though this time by two men of scholarly attainment.

That Wilder knew his Joyce very well is proved by his fine monograph on him, published a year earlier in *Poetry* (1941). There his own summation of *Finnegans Wake* is that it is a book in "sleep language," wherein the sleeper relives "the history of mankind . . . wrestling all night with the problem of original sin." Perhaps, Wilder concludes, we can agree with Joyce that it is his greatest work "when we come to know it."

Have we come to know it? More important: will we? The final judgment on Joyce's last work is not really in yet. Time will have to decide whether a book done *that way* is really a great book or despite its ambitiousness, only a literary curiosity. But, in any case, accusing Wilder of plagiarizing it is as intelligent as accusing Sophocles of plagiarizing Aeschylus in his *Electra* and Euripides of plagiarizing both in his; or Racine of plagiarizing Euripides in his *Phèdre*; or Shakespeare of plagiarizing North, Holinshed, Riche, Cinthio, Belleforest, Lodge, and many others—a thing no man of common sense would think of doing. Whatever Wilder's indebtedness to Joyce, what he may owe he has made his own, and his hand is evident everywhere in this great play—one of the greatest, I believe, in the history of the American theater. That it continues to be rated somewhat below *Our Town* I suspect to be owing to the caution of scholars who have been intimidated by the charges of Messrs. Campbell and Robinson, and dare not dismiss them, as they ought to.

Writing about *The Skin of Our Teeth* within the permitted space is a vexatious limitation; a treatise could hardly do it justice. "It was written," its author states, "on the eve of our entrance into the war and under strong emotion." He might have added: and with inspired imagination. The work is vast in both dimension and scope; its lines—which despite their being written only in *one* language may turn out to be some of the finest composed in our century—bounce with energy, sparkle with wit, and exult—for all the cataclysms involved —in the joy of living. Here at length Wilder embraces the contradictory tendencies of his talents and capitalizes on his earlier experiments, in a marvelous and complicated unity. His gift for compression is seen in a progressive series of intense events, yet the whole has a noble sweep, to which, miraculously, its farcical moments contribute no less than its somber ones. No American play is more serious, but the comic effects are as farcical as those of *The Matchmaker*. The Antrobus family is American but belongs to the whole world. The story is in the present, but it recapitulates the entire history of the human race, from glacial, prehistoric, Biblical, and classic times up through the twentieth century. Wilder's earlier skill in cheating time by deliberately confusing past and present now takes on significant philosophic meaning. But, timeless as the play is, it dramatically presents the dilemma of normal humanity faced with the recurrent systematized brutalities of fascism, nazism, and communism. Henry, the voice of such systems, cries, "I'm going to be free even if I have to kill half the world for it." At the sight of him, normal humanity exclaims: "War's a pleasure compared to what faces us now: trying to build up a peacetime with you in the middle of it." These words were first heard in 1942: they are even more desperately true in the 1970's.

The theme of this brilliantly conceived play is the ability of the human race, despite Nature's impersonally destructive powers and man's own catastrophic folly, ignorance, cruelty, indifference, and cowardice, somehow to manage to survive—and somehow, for all its readiness to forfeit all it has gained, to inch ahead of where it formerly stood. "We've come a long ways," sums up Antrobus. "We've learned. We're learning." The uphill steps by which human progress can be measured and which indicate the road still to be climbed are the great books which are the inheritance of every generation.

When we first meet the Antrobuses, representative of the race, mankind has already made its "way up from next to nothing." Antrobus (Adam, and the eternal Male) has just invented the wheel, has made great progress with the multiplication table, and is working out the alphabet. He himself is a devoted husband and father, "a pillar of the church, and has all the best interests of the community at heart." Mrs. Antrobus (Eve) "lives only for her children"; if it would help them in any way, "she'd see the rest of us stretched out dead at her feet without turning a hair." They now have two children: Henry (Cain) who, with a stone in his hand, "can hit anything from a bird to an older brother"; and Gladys, who embodies the best that Antrobus hopes for the future of the race. The other permanent member of the household is the maid Sabina (Lilith), a vain, discontented pessimist who, whenever things are running smoothly, invites Antrobus to pleasures outside the pale of respectability, but whose cowardice is forever reducing her to a servile place when extinction seems imminent.

Suddenly the ice is at their doors. Their home disappearing before her eyes, Mrs. Antrobus protects her family as best she can while her husband is busy with his inventions. He sends a message of comfort by the Telegraph Boy: "Burn everything except Shakespeare." She mutters bitterly: "Men!—He knows I'd burn ten Shakespeares to prevent a child of mine from having one cold in the head." As the glacier encroaches, Antrobus arrives, rolling in his newly invented wheel, and crying happily: "We've reached the top of the wave. There's not much more to be done." His wife reminds him that their very life is in peril. When he brings along for protection under their roof Homer, the Muses, and Moses, she consents grudgingly to allow them to share their scant food supply only on condition that their pets, the dinosaur and the mammoth, be driven out to perish. Settling down to the business of survival, Antrobus is immediately ready to give it up when he learns that Henry has been throwing stones again, and has probably killed the neighbor's boy. Alarmed at her husband's despair, Mrs. Antrobus brings forth the felicities of domestic warmth, and coaxes the Muses to sing. Gladys recites for him a poem by Longfellow which she has memorized, and shows him her excellent report card from school. There is hope in it yet, Antrobus feels, while his wife teaches Gladys the Bible, and Sabina starts burning the chairs passed up by the audience in the theater, Antrobus feverishly forces Henry to learn the multiplication table.

The second act, evoking the idea of the world as it was just before the Flood, takes place at Atlantic City, where a convention of the Honorable Order of Mammals, Subdivision Human, is being held, with all the rioting common to a Legion convention. Antrobus, its president, reviews the past smugly: "Little did my dear parents think,—when they told me to stand on my own two feet,—that I'd arrive at this point." His wife, much in the simplified style of Eleanor Roosevelt in her syndicated columns, confidently dispenses information, general and personal, on matters of interest to women in a public broadcast. The center of concern to the conventioneers is the games of chance at the Bingo Parlor; laughter and lechery are rampant; and there is only mockery for the warnings of the Fortune Teller that the Deluge is coming. Antrobus himself, his head turned by success, has begun to slip, is falling again for the wiles of Sabina, and asks his wife for a divorce. Henry hits a colored man with a stone. And even Gladys tries to imitate the garish style of the hussies about her. The race is in a bad way, and the hurricane signals are up. Mrs. Antrobus, who never loses her essential, if prosaic, balance, refuses to give her husband a divorce: she was well aware of his imperfections when she married him; what has cemented their life, she tells him, is the promise they gave each other. And it is the assurance implicit in this promise which has thus far saved mankind. Kept at the last minute from self-destruction, Antrobus-Noah sees the folly about him with clear eyes, and preserves the race again. The fools are still at the Bingo Parlor. As the Antrobuses hurry off to their boat and the tide rises, the Fortune Teller calls after them: "Think it over! A new world to make.-—think it over!"

Well, as the last act shows, it is not precisely a new world which Man has arranged. A world war has destroyed everything in sight and forced people to live underground. But there is peace again, Gladys has a baby, and Antrobus, inspired by his beloved books, begins to rebuild for a future. The last lines assure us that his family are "as confident as the day they began." Will the future be better? His optimism and determination give reason to hope so, as do his wife's steadfastness to virtues of the hearth, and his daughter's instinctive goodness and gentleness. But there will always be impediments to reckon with: the natural evil and cruelty of Henry, Antrobus' own tendency to be weak when prospering, Sabina's perpetual pessimism and preference for the line of least resistance, and Nature's unpredictable onslaughts with ice, hurricane, and flood. Yet Man's destiny is largely his own to forge—a hard task but an inescap-

able one. If he fails or takes too long, may not the Divine Intelligence, as It nearly did with the Deluge, weary of Man as an experiment and make a permanent end of him? Wilder does not ask this question, but of the larger mysteries of existence to which he calls attention this is at least one of the possible interpretations.

The dramatist's brilliant success in this play is due not only to a remarkable mingling of the serious and the comic and to a profounder use than ever of earlier devices (the telescoping of time, the diverse assignments of the Stage Manager, the simplification of scenery, and the pageantry of philosophic and poetic ideas), but also to his requiring the actors to step out of their roles to discuss with their audience their own views on the play and the problems attendant upon producing a play, and to debate and confess to one another their own personal dilemmas. In this way Wilder achives other dimensions for the work; he also is able to drive home one of his favorite convictions: that the artistic validity of a play depends to a degree upon the acknowledgment that its pursuit of truth is via make-believe.

Before writing his novel *The Ides of March*, published in 1948, Wilder had served in Italy with Air Intelligence; he had also lost a friend, the poet Lauro De Bosis, in the fight against the dictatorship of Mussolini. These experiences have been offered as an explanation of why, in this book, he was led to a consideration of the prototype of European dictators, Julius Caesar. The reader of the novel must find this a very strange conclusion. Wilder's Caesar is essentially a noble, tragic figure, and bears no resemblance to the Mussolini, Hitler, or Stalin the world has known. Wilder has never been interested in probing the psychology of the corrupt or the psychopathic; this fact alone sets him apart from many of his contemporaries. So far from having a Mussolini in mind, Wilder in creating his hero must deliberately have cast off the image of that pompous, vacuous Italian as well as the images of the dehumanized Austrian and the devious, barbaric Georgian—except insofar as their overrunning of territories had engulfed the world in destruction—in order to seek the *man*, Julius Caesar, chief architect of the Roman Empire as well as its dictator. Wilder's portrait of him is as far from those abortions of the human race, dictators of the twentieth century, as it is from the caricature Shakespeare drew of the great Julius. Shakespeare's hero was Brutus, not Caesar. It is a testimony to Wilder's unquenchable, though unsentimental, faith in humanity and to his admirable capacity to find philosophic perspective while confusion is the order of the day that he could have undertaken to reveal the tragic side of the dictator of Rome at such a time as that in which this novel was written.

The Julius Caesar whom we meet in these pages is a man of forbearance and personal charm, indulgent to enemies, fearless, incapable of self-pity, and decorous in conduct to everyone about him. His faults (and he is himself well aware of what they are) are extensions of his virtues. Unlike Shakespeare's Caesar, he is no enemy of thought—he wishes to know everything and is a great reader; but he is impatient of reflection. He must always act. Unlike, too, most of us, who deliberate or refuse to decide or else make our decisions blindly, he "embraces decision. It is as though he felt his mind to be operating only when it is interlocking itself with significant consequences. Caesar shrinks from no responsibility." On the contrary, he rejoices in the obligations of holding in his hands the destinies of the Empire. "There is no liberty save in responsibility" is his credo, and for him "the central movement of the mind is the desire for unrestricted liberty." Such a man can feel

he has achieved that desire only when he is at the top. Being at the top, and self-committed to endless responsibilities, he has in many ways less liberty than his meanest citizen.

He is unvengeful, he takes no joy in punishing those who would destroy him. No human conduct astonishes him—he can tolerate everything except bad manners—and he is not shocked when those to whom he has been magnanimous conspire against him. ("It is only dogs that never bite their masters.") He knows that someday he will be assassinated, and he feels his choice is between ignoring that eventuality ("If I were not Caesar now, I would be Caesar's assassin") and living in constant fear. He chooses the former.

Despite his unfailing courtesy, his mildness and good cheer, there is no love in his life. His physician, who completely respects him, confesses relief whenever he is able to get away from him. He is close to only two people: the matriarch Julia, his aunt, and Lucius Mamilius Turrinus, his boyhood friend and fellow soldier, thought long dead by the world but living in seclusion at Capri. But he sees very little of them, and whatever relationship he has with them is conducted chiefly through letters. His wife is a silly, superficial woman, with whom he has endless patience but no communication. He thinks he has put behind him the passion he once felt for Cleopatra, but her appearance in Rome re-awakens the old frenzy; his need of living with outward decorum, however, permits him to enjoy only clandestine moments with her. The world sees Caesar, correctly, as a man unloving and incapable of love—correctly, because the three people for whom he holds affection are nowhere near the center of his life and activities. It is true that he has retained the friendship of the women who have been his mistresses in the past, but he is too bored with them to feel their warmth. On all sides, too, he meets with adulation; the vulgar and the fanatic even insist upon considering him a god. But on all this Caesar looks with private derision. The hot hatred of the poet Catullus, whose genius is almost the only thing that holds him in awe, is more precious to him than the worship of the world.

He is a man who lives for public responsibilities. A foe to superstition, he has come to suspect religion itself. He is aware of the mystical operating in life, but with his passion for knowledge does not like to think of it; he wishes everything to be comprehensible to the rational mind. He would like to have a religion but his skepticism is too deeply rooted. "It is probable," he records, "that my last moments of consciousness will be filled with the last of many confirmations that the affairs of the world proceed with that senselessness with which a stream carries leaves upon its tide."

A lonely man, who never gives a hint of his isolation, he is cut off from humanity. His discovery that freedom involves the embracing of responsibility is an important one (and therefore Brutus and the other conspirators are, in comparison with him, small men) but his responsibilities do not include those which are the most important: those rooted in love, our chief junction with the eternal. Caesar, for all his tact, kindness, and courtesy, is a man who falls short of any spiritual illumination, though he seems to have missed it by the narrowest of margins.

The Ides of March is as authentically classic Roman as *The Woman of Andros* is classic Greek and *The Cabala* Italian. (Why does the classic Roman appear so little Italian?) Wilder's very language, limpid in *The Woman of Andros*, colloquially midwestern in *Heaven's My Destination*, takes on the sonority and intellectual weight of the Latin tongue. Never

has a writer less concerned himself with the general reader's limitations. The novel assumes some knowledge of Roman history and literature. Also, it is cast in a form perfect for the novelist's ends, but which could be guaranteed to alienate the uncultivated reader by the second page. Varying the oldest method of writing the English novel, the epistolary, Wilder tells his story through a series of often unrelated "documents," all (but the final page and the citations from Catullus) his own invention —a device enabling him to have the advantages of the "omniscient author" without seeming to be present, to be everywhere and inside everyone without intruding himself. These documents consist of edicts, letters, public communications, snatches of popular songs, scribblings on walls—and quotations from Catullus.

But he has been far from idle. A year earlier (1947) he had written an amusing three-scene skit for the Century Club's centennial, *Our Century*, issued in a limited edition; it showed the club as envisioned by members' sons, new members, and members' wives. After *The Matchmaker* he composed *The Alcestiad*, a tetralogy. The first part of it deals with the refusal of young Alcestis to marry because she wishes to devote herself to God, and then deciding to live for Admetus; the second shows her offering to die in place of Admetus; in the third she becomes spiritually one with God at her death. Only the fourth part, the satyr-play, has been published in English thus far (in the *Atlantic Monthly*), as "The Drunken Sisters"; here Apollo wins from the Three Fates the life of Admetus, by a trick. *The Alcestiad*, translated into German and published in that language, has been produced as play and as opera with great acclaim in Europe.

Wilder having early exhibited his contempt

for those concluding paragraphs which sum up what has already been said, I shall not succumb to that popular vice. Suffice to add that his hobbies never stray far from the business of writing: the study of early records of the theater, exotic languages, and the mores of distant peoples. He has always seen his occupation as a profession, and surely no American of our time seems more surely to have been born to the vocation of writer.

Selected Bibliography

WORKS OF THORNTON WILDER

The Trumpet Shall Sound, Yale Literary Magazine, 85:9–26, 78–92, 128–46, 192–207 (October, November, December 1919, January 1920).

"A Diary: First and Last Entry," *S 4 N*, No. 32, pp. 7–11 (February 1924).

"Three Sentences," *Double-Dealer*, 4:110 (September 1924).

The Cabala. New York: A. and C. Boni, 1926.

The Bridge of San Luis Rey. New York: A. and C. Boni, 1927.

The Angel That Troubled the Waters. New York: Coward-McCann, 1928.

"Playgoing Nights from a Travel Diary" (with Isabel Wilder), *Theatre Arts*, 13:411–19 (June 1929).

The Woman of Andros. New York: A. and C. Boni, 1930.

The Long Christmas Dinner and Other Plays. New York: Coward-McCann, 1931.

Lucrece. (Adapted from the French of André Obey.) Boston: Houghton, Mifflin, 1933.

"Introduction," to *Narration: Four Lectures*, by Gertrude Stein. Chicago: University of Chicago Press, 1935.

Heaven's My Destination. New York: Harper, 1935.

"Introduction," to *The Geographical History of America*, by Gertrude Stein. New York: Random House, 1936.

Our Town. New York: Coward-McCann, 1938.

The Merchant of Yonkers. New York: Harper, 1939.

"James Joyce, 1882–1941," *Poetry*, 57:370–74 (March 1941).

"Some Thoughts on Playwriting," in *The Intent of the Artist*, by Augusto Centeno. Princeton, N.J.: Princeton University Press, 1941.

The Skin of Our Teeth. New York: Harper, 1942.

Our Century. New York: Century Association, 1947.

The Ides of March. New York: Harper, 1948.

"World Literature and the Modern Mind," in *Goethe and the Modern Age*, by Arnold Bergsträsser. Chicago: Regnery, [1950]. Pp. 213–24.

"Fraternity of Man: Excerpts from Commencement Address," *Time*, 58:61 (July 2, 1951).

"Toward an American Language," *Atlantic Monthly*, 190:29–37 (July 1952).

"The American Loneliness," *Atlantic Monthly*, 190:65–69 (August 1952).

"Emily Dickinson," *Atlantic Monthly*, 190:43–48 (November 1952).

"Silent Generation," *Harper's*, 206:34–36 (April 1953).

The Matchmaker (a revision of *The Merchant of Yonkers*). New York: Harper, 1955.

"Introduction," to *Oedipus the King*, by Sophocles. New York: Heritage, [1955].

Three Plays: Our Town, The Skin of Our Teeth, The Matchmaker, with a Preface by the author. New York: Harper, 1957.

"The Drunken Sisters," *Atlantic Monthly*, 200:92–95 (November 1957).

"Childhood," *Atlantic Monthly*, 206:78–84 (November 1960).

Published since the writing of this essay.

The Eighth Day. New York: Harper, 1967.

Theophilus North. New York: Harper and Row, 1973.

The Journals of Thornton Wilder: With Two Scenes of an Uncompleted Play, "The Emporium." New Haven: Yale Univ. Press, 1985.

BIBLIOGRAPHY

Edelstein, J. M. *A Bibliographical Checklist of the Writings of Thornton Wilder.* New Haven, Conn.: Yale University Library, 1959.

BIOGRAPHICAL AND CRITICAL STUDIES

Adcock, St. John. "Thornton Wilder," *Bookman,* 69:316–19 (March 1929).

Balliett, Carl, Jr. "The Skin of Whose Teeth?" Part III, *Saturday Review of Literature,* 26:11 (January 2, 1943).

Brown, E. K. "A Christian Humanist," *University of Toronto Quarterly,* 4:356–70 (April 1935).

Brown, John Mason. "Wilder: *Our Town,*" *Saturday Review of Literature,* 32:34 (August 6, 1949).

Burbank, Rex. *Thornton Wilder.* New York: Twayne, 1961.

Campbell, Joseph, and H. M. Robinson. "The Skin of Whose Teeth?" *Saturday Review of Literature,* 25:3–4 (December 19, 1942), 26:16–18 (February 13, 1943).

Corrigan, Robert W. "Thornton Wilder and the Tragic Sense of Life," *Educational Theatre,* 13:167–73 (October 1961).

Cowley, Malcolm. *Exile's Return.* New York: Viking, 1951. Pp. 10, 239.

———. "Introduction," *A Thornton Wilder Trio.* New York: Criterion, 1956.

———, ed. *Writers at Work: The Paris Review Interviews.* New York: Viking, 1958. Pp. 99–118.

Davis, Elmer. "Caesar's Last Months," *Saturday Review of Literature,* 31:11–12 (February 21, 1948).

Edgell, D. P. "Thornton Wilder Revisited," *Cairo Studies in English,* 2:47–59 (1960).

Fergusson, Francis. "Three Allegorists: Brecht, Wilder, and Eliot," *Sewanee Review,* 64:544–73 (Fall 1956).

Firebaugh, Joseph J. "The Humanism of Thornton Wilder," *Pacific Spectator,* 4:426–28 (Fall 1950).

Fuller, Edmund. "Thornton Wilder: The Notation of a Heart," *American Scholar,* 28:210–17 (Spring 1959).

Fulton, A. R. "Expressionism Twenty Years After," *Sewanee Review,* 52:398–413 (Summer 1944).

Gassner, John. *Form and Idea in the Modern Theatre.* New York: Dryden, 1956. Pp. 14, 142–43, 256.

Gilder, Rosamond. "Broadway in Review," *Theatre Arts,* 27:9–11 (January 1943).

Gold, Michael. "Wilder: Prophet of the Genteel Christ," *New Republic,* 64:266–67 (October 22, 1930).

Guthrie, Tyrone. "The World of Thornton Wilder," *New York Times Magazine,* November 27, 1955, pp. 26–27+.

Hansen, Harry. "Three Reviews," *Woman's Radio Review,* 1935, pp. 3–21.

Hewitt, Bernard. "Thornton Wilder Says 'Yes,'" *Tulane Drama Review,* 4:110–20 (December 1959).

Hopper, Stanley R., ed. *Spiritual Problems in Contemporary Literature.* New York: Institute for Religious and Social Studies, 1952.

Kohler, David. "Thornton Wilder," *English Journal,* 28:1–11 (January 1939).

MacLeish, Archibald. "The Isolation of the American Artist," *Atlantic Monthly,* 201:55–59 (January 1958).

McNamara, Robert. "Phases of American Religion in Thornton Wilder and Willa Cather," *Catholic World,* 135:641–49 (September 1932).

"An Obliging Man," *Time,* 61:44–49 (January 12, 1953).

Parmenter, Ross. "Novelist into Playwright," *Saturday Review of Literature,* 18:10–11 (June 11, 1938).

Saltpeter, Harry. "Why Is a Best Seller?" *Outlook*, 148:643 (April 18, 1928).

Scott, Winfield Townley. *"Our Town* and the Golden Veil," *Virginia Quarterly*, 29:103–17 (January 1953).

Smith, Harrison. "The Skin of Whose Teeth?" Part II, *Saturday Review of Literature*, 25:12 (December 26, 1942).

Tritsch, Walther. "Thornton Wilder in Berlin," *Living Age*, 341:44–47 (September 1931).

Wilson, Edmund. "Thornton Wilder: The Influence of Proust," *New Republic*, 55:303–05 (August 8, 1928).

———. "The Antrobuses and the Earwickers," *Nation*, 156:167–68 (January 30, 1943).

———. *The Shores of Light*. New York: Farrar, Straus, and Young, 1952. Pp. 376–77, 384–91, 500–03, 534–39, 587–92.

—BERNARD GREBANIER

Tennessee Williams

1911-1983

TENNESSEE WILLIAMS once wrote: "My folks were pioneer Tennesseeans, mostly of a military and political disposition, some of them, such as Nollichucky Jack Sevier, having been famous Indian fighters when the South was being settled. I am also related to the late Senator John Sharp Williams who was a famous silver-tongued orator of Mississippi and also one of the State's best drinkers, who said when he retired that he 'would rather be a hound-dawg an' bay th' moon from his Mississippi plantation than a member of the United States Senate.'"

John Sevier did live on the Nolichucky River from 1783 to 1790 and the *Memphis Commercial Appeal* (September 27, 1932) did attribute to Senator Williams a quotation very like the one above. Tennessee Williams may well be descended from both men, but the quotation is given here not as a fact but as a symptom. It is part of a biographical statement which Williams sent to William Kozlenko, the editor of a collection of plays, *American Scenes* (1941), which included two early Williams one-acters—*This Property Is Condemned* and the now forgotten *At Liberty*. It is a young man's boast, a young writer's way of insisting that he is a silver-tongued, hard-drinking Indian fighter. It also identifies as a bona fide southerner the young dramatist whose two contributions carried the joint subtitle "Two Mississippi Plays."

Most of the biographical information that we have about Williams comes from him—from the introductory essays that were printed with his plays, from casual remarks made to interviewers—and it is probable that the facts of his life were occasionally sacrificed to an immediate effect. Many standard references still give 1914 as the year of Williams' birth although that fiction was exploded several years ago. A great many Williams characters, such as Mrs. Stone of the Roman spring, are haunted by encroaching age, but it was apparently practicality, and not vanity, that made Williams lie about the date of his birth. In 1939, in order to enter a playwriting contest that the Group Theatre was running for writers under 25, Williams knocked three years off his age, and, after he was awarded a special citation, he never bothered to put the years back.

Williams' biography is further complicated by the fact that many commentators go to his stories and plays to find the details of his life. Some of the details are there. We know that Williams, like Tom in *The Glass Menagerie*, worked in a shoe warehouse. It is a short step from the recognition of biographical incident to the acceptance of a fictional work as a factual statement; the short story "The Resemblance between a Violin Case and a Coffin," for instance, is usually taken as an accurate re-creation of the relationship between Williams and his sister Rose. It is quite likely that a writer as self-preoccupied as Williams is (even his most casual remarks are attempts to explain or to invent his feelings), will use himself extensively in his fictional work, but there is a danger in equating fiction with fact. Amanda in *The Glass Menagerie* is almost certainly based on Williams' mother, but that certainty should not keep us from recognizing the justice of his mother's cry, in her book *Remember Me to Tom,* "I am *not* Amanda." Williams' biography, then, like T. S. Eliot's April, is a mixture involving memory and desire. It is well to keep that in mind as you read the next few paragraphs—the short version of the Tennessee Williams story.

He was born Thomas Lanier Williams on March 26, 1911, in Columbus, Mississippi. His father was a traveling salesman who spent very little time with his family and made no permanent home for them. For the first seven years of his life, Williams and his mother and sister Rose lived with Mrs. Williams' father, an Episcopalian clergyman, either in Nashville or in the various Mississippi towns—Columbus, Canton, Clarksdale—where he held parishes. In *Remember Me to Tom* there is a family portrait, in which Mrs. Williams is reading to the two children, a studio photograph of three beautiful people, a visual equivalent of the idealization which Mrs. Williams' book makes of those early years. In her story of Tom, the shocking event in his life was the move to St. Louis in 1918, when his father, now sales manager for a shoe company, brought his family to live with him; a second son, Dakin, was born in 1919. In Mrs. Williams' account of the St. Louis years, her husband appears as something of a villain—crude, stingy, drunken. It is not necessary to accept Mrs. Williams' very defen-

sive book as completely truthful (Mr. Williams never wrote his version), but it does convey a sense of family life marked with anger, tension, separateness which might help explain the recurrent themes of Williams' plays.

If home was "not a pleasant refuge," as Williams once said, the outside world was no better. Williams recalls being teased by gangs of boys when he began to go to school. But go to school he did. He graduated from high school in January 1929, and went on to the University of Missouri that fall. He was forced to drop out after his third year and go to work for the International Shoe Company. His distaste for the job has so colored the accounts of that period that it is difficult now to know exactly what was going on in the Williams household. As the story is told, his father is once again the villain, insisting on his withdrawal from college, pushing him into the shoe company. But the year was 1932. There must have been quite a few young men who could not go to college that year and who would have considered themselves lucky to have found even a dull job which paid $65 a month. For Williams, however, his three years at the shoe company were "a living death." He escaped finally by breaking down, a collapse that is attributed variously to exhaustion, heart palpitations, and the recurrence of a childhood paralysis. After a recuperative summer with his grandparents in Memphis, he enrolled at Washington University in St. Louis, from which he was dropped in 1937. He graduated finally from the University of Iowa in 1938 and began the life of writing and wandering which has been going on—with increasing degrees of affluence—ever since.

Within the superstructure of employment and education described above, Williams was becoming a writer. He began—as what writer does not—when he was still a child; in *Remember Me to Tom,* Mrs. Williams reprints two poems which he wrote for his junior high newspaper in 1925. It is easy to call up stereotypes of the "writer" when one thinks of the young Tennessee Williams at work. Image One: the sensitive boy, uncomfortable in the public world of school and the private world of home, taking refuge in his typewriter. Image Two (borrowed from *The Glass Menagerie*): the compulsive poet, trapped by the prosaic world, scribbling lyric effusions on shoebox tops. There is probably truth in both these images. "I write from my own tensions," Williams once told a reporter from *Newsweek*. "For me, this is a form of therapy." From most of Williams' statements about his work, it is evident that for him writing is both home and healing, a way of making order out of disorder. There is, however, another, an important side to Williams the writer.

In a 1960 interview with Arthur Gelb in the *New York Times,* he speaks of his "desire for success": "I want to reach a mass audience." From the beginning, Williams has been not only the "poet," sending messages out of his own isolation, but the professional writer in search of an audience and commercial success. Amusingly enough, this side of him appears in embryonic form in the teen-age Williams. In 1927, pretending to be an unhappily married traveling salesman (a bouquet for Daddy?), the sixteen-year-old boy won third prize in a *Smart Set* contest, "Can a Good Wife Be a Good Sport?"; his entry, which answers *no* to the question, is reprinted in *Remember Me to Tom*. In 1928, his first professionally published story appeared in the August issue of *Weird Tales*. In 1929, when the university newspaper interviewed him, as a freshman whose name had already appeared in national magazines, Williams said that Louis Bromfield was his favorite author. With a best-selling novelist to look up to and with popular magazines—slicks and pulps—as his goal, Williams was obvi-

ously already thinking of himself as a professional; his announced ambition was to go to the School of Journalism.

It was later, during the Washington University years, that Williams began to read intensively in those writers whose marks can be found on much of his work—D. H. Lawrence, Hart Crane, Lorca, Rimbaud, Rilke, Melville. It was then, presumably, in his association with a group of students with literary ambitions, that his "desire for success" was transformed. Without losing the original impulse toward fame and fortune, Williams the writer acquired his double, Williams the artist. There is room in Williams the man for both figures. There is no reason why both the *Newsweek* and the *Times* quotations cannot be taken as true. The kind of revisions that he has done on his plays over the years displays both sides of him; he rewrites in an attempt to find the play implicit in the original material (as when he made *Orpheus Descending* out of *Battle of Angels*), but he also rewrites in an attempt to get the audience he would like to have (as when, following Elia Kazan's suggestions, he provided a new third act for *Cat on a Hot Tin Roof,* one which changed the meaning of the play).

Tennessee Williams' career as a playwright got under way in earnest in 1935, during the summer he spent in Memphis. He had written plays earlier when he was at the University of Missouri, but the production of *Cairo! Shanghai! Bombay!* by a small summer theater seems to have given him the immediate impetus to turn out more plays. This comedy (of which a Memphis friend, Dorothy Shapiro, was co-author), like most of his youthful plays, has never been printed. His second play to be produced was something called *The Magic Tower* which was done in 1936 by a theater group in Webster Groves, a St. Louis suburb. That year he became associated with The Mummers, a lively St. Louis theater group under the direction of Willard Holland, whom Williams warmly praises in his introduction to *27 Wagons Full of Cotton,* "Something Wild . . ." For them, he wrote a one-acter, *Headlines,* to serve as a curtain-raiser for an Armistice Day production of Irwin Shaw's *Bury the Dead.* Within the next two years, The Mummers produced two full-length Williams plays, *Candles in the Sun* and *The Fugitive Kind* (which should not, for all its title, be confused with the movie version of *Orpheus Descending*); a third play, *Not about Nightingales,* was about to be done in 1938 when the group died of economic malnutrition. From the description of these and other plays of the period, it is clear that social criticism, which runs under the surface of most of Williams' work, was presented overtly, even blatantly. *Headlines* was obviously a pacifist tract, and *Me, Vashya!,* written at the same time, was about the decade's favorite monster, the munitions maker. *Candles in the Sun,* which concerned coal miners in Alabama, was described by a reviewer on the *St. Louis Post-Dispatch* as a play about "poverty, degeneracy, accidents on the fifth level below ground, a strike and a brutal murder, ending with beans for everybody, hope and the singing of 'solidarity forever.' "

In 1939, Tennessee Williams (who had by this time dropped the Thomas Lanier) ceased to be simply a local playwright. That year, he bundled together most of his collected works, including a group of one-acters called *American Blues,* and shipped them off to the Group Theatre contest. The judges—Harold Clurman, Irwin Shaw, and Molly Day Thacher—gave him a special award, as the citation says, for "a group of three sketches which constitute a full-length play." At this point, no one seems quite certain what plays made up *American Blues,* although Mrs. Williams, in her book, mentions *Moony's Kid Don't Cry, The Dark Room,* and *The Case of the Crushed Petunias.*

All three of them appear in the Dramatists Play Service collection called *American Blues,* published in 1948, but *Petunias* carries the dateline: Key West, February 1941. In any case, they have neither stylistic nor thematic similarities and could hardly be considered as related sketches.

The most important result of the Group Theatre prize was that Williams got himself an agent, Audrey Wood, who had faith in him and worked hard for him. One of her first official acts was to get him a Rockefeller Fellowship, which gave him money enough to work comfortably, to rewrite *Battle of Angels,* which was to be his first play to receive a major theatrical production. At this time, 1940, he attended a seminar on playwriting which John Gassner and Theresa Helburn conducted at the New School in association with the Theatre Guild's Bureau of New Plays. Apparently largely as a result of Gassner's urging, the Theatre Guild produced *Battle of Angels.* It opened in Boston on December 30, 1940, with Miriam Hopkins in the lead and, after mechanical and spiritual crises, the play closed without ever getting to New York. Its opening night was a fiasco, in part because a smoke-making machine got out of control, but its chief difficulty in Boston was that it hit censorship trouble during the second week, presumably because someone decided that it was blasphemous. Although the Theatre Guild turned down a second revision of the play in 1941, Williams' career as a playwright—at least as a writer of short plays—was an active one in the early 1940's. *The Long Goodbye* was performed by students at the New School in 1940 and short Williams plays were published not only in the Kozlenko volume mentioned at the beginning of this essay, but in many of the Margaret Mayorga collections of *The Best Short Plays*—in 1940, 1941, 1942, 1944, 1945.

The Glass Menagerie opened in Chicago on December 26, 1944, and in New York on March 31, 1945. The play ran for more than a year. Tennessee Williams had arrived. From that time on, his career is a matter of public record. He has averaged rather more than a play every two years: *You Touched Me!* (1945); *A Streetcar Named Desire* (1947); *Summer and Smoke* (1948); *The Rose Tattoo* (1951); *Camino Real* (1953); *Cat on a Hot Tin Roof* (1955); *Orpheus Descending* (1957); *Suddenly Last Summer* (1958); *Sweet Bird of Youth* (1959); *Period of Adjustment* (1960); *The Night of the Iguana* (1961); *The Milk Train Doesn't Stop Here Anymore* (1963; revised 1964); *The Eccentricities of a Nightingale* (1964); *Slapstick Tragedy*, a double bill of *The Mutilated* and *The Gnädiges Fräulein* (1966); *The Two-Character Play* (1967); *Kingdom of Earth*, called *The Seven Descents of Myrtle* on Broadway (1968); *In the Bar of a Tokyo Hotel* (1969); *Small Craft Warnings* (1972). The dates are those of the Broadway or off-Broadway openings, except for *Nightingale*, which had only a summer production in Nyack, New York, and *Two-Character,* which played in London. In a note to the published *Nightingale,* a completely new play based on *Summer and Smoke,* Williams says that the new version was written shortly before the English production of the earlier play, which would seem to indicate that the *Nightingale* sat quietly in its cage between 1951 and 1964. Because of his habit of revision and his sensible desire to see his plays performed on stage before they face a New York audience, it is always difficult to place an exact time of composition. *You Touched Me!,* which Williams wrote with Donald Windham, was performed in 1944 in both Cleveland and Pasadena and certainly, in its first form, predates *The Glass Menagerie. Summer and Smoke* was performed at Margo Jones's theater in Dallas in 1947; a

version of *Sweet Bird* was put on in Florida as early as 1956; several of the other plays were tried out in Florida or at the festival in Spoleto, Italy. *Orpheus,* of course, is *Battle of Angels* done over, and *Camino Real* is an extended treatment of *Ten Blocks on the Camino Real,* first published in 1948.

If we take 100 performances as a respectable run for a play in New York, Williams had only two failures before 1963: *Camino Real* and *Orpheus Descending.* Both of these were later revived off-Broadway, and *Summer and Smoke,* which just made 100 performances in its original production, was an outstanding off-Broadway success at the Circle in the Square in 1952. His greatest commercial and critical successes have been *The Glass Menagerie, A Streetcar Named Desire, Cat on a Hot Tin Roof,* and *The Night of the Iguana.* These plays not only had the longest runs, but they all received the Drama Critics Circle Award and two of them (*Streetcar* and *Cat*) were given the Pulitzer Prize. While the reception of his plays was presumably satisfying the playwright's "desire for success" (and incidentally making him a rich man), the artist in him could take comfort in the knowledge that he had gained a reputation as one of the handful of American playwrights who could be considered serious dramatists. Beginning with *Milk Train,* however, the Williams plays were greeted by critical disdain and public indifference, and with some justice, for the plays of the 1960's—the demented *The Gnädiges Fräulein* aside—tended to be less imaginative, more discursive, less exciting than his earlier work. He was still celebrated as one of America's most important playwrights, but he found it increasingly difficult to draw audiences. A few months after the closing of *Tokyo Hotel,* which ironically enough was, as Williams said, about "the usually early and peculiarly humiliating doom of the artist," his personal and professional problems met in his own collapse, and he spent two months in a psychiatric hospital in St. Louis. Although he was back to work by early 1970, it was two years later before *Small Craft Warnings* opened in New York. It was his most successful play since *The Night of the Iguana*. At the time *Small Craft* opened, Williams told several interviewers that he would stick with off-Broadway, that he was no longer interested in Broadway production and the tensions it induces, but as I write this, *Out Cry,* a revision of *The Two-Character Play,* is scheduled for Broadway production early in 1973. Although Williams' critical reputation is based on his long plays, he has published three collections of short plays, *27 Wagons Full of Cotton and Other One-Act Plays* (1946, 1953), *American Blues* (1948), and *Dragon Country* (1970).

There is probably no American playwright since 1920—with the exception of Eugene O'Neill—who has not written for the movies as well as for the stage. Tennessee Williams spent six months in 1943 as a contract writer for MGM, turning out scripts that were never filmed; it was during this period that he wrote *The Gentleman Caller,* an original screenplay which he later turned into *The Glass Menagerie.* Since the success of that play, he has had a hand in seven films, six of them adaptations of his plays. He was co-author of the screenplays for *The Glass Menagerie* (1950, with Peter Berneis), *The Rose Tattoo* (1955, with Hal Kanter), *Suddenly Last Summer* (1959, with Gore Vidal), and *The Fugitive Kind* (1960, with Meade Roberts). He was sole author on his two most important films—*A Streetcar Named Desire* (1951) and *Baby Doll* (1956). Both of these films, which Elia Kazan directed, are works of distinction. *Streetcar* is the most successful transfer of a Williams play from stage to screen, and *Baby Doll* contains, in Archie Lee Meighan, one of the funniest

and most horrifying of Williams' comic grotesques. *Boom!* (1968), the film version of *The Milk Train Doesn't Stop Here Anymore,* although it was directed by Joseph Losey, has been one of the least successful of the Williams screen adaptations.

"I am not a good writer. Sometimes I am a very bad writer indeed." So Williams wrote in an essay published with *Battle of Angels* in *Pharos.* He was attempting to explain his attraction to the theater where, presumably, the objectivity of the genre would keep him from the romantic and subjective excess that he falls prey to in his stories and poems. His lines may be taken as an accurate summation of his talent for fiction and poetry. Yet, he has published three volumes of short stories, *One Arm* (1948), *Hard Candy* (1954), and *The Knightly Quest* (1967); a short novel, *The Roman Spring of Mrs. Stone* (1950); and a collection of poems, *In the Winter of Cities* (1956, 1964). The novel is a somewhat tiresome account of an aging ex-actress who passes from being a seller to becoming a buyer of youth and beauty; it is interesting primarily because its heroine resembles so many of Williams' stage heroines, particularly Alexandra in *Sweet Bird of Youth.* Both the stories and the poems are shot through with a kind of fuzzy mysticism which must share the page with a very specific depiction of perversion (Oliver in "One Arm" dies in the electric chair with the letters from his male lovers between his legs). Most of the stories and poems are uninteresting except as they relate to the plays. Lines from the poems find their way into the dialogue of the plays; for instance, one poem, "The Beanstalk Country," contributes a useful metaphor to *Sweet Bird of Youth.* Many of the stories are early workouts for later plays: "Portrait of a Girl in Glass" for *The Glass Menagerie,* which it greatly resembles; "Three Players of a Summer Game" for *Cat on a Hot Tin Roof;* "Man

Bring This Up Road" for *The Milk Train Doesn't Stop Here Anymore;* "The Night of the Iguana," which gave its name, its heroine, its setting, and its lizard to the play; and "The Kingdom of Earth," which provided the three characters, some of the lines and the title, minus the definite article, for the later play. Williams, then, is a literary jack-of-all-trades, sending messages of all kinds back from the beanstalk country where he has seen the ogre, but as a poet or a writer of fiction he is working with a jammed communications system. In the rest of this essay, which will attempt to describe what Williams is trying to say and how he goes about it, the plays will necessarily be center stage.

"I have never been able to say what was the theme of my play and I don't think I have ever been conscious of writing with a theme in mind." So Tennessee Williams wrote in "Questions without Answers," an article in the *New York Times* in 1948, which, as usual, was part aesthetics, part advertisement for the play about to open—*Summer and Smoke* in this case. "Usually when asked about a theme, I look vague and say, 'It's a play about life.'" The lines, of course, are defensive. No writer likes to think that a work of his can safely be paraphrased and, if it is to be summed up in a sentence or two, he does not want to do the job himself—particularly not in a situation such as the party Williams describes in the *Times* piece in which he is talking to people who have presumably seen his work. Still, to write about "life" implies the looking at it and to see it from a particular pair of eyes hooked into a particular brain involves a personal way of seeing, a vision of life. By the time the vision is embedded in a plot, made ambulatory through characters, verbalized in lines that are to be spoken by actors on a stage—by the time it has been transmuted into a play—it has become an artistic vision and that means that

themes, implicit and explicit, are walking abroad. What Williams probably means in the lines quoted above is that he does not set out to demonstrate an idea or to deliver a message in his plays. Even if we accept that as true (and we probably cannot do so for plays like *The Night of the Iguana* and *The Milk Train Doesn't Stop Here Anymore*), we must recognize that his choice of character and situation provides him with recurrent themes that turn up in his work from the earliest one-acters to *Small Craft Warnings*. A caveat: although Williams' plays all bear a family resemblance, each of them is an individual with its private strengths and weaknesses. There is no room in a work this short to do extensive analyses of his plays. In reading the discussion below of Williams' subject matter and his dramatic technique, it is well to remember that my somewhat generalized comments are only useful when they have been tried on a particular play and altered until they fit.

In 1950, Williams wrote an introduction to the New Classics Edition of Carson McCullers' novel *Reflections in a Golden Eye* in which he seems to be talking about himself as much as Mrs. McCullers. "It appears to me, sometimes, that there are only two kinds of people who live outside what E. E. Cummings has defined as 'this socalled world of ours'—the artists and the insane," he says and then he amends, "Of course there are those who are not practising artists and those who have not been committed to asylums, but who have enough of one or both magical elements, lunacy and vision, to permit them also to slip sufficiently apart from 'this socalled world of ours' to undertake or accept an exterior view of it." This is a rough definition of the kind of person who becomes the hero or the heroine of the Williams plays. The same kind of person usually fills a number of the minor roles and, in some of the plays, even acts as villain. What Williams is preoccupied with is not the artist or the insane, as such, but the man or woman who by virtue of being different can (in fact, must) stand outside and see the world clearly—which, for Williams, means to see the horror in it. Although many of his characters are artists or pseudo-artists and most of them are at least a little neurotic, a more general description of the Williams outsider is needed. Perhaps it can be found in *The Eccentricities of a Nightingale,* in which the word *eccentric* is used by the less sensitive characters as an accusatory label; in that play, Alma describes the literary club to which she belongs as "my little company of the faded and frightened and difficult and odd and lonely." The club scene is presented satirically (as it is in *Summer and Smoke*), but Williams has always recognized that his outsiders (from Amanda in *The Glass Menagerie* to Leona in *Small Craft Warnings*) are—from one angle, at least—comic characters. The laughter in them and at them need not detract from their other qualities, made all the stronger by their separateness—their courage, say, or their dignity. At the end of *The Glass Menagerie,* describing the dumb show that goes on while Tom speaks his last monologue, Williams says of Amanda: "Now that we cannot hear the mother's speech, her silliness is gone and she has dignity and tragic beauty."

In an earlier description of Williams' work (in *American Drama since World War II*), I used the label *fugitive kind* to cover all his artist-eccentrics. It still seems the most appropriate. Williams not only used the phrase as title for an early play of his, but he apparently acquiesced in its reuse as title to the movie version of *Orpheus Descending*. In *Battle of Angels,* Sandra uses the phrase to describe herself and Val, uses it too narrowly since it should be taken as a synonym of that other good label—*the dispossessed*—which Val, in the same play, uses to describe himself and

Loon, the guitar-playing Negro vagrant whom he befriends. Within the generalized term, however, there are a variety of types. It might be useful to consider the variations of the fugitive within the kind—beginning with the two categories which Williams put forward in the McCullers essay:

1. The artist. A Williams artist need never put a word to paper or paint to canvas, for it is his temperament, his inclination, that defines him. When Harold Clurman, in *Lies Like Truth,* says of Blanche in *Streetcar,* "She is a poet, even if we are dubious about her understanding of the writers she names," he is describing the artist as Williams uses him. Williams may present him seriously (as in the ponderous Val in *Battle of Angels,* writing "The Book") or satirically (as in Sebastian in *Suddenly Last Summer,* producing one poem a year after a nine-month gestation period), but whether he is serious or comic, he is a man whose special sensibility keeps him from seeing the world through its own eyes. The Williams artists form a large company. In *The Glass Menagerie,* Tom is trying to be a poet, and so is Matilda in *You Touched Me!* In *Summer and Smoke,* Alma, "The Nightingale of the Delta," sings and teaches singing and meets regularly with her bizarre literary society. Byron wanders through *Camino Real.* In *Orpheus Descending,* having put aside "The Book" to take up Loon's guitar, Val is still the central artist, although Vee Talbott, the visionary painter, shares the stage with him. Alexandra in *Sweet Bird of Youth*, like the heroine of *The Roman Spring of Mrs. Stone,* is a fading actress and Chance Wayne is an ex-chorus boy. In *The Night of the Iguana,* Hannah Jelkes, the artist, and her grandfather, "the world's oldest living and practicing poet," earn their way by making sketches or reciting in hotel dining rooms, thus managing to play both sides of the street which academic definition runs

between the fine and the performing arts. Chris Flanders in *Milk Train* is a poet and a maker of mobiles and even Mrs. Goforth is a writer of sorts since she spends her last hours dictating her autobiography. The Gnädiges Fräulein is the most grotesque of the Williams artists, although Myrtle in *Kingdom of Earth,* once one of the Four Hot Shots from Mobile, is an amiable candidate for that title. Felice and Clare are performers in *The Two-Character Play,* which is both the play we see and the play within that play. Mark, the dying artist, is central to *In the Bar of the Tokyo Hotel,* and that other bar, the one in *Small Craft Warnings* is visited not only by Quentin, a writer of sorts whose job is "to make blue movies bluer," but by the memory of Leona's violin-playing brother. To this group should probably be added Brick Pollitt of *Cat on a Hot Tin Roof,* for as an athlete he is a kind of artist, allied, in terms of his diminishing powers, to the aging actresses mentioned above. On these grounds, even Jim O'Connor, the gentleman caller of *Menagerie,* might be included, for he was a basketball star in high school; he had also sung the lead in the school production of *The Pirates of Penzance.*

2. The insane. As Williams uses the word in the McCullers essay, it is a positive restatement of the old bromide about the kinship of the poet and the madman. It is a dangerous category to try to define in Williams' plays because as soon as the label *insanity* is put on a character, part of the audience (including a number of critics) will back away from the play, muttering an incantatory word—the general *sick* or the precise *atypical*—which disassociates them from what is going on on stage. A more genteel word—*disturbed,* perhaps—might go down more easily. Yet, Blanche is carried off to an asylum at the end of *Streetcar* and Catharine, who may or may not be sane, is in an institution in *Suddenly Last Summer.* Shannon has to be tied down in *Iguana* and

Hannah, who comforts him, hints of a dark night in her own soul. The heroine of *Baby Doll* appears a little feeble-minded, at least for most of the movie, and at the end of that film Archie Lee has plainly run mad. Felice and Clare try to cope with the charge that they are insane in *The Two-Character Play,* and the breakdown of Mark in *Tokyo Hotel* is as much mental as physical. Williams' plays offer a gallery of hysterics, all little sisters to Blanche, ranging from Alma in *Summer and Smoke* and Lady in *Orpheus,* both desperate for the pills that will calm them, to poor Isabel in *Period of Adjustment,* who has to make do with Pepto-Bismol to settle her stomach. Although Williams occasionally goes clinical, at least to the extent of identifying Blanche as a "neurasthenic personality," he more often works on a metaphorical level. Think of Alexandra in the first act of *Sweet Bird,* swimming up out of sleep, crying for her oxygen tank; in a scene that is both horrifying and very funny, Williams offers an image of the man who cannot catch his breath in a world that is smothering him.

3. The cripple. This is a group which might comfortably take in the characters discussed above as "insane." It is difficult to find the line between mental and physical disturbances in a Williams character. Is Laura in *Menagerie* crippled by her limp or her shyness? Is George's tremor in *Period of Adjustment* in his head or in his hands? It hardly matters really since the diseases, the injuries, are as much metaphorical as they are real. Brick's broken ankle in *Cat,* Kilroy's weak heart in *Camino Real,* Mrs. Venable's stroke in *Suddenly Last Summer,* Trinket's missing breast in *The Mutilated,* Lot's tuberculosis in *Kingdom of Earth,* and the fatal cancer of Jabe in *Orpheus,* Big Daddy in *Cat,* and Mrs. Goforth in *Milk Train* are all devices that help indicate that they are special characters.

4. The sexual specialist. This is a hard cate-

gory to put a label on because it has to take in such disparate characters. It includes the virgins waiting to be initiated (Matilda in *You Touched Me!*, Alma in *Summer and Smoke*, Rosa and Jack in *The Rose Tattoo*, George and Isabel in *Period of Adjustment*) and those who will not be (Laura in *Menagerie*, Hannah in *Iguana*); those who have chosen chastity to escape corruption (Val in *Orpheus*, Brick in *Cat*); the professionals and those amateurs so talented they could go professional (Val, Stanley in *Streetcar*, Chance Wayne in *Sweet Bird*, Camille and Casanova in *Camino Real*, Bill in *Small Craft Warnings*); the homosexuals, explicit (Charlus in *Camino*, Sebastian in *Suddenly Last Summer*, Miss Fellowes in *Iguana*, Quentin in *Small Craft*) and implicit (Brick in *Cat*); those with a desperate need for sex as a stimulant or a punishment (Blanche in *Streetcar*, Maggie in *Cat*, Carol in *Orpheus*, Alexandra in *Sweet Bird*, Miriam in *Tokyo Hotel*). The thing that they all have in common is an extreme sensitivity.

5. The foreigner. Two things are at work here: a fact and a myth. It is a fact of American society—at least of the small-town southern society into which Williams was born—that the foreigner, even when he ceases to be foreign, is an outsider. It is a myth, one from northern Europe that was passed on to the United States, that the Mediterranean peoples live richer, wilder, more open lives than the cold, closed northerners. Thus we have Rosa Gonzales and her father, the fiery Mexicans of *Summer and Smoke*; the wild Sicilians of *The Rose Tattoo*; the corruption of *Camino Real* which, according to a Williams stage direction, recalls Tangiers, Havana, Vera Cruz, Casablanca, Shanghai, and New Orleans; the Italian Lady of *Orpheus*; the Sicilian with the riding crop of *27 Wagons Full of Cotton*, softened a little for *Baby Doll*; the Lorca-like setting for the offstage cannibalism of *Suddenly Last Summer*; and the hot-blooded Mexican

boys of *Iguana*. There are no Jews (except for some offstage names) and very few Negroes. Because these are the favorite outsiders of American writers, their absence is a bit odd. It is the missing Negro that most demands explanation since a view of the world which uses the Mississippi delta country as its microcosm would seem to have the Negro ready-made as an image of the fugitive kind. Except for Loon in *Battle of Angels*, the actual Negroes that appear in Williams' plays before *Kingdom of Earth*—the neighbor woman in *Streetcar*, the maid in *Period of Adjustment*—hardly fit this image. Williams does use the image, but by analogy. His white characters on stage recognize themselves in Negroes whom we hear about but never see. Thus, Val in *Orpheus* identifies with the runaway convict (presumably Negro) torn apart by dogs, and Chance Wayne in *Sweet Bird* feels himself menaced by the kind of envy that caused a Negro to be taken at random and castrated. I do not presume to know whether this substitution arises from a psychological defense of Williams', an artistic decision about audience identification, a guess at what the Broadway market would take, or a combination of all three possibilities. In *Kingdom of Earth*, however, the Williams hero with "*darker-than-olive skin*," unlike his counterpart in the 1954 story, admits (boasts of?) his "colored blood"; still, the character was played on Broadway by a white actor.

As the examples multiply in the categories above, it becomes clear that the concept of the outsider, the fugitive kind, is on the point of evaporating, of becoming a statement about human beings in general. After all, the list includes characters such as Jim O'Connor, whose ideas are used in opposition to those of Tom, the more conventional Williams fugitive, and such as Jabe and Miss Fellowes, who function as villains in their plays. If the outsiders get too numerous, there will be no insiders to oppose them. In a sense, this is what

Williams has begun to suggest in his more recent work. In "The World I Live In," an article for the *Observer*, in which he interviews himself, he says of people in general: "Well, I've never met one that I couldn't love if I completely knew him and understood him." Although the remark sounds both pious and folksy, a cross between "to know all is to forgive all" and Will Rogers' "I never met a man I didn't like," it contains the bridge between the outsider and the insider in the Williams plays. The insider is the man who is protected, by insensitivity or by a strong identification with the dominant group and its conventions, from knowledge of himself and the terrors around him; the outsider is the man who, by virtue of his strangeness, is particularly sensitive to horror. Williams is attracted to the second group and it is to them that he directs the sympathy of his audience.

His attitude toward the comfortable insiders has changed over the years, however; at least his fugitive kind no longer treat the others with an indifference that is a kind of contempt (as Tom did in *Menagerie*) or with open anger (as in the story "Two on a Party," in which the leading characters "loathed and despised" the "squares of the world"). It is true that Shannon in *Iguana* is still shouting out against the world that will not see what he sees (the world as a pile of excrement), but Hannah, in declaring her allegiance to him, speaks a gentle, even a pitying word for the others. "I respect a person that has had to fight and howl for his decency and his—" she begins and, then, after his interruption: "Yes, for his decency and his bit of goodness, much more than I respect the lucky ones that just had theirs handed out to them at birth and never afterwards snatched away from them by . . . unbearable . . . torments . . ." The implication of Hannah's speech is that only the degree of perception (a matter of luck) separates Shannon

from the vacationing schoolteachers whom he despises. If the fine line between the outsiders and the insiders is barely kept intact in *Iguana*, it is broken in *Sweet Bird* when Chance speaks directly to the audience, asking for "your recognition of me in you."

In *Period of Adjustment*—perhaps because he chose to write something approximating a standard Broadway marriage comedy—Williams made an attempt to create characters who displayed all the clichés of imperceptive, ordinary people and to afflict them with the desperation of the fugitive kind. It is through this play—the least typical in the Williams canon—that the playwright indicates most clearly that what he has been talking about all along is not simply the special pain of an eccentric out-group but the human condition as he sees it.

If Williams' (man)kind is fugitive, then something has to be in pursuit. His characters are menaced by three things: by other people, by themselves, and by the universe. At one level, the first of these provides whatever social comment the Williams plays contain. This can be no more than casual satire aimed at the images of what passes for the "good life" in America—the television-liquor cabinet in *Cat* and the car full of "'lectric equipment" destined for the flood waters in *Kingdom of Earth*. It is in *Period of Adjustment*, with its "'cute' little Spanish-type suburban bungalow" built in a development that is slowly sinking into the ground ("High Point over a Cavern" is the play's subtitle), that Williams' use of this kind of satire is most extensive and most conventional. Except when they "carry the banner of Bohemia" (Casanova's line from *Camino*), the Williams characters are ambivalent about American materialism and its implications. Serafina in *The Rose Tattoo* both wants a deep freeze and uses it to denounce the cold American women who do not know love as she presumably does. Amanda insists that she has remarkable children "just *full* of natural endowments," but the insistence, insofar as she believes it, is as blatant an acceptance of the American success myth as Willy Loman's in *Death of a Salesman*. Lady in *Orpheus* wants to use the confectionery, which she has decorated to suggest her father's wine garden, as an attack on those (including her husband) who killed her father and as a means to conventional success. If the trappings of American success are dangerous, they are so not because they provide an alien threat but a corruption toward which the characters yearn. The danger is shown most clearly in plays such as *Menagerie*, in which Tom must escape not only the shoe warehouse but Amanda's demands which tie him to it; *Orpheus*, in which Val, the wild one, almost becomes a shoe clerk; *Period*, in which Ralph contemplates his situation and moans: *"oh, I wish I could be the first man in a moon rocket!"*

At this level, the social comment is relatively commonplace. It is a depiction of American success and its material attributes as empty and ludicrous. In other instances, Williams' comments become much harsher, dig under the surface to turn up the avariciousness and fear that presumably motivate those who want to find and hold their place in the "good life." While Brick and Big Daddy act out their drama of truth and mendacity in *Cat*, they are surrounded by characters who want to get their hands on Big Daddy's money, from the nattering clergyman who cannot quit talking about memorial windows, to Mae and Gooper, who try to use their "no-neck monsters" as pawns in the inheritance game; even Maggie, a spitting cat on a hot tin roof, fears deprivation of money as much as she suffers deprivation of sex. Mrs. Holly and George in *Suddenly Last Summer*, loyal and lovely family types, seem willing to trade Catharine's frontal lobe

for the inheritance from Sebastian. Although these characters might be taken simply as greedy individuals, the implication is that they represent the society in which they live and function. In at least three of the Williams works—*Orpheus, Sweet Bird*, and *Baby Doll* —the playwright places his characters in a context that is political as well as social, that provides an implied attack on the self-protective nastiness (of which racism is a manifestation) that burns Val, castrates Chance, endangers Silva.

Although the social commentary here is often direct (in the revised version of *Orpheus*, one of Val's lynchers stops to rob the till), and is certainly genuine, it is finally secondary. Even Boss Finley, who holds a whole state in his control in *Sweet Bird*, is—in his political guise—only a symptom. It is the evil spirits abroad in the world that Williams wants to depict. Silva in *Baby Doll* explains what they are: "Spirits of violence—and cunning—malevolence — cruelty — treachery — destruction. . . ." Baby Doll, who is not always as simple as she is supposed to be, answers, "Oh, them's just human characteristics." The destructive cruelty that dogs the fugitive kind, then, may be social and political on occasion, but it is always human. Sometimes, it is incidental—a character like the traveling salesman who wanders through *The Rose Tattoo*, stopping just long enough to knee Alvaro in the groin. More often—particularly in the plays in which the outsider is to be destroyed —it is embodied in a central character—Boss Finley, for instance, or Jabe in *Orpheus*— and repeated in peripheral figures—Tom, Jr., and Chance's old school chums in *Sweet Bird*, Dog and Pee Wee in *Orpheus*.

The classic example, of course, is Stanley in *A Streetcar Named Desire*, the insensitive brute who drives Blanche to destruction. He would be such an example, that is, if we took

Williams' word for what the play is about: "The rape of Blanche by Stanley is a pivotal, integral truth in the play, without which the play loses its meaning, which is the ravishment of the tender, the sensitive, the delicate, by the savage and brutal forces of modern society." The quotation is from a letter Williams wrote to Joseph I. Breen, the chief censor for the Production Code, making a plea to retain the integrity of the movie version of *Streetcar*. Under such circumstances, he might be expected to overstate his case. Although Williams' sympathy plainly goes out to Blanche, *Streetcar* is too balanced a play to let her operate simply as a sensitive victim. From her first appearance, when preoccupied with her own fatigue and pain she insults the amiable Eunice, Blanche is, as Williams once called her, "a delicate tigress with her back to the wall." Her destructiveness is clear both in the immediate action on stage (her disruption of Stella's marriage) and in the expositional past (her attack on her husband Allan). In Blanche's descent into madness, we can see one of Williams' outsiders broken by one of the "others," but in much of her behavior we can see that she, too, is an "other" and that Stanley is in danger of becoming a victim.

This ambiguous sense of who is the victim and who the victimizer is used extensively in the later plays in which, to use the metaphor provided by *Suddenly Last Summer*, the eaters sometimes become the eaten. *Sweet Bird*, for all its confusion, offers one of the clearest statements of this. Both Alexandra and Chance are victims within the wide context of the play, but within the terms of their relationship they keep changing the roles of destroyer and destroyed. She describes him as "Lost in the beanstalk country, the ogre's country at the top of the beanstalk, the country of the flesh-hungry, blood-thirsty ogre" and she begs him not to leave her: "If you do I'll turn into the monster again. I'll be the first lady of the Beanstalk Country." He calls her "nice monster" and she calls him "pitiful monster." Both are amateur monsters compared to Boss Finley, but Williams plainly intends that that character should be more than caricature, that he too should be monster-ridden. That he does not come across that way is one of the artistic failures of the play, as Williams himself admitted when he said of Boss Finley's scene, "The act is weak because I couldn't really identify with Boss Finley." Couldn't, to use the terminology from the *Observer* piece quoted above, come to love him. In the revised *Sweet Bird*, Boss Finley—still unloved apparently—has almost disappeared, is given no more than a line or two to bring down an act curtain.

Although the Williams characters are constantly hurt and harried by those around them, they are also tortured by something within themselves—guilt and fear primarily. Tom in *Menagerie*, guilty at deserting Laura, can no more escape the memory of her than Blanche, guilty at having driven Allan to suicide, can stop the accusing polka music from pounding in her head. Brick in *Cat* waits for the click in his head which will turn off his suspicion that he is responsible for his friend Skipper's death. Fear cripples Laura in *Menagerie*, almost immobilizes Matilda in *You Touched Me!*, gives to George in *Period* a physical tremor. The fear here is of failure—sexual in George's case—which causes a withdrawal, a defense against the possibility of being hurt. A more important kind of fear in Williams' work is that of Alexandra in *Sweet Bird* (fear of growing old) and of Mrs. Goforth in *Milk Train* (fear of death), and with this concept of fear we get to the third and most menacing of the pursuers in the Williams plays.

That pursuer may be called the universe, or human mortality, or the absence of God, but Williams most often uses the label with which Chance ends *Sweet Bird*—"the enemy, time, in us all." An early version of that play, a one-acter, is called *The Enemy: Time*. From *Menagerie* on, time has been chasing the Williams characters. Amanda states the implacable fact when she warns Tom "that the future becomes the present, the present the past, and the past turns into everlasting regret if you don't plan for it," and Williams echoes her words in an introduction he wrote for the New Classics Edition of that play, "the monosyllable of the clock is Loss, loss, loss, unless you devote your heart to its opposition." In both these statements, there is the suggestion that time can be outmaneuvered or neutralized by some kind of activity. It is a young man's statement, one which Williams seems never to have believed. His plays are full of characters —Blanche, Marguerite in *Camino*, Alexandra and Chance, Miriam in *Tokyo Hotel*—whom the loss has made desperate. Although Williams likes to use fading beauties and aging athletes as his time-consumed characters, it is clear that it is not simply the loss of youth and beauty that preoccupies him. It is the fact of death. This can be seen in Big Daddy in *Cat* and Mrs. Goforth in *Milk Train*, both of whom try to pretend that they are not dying, and even more clearly in Jabe in *Orpheus*, a death figure who uses destruction in a vain attempt to hang onto life. Williams' conception of man is of one dogged by the knowledge of death and, hence, scarcely able to live the little life he has.

In several of his recent plays—noticeably *Suddenly Last Summer* and *Iguana*—Williams has been considering the nature of the universe in a specific manner, but it is the universe that has been implicit in all his work, one in which man is a stranger and can find comfort, if at all, only in himself and his own kind. In *Suddenly Last Summer*, there are conflicting views of God, neither designed to bring

peace to the troubled soul. Sebastian imagines that he has seen God in watching the flesh-eating birds destroy the baby turtles and, acting on that vision, he allows himself to be so destroyed. Dr. Sugar, who says that "doctors look for God, too," offers a vision which is even more horrifying, for it is described in soft and human words: the blue sky, free of Sebastian's birds, which cannot be seen until the looker has had a lobotomy. Shannon in *Iguana* shares Sebastian's cruel God, but that play makes specific what *Suddenly* only implies, that the universe is in fact an impersonal thing and that the Gods of Sebastian, of Sugar, of Shannon are all created in their own images. This is made clear in *Iguana* when the titular animal is likened to human beings ("At the end of its rope") and when Shannon goes to cut it loose, to play God "because God won't do it." The indifferent God can be seen casually, incidentally in the one-act version of *Kingdom of Earth* (1967), in which Chicken describes Mr. Sikes, who is about to blow up one of his levees, as "like God, he's got more to think about than the people below him." Williams was baptized a Roman Catholic on January 11, 1969; at that time he indicated that he considered himself a Catholic writer, having been concerned with good and evil in the half-dozen plays immediately preceding the event, but such a concern has always been his, and still is, although the post-conversion plays are not as overtly theological as *Suddenly Last Summer* and *Iguana* are.

There is no escape in a universe where there is no God and where the other inhabitants are as dangerous as one's own self. In *Orpheus*, the conjure man offers Carol a charm, the breastbone of a bird, which she rejects because it "isn't clean yet, there's still some flesh clinging to it," because until "every sign of corruption is burned and washed away" it is not a good charm; at the end, she accepts

Val's snakeskin jacket, for it is clean. Val has escaped into death. His sacrifice (he is both Orpheus and Christ) has meaning, for he has passed on to Carol the possibility of a spirit in man which lifts him out of the cruelty, the jealousy, the despair that has killed Lady and lynched the savior (Val Xavier). Here—as in *Camino Real*, in which Kilroy and Don Quixote set out for the mountains where the violets have at last broken the rocks—Williams is at his most romantic, offering the fugitive kind as a company of the elect. Most of the time, however, there are no romantic solutions. At best, the characters make do.

There are two main ways of trying to escape in the Williams plays. The first of these is by running. Williams once published an article in the *New York Times Magazine*, "A Writer's Quest for a Parnassus," which was not quite the innocent travel piece that it seemed to be. In it, he says that a writer—particularly an American writer—has to keep moving, trying to find the place in which he can feel at home, in which he can write. Williams' characters are as mobile as he is. Tom in *Menagerie* attempts "to find in motion what was lost in space." Blanche comes to New Orleans in search of sanctuary, if not Parnassus, and is about to move on when Stanley's rape brings an end to her running. Val is a wanderer in *Orpheus* and Carol is forever heading somewhere (or nowhere) in that car of hers. Sebastian is described in *Suddenly* as an unrelenting traveler. Alexandra and Chance in *Sweet Bird* break a cross-country drive and find horror in St. Cloud. George and Isabel are on a honeymoon trip in *Period*. A group of wanderers gather at Maxine's in *Iguana* and some of them—Nonno and Shannon, perhaps—come to rest. With the possible exception of Shannon, all of these characters either keep moving or are stopped by death

or disaster. Running never frees any of them from the pursuer.

The second attempt to escape is hardly that really. It is more properly a temporary surcease, a little comfort found along the road. At the end of *Menagerie*, Tom speaks of walking in a strange city, "before I have found companions." Tom's temporary companions, the lovers that Blanche or Carol finds, Sebastian's young men, Alexandra's gigolos, Mrs. Goforth's husbands, Leona's trailer mates in *Small Craft Warnings*—all these are images of attempts at human contact, "one night stands" as Shannon calls them in *Iguana*. In *Camino Real*, we hear Marguerite (Camille) playing a "love" scene with Casanova, two romantics down on their luck in a world for which *down-on-your-luck* is a descriptive term: "we stretch out hands to each other in the dark that we can't escape from—we huddle together for some dim-communal comfort." In *Milk Train*, Christopher has a long metaphorical speech in which he describes men as kittens or puppies, "living in a house we're not used to," creeping close together—"those gentle little nudges with our paws and our muzzles"—to find in contact some escape from fear. "His hand on my knee was just a human touch," says Bobby in *Small Craft Warnings*, "and it seemed natural to me to return it"; Violet, the derelict in that play who drifts from one "temporary arrangement" to another, constantly gropes for the men in search of something to hang onto, and Leona says, "She's got some form of religion in her hands." In only two of the Williams plays is there a suggestion of a conventional happy ending, of a love that is more than a momentary rest—*You Touched Me!*, in which Hadrian rescues Matilda from spinsterdom, and *The Rose Tattoo*, in which Serafina marches out to Alvaro shouting, "Vengo, vengo, amore!" Unhappy extenuating circumstances might be found to explain away the apparent endings of these two plays. Certainly Williams' most conventional happy ending—that of *Period of Adjustment*—is most unconventional. In the standard Broadway marriage comedy the complications are straightened out, which is to say glossed over, by sending the hero and heroine to bed. In his "serious comedy," Williams sends not one, but two couples to bed and just as they are about to cuddle into the familiar final curtain, there is a cracking noise as the house sinks a little farther into the cavern over which it is built; the conventional ending then follows, but it, like the house, is now a little awry. Surely, Williams, who uses sexual imagery casually, comically in all his plays, is punning on his subtitle; "High Point over a Cavern" suggests not only moving in for the sex act, but the diversion itself over the grave. In any case, the play gets the same image elsewhere: George and Isabel are on their honeymoon, driving a funeral limousine.

The sense of desperation in Williams' work seemed to be replaced by a kind of acceptance in the early 1960's. I am thinking primarily of *Iguana* and *Milk Train*, both unusual Williams plays in that each of them involves two leading characters who do not join physically. One of the two in each case acts as a spiritual guide. Hannah teaches Shannon to accept life and Chris teaches Mrs. Goforth to accept death: it is the same lesson. This apparent new calm once again gives way to desperation, but this time there is something almost comforting in the broad comedy of survival plays like *Slapstick Tragedy* and *Kingdom of Earth*. The blind but determined Gnädiges Fräulein setting out at the end of her play to fight the cocaloony birds for discarded fish must be Williams' most bizarre image of human survival, but it is rivaled by Celeste and Trinket in *The Mutilated*, on their knees in the midst of a wine-soaked Christmas Eve vision while the *a capella* choir sings of death deferred, and by Myrtle and Chicken climbing to the rooftop to sit out the flood in *Kingdom of Earth*. Not that all the Williams characters come through in his most recent plays. At the end of *The Two-Character Play*, the performers seem about to use the revolver that will end their effort to keep the show going, and *Tokyo Hotel* chronicles the death of the artist. Still, *Small Craft Warnings*, Williams' post-hospital play, is his most positive. Although Monk's bar is peopled with characters who are barely holding onto life, the play's center is Leona, who is almost Saroyanesque in her assertion: "Life! Life! I never just said, 'Oh, well,' I've always said 'Life!' to life, like a song to God, too, because I've lived in my lifetime. . . ." With a play called *Out Cry* in the offing, it is clear that in one way or another Williams will be going on with the themes that have so long obsessed him.

From the beginning of his career, Williams has been trying to tell the *real* truth (his real truth, that is) about human beings and the way they live, but he has never wanted to do that as a realist. He has made constant use of both literary and theatrical devices of a nonrealistic sort because, as he insists in the Production Notes to *The Glass Menagerie*, "truth, life, or reality is an organic thing which the poetic imagination can represent or suggest, in essence, only through transformation, through changing into other forms than those which were merely present in appearance." His use of devices ranges from the subtle to the shockingly obvious, from organic machine to pure gimmick. Williams at his most gimmicky can be seen in the screen device of *Menagerie* and in the stage assistants of *The Milk Train Doesn't Stop Here Anymore*. For *Menagerie*, he suggests that words or pictures be flashed on a screen, verbal or visual comments which, if we can believe his justification published with the play, he intends as guides to an obtuse audience, explaining each scene, and its relation to the whole. Unless his purpose in *Menagerie* is to mock his characters (which hardly seems likely), his device would be a failure, for the screened comments seem designed to reduce all the scenes—even the tenderest—to ludicrous parodies. For instance, in the dinner scene, when Laura, panic-stricken at the idea of sitting down with the gentleman caller, drags herself unwillingly toward the table, Williams calls for this legend: "TERROR!" As she stumbles and Amanda and Tom cry out, the screen says, "AH!" This would put us back with the Gish sisters in the silent movies and not, as the device suggests, with Piscator and Brecht on the edge of the Epic Theater. I use the "would" purposely because Eddie Dowling discarded the screen device in the original production of *Menagerie*, a practice since followed extensively; yet, Williams cares enough for the device to retain it in the published version of the play. In *Milk Train*, he introduces two stage assistants whose double job is to comment on what happens and to direct the point of action by removing a screen from in front of whatever playing area is to be used; since the play does not need their comments (as the Yeats plays do those of similar figures) and since lighting could spot the action, they remain arty intrusions, made foolish by Williams' distrust of the audience, which forces these non-characters to use the first scene to explain who and what they are.

If *Menagerie* is one extreme of Williams' antirealism, it also contains examples of his use of realistic technique. Despite his aesthetic stand, he is enough in the tradition of the American theater to ask his characters to move and speak realistically when he wants them to. Consider, for example, the opening of the second scene of *Menagerie* in which Amanda comes home, having discovered that Laura has dropped out of business college. Her accusation begins before she starts to speak, is apparent in the air of martyrdom with which she slowly removes her hat and gloves, drops them to the floor, digs in her purse for a handkerchief, touches it to her lips. Williams calls all this "a bit of acting," but, although the gestures are overelaborate, the scene is realistic because they are Amanda's gestures not Williams'. *Menagerie* provides Tom with the ornate and rather trying "poetic" monologue which opens the play, but at the same time it gives him a fine quarrel scene with Amanda in which both speech and action are realistic. The realistic element never disappears from the Williams plays. In *Iguana*, we see character-defining action, as in the scene in Act II in which Maxine tempts Shannon with the rum-coco; in *Period of Adjustment*, we see character-revealing speech, as in Isabel's story of her dream of serving with a handsome doctor, during which, as it becomes more clearly a movie plot, she suddenly shifts from the first to the third person. Although Williams does not write psychological drama in the conventional sense—Jim's analysis of Laura in *Menagerie* is both accurate and irrelevant, a joke about pat labels—he is psychologically sound in his choice of gesture and word. That I suppose is a way of saying that he can create character when he wants to, can put real frogs in his imaginary gardens.

Realism of a kind, then, lies at the core of his talent for creating characters (probably his greatest talent), but it would be unfair to his work to dwell heavily on that element in it. After all, he has done his best to mask it. He has used caricature extensively, sometimes in terms of Broadway convention (the clergyman in *Cat*, the businessman-father in *Period*), but more often in terms of other traditions of the theater. He calls Flora and Bessie in *The Rose Tattoo* "two female clowns" and describes them in terms of physical contrast—"tall and angular" and "rather stubby." This is the Laurel-and-Hardy bit, a standard comic contrast that circuses and music halls have found funny for years; perhaps recognizing that Bessie and Flora constituted a comic turn, Williams gave them a one-acter of their own, *A Perfect Analysis Given by a Parrot* (1958). A similar comedy team, Molly and Polly, emerge as central figures, the sustaining voices of *The Gnädiges Fräulein*. Comic caricature of another kind can be found in characters such as Alexandra in *Sweet Bird* and Archie Lee in *Baby Doll*, grotesques which suggest Ben Jonson; surely if Jonson had ever thought to do a self-deluding lesbian whose repressions had turned her into a Puritan hatchet man, he would have come up with a Zeal-of-the-hand Busy like Miss Fellowes in *Iguana*. Williams is not writing Jonsonian satire, of course; he is using his grotesques to express a condition that is at once horrible and comic.

Williams has many devices other than caricature to lift his characters out of the realistic tradition. He uses mythic identifications, for instance, as in *Orpheus*, in which Val is the titular singer, and in *Suddenly*, in which Sebastian suggests the saint of the same name; both of these characters, as well as Chance and Boss Finley in *Sweet Bird*, Shannon in *Iguana*, and Christopher in *Milk Train*, are identified by the audience or by one of the other characters as Christ figures. In *Camino Real*, the characters are borrowed directly from literature (Camille, Charlus, Don Quixote), from life (Casanova, Byron), from popular usage (Kilroy), or they are given significant names (A. Ratt, Gutman). The use of significant names is one of Williams' favorite games. Sometimes

they are used realistically, as in *Streetcar* and *Summer and Smoke*, in which the characters themselves point out that Blanche DuBois is white woods, Stella is star, Alma is soul. More often Williams uses the device himself, often comically, as in Chance Wayne, whose chances have waned, and in George Haverstick, who, through sexual fear, may be said to have no stick at all.

Mythic identifications and significant names are literary ways of stressing the nonrealistic element in character; there are theatrical means that work as well. In *Streetcar*, for instance, the nurse and the doctor are presented as ominous figures (like the nun in *Suddenly*), institutional extensions rather than individuals; when the doctor removes his hat, just before he offers Blanche his arm, Williams says "he becomes personalized." Such depersonalization can only be used with peripheral characters, but there are ways of establishing the artificiality, the theatricality of even the leading characters. The one that Williams uses most extensively is to present the long speeches as set pieces, arias almost, delivered to the audience rather than to other characters. Amanda's telephone speeches in *Menagerie* are early examples of this (Tom's soliloquies, being outside the action, are another matter), but it is in *Cat*, with Maggie's long speeches in the first act, that the device begins to take the form it will have increasingly in the latter plays. Brick is present, Maggie is presumably talking to him and he is even given occasional lines of comment, but the scene is, in fact, a kind of solo performance for the actress who plays Maggie. In the later plays, Williams stresses the special character of such speeches. Beulah's, at the beginning of *Orpheus*, should, so Williams tells us in the stage direction, "set the non-realistic key for the whole production." In *Suddenly*, Dr. Sugar leads Catharine to the forestage to describe her seduction and, when she explains what happened last summer, she is in a white spot while the other characters fade into the background. When Chance tells his story in *Sweet Bird,* he, too, moves to the forestage and when Alexandra does her telephone scene she opens it with lines that describe not only the position of the characters within the play but of the actors within the scene: "He's in the dimmed out background . . . I've taken the light again as a crown on my head . . ." Each of the characters in *Small Craft Warnings* is given his own moment in the spotlight to deliver a self-defining monologue—a confession, perhaps, since the bar is Monk's Place and the first version of the play was called *Confessional.*

In *The Life of the Drama,* Eric Bentley suggests two rules for the beginning playwright: "If you wish to attract the audience's attention, be violent: if you wish to hold it, be violent again." Williams found those rules for himself long before Bentley put them into words. How one feels about Williams depends on the emphasis (the motivation, if you like) one puts on "to attract" and "to hold." It was fashionable for a while—particularly in the late 1950's when Williams turned out a string of violent plays, *Orpheus, Suddenly, Sweet Bird* —to assume that the playwright was simply venal, tickling a sick American audience where it was most vulnerable. There may be a touch of the mercenary in what Williams calls his "cornpone melodrama," but we must assume a touch of the poet as well. In his introduction to *Reflections in a Golden Eye,* he explains that art has not the room that life has, that "the awfulness has to be compressed," that the writer is driven to "symbols of the grotesque and the violent." Although any event in a Williams play is likely to have a counterpart somewhere in fact, his lurid plots are not intended to be realistic. They are what James Thurber, in another context, called "fables of our time."

If one describes *Orpheus Descending* flatly, it may be possible to imagine it as a realistic play: a young tramp arrives in a Mississippi town, goes to work in a shoe store, impregnates his boss while her husband lies dying upstairs, and is burned to death by a gang of lynchers, spurred on by the husband who has stayed alive long enough to shoot his wife to death. In these terms, *Orpheus* would be simply a melodrama of lust and murder. Williams takes great pains to keep the audience from being hypnotized by the events of the play, from getting stuck at the realistic level. The mythic elements and the unrealistic staging—both mentioned in the paragraphs above on character—are ways of keeping an audience from taking the plot literally. It would be as well not to lean too far in the other direction, not to take the myth literally. It is amusing with the Williams plays to try to fit myth to plot— to see Orpheus (Val) with his lyre (guitar), descending into Hades (a small southern town) to rescue Eurydice (Lady) from Death (Jabe). Williams, however, does not work that neatly. His Val is identified not only with Orpheus (by the title and his guitar), but with Christ (through Vee Talbott's painting and his last name) and St. Valentine (through his first name). What Williams wants to do is to make Val's death—like Sebastian's death in *Suddenly* and Chance's castration in *Sweet Bird*—a kind of ritual that lifts the plot from the realistic to the metaphorical. The references to Greek and Christian myth that sprinkle his plays serve as distancing devices, pushing us away from a strictly realistic reading, even when they are used humorously—as with the Infant of Prague in *Period of Adjustment.*

The verbal and visual symbols that flood the Williams plays have much the same use. ". . . I have a poet's weakness for symbols," says Tom in *Menagerie.* It is a statement that Williams might well have printed on his own calling cards. Almost any Williams play could provide a plethora of symbols, but *Summer and Smoke* should give us enough to see the kind (and the quality) of symbols that he is capable of. To begin with, a stone angel, called ETERNITY, broods over the action. In this presence, a struggle between soul (Alma) and body (John) is acted out, one which lets each recognize within himself what he has seen and reached for in the other. The division is made clear through the two main playing areas (the rectory and the doctor's office) and the two points of view are made extremely explicit through Alma's speech on the Gothic cathedral ("the everlasting struggle and aspiration for more than our human limits have placed in our reach") and John's lecture, using the anatomy chart, in which he points out the brain, the belly, the sex, all of which must be fed. John as sexual figure is emphasized in his first scene with Alma when a Roman candle (seven puffs!) goes off behind them. Alma's reaching-for-the-stars theme is echoed elsewhere in the play, as in Scene 7 in which Gonzales, who has been playing poker, uses the phrase "The sky is the limit" to indicate the way he wants to lift his daughter Rosa from the dirt-floored house of her childhood ("le doy el cielo!"); or in Scene 11, when John, explaining that it is nothing physical in Alma he wants, strikes a match and cups it until it flames upward. There is a running business about a plumed hat. In Scene 1, John tells Alma to wear one when she goes riding with him and she does wear one—too late—when she comes to his office in Scene 11, ready to admit that she has been won over his view. The plumed hat is used also, and most effectively, in Scene 2 in the quarrel between Alma and her mother in which the plume is torn loose in their physical struggle.

There is a great deal too much going on symbolically in *Summer and Smoke* and all of it—from the ludicrous Roman candle to the embarrassingly obvious anatomy chart to the dramatically useful plumed hat—is presumably to be taken seriously. In other Williams plays, however, the symbols are a little tongue-in-cheek; in *The Rose Tattoo*, for instance, it must be a joke that both Serafina's husband and her lover are truck drivers who carry bananas. By making so many symbols and by overexplaining his main ones (as with the iguana in *Iguana*), Williams uses them to insist on the non-realistic quality of the plays rather than (like Chekhov with his cherry orchard) intensifying whatever realism there is.

As though pushing his characters toward caricature and his plots toward myth and decorating both with symbols were not enough, Williams makes use of every possible tool of the theater—sets, props, lights, sound—to emphasize that his plays are not realistic. The schematic set demanded by the soul-body split of *Summer and Smoke* is typical of his work. The only play in which he ever called for a conventional set is *Period of Adjustment*, which is in part a joke on the conventions it is using, but even it has some unusual features. Ralph and Isabel do not play their almost love scene in front of a very real fireplace, as Candida and Marchbanks do in Shaw's play, but in front of "a flickering red light" set in the invisible fourth wall which puts the audience into the fireplace—a device Williams also uses in *The Eccentricities of a Nightingale*. For Williams, sets are not solid indications of his characters' environment, as they are for Ibsen and Shaw. They are suggestive of a mood, often with an empty sky (a theological comment?) hanging over the action. In the "Notes for the Designer" at the beginning of *Cat on a Hot Tin Roof* (in terms of action and character, one of Williams' most realistic plays), the playwright describes the setting, using the novelistic technique familiar in playwrights like Shaw, and then withdraws the realistic implications of his remarks: "I think the walls below the ceiling should dissolve mysteriously into air; the set should be roofed by the sky;

stars and moon suggested by traces of milky pallor . . ." Perhaps the best indication of Williams' sense of what a scene on stage should look like (or feel like) is his ready use of painters and paintings to evoke a sense of the set: the lighting of *Menagerie* should suggest El Greco's religious paintings; the poker party in *Streetcar* recalls Van Gogh's billiard parlor; the fragmentary set walls of *Summer and Smoke* are out of Chirico; the porch and yard in *The Gnädiges Fräulein* are awry as though Picasso had designed them.

As with sets, so with props and costumes. The bed in *Cat*, "a functional part of the set," is raked to become a playing area itself; more than a bed—even a prop bed—it is a continual reminder of the struggle between Maggie and Brick. The mannequins in *The Rose Tattoo*, among which Williams calls for a bride and a widow, "who face each other in violent attitudes, as though having a shrill argument," are used not only to comment on Serafina's difficulties, but on occasion to harass her—as in Scene 5 where they seem to be interfering with her attempt to get to Rosa's graduation. Costumes in the early plays are often used to emphasize characters as in the white hat Blanche wears ("that suggests a moth") or the primary colors of the men's shirts in the poker scene. Such use, of course, is not a departure from the realistic tradition. In the later plays, however, Williams often emphasizes costume as costume. The most obvious instance is in *The Night of the Iguana* in which Hannah puts on her artist's smock and Shannon his clericals, each in his own cubicle: "They are like two actors in a play which is about to fold on the road . . ." Later, Hannah puts on her Kabuki robe ("as an actor puts on a costume") and in *Milk Train* both Mrs. Goforth and Chris dress up in Kabuki robes. The fine line between actress and character in Felice in *The Two-Character Play* seems to depend

on the coat that she keeps putting on and taking off; in *Kingdom of Earth*, Myrtle consciously dons her old costumes in her attempt to win Chicken, while Lot, in a transvestite act of homage, dies wearing his mother's clothes.

Williams makes extensive use of sound and light for nonrealistic effects. In *Menagerie*, he calls for a musical theme which can be identified with Laura, and in *Streetcar*, the "Varsouviana," the polka that was playing when Allan shot himself, is used both to indicate and to intensify Blanche's desperation. Street cries ("Red hots!"; "Flores para los muertos") in that play are obviously more than local color. Uncle Pleasant's Choctaw call is used twice in *Orpheus* as entrance cues for Val, and bird cries are used antiphonally in several of the plays—most notably, *Suddenly Last Summer*. Williams has always demanded that his lighting do more than illumine the stage (it was the light that was to make an El Greco madonna of Laura); he has used it not only for mood and character delineation, but also, as in *Sweet Bird* and *Small Craft Warnings*, to dim out the peripheral characters while a single one commands the audience's attention. Light can be used as a dramatic metaphor, as in *The Eccentricities of a Nightingale,* when the dead fireplace flames again, indicating that Alma and John can make love, and as a visual parallel, as in *Camino Real*, where the blue flame in the chafing dish on the Mulligans' table flares up and dies down while Marguerite and Jacques discuss dying in a sanatorium. Light and sound work together often—for instance, to create the symbolic storms that break over the Broadway version of *Cat* (Daddy's violent reaction to the news of approaching death, followed by his calm) and *Iguana* ("Here is your God, Mr. Shannon").

A random sampling, such as the one offered by the last few pages, can do no more than indicate the variety of literary and theatrical devices that Williams uses. What is clear is that a playwright who has a sharp eye for the nuances of speech and gesture which have always been of great importance to the realistic dramatist has consistently chosen to work in the nonrealistic tradition.

Selected Bibliography

WORKS OF TENNESSEE WILLIAMS

LONG PLAYS

The parenthetic dates represent the first major productions. Unless otherwise indicated, the multiple listings are for variant versions of the often rewritten plays. Paperback editions of the works, from New Directions (NDP) or New American Library (NAL), are indicated below. Four volumes of *The Theatre of Tennessee Williams* (New York: New Directions, 1971–72) have appeared; the plays in the collected edition are indicated by volume, as (T-1).

Battle of Angels (1940). In *Pharos*, nos. 1–2 (Spring 1945). Also (with no change) in *Orpheus Descending with Battle of Angels*. New York: New Directions, 1958. Pp. 119–238. (T-1)

The Glass Menagerie (1945). New York: Random House, 1945. (NDP) (T-1) New York: Dramatists Play Service, 1948.

You Touched Me! (1945), with Donald Windham. New York: Samuel French, 1947.

A Streetcar Named Desire (1947). New York: New Directions, 1947. (There are two versions of the play published under the same title page. The NAL reprint is the second version.) (T-1) New York: Dramatists Play Service, 1953.

Summer and Smoke (1948). New York: New Directions, 1948. (T-2) New York: Dramatists Play Service, 1950.

The Rose Tattoo (1951). New York: New Directions, 1951. (T-2)

Camino Real (1953). New York: New Directions, 1953. (NDP) (T-2)

Cat on a Hot Tin Roof (1955). New York: New Directions, 1955. (NAL) (T-3) New York: Dramatists Play Service, 1958.

Baby Doll (1956). New York: New Directions, 1956. (Screenplay.)

Orpheus Descending (1957). In *Orpheus Descending with Battle of Angels*. New York: New Directions, 1958. Pp. 1–118. (T-3) New York: Dramatists Play Service, 1959.

Suddenly Last Summer (1958). New York: New Directions, 1958. (T-3) In *Garden District*. London: Secker and Warburg, 1959. Pp. 27–72. (NAL)

Sweet Bird of Youth (1959). In *Esquire*, 51:114–55 (April 1959). New York: New Directions, 1959. (NAL) (T-4) New York: Dramatists Play Service, 1962.

Period of Adjustment (1960). In *Esquire*, 54:210–76 (December 1960). New York: New Directions, 1960. (T-4) New York: Dramatists Play Service, 1961.

The Night of the Iguana (1961). In *Esquire*, 57:48–62, 115–30 (February 1962). New York: New Directions, 1962. (NAL) (T-4) New York: Dramatists Play Service, 1963.

The Milk Train Doesn't Stop Here Anymore (1964). New York: New Directions, 1964.

The Eccentricities of a Nightingale. In *The Eccentricities of a Nightingale and Summer and Smoke*. New York: New Directions, 1965. Pp. 1–107. (T-2)

Slapstick Tragedy (1966). Two plays, published separately in *Dragon Country*. New York: New Directions, 1970. *The Mutilated* (pp. 77–130) and *The Gnädiges Fräulein* (pp. 215–62). Variant versions of both plays, with author's Preface. In *Esquire*, 64:95–102, 130–34 (August 1965). Of *The Mutilated*. New York: Dramatists Play Service, 1967.

The Two-Character Play (1967). New York: New Directions, 1969. Limited Edition.

Kingdom of Earth (1968). New York: New Directions, 1968. One-act version, in *Esquire*, 67:98–100, 132–34 (February 1967).

In the Bar of a Tokyo Hotel (1969). In *Dragon Country*, pp. 1–53.

Small Craft Warnings (1972). New York: New Directions, 1972. (NDP) As *Confessional*, in *Dragon Country*, pp. 151–96.

A Lovely Sunday for Creve Coeur. New York: New Directions: 1980.

The Red Devil Battery Sign. New York: New Directions, 1980.

SHORT PLAYS

American Blues: Five Short Plays. New York: Dramatists Play Service, 1948.

27 Wagons Full of Cotton and Other One-Act Plays. Norfolk, Conn.: New Directions, 1946, 1953. The 1953 edition is most complete, with 13 plays. (NDP)

At Liberty. In *American Scenes*, edited by William Kozlenko. New York: John Day, 1941. Pp. 175–82.

Lord Byron's Love Letter. New York: Ricordi, 1955. (Libretto for a one-act opera by Raffaello de Banfield; it differs from the play in *27 Wagons*.)

The Enemy: Time. In *Theatre*, 1:14–17 (March 1959).

Dragon Country. New York: New Directions, 1970. (NDP)

Stopped Rocking and Other Screenplays. New York: New Directions, 1984.

FICTION AND POETRY

The Roman Spring of Mrs. Stone. New York: New Directions, 1950. (NDP) (Novel)

One Arm, and Other Stories. New York: New Directions, 1948, reprinted 1954. (NDP)

Hard Candy, a Book of Stories. New York: New Directions, 1954, reprinted 1959. (NDP)

The Knightly Quest, A Novella and Four Short Stories. New York: New Directions, 1966.

"Happy August the 10th," In *Esquire,* 78:256–60 (December 1972).

"The Summer Belvedere." In *Five Young Poets*, Third Series. Norfolk, Conn.: New Directions, 1944. Pp. 121–70.

In the Winter of Cities. New York: New Directions, 1956. (Poetry. The 1964 paperback edition is the most complete edition.) (NDP)

"Crepe de Chine." In *New Yorker*, 45:28 (July 5, 1969).

Eight Mortal Ladies Possessed. New York: New Directions, 1974.

ESSAYS

Introductory essays also appear in a number of the volumes listed above.

"The Catastrophe of Success," *New York Times*, November 30, 1947, Section 2, p. 1. Also in the New Classics Edition of *The Glass Menagerie.* New York: New Directions, 1949. Pp. xiii–xix.

"Questions without Answers," *New York Times*, October 3, 1948, Section 2, pp. 1, 3.

"A Writer's Quest for a Parnassus." *New York Times Magazine*, August 13, 1950, pp. 16, 35.

"This Book," Introduction to New Classics Edition of Carson McCullers, *Reflections in a Golden Eye.* New York: New Directions, 1950. Pp. ix–xxi.

"The Human Psyche—Alone," *Saturday Review of Literature*, 33:19–20 (December 23, 1950).

"Facts about Me" (1952). Record Cover, Caedmon TC 100.

"Critic Says 'Evasion,' Writer Says 'Mystery.' " *New York Herald Tribune*, April 17, 1955, Section 4, pp. 1, 2.

"The World I Live In," *Observer*, April 7, 1957, p. 14. Also in *Drama on Stage*, edited by Randolph Goodman. New York: Holt, Rinehart, and Winston, 1961. Pp. 293–95.

"Author and Director: A Delicate Situation," *Playbill*, 1:9–13 (September 30, 1957).

Introduction to William Inge, *The Dark at the Top of the Stairs.* New York: Random House, 1958. Pp. vii–ix.

"Reflections on a Revival of a Controversial Fantasy." *New York Times*, May 15, 1960, Section 2, pp. 1, 3.

"Tennessee Williams Presents His POV." *New York Times Magazine*, June 12, 1960, pp. 19, 78.

"Prelude to a Comedy," *New York Times*, November 6, 1960, Section 2, pp. 1, 3.

"The Agent as Catalyst," *Esquire*, 58:216, 260 (December 1962).

"T. Williams's View of T. Bankhead," *New York Times*, December 29, 1963, Section 2, pp. 1, 3.

"Tennessee Williams: The Wolf and I," *New York Times*, February 20, 1966, Section 2, pp. 1, 5.

" 'Happiness Is Relevant' to Mr. Williams," *New York Times*, March 24, 1968, Section 2, pp. 1, 3.

" 'Tennessee, Never Talk to an Actress,' " *New York Times*, May 4, 1969, Section 2, pp. 1, 16.

"Tennessee Williams talks about his play 'In The Bar of a Tokyo Hotel,' " Letter to the cast, printed as an advertisement. *New York Times*, May 14, 1969, p. 36.

"What's Next on the Agenda, Mr. Williams?" *Mediterranean Review*, 1:15–19 (Winter 1971). (Read at the London Poetry Festival, 1970.)

"Survival Notes: A Journal." *Esquire*, 78:130–34, 166–68 (September 1972).

INTERVIEWS

Bell, Arthur. " 'I've Never Faked It,' " *Village Voice*, February 24, 1972, pp. 58, 60.

Buckley, Tom. "Tennessee Williams Survives," *Atlantic*, 206:98–108 (November 1970).

Funke, Lewis. "Williams Revival? Ask the Playwright," *New York Times*, January 8, 1970, p. 45.

Funke, Lewis, and John E. Booth. "Williams on Williams," *Theatre Arts*, 46:17–19, 72–73 (January 1962).

Gaines, Jim. "A Talk about Life and Style with Tennessee Williams," *Saturday Review*, 55:25–29 (April 29, 1972).

Gelb, Arthur. "Williams and Kazan and the Big Walk-Out," *New York Times*, May 1, 1960, Section 2, pp. 1, 3.

Glover, William. "Distress Over What People Think," *Philadelphia Bulletin*, April 30, 1972, Section 5, pp. 1, 4. (An AP interview, presumably under other titles in other newspapers).

Gruen, John. "The Inward Journey of Tennessee Williams," *New York Herald Tribune* (magazine), May 2, 1965, p. 29.

Gussow, Mel. "Williams Looking to Play's Opening," *New York Times*, March 31, 1972, p. 10.

"Man Named Tennessee," *Newsweek*, 49:81 (April 1, 1957).

Probst, Leonard. "The Shirley Temple of Modern Letters," *Village Voice*, April 13, 1972, pp. 64, 84.

Reed, Rex. "Tennessee Williams Turns Sixty," *Esquire*, 76: 105–8, 216–23 (September 1971).

Ross, Don. "Williams in Art and Morals," *New York Herald Tribune*, March 3, 1957, Section 4, pp. 1, 2.

Stang, Joanne. "Williams: 20 Years After 'Glass Menagerie,' " *New York Times*, March 28, 1965, Section 2, pp. 1, 3.

Weatherby, W. J. "Lonely in Uptown New York," *Manchester Guardian Weekly*, 81:14 (July 23, 1959).

CRITICAL AND BIOGRAPHICAL STUDIES

Donahue, Francis. *The Dramatic World of Tennessee Williams*. New York: Ungar, 1964.

Falk, Signi Lenea. *Tennessee Williams*. New York: Twayne, 1961. (Contains a descriptive critical bibliography, pp. 206–21.)

Gassner, John. *The Theatre in Our Times*. New York: Crown, 1954. Pp. 342–59.

Hurrell, John D., ed. *Two Modern American Tragedies*. New York: Scribners, 1961.

Jackson, Esther M. *The Broken World of Tennessee Williams*. Madison: University of Wisconsin Press, 1965.

Maxwell, Gilbert. *Tennessee Williams and Friends*. Cleveland: World, 1965.

Nelson, Benjamin. *Tennessee Williams: The Man and His Work*. New York: Ivan Obolensky, 1961.

Steen, Mike. *A Look at Tennessee Williams*. New York: Hawthorn, 1969.

Tischler, Nancy M. *Tennessee Williams: Rebellious Puritan*. New York: Citadel Press, 1961.

Weales, Gerald. *American Drama since World War II*. New York: Harcourt, Brace, and World, 1962.

———. *The Jumping-Off Place, American Drama in the 1960's*. New York: Macmillan, 1969.

Williams, Edwina Dakin (as told to Lucy Freeman). *Remember Me to Tom*. New York: Putnam's, 1963. (Contains many Williams letters.)

—GERALD WEALES

William Carlos Williams

1883-1963

Among the poets of his own illustrious generation, William Carlos Williams was the man on the margin, the incorrigible maverick, the embattled messiah. During the years when T. S. Eliot, Ezra Pound, Wallace Stevens, Marianne Moore, and E. E. Cummings were departing from traditional English practice in ways that stamped the character of American poetry in the twentieth century, Williams quite by himself was trying to impart to poetry a new substance and a violent new orientation. Something in his blood that was not in theirs had already made him the more congenial fellow of strangers who, unknown to him, were shaping in the rickety garrets of Montmartre the artifacts and totems of a new era. In secret alliance with little known painters, he nevertheless became famous along with his literary contemporaries and still tends to be indiscriminately categorized with them in the annals of poetry. But as modern poetry consolidates its academic position and ceases to challenge the young and adventurous, the singularity of Williams' contribution is being discovered, rediscovered, and put to uses that presage the most striking development in American poetry since J. Alfred Prufrock rolled the bottoms of his trousers and listened to the mermaids.

From the moment of his first adult recognition of himself as a poet, Williams built his career on opposition—opposition to every form of poetry that depends on meter or rhyme or any other device that, to his mind, served only to falsify the experience it would transcribe—opposition to every kind of thinking that orders itself in generalities rather than submits to the hazards of unwieldy particulars. He continually put forth theories that sounded like sweeping new programs for the whole art of poetry but which turned out to be merely new formulations of the private practice of William Carlos Williams. He railed against T. S. Eliot as though he were disaster incarnate, and against the scholars who explicated Eliot as though they were members of some nefarious academic cabal. His poetic disciples included from time to time such younger masters as Theodore Roethke and Robert Lowell, as well as a whole rag, tag, and bobtail succession of meagerly talented iconoclasts who thought that by assuming his freedom they might somehow inherit his integrity. In either case, Williams greeted them all with the zeal of a salvationist embracing new converts. In pursuit of the antagonisms that kept him young through a creative span of more than fifty years, he fumed, proclaimed, and shook his head with an air of nettled divinity. But while his theories indicate that, as critic and prophet, he was often narrow in outlook, preoccupied with repetitions of the obvious, old-fashioned in his persistent "newness," his poems unequivocally excuse and justify all his talk. As an aesthetic achievement in itself, the body of his work cannot be accorded less than major status. As an influence upon the development of a native American idiom, it stands beside, and will probably loom above, the celebrated contributions of Ezra Pound and T. S. Eliot.

The quest to which Williams addressed himself as early as 1912 is essentially the same as that to which his attention was turned five decades later: What is the measurable factor in language that will replace metrics as a basis for poetic composition? An apparently simple and exclusively technical point of inquiry, this question nevertheless involved for Williams the whole meaning of poetry. Since he believed that experience does not objectively exist until it is embodied in language, the nature of that language—its ability to convey actuality without distorting it through the crippling biases of "literary" means—is all-important. Far more by example than by precept, Williams demonstrated that there are moments and phases of experience that, by an economy of means so strict as to defy analysis, can be lifted from the meaningless flux of actuality into reality and significance. When this happens, all the ways and means that remain tangled and unresolved in his pronouncements are quite simply and convincingly documented in his poems.

The primary concerns of Williams—too clearly the applications of naive good sense and native intelligence to be canonized—were constant: to devise the poetic structure that would formalize experience without deforming it; to let the beat of speech determine the measure; to rinse the language of ornament and encrustation; to be scrupulously selective but to allow for accident and impingement. Philosophy and metaphysics to Williams had no place and no meaning apart from the structures by which they were expressed or could be deduced. "No ideas but in things," he said, and he believed that the poet's business is "not to talk in vague categories but to write particularly as a physician works, upon a patient, upon the thing before him, in the particular to discover the universal." *Discovery* is a key word in anything he undertakes— discovery of the relationship between actuality and the mind confronting it, discovery of the language that would in turn make that discovery "true" and communicable. Where his contemporaries adapted or re-channeled old forms of poetry, Williams, ignoring the shapes in which poetry had been cast, sought always to rediscover poetry itself. And yet his dismissal of entrenched forms of English poetry—his lifelong crusade against the iambic pentameter, for instance, and his endlessly burning scorn for the sonnet—should not blind his readers to the fact that his searchings and his concerns were exclusively directed toward formal solutions. Where other poets achieved a homespun celebrity by exploiting regional or "Americanese" subject matter, Williams pursued a far more difficult and less rewarding path. Taking his native scene as much for granted as the view from his office window, he used his gifts of perception to reconstitute it freshly. He resisted the antiquarian charms of folklore and the chauvinist pleasures of Americana to search for the rhythm in the American grain, the timeless in the momentary, the universal in the immediate and local. He thus escaped the sort of provincialism that might guarantee him a place in the academies and joined an international company of geniuses whose astonishing innovations in literature and the plastic arts parallel the twentieth century's great discoveries in physics.

William Carlos Williams was born on September 17, 1883, in Rutherford, New Jersey. His father was of pure English ancestry; his mother's family, settled on various islands of the Caribbean, contained elements of French, Spanish, and Jewish cultures. With his younger brother, Edward, Williams went to public schools in his home town, attended the Unitarian church, of which his father was a staunch pillar, and, when he was fourteen, went with his family to Europe for two years. There he attended the Château de Lançy near Geneva and, later, the Lycée Condorcet in Paris. Upon the family's return to the United States, he was sent to Horace Mann High School in New York City, to which he commuted daily by streetcar and Hudson River ferryboat. When he had decided on a career in medicine, he took the entrance examinations and, since in those years it was still possible to enter medical school without a degree, was admitted to the University of Pennsylvania Medical School. In Philadelphia his interest in poetry led him into acquaintance with the poets Ezra Pound and H. D. (Hilda Doolittle), and the painter Charles Demuth, all of whom became his lifelong friends.

After his graduation in 1906, he interned at the old French Hospital in New York City and later at the Nursery and Child's Hospital. His first poems, published at his own expense, appeared in 1909, and shortly afterwards he went abroad again, to Leipzig where he did postgraduate work in pediatrics. In Europe he renewed his friendship with Ezra Pound and through him was introduced to the literary life of prewar London and, on more than one occasion, to William Butler Yeats. After a brief period of travel in Italy and Spain, he returned to Rutherford to marry a local girl, Florence Herman, the "Flossie" of his poems, and to begin the practice of medicine. He became the father of two boys, William and Paul, during the next few years and when he bought the big old house at 9 Ridge Road his lifetime residence was established. A very active pediatrician with a wide practice among the industrial population of the region, Williams continued to be a deeply committed poet and a literary man happily caught up in the various cliques, publishing ventures, and general creative ferment that charged Greenwich Village in the years of World War I and after.

In 1924 he went to Europe with his wife for six months, a period of dazzling introductions and exhausting participation in the expatriate life of the movers and shakers of the American "lost generation" and their French counterparts. Ezra Pound was again his cicerone, along with the young publisher Robert McAlmon, and through them Williams associated with such people as Hemingway, Gertrude Stein, Sylvia Beach, Kay Boyle, Man Ray, George Antheil, and such members of the French literati as Valéry Larbaud and Philippe Soupault. In 1927 he made another European visit when he and his wife escorted their sons to school in Switzerland. He wrote a novel, *A Voyage to Pagany*, based on these visits, and in the course of it recorded his response to Paris: "Where *la France?* he cried within himself, as if expecting to see some symbolic image of joy rise from the ground and stride forward carrying flowers in her hand triumphantly. . . . Paris as a serious city, the beloved of men; Paris that releases what there is in men—the frivolity that means a knife cut through self-deception."

A prolific writer, Williams continued in the following years to apportion his talents among prose—short stories, essays, novels, an autobiography—poetry, and plays and, seemingly unaffected by constant professional demands and intrusions, to publish volumes eventually counted by the score. Turning over his medical practice to his son William in the middle 1950's, he devoted himself wholly to writing, with frequent appearances at colleges and universities to lecture and to read his poems. In 1949 he received an appointment to the Chair of Poetry at the Library of Congress. But this was withdrawn before he could assume his duties in Washington, partly because of accusations concerned with his supposed leftist sympathies, partly because of his old association with Ezra Pound who by then was committed to a psychiatric hospital after having been returned to America to stand trial as a traitor and propagandist for Italian fascism. In the same year he suffered the first of a series of strokes that eventually made him a semi-invalid. But in spite of consequent periods of difficulty with his vision and his speech, he continued to live a vigorous creative life and to travel in the United States and, on two occasions, to the Caribbean. He died at the age of seventy-nine, on March 4, 1963. Two months later he was posthumously awarded the Pulitzer Prize and the Gold Medal for Poetry of the National Institute of Arts and Letters.

While he always had the great admiration of many of his contemporaries, some of whom were highly influential in the literary world, general recognition came slowly to Williams. When it did come, however, he was the recipient of many awards, honorary degrees, and extensive critical appraisals—honors that merely certified in a public way the distinction for which he had been recognized by independent readers, by critics, and, even anti-academic Williams himself had finally to admit, by the many members of the teaching profession who for years sympathetically expounded his cause and promoted his reputation.

Keats was the first influence in Williams' career forceful enough to induce imitation; Whitman was the second. By the time he came to know Ezra Pound (during his freshman year at medical school), he had already completed a bulky manuscript of "studied Keatsian sonnets," an imitation of *Endymion*, and eighteen copybooks full of "quick spontaneous poems" whose free forms were derived from *Leaves of Grass*, which he didn't really like except for "Song of Myself." "Before meeting Ezra Pound," Williams said, "is like B.C. and A.D.," even though Pound showed notably little enthusiasm for the poems Williams offered for criticism. Pound's influence on Williams seems to have been mainly the communication of an attitude—an aesthete's concern for the primacy of art and a craftsman's concern for poetry as direct as speech and for lean, fresh expression at all costs, even at the cost of clarity. In other ways Pound influenced Williams by directing him to books that had formed Pound's own taste, and by praising Williams for his commendable independence, his "opacity" which he considered an un-American virtue, his refusal to cultivate "the magazine touch" and to accede to the demands of editors. Under Pound's influence and other stimuli, Williams was soon ready to close the door on the "studied elegance of Keats on one hand" and "the raw vigor of Whitman on the other." Keats had begun to seem intolerably archaic and Whitman, he came to feel, had foundered on an abstract idea of freedom, "an idea lethal to all order, particularly to that order which has to do with the poem" and had consequently "resorted to a loose sort of language with no discipline about it of any sort." Casting off his mentors, Williams continued to listen to Pound and to rummage through *Palgrave's Golden Treasury*, studying the models of the past, yet certain in his own mind that "If poetry had to be written, I had to do it my own way."

Many of his very early poems are almost indistinguishable from some of Pound's written during the same period. Both poets tended to write short aphoristic pieces studded with classical names and colored by an assumed mood of Alexandrian weariness. Frequently they adopted a courtly tone—sometimes daintily romantic, sometimes bluffly mocking—in poems addressing real or imaginary ladies; and in other poems they spoke with a roguish forthrightness, as though they were heroes out of some picaresque novel rather than modern men attempting to cut through the lacy conventions of parlor poesy. But within a very short time neither poet sounded like the other. Pound kept his wryness, his astringent understatement, his satire, and his cantankerousness. Williams maintained his capacity for surprise, his determination to meet life head-on; his naiveté remained fresh, his subject matter homely, his speech underlined for emphasis and riddled with punctuation marks.

The reformist movement known as Imagism had cleared the air at this period and its emphasis on direct apprehension of natural things and minor social phenomena was attractive to a man who had aleady foreseen that his best poetic strategy would be simply the deft, uncalculated transcription of what he saw and felt. Williams later looked upon his Imagist phase as a passing and tangential involvement, yet no other American poet—with perhaps the exception of H. D.—has written so many poems that can serve as models illustrating the Imagist canon. Concretion, exactitude, observation without comment, vulgar subject matter, common speech, homely details glittering with a mineral clarity—Williams exhibits them all and achieves over and over again that complexity of emotion within an instant of time that was the goal of the true Imagist. The tenets of Imagism gave him a sanction, and the loosely constituted Imagist "school" afforded him his first association with a group of poets consciously trying to find an idiom to oppose the stale metrics and mellifluous rhythms of the popular Georgian poets. But he soon became impatient with the limitations on structure that Imagism imposed. He believed that a focus on concrete imagery was a necessary step toward the rehabilitation of the poem, yet he felt that Imagism "lost its place finally because as a form it completely lacked structural necessity. The image served for everything so that the structure, a weaker and weaker free verse, degenerated into a condition very nearly resembling that of the sonnet."

Imagism was never for American poets quite the doctrinaire thing it was for a small group of English poets, notably those under the aegis of T. E. Hulme, its unofficial philosopher. Imagism nevertheless provided a healthy climate for a man of Williams' persuasions and a mode of expression in which his nervous sort of poetic shorthand seemed less idiosyncratic. He perhaps contributed to the movement as much as he learned from it, and helped to make it the crucible in which many talents far different from his own were refined. In any case, the spare hard smack of Imagist language is a note that echoes throughout his career. On poetry that had become muddy and stagnant, Imagism acted like an agent that clarifies a solution without seriously changing its chemical structure. While it undoubtedly helped Williams to define his own peculiar language, it did not serve his greater need for a broader and more viable sense of structure, a means of moving on from the miniature, Japanese-y organization of the typical Imagist poem. At the very time of his strongest Imagist affinities, a more important and longer lasting influence was already working in his poetic bloodstream. This influence came from the plastic arts—the American paintings from Philadelphia's "Black

Gang" and from New York that foreshadowed a revolution in taste and subject matter, the Parisian paintings that pointed to a revolution in technique established by Impressionism and strengthened by the related developments of Fauvism, Cubism, and the various splinter movements to which the latter gave rise. "As I look back," Williams wrote decades later, "I think it was the French painters rather than the writers who influenced us, and their influence was very great. They created an atmosphere of release, color release, release from stereotyped forms, trite subjects." The impact of painting on many of Williams' poems dates from 1913, the year of the famous Armory Show which opened for Americans a broad window on the blocked-in landscapes of Cézanne, the swabbed-on colors and visual rhythms of Matisse, the constructions of Picasso. Meanwhile, he was swiftly evolving the technique which, once he had it wholly in his control, would make it register as uniquely as a signature.

When he dispensed with measure by count, with the assured music of rhyme and metrics that can buoy a poet's natural cadences, Williams had to depend completely on the simple rightness of his eye and ear. The success of any one of his poems came to depend on its movement, its line-to-line tensions, the tightrope-walking progress of an idea. In a typical Williams poem a notion is introduced, then sent off on a balancing act that involves interruptions, sudden twists and turns, moments of jeopardy when the wire goes slack, brief shifts of weight, tripping steps and sudden stops, and, finally, rest and poise. When this sense of performance is most alive in Williams, his poems give the illusion of the mind in the process of thinking. The reader has no sense of emotion recollected in tranquillity, but rather of emotion as a process—a living document of experience rather than a delayed report of experience. But when this sense of performance is least alive, he fails to keep the delicate relationship between actuality and reality on which the success of the poem depends and the result is a note instead of a composition. The poem then becomes an item of marginalia, something picked up and dropped by the poet as easily as it is scanned and discarded by the reader.

One of the earliest poems bearing the unmistakable Williams signature is "Le Médecin Malgré Lui." Here he steps away from Pound and drops the little stances and postures that gave many of his early poems a naively transparent literary gloss. The French title is perhaps a concession to "poetic" orientation, and "my Lady Happiness" is a prettier phrase than any the poet would soon care to entertain. Otherwise the poem consists of the homely, nervous lines that are already his stock in trade:

LE MÉDECIN MALGRÉ LUI

Oh I suppose I should
wash the walls of my office
polish the rust from
my instruments and keep them
definitely in order
build shelves in the laboratory
empty out the old stains
clean the bottles
and refill them, buy
another lens, put
my journals on edge instead of
letting them lie flat
in heaps—then begin
ten years back and
gradually
read them to date
cataloguing important
articles for ready reference.
I suppose I should
read the new books.
If to this I added

a bill at the tailor's
and at the cleaner's
grew a decent beard
and cultivated a look
of importance—
Who can tell? I might be
a credit to my Lady Happiness
and never think anything
but a white thought!

When he had found his way to this free speech with its rough prose measure, Williams was on his own. Forty years later he would be ready to come to a complicated long poem, epical in dimension and intention, but until then his technique, in spite of various dispositions of measure, is remarkably all of a piece. Unlike the poet whose lifework is clearly segmented in periods, Williams wrote poems in the 1960's, as he had in every other decade of his career, very much like those he wrote in 1914. One cannot study him with the expectation of tracing gradual changes in structure and diction that signify successive methods. He did not so much develop a technique as he exploited a general attitude which determinedly avoided the repetitions on which technique is based. "What Williams sees he sees in a flash," wrote Kenneth Burke. "[He] is the master of the glimpse. A line of his . . . will throw the reader into unexpected intimacy with his subject, like pushing open a door into some foreign face. . . . It would be mere idleness to give his *ars poetica* in more presumptuous terms. The process is simply this: There is the eye, and there is the thing upon which the eye alights; while the relationship existing between the two is the poem."

Consequently, Williams' technical development was largely a matter of canny dispositions of language within a limitless area; his philosophical development mainly a matter of the representation of ideas elaborating the view of life with which he began. His technique per se remained comparatively static, allowing for intensification and extension but not for complication. The philosophy reflected Williams' zealous involvement in his personal poetic mission and, to a lesser extent, in the life of his times—occasionally in overt concern with politics, economics, and the global dilemmas of the nuclear age, but mostly as the effects of contemporary history were manifest in purely local instances. Just as his technique inhibited development, his philosophy precluded systematization. Since immediately present sensation was the only thing he wholly trusted, the work produced by such impetus was necessarily an index of feeling rather than a register of thought. "A work of art," Williams once wrote, "is important only as evidence, in its structure, of a new world which it has been created to affirm. . . . A life that is here and now is timeless. That is the universal I am seeking: to embody that in a work of art, a new world that is always 'real.' " Since he conceived the poem "as a field of action, at what pitch the battle is today and what may come of it," one does not look toward Williams for considered conclusions and summations. In catching the tilt and shine of his observations, however, and by participating in his endless forays into the immediate, one can deduce attitudes and convictions. These give little substance to a philosophical position normally embodied in statements and tenets. Instead they reveal a pragmatic vision continually energized by action and reaction.

In the years just before World War I, Williams' associates were just as often painters as they were writers. In the New York studio of Walter Arensberg he met Marcel Duchamp, whose "Nude Descending a Staircase" became the *cause célèbre* of an era, and there he saw the new works from Paris that were to rechannel the course of American painting. "I bumped through these periods like a yokel," he said, "narrow-eyed, feeling my own inadequacies, but burning with the lust to write." His conviction that American poetry had to be new, that it had to find a way to cast off the heavy pall of gentility and servile provincialism, to find the means to use the advance that Whitman presaged but, according to Williams, did not develop, was passionate. In the new paintings, not only those from Montmartre and Montparnasse, but those by such Americans as Charles Sheeler, Marsden Hartley, and Stuart Davis who had already absorbed the spirit of Paris, Williams sensed a spirit that promised to generate a method. "Here was my chance," he wrote, "that was all I knew. There had been a break somewhere, we were streaming through, each thinking his own thoughts, driving his own designs toward his self's objectives. Whether the Armory Show in painting did it or whether that also was no more than a facet—the poetic line, the way the image was to lie on the page was our immediate concern. For myself all that implied, in the materials, respecting the place I knew best, was finding a local assertion—to my everlasting relief." When Williams came to make his "local assertion," it was phrased in modes suggesting he had borrowed from two kinds of painting, both of which were importantly represented in the Armory Show.

One was the native product of what was popularly known as the "Ash Can" school—the group of artists who brought into the forefront unsentimentalized versions of the ugly vitality of American city life. In scores of poems, Williams catches the same hitherto neglected fragments of observation as those with which the painters were dealing, letting his figures and his city-scapes speak for themselves, unencumbered by academic notions of design or the rehearsed pathos of the genre painter or poet.

The other kind of painting to which Williams responded with instinctual shocks of recognition was the Parisian import in which the pre-eminent thing was stress on new forms, new apprehensions and constructions of reality. Mainly this was Cubism which, in all of its forms, placed emphasis upon construction rather than upon representation. As a technique it offered Williams that release for which he was always searching and he borrowed it and used it with such easy authority that he might have invented it. One of the poems that best illustrates his use of Cubist techniques is the following:

ST. FRANCIS EINSTEIN OF THE DAFFODILS

*On the first visit of Professor Einstein
to the United States in the spring of 1921.*

"Sweet land"
at last!
out of the sea—
the Venusremembering wavelets
rippling with laughter—
freedom
for the daffodils!
—in a tearing wind
that shakes
the tufted orchards—
Einstein, tall as a violet
in the lattice-arbor corner
is tall as
a blossomy peartree

O Samos, Samos
dead and buried. Lesbia
a black cat in the freshturned
garden. All dead.
All flesh they sung
is rotten
Sing of it no longer—
Side by side young and old
take the sun together—
maples, green and red
yellowbells

and the vermilion quinceflower
together—

The peartree
with foetid blossoms
sways its high topbranches
with contrary motions
and there are both pinkflowered
and coralflowered peachtrees
in the bare chickenyard
of the old negro
with white hair who hides
poisoned fish-heads
here and there
where stray cats find them—
find them

Spring days
swift and mutable
winds blowing four ways
hot and cold
shaking the flowers—
Now the northeast wind
moving in fogs leaves the grass
cold and dripping. The night
is dark. But in the night
the southeast wind approaches
The owner of the orchard
lies in bed
with open windows
and throws off his covers
one by one.

Discussing the content, but not the technique, of the poem, Williams made this comment: "It is always spring time for the mind when great discoveries are made. Is not Einstein, at the same time, saintly in the purity of his scientific imagining? And if a saint it seems to me that the thorough logic which St. Francis saw as sparrows or donkeys, equally to be loved with whatever other living aspect of the world, would apply equally to Einstein's arrival in the United States a number of years ago to celebrate the event in the season's shapes and colors of that moment." This indicates the theme and general feeling, yet the real difficulty of the poem lies in the tenuous conjunctions and loose order of its images and allusions. A place must be found for each of these things: Einstein, St. Francis of Assisi, a black cat named Lesbia, a pear tree, peach trees, an old Negro who sets cat-traps, and a man who can't sleep. The challenge of discerning a logical order in a sequence so disparate is modified only when the reader becomes aware that the poem has been conceived in terms of a kind of painting in which all of these things must be apprehended at a glance.

The elements of the poem are necessarily presented in a series—in time. But their relationships to one another are perceived only when they are viewed simultaneously—in space. As the Cubist painter adds the dimension of time to his composition—enabling him to present in one picture not only the observed surface of a table, for instance, but its undersides, legs, and many possible angular views of it—Williams adds the dimension of space, thereby establishing a panoramic surface on which everything can be seen at once. Einstein and St. Francis, whose lives were separated by hundreds of years, become one composite agent of discovery in an actual springtime that is also the springtime of the mind. A tag— "Sweet land"—from the hymn "America," immediately superimposed upon "the Venusremembering wavelets," produces a montage: America and all the brave clichés of its anthem mingle intimately with Botticelli's "The Birth of Venus"—a figure from the classical past borne shoreward like Einstein, but on a great scallop shell instead of on an ocean liner. When these central evocations have set the historical time and imaginative space in which the poem is composed, its other elements become relevant to them. Samos, another reminder of the classical past, is "dead and buried"; Lesbia survives—only as a namesake —in the figure of the black cat that scavenges in the blossoming season and presumably meets her death in the course of her pursuit. "The old negro," involved in everything without knowing it, causes the cat's death simply by pursuing, like her, a set way of existence. The little conflict of hunger and survival, dispassionately regarded in terms of history, is really a deadly backyard drama, enacted within the flowering orchards of a man who feels the season's change—not only a change in the weather but a nameless change in the conditions of his life made inevitable by the discoveries of Einstein, the saint-scientist. Throwing off his blankets, he makes his meek, entirely human adjustment to warmer weather and a new life. The devious logic of the poem is merely a thread and a new life. The devious logic of the poem is merely a thread on which its visual sequence is strung. The meaning of the poem lies in simultaneity—the comprehension in an instant of tenuously related elements which, on the flat surface of a canvas, could be taken in at a glance.

Of the many painters whose works have influenced Williams—from the realist Americans like George Luks, Robert Henri, and John Sloan through the Parisian Cubists, the surrealists, and on to "action" painters like Jackson Pollock—the one with whom he has the clearest technical and thematic affinities is the American Edward Hopper. Williams never mentions Hopper in his essays and memoirs, and seems curiously unaware of a contemporary whose career parallels his own. Yet a joint exhibition featuring their paintings and poems would present a view of experience remarkably cohesive in substance and attitude. Many of Williams' poems might be anecdotes drawn from the particular seam of American life Hopper records on canvas; many of Hop-

per's paintings might be visual realizations of a mood, a situation, or a figure from the poetic documentation of Williams. Both men listen to the human pulse that beats beneath urban squalor, both are moved by the pathetic self-sufficiency of lives eked out in the isolation of steel and stone, and both detect the muted beauty that lurks in the tawdry, vulgar, even in the grotesque. Hopper's paintings are as free of "painterly" techniques as photographs, yet they are emotionally charged in ways no photograph could match. Like Williams' poems, they say what they have to say in a glimpse, leaving the observer to provide the human frame and, within his capacities, to feel the human resonance. Their successes are of the same nature; pigment or words convey the illusion of actuality passing into art without deformation. Their failures are also similar: actuality is merely recorded, without the accompaniment of that aesthetic benison that makes an observed fact part of an imposed vision. Williams' incorrigible zest for life as a going concern, the way in which, as Randall Jarrell remarked, he "spins willingly on the wheel of things," and his indiscriminate acceptance of its heinous injustices and incongruities tend to separate him from Hopper, whose temperament is far more selective. But on nearly all other grounds, painter and poet, through the greater part of their respective careers, share a proximity that is unique in American art.

One of the shortest, and perhaps the most famous, of Williams' poems is "The Red Wheelbarrow." Since it has long been recognized as a staunch contribution to modern poetry, and can now be accommodated without strain among many other similar poems by Williams and by others, a contemporary reader can gain a sense of its original impact only by putting himself in the position of the reader of some forty years ago. Then, most poetry, American as well as English, was comfortably couched in Georgian nostalgias, measured in lines that ticked off rhymes at predictable intervals, and furnished with the dainty figurations that certified the license of its authors. Confronted by an odd-looking book from an obscurely private publisher, what was the cultivated reader to make of these sixteen words that might just somehow have fallen from the typesetter's font?

THE RED WHEELBARROW

so much depends
upon

a red wheel
barrow

glazed with rain
water

beside the white
chickens

About similar poems of Williams', Hugh Kenner remarked, "If you are obliged to *talk* about poetry of this kind, your only recourse is to provide it with a theoretical scaffolding. Of such an enterprise, it may be noted that the function of theory is to make the cautious mind feel that the poems so located exist by some right, and after that to disappear." Against the temptation to let the little poem stand in its own realized moment, there is also the temptation to ask, What possibly "happens" in his poem to make it so durable? Because it is, after all, a composition and not a typographical accident, the poem, like others of its kind, *can* be talked about as long as the talk is an account of a response and not an attempt to grind it fine in the mills of a system. First: "so much depends . . ." This deliberately vague but enormously suggestive phrase leads the reader to expect, at least, a subject open to

contrary possibilities and, at most (*what* is contingent upon *what?*), some relaxation of the little thrust of tension the phrase sets up. Except for the slight metaphorical lift of the word "glazed," what the reader gets is flat actuality, ignoring his rising expectation and answering in its own disinterested and incontrovertible terms. The movement of the poem is in the nature of a reversal: a yearning toward what might or could be is quietly checked by the homely beauty of what *is*.

While his subjects include almost anything that would normally come within the purview of a busy physician on his rounds, Williams' whole and very ample theme is himself—a feeling man who charges the commonplace with his own uncommon ardors and who makes of his relations with the ordinary an idyll and a romance. By isolating details, magnifying them, or cinematically "freezing" them, he gives to the average and quotidian a significance that would otherwise go unnoticed. By imposing his own *joie de vivre* on the life within his house, on his street, and across the breadth of his home town, he makes lyrics out of circumstances that would often seem more ripe for the sociological casebook or for the chilling satire of a Daumier etching. The following poem is an instance of Williams in his role as the poet of domesticity:

DANSE RUSSE

If when my wife is sleeping
and the baby and Kathleen
are sleeping
and the sun is a flame-white disc
in silken mists
above shining trees,—
if I in my north room
dance naked, grotesquely
before my mirror
waving my shirt round my head
and singing softly to myself:

"I am lonely, lonely,
I was born to be lonely,
I am best so!"
If I admire my arms, my face,
my shoulders, flanks, buttocks
against the yellow drawn shades,—

Who shall say I am not
the happy genius of my household?

In moments of pure observation he takes scenes that anyone might witness a hundred times without a thought and invests them with a pathos that is as real as it is intangible. In "The Lonely Street," which might be a poet's transcription of a typical subject of Edward Hopper, words merely annotate a situation that must, for the most part, be inferred. Since Williams comes clean, so to speak, without a frame and without any tradition but his own, much of his work demands unusually close participation on the part of the reader: the poet provides a picture, sets a mood with gravity and economy, but the meaning of the poem is heard only in its reverberations.

THE LONELY STREET

School is over. It is too hot
to walk at ease. At ease
in light frocks they walk the streets
to while the time away.
They have grown tall. They hold
pink flames in their right hands.
In white from head to foot,
with sidelong, idle look—
in yellow, floating stuff,
black sash and stockings—
touching their avid mouths
with pink sugar on a stick—
like a carnation each holds in her hand—
they mount the lonely street.

In the simplicity and starkness of his recordings of an observed action or a figure, Williams throws away many of the conventional advantages of poetry as a form of expression and thereby takes chances few poets are willing to hazard. Other poets depend largely on craft, maneuver, and all the learned strategies of an art with a long history. Williams depends on little more than the feeling that can be evoked, or conveyed, by a spontaneous sequence of words arranged in a manner meant to echo the artlessness of ordinary speech. When he succeeds, the result is an impact and a surprise, a sudden, sometimes shocked awareness on the part of the reader that affirms the reality of what he records. In a poem such as the following, the separating distance between an event and its report falls away; reality and its poetic apprehension are joined in a compatibility that seems absolute.

COMPLETE DESTRUCTION

It was an icy day.
We buried the cat,
then took her box
and set match to it

in the back yard.
Those fleas that escaped
earth and fire
died by the cold.

But there are frequent occasions in the body of Williams' work where his exclusive dependence on the sort of poetic shorthand that might catch actuality *in situ* leads him into banality and even into the overweening poetic fancy he most abhors. In a passage from his autobiography, he pinpoints the occasion of a particular poem: "Once on a hot July day coming back exhausted from the Post Graduate Clinic, I dropped in as I sometimes did at Marsden's [Hartley] studio on Fifteenth Street for a talk, a little drink maybe and to see what he was doing. As I approached his number I heard a great clatter of bells and the roar of a fire engine passing the end of the street down Ninth Avenue. I turned just in time to see a golden figure 5 on a red background flash by. The impression was so sudden and forceful that I took a piece of paper out of my pocket and wrote a short poem about it." Here it is:

THE GREAT FIGURE

Among the rain
and lights
I saw the figure 5
in gold
on a red
firetruck
moving
tense
unheeded
to gong clangs
siren howls
and wheels rumbling
through the dark city.

Clearly a case where Williams' material remains quite where he found it, this poem neither heightens the prose account nor extends the perception it reports. The poetic version, in fact, muddies the simplicity of the prose statement, "just in time to see a golden figure 5 on a red background flash by." The attempt to give significance to an observation that had no significance beyond the fact that he made it leads Williams into sophomoric poetic straining. The possibility that the figure 5, or any other figure, on a fire engine might be "tense" is absurd; the statement that it is "unheeded" is, in the testimony of the poem itself, patently false. After these sentimentalities, the spuriously ominous note of "wheels rumbling/ through the dark city" is as phony as a tumbrel in Times Square.

Alternation of happy accident and bad chance is necessarily the lot of any poet, no matter how great his talent, who is a personality gifted with a knack more than he is a craftsman pledged to a profession. Because of his preoccupation with finding the measure that would dictate the form and the demonstrated dexterity with which he pursued it, and because of the great number of his poems that exist without the support of convention, Williams was not quite either. He was a phenomenon: a master whose precepts, dutifully followed, led almost always to disaster; a poet whose example, on the other hand, had tonic effect on a generation of poets not remotely like him. When Williams wrote criticism, he often unconsciously parodied the academic lingo he officially deplored, and when he gave advice, he tended to ignore the personal temperament and private circumstance that made his own working methods special. He admitted, for instance, that "I didn't go in for long lines because of my nervous nature," and that, from his beginnings as a poet, he felt he was "*not English,*" and that rhyme and other means of organizing a poem seemed to him intolerably restrictive. Consequently, when he came to use his personal limitations as the basis of a general program, he was guilty of an exclusiveness his nature otherwise seemed to deny. Many modern poets are able to compose a long line in an equilibrium of spirit as well as of metrics, and many have found the old devices of poetry flexible, capable of entirely new variations, and more advantageous than obstructive. As a practicing physician, continually working long hours day and night, Williams usually had to write in moments stolen between appointments, in snatches and fragments, on prescription blanks sometimes, or any other writing surface at hand. This necessity should not be discounted as a very large factor in his particular development. The wonder is that so many hurried notations and seized moments should have become part of the permanent record of a career and a poetic era.

The only "official" program with which Williams was identified was the one that went by the name of Objectivism. This was a term devised to give emphasis to certain notions he and others shared with Gertrude Stein about the literal and structural qualities of "words being words," and came to signify a short-lived movement confined to himself, the poet Louis Zukofsky who was a disciple of Ezra Pound's, Charles Reznikoff, and George Oppen. Together these men organized and financed the Objectivist Press from which, in a short career, issued a handful of books including Williams' *Collected Poems*. In Williams' own words, Objectivist theory was this:

"We had had 'Imagism' . . . which ran quickly out. That, though it had been useful in ridding the field of verbiage, had no formal necessity implicit in it. It had already dribbled off into so called 'free verse' which, as we saw, was a misnomer. There is no such thing as free verse! Verse is measure of some sort. 'Free verse' was without measure and needed none for its projected objectifications. Thus the poem had run down and became formally non extant.

"But, we argued, the poem, like every other form of art, is an object, an object that in itself formally presents its case and its meaning by the very form it assumes. Therefore, being an object, it should be so treated and controlled— but not as in the past. For past objects have about them past necessities—like the sonnet— which have conditioned them and from which, as a form itself, they cannot be freed.

"The poem being an object (like a symphony or cubist painting) it must be the purpose of the poet to make of his words a new form: to invent, that is, an object consonant with his day. This was what we wished to imply by Objectivism, an antidote, in a sense, to the bare image haphazardly presented in loose verse."

Most poets who reach an artistic maturity as advanced as Williams' define for themselves an area in which poems inspired by new experience and the surprise encounters of everyday existence quite naturally find a place. If they do not come to a settled view of life, they at least are marked by attitudes that color their thinking and lend a consistent tone to its expression. These poets achieve a style of language that identifies them as surely as the clothes they wear. When their individual interests are repeated and developed in the course of many poems, their predilections, like their uses of language, tend to fall into patterns. Once a pattern has become clear, its rhythms obvious and its figures familiar, it takes on the character of a territory staked out and settled. The poet's authority there is both natural and appropriate: he has found a local habitation and created a world of such distinctive character that any sensitive reader knows at once just what territory he has ventured. The worlds of Frost and Stevens and Cummings can be recognized at the threshold; and while, in each case, objects that loom beyond may vary enormously, they are always harmonious with their settings and obedient to laws of sensibility that are seldom relaxed.

In the case of Williams, the sense of a large controlling spirit, on the one hand, and of an essentially homogeneous landscape, on the other hand, is comparatively minor. He maintained a refreshing ability to surprise himself as often as he was surprised by what he met, but since the element of chance was the liveliest agent in his purview, Williams' vision remained expectant and unsettled. Where other poets tend to dwell in wonder, Williams, refusing to stay put, made wonder the vehicle on which he rode. His creative life depended upon his being alive to contingencies; and since these recurred with a relentlessness that kept him always newly addressed to his task, he gave the appearance of a man forever trying to transmute base metals into gold or to re-invent the umbrella. He never gave up the attempt to capture the thing that cannot be captured, to do the work that is never done. Unlike the master craftsman who apportions his energies with an inherent sense of economy, Williams spent his with profligacy. Since he was less interested in arriving anywhere than he was in maintaining the journey at a high pitch of movement and purposiveness, his career had the quality of a vector that continually points a direction that needs no goal.

Tracking Williams' progress is a remarkably brief operation. When he had broken with the poets of the past and those of his contemporaries whose disposition, he felt, was to make accommodation rather than revolution, he had taken the one stride within which all his lesser steps are subsumed. The progress is begun and ended almost at once; there remains the development. Technically speaking, Williams' creative life can be conveniently viewed in at least five distinct phases. Beginning as an imitator of nineteenth-century forms inherited from the romantics, particularly Keats, but including also small persistent echoes of Browning, he moves on toward a Whitmanesque free verse somewhat incongruously modified by the classic stances and *fin de siècle* sophistications that crop up in the early work of Ezra Pound. Imagism later provides a salubrious climate for his hard clear transcriptions of natural, urban, and domestic life, and for the pithy short forms into which his poetic thought characteristically falls. But through each of these phases he is searching for the measure that will afford him greater freedom and, at the same time, tighter

control—a measure replacing the strict count of metrics that will open to him, and all the other poets of the new age, a means of getting through to the American idiom that is recognized as a cultural fact but persists as a poetic anomaly. This search takes on the obsessive power of a mystique for Williams and through many variations in free form he eventually comes to the notion of the "variable foot," his name for a vague entity meant to delineate a unit of language that might carry into formal expression the tilt and accent of natural speech. In a letter to Richard Eberhart in 1954, Williams explains:

"I have never been one to write by rule, even by my own rules. Let's begin with the rule of counted syllables, in which all poems have been written hitherto. That has become tiresome to my ear.

"Finally, the stated syllables, as in the best of present-day free verse, have become entirely divorced from the beat, that is the measure. The musical pace proceeds without them.

"Therefore the measure, that is to say, the count, having got rid of the words, which held it down, is returned to the *music*.

"The words, having been freed, have been allowed to run all over the map, 'free' as we have mistakenly thought. This has amounted to no more (in Whitman and others) than no discipline at all.

"But if we keep in mind the *tune* which the lines (not necessarily the words) make in our ears, we are ready to proceed.

"By measure I mean musical pace. Now, with music in our ears the words need only be taught to keep as distinguished an order, as chosen a character, as regular, according to the music, as in the best of prose.

"By its *music* shall the best of modern verse be known and the *resources* of the music. The refinement of the poem, its subtlety, is not to be known by the elevation of the words but—

the words don't so much matter—by the resources of the *music*.

"To give you an example from my own work—not that I know anything about what I have myself written:

(count):—not that I ever count when writing but, at best, the lines must be capable of being counted, that is to say, *measured*—(believe it or not).—At that I may, half consciously, even count the measure under my breath as I write.—

(approximate example)

(1) The smell of the heat is boxwood

 (2)when rousing us

   (3) a movement of the air

(4) stirs our thoughts

 (5) that had no life in them

   (6) to a life, a life in which

(or)

(1) Mother of God! Our Lady!

 (2) the heart

   (3) is an unruly master:

(4) Forgive us our sins

 (5) as we

   (6) forgive.

(7) those who have sinned against

"Count a single beat to each numeral. You may not agree with my ear, but that is the way I count the line. Over the whole poem it gives a pattern to the meter that can be felt as a new measure. It gives resources to the ear which result in a language which we hear spoken about us every day."

As an explanation, and an attempted demonstration of the "variable foot" as meticulous as any Williams made, this account nevertheless gives a reader or critic little more than a statement of intention. Williams anticipates the difficulty when he says, "You may not agree with my ear, but that is the way I count the line." His count is arbitrary, applied to lines that may ring with an authentic music in his ears, but which are apt to register with an entirely different measure, and consequently a different music, on the ears of anyone else. The way in which one hears naturally determines the way one writes, but the enormous variability in the capacity to hear, plus all the intricacies of selection that set one hearer apart from another, gives Williams' theory so much latitude that it becomes all but useless for analysis or for emulation. That this method worked for him is indisputable. But if it is to work for anyone else, its pretensions as theory and method must be put aside in favor of the unique pragmatic ingenuity which gives his poetry its character.

There are distinguishing aspects of American speech on many levels—regional, societal, occupational, cultural; the phonetic emphases that Americans make in the thousands of phrases they use in their everyday exchanges—shorthand expressions that signify a mood or an attitude—are distinctively different from British usage as well as from general literary or journalistic usage; the poet who can hear these streamlined expressions, who can catch the relationship between a thought and the gesture of words that carries it, should find a way to use them. When Williams does not try to make a limiting formula of a spontaneous practice, his explanation of the way he works is succinct and clarifying: ". . . in some of my work all I have to do is to transcribe the language when hot and feelingly spoken. For when it is charged with emotion it has a tendency to be rhythmic, lowdown, inherent in the place where it is being used. And that is, to me, the origin of form, the origin of measure. The rhythmic beat of charged language." Poets other than Williams have used such moments of charged vernacular speech, sometimes as embellishments or variations on formal passages, sometimes in verse somewhat freely conceived as a nice succession of cadences, but also at times within the strictures of iambic or trochaic meter. Williams must be credited with knowing the source and strength of his own endeavors, but when he attempts to fit them into a formula, he appears unnecessarily determined to predicate a system and to offer it as generally applicable when, actually, it is based on practices congenial only to himself.

In his final phase, Williams carries forward his innovations and expands their range in several individual volumes of lyrics and in one of the longest poems of modern times, *Paterson*. The lyrics, more subdued and mellow in feeling than most of the earlier poems, are technically as free but handled with notably more consistency and assurance as Williams exploits his congenial personal discovery, the "variable foot." In *Paterson*, recapitulating the adventure of his poetic and personal history, Williams tests the adequacy of his techniques in the light of the special demands of epic expression.

As an epic, *Paterson* shares with a number of other modern poems the fact that its structure, suggested partly by an available cultural situation, is nevertheless mostly the device of an author who, in despair, creates what he has failed to inherit—a body of myth, a roster of dramatis personae, a religious sanction. The official façades of democracy and Christianity cannot disguise the fact that the contemporary world is characterized more by disparity than by unity. Consequently, the poet is denied the advantage of a homogeneous community where the deeds of religious and political heroes reflect common ideals. While it is likely that he knows his heritage better than most people, the poet who wants to write an epic today tends to ignore the possibilities still available to him in the legends of Christianity and the annals of democracy, and to look for, or to make, some over-all structure that may include aspects of both but which does not pretend

wholly to represent either. Usually this structure takes the form of a "model of confusion" that reflects the contradictions implicit in a society that is at once intensely self-conscious and self-deceptive. All but the thinnest line of narrative is dispensed with. In its place the poet offers a polyhedral view of experience, forcing the reader to witness as a fact the historical and spiritual dislocation that not only provides the poem with its theme but suggests its shape.

Readers familiar with the mythical structures of Joyce's *Ulysses* and *Finnegans Wake*, Eliot's *The Waste Land*, or Hart Crane's *The Bridge* will discern in *Paterson* methods with which they are already acquainted, and a few that belong uniquely to Williams. The theme of his epic is, almost inevitably, another dramatized statement of his long quest for the language that will record actuality with the natural force of actuality—"the redeeming language by which a man's premature death . . . might have been prevented." As he moved gradually toward the undertaking of a long poem, Williams knew that his theme was set and understood that he was challenged to find a symbolical situation—some tangible equivalent of a myth built like a coral formation, cell by cell, through the cultural phases of a people or a nation—that might embody his theme locally and yet allow for its universal application. In a half-conscious, almost subliminal way, Williams had for many years been aware of just such a reticulum of ideas and had in fact used some of these ideas in poems where landscape is treated as a kind of emotional topography. Persistently ambitious to write a long poem, he continued to lack any clear notion of its architecture. As a saint's spiritual exercises prepare him for revelation, Williams' long poetic life had prepared him to recognize at once the idea that would serve him. When suddenly it came, it was set down as a modest three lines first appearing in a pamphlet of poems, *The Broken Span,* published in 1941:

A man like a city and a woman like a
flower—who are in love. Two
women. Three women. Innumerable
women, each like a flower. But only
one man—like a city.

From this kernel—"A man like a city"—the whole poem flowered.

But, first, there was the question of *what* city. "Like what baby when I decided to write about babies," said Williams. "The problem of the poetics I knew depended upon finding a specific city, one that I knew, so I searched for a city. New York? It couldn't be New York, not anything as big as a metropolis. Rutherford wasn't a city. Passaic wouldn't do. I'd known about Paterson, even written about it . . . Suddenly it dawned on me I had a find. I began my investigations. Paterson had a history, an important colonial history. It had, besides, a river—the Passaic, and the Falls. I may have been influenced by James Joyce who had made Dublin the hero of his book. . . . But I forgot about Joyce and fell in love with my city. The Falls were spectacular; the river was a symbol handed to me. I began to write the beginning, about the stream above the Falls. I read everything I could gather, finding fascinating documentary evidence in a volume published by the Historical Society of Paterson. Here were all the facts I could ask for, details exploited by no one. This was my river and I was going to use it. I had grown up on its banks, seen the filth that polluted it, even dead horses. . . . I took the river as it followed its course down to the sea; all I had to do was follow it and I had a poem."

The virtue of Williams' idea was its viability. As soon as he had begun to give it full expression he found that everything was inter-active and relevant: history from local archives gave identity to a population in general and to one man in particular; the mutations of geology gave spaciousness to a concept and recognizable silhouettes to giant figures; the composite City-Man was a hero of many parts, each of which caught and objectified some facet of truth about the other; the sweep of actuality—a Babel of speech and brute action—resounded like the Falls, overheard but not interpreted; like existence into time, the Passaic River flowed every day, eternally, toward the ocean.

An extended meditation on an idea that cannot be reduced to a statement, the poem makes a continuous graph-like recording of a process of discovery and affirmation, flux and stasis, permanence and mutability. In a vast collocation of fragments—a sort of mosaic of the contents of consciousness—poetry is interspersed with long and short passages of prose. Over these the poet's imagination moves like a flame sporadically burning, fed by the debris of old letters personal and anonymous, old journals, newspaper reports, advertisements, and passages from historical documents. In certain of these the language is inchoate, flat, choked with sentiment or cloyingly prettified by flourishes of fine writing. In others, the prose account serves to introduce matters that underline, counterpoint, or in some way vary the central theme. These interpolations serve for *Paterson* as Eliot's appended annotations served for *The Waste Land* and as Hart Crane's marginal commentaries served for *The Bridge.* What in another poem would be regarded as addenda, or the dross of the author's investigations, become in *Paterson* an essential part of the process of the poem.

The dramatis personae consists of scores of characters who drift in and out of its five books, a few whose problems are persistent, many who make one brief contribution, then disappear, and one all-embracing figure, the Man-City, Paterson, Dr. Paterson, Noah Faitoute Paterson who is, first, William Carlos Williams and all the factors of environment, heritage, and history of which he is composed. In his mythological role, he is a geological giant who lies sleeping on his right side on the bank of the Passaic River with the noise of the great Falls tumbling in his ear, facing the recumbent figure of another geological giant, Garrett Mountain, his female counterpart. The river flows between them, a stream of consciousness, a stream of language which, at the spillway of the Great Falls, speaks in torrential dialects which the poet must unravel, must comb "into straight lines/ from that rafter of a rock's/ lip ."

Having conceived *Paterson* as a poem primordially involved in history and, at the same time, overwhelmed by the thousand voices of immediacy, Williams arrived at two distinct methods of dealing with his materials: a method of contrast and a method of dispersion. In the former he follows one of the devices used in *The Waste Land* and, to a lesser extent, in *The Bridge*. The present is compared with the past in terms of spiritual grace and spiritual vulgarity; pastoral charm and urban tawdriness; the human capacity for awe and its debasement to an appetite for sensation. This is all familiar, amounting to something like a concession on Williams' part to the academically certifiable poetry to which he normally gives no quarter. The second of his methods, dispersion, finds him quite in character and on his own. Truth lies in the search for truth, he seems to say; the energy with which the mind deals with experience is the thing, and not the little conclusions about experience that the mind might sort out. In this method he gives up any pretension toward the intellectual's drive to fuse and unify. Differing from poets who seek, like Eliot, the recovery of the wholeness that religious faith once made possible, or those, like Crane, who seek a recovery of faith in the generative power of love, Williams seeks the key to that awareness that would make all life transcendent. This pursuit leads him away from dependence on the consolations of philosophy and into the belief that, as the physicist unlocks the structure of matter, the poet may find the measure that identifies the human.

In the method he adopts he is characteristically closer to the painters than he is to the poets, especially to those comparatively recent American artists known as "action" painters. Williams' goal, like theirs, is the release of energy rather than the reassembling of familiar counters; he strives for a poem that will, in its own process, answer the question it continually poses. Like the abstractionist painter who gives up identifiable shapes and forms for visual rhythms, Williams dispenses with poetic modes that might unify his poem, hopeful that incursions of indiscriminate subject matter may find their place in his over-all design. His aim is similar to that of the painter who expects that his rhythmic emphases will find their functional place in the over-all "writing" that covers his canvas. The massed dispersions of a late Jackson Pollock—energies flowing from and ordered by one consciousness—are duplicated in the thrusts and charges by which Williams creates a field of action. The achievement in both cases is a styleless style in which energy and force take precedence over organization and the graceful disposition of subject matter.

Release of energy in *Paterson* is both a theme and a technique. As a technique it operates continually; as an explicit theme it occurs sporadically throughout the poem, and most importantly in *Book III*, in relation to the figure of Marie Curie who, with her husband Pierre, discovered radium in 1898. In an early typescript of *Paterson,* Williams notes the ways in which a lecture on atomic fission suggested to him how the antennae of the poet and the yardstick of the scientist work on the same subject: "The lecture on uranium (Curie), the splitting of the atom (first time explained to *me*) has a literary meaning . . . in the splitting of the foot . . . (sprung meter of Hopkins) and consequently is connected thereby to human life or death. . . . Three discoveries here: 1. radium. 2. poet's discovery of modern idiom. 3. political scientist's discovery of a cure for economic ills." In her book *The Metamorphic Tradition in Modern Poetry,* Sister M. Bernetta Quinn further delineates these concepts as they are used in *Paterson*:

"The analogy between the poet's business and the physicist's is treated at length. Madame Curie's discovery—and by implication the poet's also—being compared to that of Columbus. Both Madame Curie and Paterson were seeking the radiant gist, the luminous stain:

> *A dissonance*
> *in the valence of Uranium*
> *led to the discovery*
>
> *Where dissonance*
> *(if you are interested)*
> *leads to discovery*

"Through the experience of twentieth-century scientists like the Curies, a man's old dream of transmuting the elements . . . has indeed come true. . . . Basic to such metamorphoses is the conversion of mass into energy, as predicted by Einstein, whose work revised the traditional concept of the indestructibility of matter to the present law of conservation of mass and energy. Because of physical research in this direction, scientists can now go through the Mendeleev molecular weight table, explicitly referred to by Williams, changing one element into another—for instance, mercury to gold—by capturing into

a nucleus such extra particles as protons, neutrons, deuterons, and alpha particles. Another aspect of artificial transmutation is the splitting of the uranium 235 atom. Man-made devices, such as the cyclotron, can today achieve a metamorphosis which will set up chain reactions of incredible power.

"By the inevitable laws of nature itself, uranium transmutes into radium and finally to the stable substance of lead: 'Uranium (bound to be lead)/throws out the fire.' The important part of this process, however, is not the lead, its conclusion, but the enormous forces for good or evil which the giving off of radioactive emanations (Gamma rays) means for the human race. All these implications Williams weaves into his poem."

The idea of *Paterson* is superb, clearly equal in its dimensions to the other celebrated modern poems based on myth structures, elastically appropriate to Williams' temperament and practice, and charged heroically with purpose. But the idea on which this and any other epic is based is, unfortunately, merely the abstract, the blueprint, and the non-poet can devise an impressive one as easily as the poet. The enormous accommodation provided for in a method of dispersion gives *Paterson* an all-of-a-piece consistently on an intellectual level, but on an emotive level the poem is vastly uneven and at times hopelessly fragmented. Like Joyce in some of the most clotted arcana of *Finnegans Wake,* Williams appears to be guilty of a fetishism of the very instrument he has taken great pains to perfect. An obsession with freedom has resulted in anarchy; the poem becomes more accident than design. Moments of brilliance are succeeded by stretches of dullness and the whole work seems clogged in its own machinery. These failures would not seem so great if the successful parts of the poem were not so luminous. *Book I* is the paragon. Here idea and illustration are electrically related;

prose informs the poetry and poetry enhances the prose; the vertical plane of the past and the horizontal plane of the present intersect in bursts of illumination. Everything strikes fire from everything else and the effect is that of a crystalline substance that can be turned endlessly, facet by facet catching the points of light that shed a radiance.

But where, in *Book I*, the idea serves to polarize all the materials in its field, in successive books the materials refuse to respond to any magnet and often lie curiously inert. The structure consequently begins to seem hammered together and rickety. When the energy of the idea holds things together, the result is a miraculous appositeness that extends to the most disparate conjunctions of material. When the energy flags, however, waywardness takes over and the will tries desperately to do the work of the imagination. Randall Jarrell, who felt that the term Organization of Irrelevance might describe Williams' type of structure, posed questions that may occur to other readers who have ventured into the interior of *Paterson*: "Such organization is *ex post facto* organization: if something is somewhere, one can always find Some Good Reason for its being there, but if it had not been there would one reader have missed it? if it had been put somewhere else, would one reader have guessed where it should have 'really' gone?" According to Jarrell, Williams was not able to resist the dangerous license that his structure permitted and was guilty of a crippling arbitrariness. "Sometimes these anecdotes, political remarks, random comments seem to be where they are for one reason: because Dr. Williams chose—happened to choose—for them to be there. One is reminded of that other world in which Milton found Chance 'sole arbiter.' "

Nearly ten years after *Paterson* had been published as a completed poem in four books, Williams added a fifth book in the nature of an afterword or coda. Included in this book were sections published as single lyrics, or under the title "Work in Progress," in his *Desert Music* and *Journey to Love*. *Book V*, more relaxed in tone than the rest of the poem and more consistent in its employment of the loose "step down" measure of the "variable foot," recovers some of the magic of the best sections of the earlier books. Here, from the vantage point of old age and the height of achievement, the poet looks back and down upon his life and his poems. Two themes are woven through his meditation: (1) the endurance of art as an immortal seam of reality and (2) the Virgin and the Whore—the female principle, existing beyond the discriminations of morality, that ensures the continuity of the race of man. In this last book, the methods of contrast and dispersion are somewhat relaxed in favor of a sense of quietly unifying reflection. Speaking more clearly in his own person than in the terms of his multi-faceted projection, Dr. Paterson, Williams recounts his involvements in art and his involvements in love. Together they make affirmations of what he always believed and what he instinctively knew. As *Paterson* begins with a question, it ends with an answer.

This is the question:

"Rigor of beauty is the quest. But how will you find beauty when it is locked in the mind past all remonstrance?"

This is the answer:

The measure intervenes, to measure is all we
    know,
        a choice among the measures . . .
               the measured dance

"unless the scent of a rose
    startle us anew"

Equally laughable
>is to assume to know nothing, a
>>chess game
Massively, "materially", compounded!
>Yo ho! ta ho!

We know nothing and can know nothing
>>but

the dance, to dance to a measure
contrapuntally,
>>Satyrically, the tragic foot.

The question poses the grand attempt; the winning of wisdom, the answer suggests, involves not the comfort of conclusion but the discovery of a means.

Selected Bibliography

WORKS OF
WILLIAM CARLOS WILLIAMS

Poems. Rutherford, N.J.: Privately printed, 1909.

The Tempers. London: Elkin Mathews, 1913.

Al Que Quiere! Boston: Four Seas Co., 1917.

Kora in Hell: Improvisations. Boston: Four Seas Co., 1920.

Sour Grapes. Boston: Four Seas Co., 1921.

Spring and All. Dijon: Contact Publishing Co., 1923.

Go Go. New York: Monroe Wheeler, 1923.

The Cod Head. San Francisco: Harvest Press, 1932.

Collected Poems 1921–1931. New York: Objectivist Press, 1934.

An Early Martyr and Other Poems. New York: Alcestis Press, 1935.

Adam & Eve & The City. Peru, Vt.: Alcestis Press, 1936.

The Complete Collected Poems of William Carlos Williams 1906–1938. Norfolk, Conn.: New Directions, 1938.

The Broken Span. Norfolk, Conn.: New Directions, 1941.

The Wedge. Cummington, Mass.: Cummington Press, 1944.

Paterson, Book One. New York: New Directions, 1946.

The Clouds. Aurora, N.Y., and Cummington, Mass.: Wells College Press and Cummington Press, 1948.

The Pink Church. Columbus, Ohio: Golden Goose Press, 1949.

Selected Poems. New York: New Directions, 1949.

Paterson, Book Two. New York: New Directions, 1948.

Paterson, Book Three. New York: New Directions, 1949.

The Collected Later Poems. New York: New Directions, 1950.

The Collected Earlier Poems. New York: New Directions, 1951.

Paterson, Book Four. New York: New Directions, 1951.

The Desert Music and Other Poems. New York: Random House, 1954.

Journey to Love. New York: Random House, 1955.

"The Lost Poems of William Carlos Williams or The Past Recaptured," in *New Directions 16.* New York: New Directions, 1957. Pp. 3–45.

Paterson, Book Five. New York: New Directions, 1958.

Pictures from Brueghel and Other Poems. Norfolk, Conn.: New Directions, 1962. (Includes *The Desert Music* and *Journey to Love.*)

Paterson. Norfolk, Conn.: New Directions, 1963.

The Collected Later Poems of William Carlos Williams. Norfolk, Conn.: New Directions, 1963.

The Selected Poems of William Carlos Williams, with an Introduction by Randall Jarrell. Norfolk, Conn.: New Directions, 1963.

Autobiography of William Carlos Williams. New York: New Directions, 1967.

BIBLIOGRAPHIES

Engels, John. *Checklist of William Carlos Williams.* Columbus, Ohio: Charles E. Merrill, 1969.

Heal, Edith, ed. *I Wanted to Write a Poem.* Boston: Beacon Press, 1958.

Wallace, Emily M. *A Bibliography of William Carlos Williams*. Middletown, Conn.: Wesleyan University Press, 1968.

White, William. "William Carlos Williams: Bibliography Review with Addenda," *American Book Collector*, 19, vii: 9–12 (1969).

CRITICAL AND BIOGRAPHICAL STUDIES

Blackmur, R. P. *Form and Value in Modern Poetry*. New York: Doubleday, 1957.

——. *Language as Gesture*. London: Allen and Unwin, 1954.

Breslin, James E. *William Carlos Williams: An American Artist*. New York: Oxford University Press, 1970.

Burke, Kenneth. "The Methods of William Carlos Williams," *Dial*, 82:94–98 (February 1927).

Cambon, Glauco. *The Inclusive Flame: Studies in American Poetry*. Bloomington: Indiana University Press, 1963.

Ciardi, John. "Epic of a Place," *Saturday Review*, 41:37–39 (October 11, 1958).

Coffman, Stanley K. *Imagism: A Chapter for the History of Modern Poetry*. Norman: University of Oklahoma, 1951.

Conarroe, Joel O. "A Local Pride: The Poetry of *Paterson*," *PMLA*, 84:547–58 (May 1969).

Cook, Albert. "Modern Verse: Diffusion as a Principle of Composition," *Kenyon Review*, 21:208–12 (Spring 1959).

Deutsch, Babette. *Poetry in Our Time*. New York: Holt, 1952.

Dijkstra, Abraham. "William Carlos Williams and Painting: The Hieroglyphics of a New Speech." Unpublished dissertation. University of California, Berkeley, 1967.

Donoghue, Denis. "For a Redeeming Language," *Twentieth Century*, 163:532–42 (June 1958).

Ellmann, Richard, "William Carlos Williams: The Doctor in Search of Himself," *Kenyon Review*, 14:510–12 (Summer 1952).

Engels, John. *Guide to William Carlos Williams*. Columbus, Ohio: Charles E. Merrill, 1969.

Garrigue, Jean. "America Revisited," *Poetry*, 90:174–78 (June 1958).

Guimond, James. *The Art of William Carlos Williams: A Discovery and Possession of America*. Urbana: University of Illinois Press, 1968.

Hoffman, Frederick J. "Williams and His Muse," *Poetry*, 84:23–27 (April 1954).

Honig, Edwin. "City of Man," *Poetry*, 69:277–84 (February 1947).

Hoskins, Katherine. "Sweating Out a Birthright," *Nation*, 185:226–27 (October 5, 1957).

Jarrell, Randall. "A View of Three Poets," *Partisan Review*, 18:691–700 (November-December 1951).

——. *Poetry and the Age*. New York: Vintage (Knopf), 1955.

Kenner, Hugh. "To Measure Is All We Know," *Poetry*, 94:127–32 (May 1959).

Koch, Vivienne, *William Carlos Williams*. Norfolk, Conn.: New Directions, 1950.

——. "William Carlos Williams: The Man and the Poet," *Kenyon Review*, 14:502–10 (Summer 1952).

——. "Williams: The Social Mask," *Poetry*, 80:89–93 (May 1952).

Lechlitner, Ruth. "The Poetry of William Carlos Williams," *Poetry*, 54:326–35 (September 1939).

Lowell, Robert. "Paterson II," *Nation*, 166:692–94 (June 19, 1948).

——. "William Carlos Williams," *Hudson Review*, 14:530–36 (Winter 1961–62).

Miller, J. Hillis, ed. *William Carlos Williams: A Collection of Critical Essays*. Englewood Cliffs, N.J.: Prentice-Hall, 1966.

Moore, Marianne. "A Poet of the Quattrocento," *Dial*, 82:213–15 (March 1927).

——. "Things Others Never Notice," *Poetry*, 44:103–06 (May 1934).

Morgan, Frederick. "William Carlos Williams: Imagery, Rhythm, Form," *Sewanee Review*, 55:675–90 (1947).

Paul, Sherman. *The Music of Survival: A Biography of a Poem by William Carlos Williams*. Urbana: University of Illinois Press, 1968.

Peterson, Walter S. *An Approach to Paterson*. New Haven, Conn.: Yale University Press, 1967.

Pound, Ezra. "Dr. Williams' Position," *Dial*, 75:395–404 (November 1928).

——. *Polite Essays*. London: Faber and Faber, 1937.

Quinn, Sister M. Bernetta. *The Metamorphic Tradition in Modern Poetry*. New Brunswick, N.J.: Rutgers University Press, 1955.

Rosenfeld, Paul. *Port of New York.* New York: Harcourt, Brace, 1924.

Rosenthal, M. L. "Salvo for William Carlos Williams," *Nation,* 186:497, 500 (May 31, 1958).

———. *The Modern Poets: A Critical Introduction.* New York: Oxford University Press, 1960.

Shapiro, Karl. *In Defense of Ignorance.* New York: Random House, 1960.

Taupin, René. *L'Influence du symbolisme français sur la poésie américaine (de 1910 à 1920).* Paris: Champion, 1929.

Thirlwall, John C. "William Carlos Williams' 'Paterson,'" in *New Directions 17.* New York: New Directions, 1961. Pp. 252–310.

Wagner, Linda Welshimer. *The Poems of William Carlos Williams.* Middletown, Conn.: Wesleyan University Press, 1963.

Weatherhead, A. Kingsley. *The Edge of the Image.* Seattle: University of Washington Press, 1967.

Weaver, Mike. *William Carlos Williams. The American Background.* London: Cambridge University Press, 1971.

Wilson, T. C. "The Example of Dr. Williams," *Poetry,* 48:105–07 (May 1936).

Winters, Yvor. *Primitivism and Decadence in Contemporary Poetry.* New York: Arrow, 1937.

SPECIAL ISSUES OF MAGAZINES

Briarcliff Quarterly, vol. 3 (October 1946). (Contains articles, letters, and comments on Williams by various hands.)

Massachusetts Review, vol. 3, no. 2 (Winter 1962). (Contains "A Gathering for William Carlos Williams" pp. 277–344, with contributions by Clinton J. Atkinson, Carlos Baker, Cid Corman, H. E. F. Donohue, Raymond A. Kennedy, Hugh Kenner, David Leviten, Gosta Peterson, Seldon Rodman, Charles Sheeler, Mary Ellen Solt, John Thirlwall, Gail Turnbull, and Louis Zukofsky.)

Perspective, vol. 6, no. 4 (Autumn-Winter 1953). (Contains articles by Robert Beum, Gary Davenport, Sanford Edelstein, Hugh Kenner, Ralph Nash, and George Zabriskic.)

Western Review, vol. 17, no. 4 (Summer 1953). (Contains "American Letters: A Symposium," which is an article by Russell Roth followed by comments by Elizabeth Hardwick, Robert B. Heilman, and William Van O'Connor.)

JOHN MALCOLM BRINNIN

Edmund Wilson

1895-1972

*T*HE American literary critic and journalist Edmund Wilson was born May 8, 1895, at Red Bank in the Atlantic Highlands–Asbury Park angle of the New Jersey coast, a district originally composed of independent towns and villages but during his early life being steadily absorbed into the suburban, summer-resort sprawl of metropolitan New York. The transformation seems prophetic; it presents in miniature the pattern of all those developments and changes in society at large which have produced the distrustful outlook on modern progress that Wilson has held to most of his life. One may feel that this outlook was his chief inheritance. His father, for whom he was named, was a lawyer and civil servant of distinction who became attorney general of New Jersey under both Republican and Democratic administrations but refused various federal appointments: a moody, self-absorbed man, as Wilson describes him, tending to be impatient and peremptory with others and subject in his later life to "neurotic eclipses" requiring periodic withdrawals and retreats. The family background was upper middle class, college oriented, and professional—lawyers, doctors, ministers, and, later, board members and museum managers—with a sprinkling of more exotic figures: the Seabright cousins whom

Wilson subsequently identified with the charming, aimless aristocrats of *The Cherry Orchard*; an aunt who married a French painter descended from the Egyptologist Champollion and killed on the Western Front in 1915.

Two autobiographical sketches, "The Author at Sixty" in *A Piece of My Mind* (1956) and "Family" in the recently published volume of early journals, *A Prelude* (1967), delineate very precisely the qualities of this life and background—the tangle of family relationships, intense, self-nourishing, untranslatable to outsiders; the cultural snobbery; the insulation and stuffiness of a clan easily scandalized yet tolerant and protective with its own delinquents, being finally indifferent to general opinion; the combination of outward assurance and parlor hysterics and melancholia; the erratic blend of sexual and imaginative repression and leisure-class self-indulgence; the custom of marrying within a limited circle of social familiars but on perhaps no other basis of compatibility, "because there was no one else"; and, at the root, the loss of contact in an investment-trust era with the traditional functions of a property-owning gentry. For people of this class, privilege was no defense against instability and disorientation. "Of my father's close friends at college," Wilson has written, "but a single one was left by the time he was in his thirties: all the rest were dead— some had committed suicide."

After a family tour of Europe in 1908 Wilson entered the Hill School in Pottstown, where he endured a cramping regime devoted to evangelical uplift and the avoidance of unclean thoughts but where he also received sound training in Greek and Latin. In 1912 he went on to Princeton, concentrating there on modern literature and language and writing essays, poems, stories, and parodies for the *Nassau Lit*. At each school he found a teacher of superior character and gifts—Alfred Rolfe at the Hill, Christian Gauss at Princeton— whose influence upon him he would later handsomely acknowledge. Wilson's memoirs of these humanely principled men are in fact outstanding among his portrait-essays, having that core motive of personal attachment and identification that regularly distinguishes his best work as a critical observer. At Princeton, too, he fell in with an exceptionally gifted and ambitious company of undergraduate writers. T. K. Whipple, John Bishop, and Scott Fitzgerald were close friends and collaborators on the *Lit*; for each of them too Edmund Wilson would eventually serve as memoirist and posthumous editor.

After Princeton he worked as a cub on the *New York Evening Sun* and then, in the summer of 1917, enlisted in a hospital unit and was in France for a year and a half. "My experience of the army," he writes in *A Prelude*, "had had on me a liberating effect. I could now get on with all kinds of people and could satisfy my curiosity about aspects of life that otherwise I should not perhaps so soon have known." It was a disillusioning and angering experience as well, with an impact much like that recorded in the war books of Wilson's American contemporaries, Dos Passos, Hem-

ingway, E. E. Cummings, Thomas Boyd. Besides a few deromanticizing stories of his own— one, "The Death of a Soldier," appeared in *The Undertaker's Garland*, a miscellany of apprentice work in prose and verse published with John Peale Bishop in 1922—Wilson's literary response to the war took the form of a manifesto, composed at an occupation GHQ in Germany, which "indicted the institutions of the Western world and suggested a way out in the direction of socialism." At the same time (as he later wrote in *The American Jitters*, in 1932) he had decided that he "could never go back to the falseness and dullness of my pre-war life again. I swore to myself that when the War was over I should stand outside society altogether." It was not the last time he would sound a secessionist note.

In the early 1920's, confident that the arts were thriving despite all the restlessness and disorder of postwar society, Wilson committed himself to a career in literature and settled down to writing essays, reviews, and sketches for various New York papers: among others *Vanity Fair*, of which he was managing editor during 1920–21, the *Liberator* and the *Dial*, and finally the *New Republic*, which he joined as an associate editor in 1926. His writings of this period, including plays and fictional sketches, are brimful of literary attitudes and circumstances characteristic of the American twenties. Continually, despite his resolve to "stand outside society" and devote himself to the great transcendent human interests, he returns to that preoccupation with the issue of American cultural maturity which Van Wyck Brooks in particular, in studies like *America's Coming-of-Age*, had defined for this era. At the same time, in discussing new work, Wilson showed himself an alert and precisely sympathetic advocate of the creative revolution of his time; he was far freer in greeting all its remarkable innovations and triumphs than Brooks, only nine years his senior, ever learned to be. Wilson's first important book, the novel *I Thought of Daisy* (1929), joins these two period concerns. The form of his novel he thought of as experimental, in the art-fashion of the day—he later described it as "a sort of symphonic arrangement . . . like *Ulysses* and *A la Recherche du Temps Perdu*"—while the theme is the effort of the narrator, an American intellectual whose literary friends represent various characteristic attitudes and philosophies of the era, to make invigorating connections with common American life (represented by Daisy) and so close the disabling gap between common reality and abstract literary ideas about it, between "the self that experiences and the self that writes."

I Thought of Daisy resolves this theme satisfactorily in the moving peroration that closes the last chapter, with its vision of a universal acceptance of the reality created and shared by all who are alive together in one place and time. But Wilson himself, three years later at the end of his Depression chronicle, *The American Jitters*, was very much less sanguine about the twenties milieu he had commemorated in his novel: "I always felt so little at home in the American prosperity era, though I made earnest efforts to enjoy it and to believe that it was beneficial to other people (not exercising enough insight to know that it was bound for the rocks), that I am not sorry to see it all go glimmering." He closed this testament with an affirmative credo, but what is affirmed is as materialistic in its premises, and as vague, as the reassurances of any Chamber of Commerce publicist: a belief in "progress" (symbolized by the convenience-enhancing achievements of modern technology) and, more generally, in "human evolution," leading to the bracing thought that "we" as "beings" are sure to develop "into something higher still." It was

an anachronistic, "eighteenth-century" belief, Wilson confessed, and it merged rather wishfully into a vision of some purified future of renewed human nobility. Seemingly, Wilson's voiced confidence in the vocation of letters and its uses, though primed by the heady victories of contemporary art, could now find broader social confirmation only in carefully nourished visionary states: in a simplified picture of certain epochs in the past which had produced great literature, and in the regenerate historical future promised by ideological Marxism—to the study of which, as the crisis of the Depression deepened, he had begun to direct his attention.

At no point in his long career does Edmund Wilson strike us as profound or original in his presentation of systems of thought and imagination, yet this persistent element of serious, thoroughgoing, personal concern gives his reports a vividness and an urgency that fix them in the mind. From his earliest reviews he had known how to make his subjects interesting—the *sine qua non* of effective journalism. In the late twenties, alongside an undiminished output of shorter pieces, he had begun to write more extended critical studies characterized by a richer blend of historical consideration, a fuller review of each author's career, and a more sustained effort of consecutive description. These studies, brought together under some attention-focusing title, became the books that in the next ten years gained Wilson a place of his own in his time's literature.

In *Axel's Castle* (1931) a whole new American generation of students learned about Symbolism and its central role in modern writing, and discovered for perhaps the first time something of the artistic logic behind the work of authors like Valéry, Joyce, and Proust. In *The Triple Thinkers* (1938) Wilson helped to keep current the Flaubertian doctrine of the disinterestedness and sacrificial heroism of the true artist. In the essays composing *The Wound and the Bow* (1941) he used, with intelligence and discrimination, Freudian insights as well as a consciousness of the political malaise of the thirties to show off both the inward complexity in the writings of several mostly out-of-fashion authors—the essays on Dickens and Kipling are outstanding in this respect—and also the relevance of their work to fundamental situations in common life; he emphasized, too, the personal courage, despite afflictions, with which these authors had persisted in their careers.

A steady widening of horizons and perspectives shows in other ways at this time and principally, as the thirties advanced, in his study of Marxism. In the disorder and confusion of literary thought during this decade—its political side is well described in Daniel Aaron's *Writers on the Left*—Wilson's personal course seems of a singular steadiness and integrity. A concern for social justice rises strongly to the surface. He traveled widely through the country filing on-the-scene reports of the suffering and violence of the Depression years, the labor struggles, relief offices, congressional hearings, the varied scenes of a nationwide demoralization. Sympathetic toward the Soviet Russian experiment, he was sharply critical of the hostility it aroused among Western liberals, a hostility, he felt, based on ignorance—or worse. There was an abrasive virtue in his recognition ("An Appeal to Progressives," 1931) that not only business leaders and politicians but liberal and progressive intellectuals —including the most honored recent spokesmen of the American public conscience, men like John Dewey, Charles Beard, Walter Lippmann, Justice Holmes—had all been "betting on capitalism" and were all implicated in the world crisis following on its huge civil failures in World War I and the Depression.

Wilson did not, however, become a Communist himself. Some unshakable critical fidelity to the fitness of word and occasion, and behind it that independence of judgment which has always, so to speak, made his yea, yea and his nay, nay, kept him from serving time as either party member or fellow traveler. (So, later, he was spared the necessity of apostasy and recantation over the Moscow trials and the Nazi-Soviet pact). What he did instead was characteristic. He went to Russia to study and to look around for himself (it was his first trip abroad since 1919, for Wilson was one of the few important new writers of the twenties who had not joined in person the expatriate scramble to Paris); and he undertook a prolonged examination of the basic literature of revolutionary socialism, in particular the writings and memoirs of Marx, Engels, Lassalle, Bakunin, Trotsky, and Lenin. Out of this he produced, at the end of the decade, his ambitious "Study in the Writing and Acting of History," *To the Finland Station* (1940).

From this point forward there is a certain miscellaneousness about the profusion of Edmund Wilson's writing. He continued, as before, turning out occasional plays and stories that document the literary life of the period he himself had lived through; and with the story collection *Memoirs of Hecate County* (1946), one of the better books of American fiction in the lean forties, he had an unlooked-for succès de scandale by way of the sexual explicitness in his portraits of modern "damned souls." He was staff book reviewer for the *New Yorker* from 1944 to 1948 and continued after 1948 to publish literary articles there, also travel essays and personal memoirs. His caustic, disillusioned postwar report from "the ruins of Italy, Greece, and England," *Europe without Baedeker* (1947), was carried by the *New Yorker* as foreign correspondence, and later books like *The Scrolls from the Dead Sea* (1955), *Apologies to the Iroquois* (1960), *O*

Canada (1965), and *A Prelude: Landscapes, Characters and Conversations from the Earlier Years of My Life* (1967) also appeared first in the *New Yorker*. (An exception was *The Cold War and the Income Tax* of 1963, the latest of his pamphlets dissociating himself from contemporary society.)

The manner of Wilson's casual book reviewing in the forties and fifties was, if anything, more assured than ever. It remained one of the pleasures of his critical style that he had nothing at all of the pontifical solemnness then flourishing in the Eliot-infected literary quarterlies. Yet if any American reviewer seemed to speak *ex cathedra*, it was he. The price of this authority, however, was for the first time a certain remoteness from current developments. He continued to write on new books and authors as well as established names. But his work was less and less an inclusive record of the literary temper and achievement of the present moment. (The new era, it must be said, was a less distinguished one than the twenties and much less in need of critical translation.) By his seventh decade—introduced with the crusty miscellany *A Piece of My Mind: Reflections at Sixty* (1956)—Wilson had become not so much a critic among other critics, other working contemporaries, as a public institution: an honorable but always rather saddening American fate.

There was no softening, however, of personal attitudes and no appearance of compromise or accommodation with the ethos of what he plainly felt to be a bad time, a deteriorating social order. In this most recent phase we still find Edmund Wilson, as in 1919 and 1932, affirming his disaffection from modern society as he regularly encounters it and as he understands its historical formation. He has done this in so many words and also, increasingly, through choice of subject. His last large-scale undertaking, *Patriotic Gore: Studies in the Literature of the American Civil War* (1962), is an examination of that time in earlier history when the American nation came closest to dissolution and of the effects of this ordeal on battle-shocked survivors; one may feel that nothing has yet been written of greater relevance to the civil-rights ordeal of the 1960's, and hardly anything that is more despairing in its implications. (The book's introduction, which bluntly compares the actions of national societies, democratic or otherwise, to the unreasoning behavior of sea slugs and insects, establishes a mood that suffuses all that follows.)

Even when he writes on subjects far removed from contemporary preoccupations, a relevance is suggested. The historical and textual origins of Christianity, the distinctive quality of Hebrew and Russian as instruments of expression, the morally suggestive findings of entomologists and mycologists, the struggles of fringe cultures (the New York State Iroquois) and minority languages (Hungarian) to survive in the modern mass-world—all furnish perspectives on the confusions of the present moment. Wilson even makes a show of out-and-out pedantry, though in a constructive vein. He studies dictionaries and grammars and laments their declining usefulness; he compiles lists of fashionable clichés, "words of ill omen," particularly the murderous euphemisms of the Cold War dialect and the huckster-jargon of slick literary and political journalism; he offers intelligent proposals for the teaching of classical literature and language, to stem the decline of old-fashioned humanistic education.

We also still find him, though less systematically than before, rummaging about on the open shelves of contemporary letters—reading Kingsley Amis, Lawrence Durrell, Edward Gorey, the later Angus Wilson, W. H. Auden in his American phase, Mario Praz, Stephen Potter, Robert Lowell, John Berryman—and as usual pointing out virtues that others might have noticed but had not brought into general consciousness or defining careers where nothing so prestige-laden had yet been seen to exist. Among active critics and journalists Wilson retains an unsurpassed ability not only to make one want to read the books he discusses but to compose believable pictures of continuing literary history. Past seventy, he remains what he has always been, a critical touchstone by which other readers and writers may better understand their own attitudes and findings, their own progressive experience of literature.

This practical devotion to the existing community of authors and readers and to the common mental life of his age has been the great sustaining virtue of Edmund Wilson's performance as a critic. It has not fallen to him to redirect fundamental literary history or to bring about momentous changes in taste and understanding—a fact that overenthusiastic assessments of his work (comparisons, for example, of *Axel's Castle* to Eliot's *The Sacred Wood*) fail to take into account. He has not been a lawgiver or theorist (his essay "The Historical Interpretation of Literature," 1940, is hardly more than a confession of personal interests); no critical school, no new lines of creative achievement, have developed from his work; nor have his books noticeably affected understanding of the essential nature of literary expressiveness and the "meaning of meaning," as did (to cite volumes of criticism published at the same moment as *Axel's Castle* but based on more sophisticated theoretical interests) William Empson's *Seven Types of Ambiguity* and Kenneth Burke's *Counter-Statement*. His own frequent assessments of his role and function have always been attractively modest. Where Eliot would write essays defining the universal "function of criticism" or the qualities of "the perfect critic," Wilson typically issued a set of

practical instructions for authors and editors which he called, with multiple irony, "The Literary Worker's Polonius" (1935). Short of positive insult, a flatter term than "literary worker" would be hard to find. In an earlier piece on "The Critic Who Does Not Exist" (1928) he was principally concerned with the simple lack of communication among authors and literary groups in the United States and with the failure of creative ideas to circulate productively. It is as a bringer of news, preferably good news, that he has seen himself; as a journalist in the most honorable sense; as a contributor to "the general cross-fertilization" ("A Modest Self-Tribute," 1952).

He has been quite explicit about this. Writing once of his disappointment when, full of the last installment of Proust's great novel and a swelling sense of the grandeur of the whole, he found that Thornton Wilder knew as much about it as he did, and knew it also at first hand, Wilson confessed: "There are few things I enjoy so much as talking to people about books which I have read but they haven't, and making them wish they had—preferably a book that is hard to get or in a language that they do not know" ("A Weekend at Ellerslie," 1952). In the 1948 Foreword to *The Triple Thinkers*, defending himself against the complaint that he sometimes had little to say about his subjects' most prominent or most characteristic qualities, he wrote, "my purpose has always been to try to contribute something new: I have aimed either to present some writer who was not well enough known or, in the case of a familiar writer, to call attention to some neglected aspect of his work or his career." Perhaps "Boswell" would be closer to the mark than "Polonius," if we can imagine a Boswell for an entire era, taking "literature as a whole" (as he wrote in the 1938 essay "Is Verse a Dying Technique?") for his field.

What Wilson has meant by "journalism" is

nothing degrading or commonplace. From the start he chose impressive masters to guide his ambition, writers who in various ways had found scope in their journeywork for serious individual reflection and judgment. "We had grown up," he wrote of the situation of the twenties, "on the journalism of Shaw and Chesterton, Belloc and Max Beerbohm, and later, in the United States, of the Mencken and Nathan of the *Smart Set* and the Woollcott and Broun of the *World*. All these writers were everlastingly saying 'I': the exploitation of personality had become an integral part of criticism" (Foreword, *The Shores of Light*). And in ways that unfailingly give dramatic movement and suspense to his best longer essays, Wilson uses this first-person method himself. Returning to a familiar name or taking up some widely discussed new topic, he tells us what he has heard and been led to expect, and then how his expectation has been satisfied, disappointed, surprised, or overturned.

But the list of his early admirations gives only a part of his picture of himself as "literary worker"—unless Shaw's name in particular reminds us that an easy practical mastery of the subjects treated, and the hard work required to gain this mastery, are to be included by definition. "Reviewer critic" was another name for Wilson's conception of his role—an "extremely rare" being, he noted in the "Polonius" article—and the description offered there may be taken as an accurate summary of his own working program: "Such a reviewer should be more or less familiar, or be ready to familiarize himself, with the past work of every important writer he deals with and be able to write about an author's new book in the light of his general development and intention. He should also be able to see the author in relation to the national literature as a whole and the national literature in relation to other literatures. But

this means a great deal of work, and it presupposes a certain amount of training." The article goes on to describe the minimum responsibility that goes with each new critical task: "The reviewer, at the very least, should be expected to supply information. The retelling of the story of a novel, the summary of an historical or philosophical book, the selection of representative passages and the attempt to communicate the quality of a poet, is the most boring part of the reviewer's business, that it is an absolutely essential part. The reader should be given a chance to judge whether or not he would be interested in the book, irrespective of what the reviewer may think of it; and it is an indispensable discipline for the reviewer, or any critic, to give the gist of the book in his own words. . . . It is as vitally important for the critic to establish definite identities for the books that he discusses in an essay as it is for the novelist to establish them for the characters who figure in his story." Sainte-Beuve is the example Wilson gives of this ideal reviewer-critic—though elsewhere ("A Modest Self-Tribute") he has said that he knows very little of Sainte-Beuve's writing and was not directly influenced by him; Poe, that American "literary worker" *tout court*, is the nineteenth-century predecessor more frequently invoked.

The success he has had with this plan of work is a matter of record. When in the early 1950's he took the risk of reprinting in two fat volumes nearly two hundred periodical pieces written between 1922 and 1949, and written each time with the steadfast journalistic purpose of producing something readable and immediately interesting, the result impressively confirmed the rough sense that had been gathering in the minds of readers for a quarter of a century: that for nearly every important development in contemporary literature Edmund Wilson was in some way a spokesman—an arbiter of taste, a supplier of perspective, at the least (to adapt his own phrase for Hemingway) a gauge of intellectual morale. Time and again, reading *Classics and Commercials* (1950) and especially *The Shores of Light* (1952), one would find that judgments formulated under pressure of the weekly deadline had proved to be both just and durable; that they somehow contained that sense of the matter which academic historians of literature, with all the advantages of hindsight, were still groping after. In *The Shores of Light*, for example, one could notice his comments on Pound in 1922 ("at heart . . . an incurable provincial"), on Sherwood Anderson's "queer and disquieting impressiveness" (1923), on the artistic intelligence and originality of Ring Lardner (1924), on E. E. Cummings' lyric integrity (1924, 1927), on the "buried streak of hysteria" in Dos Passos (1929), on John Crowe Ransom's "metaphysical" charm and Allen Tate's "special vein of macabre imagination" (1928), or—in a review of *The Pilgrimage of Henry James* (1925)—on how James's last three novels are "not, as Mr. Brooks asserts, fundamentally unreal and weak" but "perhaps the most vigorous, the most heroically conceived" in all his work.

One could notice, too, the unfailing freshness of his testimony. Despite, inevitably, a certain use of journalistic formulas, Wilson rarely seemed to have repeated himself, in the tiresome manner of the special pleader, the performer with only one string to his fiddle. His stance was rather that of the attentive and openminded common reader, equipped with nothing more nor less than his own version of that ideal civil intelligence to which every actual phenomenon is in some way significant, deserving to be looked into with an appropriate respect and concern. At the same time it was also clear that in so operating Wilson had never bothered to disguise his prejudices and

the play of personal taste and distaste in his reactions. More than once he had been led to assert unfashionable judgments which he was quite unable to carry off in the detail—on the poetry of Edna St. Vincent Millay, for example—and to make a point of persisting in them when they met with general incredulity. But this stubbornness had one virtue: it seemed a further guarantee of that personal engagement with his subjects which might commend his opinions even to those who found them unsatisfactory. In just this respect it gave his work an air of greater relevance to the actual conditions in which literature has its existence —as an affair of *these* writers and *this* reader, struggling within such and such practical circumstances—than, say, the more methodically conceived practice of American university critics in the heyday of the "new criticism."

For what Edmund Wilson's writing has always served—and here again we may think of all he has contributed besides criticism proper —is nothing less than Literature itself, in the broadest sense. He believes in literature as a humane activity, an index to civilization; or, if "belief" seems the wrong sort of word, he trusts it to the point of choosing to live by it. (We may recall his celebration, in "The Historical Interpretation of Literature," of all those before him who truly revered "the priesthood of literature," whatever their special notions.) He takes pride in its successes; he is endlessly curious about its tribal customs and the character, the idiosyncrasies, of its practitioners; out of the same practical dedication he even concerns himself with the outward dress and appearance of books, insisting in the latter part of his career that his own be published in a size and shape that make holding them and turning their pages a sensible pleasure. And in so doing he continually bestows upon the whole institution of literature, and reasserts for it, within the fabric of civilization, something of that vital efficacy the idea of which we usually think to associate only with the "great" books but which must survive at a common level of everyday effort and collaboration if it is to survive at all. For Wilson has never limited "literature," in the manner of university reading lists and publishers' anthologies, to the acknowledged masterpieces. He spreads his net to anything written in such a way, by whatever means, that it conveys some portion of accurate knowledge or fosters some sort of useful understanding; in such a way, too, that it helps to maintain the serviceability of ordinary written English to these practical ends. He is genuinely interested in what is being done, and whether it is being done well. He can even grant a virtue of sorts ("a certain purity" that demands "a certain respect") to a best seller like *The Robe*, Dr. Lloyd Douglas' interminable parsonage fable of 1942, when he unexpectedly finds that its author, though in a labored, cliché-ridden way, has done what the best of writers must also do with each new work: "he has imagined the whole thing for himself." But when, infrequently, some truly major occasion presents itself, Wilson can rise to it. A tangible pleasure and exhilaration overtake him when a work of the first rank appears, of almost any kind. He reports it as an occasion for general rejoicing. So he greeted *Lady Chatterley's Lover* in 1920 and so, thirty years later, *Doctor Zhivago*; so, too, after World War II, he celebrated the completion of Malraux's *Psychology of Art*, "one of the really great books of our time."

This generosity of attention deserves the gratitude and praise it has received. Is there anyone among Edmund Wilson's contemporaries who has done so much to keep the general literary establishment critically aware of its own passing history and of its inheritances and opportunities? His great service is to have been (to borrow a phrase) a museum without walls: a museum of idiosyncratic design in some respects but open to all and generally reliable in what it mounts for public view. It may well be that Wilson's long persistence in this service has taken a certain obtuseness and vanity on his part—the same amount needed to support his pretensions as a writer of verse and drama or to permit him, as we have seen, to group *I Thought of Daisy* (and not in 1929 when it was new but twenty-five years later when he reissued it) with the mature masterpieces of Proust and Joyce. Certainly he has had need in some form of that complete self-assurance in opinion and judgment that Alfred Noyes would remember from Princeton in 1914–15, which made Noyes doubt "whether it had ever occurred to him that he could possibly be wrong." (In *A Prelude* Wilson disputes the accuracy of Alfred Noyes's recollections.) The defects of Wilson's singular virtues must be considered. But the essential fact remains: that he has served the collective enterprise of literature in his day with an extraordinary practical energy and faithfulness. By continuing to act as if it really was alive and kicking, he has helped it as much as any critic of his time actually to remain so. His whole career has been a kind of optimistic gamble: he has bet on literature and on its survival—literature as it was in those rich epochs of human history that produced the work his own strong appetite as a reader was nurtured on—and he has never seriously hedged this bet.

It may be added that he has carried through this lifelong gamble with a contagious show of willingness and spirit. The way he characterized himself in his "All-Star Literary Vaudeville" of 1926 identifies his outlook still. He is one who has felt "a certain human sympathy" with all manifestations of literary activity, "even with those of which, artistically, he disapproves." It is a source of deep gratification to him when literature is "sold" to the public, and he is happy to be known as one who "on principle, in the face of alien attack . . . will stand by even the least intelligent, the least disinterested, of its salesmen: he has served in that army himself."

The word Wilson has used for his general attitude is "humanistic." It is not an attitude he has ever troubled to define precisely or to formalize as an objective standard. (But it is not to be confused with the so-called "New Humanism" that was the focus of aggressive controversy in the United States around 1930, a movement of censorious academicians which, because of its arrogant dismissal of nearly everything in literature but the greatest of established classics, Wilson himself attacked with unusual polemic sharpness—see his "Notes on Babbitt and More" of 1930.) Wilson's "humanism" involves first of all an attitude toward the intensity and confusion of ordinary human life. "Poor male and female human beings," he wrote in one of his earliest reviews, of Byron's letters (1922), by way of rejecting the easy moralism that, finding an author like Byron to have been disorderly in his private life and to have brought suffering to others, occupies itself with calling him names—"Poor male and female human beings, who, understanding life in different fashions and unfitted to live together, yet cannot leave each other alone!" (This same outlook is strikingly voiced on the last page of *I Thought of Daisy*.) To be both truthful and sympathetic in one's response to life as it really unfolds, according to the common exactions of human nature, is for Wilson indispensable to a healthy interest in literature, which in turn has value not only as it stays close to concrete experience but as it teachers us this magnanimity of outlook. If, behind particular works of literature seemingly eloquent and well formed, we discover lives and feelings that are sordid, undisciplined, even criminal, we have no reason to turn against these works themselves, or to find fault with the extravagance, perhaps the insincerity, of the imaginative countermeasures they are seen to contain. For art, the Byron piece affirms, "has its origin in the need to pretend that human life is something other than it is, and, in a sense, by pretending this, it succeeds to some extent in transforming it."

This generalized "humanism," as it finds expression in particular critical judgments, is traditional and familiar to a fault. The positivistic Victorian conception of literature as a "criticism of life," basically uplifting in purpose, is still at the core of it; the sense of what "life" is has simply been brought up to date, to fit the greater freedom and outspokenness of post-Victorian literary manners. It is a measure of value which Wilson tends to make explicit, however, only at odd moments, as when he wishes to round out an argumentative sequence or give special weight to some particularly mettlesome opinion. Then we may find it stated quite boldly, even primly, as if for a moment we were listening not to a free-minded partisan of modernism in art and thought but to one of those moralizing schoolmasters whose habit of literary judgment Edmund Wilson claimed to have shaken off in his adolescence.

Trying to formulate his distaste for Aldous Huxley's later work, which he saw as rising out of a rootless detachment from common human experience, he casually proposed this criterion: the writing we support must help us "to find out something of value for the control and ennoblement of life" (1941). "It is the part of an educated man," he remarked in criticizing (as well he might) the reductive cynicism of the reporting in the magazine *Time*, "to try to give life some value and point" ("Thoughts on Being Bibliographed," 1943). Writing with delight and approval of the "malevolent gusto" of caricature in Angus Wilson's stories, he nevertheless was finally critical of a vision that never showed anything but "ugliness and humiliation," that seemed to withhold even pity: "There ought to be some noble value somewhere" (1950). At times, on this ground, Wilson can bluster like the rankest Philistine. How little Picasso's art has to offer, he declares, "towards the vindication of human dignity" (1965).

As a memoirist, too, Wilson has regularly spoken the same language, and spoken it effectively; he falls back on words of old-fashioned moral approbation with an unembarrassed bluffness that, following some cogent recital of leading details, can positively rescue these words from cant and preachiness. A piece on the death of Elinor Wylie (1929) moves from a straightforward assessment of his subject's artistic virtues and limitations to praise of her personal nobility, her grace and perseverance through emotional dislocations and against the threat of death, and then to a peroration (moving despite its audibly Proustian origin) on what such a spirit means to the rest of us—"doubtful human creatures, all quarrelling or herding together, knowing little and thinking less, vague, pig-headed, purblind and violent"—when we come upon it in life or in a book. His direct sense of Edna Millay's gallantry as a person, of some "invincible magnanimity" and "impartiality" of mind that distinguished her from the run of assertive talents in her time and that made it impossible not to fall in love with her, surely underlies his obstinate overvaluation of her poems. Correspondingly, he several times attacked not only as inappropriate and misleading but as "unhumanistic" the formulas of "ironic belittlement" that biography in the Lytton Strachey manner had made fashionable, though he recognized the individual brilliance of Strachey's own work. This attitude is a leitmotif in his major books as well. Perhaps the solidest impression

we carry away from *To the Finland Station* is of the individual moral heroism of the great Marxist leaders and its ultimate ascendancy in the convulsions of modern history—the tenacious idealism of Marx himself, surmounting all his human failures and weaknesses; the disinterested passion of Lenin, the truly "good-natured man" turned world revolutionary.

There is in fact a good deal of the hero-worshipper in Edmund Wilson. For a critic whose purpose has been to make what he admires accessible to others, one must say that there are far worse things to be. The fine essays on John Jay Chapman, on "Mr. Rolfe," on Justice Holmes, which are among his most satisfying performances, testify to the usefulness to him of this particular moral attitude. Indeed the bulk of Wilson's work in criticism can plausibly be seen as the record of a quest for a legitimate authority; its root impulse a yearning for the reassurance offered by a certain kind of completed, independent, authoritative image of personality, to which his critical intelligence could honorably attach itself. (Thus his passing allegiance to Marxism seems biographical and literary in inspiration rather than philosophically reasoned.) But for the most part there has been nothing narrow-minded, nothing foolishly restrictive, about the way this impulse has been expressed. Anyone "who works in good faith in his own field," however precious or marginal or even perverse the result may be, anyone who is professionally committed to the thing he does and who goes about it with integrity and, so to speak, professional courage, is likely to win some kind of commendation from him. Early and late, some of Wilson's most characteristic studies are of minor artists and popular entertainers who have caught his attention in this way—Firbank, Max Beerbohm, Genevieve Taggard, Herbert Croly as an editor, the cartoonists Art Young and Sem, Edward Gorey, or the magician

Houdini ("an audacious and independent being, whose career showed a rare integrity"). It was in writing about Houdini that Wilson candidly described the radically subjective response that regularly lends feeling and conviction to his exercise of critical judgment: "It is exhilarating, even in a juggler, even in a trapeze performer, to see some human skill or faculty carried to its furthest point, to a point where its feats seem incredible" (1928).

We may say that Wilson's "humanism," whatever its limitations, has finally this virtue: it rests on the knowledge that efforts to derive systems of value from anything but discoverable human experience, or in disregard of any part of discoverable human experience, will fail. The breadth of his tolerance and curiosity as a critic has beneath it this principled concern for admitting the unpleasantest truth about man's life, as does also his special appreciation of works, including diaries and collections of letters, which in any way bring to light the more remarkable conditions of human life and demonstrate its latent further possibilities. So, choking down his revulsion, he labors through the documents in the case of the Marquis de Sade, stopping now and then to note the disingenuousness of attempts to softpedal the real horror of Sade's mind and work, earnestly hoping that his vogue is passing, but granting him the "queer distinction" of having expressed "the ultimate blasphemy" of his (and modern history's) "contempt for human life" with an "ultimate audacity" (1952). It is a point of honor with Wilson, as a critical journalist, to follow to whatever atrocious extreme an accomplished writer may have chosen to lead him.

But every so often Wilson's generosity of attention, his fine critical alertness and receptivity, stop curiously short and are succeeded by obstinate disapproval. An interesting case is his response in the 1940's to Kafka. The chief document here is a *New Yorker* essay of 1947, "A Dissenting Opinion on Kafka." Its journalistic occasion was the appearance of a collected edition of Kafka's writings (which Wilson welcomed as a publishing venture) along with a number of secondary works representing the sudden flaring of a cult-fashion in which as sensible a writer as Delmore Schwartz could suggest that every word Kafka had written was sacred.

Wilson's main objection is to the cult, and to the evidence that Kafka is being "wildly overdone" by demoralized intellectuals who, in their contempt for themselves and for human life in general, are "building him up as a theologian and saint," probably as part of some sinister religious revival. But the full essay, in its zeal to make a case, becomes a gross parody of Wilson's usual humane attentiveness of consideration. Debater's absurdities of innuendo give the argument away. If Kafka is religious, as his devotees say, why don't his characters show the "moral fortitude" of Bunyan's Christian? Where is the "control and direction" shown by a religious poet like Dante? And how in any case can Kafka's books be called religious in implication when it is obvious that he himself "could never let go of the world— of his family, of his job, of his yearning for bourgeois happiness— in the interest of divine revelation"? There *was* a certain "spiritual charge" in Kafka, but "you cannot have a first-rate saint or prophet [!] without a faith of a very much higher potential than is ever to be felt" in his work.

The coarseness and confusion of argument in this are shocking—and may seem, when they take the form of suggesting that Kafka's mistake was to make writing "not merely an art but also somehow a pursuit of righteousness" and "a form of prayer," positively dishonest to anyone who remembers Edmund

Wilson as a sympathetic historian of Symbolism, where such doubleness of purpose was fundamental; in *Axel's Castle* Wilson had noted reactionary and anti-humanist elements in the writers examined but had celebrated them all for waking us through their artistic mastery "to the hope and exaltation of the untried, unsuspected possibilities of human thought and art." So one hastens to point out that elsewhere ("A Treatise on Tales of Horror," 1944) Wilson had already spoken of Kafka as "a master," at least the equal of Gogol and Poe, whose narratives, at once "satires on the bourgeoisie and visions of moral horror," are always compellingly logical and go straight to the imaginative heart of their subjects "with none of the puppetry of specters and devils" used by run-of-the-mill fantasists. And in praising George Grosz only a few months before the Kafka diatribe, Wilson had used the term "Kafkaesque"—like everybody else in the forties—to sum up Grosz's vision of Germany on the threshold of Hitlerism.

In 1944 he had been unsure whether Kafka's work and the popular taste for it represented "a retrogression or a progress in the development of modern literature in general," but in 1947 he seems merely priggish, and worse. Kafka—who is somehow to blame for being "denationalized, discouraged, disaffected" as a person: as if a consumptive Czech Jew working as a clerk in a disability claims office during the last decade of the Austro-Hungarian empire was likely to be anything else—"can in the end only let us down. He is quite true to his time and place, but it is surely a time and place in which few of us will want to linger . . ." A cash prize, one thinks, to the reader who can tell that this is not J. Donald Adams but Edmund Wilson. If a critic's "humanism" is finally a matter of not wanting to be "let down" or made to linger in discouraging situations, what virtue is there in it?

What happened in this instance? Leaving aside the provocations of cult-worship (Kafka fanatics *could* be unnerving in 1947), one suspects that Kafka's very artistry, his seamless rendering of an appallingly complete and self-authenticating vision, came too close to certain of Wilson's own fears and cherished fantasies. One point in Wilson's indictment is that unlike Dante, who asserts the classical standard of virtue, "Kafka is at his most characteristic when he is assimilating men to beasts —dogs, insects, mice and apes." But this (which will hardly pass as a description of the moral logic of "Metamorphosis" or even "Investigations of a Dog") is precisely what Wilson himself has regularly done in his satires and polemics, from the moralized dialogue between zoologist and iguana that he wrote in 1925 to the behaviorist swagger of the chapter on sex in *A Piece of My Mind* in 1956 or the wastefully overwritten "Introduction" to *Patriotic Gore* in 1962. There is also the fact that Kafka's work *is* religious in its accomplished grasp: it is religious—rabbinical and Kierkegaardian derivations apart—in the root sense of binding together and sustaining with a rapt simplicity of style a fully apprehended and endured totality of events and impressions which are absolute to experience but remain separately inexplicable. With Kafka as with Biblical narrative, or with a work like *Doctor Zhivago* that Wilson rightly venerates, narrative substantiation of a folklorish definiteness and transparency (including dialogue) is always primary. And what may have been most subtly offensive about Kafka's writings to Edmund Wilson, who has never ceased to boast of the fact that he saw through religion when he was in prep school ("a delusion entertained by other people which one has to try to allow for and understand"), was their undistractible confirmation of the possibility that the religious apprehension of experience is as "real" as the rationalistic, and as absolute an expression of free creative human consciousness. Exposing the doctrinal absurdities advanced in the name of religion (the great game of the fundamentalist freethinkers of Wilson's youth) hardly touches the question of its normative place in human life and history.

The Kafka episode raises with particular sharpness the problem of Wilson's lasting value as a critic and literary worker. There is the question of his working method, and there is the question of the quality of his intelligence, the depth and freedom of mind from which his humanistic judgment proceeds.

As we have seen, Wilson's approach to his subjects is essentially descriptive: he tells the story of careers (his remarks on Kafka are, as usual, chiefly biographical); he summarizes plots, paraphrases arguments, tabulates symbols; he practices psychological description, classification of genres, structural comparison, and various other incidental skills. But he does not analyze, or sufficiently persist in analysis; he does not measure and weigh the constituent ideas; he does not inquire, except biographically, into the whole logic and mode of existence of the works surveyed. In short, for all his devotion to the idea of literature, he does not examine and plainly define the specifically literary, architectonic virtues his arguments assume. His interest regularly turns off to the special matter of the psychology of literary behavior, to what he speaks of in "The Historical Interpretation of Literature" as "the attitudes, the compulsions, the emotional 'patterns' that recur in the work of a writer." What was it like, in terms of familiar human emotions, to have been this or that author at the moment of composing such and such a work?—a legitimate question but incidental to the primary and distinguishing concerns of literary criticism. (In *Axel's Castle,* for example, we find

this rare formulation of critical theory: "The real elements, of course, of any work of fiction, are the elements of the author's personality." It is a notion, one must say, which crops up strangely in a chapter, on Proust, that has been largely occupied with commenting on a controlled artistic structure of an extraordinary compositional complexity, and in a book that has set out to demonstrate the existence of a broad historical "movement" characterized by various "common tendencies.") On this ground, viewing literature as a species of personal expression, Wilson takes what appears before him, what is given and describes it according to his lights. But he is without the disciplined interest in what could be or might be or even should be that makes the great critic, the writer on literature who will alter the very foundations of critical judgment and who may even project (as, in earlier American criticism, Poe did) new images of creative personality for literary history to advance by.

There is point to such reservations—certainly we have to distinguish between the service of an Edmund Wilson to critical understanding in his time and the service of a Poe, a James, an Eliot—but first the virtues of his manner may be considered. Who his closest practical models have been is not difficult to discover. He has been explicit about them, and insofar as they have also served as models for his justly admired prose style, with its clarity, efficiency, and steady forwarding energy, we cannot say offhand that they have been bad models. One of the most important was his teacher at Princeton, Christian Gauss; and in Wilson's memorial account of the method of Gauss's teaching we find a clear statement of his own chosen procedure as a critic. The special quality in Gauss, Wilson writes, was "the unusual fluidity of mind that he preserved through his whole career." As against a dogmatist like Irving Babbitt, Gauss was the kind of teacher "who starts trains of thought that he does not himself guide to conclusions but leaves in the hands of his students to be carried on by themselves." Moreover, "his own ideas on any subject were always taking new turns: the light in which he saw it would be shifted, it would range itself in some new context." Gauss knew a great deal about a great many things, and had the knowledge of languages to back up his literary and historical learning. But he carried this learning unostentatiously. His easy manner, his level voice, Wilson says (apparently without irony), "made a kind of neutral medium in which everything in the world seemed soluble."

The result was an impression of "extreme flexibility and enormous range"—of a mind whose powers could be brought to bear with equal force on any important subject—and in describing Gauss's method Wilson is clearly projecting a view of his own. Gauss, he writes, was "able to explain and appreciate almost any kind of work of literature from almost any period. He would show you what the author was aiming at and the methods he had adopted to achieve his ends." And he had "a knack of fixing in one's mind key passages and key facts." At the same time he was distinctly at his best in presenting an established figure whose relative stature and significance might be open to more questions than he cared to deal with but whose claim to attention was beyond dispute. Rousseau is the example Wilson cites, and in his account of how Gauss would highlight the main incidents in Rousseau's career —a writer whom students were likely to find boring—"by a series of incisive strokes that [nevertheless] involved no embroidery or dramatics," we see what the technique was. Gauss would bring Rousseau forward to the turning point; the moment when, going to visit Diderot in prison, he decided to compete for the essay prize on the question of whether progress in the arts and sciences had tended to corrupt or to purify society; the moment when he set out for the "Finland station" of his life's progress. Gauss also set a standard for style that Wilson respected and mastered. "He made us all want to write something in which every word, every cadence, every detail, should perform a definite function in producing an intense effect."

Another of Wilson's models of critical procedure (leaving aside models of style and intellectual temper like Shaw, Samuel Butler, Renan, H. L. Mencken) was Saintsbury, and again, professing admiration for Saintsbury's *Encyclopaedia Britannica* articles, he gives us a passage of self-definition, praising those "wonderful feats of condensation that manage, in summarizing a lifetime, to include a maximum of detail and, in their briefly expressed comments, to hit all the nails on the head." Saintsbury was "perhaps the only English critic, with the possible exception of Leslie Stephen, whose work is comparable, for comprehensiveness and brilliance, to the great French critics [Taine in particular] of the nineteenth century." But Wilson also remarks that unlike these latter, Saintsbury "has no interest in ideas"—and we recall our reservations about Wilson's own performance. He himself clearly has had an *interest* in ideas, but it has been an oddly acquiescent and derivative interest. He observes them, like natural phenomena; he wonders what drives men to take them up, and he is impressed by the power that derives from them; but he does not seem to *think* with them, or about them, or make them—at least provisionally—his own. He does not seem to have imagined what exactly it means to say that thought, in our own case as well as for those history presents, must be proved in experience.

Wilson has always seemed admirably free of ideological dogmatism and pre-commitment and especially alert to how other minds and lives may be warped by them—one reason why he has been so effective as a natural historian of the literary life. But there is something static about this liberal curiosity of his, something curiously automatic and self-enclosed. What Santayana said once about American open-mindedness in general applies to it: that it can too easily turn into "a habit of doting on everything"—everything, that is, that happens to have caught its attention; that it derives from a personal assurance it never stops to test, which is that "the forces that determine fortune are not yet too complicated for one man to explore"; that it trusts its own accumulated habituations as it trusts nothing else, because it has always been able to do so "safely and prosperously." If we read a lot of Edmund Wilson's criticism at one time, what we may come to notice is less and less the free play of this curiosity and the insights and discoveries it leads him to, and more and more the a priori assurance it rests upon—and in this regard the mind which most resembles his own or which his own most resembles is that of his father, the Red Bank, New Jersey, lawyer to whom he devoted the last section of his book of "reflections at sixty," *A Piece of My Mind.*

For it is very much a *type* of mind that Wilson's writing gives voice to, a distinctly American type perhaps, at least a familiar and important one in both American literature and American public life. An otherwise excellent study of his career written some years ago by Norman Podhoretz labeled him "the last patrician," which is of course inaccurate; whoever our American patricians may be, they have had little to do with our serious literature. His mold is rather his father's—the mold of the independent, freethinking professional man, in this case of the type of the town or small-city lawyer (a newspaper editor or certain types of businessman would do about as well; a doctor, teacher, minister less well); the man of broad but not particularly fine taste, with a strong

and confident habit of mind and with pride in his judgment, who is skillful at dossiers, presentations of essential evidence, summings-up; something of a dissenter but according to no easily predictable pattern, and certainly not one of shallow self-interest; conservatively radical, out of an unshakable assurance about his own privileged position; a leader of opinion used to making himself listened to (but not likely to be aware that among those who have come to know him well, as opposed to the public at large, a silent resistance is steadily building up); a champion of seemingly unpopular causes, but not so much lost causes as certain ones not yet effectively taken up; one whom we visualize finally rather as Edmund Wilson portrays his father, "explaining at length, but with an expert lucidity, some basic point of law or government."

This breed of mind, which seems raised to a virtuoso perfection in the two Edmund Wilsons, has substantial virtues. It is intelligent and accurate. It can be trained into great practical skill. It will give steady, efficient, profitable performance. It admires things worth admiring; it has a sense of "excellence" (a favorite word); it is alert to prevailing tendencies. It understands Darwinism and Freudianism—it used to understand Marxism—and modern anthropology and, nowadays, the theory of the genetic code and the notion of complementarity and perhaps the eightfold way. It is at ease with literary and philosophical classics and is given to more or less appropriate citations from them in support of its point of view. It only lacks the ability to see beyond itself. And it is not so much without the power to do this as without the inward incentive, the imaginative will. For it is finally an arrogant and airless mind. It is acquainted with a great many ideas, but ideas become things to it, counters to score with. Its besetting sin is in fact *knowingness,* which is its substitute for imaginative freedom and the passion of irreversible creative conviction. And whatever else knowingness is good for, it cannot cure itself; it cannot intercede against those particular afflictions, "complacency and resentment," which Camus in a late essay identified as peculiar to the writer's, the intellectual's, course of life.

Far more than any particular miscarriage of critical judgment, it is this element of knowingness that disturbs us in Edmund Wilson's writing. We come to sense a kind of incapacity to imagine that what he knows or has found out is not always the whole essential story, and that what others see, which he himself cannot see, may nevertheless really be there. We see finally that his curiosity and liberality are of a special kind. Like his father, Wilson accepts the system he works within, in this case the literary establishment and its received custom—about which he makes it his business to keep very well informed. He does not fundamentally question this system. He only aspires to master it (which he is willing to work hard to do) and then to have his mastery acknowledged. When something comes into view that does not fit the measure of this system or that would expose the accommodations it is built on to some ulterior judgment—the Kafka case is one instance; Eliot's writing, with its inner burden of religious nostalgia and reversion, is another —liberal curiosity may give way abruptly to irritation and withdrawal.

Irritability, resentment, the impatient dismissal of what cannot be absorbed without a basic recasting of his own fixed attitudes, appear to be Edmund Wilson's characteristic vices; and the point to be made about them is that they are not merely personal failings but the intellectual expedients of a whole identifiable class. His postures as a critic are those of the privileged and established old resident, American style—we picture him on a balcony or at an upstairs window overlooking the town, a county seat perhaps (for he is a man of the world)—beset by uneasiness at some of the changes taking place before him but not compelled to add them all up and arrive at a genuinely new sum. The system he contemplates he imagines to be for him and he does not mean to see it fundamentally changed, but in his own mind he stands outside it. There he perches, coolly examining the credentials of oldtimers and newcomers alike as they pass in review; examining them shrewdly and fairly, to be sure, but nevertheless with the limited purposes of a chronicler of settlement. He is interested in much that is irregular and judged by others to be unworthy of a reputable mind's concern: burlesque shows, popular cartoonists, sentimental best sellers, the Marquis de Sade. But he tends to give his full attention and approval only to those who lend themselves to his developed methods of treatment, who provide him with a trustworthy professional occasion.

Here again Wilson's portrait of his lawyer-father mirrors his own professional character and identifies something central to his whole effort as a critic. "The reason for his success [in the practice of law] was undoubtedly that he never undertook a case which he did not think he could win, and that his judgment about this was infallible. In court, he attacked the jury with a mixture of learning, logic, dramatic imagination and eloquence which he knew would prove irresistible. He would cause them to live through the events of the crime or supposed crime, he would take them through the steps of the transaction, whatever this was, and he would lodge in their heads a picture that it was difficult for his opponent to expel." Such a man is hard to argue with. One can only point to what has been left out, provided one has sufficient knowledge of the case oneself and has not been charmed into overlooking the omissions.

And in all of Wilson's writing, most strikingly in his three major works of sustained exposition—*Axel's Castle, To the Finland Station, Patriotic Gore*—there are, given the designated subject, notable omissions. We must be fair to Wilson on this point and grant that the format of these books—each is presented as a "study" or set of "studies" and not as a definitive history—allows him a broad margin for choice and special emphasis within the scope of the subject as a whole. As it happens, however, the pattern of emphasis and omission significantly affects the historical case each book develops. The broad criticism climaxing *Axel's Castle*, that the Symbolist tradition encourages an ivory-tower withdrawal from the objective world and in particular from society, is made easier to sustain by the fact that the field has been limited to French- and English-speaking examples (easier, also, through the inclusion of Gertrude Stein, who is in no proper sense a Symbolist). The story would be interestingly different if important Russian and German Symbolists had been introduced—Blok, George, even Rilke, who once eloquently defined his work as proceeding "from the conviction that it is possible to give a pure demonstration of the width, variety, and even the fullness of the world." (Wilson's unfamiliarity with German literature is perhaps the chief defect in his ambitious scheme to be an agent of "general cross-fertilization"; he himself has noted, as his "own worst disqualification," his lack of Spanish and Portuguese, but his disregard of the leading German writers of the modern era has left the more serious gap in the kind of "synoptic" record he has spoken of wanting to establish.)

More important, for *Axel's Castle,* is his disregard of one of the key developments in the ideology of classical French Symbolism: its extreme and uncompromising case against literature itself as a justifiable activity. Surely it was this, and not, as Wilson argues, "a personal crisis" precipitated by "an unhappy love affair," that silenced Valéry as a poet for twenty years. The real choice posed by the pairing off of Axel and Rimbaud in the last chapter is not between the ivory tower and common life but between literature and silence—and in concentrating on the sensational facts of Rimbaud's personal behavior rather than on the critical matter of his furious rejection of the time-serving life of letters in any form, including the visionary, Wilson managed to avoid the profound challenge thrown out by the very tradition he was examining against the whole system of literature he had made it his vocation to serve.

Even within the individual chapters of *Axel's Castle,* one's initial admiration for the fullness and panoramic clarity with which, say, the immense structure of Proust's masterpiece is described and put in order may be modified by second thoughts. Being invited to consider a writer like Proust "in a large context of ideas and history, after so many purely exegetical commentaries," is indeed novel and exhilarating, as Richard Chase remarked on rereading the book in the late 1950's. But one is also more likely upon a rereading to notice, for example, the absence of any reference whatsoever to the painter Elstir and to the great speculative disquisitions on his art and his progress as an artist. It is like reading an account of the design of *Doctor Zhivago* that failed to mention that novel's moving, simple, and absolutely crucial evocation of the creative process, in its climactic fourteenth chapter.

Again, with *To the Finland Station,* the concentrated studies, which are the core of the book's argument, of Marx, Engels, and Lenin as individual agents are vividly persuasive and add a dimension to our knowledge of this great chapter in modern history that we may not have gotten so well from ordinary historians. But the scheme Wilson worked out for the book as a whole calls for an opening section on the decline of the bourgeois revolutionary tradition—against this decline and "disintegration" the emergence of revolutionary socialism in the extreme Marxist-Leninist mold appears both the more heroic and the more inevitable—and here we feel that the scheme derives not from an objective grasp of these momentous developments in modern history but from the accidents of the author's earlier reading; for the figures chosen to represent bourgeois revolutionary decadence are, surprisingly, Renan, Taine, and Anatole France, men of letters all and, as it happens, key figures (they have remained critical touchstones all his life) in the study of French literature he carried out under Christian Gauss at Princeton.

With *Patriotic Gore*, built up more obviously piecemeal during ten years of book-reviewing, the pattern of emphasis and omission can better afford to be irregular and somewhat arbitrary. Yet in a work that presents itself as dealing with the *literature* of the Civil War and that includes a bold hypothesis about the effects of the war on American style and diction, the absence of anything but the most cursory references to Whitman and Melville—each of whom created an imaginative record of the progress of the war that is without parallel in modern literature—is remarkable, to say the least. They are mentioned, and warily praised (*Drum-Taps*, Wilson writes, "certainly contained the best poetry that was written during the war on the subject of the war"), but the possibility that their extraordinary creative originality might provide a deeper insight into the whole experience of the war and contribute

a more profoundly truthful response to the book's record of the war's progressive impact is passed over. One begins to appreciate the point of an English reviewer's waspish remark, in another context in the early 1950's, that "Mr. Wilson, as a commentator, seems in his heart to prefer small perishable books to large enduring ones."

It is disappointing, too, considering the detailed attention given to Frederick Goddard Tuckerman and Sidney Lanier, that Emily Dickinson is passed over in half a page. Perhaps this is stretching the point: though the bulk of her finest poetry was in fact written during the first years of the war crisis, the great productive interval in her life, Wilson is correct in saying that she does not allude directly to the war, and we have also to remember his principle of not writing at length on authors who have already been widely discussed, or "overdone." Yet a critic of Wilson's determined sensitivity to the way historical forces impinge on individual imaginations might reasonably be expected to make something out of Emily Dickinson's special eloquence through this period (when New England, its conscience roused, poured out its regiments of volunteers), with her themes of parting, spiritual division, the transforming shock of death, and with her imagery, direct and oblique, of souls at Armageddon. It would be something critically "new," and it would throw a clarifying light on the other testimonies *Patriotic Gore* presents.

Scanting the three great poets of the era (who alone among American authors could fully articulate the same tragic and purgatorial sense of the terrible experience of their time that is expressed in Lincoln's second inaugural) simplifies Wilson's task in psychologizing the conduct and the consequences of the war, North and South. It makes easier the job of imposing a general view of war (given directly in the "Introduction" and strongly insinuated in the stress laid on Calvin Stowe's apocalyptic fantasies or Sherman's manic ruthlessness) as a wholly irrational embodiment of unconscious power drives yielding best to essentially zoological behavior analysis. Clarity and firmness of opinion seem here to have been purchased at too dear a cost. One does not have to be a secret war-lover, or any less opposed to the self-righteousness and hypocrisy that always seek to justify aggressive violence, to feel that Wilson has prejudged the case and that criticism has given way to distemper and invective. Or is it that a desire to separate himself from what to reasoned calculation will always be most disturbing in any great convulsion of human experience, being most problematical and obscure, seems stronger than the wish to know all that may be known?—a desire above all to guard himself against the possibility that for those fully caught up in life, even for the wisest, there may always be something they must do that cannot be properly prepared for or explained, and, moreover, that such moral disorder may be normative for man and not the result of somebody else's having panicked. Some fundamental deficiency in his address to human experience, some incapacity to carry on where the way is not wholly clear, severely inhibits the thrust of Wilson's critical inquiry just as it approaches deep waters. That queer pleasure he has always taken in listing the superficial resemblances of men to animals and insects begins, in its indiscriminate repetitiveness, to appear less and less the expression of a ruthless iconoclasm or moral honesty and more and more a whistling in the dark to keep his courage up.

But once again we find that Wilson himself has given the plainest account of his own case. In *A Prelude*, looking back over his whole life, he writes: "The most painful moments of my life have been due to indecision. I usually know exactly what I want to do, and it has been only when I could not make up my mind that I have really gone to pieces." (What is strangest about wartime conditions in his early story, "The Death of a Soldier," is learning "the habit of not making plans and surrendering the direction of his life"; this becomes in fact the first step in the young soldier's progress toward death.) Correspondingly, in the essay "The Historical Interpretation of Literature," Wilson's final stress is on the "relief" that great works of literature bring us—relief from the element of change and disruptive novelty in our experience, and from the confrontation with those emergent conditions of life which nobody has yet mastered: "With each such victory of the human intellect, whether in history, in philosophy or in poetry, we experience a deep satisfaction; we have been cured of some ache of disorder, relieved of some oppressive burden of uncomprehended events." A negative satisfaction, one is bound to say. Surely the best part of our response to the literature that seems important to us is to the sustained act of original creation it comprises, its surprising augmentation of the life and fortune we must endure in any case, and not merely to some soothing feat of homeopathic exorcism.

Yet we must grant that this appropriation of literature for purposes of creaturely self-defense is related to what has always been most interesting and rewarding in Edmund Wilson's work, and that is his exceptional shrewdness in catching the distinctive character and use of the document before him and in establishing for it (to use his own phrase) a definite literary identity. For the kind of serious journalistic accounting that his work regularly proposes, this is the indispensable virtue. Wilson is consistently quick and definite as a judge of the special quality of individual men. More exactly, he is a good judge of the *testimony* of individual men. (In this respect, too, he is his father's son.) He is a good judge, that is, of men according to their manner of expression in words. In *Patriotic Gore* what he writes about Grant and Sherman on the basis of their written memoirs is perceptive and just. But the kind of panoramic historical criticism he seems to be attempting in this as in his other major books has to be something more than cross-examination and the description of documents—and we notice that what Wilson says of these same men by inference from their conduct in the field and from the general evidence of their behavior in life or of their children's behavior (see the ten pages on Tom Sherman's tormented life) is very much less satisfactory. When it is not the cliché of common gossip and memory, of hero-worship or collective slander, it is mostly behaviorist fantasy. Wilson has a sharp ear for the points at which a man's casual language may have revealed or betrayed him, and he can usually be trusted in descriptions of where and in what ways a writer has put some part of himself into his books. But this is not the same thing as understanding the full historical life such books and documents have emerged from and ambiguously refer to, in which respect Wilson's effort of judgment tends regularly to lapse into a kind of sophisticated sloganeering or namecalling. Again, we feel the lack of any controlling idea that is appropriate, and sufficient, to the full dimensions of the subject.

We see, in short, that Edmund Wilson's critical intelligence operates most persuasively on the words people leave behind them, but that as his inquiry draws him on into speculation about the reasons for these words and the human motives, actions, necessities they incorporate, this verbal positivism—the very quality that gives his literary chronicling its admirable particularity and common sense—becomes more obstruction than asset. We notice in *To the Finland Station* and *Patriotic Gore* that his comparisons and definitions are nearly always in terms of other books, and that he is most effective in comparing minor and uncomplicated matters to familiar situations in guaranteed classics: thus the South Carolina Chestnuts are like the Bolkonskys in *War and Peace*, an episode in their life is like Chekhov, and so on. (So he himself wrote in 1922 of the insulated bookishness of Ezra Pound: "everything in life only serves to remind him of something in literature.") When such comparisons do not turn up, he seems at a loss to know what to think. And the suspicion rises again that perhaps this praiseworthy belief in the efficacy and validity of literature-as-such is damagingly related, in Edmund Wilson's case, to some profound distrust of life and all its disconcerting profusion of motives and appearances; a constitutional distrust of the mind's freedom to act, its power to keep balance, against such profusion; a chronic personal insecurity that issues in these strained countermeasures of hero-worship and aggressive irritability. It may be sound tactics for a journalist on roving commission to work from such motives. It can be a guarantee of directness and authenticity of relation. But it is a handicap, one must say, in the serious prosecution of a sustained historical argument.

But that being said, the fact remains that Edmund Wilson's service as a writer on literature and contemporary events has been for nearly half a century a singularly valuable and important one. Again and again, returning to his essays, we are reminded how much we depend on first-rate critical journalism of the kind he has provided and how rare a thing it is, how poor we are without it. Even more than readers, writers need it—need from their apprenticeship a reliable court of appeals, sympathetic yet discriminating, tireless in its devotion to special cases, liberally informed, indifferent to ideological clamor and extraneous systems of valuation; a court that can be trusted to respond to their work directly and on its own presented terms but that can also remember its developing character from one effort to the next and so help gain for each author treated the status, the clarifying dignity and coherence, of a recognizable career.

That is to say, literature itself—whatever further history lies in store for it—needs such writing. And it is hard to imagine American literature in all the decades since 1920 without the assisting presence of Edmund Wilson. For several successive literary generations he has continued as a critical observer to make the whole enterprise of literature seem an enterprise immensely worth participating in and extending further. It has been a worthy service, richly deserving the honor and respect it has brought him. And nothing, now, seems more agreeably in character than Wilson's businesslike way of playing his part as a literary elder statesman. Refusing to retire into a merely ceremonial eminence, he continues to observe and to offer his affirmative comment: a still reliable measure of present value, a practical source of encouragement for any future we can bear to imagine.

* * *

Edmund Wilson died in Talcottville, New York, June 12, 1972, at the old family summer home described in his absorbing memoir-journal, Upstate *(1971). His ashes were buried in Wellfleet, Massachusetts. In the last year of his life he completed work on a memoir of the 1920's and two further books of criticism, one* of these being a collection of his writings on Russian literature and the Russian language. These posthumous volumes incorporate the principal interests of the first and last phases of his life as a man of letters, the singular integrity of which, over half a century, is perfectly exemplified by his thus clearing his desk, so to speak, as its end approached.*

Selected Bibliography

WORKS OF EDMUND WILSON

The Undertaker's Garland (with John Peale Bishop). New York: Knopf, 1922.
Discordant Encounters: Plays and Dialogues. New York: Boni, 1926.
I Thought of Daisy. New York: Scribners, 1929.
Poets, Farewell! New York: Scribners, 1929.
Axel's Castle: A Study in the Imaginative Literature of 1870 to 1930. New York and London: Scribners, 1931.
The American Jitters: A Year of the Slump. New York and London: Scribners, 1932.
Travels in Two Democracies. New York: Harcourt, Brace, 1936.
This Room and This Gin and These Sandwiches: Three Plays. New York: New Republic, 1937.
The Triple Thinkers: Ten Essays on Literature. New York: Harcourt, Brace, 1938.
To the Finland Station: A Study in the Writing and Acting of History. New York: Harcourt, Brace, 1940.
The Boys in the Back Room: Notes on California Novelists. San Francisco: Colt Press, 1941.
The Wound and the Bow: Seven Studies in Literature. Boston: Houghton Mifflin, 1941.
Note-Books of Night. San Francisco: Colt Press, 1942.
The Shock of Recognition: The Development of Literature in the United States Recorded by the Men Who Made It (anthology). Garden City, N.Y.: Doubleday, Doran, 1943.
Memoirs of Hecate County. Garden City, N.Y.: Doubleday, 1946.

Europe without Baedeker: Sketches among the Ruins of Italy, Greece, and England. Garden City, N.Y.: Doubleday, 1946.

Classics and Commercials: A Literary Chronicle of the Forties. New York: Farrar, Straus, 1950.

The Shores of Light: A Literary Chronicle of the Twenties and Thirties. New York: Farrar, Straus and Young, 1952.

Eight Essays. Garden City, N.Y.: Anchor Books (Doubleday), 1954.

Five Plays. New York: Farrar, Straus and Young, 1954.

The Scrolls from the Dead Sea. New York: Oxford University Press, 1955.

Red, Black, Blond and Olive: Studies in Four Civilizations: Zuni, Haiti, Soviet Russia, Israel. New York: Oxford University Press, 1956.

A Piece of My Mind: Reflections at Sixty. New York: Farrar, Straus and Cudahy, 1956.

The American Earthquake: A Documentary of the Twenties and Thirties. New York: Doubleday, 1958.

Apologies to the Iroquois. New York: Farrar, Straus and Cudahy, 1960.

Night Thoughts. New York: Farrar, Straus and Cudahy, 1961.

Patriotic Gore: Studies in the Literature of the American Civil War. New York: Oxford University Press, 1962.

The Cold War and the Income Tax. New York: Farrar, Straus, 1963.

O Canada: An American's Notes on Canadian Culture. New York: Farrar, Straus and Giroux, 1965.

The Bit Between My Teeth: A Literary Chronicle of 1950–1965. New York: Farrar, Straus and Giroux, 1965.

A Prelude: Landscapes, Characters and Conversations from the Earlier Years of My Life. New York: Farrar, Straus and Giroux, 1967.

The Fruits of the MLA. New York: New York Review of Books, 1968.

The Duke of Palermo and Other Plays, With an Open Letter to Mike Nichols. New York: Farrar, Straus and Giroux, 1969.

The Dead Sea Scrolls 1947-1969. New York: Oxford University Press, 1969.

Upstate: Records and Recollections of Northern New York. New York: Farrar, Straus and Giroux, 1971.

A Window on Russia: For the Use of Foreign Readers. New York: Farrar, Straus and Giroux, 1972.

The Devil and Dr. Barham. New York: Farrar, Straus and Giroux, 1973.

The Twenties: From Notebooks and Diaries of the Period. New York: Farrar, Straus and Giroux, 1973.

Published since the writing of this essay

The Thirties. New York: Washington Square Press, Inc., 1982.

The Forties: From Notebooks and Diaries of the Period. New York: Farrar Straus and Giroux, 1983.

The Fifties: From Notebooks and Diaries of the Period. New York: Farrar, Straus and Giroux, 1986.

BIBLIOGRAPHY

Ramsay, Richard David. *Edmund Wilson: A Bibliography.* New York: David Lewis, 1971.

CRITICAL AND BIOGRAPHICAL STUDIES

Aaron, Daniel. *Writers on the Left.* New York: Harcourt, Brace and World, 1961.

Adams, Robert M. "Masks and Delays: Edmund Wilson as Critic," *Sewanee Review,* 16:272–86 (Spring 1948).

Berthoff, Warner. "Edmund Wilson and His Civil War," *Fictions and Events.* New York: Dutton, 1971.

Brown, E. K. "The Method of Edmund Wilson," *University of Toronto Quarterly,* 11:105–11 (October 1941).

"A Critic and His Time," *Times Literary Supplement,* 2877:240 (April 19, 1957).

"Edmund Wilson and the End of the American Dream," *Times Literary Supplement,* 3664: 561–64 (May 19, 1972).

Frank, Charles P. *Edmund Wilson.* New York: Twayne, 1970.

Graves, Robert. "Edmund Wilson, A Protestant Abroad," *New Republic,* 134:13–16 (April 30, 1956).

Hicks, Granville. "The Intransigence of Edmund Wilson," *Antioch Review,* 6:550–62 (Winter 1946–47).

Howe, Irving. "Edmund Wilson: A Revaluation," *Nation,* 167:430–33 (October 16, 1948).

Hyman, Stanley Edgar. "Edmund Wilson and

Translation in Criticism," *The Armed Vision.* New York: Knopf, 1948.

"The Influence of Edmund Wilson," *Nation,* 186:159–70 (February 22, 1958). (Essays by Robert E. Spiller, Richard Chase, Robert Cantwell.)

Kaufmann, R. J. "The Critic as Custodian of Sanity," *Critical Quarterly,* 1:85–98 (Summer 1959).

Kermode, Frank. "Edmund Wilson's Achievement," *Encounter,* 26:61–70 (May 1966).

Kriegel, Leonard. *Edmund Wilson.* Carbondale: Southern Illinois University, 1971.

Paul, Sherman. *Edmund Wilson: A Study of Literary Vocation in Our Time.* Urbana: University of Illinois, 1965.

Perényi, Eleanor. "Wilson," *Esquire,* 60:80–85, 188 (July 1963).

Podhoretz, Norman. "Edmund Wilson: Then and Now," *Doings and Undoings.* New York: Farrar, Straus and Giroux, 1964.

Schwartz, Delmore. "The Writing of Edmund Wilson," *Accent,* 2:177–86 (Spring 1942).

Snell, George. "Edmund Wilson: The Historical Critic," *Rocky Mountain Review,* 8:36-44 (Winter 1944).

Wain, John. "Edmund Wilson," *Essays on Literature and Ideas.* London: Macmillan, 1963.

—*WARNER BERTHOFF*

Thomas Wolfe

1900-1938

THOMAS WOLFE grappled in frustrated and demonic fury with what he called "the strange and bitter miracle of life," a miracle which he saw in patterns of opposites. The elements of life and art seem to have existed for him as a congeries of contradictions, and he could not understand a thing until its negation had been brought forth. The setting down of those opposites is the most obvious single characteristic of his work, the significant parts of which are four vast novels, seven short novels, two collections of short stories, and an essay in criticism—all fragments of an incomplete whole, only the most shadowy outlines of which are discernible.

Even the titles of his books—*Look Homeward, Angel*, with its suggestion of near and far; *Of Time and the River*; *From Death to Morning*; *The Web and the Rock*; *You Can't Go Home Again*, with its idea of home and exile; *The Hills Beyond*, with its suggestion of movement, of extension—reflect this view of experience. So do his geographical oppositions—South and North, country and city, plain and "enfabled rock," America and Europe—and the contrasting pairs into which he regularly grouped his characters—father and mother, Jew and Gentile, South and North Carolinian, poor and rich, true artist and aesthete. Wolfe's vision of himself carried the

same pattern of oppositions; in *The Web and the Rock* Esther Jack sums up the autobiographical hero with these words: "He has the face of a demented angel . . . and there is madness and darkness and evil in his brain. He is more cruel than death, and more lovely than a flower. His heart was made for love, and it is full of hate and darkness."

There is also a basic conflict of themes in Wolfe's work. He declared, "I have at last discovered my own America. . . . And I shall wreak out my vision of this life, this way, this world and this America, to the top of my bent, to the height of my ability, but with an unswerving devotion, integrity and purity of purpose." He saw himself as one with Walt Whitman, Mark Twain, and Sherwood Anderson, whom he called "men who have seen America with a poet's vision." The "epic impulse," the desire to define in fiction the American character and to typify the American experience, was obsessively present in his work. Yet another theme, contradictory but equally persistent in his work, was loneliness and the isolation of the incommunicable self. In a major sense, his subject matter was himself, his self-discovery and his groping toward self-knowledge; his forte was the lyrical expression of personal emotion and the rhetorical expression of personal attitudes. Aside from Whitman, no other major American writer ever celebrated himself at such length, with such intensity, or with so great a sense of his own importance as Wolfe did. The private self and the public seer were roles that he was never quite able to harmonize, and yet he persisted in playing them both.

This fundamental concern with opposites is reflected in Wolfe's literary style itself—in the balanced antitheses that abound in his writing, in his shocking juxtaposition of images, in his use of contradictory phrases, such as "changeless change," "splendid and fierce and weak and strong and foolish," "of wandering forever and the earth again," and "the web and the rock." In fact, Wolfe was a writer with two distinctive and contrasting styles. On one level he wrought with lyrical intensity a web of sensuous images capable of evoking from his readers a response almost as intense as that resulting from direct experience. Of American writers in this century, Ernest Hemingway is Wolfe's only equal at the evocative representation of the physical world through images so startlingly direct that they seem to rub against the reader's raw nerve ends. Wolfe said, "The quality of my memory is characterized, I believe, in a more than ordinary degree by the intensity of its sense impressions, its power to evoke and bring back the odors, sounds, colors, shapes, and feel of things with concrete vividness." At its best his style was superbly suited for transferring this concrete vividness to the reader.

Yet Wolfe was seldom content to let the scene or the senses speak for themselves; rather, he felt an obligation to define the emotion which he associated with the scene and to suggest a meaning, a universality, a significance through rhetorical exhortation. The resulting passages are marked by extravagant verbal pyrotechnics—by apostrophe, by incantation, by exhortation, by rhapsodic assertion,

and, all too often, by rant and bombast. The lyric style evokes in the reader the ineffable emotion called forth in Wolfe by the scene; then the rhetorical assertion attempts to utter the ineffable and to articulate the transcendent aspects of the scene which Wolfe fears that the reader otherwise may miss. While passages in this second style often succeed magnificently in lifting the reader with their cadenced chants to glimpse Wolfe's ultimate visions, it is also true that such passages sometimes degenerate into dithyrambic incantations that become strident, false, and meaningless. Few writers have been so clearly at the same time both the masters and the slaves of language.

The same contrasts are apparent in the structural qualities of Wolfe's fiction. On the level of dramatic scene, fully realized and impacted with immediacy, Wolfe could construct magnificently. Single episodes of his work, published separately as short stories, are powerful narrative units. "The Child by Tiger," first a short story in the *Saturday Evening Post* and later an episode in *The Web and the Rock*, is a clear example; so are "Only the Dead Know Brooklyn," "The Lost Boy," and "An Angel on the Porch." In the middle length of the short novel he worked with perhaps his greatest effectiveness. He produced seven pieces in this middle length, all of them originally published in magazines as independent entities, although five were later fragmented and distributed through the full-length novels. They include *The Web of Earth*, in a structural sense his most completely successful work; *A Portrait of Bascom Hawke*, which was later fragmented and distributed through *Of Time and the River* as a portrait of Bascom Pentland; *No Door*, whose thematic organization was a microcosm which he later expanded into *Of Time and the River*; and *The Party at Jack's*, which, in an expanded form, was incorporated into *You Can't Go Home Again*. These short novels represent strong dramatic and narrative writing, rich in subject matter, firm in control, often objective in point of view.

Furthermore, Wolfe projected ambitious plans for his books. Out of the experiences which were to be the material of his fiction he wished to weave a myth of his native land, an embodiment of its nature and its spirit. At a time when the American critic was just beginning to be concerned with the newer concepts of myth, Wolfe wrote, in the manuscript later published as the title piece of *The Hills Beyond*: "The Myth is founded on *extorted* fact; wrenched from the context of ten thousand days. . . . For it is not a question of having faith, or lack of it. It is a simple fact of seeing." In order to contain and define this mythic aspect of human experience, Wolfe sought in old myths and in fable, as well as in the structure of his own experience, the enclosing form for his utterance. *Of Time and the River* in one of its earlier projections was to be called *Antaeus*, and its characters were to symbolize Heracles, Poseidon, Gaea, Helen, Demeter, Kronos, Rhea, Orestes, Faustus, Telemachus, Jason. After outlining the proposed plot in a letter to Maxwell E. Perkins, his editor, he wrote: "Now, don't get alarmed at all this and think I'm writing a Greek myth. All of this is never mentioned once the story gets under way, but . . . it gives the most magnificent plot and unity to my book." Such projects are one of the staples of Wolfe's correspondence with the editors at Scribners and at Harpers and with his agent.

Yet, in sharp contrast to the dramatic power in individual scenes and the magnificent and mythic scope in plan, the realized larger units of his work show a formlessness and plotlessness that have baffled and perplexed the critic of Wolfe since he first published a novel. The structure of his works, at least on the surface, seems to be the simple chronological pattern of his own life, their incidents those participated in or witnessed. Scholars and critics have explored the close relationship of Wolfe's work to his life, and they have found that, despite his frequent disclaimers that his work is no more autobiographical than that of other novelists, the use of direct experience and the representation of actual persons and events are very great in his novels. Floyd C. Watkins, who examined Wolfe's use of materials drawn from his home town, Asheville, concluded, "there are many more than 300 characters and places mentioned by name or described in *Look Homeward, Angel*, and probably there is not an entirely fictitious person, place, or incident in the whole novel." Wolfe's disarming statement, "Dr. Johnson remarked that a man would turn over half a library to make a single book: in the same way, a novelist may turn over half the people in a town to make a single figure in his novel," is no defense at all when the people of the town are merely represented under the thinnest and most transparent disguises, and when the changes in name are as slight as "Chapel Hill" to "Pulpit Hill," "Raleigh" to "Sydney," "Woodfin Street" to "Woodson Street," or "Reuben Rawls" to "Ralph Rolls." His father's name is changed from "W. O. Wolfe" to "W. O. Gant," his mother's from "Julia Elizabeth Westall Wolfe" to "Eliza Pentland Gant," his brother's from "Ben Wolfe" to "Ben Gant."

Wolfe's artistic method was a combination of realistic representation and romantic declaration; and it seems to have reflected accurately a contradictory—or perhaps double—view of the nature of art. On one hand, he was committed to the detailed, exact, accurate picturing of the actual world—committed to such an extent that he found it hard to represent anything that he had not personally experienced. On the other hand, his view of the nature and function of art was essentially that of the nineteenth-century Romantic poets and critics.

In one sense this aesthetic view was a natural outgrowth of his education. Six teachers had major influences on Wolfe, and five of them were clear-cut romantics. Margaret Roberts, who taught him for years in a boys' preparatory school, made an indelible impression upon him with her love for the English poets; Mrs. Roberts, represented in *Look Homeward, Angel* as Margaret Leonard, filled the boy with a corresponding love of Wordsworth, Burns, Coleridge, Herrick, Carew, Jonson, Shakespeare, Poe, Hawthorne, Melville, and Scott. At the University of North Carolina he studied under Horace Williams, a philosophy professor whom he represented as Vergil Weldon and whom he called "Hegel in the Cotton Belt." Williams, who was a mystic, taught him a rather loose form of the Hegelian dialectic, in which a concept, or thesis, inevitably generates its opposite, or antithesis, and the interaction of the two produces a new concept, or synthesis. He also studied under Frederick Koch, who was beginning his work with the Carolina Playmakers and was encouraging his students to write folk plays, finding and underscoring the strange in the commonplace. Wolfe's first successful literary efforts were one-act plays written for Koch and produced by the Playmakers with Wolfe acting in them. At Chapel Hill he was also greatly influenced by the teaching of the Spenserian scholar Edwin A. Greenlaw and by his theories of the inseparable relationship of "literature and life." At Harvard an important influence was John Livingston Lowes, who was writing *The Road to Xanadu* while Wolfe was a graduate student in his classes and whose view of the nature of Coleridge's imagination remained for Wolfe until his death a truthful picture of the workings of the artist's mind. At Harvard, too, he was influenced by George Pierce Baker, famous as the director of the "47 Workshop" in drama, although he later broke with Baker, at least partially as a result of dissatisfaction with the brittle and essentially anti-romantic views of students whom Baker applauded.

The marked romanticism of his aesthetic theory, with its pronounced distrust of almost all forms of intellectualism and its emphasis on the expression of the artist's feelings as the highest objective of a work of art, was at a polar extreme from the view Wolfe later developed of the novelist as national prophet obligated to represent the social scene; and his own novels are caught between the tug of the representation of the nation and the expression of the self.

Wolfe's tendency to see and to express things in terms of oppositions may have been learned at the feet of Horace Williams; it is possible that, as some critics have asserted, it represented a failure of his mind adequately to grapple with the problems before it; certainly it was, to some extent, an expression of his southern qualities, for the typical native of the southern states is fascinated by paradox, enamored of ambiguity, devoted to the particular and the concrete, and, although a dreamer of grandiose dreams, seldom the articulator of effective larger structures. The men of Wolfe's region were, like Wolfe himself, caught between the romantic view of their own past and the realistic fact of their present poverty. And over the years they have proved themselves capable of living with unresolved contradictions. Yet Thomas Wolfe was marked almost from his birth by certain unique paradoxes, which formed a peculiar aspect of his life, and therefore an inevitable aspect of his autobiographic art.

Thomas Wolfe was born in Asheville, North Carolina, which he was to call Altamont and Libya Hill in his novels, on October 3, 1900.

He was, therefore, a southerner, yet his native state in 1900 was in the midst of its espousal of the Populist movement that has left a heritage of liberalism in educational, social, and economic matters quite different from that in most of the rest of the South. Furthermore, Wolfe came from a mountain town far removed from even the dream of a South of tall white columns and banjo-strumming darkies, a town which was to be caught in a real estate fever and go on a middle-class speculative binge, keyed, as Wolfe lamented, to Yankee materialism and dollar greed. In *You Can't Go Home Again* he described that binge and its painful aftermath in coruscating detail. It would have been hard to find a southern town more thoroughly middle class than Asheville in the years of Wolfe's childhood; yet it was a town still of its region, tasting on its tongue the bitterness of defeat, the sharp sting of southern poverty, and the acrid flavor of racial injustice. This middle-class world was his particular subject throughout his career, although he qualified its customary "booster" optimism by the more pessimistic approach natural to a poverty-stricken region still conscious—as no other part of America is—of defeat.

His mother was Julia Elizabeth Westall Wolfe, a member of a mountain clan memorialized by her son as the "time-devouring" Joyners and Pentlands, and she symbolized for him the protean texture of the South, which was always feminine in his view, "the dark, ruined Helen of his blood." The Westalls were people of some prominence in their region, men and women of medium standing in Asheville and its encircling hills. His mother had been a schoolteacher and a book saleswoman before she became the third wife of William Oliver Wolfe, a native of Pennsylvania. W. O. Wolfe was a stonecutter by profession, owning his own business, and he was a powerful man of great gusto, vast appetites, and a tor-

turing need to assert himself vividly against his drab world. Wolfe's representations of his parents as Eliza and W. O. Gant are among his greatest portraits, and their chance meeting and marriage in a southern hill town were central to his view of the "bitter mystery" of his life. He opens his first novel, *Look Homeward, Angel*, with a speculation on "that dark miracle of chance which makes new magic in a dusty world" and symbolizes it through "A destiny that leads . . . from Epsom into Pennsylvania, and thence into the hills that shut in Altamont." He saw Eugene Gant, the hero of that novel, as "the fusion of two strong egotisms, Eliza's inbrooding and Gant's expanding outward."

Thomas was the youngest of the Wolfes' eight children, of whom two died in infancy. During his childhood his mother bought a boardinghouse and moved into it, taking Thomas and his brother Ben with her and leaving W. O. Wolfe and their daughter Mabel in the old house. (The other two sons and a daughter were no longer living at home.) Wolfe's childhood was spent in a family divided between two home establishments, with itinerant boarders as his closest companions, except for his brother Ben, whom he idolized and whose death left upon Thomas' spirit a scar that never healed. Wolfe regarded himself in later life as "God's Lonely Man," and he attributed that loneliness to the experiences of his childhood. In 1933 he wrote his sister, "I think I learned about being alone when I was a child about eight years old and I think that I have known about it ever since."

He attended public school until he was eleven; then he entered a small private school operated by Mr. and Mrs. J. M. Roberts. Wolfe was a bright and perceptive boy, and during the four years he spent at the Roberts' school he was almost totally absorbed in learning. At the age of fifteen—three years ahead of his contemporaries—he entered the University of North Carolina at Chapel Hill.

At the time he entered it, the university was undergoing the changes that converted it from a leisurely undergraduate liberal arts college into a university engaged in research and graduate instruction and that made it the focal point of the New South movement, the center of southern liberalism. Once more the southern boy was caught up in the fabric of change, confronted by the oppositions of the old and the new. In the university Wolfe proved to be a good student and a "big man on the campus," being active in debate, publications, and fraternities, as well as working with the Playmakers. He was graduated at the age of twenty, with an urge to study further and the desire to become a playwright.

Borrowing from his mother against his anticipated share in his father's estate, Wolfe went to Harvard, where he studied for three years, and earned the Master of Arts degree in English literature. But the central interest of his Harvard years was in the "47 Workshop" in drama and the furtherance of his projected career as a playwright. The picture he paints of the Workshop in *Of Time and the River* is a satiric attack on pretension and lifeless aestheticism, although his portrait of Professor Baker as "Professor Hatcher" (in the original notes for the novel he had called him "Butcher"), while tainted with malice, is still drawn with respect.

Although teachers as eminent as John Livingston Lowes praised Wolfe's "very distinct ability" as a scholar, he had chosen playwriting for his career, and he vainly tried his fortunes peddling his plays in New York City in the fall of 1923 before he accepted appointment as instructor in English at New York University in January 1924. Wolfe taught at the university, satirically represented as the School of Utility Cultures in *Of Time and the River*, intermittently until the spring of 1930. During this period he made several European tours, met and had a violent love affair with Mrs. Aline Bernstein, a scene and costume designer seventeen years his senior and a married woman with two children. She is the "Esther Jack" of his later novels.

It was in London in the autumn of 1926 that Wolfe began committing to paper in the form of a huge novel the steadily accelerating flood of his childhood memories. The mounting manuscript bore the stamp of the immersion in literature and poetry which had been a major element of Wolfe's life up to that point, but above all it bore, by his own testimony, the mark of Joyce's *Ulysses*. Discernible in it too were traces of H. G. Wells and Sinclair Lewis. When he returned to New York, he continued the writing of the book, while his love affair with Mrs. Bernstein waxed and waned and waxed again. Both have left records of the affair, Mrs. Bernstein in *The Journey Down*, an autobiographical novel, and Wolfe in *The Web and the Rock*. The exact measure of Mrs. Bernstein's influence in disciplining Wolfe's monumental flow of memory, energy, and words into the form which *Look Homeward, Angel* had taken by its completion in first draft in March 1928 is a matter of debate but it was certainly great. The manuscript of the book was complete, in any case, when, after a violent quarrel with Mrs. Bernstein, Wolfe went again to Europe in July, leaving it with an agent. When he returned to New York in January 1929 it was to find a letter from Maxwell E. Perkins, editor of Charles Scribner's Sons, publishers, expressing an interest in the novel, if it could "be worked into a form publishable by us."

Wolfe renewed the affair with Mrs. Bernstein, to whom *Look Homeward, Angel* is dedicated, and worked desperately to cut and arrange the material of his manuscript into a publishable book. In its original form, *Look Homeward, Angel* was the detailed and intense record of the ancestry, birth, childhood, adolescence, and youth of Eugene Gant. It began with a ninety-page sequence on Eugene's father's life, and it concluded when, after Eugene's graduation from college, he discovers, in an imaginary conversation with the ghost of his brother, that "*You* are your world," and, leaving home, "turns his eyes upon the distant soaring ranges." Perkins insisted on the deletion of the historical opening, on the removal of some extraneous material, and on minor rearrangements, but the novel when it was published on October 18, 1929, probably had undergone little more editorial supervision than long manuscripts by exuberant but talented first novelists generally undergo. As it was to work out, *Look Homeward, Angel* was more unqualifiedly Wolfe's in conception, writing, arrangement, and execution than any other work of long fiction that was ever to be published under his name.

Its lyric intensity and its dramatic power were immediately recognized and hailed; even before Sinclair Lewis, in accepting the Nobel Prize in 1930, praised him highly, Wolfe was recognized as a figure to be reckoned with in the literary world. His native Asheville paid him the tribute of being collectively indignant at the portrait of itself in the novel. A novelistic career of great promise was launched, and Wolfe, who had hungered for fame, suddenly found that he didn't want it. Not only were the members of his family hurt and the people of Asheville angry, but he also felt the obligation of producing a second work that represented an advance over the first. This proved to be one of the major struggles of his life.

He resigned from New York University, ended the affair with Mrs. Bernstein, and went to Europe for a year on a Guggenheim fellowship. When he returned to America, he established himself in an apartment in Brooklyn and took up the lonely vigil with himself and his writing which he describes in *The Story of a Novel* and portrays in *You Can't Go Home Again*. Before *Look Homeward, Angel* was published, he had begun planning the new novel and writing parts of it. During the lonely years in Brooklyn, he struggled in growing desperation to produce the second book. The short novel *A Portrait of Bascom Hawke* in 1932 shared a short novel contest prize of $5000 offered by *Scribner's Magazine*. Another short novel, *The Web of Earth*, was written and published in *Scribner's Magazine* during the early Brooklyn years. A reminiscence of her early life by Eliza Gant, *The Web of Earth* is one of his most successful pieces of work. Nowhere else does the Joycean influence on Wolfe find as direct and as satisfying an expression as it does here.

The success of these two short novels encouraged Wolfe to continue to work in this form, and between 1932 and 1934 he produced *Death the Proud Brother*, which was reprinted in *From Death to Morning*; *Boom Town*, which appears in greatly modified form in *You Can't Go Home Again*; and *No Door*. Scribners planned at one time in 1934 to issue *No Door* as a separate volume, but the short novel was finally broken into two parts and published in *Scribner's Magazine* as "No Door" and "The House of the Far and Lost." The work was first published in its complete short novel form in 1961 in *The Short Novels of Thomas Wolfe*. However, Wolfe's accomplishment in this work was by no means lost, for the thematic structure which he evolved in *No Door* became the model which he followed in organizing *Of Time and the River*.

Despite the fact that Wolfe was living almost entirely on the rather slender proceeds from the sale to magazines of his short stories and his short novels, when he was approached by a representative of Metro-Goldwyn-Mayer about the possibility of his doing motion picture writing at $1000 to $1500 a week, he declined it on the grounds that he had "a lot of books to write."

He was struggling with a vast novel, to be entitled "The October Fair," which would be in at least four volumes and would have a time span from the Civil War to the present, with hundreds of characters and a new protagonist, David Hawke, replacing Eugene Gant. Maxwell Perkins was working with him every night and on weekends in an attempt to give the new work an acceptable structure and symmetry. It is difficult to separate in Wolfe's letters what is defensible judgment based on fact and what is the frenzied product of his febrile imagination; yet, if his versions are to be trusted even in minor part, Maxwell Perkins had a truly major role to play in the formulation of his second novel. It was Perkins, Wolfe said, who suggested what Wolfe took to be the theme of the new novel, "the search for a father." Seemingly it was Perkins who turned him back to Eugene Gant and away from David Hawke; it was Perkins who discouraged his attempts at formulations of his vision of America in other terms than those of the autobiographical "apprenticeship novel," for Wolfe had worked out a number of elaborate schemes for his new novel. And it was Perkins who insisted that *Of Time and the River* was ready to be published and in 1935 sent it to the printers despite Wolfe's protest.

Of Time and the River was a mammoth book, continuing the chronicle of Eugene Gant's sensibility. It opens as he leaves Altamont for Harvard, follows him there, to New York City where he teaches in the School of Utility Cultures, to Europe, where he begins the writing of a novel and has a frustrating love affair with a girl named Ann, and concludes as he meets Esther on the boat back to America.

Look Homeward, Angel, although it had lacked the traditional novelistic structure, had a certain unity through its concentration on a family, a mountain town, and a way of life. In reading it one was caught up in the sharp impressions of youth and somehow rushed along to that moment of self-realization with which it ended. *Of Time and the River* had less plot, more introspection, less structural cohesion, more rhetoric. Large segments of the book exist without thematic or plot relevance; some of the best scenes and most effective portraits seem to be dramatic intrusions; and it is only when one knows the rest of the story as it is revealed in *The Web and the Rock* that one is able to appreciate the climactic significance of the meeting with Esther with which the book closes.

That these events have meaning for Wolfe beyond their merely personal expression—indeed, that Eugene Gant is in an undefined way the generic Everyman of Whitman's poems or the racial hero of the national epic—one senses from the amount of rhetorical extrapolation by which the hero becomes one with the world, his experiences one with the national experience. Sometimes the rhetoric is wonderfully handled. Indeed, *Of Time and the River* is unusually rich in Wolfe's "poetic passages," but the organization of the materials of the story so that they speak a national myth through self-sufficient action is not attempted with any consistency in the book.

It was greeted with mixed reactions. Many hailed it as a fulfillment of the earnest given by *Look Homeward, Angel*; but its formlessness, its lack of story, and its rhapsodic extravagance were also inescapable, and the really serious critical questions which have been debated about Wolfe's work ever since were first clearly expressed about this novel. These questions are whether it is legitimate in fiction to substitute autobiography and reporting for creation; whether rhetorical assertion, however poetic, can be an acceptable substitute for dramatic representation; whether immediacy can ever be properly bought at the expense of aesthetic distance; and, inevitably, what constitutes form.

In the fall of 1935 a group of stories and sketches originally written as parts of the novel but published in periodicals and excluded from the completed work was assembled and published under the title *From Death to Morning*. This volume, which was attacked by the critics when it appeared and which sold poorly, has never received the attention it deserves. The stories reprinted in it are extremely uneven in quality, but they show Wolfe as a serious experimenter in fiction. His mastery of the short and middle forms of fiction is demonstrated here in such works as *Death the Proud Brother*, "Only the Dead Know Brooklyn," "In the Park," and *The Web of Earth*. That the book would take a critical pounding Wolfe knew, but he said, "I believe that as good writing as I have ever done is in this book." The judgment is startlingly accurate.

Yet if this volume demonstrated a technical virtuosity with which Wolfe is seldom credited, it also showed through its characters and incidents the essential unity and hence the basic autobiographical tendency in his total work. When, in 1936, Wolfe published an essay in criticism, *The Story of a Novel*, originally a lecture given at a writers' conference at Boulder, Colorado, this record of how he wrote *Of Time and the River*, told with humility and straightforward honesty, seemed to many critics to prove that he simply was not a novelist: in two long novels and a volume of short stories, Wolfe had written out of his direct experience, seemingly without a sense of form, and under the direction of the editors at Scribners. More than one critic found this situation less than admirable. Robert Penn Warren

summed up the case: ". . . despite his admirable energies and his powerful literary endowments, his work illustrates once more the limitations, perhaps the necessary limitations, of an attempt to exploit directly and naïvely the personal experience and the self-defined personality in art." And Bernard De Voto, in a savage attack, declared Wolfe to possess great narrative and dramatic talents but to be unable to realize them in novelistic form; he was guilty of leaving coexisting with true fictional materials too much "placental" matter "which nature and most novelists discard." De Voto also charged that Wolfe's novels were put together by "Mr. Perkins and the assembly-line at Scribners." That Wolfe was a genius he conceded, but he added that "genius is not enough."

The De Voto article hurt Wolfe deeply. In 1936 a desire to prove De Voto wrong (perhaps heightened by an unconscious awareness that in certain respects at least he was right) joined with many other factors to make Wolfe wish to change his publisher. Among the reasons were a dispute with Perkins about Wolfe's representation of Scribners people in a story, a disagreement over the cost of corrections in *Of Time and the River*, a group of libel suits which Scribners wanted to settle out of court, and, most important of all, Wolfe's awareness that his attitudes were incompatible with those of Perkins and that he wanted to go in directions in which Perkins did not wish him to travel. The long and agonizing break with Scribners, begun in mid-1936, was finally effected in 1937, when Wolfe formed a publishing arrangement with Harper and Brothers, with Edward C. Aswell to act as his editor.

He spent the summer of 1937 working in a cabin in the North Carolina mountains and was happy to find that he was received by his people with pride and pleasure, that they had forgiven him; but he also learned from the experience that "you can't go home again," an idea that loomed large in his thinking and which symbolized for him the fact that we move onward not backward. He was working hard, with the frenzied expenditure of energy of which he was capable, getting material ready to show Aswell as the beginning of a book. At that time he was again projecting a story of great magnitude in at least four volumes, and he was seeking forms and structures through which it could be made into a mythic record of "an innocent man's discovery of life and the world." At one time the book was to be called "The Vision of Spangler's Paul," with the subtitle "The Story of His Birth, His Life, His Going To and Fro in the Earth, His Walking Up and Down in It: His Vision Also of the Lost, the Never-Found, the Ever-Here America." At another time he changed his protagonist's name to Doaks, in an effort to symbolize his typical nature, and wrote "The Doaksology," a history of his family. Finally, he selected George Webber as his protagonist—a character physically very much like the David Hawke whom he had wished to make the hero of *Of Time and the River*—and wrote of him: "The protagonist becomes significant not as the tragic victim of circumstances, the romantic hero in conflict and revolt against his environment, but as a kind of polar instrument round which the events of life are grouped, by means of which they are touched, explained, and apprehended, by means of which they are seen and ordered."

In May 1938 he delivered a great mass of manuscript, perhaps a million words, to Aswell. It represented an ordering of the materials on which he was working, but not a book ready for the press. He himself estimated that more than a year's work remained to be done before the first volume of the new work would be ready. Then he left on a tour of the West which ended with his serious illness from pneumonia in Vancouver, followed by a worsening of his condition in Seattle, and the discovery, after he had been moved to the Johns Hopkins hospital in Baltimore, that the pneumonia had released old sealed-off tuberculosis bacteria in his lungs and that these bacteria had gone to his brain. On September 15, 1938, eighteen days before his thirty-eighth birthday, he died.

Edward Aswell extracted the materials for three books from the mountain of manuscript which Wolfe left. The first, *The Web and the Rock* (1939), is apparently in a form not too different from that which Wolfe had planned, although the last 400 pages of it are still in the earlier and more extravagant style of *Of Time and the River*, rather than the sparser and more controlled style of the opening sections. The new protagonist, George Webber, is surprisingly like Eugene Gant, although his physical characteristics and his family life have changed. The early sections of the book take him through childhood, to college, and then to New York City. There he meets Esther Jack and the novel becomes the record of a tempestuous love affair. Then Webber goes to Germany, is badly beaten in a riot at a festival, the *Oktoberfest*, in Munich, and, through a monologue between his body and his soul, Webber understands that he must turn from his immersion in himself and his past. "He knew and accepted now its limitations" and ". . . looked calmly and sanely forth upon the earth for the first time in ten years." *The Web and the Rock* is a very imperfect book, seeming to be the forced union of two inharmonious parts. Yet it is much more nearly a novel than *Of Time and the River*, and in the early parts, prepared for publication during the last year of Wolfe's life, it shows a groping toward the control of material and a desire to represent dramatically rather than to assert rhetorically. Wolfe was still grappling with the problem of novelistic form and language, and grappling with at least limited success.

The second of the books which Aswell assembled is much less a novel than *The Web and the Rock*. *You Can't Go Home Again* (1940) is a bringing together in a narrative frame of large units of material which Wolfe had completed but only partially arranged at the time of his death. It continues the story of George Webber, but in it what Wolfe meant when he said that the protagonist was to be a "kind of polar instrument, round which the events of life are grouped," becomes clearer. The book—it is hardly a novel at all—has the very loose narrative structure of George Webber's life: he returns from Europe, writes his book, goes to Libya Hill (Asheville) for his aunt's funeral, travels in Europe, sees the emptiness of fame in the person of Lloyd McHarg (Sinclair Lewis), travels in Germany and comprehends the horror of the Nazi regime, and writes a long letter setting forth his credo. Yet what gives the book vitality is not George and his experiences—although those dealing with the publication and reception of his novel *Look to the Mountains* are extremely interesting to the Wolfe student— but the view of life which is seen through George. Mr. Katamoto, Mr. Jack and the party at his house, Judge Bland and the satiric picture of the moral and material collapse of Libya Hill, Daisy Purvis, Lloyd McHarg, Foxhall Edwards and his family, Mr. C. Green, who jumps from the twelfth story of the Admiral Francis Drake Hotel, the frightened little Jew on the train out of Germany—it is in such materials as these that the dramatic strength of the book resides.

You Can't Go Home Again is freer than his other books of the rhapsodic assertion that so often replaces dramatic statement. Those who have found Wolfe's strength in his ability to depict character and to invest scenes with life and movement are likely to find in *You Can't Go Home Again* both his best writing and a discernible promise of greater work and greater control to come. On the other hand, those who see Wolfe's strength to be peculiarly his power with words are likely to feel that the dramatic and narrative success of *You Can't Go Home Again* was bought at the price of his most distinctive qualities. As a novel it is the least satisfactory of his works, yet in its pages are to be seen, dimly and afar off it is true, the faint outline of what he was striving for in his vast and unrealized plans for the "big book."

The third volume that Aswell mined from the manuscript was *The Hills Beyond* (1941), a collection of fragments and sketches. A few of the stories were published in magazines after 1935, but most of them were previously unpublished units of the manuscript. Two distinguished short stories are here, "The Lost Boy" and "Chickamauga," together with a 150-page fragment, "The Hills Beyond," which is a narrative of the Joyners and would have been the early introductory material to the big book. "The Hills Beyond" parallels, in subject matter, material which Wolfe tried to introduce at the beginning of each of his major stories. In this fragment Wolfe's efforts at being an objective novelist have more immediately apparent success than they do elsewhere, and he seems to be moving much more toward the realism of the southern frontier and away from the romanticism of his early career. Valuable though it is to have as many of the self-contained fragments of the Wolfe manuscripts as we can get, *The Hills Beyond* adds very little to Wolfe's stature as a novelist.

In 1948 *Mannerhouse,* one of the plays which Wolfe had tried very hard to peddle to professional producers but without success, was published from the manuscript. An abbreviated version of his ten-scene play *Welcome to Our City* was published in *Esquire Magazine* in 1957. Both the one-act and the three-act versions of his play *The Mountains* were published in 1970. All are documents purely of historical importance. With the publication of *The Hills Beyond* most of Wolfe's significant work was in print, and, incomplete though it is as a record of his vast and ambitious project, it is all that remains of his efforts to formulate in fiction a vision of himself and his world. The manuscripts out of which Aswell quarried the last three books are now in the William B. Wisdom Collection at Harvard. They contain many scenes, characters, and sections that have never been published, but the unpublished materials will probably have to await a completely new editing of the total manuscripts before they will find an audience.

Wolfe's career, like his works, became a matter of debate before his death; and his untimely demise, when seemingly the world was all before him and his prodigious talent was still groping toward an adequate mode of expression, increased the debate without giving appreciable weight to any of the answers. He remains, despite his thirty-seven years, a "golden boy" cut off in the moment of the flowering of his talent, and the issue of whether he had already done all that he was capable of and was, therefore, saved by death from tasting the fruits of a certain diminution of power or whether a major talent went unrealized through the cruel accident of time will remain as unresolved with him as it has been with all the other "golden boys" who tasted too early "the bitter briefness of our days."

The remark of William Faulkner, "I rated Wolfe first [among modern American writers] because we had all failed but Wolfe had made the best failure because he had tried hardest to say the most," is a peculiarly unsatisfying and unrewarding comment which merely restates the question; although his added remark, "He may have had the best talent of us, he may have been 'the greatest American writer' if he had lived longer, though I have never held much with the 'mute inglorious Milton' theory," helps a little.

One of the principal facts of Wolfe's career is summed up in his statement to Edward Aswell: "I began life as a lyrical writer . . . I began to write with an intense and passionate concern with the designs and purposes of my own youth; and like many other men, that preoccupation has now changed to an intense and passionate concern with the designs and purposes of life." This extension of interest to the surrounding world, to "life," was obsessively present with Wolfe from the time of the publication of *Look Homeward, Angel* to his death. In 1929, when the new book was to be "The October Fair," he described it to the Guggenheim Foundation: "It tries to find out why Americans are a nomad race (as this writer believes); why they are touched with a powerful and obscure homesickness wherever they go, both at home and abroad." In 1930 he wrote Perkins: "I believe I am at last beginning to have a proper use of a writer's material: for it seems to me he ought to see in what has happened to him the elements of the universal experience." He wrote John Hall Wheelock, another editor at Scribners, enthusiastically about a section of "The October Fair" which he had just completed: "In *Antaeus*, in a dozen short scenes, told in their own language, we see people of all sorts *constantly in movement*, going somewhere." But in the same letter he also says, "God knows what Maxwell Perkins will say when he sees it." He was always toying with ideas like his largely unwritten "The Hound of Darkness," of which he said,

"It will be a great tone-symphony of night—railway yards, engines, freights, deserts, a clopping hoof, etc.—seen *not by a definite personality*, but haunted throughout by a *consciousness* of personality."

After *Look Homeward, Angel*, he wanted to abandon Eugene Gant for a less autobiographical protagonist, David Hawke, and to write his next novel in the first person—apparently realizing that a first-person narrator is less in the forefront of a story and is more a transmitting vehicle than the third-person protagonist. But during the years of agonized labor by himself and with Perkins most of these plans went by the wayside. Maxwell Perkins believed that Wolfe's second novel should continue the story of Eugent Gant and should center itself exclusively in Gant's consciousness. Perkins wrote, "The principle that I was working on was that this book, too [as *Look Homeward, Angel* had], got its form through the senses of Eugene," and he told how he objected to scenes in the novel that were not recorded through Eugene's perceptions; he tried, for example, to exclude the episodes about Gant's death—one of the most memorable sequences that Wolfe ever wrote. The struggle by which *Of Time and the River* achieved publication over Wolfe's protest is well known; but the depth of Wolfe's dissatisfaction with the book became clear only with the publication of the *Letters* in 1956. When *Of Time and the River* appeared, he wrote Perkins, ". . . as I told you many times, I did not care whether the final length of the book was 300, 500, 1000 pages, so long as I had realized completely and finally my full intention—and that was not realized. I still sweat with anguish—with a sense of irremediable loss—at the thought of what another six months would have done to that book—how much more whole and perfect it would have been. Then there would have been no criticism of its episodic character—for, by God, in purpose and in spirit, that book was not episodic, but a living whole and I could have made it so."

There is certainly the possibility that Wolfe was too competely lost in the deluge of his own memories and words to form them into an intelligent large whole in the years between 1930 and 1935—although his most distinguished short and middle-length fiction was done in this period—and the sometimes violent midwifery of Perkins may have been essential to getting anything publishable from the laboring author. On the other hand, when one examines the first 300 pages of *The Web and the Rock* and recalls that it is Wolfe's own work done without editorial assistance or thinks of the power and directness of the first two books of *You Can't Go Home Again*, it is difficult not to wish that Wolfe had been free to try.

To the imponderable *if's* which haunt the mind in the case of an artist too youthfully dead must be added in Wolfe's case this one: what might his career have been if he had struggled through toward the realization of form without the assistance of Perkins? Certainly if Wolfe had written *Of Time and the River* without Perkins' aid, it would have been a radically different book and possibly a much better one. But he did not, and so the fact remains that only as the lyric recorder of his youth was Wolfe truly successful in the longer fictional forms. His great vision of being the critic of his society and the definer of his nation can be seen in fragments but its large outline is shadowy and incomplete.

It is for this reason that the central problems concerning Wolfe as a writer are as intimately tied up in his personality and his career as they are in his work. Louis D. Rubin, Jr., in an excellent critical study of Wolfe, has asked that the autobiographical quality of the novels be accepted as clear fact and they then be examined as novels, as works of art. When this is done—and Mr. Rubin does it with great skill —*Look Homeward, Angel* emerges as Wolfe's only satisfactory full-length novel, and in his other book-length works one almost has the feeling of an expense of talent in a waste of formlessness. Perhaps such a conclusion is proper—certainly it is the one reached by many of the best and most rigorous of American critics—but it leaves untouched the question of Wolfe's power and the continuing and mounting success which he has with readers.

Wolfe's failure to write his own books as he wanted them written cannot ultimately be laid at any door other than his own. The causes of this failure are complex: they include his own lack of security (his extreme sensitivity to reviews shows that such a lack was there), his desire to achieve publication at whatever cost (there is evidence of this quality in his letters), and a deep-seated affection for Perkins and gratitude to him. As William Faulkner once declared, "The writer's only responsibility is to his art. He will be completely ruthless if he is a good one . . . If a writer has to rob his mother, he will not hesitate." Paradoxically, Thomas Wolfe devoted his life and his energies to the creation of art with a single-mindedness not surpassed in this century—he is almost archetypally the "dedicated writer"—and yet he lacked that ultimate ruthlessness of which Faulkner speaks. For a writer whose talent is of the magnitude of Wolfe's and whose plans have the scope and importance that his do, such a failing cannot be easily brushed aside. On this point he was highly culpable—he did not make the longer forms of fiction, at whatever cost, the adequate vehicles of his vision and his talent; he did not subject his ego to the discipline of his own creative imagination— and the price he has paid for the failure has

been very great indeed. It is the price of being a writer of inspired fragments and of only one satisfying larger work and that an imperfect one.

Here the oppositions in Wolfe reach a crucial test. He seemed always to feel that when the contrasting opposites were defined the synthesis would result automatically; he was always stating a thing and its opposite and allowing the "miracle" of their coexistence to stand. Here in his own work the fact of his great talent and the fact of his ambitious projects were never submitted to the discipline which would have made a synthesis of them; they were allowed to coexist without serious efforts at fusion.

This aspect of Wolfe's work points to its essential romanticism, to the extent to which it is embedded in the doctrine of self-expression and self-realization. Whitman once wrote: " 'Leaves of Grass' . . . has mainly been the outcropping of my own emotional and other personal nature—an attempt, from first to last, to put a *Person* . . . freely, fully and truly on record." This is basically Wolfe's accomplishment, although he was clearly striving toward something else in the last seven years of his life.

Wolfe's work is not, therefore, of primary value as a group of novels, or even in terms of his shadowy larger plan. His total work stands, as do so many other monuments of romantic art, as a group of fragments imperfectly bodying forth a seemingly ineffable cosmic vision in terms of the self of the artist. Although it contains large areas of poor and even bad writing, scenes that do not come off or that bear no relevance to what has gone before, and rhapsodies that fail utterly to communicate, it also contains some of the best writing done by an American in this century, and it merits our thoughtful examination.

The most obvious of Wolfe's strengths is his ability with language. The word has for him unique powers; he was fascinated by language, enchanted with rhythms and cadences, enamored of rhetorical devices. Language was the key he sought to unlock mysteries and to unloose vast forces; he approached it almost in the spirit of primitive magic. This aspect of language he expressed in the paragraph printed as a prologue to *The Web and the Rock*: "Could I make tongue say more than tongue could utter! Could I make brain grasp more than brain could think! Could I weave into immortal denseness some small brede of words, pluck out of sunken depths the roots of living, some hundred thousand magic words that were as great as all my hunger, and hurl the sum of all my living out upon three hundred pages— then death could take my life, for I had lived it ere he took it: I had slain hunger, beaten death!"

Another aspect of his effective use of language is his accurate and vivid dialogue. Wolfe had a remarkable ear for folk speech, and his people speak personal dialects set down with great verisimilitude. His characters sometimes seem to talk forever, but their speech is always marked by distinctiveness in diction, syntax, and cadence. Accuracy, however, is a less obvious quality of their speech than gusto and vigor are. There is a feeling of great energy in the speech of most of them. The clearest example of Wolfe's mastery of the spoken language is to be seen in *The Web of Earth* but it is apparent in almost everything that he wrote.

He declared that he sought a language, an articulation: "I believe with all my heart, also, that each man for himself and in his own way, each man who ever hopes to make a living thing out of the substances of his one life, must find that way, that language, and that door— must find it for himself." He sought this language, this tool of communication, not only in the rolling periods of rhetoric but also in the sensuous image drawn from the "world's body," which is a distinctive aspect of the language of lyric and dramatic writing. And here, in the concrete and particularized representation of the sensory world, he was triumphantly the master. It is Wolfe's ability to evoke the world's body which is responsible for the sense of total reality which his work produces in the young and impressionable, and it is this seeming immersion in the sensuous which makes him sometimes appear to be more the poet of the senses than of sense.

This concern with language, one so great that he might have said of his total work, as Whitman did of *Leaves of Grass*, that it was "only a language experiment," is the logical expression of one of Wolfe's major themes, the loneliness at the core of all human experience. He saw each individual in the world as living in a compartment in isolation from his fellows and unable to communicate adequately with them. It is this tragedy of loneliness that is at the heart of Eugene Gant's experience and makes *Look Homeward, Angel* a book which can appropriately bear the subtitle "A Story of the Buried Life." The desire to break down the walls keeping him from communion with others is at least a part of "man's hunger in his youth," in *Of Time and the River*. The need Wolfe's characters have for a language with which to breach the isolating walls is very great. In a scene in *Of Time and the River*, Helen, Eugene Gant's sister, is lying awake in the darkness: "And suddenly, with a feeling of terrible revelation, she saw the strangeness and mystery of man's life; she felt about her in the darkness the presence of ten thousand people, each lying in his bed, naked and alone, united at the heart of night and darkness, and listening, as she, to the sounds of silence and of sleep. . . . And it seemed to her that if men would only listen in the darkness, and send the language of their naked lonely spirits across the silence of the night, all of the error, falseness and confusion of their lives would vanish, they would no longer be strangers, and each would find the life he sought and never yet had found." There are few lonelier people in fiction than W. O. and Eliza Gant. Each is lost in an envelope of private experience and each tries vainly to express himself—W. O. through rhetoric, invective, alcohol, and lust; Eliza through garrulity, money, and real estate. The terrible incompatibility in which they live reaches its almost shocking climax when, in the last moments of Gant's life, they finally speak across the void to each other, and Gant's expression of kindness dissolves Eliza into tears.

Wolfe described the controlling theme of all his books as "the search for a father"—the theme he said he consciously made central in *Of Time and the River* at Perkins' suggestion. Perkins had intended merely to suggest a type of plot, but Wolfe took the suggestion as a statement of philosophical theme, and he defined that search as a search for certainty, an "image of strength and wisdom external to his [man's] need and superior to his hunger." In one sense, this search is the seeking for an individual with whom communication can be established and maintained. The search grows out of Eugene's loneliness in his childhood and the sense of isolation which he has in his world. It is intensified by his inability to communicate his love to his brother Ben. In his later life, whether for Gant or for George Webber, it finds expression in the relationships established and broken with Francis Starwick, Esther Jack, and Foxhall Edwards, to name only the major figures. About all these relationships there is a recurrent pattern: the new person is approached with eagerness; an intense relationship is established; then a failure of communication and understanding occurs; and Gant-Webber rejects the friendship. The affair with

Esther Jack is, perhaps, the clearest example of this pattern. It is debatable whether the idea of the search for the father, with its suggestion of myth and of fable, defines, as well as does the representation of loneliness the fundamental theme of Thomas Wolfe, whether that loneliness be described as the search for "a stone, a leaf, an unfound door," as the urge to wandering and the counter tug of home (so well articulated in *The Web of Earth* and parts of *Of Time and the River*), or as the desire vicariously to be one with and to understand "ten thousand men" in the cities, the towns, and the hamlets of America.

Here Wolfe's concern with oppositions takes on its tragic overtone. The essentially contradictory aspect of life creates barriers of race, of place, of heritage, of language, and as he portrays these barriers, he tries to lead us to say at the end of the Gant-Webber chronicle, as he says at its beginning: "Naked and alone we came into exile. In her dark womb we did not know our mother's face: from the prison of her flesh have we come into the unspeakable and incommunicable prison of this earth." Thus, as Wolfe sees it, all human experience seeks the "great forgotten language, the lost lane-end into heaven." Certainly, as several critics have pointed out, there are Wordsworthian suggestions here. Out of some transcendent glory of childhood, we gradually are hemmed in by the growing prison house of the world, the luster and glory of life are gradually tarnished, and we are forced further away from communion. But there are also suggestions of a book which Wolfe knew and praised and whose formlessness he defended, Laurence Sterne's *Tristram Shandy*. Sterne's novel is concerned with the education of the young through the impact of the world outside upon the young mind. It is told through the memories in maturity of Tristram, and it is the associational pattern of those memories which determines the form of the book. At the core of *Tristram Shandy* is the tragedy of isolation. W. O. Gant has in one sense a recognizable ancestor in "My Father" Walter Shandy, who sought in vain for a word to communicate with wife and brother. Loneliness, memory, and time are intertwined in the sad comedy of the Shandean world. And so they are in Wolfe's.

For while the Wolfean character cannot find a language through which to speak, cannot break through "the incommunicable prison of this earth," he is the victim of more than silence and the lack of a language—he is also the victim of time. And the entity time is for Wolfe the great factor in life and in his books and the only really serious philosophical concept which he uses in his fiction. One of the structural problems with which he grappled seriously throughout his novelistic career was the finding of a means by which to represent adequately his views of time, which he saw as threefold.

The first and most obvious element of time, he believed, is that of simple chronology, the element that carries a narrative forward; this may be called "clock time." The second element is past time, the "accumulated impact of man's experience so that each moment of their lives was conditioned not only by what they experienced in that moment, but by all that they had experienced up to that moment." This past time exists in the present principally through the action of the memory, being triggered by a concrete sensory impression which in some way recalls the past. However, as Margaret Church has pointed out, memory in Wolfe merely recalls this past; it does not re-create it or actually assert its continued existence, as Bergson's and Proust's theories of time tend to do. All this action—the present and the recollections of the past in the present—takes place against what Wolfe calls "time immutable, the time of rivers, mountains, oceans, and the earth; a kind of eternal and unchanging universe of time against which would be projected the transience of man's life, the bitter briefness of his day." It is this inexorable forward flow of time, pictured as a river or more often as a train, which constantly carries man away from his golden youth, which is "lost and far" and can exist again only in memory. It is Wolfe's repeated representation of his protagonist as a narrator reporting his present emotions as he remembers the past in sensuous detail which, at least in part, creates the nostalgic quality of his writing.

Wolfe's problem was the picturing of scenes so that an awareness of these three elements of time was created. In a given situation a man caught in his particular instant in time has it enriched and rendered more meaningful as the past impinges upon him through memory, and he gets thereby a sense of the absolute time within which his days are painfully brief. Wolfe gives this concept fictional expression in his four-part story "The Lost Boy." In the first part, a boy, Grover, passes an initiation point in life, as his father intercedes for him with a candy store keeper. " 'This is Time,' thought Grover. 'Here is the Square, here is my father's shop, and here am I.' " The second part is the mother's reminiscence years later about Grover on a train trip to the St. Louis Fair. Her monologue ends, "It was so long ago, but when I think of it, it all comes back . . . I can still see Grover just the way he was, the way he looked that morning when we went down through Indiana, by the river, to the Fair." The third part is a monologue by the sister, recounting Grover's death. It ends, "It all comes back as if it happened yesterday. And then it goes away again, and seems farther off and stranger than if it happened in a dream." In the fourth part, the brother, who was a very small boy when Grover died, goes to the house in St. Louis where it happened and tries by the use of memory to bring back the "lost boy." This section ends: "And out of the enchanted wood, that thicket of man's memory, Eugene knew that the dark eye and the quiet face of his friend and brother—poor child, life's stranger, and life's exile, lost like all of us, a cipher in blind mazes, long ago—the lost boy was gone forever, and would not return." The ultimate meaning of the statement "You can't go home again," which Wolfe used over and over in the last year of his life, is to be found here. "Home" is a symbol of the past, of what has been lost; for the holder of a romantic view of childhood, it is a peculiarly effective and revealing symbol. None of us, it says, can return to the lost childhood, the lost community, the fading glory; for time carries us inexorably away. We can't go home again.

In Wolfe's work this vision of time is always associated with the sense of being alone, of being isolated. In *Of Time and the River* he tries to enumerate the concrete memories which taken together make up the remembered past for America, and then he says: "But this was the reason why these things could never be forgotten—because we are so lost, so naked and so lonely in America. Immense and cruel skies bend over us, and all of us are driven on forever and we have no home. Therefore, it is not the slow, the punctual sanded drip of the unnumbered days that we remember best, the ash of time; nor is it the huge monotone of the lost years, the unswerving schedules of the lost life and the well-known faces, that we remember best. It is a face seen once and lost forever in a crowd, an eye that looked, a face that smiled and vanished on a passing train." And a little later, he describes the way in which the past almost forcefully entered the present for him: ". . . always when that lost world would come back, it came at once, like a sword thrust through the entrails, in all its panoply of past time, living, whole, and magic as it had always been." It is like a sword because it cuts

sharply and deeply and hurts very much. Perhaps the one emotion which Wolfe describes most effectively is this pain from which comes the sudden hunger for a lost and almost forgotten aspect of life, for "the apple tree, the singing, and the gold." Wolfe succeeds in giving us this sense of the onward rush of time and the death of the morning's gold, an awareness of the price that is paid before the "years of philosophic calm" can come. Since this feeling is very much a part of youth and its pain and *Weltschmerz*, its inarticulate melancholy, he speaks with peculiar authority to the very young and to those older chiefly through their memories of having been very young.

Wolfe did not theorize about these concepts of time, or, except in passing, discuss them. He probably did not know the works of Proust at all well, despite the degree to which the sense impressions in the present restored the lost past for both of them. Karin Pfister has suggested that Wolfe's time theories may owe something to those of Bergson, to whom Proust was also a debtor. As a novelist Wolfe seemingly was fascinated by the mystery rather than the metaphysics of time. In *The Web and the Rock* he wrote: "Time is a fable and a mystery . . . it broods over all the images of earth . . . Time is collected in great clocks and hung in towers . . . and each man has his own, a different time."

The river and the ocean he used as large symbols for "time immutable," yet his clearest figure for the ceaseless motion and the inexorable passage of time is the train. No American in the past fifty years has been more the poet of trains. Their rushing across the face of the earth, the glimpses of life to be seen flashing past their speeding windows, the nostalgic and lonely wail of their whistles in the night, even their sounds echoing in depots, which in *Of Time and the River* he imagines to be the very sounds of time itself—all these characteristics Wolfe associates with loneliness and movement and the sad passage of time.

Yet in one sense Wolfe's characters transcend his themes. The paradox here is a very great one: Wolfe, who asserted that no man could know his brother, described his fellowmen with deep understanding; Wolfe, whose subject seemed always to be himself, whose characters are drawn in large measure from real life rather than imagined, and who presented his world chiefly through the consciousness of an autobiographical hero, created a group of characters so fully realized that they live with great vigor in the reader's mind. *Look Homeward, Angel* is perhaps the most autobiographical novel ever written by an American, yet the protagonist, Eugene Gant, is a much less vivid person than the members of his family. It is W. O. Gant, Eliza, Helen, and brother Ben who glow with life and absorb our imaginations. Eugene himself is more a "web of sensibility" and a communicating vehicle than a person, or perhaps it is that he seems to us more nearly ourselves and less someone whom we are observing. In *Of Time and the River* the Gant family, Bascom Pentland, Francis Starwick, Abraham Jones, and Ann are more convincingly persons than the hero is. In *The Web and the Rock*, there is less centering in the consciousness of the protagonist and George Webber exists more as an individual than Eugene does. The result is that the other characters of this novel and *You Can't Go Home Again* are seen in relation to the protagonist rather than through him. Yet in these books too Wolfe's gift for creating believable people of unbelievable gusto is very impressive. Certainly among all his memorable creations Esther Jack, Dick Prosser, Nebraska Crane, Judge Rumford Bland, and Foxhall Edwards would stand high.

Wolfe's concentration upon people of excessive vigor may be the result of his vitalism, his worship of life as a pervasive force and a supreme value in itself. Certainly, whether as the result of philosophical attitude or of mere artistic excess, the characters in Wolfe's work loom larger than life and are possessed of an awesome and sometimes awful dynamism. They are large in body, appetite, feeling, disease, and suffering. They crowd the canvas to the exclusion of the background and even of the context of action. Possibly this lack of aesthetic distance, which is one of the most obvious qualities of Wolfe's work, results from his extreme subjectivity, but it is also attributable in part to his view of life. Bella Kussy thinks that the example of vitalism run rampant which Wolfe saw in Nazi Germany cured him, and that the German experience caused his concern in his last years with social rather than personal consequences. The tendency toward social criticism, however, was present in his work some time before he was made shockingly aware of the direction that Nazi Germany was taking.

Among the important influences on the social aspect of Wolfe's work was that of Sinclair Lewis, whose satiric condemnation of materialistic society dedicated to bulk, glitter, and the conscious disregard of beauty made a powerful impact on the younger writer. As early as 1923 Wolfe wrote his mother contemptuously of "those people who shout 'Progress, Progress, Progress'—when what they mean is more Ford automobiles, more Rotary Clubs, more Baptist Ladies Social unions." This attitude is just about the extent of the social criticism in *Look Homeward, Angel,* although it is often expressed in that novel. Wolfe's tendency toward satire is clearly present in the book, but it is satire aimed at Main Street and Booster's Club targets; in the name of beauty it is attacking blatant commercialism and its attendant ugliness.

The years that Wolfe spent in Brooklyn

during the depths of the depression were filled with social lessons for him. "Everywhere around me," he wrote later, "during these years, I saw the evidence of an incalculable ruin and suffering. . . . universal calamity had somehow struck the life of almost every one I knew." He became convinced that something was basically wrong with such a social order. His letters show that he had wanted to make what he and Perkins regarded as a "Marxist" interpretation of the social scene in *Of Time and the River,* although Perkins dissuaded him from doing it. The egalitarianism and the essentially middle-class economic radicalism of his native region reasserted themselves in his thinking during this period, and in *You Can't Go Home Again* they find expression. A sense of primary social injustice in the world is an operative force in Book II, "The World That Jack Built," which was originally published as the short novel *The Party at Jack's* and which contrasts the world of the very wealthy with that of the laboring classes that serve it; in the section "The Hollow Men," dealing with the suicide of C. Green and asserting the primary worth of the individual in a society that would reduce him to a mere statistic; in Book IV, " 'I Have a Thing to Tell You,' " also originally a short novel, with its angry picture of Nazi Germany; and in the revised segments from the short novel "Boom Town," with its satiric pictures of Libya Hill in the grip of the real estate boom and in the disaster of the crash, where ignoble motives of little men play destructively upon the common greed of their fellow citizens.

One of the repeated charges that Wolfe made against Perkins was that he was a "conservative," whereas Wolfe had become what he called a "revolutionary." Yet his social thinking is lacking in depth and significance. Pamela Hansford Johnson is probably too harsh when she says, "His is a young man's

socialism, based on the generous rage, the infuriated baffled pity; like the majority of young, middle-class intellectuals, he looked for 'the people' in the dosshouse and upon the benches of the midnight parks." But, as E. B. Burgum has noted, ". . . he was so constituted that he must fight alone." In that aloneness he was unable to act as a part of any coordinated social scheme. The future of America which he asserts at the conclusion of *You Can't Go Home Again* is really an act of faith—and of a faith still based on the spiritual as opposed to the material, on the reawakening of "our own democracy" within us. Here, as a social critic, he again reminds us most of Whitman. For Whitman in *Democratic Vistas* saw with mounting alarm the pattern that his nation was following and opposed it to the expanding realization of the self, of "Personalism," which it was the poet's program to advance. This is a defensible and even an admirable position, but the work of those who hold it can seldom bear the logical scrutiny of those who espouse specific social programs. As contrasted with Maxwell Perkins, Wolfe properly regarded himself as a "revolutionary," yet he remained the most persuasive advocate of an enlightened middle-class democracy that America has produced in this century.

It was inevitable that the centrality of loneliness and separateness in Wolfe's experience and his writing, coupled with the social problems and the human suffering of the years of his active career, should have fostered in him a sense of evil in the world and have given a tragic quality to his writing. His very method of oppositions would lead him to a Manichaean cosmic view. Furthermore, he was a product of a region steeped in defeat, suffering, and the acceptance of an unthinkable inevitability. As C. Vann Woodward has stated it, "Nothing about [its] history is conducive to the theory that the South was the darling of divine providence." Something of this attitude—which, in Wolfe, E. B. Burgum inaccurately called "reconciliation with despair"—is a part of the heritage of all southerners, even in the liberal areas of the South such as the one in which Wolfe grew up.

Wolfe wrote of the shock he experienced in Brooklyn during the depression at the "black picture of man's inhumanity to his fellow man . . . of suffering, violence, oppression, hunger, cold, and filth and poverty," and added, "And from it all, there has come the final deposit, a burning memory, a certain evidence of the fortitude of man, his ability to suffer and somehow to survive." Loneliness and suffering and pain and death—these are the things which man—frail, weak, hauntingly mortal—can expect. Yet man, for Wolfe, is also a noble creature. The despair of the literary naturalist, so common in America in the twentieth century, is not a part of his thinking. In a too obvious extension of speeches by Hamlet and Jaques, in the twenty-seventh chapter of *You Can't Go Home Again*, Wolfe attempts to answer the question "What is man?" and in his answer states as clearly as he was ever to do the basic contradiction and the tragic magnitude of the earthly experience. Man is "a foul, wretched, abominable creature . . . it is impossible to say the worst of him . . . this travesty of waste and sterile breath." Yet his accomplishments are magnificent. The individual, viewed as physical animal, is a "frail and petty thing who lives his days and dies like all the other animals and is forgotten. And yet, he is immortal, too, for both the good and the evil that he does live after him." In the teeming, uneven pages of Wolfe's work this vision of man possessed of tragic grandeur—essentially the vision of the nineteenth-century Romantic—is presented with great intensity.

Wolfe believed that the American experience demanded a new art form and a new language for the expression of this view, however. Like Whitman, he invited the Muse to "migrate from Greece and Ionia," and

> Making directly for this rendezvous,
>   vigorously clearing a path for herself,
>   striding through the confusion,
> By thud of machinery and shrill
>   steam-whistle undismay'd,
> Bluff'd not a bit by drain-pipe, gasometers,
>   artificial fertilizers,
> Smiling and pleas'd with palpable intent
>   to stay,
> She's here, install'd amid the kitchen ware!

Wolfe wrote: ". . . in the cultures of Europe and of the Orient the American artist can find no antecedent scheme, no structural plan, no body of tradition that can give his own work the validity and truth that it must have. It is not merely that he must make somehow a new tradition for himself, derived from his own life and from the enormous space and energy of American life . . . it is even more than this, that the labor of a complete and whole articulation, the discovery of an entire universe and of a complete language, is the task that lies before him."

In his attempt to accomplish that task Wolfe strove with unceasing diligence. That he failed to realize the full structural plan of his work in the years in which he lived is obvious; that he made no whole articulation of the space and energy of American life is obvious; that he failed to formulate a completely adequate language for the singer of America in fiction is also obvious. What he might have done and even why he did not accomplish more of it become finally unanswerable questions; they tease the mind without enlightening it. We must ultimately accept or reject what he did accomplish.

Wolfe's kind of imagination and his artistic attitudes and methods equipped him well for the depiction of character and the portrayal of action in self-contained but isolated sequences. He seems to have functioned most naturally and best when he was depicting his recollections of individual people and specific actions, when he was making the effort which F. Scott Fitzgerald praised in him and called "the attempt . . . to recapture the exact feel of a moment in time and space, exemplified by people rather than by things . . . an attempt at a mature memory of a deep experience."

Hence he showed a control and an objectivity in his short stories and his short novels that effectively belie the charge of formlessness. Yet his desire to find a new "structural plan" and as a kind of national epic-maker to create the "complete and whole articulation" of America led him to fragment these effective short fictions and use them as portions of the record of the total experience by which his Whitmanesque narrator knows and expresses his native land. He never succeeded completely in this effort, and the result is that the parts of his books are often better than the wholes which they go together to create. Despite his bardic effort and his epic intention, his total work—however flawed, imperfect, fragmentary—is ultimately the record of a self and only very partially that of a nation. Wolfe himself described its strength and suggested its great weakness when he called it "a giant web in which I was caught, the product of my huge inheritance—the torrential recollectiveness, derived out of my mother's stock, which became a living, million-fibered integument that bound me to the past, not only of my own life, but of the very earth from which I came, so that nothing in the end escaped from its inrooted and all-feeling explorativeness." To the end Thomas Wolfe retained a childlike, pristine delight in the manifold shapes, colors, odors, sounds, and textures of experience and his work communicates this delight—shadowed with a nostalgia for things past—with almost total authority.

The measure of this accomplishment is not small. *Look Homeward, Angel* is a richly evocative account of the pains and joys of childhood and youth, peopled with a host of living characters. With all its flaws, it is a fine novel, and one that gives promise of enduring. In Wolfe's total work a personality is set down with a thoroughness and an honesty, with an intensity and a beauty of language unsurpassed by any other American prose writer, even though, aside from *Look Homeward, Angel*, it is only in the short novels that we find really sure artistic control, and sprinkled through the other books are passages of very bad writing and of irrelevant action.

Wolfe began obsessed with paradox and contradiction; the shape of his whole career reflects startling contrast. He who would have written the definition of his nation left primarily the definition of a self; he who would have asserted that though we "are lost here in America . . . we shall be found" was from birth to death a lonely man, vainly seeking communion. He survives—and probably will continue to survive—as the chronicler of a lost childhood, a vanished glory, the portrayer of an individual American outlined, stark and lonely, beneath a cruel sky.

Selected Bibliography

*WORKS OF
THOMAS WOLFE*

Look Homeward, Angel. New York: Scribners, 1929.
Of Time and the River. New York: Scribners, 1935.

From Death to Morning. New York: Scribners, 1935.

The Story of a Novel. New York: Scribners, 1936.

The Web and the Rock. New York: Harper, 1939.

You Can't Go Home Again. New York: Harper, 1940.

The Hills Beyond. New York: Harper, 1941.

Thomas Wolfe's Letters to His Mother Julia Elizabeth Wolfe, edited with an Introduction by John Skally Terry. New York: Scribners, 1943.

Mannerhouse: A Play in a Prologue and Three Acts. New York: Harper, 1948.

A Western Journal. Pittsburgh: University of Pittsburgh Press, 1951.

The Correspondence of Thomas Wolfe and Homer Andrew Watt, edited by Oscar Cargill and Thomas Clark Pollock. New York: New York University Press, 1954.

The Letters of Thomas Wolfe, collected and edited by Elizabeth Nowell. New York: Scribners, 1956.

Welcome to Our City: A 10-Scene Play, Esquire Magazine, 48:58–83 (October 1957).

The Short Novels of Thomas Wolfe, edited with an Introduction and Notes by C. Hugh Holman. New York: Scribners, 1961. (Contains the original versions of *A Portrait of Bascom Hawke, The Web of Earth, No Door,* "*I Have a Thing to Tell You,*" and *The Party at Jack's.*)

Thomas Wolfe's Purdue Speech, edited by William Braswell and Leslie A. Field. Lafayette, Ind.: Purdue University Studies, 1964.

The Letters of Thomas Wolfe to His Mother, newly edited from the original manuscripts by C. Hugh Holman and Sue Fields Ross. Chapel Hill: University of North Carolina Press, 1968.

The Mountains, A Play in One Act; The Mountains, A Drama in Three Acts and a Prologue, edited with an introduction by Pat M. Ryan. Chapel Hill: University of North Carolina Press, 1970.

The Notebooks of Thomas Wolfe, edited by Richard S. Kennedy and Paschal Reeves. Two volumes. Chapel Hill: University of North Carolina Press, 1970.

BOOKS OF SELECTIONS

The Face of a Nation: Poetical Passages from the Writings of Thomas Wolfe, selected by John Hall Wheelock. New York: Scribners, 1939.

A Stone, a Leaf, a Door: Poems by Thomas Wolfe, selected and arranged in verse by John S. Barnes. New York: Scribners, 1945.

The Portable Thomas Wolfe, edited by Maxwell Geismar. New York: Viking, 1946. (Contains *The Story of a Novel,* episodes from each of the novels, and six short stories.)

The Thomas Wolfe Reader, edited with an Introduction and Notes by C. Hugh Holman. New York: Scribners, 1962. (Contains *The Story of a Novel* and selections from all of Wolfe's other books.)

BIBLIOGRAPHIES

Beebe, Maurice, and Leslie A. Field. "Criticism of Thomas Wolfe: A Selected Checklist," *Thomas Wolfe: Three Decades of Criticism,* edited by Leslie A. Field. New York: New York University Press, 1968. Pp. 273–93.

Holman, C. Hugh. "Thomas Wolfe," *Fifteen Modern American Authors: A Survey of Research and Criticism,* edited by Jackson R. Bryer. Durham, N. C.: Duke University Press, 1969. Pp. 425–56.

Johnson, Elmer D. *Thomas Wolfe: A Checklist.* Kent, Ohio: Kent State University Press, 1970.

Kennedy, Richard S. "Thomas Wolfe (1900–1938)," *A Bibliographical Guide to the Study of Southern Literature,* edited by Louis D. Rubin, Jr. Baton Rouge: Louisiana State University Press, 1969. Pp. 328–32.

Preston, George R., Jr. *Thomas Wolfe: A Bibliography.* New York: Charles S. Boesen, 1943.

Reeves, Paschal. *Checklist of Thomas Wolfe.* Columbus, Ohio: Charles E. Merrill, 1969.

CRITICAL AND BIOGRAPHICAL STUDIES

Most of the good critical and biographical essays of less than book length are reprinted in Field, *Thomas Wolfe: Three Decades of Criticism;* Holman, *The World of Thomas Wolfe;* Reeves, *The Merrill Studies in Look Homeward, Angel;* and in Walser, *The Enigma of Thomas Wolfe.* This listing is confined to these and other book-length works.

Adams, Agatha Boyd. *Thomas Wolfe: Carolina Student*. Chapel Hill: University of North Carolina Library, 1950.

Austin, Neal F. *A Biography of Thomas Wolfe*. Austin, Texas: Roger Beacham, 1968. [For teenagers.]

Beach, Joseph Warren. *American Fiction: 1920–1940*. New York: Macmillan, 1941. Pp. 173–215.

Champion, Myra. *The Lost World of Thomas Wolfe*. Asheville, N. C.: Thomas Wolfe Memorial, 1970. [Photographs of Asheville and quotations from *Look Homeward, Angel*.]

Daniels, Jonathan. *Thomas Wolfe: October Recollections*. Columbia, S.C.: Bostick and Thornley, 1961.

Delakas, Daniel L. *Thomas Wolfe, la France, et les romanciers français*. Paris: Jouve & Cie., 1950.

Field, Leslie A., ed. *Thomas Wolfe: Three Decades of Criticism*. New York: New York University Press, 1968. [Selected essays.]

Geismar, Maxwell. *Writers in Crisis*. Boston: Houghton Mifflin, 1942. Pp. 185–236.

Helmcke, Hans. *Die Familie im Romanwerk von Thomas Wolfe*. Heidelberg: Carl Winter, 1967.

Holman, C. Hugh. *Three Modes of Modern Southern Fiction: Ellen Glasgow, William Faulkner, Thomas Wolfe*. Athens: University of Georgia Press, 1966.

————, ed. *The World of Thomas Wolfe*. New York: Scribners, 1962. [Selected essays.]

Johnson, Pamela Hansford. *The Art of Thomas Wolfe*. New York: Scribners, 1963. (A reprint of *Hungry Gulliver* [New York: Scribners, 1948], which was an American edition of *Thomas Wolfe: A Critical Study* [London: William Heinemann, 1947].)

Kennedy, Richard S. *The Window of Memory: The Literary Career of Thomas Wolfe*. Chapel Hill: University of North Carolina Press, 1962.

McElderry, B. R., Jr. *Thomas Wolfe*. New York: Twayne, 1964.

Muller, Herbert J. *Thomas Wolfe*. Norfolk, Conn.: New Directions, 1947.

Norwood, Hayden. *The Marble Man's Wife: Thomas Wolfe's Mother*. New York: Scribners, 1947.

Nowell, Elizabeth. *Thomas Wolfe: A Biography*. Garden City, N.Y.: Doubleday, 1960.

Payne, Ladell. *Thomas Wolfe*. Austin, Texas: Steck-Vaughn Co., 1969.

Pfister, Karin. *Zeit und Wirklichkeit bei Thomas Wolfe*. Heidelberg: Carl Winter, 1954.

Pollock, Thomas Clark, and Oscar Cargill. *Thomas Wolfe at Washington Square*. New York: New York University Press, 1954.

Raynolds, Robert. *Thomas Wolfe: Memoir of a Friendship*. Austin: University of Texas, 1965.

Reeves, George M., Jr. *Thomas Wolfe et Europe*. Paris: Librairie Marcel Didier, 1955.

Reeves, Paschal, ed. *The Merrill Studies in Look Homeward, Angel*. Columbus, Ohio: Charles E. Merrill, 1970.

————. *Thomas Wolfe's Albatross: Race and Nationality in America*. Athens: University of Georgia Press, 1968.

————, ed. *Thomas Wolfe and the Glass of Time*. Athens: University of Georgia Press, 1971.

Rubin, Louis D., Jr. *Thomas Wolfe: The Weather of His Youth*. Baton Rouge: Louisiana State University Press, 1955.

————. *The Faraway Country*. Seattle: University of Washington Press, 1963. Pp. 72–104.

Snyder, William U. *Thomas Wolfe: Ulysses and Narcissus*. Athens: Ohio University Press, 1971. [Psychological study.]

Thomas Wolfe Special Number. *Modern Fiction Studies*, 11:219–328 (Autumn 1965).

Turnbull, Andrew. *Thomas Wolfe*. New York: Scribners, 1967.

Walser, Richard. *Thomas Wolfe: An Introduction and Interpretation*. New York: Barnes and Noble, 1961.

————, ed. *The Enigma of Thomas Wolfe: Biographical and Critical Selections*. Cambridge, Mass.: Harvard University Press, 1953.

Watkins, Floyd C. *Thomas Wolfe's Characters: Portraits from Life*. Norman: University of Oklahoma Press, 1957.

Wheaton, Mabel Wolfe, and LeGette Blythe. *Thomas Wolfe and His Family*. Garden City, N.Y.: Doubleday, 1961.

—C. HUGH HOLMAN

Richard Wright

1908-1960

RICHARD WRIGHT was born in 1908 on a cotton plantation not far from Natchez, Mississippi. His father was a sharecropper, a man of casual affections who deserted wife and family when Wright was only five. His mother struggled ineffectively as cook or housemaid to raise two growing boys. When Wright was ten or twelve she suffered a series of paralytic strokes. Her chronic illness set the emotional tone of his life and imbued his writing with a somber cast. Anguish is Wright's characteristic note; four of his epigraphs are taken from the Book of Job.

Hunger and violence were his family heirlooms. A hunger that dominates his childhood memories; that aroused a deep, biological bitterness; that drew him to the ranks of the Communist party, and left him with an enduring sympathy for the dispossessed. And a violence, inflicted by his immediate family, but stemming from the larger violence of southern life. Surrounded by a latent terror, which might be called forth by any act of self-assertion, the Negro family tried to beat the dangerous assertiveness out of its wayward members. Never lacking in waywardness, Wright was severely beaten, his spirit branded with the images of violence that crowd the pages of his fiction.

Wright's rebellious tendencies were reinforced by an early exposure to Seventh-Day Adventism. His grandmother's household, where he spent a crucial portion of his childhood, was pervaded by a stern evangelism. Half a dozen daily prayers were supplemented by all-night revival meetings. Dietary restrictions further reduced an already meager food supply. Boyish recreations such as baseball and marbles were forbidden. Books on nonreligious subjects were proscribed as "the Devil's work." This pious woman, in short, tried by every stratagem to save her grandson from the world. Wright's response, in his mature years, was to embrace a humanist philosophy, militantly secular and implacably hostile to any brand of otherworldliness.

Wright's boyhood was too turbulent to permit of much formal schooling. Shunted back and forth among his mother's relatives, moving constantly from one southern town to the next, he was seldom able to complete a year of unbroken study. At the age of sixteen he graduated from the ninth grade, without having undertaken anything that might be called a high-school education. This lack of formal study, which Wright shares with an earlier generation of American naturalists, cannot be ignored in any just appraisal of his work. If it compels a tribute to his raw power, it explains a persistent awkwardness that mars all but his finest efforts.

Against heavy odds, and on rations as slender as his daily plate of greens, Wright's imagination flickered into life. Sunday supplements, cheap pulp tales, and vivid country sermons fed the flame. During an enforced hour of prayer the lonely boy amused himself by writing poetry and fiction. At the age of fifteen he published a story in the local Negro press. Such ambitions in a black boy were a challenge and affront to the southern way of life. In them may be found the seeds of Wright's conflict with the white South.

Richard Wright grew to manhood in the afterglow of human slavery. A generation from absolute power, the whites were determined to restore their traditional prerogatives. A generation from the auction block, the blacks clung for protection to their ancient, servile ways. Wright wanted no part of this accommodation. His insistence on behaving like a man, his stubborn refusal to know his place, and above all his expanding sensibility brought him into deadly conflict with the closed society. Knowing that his life depended on it, in his seventeenth year he fled to Memphis, Tennessee, the first stop on his northern journey.

It was in Memphis that his intellectual awakening occurred. Having read in the local press an editorial attacking H. L. Mencken, he resolved to examine for himself the writings of a man who could so enrage the southern whites. Barred from access to the public library, he finessed the Jim Crow laws by forging a note: "Dear Madam: Will you please let this nigger boy have some books by H. L. Mencken?" Mencken's essays were the gateway to a new world. What appealed to Wright was the man's irreverence, his open mockery of human and divine authority. Mencken was

his introduction to the modern temper; his link to the muckraking spirit and the naturalist tradition; his preparation for the fiction of Sinclair Lewis, Theodore Dreiser, and Stephen Crane.

In the winter of 1927 Wright and his family migrated to Chicago, the city where he was to pass the next decade of his life. For several hard-pressed years he worked as porter, dishwasher, part-time postal clerk, life-insurance salesman. During the depression he suffered the humiliations of unemployment and relief. At one point a relief agency placed him in the South Side Boys' Club, where he met the living models from whom he was to sketch Bigger Thomas. In the end he found a refuge, like many writers of his generation, preparing guidebooks for the Federal Writers' Project.

Chicago captured Wright's imagination. He responded to its massive scale and quickened tempo, its toughness, vitality, and raw beauty. A newcomer to the urban scene, he sought to understand the social transformation in which he was caught up, to gain perspective on his life experience. He turned at first to social science: "The huge mountains of fact piled up by the Department of Sociology at the University of Chicago gave me my first concrete vision of the forces that molded the urban Negro's body and soul."

Social science became a permanent feature of Wright's world view. From the work of Robert Park, Robert Redfield, and Louis Wirth, he absorbed the concepts of industrialization, secularization, urbanization, and social class. From Horace Cayton he absorbed the social science ethos, with its emphasis on field study, statistical methods, and empirical research. Wright acknowledges his debt to the social sciences in his introduction to *Black Metropolis,* a monumental study of the South Side ghetto by Cayton and St. Clair Drake.

Wright's second attempt to achieve perspective led him to contemplate the October Revolution. Had the Bolsheviks not organized an inert peasant mass into an effective instrument of social change? Were they not transforming a static, tradition-bound, and absolutist feudal order—not unlike rural Mississippi—into a modern industrial society? And was the capitalist order not visibly disintegrating in 1932? A revolutionary movement that promised to organize the outcast and rejected; that provided outlets for rebelliousness and thwarted self-expression; that countered loneliness with fraternity, and self-hatred with a universal vision: this was irresistible.

Wright joined the Communist party in 1932 and maintained his membership for twelve years. In Chicago he was executive secretary of the local John Reed Club and an activist in his South Side party cell. In New York he was Harlem editor of the *Daily Worker,* a member of the executive board of the League of American Writers, and a vice-president of American Peace Mobilization. At the same time, inclined by nature to a crusty individualism, he chafed under party discipline, resented interference with his writing, and was repelled by the atmosphere of paranoia that prevailed during the Stalin era. These disaffections led to his expulsion in 1944.

Richard Wright served his literary apprenticeship under the tutelage of the Communist party. As a member of the John Reed Club, he contributed poetry and fiction to *Left Front, Anvil,* and *New Masses.* As a party activist, he· acquired a variety of journalistic and editorial skills. His party contacts, moreover, were a source of material for his first book. In his South Side unit Wright met a Negro Communist whose early life in Mississippi inspired him to attempt a series of novellas. These stories won first prize in a competition among WPA writers. They were published in 1938 under the title *Uncle Tom's Children.*

Wright moved from Chicago to New York in 1937. Ten years later, he became a permanent expatriate in Paris. During most of the intervening decade he lived in Brooklyn or in Greenwich Village. These were the years of Wright's most enduring literary work. They witnessed the publication of his first four books and the establishment of his worldwide reputation. They were also the years of an ill-fated first marriage, and of an enduring union with Ellen Poplar, a Brooklyn girl of Jewish antecedents. Two daughters were born of this union.

New York did not engage the deepest layers of Wright's imagination. It is at most, in his later fiction, a thinly painted backdrop for some drama of the soul. The city served him rather as a vantage point from which to view the past. These were retrospective years, in which Wright attempted to assimilate the traumas of his youth and early manhood and impose on this material a literary form. He became, in the process, consciously concerned with matters of technique. Searching for clues among the masters, he ransacked the letters of Dostoevski, the prefaces of Conrad and of Henry James. His reward was the triumph of his first novel.

Published in the spring of 1940, *Native Son* was an instantaneous success. A best seller and Book-of-the-Month Club selection, it was subsequently adapted for the stage by Orson Welles and for the cinema by Wright himself. After years of personal hardship Wright's career was launched: serious attention, financial independence, and professional status were assured. At the same time, *Native Son* was a major breakthrough for the Negro writer. With one powerful thrust, Wright had breached the ghetto walls. He had gained a hearing, claimed a territory, challenged the conscience of a nation. In recognition of this achievement, he was awarded the coveted Spingarn Medal by the National Association for the Advancement of Colored People.

Wright's third book, *Twelve Million Black Voices,* appeared in 1941. Conceived as a folk history of the American Negro, the book consists of photographs by Edwin Rosskam and a text by Richard Wright. This was followed in 1945 by *Black Boy,* whose sales exceeded even those of *Native Son.* It is Wright's best book. By virtue of its depth of feeling, its sustained dramatic power, its relentless unmasking of the self, and still more naked exposure of the social order, *Black Boy* is an American classic.

Black Boy was followed by a long period of public silence. It was a time of introspection, of honest effort to replace the god that failed. When Wright resumed his career in the 1950's he was working in a different vein. But the Richard Wright of *Native Son* and *Black Boy* had become a culture hero. He inspired a host of imitators, both novelists and poets, who flourished in the postwar years. No Negro writer was entirely immune from Wright's influence. Even the most original of his contemporaries were forced to reckon with his presence and somehow circumvent it, in order to protect their own careers.

Some months after the liberation of Paris, Gertrude Stein published an account of the Nazi occupation called *Wars I Have Seen.* The book was reviewed by Richard Wright in the pages of *PM.* Pleased by the review, Miss Stein initiated a correspondence, in the course of which Wright expressed a desire to visit France. The upshot was a formal invitation, issued by the French government over the signatures of France's most distinguished men of letters. In the spring of 1946, when the Wrights arrived in Paris, Gertrude Stein helped them to arrange for housing and introduced them to her circle of Parisian friends.

In spite of a growing affection for Paris, the Wrights did not decide at once to emigrate. After a pleasant sojourn of six months they returned to New York with every intention of resuming their accustomed lives. They had not reckoned with the strength of Wright's expatriate impulse. He embarked once more for Paris in the summer of 1947 and remained until his death in 1960. His principal residence, during these final years of exile, was a spacious apartment in the rue Monsieur le Prince, adjacent to the Jardin du Luxembourg. In 1956 he bought a country house in Normandy, near the village of Ailly, where he retired to write or, confessing to his friends that he was still a country boy, to grow potatoes, corn, and collard greens.

Throughout his Paris years Wright enjoyed the status of an *homme célèbre.* He was invited to lecture in the major European capitals, was widely quoted in the press, and made frequent guest appearances on radio and television. His private life was invaded by a constant stream of visitors to his Left Bank apartment. African diplomats, Parisian intellectuals, eminent American Negroes, writers of international repute, luminaries of the democratic left, were among his honored guests. Foremost among these personages, in terms of their influence on Wright's work, was the group of French existentialists which included Jean-Paul Sartre and Simone de Beauvoir.

What attracted Wright to existentialism was its tendency to make a virtue out of rootlessness, to conceive of the human condition as a kind of cosmic exile. Himself an exile, twice removed from Mississippi soil, he responded by exulting in his fate, by glorifying heroes who are cut off from the past and dependent on the self alone. Wright explores these themes in three novels: *The Outsider* (1953), *Savage Holiday* (1954), and *The Long Dream* (1958). The novels are intended as a celebration of the rootlessness of modern man. Unhappily, for reasons that have everything to do with rootlessness, the fiction of the fifties is a travesty of Wright's best work.

Meanwhile, in the decade following World War II, a series of colonial wars and revolutions shook the foundations of European empire. With the defeat or withdrawal of imperialist power, nation after new nation emerged in Africa and Asia. Fascinated by this confrontation of a civilization and its former subject peoples, Wright determined to witness it at first hand. He traveled to Ghana in 1953, to Indonesia in 1955, and, by way of contrast, to Spain in 1954. Each journey produced a book: *Black Power* (1954), *The Color Curtain* 1956), and *Pagan Spain* (1957). To these must be added *White Man, Listen!* (1957), a summary statement of Wright's concern with the colonial revolution.

Richard Wright died of a heart attack in 1960 at the age of fifty-two. He had published eleven books in the course of a short lifetime. Two more were brought out by the Wright estate. One of these, *Lawd Today* (1963), adds nothing to his reputation. It is an apprentice novel, written during his Chicago years and dealing with the sordid milieu of a Negro postal clerk. The other, *Eight Men* (1961), is a collection of short stories, written at various stages of Wright's career. Uneven, badly edited, and containing only two unpublished stories, the book does serve to rescue from oblivion some of Wright's most impressive fiction.

The life of Richard Wright unfolded in progressive stages. Mississippi, Chicago, New York, Paris: these were the milestones of a picaresque journey. Moving instinctively toward greater freedom, wider horizons, more cosmopolitan perspectives, Wright attempted to transcend the narrow and the local, the pinched and straitened outlook of the tribal soul. His life was a persistent quest for meaning: of the South, of industrial America, ultimately of the Western world. To share with others a liberating knowledge of the white man's ways is the motivating force of his career. To this end he invades the silent places of the human heart and bruits his discoveries to the world.

We turn now to the tasks of literary criticism: the exposition of principal themes and the evaluation of individual works. Richard Wright's output is readily divided into two periods. The first encompasses the writing done in the United States, roughly from 1935 to 1945; the second, the writing done in France, roughly from 1950 to 1960. These two productive decades, separated by a period of personal and political crisis, are quite distinct in subject matter and philosophic ambience.

Wright's early subject is the Great Migration: that vast demographic shift of the Negro population from rural South to urban North. His most explicit treatment of the subject is the documentary study *Twelve Million Black Voices*. This book, which remains a useful summary of Negro folk experience, forms the programmatic basis of Wright's American period. Thus *Uncle Tom's Children* and *Black Boy* are set in rural Mississippi. They deal with the conditions of injustice and oppression which motivate the Great Migration. *Lawd Today* and *Native Son* are set in metropolitan Chicago and are concerned with the Negro migrant's adjustment to the urban scene.

From a literary point of view, which of Wright's early works are likely to endure?

Surely *Black Boy,* his solid contribution to the art of autobiography. Surely *Native Son,* his most successful full-length novel. And surely "The Man Who Lived Underground," that remarkable novella which explores the innermost recesses of the black man's soul. It is to these three works that we must turn to discover the central thrust of Wright's imagination.

Black Boy forces us, in the first instance, to imagine southern life from a Negro point of view. What we discover from this harrowing perspective is that the entire society is mobilized to keep the Negro in his place: to restrict his freedom of movement, discourage his ambition, and banish him forever to the nether regions of subordination and inferiority. This attempt to mark off in advance the boundaries of human life is Wright's essential theme. "The white South said that I had a 'place' in life. Well, I had never felt my 'place'; or, rather, my deepest instincts had always made me reject the 'place' to which the white South had assigned me."

The spiritual deprivations suffered under such a system are embedded in the language of the book. Wright describes himself as trapped, imprisoned, stifled, stunted, curbed, condemned. At the most elementary levels of human existence he is forbidden to touch, to look, to speak, to eat, to play, to read, to be curious, to dream, aspire, expand, or grow. Ringed about with prohibitions and taboos, he is denied access to experience, the catalyst of spiritual growth. Assigned by tradition to a demeaning role, he is deprived of possibility, of what he might become. Defined by others, and manipulated by means of these twisted definitions, he is robbed of personality, identity, a sense of self.

Wright's response to the straitened circumstances of his life was implacable rebellion. The more his society insisted on setting arti-ficial bounds to his experience, the greater his compulsion to trespass, to taste forbidden fruit. The more his society conspired against his human weight and presence, the more determined he became to assert himself, to compel the recognition of his individuality. Hence his urge to write, which was born of a fierce desire to affirm his own reality. What obsessed him was a fear of nothingness, of becoming in the end what the white South proclaimed him to be: a non-man.

The linguistic equivalent of nothingness is silence. Throughout *Black Boy* we can observe Wright's obsessive fear of speechlessness: "I was frightened speechless"; "I wanted to speak, but I could not move my tongue." Southern Negroes are forced to accommodate their speech habits to the expectations of the whites. To be "sassy," after all, is to be *outspoken.* But Wright could never master the language of self-effacement. His career as a writer was in fact a rejoinder to the repression of Negro speech. To speak out at all costs; to refuse to be intimidated into silence: this is the force behind the stridency and clamor of his prose.

Wright's literary aspirations were profoundly subversive of his social order. "My environment," he observes, "contained nothing more alien than writing or the desire to express one's self in writing." Nor was this a matter primarily of race. In traditional societies, sensibility itself is regarded with suspicion. Truth and wisdom are thought to be transmitted from the past, rather than discovered by the exploring self. *Black Boy* may thus be read as a drama of sensibility, in which the individual perceptions of the artist-hero are pitted against the inherited codes and a priori judgments of a closed society.

A closed society and a quest for self-realization: these are the preconditions of the picaresque. The form appeared in European letters toward the end of the feudal and beginning of the bourgeois epoch. It reflects the breakdown of static social relations and their replacement by more fluid forms. The picaresque tradition, with its thrust toward a greater personal and social freedom, is readily adapted to the needs of the black writer.

The picaresque hero is a rootless man, a wanderer. No longer an organic part of a stable social order, he undertakes a symbolic journey, whose aim is the emancipation of the self. On the open road, he has a series of adventures which test his capacity for improvisation. Living by his wits, he often employs questionable methods. If he is something of a rogue and mischief maker, it is because his energies cannot be absorbed within the legal order. His society is closed against him; it drives him out; it threatens him with spiritual death. To survive he becomes a hustler, a confidence man, an outlaw, a criminal.

Black Boy conforms in all essentials to the pattern of the picaresque. The book consists of a series of encounters with the closed society which lead to an overwhelming conclusion: flight. The last five chapters are devoted to the early stages of the author's northern journey. This symbolic journey, moreover, is crime-tinged. In order to finance his flight to Memphis, Wright turns to petty crime. He begins by selling bootleg liquor to white prostitutes, proceeds to a complicated ticket swindle at a local movie house, and ends by stealing cans of fruit preserves from the commissary of a Negro college.

Wright insists upon his criminality, for it reveals the hidden meaning of his life. At the same time, he insists on his essential innocence. The explanation of this paradox lies in the domain of the picaresque. What motivates the rogue-hero, what pushes him beyond the pale, is a disillusioning encounter with *legal wrong*: "I had now seen at close quarters the haughty white men who made the laws; I had seen how they acted, how they regarded black people, how they regarded me; and I no longer felt bound by the laws which black and white were supposed to obey in common. I was outside those laws; the white people had told me so."

This sense of being outside or above the law is characteristic of Wright's fictional heroes. Typically they are innocent outlaws, ethical criminals, who murder with a deep conviction of their own blamelessness. Despite the horror of their crimes, they can never muster a convincing show of remorse. In effect, Wright claims immunity from ordinary standards of justice and morality. Whatever the philosophical validity of such a claim, its emotional source is plainly Wright's experience as a Negro in the deep South. The ultimate crime, for which he cannot bring himself to acknowledge any guilt, but for which he knows that he will nonetheless be punished, is the crime of being black.

The secondary theme of *Black Boy* is Wright's emphatic rejection of southern Negro values. A stubborn individualism was the basis of this conflict. For the ethos of the black South, conditioned by generations of slavery, was pre-individualistic. Instinctively the black community sought to suppress individuality, discourage competition, and restrain aggressiveness. Insofar as the black South opposed his efforts at self-realization, Wright did not hesitate to attack its value system. Like Huck Finn, who fled as much from Pap as from the Widow Douglas, he was forced to number his own kin among his enemies.

Wright's estrangement from communal values can be traced to his affiliation with Seventh-Day Adventism. To keep the Sabbath on Saturday, after all, is a deeply divisive ritual in a community of Methodists and Baptists. When his mother, hoping to reduce the boy's sense of being different, brought him to a

Methodist Sunday school, it was already too late: "I had been kept out of their world too long ever to be able to become a real part of it." This sense of not belonging would persist throughout Wright's career. He remained an outsider, a solitary artist whose supreme value was not the welfare of the group but the realization of the self.

Of all the communal rituals demanded of a Negro adolescent, none was more compelling than church membership. This was the supreme test of racial loyalty: "We young men had been trapped by the community, the tribe in which we lived and of which we were a part. The tribe, for its own safety, was asking us to be at one with it." Wright would never give the sign of allegiance. With all his being he resisted the tribal spirit. A certain independence and aloofness, a firm rejection of nationalism and negritude, an insistence on broader loyalties than race, would be characteristic of his life and art.

What alienated Wright above all from the black community was the southern Negro's complicity in his own abasement. Thus the boy's symbolic confrontation with his Uncle Tom, who undertakes to teach him with a hickory switch "to grin, hang my head, and mumble apologetically when I was spoken to." The Negro family, hoping to protect the child from violent reprisal, agrees to serve as a surrogate of the white power structure. To be an Uncle Tom, in short, is to enforce the white man's discipline against your own.

But still more shameful is the effort to enforce that discipline against the self; still more sinister the Uncle Tom within. Wright marvels at the willingness of southern Negroes to police themselves; to curb their natural impulses, their speech and gestures, aspirations, hopes, and dreams. Here is the ultimate betrayal: the collusion of the self in its own annihilation.

The archetype of self-annihilation is the Sambo figure, the Negro who approximates in his behavior the clownish role assigned him by the whites. This figure appears in *Black Boy* in the episode of Shorty, the elevator boy who invites a white man to kick him for a quarter. We shall encounter this symbolic clown elsewhere in the Wright canon, notably in *The Outsider*. For the moment it will suffice to recognize in Shorty a symbol of psychic nothingness. This is the inauthentic self that Wright repudiates, the role that he would rather die than play, the void from which he flees in order to establish an identity.

Wright's response to the self-limiting tendencies in Negro life was a profound disgust. That disgust, so perilously close to self-hatred, was scarcely to be acknowledged by the conscious self. Yet it forms the basis, in Wright's fiction, for his uncomplimentary images of Negro life. On the intellectual plane, it leads him consistently to underestimate his Negro heritage. In a famous passage in *Black Boy*, too long to quote, he deplores the bleakness and barrenness of Negro culture. This mistaken judgment, which tempted him to flee rather than explore the Negro past, has had disastrous consequences for his art.

That art, at its most robust, is to be found in *Black Boy*. Most of Wright's work is seriously flawed, marred by a tendency to preach and editorialize. The long courtroom speech in *Native Son* is only the most regrettable instance of this fault. In *Black Boy*, however, Wright entrusts his meaning entirely to his images. The didactic tendency is suppressed, and the narrative element allowed to speak for itself. The result is writing of unusual imaginative force.

The artistic strength of *Black Boy* lies in its power to evoke the spiritual realities of southern Negro life by means of parable. The structure of the book, deriving from the tradition of the picaresque, consists of a series of dramatic episodes. Each episode, moreover, is parabolic: it comes to stand for something larger than itself. Thus we have parables of blasted hope, inauthentic selfhood, social stagnation, embattled individuality. Toward the end these parables coalesce into a single vision. They are seen to represent the options of the artist-hero. He must choose between the terrible alternatives of martyrdom or exile.

Black Boy is at bottom a parable of extrication. Its theme is the judgment and rejection of a narrow world. The nature of that world is hinted at in Wright's explicit tribute to H. L. Mencken. The American South, after all, is a part of the Bible Belt, a stronghold of rural fundamentalism. Like Mencken, Dreiser, Anderson, and Lewis, Wright felt compelled to disengage his sensibility from the stifling atmosphere of a provincial, puritanical, and philistine America. This is Wright's American tradition: the revolt from the village. That his village is southern rather than midwestern simply adds a racial dimension to a fundamental impulse toward cultural freedom.

Native Son appeared in 1940, five years in advance of *Black Boy*. Wright had not yet fully plumbed the meaning of his Mississippi youth, and the outlaw bent of his imagination had not yet found its proper form. Nonetheless, the pattern of the picaresque is plainly visible in *Native Son*. Here the closed society is the northern ghetto, but it is equally restrictive of Negro life. The symbolic journey is internalized: it is not so much geographical as spiritual or moral. Instead of flight from an oppressive social order we have an open foray into criminality.

Book I presents a northern version of the closed society. In a crucial episode Bigger Thomas and his gang are "playing white." To amuse themselves they assume the roles of generals, financial magnates, and government officials. Barred in real life from the military, industrial, or political hierarchies, their fantasy dwells on these forbidden roles. The limits and restrictions that push them toward a social marginality are deeply resented by Bigger and his friends: "We blacks and they white. They got things and we ain't. They do things and we can't. It's just like living in jail. Half the time I feel like I'm on the outside of the world peeping in through a knot-hole in the fence."

What is missing in Bigger's world is the element of exploit or heroic action. Yet if all legitimate outlets for exploit and adventure are closed to him, the black man will assert his claim to heroism through extralegal means. That is the symbolism of Bigger's name: he aspires to action on the epic plane; he seeks a challenge worthy of his manhood; he insists on something "bigger" than the cramped horizons of ghetto life. The central irony of *Native Son* is that he can find a larger and more meaningful existence only through violence and crime.

Bigger's murder of a white girl, Mary Dalton, is philosophical in motive. All his life he has been treated like a cipher, made to feel his nothingness. Reduced to a shadowy presence in the white man's mind, he has been drained of all substantiality. Bigger murders in order to become real, to make the white world acknowledge his existence. The whites conspire to ignore his human presence. Very well, then: let them ignore the presence of a white corpse! It is an act of metaphysical reprisal. If the white world *blots out* his reality, he will blot out the reality of the white world.

Book II develops Bigger as an outlaw hero. In the fiery crucible of crime he discovers a new sense of purpose and a new freedom of action. As a murderer he acquires a new conviction of his own worth, even his superiority. The people around him seem blinded by illusion, by conventional notions of reality, but Bigger has experienced a form of transcendence. He has moved beyond the law, beyond convention, beyond good and evil, and he is now able to see beyond the surfaces of things. His sudden release from the invisible forces that oppress him propels him toward a deeper vision of reality.

Bigger's heightened powers are displayed in the episode of the kidnap note. He emerges as a kind of artist, creating fictive worlds, inventing scenarios, manipulating others as he himself was formerly manipulated. He combines, in short, those qualities of creativity and illegality that are typical of the picaresque hero. For the creative impulse, denied legitimate expression, will seek an antisocial outlet. In Bigger's case, the result is an inspired criminality; in Wright's, a revolutionary art.

Book III is a quest for values. As Bigger faces death in the electric chair he seeks desperately for something to believe in, something that will give his life, and therefore death, a meaning. Traditional religious values no longer can sustain him. An old preacher visits Bigger's cell to comfort him. In praying for his soul he summons "images which had once given him a reason for living, had explained the world." But Bigger emphatically repudiates his ministry.

The visit of the old preacher is followed by that of the young Communist, Jan Erlone. Jan is the apostle of a secular religion, and together with the lawyer, Max, he represents an alternative to Christian values, a new evangelism capable of explaining the world. Jan and Max offer Bigger a vision of human fraternity from which no one is excluded on grounds of race. But Bigger rejects their vision as inauthentic, false to his experience. The political commitment that saved Wright from nothingness is not available to Bigger. He is thrown back on himself and what he has become.

The novel moves, in its denouement, toward values that we have learned to recognize as existentialist. Having rejected Christianity and Communism Bigger finds the strength to die in the courageous acceptance of his existential self: "What I killed for, I *am*!" In embracing his own murderous instincts, however, Wright's hero is compelled to sacrifice other and perhaps more basic values. He has established an identity through murder, but that identity, by virtue of its horror, has cut him off from the human community of which he longs to be a part. That is the meaning of Max's profound revulsion in the final scene.

The triumph of authenticity, in short, is offset by the defeat of love. For beneath Bigger's posture of defiance is a desperate craving to be loved. What he has hoped for all along from those who have rejected him is some gesture of affection, some mutual exchange if not of love at least of recognition. Now these hopes are doomed. In accepting the brand of Cain he confirms his outcast state. The novel thus concludes on an unresolved chord. Bigger achieves a partial affirmation, but only at the expense of his deepest needs.

As a work of art *Native Son* is seriously flawed. The first two books are solidly designed and fully realized, but in Book III Wright has allowed his statement as a Communist to overwhelm his statement as an artist. Plot dissolves into improbability as fictional events are manipulated to score propaganda points. Characterization descends to caricature, and Bigger alone persuades us of his authenticity. Stylistically there is a sharp decline, all the more surprising after the sure control of Books I and II. Capping these disasters is the long speech of Bigger's lawyer, who is at once a mouthpiece for the author and a spokesman for the party line.

Beyond the obvious flaws of agitprop there is a philosophical confusion at the heart of *Native Son*. As a naturalist, an amateur social scientist, and a Communist, Wright is committed to the concept of determinism. His approach to Bigger's crime, for example, is environmentalist: "Men like you made him what he is." That is the entire burden of the lawyer's speech, and its purpose is to minimize the element of choice in Bigger's criminal behavior. It is a question of conditioning, of automatic reflexes. Bigger's actions are presented as inevitable, compulsive, beyond conscious control or, in a word, unfree.

At the same time Wright is moving toward a concept of existential freedom. As we have seen, the picaresque hero journeys toward the realm of possibility, and away from the tyranny of predetermined forms. The object of his quest is an unprecedented freedom of action, though he turn outlaw to achieve it. Thus with Wright's hero, who attains the desired degree of indeterminacy through murder: "Bigger had murdered and created a new life for himself." Such a concept must bring into play the elements of decision, purpose, choice, and moral agency. The emphasis is on the creative act, which by definition cannot be unfree.

The language of the novel reflects the author's philosophical confusion. For each of his perspectives Wright employs a distinct rhetorical style. On occasion the two rhetorics collide: "The actions that resulted in the death of those two women were as instinctive and inevitable as breathing or blinking one's eyes. It was an act of *creation*!" But murder is either inevitable or creative. Only by conjuring trick, by a rigorous separation of Bigger No. 1 from Bigger No. 2 can Wright maintain the semblance of novelistic unity.

Two philosophical perspectives and two literary traditions meet and clash in *Native Son*. The one stems from Dreiser, and more precisely *An American Tragedy*; the other from Dostoevski, and particularly *Crime and Punishment*. Dreiser appealed to Wright's rationalist side; Dostoevski to his demonic urges. At this stage of his career he was under the illusion that Clyde Griffiths and Raskolnikov could be incorporated in a single hero. Increasingly the Dreiserian strain in Wright gave way to the Dostoevskian. After his break with the party, and hence with socialist realism, he was free to follow the demonic promptings of his deepest nature.

Despite its serious shortcomings *Native Son* must be counted among the major American novels. If the function of the literary imagination is to conquer new frontiers, to prepare unpopulated regions of the soul for permanent settlement, then Wright must be honored for his pioneering role. He has shown us a nation divided against itself; a gulf so vast between the white suburb and the black ghetto that no kindly paternalism can span it. He has revealed the hatred and resentment of the ghetto masses and exposed a psychic wound so deep that only violence can cauterize it. He has given us, in short, the first authentic portrait of the stranger in our midst.

Urban nihilism is the real subject of *Native Son*. Wright confronts us with a segment of the nation that believes in nothing. His hero, in the last analysis, can affirm no values other than his own acts of violence. Bigger Thomas now is legion, and his nihilism threatens not only the tranquillity but the very foundations of the republic. This is the substance of Wright's prophetic vision. We have spawned in the city slums a breed of men who are radically alienated from the dominant values of their culture. And this rough beast, its hour come round at last, slouches toward the ghettos to be born.

At the height of his artistic powers, between the publication of *Native Son* and *Black Boy*, Wright conceived and executed his most flawless work of fiction. "The Man Who Lived Underground" is a minor masterpiece, deserving of an honored place in American literary history. An early version of the story appeared in *Accent* (Spring 1942); an enlarged version in Edwin Seaver's *Cross-Section* (1944). The finished product, a novella of some fifty pages, may most conveniently be found in Abraham Chapman's anthology, *Black Voices* (Mentor Books, 1968).

The image of the Negro as underground man had its origin in Wright's personal experience. During the winter of 1932, he was employed by a Chicago hospital to look after the experimental animals. He and his fellow porters were confined to the basement corridors of the institution, restricted to what might be called an underground point of view: "The hospital kept us four Negroes as though we were close kin to the animals we tended, huddled together down in the underworld corridors of the hospital, separated by a vast psychological distance from the significant processes of the rest of the hospital—just as America had kept us locked in the dark underworld of American life for three hundred years. . . ."

This germinal idea was subsequently deepened and enriched through Wright's discovery of *Notes from the Underground*. In the Dostoevski novella he encountered a familiar state of soul, a spiritual plight bearing an uncanny resemblance to that of the American Negro. For Dostoevski's hero is a man of morbid sensitivity who feels himself to be rejected by the world. Convinced that he excites aversion, he broods on his humiliations and harbors violent fantasies of revenge. He is a man possessed

by the demons of shame, self-hatred, and vindictiveness. The negative quality of his existence is symbolized by his withdrawal to an underground den.

Wright's subterranean world is a symbol of the Negro's marginality. Thrust from the upper world by the racial exclusiveness of whites, he is forced to lead an underground existence. Wright was groping for a spatial metaphor that would render the Negro's ambiguous relationship to Western culture. In *Native Son*, seeking to express the same reality, he hit upon the metaphor of No Man's Land. It conjures up a bleak and sterile landscape in which a hapless soldier crouches, in constant danger of annihilation by enemy or friend. Some of the same qualities of desolation, abandonment, and vulnerability will be found in the bizarre world of Wright's underground hero.

"The Man Who Lived Underground" is a variation on the theme of nihilism. To be driven underground is to suffer spiritual death, to be the victim of metaphysical annihilation. The social reality here expressed has to do with anti-Negro stereotypes. For the stereotype, which is a projection of the white man's mind, drains the Negro of reality. It draws attention to itself, and away from the black man's humanity. What is left him is a shadow-world, an underground existence in some murky region of the white man's soul. A fear of nothingness is thus the key to Negro personality.

At the bottom of the Negro's metaphysical dread is his fear of rejection. This is the emotional core of Richard Wright's art. Whether we recall that his own mother beat him half to death at the age of four, or focus on the racial traumas of his later years, it is evident that this excruciating pain is his chief preoccupation. Wright's essential contribution as an artist is his understanding of the link between emotional rejection and philosophic nothingness. He is indebted for this insight to the work of William James, whose devoted reader he remained throughout his adult life.

In his introduction to *Black Metropolis* Wright quotes a crucial passage from William James: "No more fiendish punishment could be devised . . . than that one should be turned loose in society and remain absolutely unnoticed by all the members thereof. If no one turned round when we entered, answered when we spoke, or minded what we did, but if every person we met 'cut us dead,' and acted as if we were non-existent things, a kind of rage and impotent despair would ere long well up in us, from which the cruelest bodily tortures would be a relief; for these would make us feel that, however bad might be our plight, we had not sunk to such a depth as to be unworthy of attention at all."

It is the pain so vividly conveyed by James that we must seek to understand. Wright's entire career may be regarded as a search for ways of dealing with this pain. He comes closest to realizing his essential theme in "The Man Who Lived Underground." Here the fabulous plot and surrealistic style serve as a kind of mask or veil, drawn over the nakedness, the raw and quivering wounds of the Negro psyche. We are dealing with veiled confession, with experiences too painful to approach directly, with meanings that can only be expressed in symbolic language. The novella confronts us with underground (i.e., repressed) material. It can only be retrieved by a strenuous effort of imagination.

Wright's fable is best conveyed through a series of images. We begin with a Negro fugitive, running from the police. He dodges down a manhole and finds himself in the municipal sewer system. Now a sewer is a place for discarded and rejected things, a place of filth and excrement, bad odors, revulsion and disgust. Wright employs it as a symbol of Negro life. For white people shrink from the black man as if he were a filthy thing. They respond to his dark skin as if it were dirty. He is made to feel repulsive, and Wright's sewer is a brilliant projection of this feeling.

The fugitive explores the sewer until he finds a dry cave. From the other side of this excavation he hears human voices. Pulling himself up to a small hole he looks into the basement of a Negro church. It is a symbol of segregation-in-Christ: the Jim Crow Christianity that offers salvation without human brotherhood. The hero's angle of vision is also symbolic. He is forever the outsider, looking at the world through a knothole in the fence. To see without being seen, to overhear without being heard, is the daily fate of a servant class. How many black maids and cooks and waiters look out upon America from this underground perspective?

Pushing deeper into the sewer, Wright's hero comes upon "a tiny nude body of a baby snagged by debris and half submerged in water." Some desperate mother has killed her child and disposed of the body in a sewer. The discarded infant is emblematic of the Negro as the unwanted child of his culture. Still more it is a symbol of what has been killed, and thrust down out of sight, in the Negro's heart. That something is newborn hope, or possibility. The child, as yet unshaped by his environment, represents potentiality. But the Negro's humanity is nipped in the bud. What-might-have-been is systematically destroyed by white oppression.

Returning to his cave he finds an iron pipe and begins to dig. Soon he is tunneling through walls into a maze of basements and cellars. Symbolically these walls represent the fixed boundaries of Negro life which he proceeds to violate. He next comes upon a peculiar scene. A human figure is stretched out on a white table, above which is suspended a glass container filled with a blood-red liquid. It is an undertaker's establishment, and it symbolizes the lethal power of the anti-Negro stereotype. These stereotypes drain the black man's blood and replace it with embalming fluid. They dehumanize him; turn him into a nonexistent thing.

Eventually Wright's outlaw-hero burglarizes a jewelry store, taking money, rings, watches, and precious stones. This criminal act gives meaning to his underground existence. It represents the element of exploit (in particular financial exploit) that is ordinarily forbidden by the whites. He also steals a typewiter, on which he laboriously spells his name: *freddaniels*. This elementary act of self-definition is an emblem of the writer's art. As in *Native Son*, criminality and art are placed in metaphorical relation. Both are forms of metaphysical revolt: in the myth, Prometheus steals the sacred fire.

The crime is followed by a fantastic sequence. Daniels returns to the cave with his loot, and undertakes a project in interior decorating. He papers the dirt walls of his den with hundred-dollar bills. He drives nails everywhere and hangs up watches and rings. He dumps out all the metal coins in heaps on the ground and strews the earth with handfuls of precious gems. Finally, he hangs up a gun and cartridge belt taken from a night watchman, and a bloody meat cleaver stolen from a butcher shop.

Wright's hero has perceived, in short, the absurdity at the heart of white civilization. Once you grasp the joke, once you perceive Western culture as a combination jewelry store and butcher shop, you need no longer feel ashamed. By constructing this mocking symbol of the white man's most cherished values, Fred Daniels has set himself free.

From this point on the story is concerned with the hero's attempt to return to the upperworld. He wants to share his vision with the whites, disclose his underground reality, make his darkness visible. But words fail him; it is an incommunicable vision. When he first emerges from the sewer he expects to be seized by the police. Instead he is taken for a sewer workman and ignored. In desperation he approaches a Negro church where the congregation is singing a hymn: "The Lamb, the Lamb, the Lamb/Tell me again your story." The ushers take one look and toss him out.

At last he turns himself in to the police, only to discover that he has been cleared of his alleged crime. Unable to give credence to his story, and thus acknowledge his reality, the police handle matters in their own inimitable way. Pretending to believe his mad tale, they accompany him to his manhole, where they shoot him down in cold blood. This ritual murder is an emblem of American racism. Its object is the obliteration of the Negro's existenial reality. For the black man is a scapegoat, and as such, an actor in someone else's drama. To prepare him for the role, his claim to an autonomous existence is ruthlessly denied.

"The Man Who Lived Underground" is an existentialist fable based on the absurdities of American Negro life. The point must be made if only to correct a misconception concerning Wright's subsequent career. When Wright published an overtly existentialist novel in 1953, he was accused in certain quarters of abandoning his "true" subject and succumbing to an alien philosophy. But Wright's existentialism is not a foreign graft. Long before he met Sartre or read Camus he was working in this vein. What occurred in France was the vindication of his early intuitions.

Before closing our discussion of Wright's American period, a few words must be said about his first book. *Uncle Tom's Children* is a collection of five novellas which conform in essence to the pattern of the picaresque. At the center of each story is a brutal wrong, which is, however, sanctioned by southern law or custom. These incidents are designed to produce in the reader a sense of moral outrage. Wright's purpose is to portray a closed society so flagrantly unjust as to warrant the adoption of an outlaw code. His heroes are hunted men, driven to extremities of violence, who face the grim alternatives of flight or martyrdom.

Certain critics have claimed for *Uncle Tom's Children* a place in the Wright canon not inferior to that of *Black Boy* and *Native Son*. It is this exaggerated claim that invites a brief comment. The last two stories, "Fire and Cloud" and "Bright and Morning Star," are crude propaganda pieces. They were written, as Wright himself admits, for the greater glory of the Communist party. The other three are marred by melodrama. They are action-centered, and everything is sacrificed to a certain speed and tautness. We are clearly in the presence of a talented apprentice, but a period of seasoning is just as clearly needed before this writer will acomplish his mature work.

Between the publication of *Black Boy* in 1945 and *The Outsider* in 1953 Wright was overtaken by the famous spiritual crisis of the ex-Communist. This crisis is in part political, necessitating a new orientation in world affairs; in part philosophical, necessitating a new conception of the universe; and in part psychological, necessitating a new identity. In his writings of the 1950's, Wright attempts to surmount this crisis: politically by a new concern with the Third World; philosophically by a new interest in existentialism; and psychologically by adopting a new mask or persona, that of the outsider.

The work of Wright's French period consists of two distinct streams. His political concerns are expressed for the most part in four books of nonfiction. *Black Power, The Color Curtain, Pagan Spain*, and *White Man, Listen!* are a combination of travelogue, journalism, and inspired political and historical commentary.

Wright's philosophical and literary interests are pursued in three novels and a handful of short stories. *The Outsider* is the most ambitious of these efforts. It is an artistic failure, and a key to the deterioration of Wright's later style. *Savage Holiday* was written for the pulp market and need not detain us here. *The Long Dream* is a desperate attempt to rejuvenate his art by returning to his Mississippi youth. The more recent stories published in *Eight Men* all show symptoms of the curious unreality that permeates his late fiction.

The two streams converge in Wright's conception of the outsider. His new political heroes are the Westernized elite of Africa and Asia, "lonely outsiders who exist precariously on the margins of many cultures." His new fictional heroes are likewise lonely men, metaphysical rebels who exist precariously on the margins of the universe. There is thus a continuity of theme and image in Wright's French period. We shall begin with his political and historical theories, proceed to his search for an identity in *The Outsider*, and conclude by exploring the reasons for his artistic decline.

Richard Wright spent the spring and summer of 1945 on a small island in the St. Lawrence River, about fifteen miles from the city of Quebec. His immediate task was to write an introduction to *Black Metropolis* for his friend Horace Cayton. As he turned to this exhaustive study of Negro urbanization, a fruitful tension arose between his subject matter and his pastoral surroundings. Before him on the printed page were images of the Chicago ghetto that he knew so well. But just beyond the window of his study was a rural world reminiscent of his Mississippi boyhood. In this dramatic contrast of urban and rural cultures were the beginnings of a theory of history.

Quebec made a permanent impression on Wright's imagination. His first encounter with Old World values, it served him as a link to the European past. "The Province of Quebec," he writes in *White Man, Listen!*, "represents one of the few real surviving remnants of feudal culture on the American continent." What struck him was the contrast between the rural, traditional, Catholic culture of French Canada and the urban, industrial, Protestant culture of the United States. Out of these polarities he designed a conceptual model with which he might interpret contemporary history:

"Let us imagine an abstract line and at one end of this line let us imagine a simple, organic culture—call it Catholic, feudal, religious, tribal, or what you will. . . . At the opposite end of our imaginary line, let us imagine another culture, such as the one in which we live. In contrast to entity, in which the personality is swallowed up, we have a constant striving for identity. Instead of pre-individualism we have a strident individualism. Whereas French Quebec has holy days, we have holidays. Church bells toll the time of day in French Quebec; we look at our watches to see the hour."

If we listen carefully to this refrain we will recognize the central theme of *Black Boy*. Not entity but identity; not pre-individualism but individuality: this is the language of the picaresque. What is at stake for Wright in the transformation from a rural to an urban culture is freedom from the curbs and restrictions of traditional society. Everything in his Mississippi background predisposed him to repudiate tradition. For the black man was consigned, by

the power of tradition, to an inferior role in southern life. Conversely, everything in his Chicago environment led him to embrace industrialism as the scourge of traditional values.

Having himself been liberated by the Great Migration, Wright sought to endow his personal history with universal meaning. When he arrived in Paris he found a culture in the throes of rapid change. France, like much of postwar Europe, was in process of discarding the remnants of her feudal past. Nor was this exclusively a European phenomenon. Everywhere that Wright traveled in Africa and Asia he saw mankind struggling to rise above an ancient, rural way of life, and to establish a foothold in the modern wold. Everywhere a spiritual outlook steeped in poetry and mysticism, folklore and superstition, yielded to the forces of science and technology, rationalism, logic, and objective truth.

In the early 1950's Wright delivered a series of lectures on this theme to European audiences. Published under the title *White Man, Listen!*, these lectures contain the essence of his postwar thought. The centerpiece of the collection is an essay called "Tradition and Industrialization." Here Wright develops a capsule history of Western rationalism, an analysis of its impact on the traditional cultures of Asia and Africa, and a suggestive approach to the politics of the Third World which stresses the emergence of a Westernized elite.

Wright begins by stating his biases. He is a black man, and on that account estranged from certain Western values, namely those of racism. Nonetheless he stands before us as a child of the Enlightenment: a humanist and scientific rationalist, an incorrigibly secular and unalterably Western man. From this perspective he attacks the irrationality of medieval Christian culture. Throughout the Middle Ages, European man was wrapped in a subjective dream. As long as he pursued his mystic vision of the cosmos, so long was he prevented from dealing effectively with the external world.

The Protestant Reformation dealt a fatal blow to Western irrationality. Calvin and Luther, while preoccupied with metaphysical concerns, unwittingly created the conditions of emotional autonomy essential to scientific work. "As a result of Calvin's and Luther's heresy, man began to get a grip upon his external environment." The Reformation, however, did not go far enough. The secular philosophers of the Enlightenment were required to complete the emancipation of the Western mind. It was they who created what might be called the philosophical foundations of modern industry.

In the midst of this transition from a sacred to a secular society, Western Europe undertook a series of imperialist conquests. As European man overran the continents of Africa and Asia, "irrationalism met irrationalism." Acting in the faith that he was the agent of a cosmic power, the white man demolished or subdued all rival cultures and religious forms. While Wright condemns the predatory motives of the Europeans, he is not entirely displeased with the objective consequences: "What rivets my attention . . . is that an irrational Western world helped, unconsciously and unintentionally to be sure, to smash the irrational ties of religion and custom and tradition in Asia and Africa."

Western imperialism, despite its crimes, has made possible the rise of rational societies for the vast majority of mankind. Already beachheads of rationality have been established in the form of the Westernized elite. This elite, by virtue of its marginality, enjoys an unprecedented existential freedom. Torn from their roots in traditional or tribal cultures, these men are alienated from the values of their ancestors and eager to build industrial

civilizations. "What does this mean? It means that the spirit of the Enlightenment, of the Reformation, which made Europe great, now has a chance to be extended to all mankind!"

How does Wright's analysis comport with the facts of contemporary history? One must concede at once that he has been uncommonly deceived in his choice of heroes. He hoped for much from such figures as Nkrumah, Nasser, Sukarno, and Nehru, and if he had survived another decade he might have died a disillusioned man. On the other hand, he has not mistaken the decisive issues. He predicted a bitter struggle beween Nkrumah and Ashanti tribalism; Nehru and Hindu nationalism; Sukarno and Moslem orthodoxy—in short, between the forces of tradition and industrialization.

To offer a detailed critique of Wright's political ideas is beyond the scope of this essay. It will suffice to note a serious discrepancy between his intellectual system and the reality that he professes to describe. The system calls for a remorseless war upon tradition by the Asian-African elite. But on two occasions when the leaders of the Third World recorded their opinions, they did not behave according to the script. At Bandung, as Wright himself reports, the delegates approved a resolution calling for the rehabilitation of their ancient cultures and religions. At the Congress of Black Writers and Artists held at the Sorbonne in 1956, a similar resolution won the day.

How is it that these statesmen and artists cannot see, with the clarity of Richard Wright, that they must wage an implacable war against tradition? Perhaps Wright underestimates what he refers to so contemptuously as "the subjective illusions of mankind." Perhaps the Westernized elite understands, as Wright does not, the efficacy of myth and legend in providing cohesiveness, direction, and morale to a nation emerging from colonialism. It is

Wright's dogmatic rationalism that blinds him to these realities. Intent on attacking tradition wherever he encounters it, he cannot concede that cultural nationalism might play a constructive role in the independence struggle.

Whatever the limitations or excesses of Wright's world view, he must be acknowledged as a major spokesman of contemporary humanism. No writer of the present century has celebrated the values of the Enlightenment on such a global scale. None has dealt more comprehensively with the momentous issues of tradition and industrialization. Wright is the principal challenger of T. S. Eliot in this regard. If Eliot has put the case for tradition at its most persuasive, Wright has been the most thoughtful partisan of modern industry as a progressive force.

Wright's grand theme has been tradition and industrialization. Linking the work of his American and French periods, these polar concepts have served to unify his art. They have been implicitly the subject of his fiction and explicitly of his expository prose. From the first they have provided him with his essential form: the pattern of the picaresque. In *The Outsider* this form is carried to its logical extremity. Wright's hero has discarded all tradition, and with it all restraint. He is a symbol of modern, industrial, and post-Christian man.

The Outsider is Richard Wright's major failure. His first novel since *Native Son*, it is his last serious attempt to employ the form as an instrument of spiritual growth. At bottom he is trying to exorcise a demon, to discover and cast out whatever bad angel led him into the totalitarian labyrinth. That demon is the will to power: it is at once the malaise of his century and the source of his personal corruption. Wright does not defeat his bad angel, for he cannot finally be honest with himself.

The novel has its origin in a crisis of iden-

tity, precipitated by Wright's break with the Communists and aggravated by his Parisian exile. In what voice, through what mask, from what point of view will he address us? That is the most urgent requirement of his art. In *The Outsider* he is putting to death the Richard Wright that was, destroying the Communist self of former years, and replacing it with a new persona, that of the outsider. This new identity will consist precisely of his marginality, whether conceived in cultural or cosmic terms.

Wright's new sense of self is reinforced by his readings in philosophy. In the work not only of the French existentialists, who have become his personal friends, but of Jaspers and Heidegger, Husserl and Kierkegaard, Nietzsche and Dostoevski, he finds images of man and of the modern condition that confirm his deepest intuitions. Within the ambience of existentialism he discovers new directions for his art. Themes and emotions strongly felt but dimly understood are given fuller exposition. His self-loathing, his rootlessness, his nihilism are examined for their formal possibilities. What remains is the creation of a hero.

The hero of *The Outsider* is intended as a symbol of contemporary man. His central traits are rootlessness and amorality. He is rootless because of the impact of science and technology on the ancient worlds of ritual and myth; he is amoral by virtue of the death of God. Accountable to nothing but his own desire, he is capable of all brutalities. He is a man for whom ethical laws are suspended; who acts in unrestricted freedom; who usurps, in short, the prerogatives of God. Hence his ironic name, Cross Damon, to remind us that he is possessed.

This is the moral universe of Dostoevski's novels: its central feature is gratuitous murder. Cross Damon kills four people in wanton fulfillment of his own desire. His motives are philosophical: he kills in order to assert his claim to absolute freedom. Wright is testing the consequences of Ivan Karamazov's dictum, "If God is dead, everything is allowed." The death of God, he perceives, has precipitated a cultural crisis, bringing to the fore the elementary question "What is man?" Damon answers, in the spirit of the age, "Man is nothing in particular."

The theme of nihilism has always haunted Wright's imagination. From his early explorations of Negro nothingness and slum nothingness, he now proceeds to a fuller treatment of the theme. Cosmic nothingness, and its implications for technological society, is his present concern. If the universe is empty of a guiding intelligence, what force will restrain the Faustian urge of Western man? Power without limit or restraint is the legacy of the post-Christian era. Having stripped himself of all traditional defenses against his own will to power, modern man will move toward a new barbarism, incorporated in totalitarian political forms.

Wright's response to the nihilism of the age has been a persistent quest for enduring values. His career consists of a progression of identities, a perpetual sorting of values, a desperate search for meaning, conducted always on the edge of the abyss. Viewed in this perspective, *The Outsider* may be read as a recapitulation of the author's spiritual journey. Books I and II are concerned with Wright's identity as Negro; Books III and IV with his identity as Communist; Book V with his identity as lonely intellectual, disillusioned outsider, marginal man.

When we first meet Wright's hero he is employed as a clerk in a Chicago post office. His work consists of an absurd routine and his private life is in total disarray. He is separated from his wife and children, but obliged to contribute to their support. His teen-age mistress is pregnant, and in a desperate attempt to force him into marriage she threatens to send him to prison on a charge of statutory rape. He is heavily in debt. In short, he is trapped in an inauthentic existence, a life of *mauvaise foi*.

One evening fate presents him with a second chance. He is involved in a subway disaster in which it is supposed that he has lost his life. He seizes the occasion to disappear, to terminate his legal existence, and to escape from the web of promises and pledges in which he is ensnared. He emerges from the subway into a realm of absolute freedom. By a brutal act of will he has severed all connection with the past; his reward is an undetermined future. Viewed symbolically his freak accident represents a cultural trauma: the severing of modern man, by the forces of science and technology, from the myth-worlds of the past.

Throughout this episode, and for that matter throughout the novel, Wright emphatically denies that his hero's actions are in any way determined by his race. "Being a Negro," he assures us, "was the least important thing in his life." Yet the world that Cross Damon inhabits before his accident is a Negro world; the nothingness he flees is a Negro nothingness; the nonidentity that he resents is a Negro nonidentity. It is in fact the very world of the Chicago postal clerk that Wright describes with such obvious loathing in *Lawd Today*. In denying the racial implications of *The Outsider* he denies the basic continuity of his fiction.

The subway scene, for example, is linked in Wright's imagination to "The Man Who Lived Underground." As we have seen, he employs the underground motif as a symbol of Negro self-immolation. In effect, Cross buries his Negro past; hereafter his important ties will be with whites. Similarly with the murder of Joe Thomas, the postal clerk who recognizes

Cross in a dingy hotel. Joe is a variation of the Sambo figure, the clown who embodies the self-limiting tendencies of Negro life. In order to be free, Cross must put to death his clown, or Negro self.

Cross Damon's self-hatred, Wright would have us believe, is merely the famous nausea of Jean-Paul Sartre. But in denying the racial dimension of his hero's anguish he deceives both himself and his readers. The result is a fatal emotional blockage: we are asked to experience Cross Damon's emotions abstracted from their racial source. Anxiety, self-hatred, and a sense of nothingness are the daily psychological realities of Negro life. If these emotions are examined in clinical isolation we are left without so much a novel as a textbook in existentialist philosophy.

After the murder of Joe Thomas, Wright's hero flees to New York, where he is drawn into the orbit of the Communist party. Soon he is living in the Greenwich Village flat of a party leader, Gilbert Blount, and his wife, Eva. One night there is a bitter quarrel between Blount and his landlord, who is a racial bigot. A violent fight ensues between Communist and Fascist, and entering the room, Cross kills them both. He acts in such a way as to avert suspicion, and the police are forced to conclude they have killed each other. But Cross has been detected by a second party leader, whom he murders to protect his legal innocence.

Wright uses the long middle section of the novel to probe the wounds of his own political past. Above all he is struggling with the experience of being duped, an exceptionally painful fate for a proud man. As a result of having been deceived Wright attains a new philosophic depth. What evolves in his mind might be called the metaphysics of the disillusioned. He now realizes that it is necessary "to

peel off layer after layer of pretense, uncover front after front of make-believe" in order to apprehend reality. "Modern life is a kind of confidence game."

This new perception, which represents the growing edge of Wright's art, bears a striking resemblance to the concurrent discoveries of Ralph Ellison. The dissolving shapes of reality, the figure of the confidence man, the tactic of manipulative "masking": these are the major themes of *Invisible Man*. Wright, however, is unable to consolidate these gains linguistically; his philosophical discoveries are not accompanied by an appropriate stylistic growth. Where symbolism or surrealism would best serve his emerging metaphysic, he continues to depict, in the naturalistic mode, the solid surfaces of things.

Unable to transcend the limitations of socialist realism, Wright fails equally to outgrow the polemical habits of his Communist past. There is too much soapbox oratory in *The Outsider*. As Wright's imagination falters he virtually abandons narrative for arid stretches of expository prose. A fourteen-page speech toward the end of Book IV is the measure of his novelistic failure. As in *Native Son*, ideology preempts the craft of fiction. That the ideology has changed from pro- to anti-Communist does not make it any less a betrayal of the writer's art.

Book V is dominated by images of abandonment. Isolated from the world by his criminality, Cross has managed to preserve two vital human ties. The first is with Eva Blount, whose husband he has killed, and whom he subsequently comes to love. The second is with Ely Houston, the hunchback district attorney whose gifted imagination penetrates the secret of his crimes. Now, in effect, both abandon him. Eva commits suicide when she discovers his deceptions, and Houston deprives him of his last emotional prop by setting him free. Utterly alone, Cross is shot to death by the hired gunmen of the Communist party.

Abandonment, in the imaginative universe of Richard Wright, is the psychological equivalent of Hell. He thus administers to his hero the ultimate rebuke. Cross Damon represents the Faustian urge in Western man, his desire to become God. The penalty for such a crime is damnation. Eva and Houston represent the values that might have led to his salvation. Eva is a symbol of trust and love, of promises kept and pledges honored, of the will to power willingly surrendered. Houston is a symbol of restraint, humility, and the acceptance of limits: "I'm not a god and do not claim to be one, or want to be one. I curb my desires, you see?"

Together Eva and Houston are intended to bear the weight of Wright's disaffection from his hero. If the strategy succeeds, we will shift our allegiances from one value system to another. Cross Damon's moral nihilism will be discredited, while love and a sense of limits will emerge as the redeeming virtues of modern man. Such are Wright's intentions, but he fails to accomplish the necessary transfer of emotion. Eva is the weakest figure in the novel, and Houston, who is nine parts rhetoric, does not enlist our deepest sympathies. Sensing Wright's ambivalence, we withhold assent. He renounces demonism, but we suspect that the renunciation is insincere.

Nothing confirms these suspicions more than Wright's subsequent career. What has he learned of limits or of love? In *Black Power* we find him playing god to the continent of Africa, dispatching an arrogant letter of advice to Nkrumah which calls for the militarization of African life. In *White Man, Listen!*, he strikes a pose entirely worthy of Milton's Satan: "I declare unabashedly that I like and even cherish the state of abandonment, of aloneness; it does not bother me; indeed, to me it seems the natural, inevitable condition of man, and I welcome it."

When a writer can describe the amosphere of Hell as positively bracing, he counts himself among the damned. The price exacted from the radically disoriented soul is the loss of creativity. Stagnation is thus the keynote of Wright's late career. There is much backing and filling; a desperate casting about for suitable projects; various gimmicks, stopgaps, and evasions; but no growth. His last published novel, *The Long Dream*, is a reworking of material thoroughly explored in *Black Boy*. His last few stories, collected in *Eight Men*, are promising in theme but slovenly in execution.

Comparing the work of Wright's French period with his earlier achievement, we must acknowledge a precipitous decline. To account for this decline is our concluding task. The standard explanation has been Wright's Parisian exile. In moving to France, it is argued, he cut himself off from his roots in American Negro experience. Not without a certain plausibility, this explanation ignores the fact that many American writers, including some Negroes, have done their finest work in exile. If geography is not the point, we must seek the causes of Wright's aesthetic failure in his inner life.

The symptoms of a spiritual crisis will be found above all in a writer's language. It is true that Wright's dialogue, his rendition of living speech, suffers when he moves to France. Attuned now to a foreign tongue, his ear is deadened to the cadences of Negro speech. But the disease is far more serious. There is in Wright's late manner a stilted quality, a pompousness, a lack of observation, an absence of the smells and savors and juices of existence. The style becomes grandiose, abstract. It is Wright's surrender to abstraction that betrays his spiritual sickness.

Wrights suffers, no doubt, from rootlessness, but the source of that rootlessness is self-hatred. From the first, he adopts a negative attitude toward Negro life. He finds no sustaining values in the Negro past, but on the contrary equates being black with being nothing. He then proceeds to flee from that putative nothingness. Abandoning a concrete sense of time and place and circumstance, he espouses a specious and abstract universalism. He writes in *Pagan Spain*, "I have no religion in the formal sense of the word. I have no race except that which is forced upon me. I have no country except that to which I am obliged to belong. I have no traditions. I'm free."

Freedom thus conceived amounts to a process of purgation. Systematically the writer empties his consciousness of the past, of tradition, of culture itself—of all that is concrete, unique, distinctive. What remains is windy abstraction and grandiose system-building. Wright's universalism leads him, in short, to abandon his experience. As a substitute he turns to ideology, which is reassuringly abstract. Or he turns to the experience of others, whether Asians, Africans, or Europeans. Or he turns from America to France. But always there is an *aversion*, a turning from his own to another, and presumably a better world.

It is a strategy inherited from the Seventh-Day Adventists of his Mississippi boyhood. Born into a world where white was right and black was nothing, they responded with a classical defense. They denied the reality of their earthly existence and turned for solace to the Promised Land. This otherworldliness, this denial of the flesh, this Platonic and Utopian strain, is the philosophical foundation of Wright's universalism. It explains his lifelong fascination with abstract systems of reality, held in defiance of experience and impervious to anything so earthy as a fact.

If Wright is unable to transcend his self-hatred, he fails equally to cope with his compulsion to rebel. This compulsion, which is Wright's demon, is the source of the violence and criminality that dominate his fiction. It is plainly rooted in his relations with his mother, who beat him so unmercifully in his boyhood. To rebel against maternal authority is to establish a sense of self, but also to risk abandonment, the loss of mother love. The problem, as neurotic as it is insoluble, is how to fulfill both needs at once: how to combine demonism with love.

This psychological dilemma is projected in Wright's major novels. It is precisely the dilemma of Bigger Thomas in the last book of *Native Son*, and of Cross Damon in the last book of *The Outsider*. Cross and Bigger have committed monstrous crimes, and the price that they must pay is the loss of love. As Max recoils in horror from Bigger, so Eva from Cross. Demonism, in short, leads to the state of abandonment. Finally, Wright perceives, one must choose between the need to rebel and the need to be loved. In *Native Son*, by endorsing Bigger's existential self, he chooses demonism. In *The Outsider*, by disclaiming Cross, he chooses love.

Wright cannot, however, convincingly exorcise his demon. His sense of self is too deeply rooted in revolt. To opt for love is to give up his identity as picaresque saint, metaphysical rebel, lonely outsider. The compulsion to rebel is too firmly embedded in his personality structure: he is like a life prisoner who organizes an escape attempt that fails. In the end he embraces demonism and its consequence, abandonment. As a result, his art dries up. He understands, but cannot choose, the higher way. After such knowledge, what forgiveness?

Such is the parabola of Richard Wright's career. An impulse to cast off all servitude, including metaphysical servitude, runs its course and then subsides. What begins in self-assertion ends in self-parody. It would falsify the record, however, to dwell on Wright's defeat to the neglect of his accomplishment. He has created, out of his flight from nothingness and his compulsion to rebel, a memorable art.

"The Negro," Wright once observed, "is America's metaphor." He is the supreme example of an uprooted people, torn from a traditional culture and confronted in the new world by an existential void. This spiritual state, as our major writers will attest, is quintessentially American. Richard Wright is an artist in the American grain. His work, in a phrase he liked to quote from William James, is a celebration of "the unguaranteed existence." He will be remembered as a pioneer, an explorer of the territory ahead, a pilot on the unknown waters that the nation now must learn to sail.

Selected Bibliography

WORKS OF
RICHARD WRIGHT

BOOKS
Uncle Tom's Children. New York: Harper, 1938.
Native Son. New York: Harper, 1940.
Twelve Million Black Voices. New York: Viking, 1941.
Black Boy. New York: Harper, 1945.
The Outsider. New York: Harper, 1953.
Savage Holiday. New York: Avon, 1954.
Black Power. New York: Harper, 1954.
The Color Curtain. Cleveland and New York: World, 1956.
Pagan Spain. New York: Harper, 1957.
White Man, Listen! New York: Doubleday, 1957.
The Long Dream. New York: Doubleday, 1958.
Eight Men. Cleveland and New York: World, 1961.

Lawd Today. New York: Avon, 1963.
Published since the writing of this essay
American Hunger. New York: Harper & Row, 1977.

PRINCIPAL ESSAYS
"The Ethics of Living Jim Crow," *American Stuff: A WPA Writers' Anthology.* New York: Viking, 1937. Pp. 39–52.
"Blueprint for Negro Writing," *New Challenge,* Fall 1937. Pp. 53–65.
How Bigger Was Born (pamphlet). New York: Harper, 1940.
"I Tried to Be a Communist," *Atlantic Monthly,* 174:61–70 (August 1944); 174:48–56 (September 1944).
"Early Days in Chicago," *Cross-Section,* edited by Edwin Seaver. New York: L. B. Fischer, 1945. Pp. 306–42.
"Introduction" to *Black Metropolis,* by Horace Cayton and St. Clair Drake. New York: Harcourt, Brace, 1945. Pp. xvii-xxxiv.

BIBLIOGRAPHY
Fabre, Michel, and Edward Margolies. In *Bulletin of Bibliography and Magazine Notes* (Boston), 24:131–33, 137 (January-April 1965). This comprehensive bibliography is also available as an appendix to the biography by Constance Webb.

CRITICAL AND
BIOGRAPHICAL STUDIES
Baldwin, James. "Many Thousands Gone," in *Notes of a Native Son.* Boston: Beacon Press, 1955. Pp. 24–45.
————. "Alas, Poor Richard," in *Nobody Knows My Name.* New York: Dial Press, 1961. Pp. 181–215.
Brignano, Russell. *Richard Wright: An Introduction to the Man and His Work.* Pittsburgh: University of Pittsburgh Press, 1970.
Ellison, Ralph. "Richard Wright's Blues," in *Shadow and Act.* New York: Random House, 1964. Pp. 77–94.
Fabre, Michel. "Richard Wright: The Man Who Lived Underground," *Studies in the Novel,* 3:165–79 (Summer 1971).
Hill, Herbert, ed. "Reflections on Richard Wright: A Symposium on an Exiled Native Son," in

Anger and Beyond. New York: Harper and Row, 1966. Pp. 196–212. (Participants include Arna Bontemps, Horace Cayton, and Saunders Redding.)

Howe, Irving. "Black Boys and Native Sons," in *A World More Attractive*. New York: Horizon Press, 1963. Pp. 98–122.

Isaacs, Harold. "Five Writers and Their African Ancestry," *Phylon,* 21:254–65 (Fall 1960).

Margolies, Edward. *The Art of Richard Wright*. Carbondale: University of Southern Illinois Press, 1969.

McCall, Dan. *The Example of Richard Wright*. New York: Harcourt Brace and World, 1969.

Redding, Saunders. "The Alien Land of Richard Wright," in *Soon, One Morning,* edited by Herbert Hill. New York: Knopf, 1963. Pp. 50–59.

Scott, Nathan. "Search for Beliefs: Fiction of Richard Wright," *University of Kansas City Reviews,* 23:19–24 (Autumn 1956); 23:131–38 (Winter 1956).

Special Richard Wright Number, *CLA Journal,* Vol. XII, No. 4 (June, 1969).

Webb, Constance. *Richard Wright*. New York: G. P. Putnam's Sons, 1968.

Williams, John A. *The Most Native of Sons*. New York: Doubleday, 1970.

—*ROBERT BONE*

Index

*Arabic numbers printed in bold-face type refer
to extended treatment of a subject*

"Elementary Scene, The" (Jarrell), II, 387, 388, 389

"Eleonora" (Poe), III, 412

Eleothriambos (Lee), IV, 158

"Elephants" (Moore), III, 203

Eleven Poems on the Same Theme (Warren), IV, 239–241

Elias, Robert H., I, 520

Elijah (biblical person), III, 347

Eliot, Charles W., I, 5; II, 345

Eliot, Charlotte Champe Stearns, I, 567

Eliot, George, I, 375, 458, 459, 461, 467; II, 179, 181, 191–192, 275, 319, 324, 338, 577; IV, 311, 322

Eliot, Henry Ware, I, 567

Eliot, T. S., I, 48, 49, 52, 59, 60, 64, 66, 68, 105, 107, 215–216, 236, 243, 256, 259, 261, 266, 384, 386, 395, 396, 399, 403, 430, 433, 441, 446, 475, 478, 479, 482, 521, 522, 527, **567–591**; II, 65, 96, 158, 168, 316, 371, 376, 386, 529, 530, 532, 537, 542, 545; III, 1, 4, 5, 6, 7–8, 9, 10, 11, 14, 17, 20, 21, 23, 26, 34, 174, 194, 195–196, 205–206, 216, 217, 220, 236, 239, 269, 270–271, 277–278, 301, 409, 428, 432, 435, 436, 453, 456–457, 459–460, 461–462, 464, 466, 471, 476, 478, 485, 488, 492, 493, 498, 504, 509, 511, 517, 524, 527, 539, 572, 575, 586, 591, 594, 600, 613; IV, 27, 74, 82, 83, 95, 122, 123, 127, 129, 134, 138, 140, 141, 143, 191, 201, 213, 237, 331, 379, 402, 403, 418, 419, 420, 430, 431, 439, 442, 491

Eliot Mrs. T. S. (Valerie Fletcher), I, 568, 583

Eliot, Mrs. T. S. (Vivienne Haigh Haigh-Wood), I, 568

Elisha (biblical person), III, 347

Elizabeth I, Queen, I, 284; II, 139

"Elizabeth" (Longfellow), I, 502

Elizabeth Appleton (O'Hara), III, 362, 364, 375–377

Elizabethan literature, I, 177, 384, 569; II, 14–15, 18, 74; III, 77, 83, 145, 152, 397; IV, 155, 309

Ellen Rogers (Farrell), II, 42–43

Ellerman, Winifred, *see* McAlmon, Mrs. Robert (Winifred Ellerman)

Elliott, George B., III, 47, 289, 478

Elliott, Karin, III, 407

Ellis, Havelock, II, 276

Ellis, Katherine, IV 114

Ellison, Ralph, I, 426; IV, 250, 493, 496

Ellmann, Richard, IV, 424

Elman, Richard M., IV, 23

Elmer Gantry (Lewis), I, 26, 364; II, 447–449, 450, 455

Elmer the Great (Lardner), II, 427

"Eloquence of Grief, An" (Crane), I, 411

Elsasser, Henry, I, 226

Eluard, Paul, III, 528

Elwood, Douglas J., I, 565

"Emancipation in the British West Indies" (Emerson), II, 13

"Emancipation Proclamation, The" (Emerson), II, 13

Embree, Lester E., II, 366

Emerson, Donald, II, 697

Emerson, Edward Waldo, II, 22, 23; IV, 189

Emerson, Everett, IV, 166

Emerson, Mary Moody, II, 7, 8; IV, 172

Emerson, Ralph Waldo, I, 98, 217, 220, 222, 224, 228, 239, 246, 251, 252, 253, 257, 260, 261, 283, 386, 397, 402, 424, 433, 444, 447, 455, 458, 460–461, 463, 464, 485, 561; II, **1–24**, 49, 92, 127–128, 169, 170, 226, 233, 237, 273–274, 275, 278, 289, 295, 301, 313, 315, 336, 338, 344, 402, 491, 503; III, 53, 82, 171, 174, 260, 277, 409, 424, 428, 453, 454, 507, 576–577, 606, 614; IV, 60, 167, 169, 170, 171, 172, 173–174, 176, 178, 183, 186, 187, 192, 201, 202, 211, 335, 338, 340, 342, 350

Emerson, Mrs. Ralph Waldo (Lydia Jackson), II, 7; IV, 171, 177

Emerson, Mrs. Ralph Waldo (Ellen Tucker), II, 7, 11

Emerson, Reverend William (father), II, 7

Emerson, William (brother), II, 7

Emerson family, IV, 177, 178

Emery, Clark, III, 478

"Emma and Eginhard" (Longfellow), II, **505**

"Emperor of Ice Cream, The (Stevens), IV, 76, 80–81

Emperor Jones, The (O'Neill), II, 278; III, 391, 392

"Emperor's New Clothes, The" (Anderson), I, 441

"Empire Builders" (MacLeish), III, 14

Empson, William, I, 522, 533; II, 536, III, 286, 497, 498, 499; IV, 136, 431

"Empty Threat, An" (Frost), II, 159

"Encantadas, The" (Melville), III 89

Enck, John, I, 143, 165; IV, 95

"Encomium Twenty Years Later" (Tate), I, 381

"Encounter, The" (Pound), III, 466

Encyclopaedia Britannica, The, IV, 91, 440

"End of the Line, The" (Jarrell), III, 527

"End of the Rainbow, The" (Jarrell), II, 386

End of the Road, The (Barth), I, 121, 122, 126–131

"End of Season" (Warren), IV, 239–240

"End of Something, The" (Hemingway), II, 248

"End of the World, The" (MacLeish), III, 8

Endecott and the Red Cross (Lowell), II, 545

Endor (Nemerov), III, 269, 270, 279

"Enduring Chill, The" (O'Connor), III, 349, 351, 357

Endymion (Keats), IV, 405

Enemies—A Love Story (Singer), IV, 1

Enemy, The: Time (Williams), IV, 391

Enemy of the People, An (adapt. Miller), III, 154–156

Electricity (Franklin), **II**, 102, 114–115

"Explanation" (Stevens), **IV**, 79

"Exploit" (Wharton), **IV**, 324

Expositor's Bible, The (Smith), **III**, 199

Extract from Captain Stormfield's Visit to Heaven (Twain), **IV**, 299–210

Extracts from Adam's Diary (Twain), **IV**, 208–209

"Exulting, The" (Roethke), **III**, 544

Eye, The (Nabokov), **III**, 251

"Eye of Paris, The" (Miller), **III**, 183–184

"Eye of the Story, The" (Porter), **IV**, 279

"Eyes, The" (Wharton), **IV**, 315

"Eyes to See" (Cozzens), **I**, 374

Ezekiel (biblical book), **II**, 541

Ezekiel (biblical person), **III**, 347

Ezra Pound's Mauberley (Espey), **III**, 463

Fable, A (Faulkner), **II**, 55, 73

"Fable of the War, A" (Nemerov), **III**, 272

Fables (Gay), **II**, 111

Fables of La Fontaine, The (Moore), **III**, 194, 215

"Fables of the Moscow Subway" (Nemerov), **III**, 271

Fabre, Michel, **IV**, 496

Fabricius, Johannes, **I**, 590

Face of Time, The (Farrell), **II**, 28, 34, 35, 39

Fackre, Gabriel J., **III**, 312

"Fact in Fiction, The" (McCarthy), **II**, 562

"Facts, The" (Lardner), **II**, 431

"Facts in the Case of M. Valdemar, The" (Poe), **III**, 416

Fadiman, Clifton, **I**, 213; **II**, 430, 431, 443, 591–592; **III**, 384

Faerie Queen, The (Spencer), **III**, 487; **IV**, 253

Fagin, N. Bryllion, **III**, 432

Faith and History (Niebuhr), **III**, 308

Faithful Narrative of the Surprising Works of God in the Conversion of Many Hundred Souls in Northampton, and the Neighbor-ing Towns and Villages of New-Hampshire in New-England, A (Edwards), **I**, 545, 562

"Falcon of Ser Federigo, The" (Longfellow), **II**, 505

Falk, Doris V., **III**, 407, 408

Falk, Signi Lenea, **III**, 25; **IV**, 401

Falkner, Dean, **II**, 55

Falkner, John, **II**, 55

Falkner, Murray, **II**, 55

Falkner, Murray C., **II**, 55, 76

Falkner, Mrs. Murray C. (Maud Butler), **II**, 55

Falkner, William C., **II**, 55

Fall of the City, The: A Verse Play for Radio (MacLeish), **III**, 20–21

"Fall of the House of Usher, The" (Poe), **III**, 412, 414, 415, 419

"Fall 1961" (Lowell), **II**, 550

"Falling Asleep over the Aeneid" (Lowell), **II**, 542

"Family" (Wilson), **IV**, 426

Family Moskat, The (Singer), **IV**, 1, 4–6, 17, 20

Family Party, A (O'Hara), **III**, 362

Family Reunion, The (Eliot), **I**, 570–571, 572, 581, 584, 588

"Famous Gilson Bequest, The" (Bierce), **I**, 204

"Fancy and Imagination" (Poe), **III**, 421

"Fancy's Show Box" (Hawthorne), **II**, 238

Fanshawe (Hawthorne), **II**, 223–224

"Fantastic Fables" (Bierce), **I**, 209

Far Field, The (Roethke), **III**, 528, 529, 539, 545, 547–548

"Far Field, The" (Roethke), **III**, 537, 540

Far from the Madding Crowd (Hardy), **II**, 291

Faraday, Michael, **I**, 480–481

"Farewell" (Emerson), **II**, 13

Farewell to Arms, A (Hemingway), **I**, 212, 421, 476, 477; **II**, 68–69, 248–249, 252–253, 254, 255, 262, 265

"Farewell to Miles" (Berryman), **I**, 173

Farewell—Sermon Preached at the First Precinct in Northampton, after the People's Publick Rejec-tion of their Minister, A (Edwards), **I**, 548, 562

Farley, Abbie, **I**, 458

Farmers Hotel, The (O'Hara), **III**, 361

Farnham, James F., **III**, 360

Farrand, Max, **II**, 122, 124

Farrar, John, **II**, 191

Farrell, James, **II**, 25–26

Farrell, James Francis, **II**, 25, 26

Farrell, James T., **I**, 97, 288, 475, 508, 517, 519; **II**, **25–53**, 416, 424; **III**, 28, 114, 116, 118, 119, 317, 382; **IV**, 211, 286

Farrell, Mrs. James T. (Hortense Alden), **II**, 26, 27, 45, 48

Farrell, Mrs. James T. (Dorothy Butler), **II**, 26

Farrell, John, **II**, 26

Farrell, Kevin, **II**, 26

Farrell, Mary, **II**, 25

Fascism, **I**, 172, 588; **II**, 44, 454, 480

"Fastest Runner on Sixty-first Street, The" (Farrell), **II**, 45

Fatal Interview (Millay), **III**, 128–129, 130

"Fate" (Emerson), **II**, 2–3, 4, 16

"Father and Daughter" (Eberhart), **I**, 539

"Father and Son" (Eberhart), **I**, 539

Father and Son (Farrell), **II**, 34, 35, 290, 291

Fathers, The (Tate), **IV**, 120, 127, 130, 131–133, 134, 141

"Fathers and Sons" (Hemingway), **II**, 249, 265–266

Fatout, Paul, **I**, 213

Faulkner, William, **I**, 54, 97, 99, 105, 106, 115, 117, 118, 119, 120, 123, 190, 204–205, 211, 288, 289, 291, 292, 297, 305, 324, 374, 378, 423, 480, 517; **II**, 28, 51, **54–76**, 131, 174, 194, 217, 223, 228, 230, 259, 301, 306, 431, 458–459, 542, 594, 606; **III**, 45, 70, 108, 164, 218, 220, 222, 236–237, 244, 292, 334, 350, 382, 418, 453, 454, 482, 483; **IV**, 2, 4, 33, 49, 97, 98, 100, 101, 120, 131, 203, 207, 211, 217, 237, 257, 260, 261, 279, 280, 352, 461, 463

Glory of Hera, The (Gordon), II, 196–197, 198, 199, 217–220
Glover, William, IV, 401
Gluck, Christoph Willibald, II, 210, 211
Gnädiges Fräulein, The (Williams), IV, 382, 395, 398
Gnomes and Occasions (Nemerov), III, 269
Gnomologia (Fuller), II, 111
"Gnothis Seauton" (Emerson), II, 11, 18–19
"Go Down, Moses" (Faulkner), II, 71–72
Go Down, Moses and Other Stories (Faulkner), II, 71
"Go to the Shine That's on a Tree" (Eberhart), I, 523
"Goal of Intellectual Men, The" (Eberhart), I, 529–530
God of His Fathers, The (London), II, 469
"God is a distant-stately Lover" (Dickinson), I, 471
"God Rest Ye Merry, Gentlemen" (Hemingway), IV, 122
God without Thunder (Ransom), III, 495–496, 499
God of Vengeance (Asch), IV, 11
Godkin, E. L., II, 274
Gods Arrive, The (Wharton), IV, 326–327
Gods Determinations touching his Elect: and the Elects Combat in their Conversion, and Coming up to God in Christ together with the Comfortable Effects thereof (Taylor), IV, 155–160, 165
God's Country and My People (Morris), III, 238
God's Little Acre (Caldwell), I, 288, 289, 290, 297, 298–302, 305–306, 309, 310
God's Man: A Novel in Wood Cuts (Ward), I, 31
God-Seeker, The (Lewis), II, 456
Godwin, William, II, 304; III, 415
Goebbels, Josef, III, 560
Goen, C. C., I, 560, 564, 565
Goethe, Johann Wolfgang von, I, 181, 396, 587–588; II, 5, 6, 320, 344, 488, 489, 492, 502, 556; III, 395, 453, 607, 612, 616; IV, 50, 64, 173, 326

Gogol, Nikolai, I, 296; IV, 1, 4
"Going to Naples" (Welty), IV, 278
"Going to Shrewsbury" (Jewett), II, 393
Going South (Lardner and Buck), II, 427
Gold, Michael, II, 26; IV, 363, 364, 365, 376
Gold (O'Neill), III, 391
"Gold Bug, The" (Poe), III, 410, 413, 419, 420
Goldberg, Isaac, III, 121
Golde, Miss., (Mencken's Secretary), III, 104, 107
Golden, Harry, III, 579, 581, 598
Golden Apples, The (Welty), IV, 261, 271–274, 281, 293
Golden Bough, The (Frazer), II, 204, 549; III, 6–7
Golden Bowl, The (James), II, 320, 333, 335
Golden Era (publication), IV, 196
"Golden Honeymoon, The" (Lardner), II, 429–430, 431
"Golden Lads" (Marquand), III, 56
Golden Legend, The (Longfellow), II, 489, 490, 495, 505, 506, 507
Golden Mean and Other Poems, The (Tate and Wills), IV, 122
Goldhurst, William, II, 100
Golding, Arthur, III, 467, 468
Goldini, Carlo, II, 274
Goldman, Emma, III, 176, 177
Goldman, Sherli Evans, II, 584
Goldring, Douglas, III, 458
Goldschmidt, Eva M., III, 25
Goldsmith, Oliver, II, 273, 282, 299, 304, 308, 314, 315, 514
Goldwater Barry, I, 376; III, 38
Golem, The (Leivick), IV, 6
Goncourt, Edmond de, II, 325, 328
Goncourt, Jules de, II, 328
Goncourt brothers, III, 315, 317–318, 321
Gone with the Wind (Mitchell), II, 177
Gongora y Argote, Luis de, II, 552
Good, Robert C., III, 312
"Good Anna, The" (Stein), IV, 37, 40, 43
"Good Country People" (O'Con-

nor), III, 343, 350, 351, 352, 358
Good Housekeeping (magazine), II, 174
Good Man Is Hard to Find, A (O'Connor), III, 339, 343–345
"Good Man Is Hard to Find, A" (O'Connor), III, 339, 344, 353
Good Morning, America (Sandburg), III, 592–593
"Good Morning, Major" (Marquand), III, 56
"Good-bye" (Emerson), II, 19
Goodbye to All That (Graves), I, 477
"Good-Bye My Fancy" (Whitman), IV, 348
Goode, Gerald, III, 24
Goode, James, III, 169
Goodheart, Eugene, IV, 23
Goodman, Henry, I, 95
Goodman, Paul, I, 218, 261; III, 39
Goodman, Philip, III, 105, 108
Goodman, Randolph, IV, 400
Goodwin, K. L., III, 478
"Goose Fish, The" (Nemerov), III, 272, 284
Gordan, John D., I, 426
Gordon, A. R., III, 199
Gordon, Andrew, III, 48
Gordon, Caroline, II, **196–222**, 536, 537; III, 360, 454, 482; IV, 123, 126–127, 139, 142, 282
Gordon, Charles G., I, 454
Gordon, James Morris, II, 197
Gordon, Ruth, IV, 357
Gordon, William A., III, 191, 192
Gorey, Edward, IV, 430, 436
Gorki, Maxim, I, 478; II, 49; III, 402; IV, 299
Gorman, Herbert, II, 509
Gosse, Edmund, II, 538; IV, 350
Gossett, Louise Y., I, 311; III, 360; IV, 119
Gottlieb, Elaine, IV, 22, 23
Gould, Edward Sherman, I, 346
Gould, Jay, I, 4
Gould, Jean, I, 95
Gourmont, Rémy de, I, 270, 272; II, 528, 529; III, 457, 467–468, 477
Grabo, Norman S., IV, 165, 166
Graham, Billy, I, 308

Hemingway, Dr. Clarence Edwards, II, 248, 259

Hemingway, Ernest, I, 28, 64, 97, 99, 105, 107, 117, 150, 162, 190, 211, 221, 288, 289, 295, 367, 374, 378, 421, 423, 445, 476, 477, 478, 482, 484–485, 487, 488, 489, 491, 495, 504, 517; II, 27, 44, 51, 58, 68–69, 78, 90, 97, 100, 127, 206, **247–270**, 289, 424, 431, 456, 457, 458–459, 482, 560, 600; III, 2, 18, 20, 35, 36, 37, 40, 61, 108, 220, 334, 363, 364, 382, 453, 454, 471–472, 476, 551, 575, 576, 584; IV, 27, 28, 33, 34, 35, 42, 49, 97, 108, 122, 126, 138, 190, 191, 201, 216, 217, 257, 297, 363, 404, 427, 433, 451

Hemingway, Mrs. Ernest (Martha Gellhorn), II, 260

Hemingway, Mrs. Ernest (Pauline Pfeiffer), II, 260

Hemingway, Mrs. Ernest (Hadley Richardson), II, 257, 260, 263

Hemingway, Mrs. Ernest (Mary Welsh), II, 257, 260

Hemingway, Leicester, II, 270

Hemley, Cecil, IV, 22, 23

Henderson, Archibald and Barbara, II, 365

Henderson, F. C., III, 121

Henderson the Rain King (Bellow), I, 144, 147, 148, 152, 153, 154, 155, 158, 160, 161, 162–163

Hendin, Josephine, III, 360

Hendricks, King, II, 484

Henfrey, Norman, III, 622

Henle, James, II, 26, 30, 38, 41

Henri, Robert, IV, 411

Henry VI, King, II, 379

Henry VIII, King, I, 12; III, 101; IV, 201

Henry, Arthur, I, 515

Henry, O. (pseudonym), *see* Porter, William Sydney

Henry IV (Shakespeare) III, 166

"Henry James, Jr." (Howells), II, 289

Henry Miller Reader, The (ed. Durrell), III, 175, 190

"Henry's Confession" (Berryman), I, 186

"Her Own People" (Warren), IV, 253

"Her Quaint Honour" (Gordon), II, 196, 199, 200

Heraclitus, II, 1, 163; IV, 86

Herakles: A Play in Verse (MacLeish), III, 21, 22

Herberg, Will, III, 291

Herbert, Edward, II, 11; III, 408

Herbert, George, II, 12; IV, 141, 145, 146, 151, 153, 156, 165

Herbert of Cherbury, Lord, II, 108

Herbst, Josephine, I, 119; III, 455

Herford, Reverend Brooke, I, 471

Herman, Florence, *see* Williams, Mrs. William Carlos (Florence Herman)

Herman, William (pseudonym), *see* Bierce, Ambrose

Hermit and the Wild Woman, The (Wharton), IV, 315

Herne, James A., II, 276

"Hero, The" (Moore), III, 200, 211, 212

Hero, The (Raglan), I, 135

Hero in America, The (Van Doren), II, 103

Herod, King, III, 353; IV, 138

Hérodiade (Mallarmé), I, 66

"Heron, The" (Roethke), III, 540–541

Herrick, Robert, II, 11, 18, 444, 484; III, 463, 592; IV, 453

Herring, Paul D., III, 241

Hersey, John, IV, 4

Herzog (Bellow), I, 144, 147, 149, 150, 152, 153, 154, 155, 156, 157, 158, 159–160

Heseltine, H. P., IV, 259

Hetherington, H. W., III, 97

Hewitt, Bernard, IV, 376

Hewlett, Maurice, I, 359

Hey Rub-a-Dub-Dub (Dreiser), I, 515; II, 26

Hiatt, David F., II, 294

Hicks, Granville, I, 254, 259, 374, 380, 520; II, 26; III, 72, 240, 241, 242, 336, 342, 355, 359, 360, 407, 452; IV, 448

Higgins, David, I, 473

Higginson, Thomas Wentworth, I, 451–452, 453, 454, 456, 458,

459, 463, 464, 465, 470, 472; II, 509

"High Tide" (Marquand), III, 56

Hike and the Aeroplane (Lewis), II, 440–441

Hildebrand, Al, III, 118

Hilen, Andrew, II, 509

Hilfer, Anthony Channell, I, 95

Hill, Joe, I, 493

Hill, Hamlin, IV, 212, 213

Hill, Herbert, IV, 496

Hill, Patti, I, 289

"Hill Wife, The" (Frost), II, 154

"Hillcrest" (Robinson), III, 504

Hiller, Hilaire, III, 191

Hiller, Wendy, III, 404

Hills, L. Rush, III, 573

Hills Beyond, The (Wolfe), IV, 450, 451, 460, 461

"Hills Beyond, The" (Wolfe), IV, 460

Hillway, Tyrus, III, 97

Hillyer, Robert, I, 475

"Hilton's Holiday, The" (Jewett), II, 391

Him (Cummings), I, 429, 434–435

Hindemith, Paul, IV, 357

Hindus, Milton, I, 286; IV, 23

Hippolytus (Euripides), II, 543

Hirsch, Sidney, *see* Mttron-Hirsch, Sidney

"His Chest of Drawers" (Anderson), I, 113, 114

"His Shield" (Moore), III, 211

His Thought Made Pockets & the Plane Buckt (Berryman), I, 170

His Toy, His Dream, His Rest (Berryman), I, 169, 170, 183, 184–186

"His Words" (Roethke), III, 544

Histoire comparée des systèmes de philosophie (Gérando), II, 10

"Historical Conceptualization" (Huizinga), I, 255

"Historical Interpretation of Literature, The" (Wilson), IV, 431, 433, 445

"History" (Emerson), II, 13, 15

History of English Literature (Taine), III, 323

History of Fortus, The (Emerson), II, 8

History of Henry Esmond, The (Thackeray), II, 91, 130

"Jan, the Son of Thomas" (Sandburg), III, 593–594

Janet, Pierre, I, 248, 249, 252

"Janet Waking" (Ransom), III, 490, 491

Jarrell, Randall, I, 167, 169, 173, 180, 189; II, **367–390**, 539–540; III, 134, 194, 213, 217, 268, 289, 527; IV, 352, 411, 422, 423, 424

Jarrell, Mrs. Randall (Mary von Schrader), II, 368, 385

"Jason" (MacLeish), III, 4

Jaspers, Karl, III, 292; IV; 491

Jay, William, I, 338

"Jazz Age Clerk, A" (Farrell), II, 45

"Jazz Fantasia" (Sandburg), III, 585

Jeffers, Robinson, I, 66; III, 134

Jefferson, Thomas, I, 1, 2, 5, 6–8, 14, 485; II, 5, 6, 134, 217, 300, 301, 437; III, 3, 17, 18, 294–295, 306, 310, 473, 608; IV, 133, 243, 249, 334, 348

Jelliffe, Robert A., II, 75

"Jelly-Bean, The" (Fitzgerald), II, 88

"Jellyfish, A" (Moore), III, 215

Jenkins, J. L., I, 456

Jenkins, Kathleen, III, 403

Jenkins, Susan, IV, 123

Jennie Gerhardt (Dreiser), I, 497, 499, 500, 501, 504–505, 506, 507, 519

"Jenny Garrow's Lover" (Jewett), II, 397

"Jerboa, The" (Moore), III, 203, 207, 209, 211–212

"Jericho" (Lowell), II, 536

Jerome, Judson, III, 289

"Jersey City Gendarmerie, Je T'aime" (Lardner), II, 433

Jesus, I, 27, 34, 68, 89, 136, 552, 560, II, 1, 16, 197, 198, 214, 215, 216, 218, 219, 239, 373, 377, 379, 537, 538, 539, 549, 569, 585, 591, 592; III, 39, 173, 179, 270, 291, 296–297, 300, 303, 305, 307, 311, 339, 340, 341, 342, 344, 345, 346, 347, 348, 352, 353, 354, 355, 436, 451, 489, 534, 564, 566, 567, 582; IV, 51, 69, 86, 107, 109,

117, 137, 138, 141, 144, 147, 149, 150, 151, 152, 155, 156, 157, 158, 159, 163, 164, 232, 241, 289, 293, 294, 296, 331, 364, 392, 396, 418, 430

"Jeune Parque, La" (Valéry), IV, 92

Jewett, Caroline, II, 396

Jewett, Mary, II, 396, 403

Jewett, Sarah Orne, I, 313; II, **391–414**

Jewett, Theodore Furber, II, 395

Jewett, Mrs. Theodore Furber (Sarah Orne), II, 395

Jewett, Dr. Theodore Herman, II, 396–397, 402

Jewett family, II, 391

Jewish Daily Forward (newspaper), IV, 2

Jews of Shklov (Schneour), IV, 11

Jig of Forslin, The: A Symphony (Aiken), I, 50, 51, 57, 62, 66

"Jilting of Granny Weatherall, The" (Porter), III, 434, 435, 438

Joan, Pope, IV, 165

Joan, Saint, IV, 241

Job (biblical book), II, 165, 166–167, 168; III, 21, 199, 512; IV, 13, 158

Job, The: An American Novel (Lewis), II, 441

John the Baptist, I, 389; II, 537, 591

John of the Cross, Saint, I, 585

John (biblical book), I, 68

John Addington Symonds: A Biolographical Study (Brooks), I, 240, 241

John Barleycorn (London), II, 467, 481

"John Brown" (Emerson), II, 13

John Brown: The Making of a Martyr (Warren), IV, 236

John Brown's Body (Benét), II, 177

John Bull in America; or, The New Munchausen (Paulding), I, 344

"John Carter" (Agee), I, 27

John Deth: A Metaphysical Legend and Other Poems (Aiken), I, 61

John Endicott (Longfellow), II, 505, 506

"John Evereldown" (Robinson), III, 524

John Keats (Lowell), II, 530–531

"John Marr" (Melville), III, 93

John Marr and Other Sailors (Melville), III, 93

John Sloan: A Painter's Life (Brooks), I, 254

"John Smith Liberator" (Bierce), I, 209

"Johnny Bear" (Steinbeck), IV, 67

Johnson, Alvin, I, 236

Johnson, Carl L., II, 509

Johnson, Eastman, IV, 321

Johnson, Edward, IV, 157

Johnson, Elmer D., IV, 472

Johnson, George W., II, 148

Johnson, Gerald W., III, 121

Johnson, J. W. III, 455

Johnson, Lyndon B., I, 254; II, 553, 582

Johnson, Martin, II, 484

Johnson, Merle, IV, 212

Johnson, Pamela Hansford, IV, 469, 473

Johnson, Richard Colles, I, 120

Johnson, Dr. Samuel, II, 295; III, 491, 503; IV, 452

Johnson, Thomas H., I, 470–471, 473, 564, 565; II, 125, 533; IV, 144, 158, 165

Johnson, W. R., III, 289

Johnson, Walter, II, 422

Johnsrud, Harold, II, 562

Johnston, Mary, II, 194

"Jolly Corner, The" (James), I, 571

Jonah (biblical person), III, 347, 348; IV, 152

"Jonah" (Lowell), II, 536

"Jonathan Edwards in Western Massachusetts" (Lowell), II, 550

Jones, Claude E., III, 431

Jones, David E., I, 590

Jones, E. Stanley, III, 297

Jones, Edith Newbold, *see* Wharton, Edith

Jones, Ernest, II, 365

Jones, Genesius, I, 590

Jones, George Frederic, IV, 309

Jones, Howard Mumford, I, 119, 263, 353, 357; II, 509

Jones, James, III, 40; IV, 98, 118

Jones, John Paul, II, 405–406

Jones, Lucretia Stevens Rhinelander, IV, 309

Pierrepont, Sarah, *see* Edwards, Sarah

Pierrot Qui Pleure et Pierrot Qui Rit (Rostand), II, 515

Pigeon Feathers (Updike), IV, 214, 218, 219, 221–223, 226

"Pigeons" (Rilke), II, 544

"Pilgrim Makers" (Lowell), II, 541

Pilgrimage of Festus, The (Aiken), I, 50, 55, 57

Pilgrimage of Henry James, The (Brooks), I, 240, 248, 250; IV, 433

Pilgrim's Progress (Bunyan), I, 92; II, 15, 168, 572

Pilot, The (Cooper), I, 335, 337, 339, 342–343, 350

"Pilot from the Carrier, A" (Jarrell), II, 374

"Pilots, Man Your Planes" (Jarrell), II, 374–375

Pindar, I, 381; II, 543; III, 610

Pinker, James B., I, 409

Pinter, Harold, I, 71

Pioneers, The (Cooper), I, 336, 337, 339, 340–341, 342, 348; II, 313

Pious and Secular America (Niebuhr), III, 308

Pipe Night (O'Hara), III, 361, 368

Piper, Henry Dan, II, 100

Pippa Passes (Browning), IV, 128

Pirate, The (Scott), I, 339

Pirates of Penzance, The (Gilbert and Sullivan), IV, 386

Pisan Cantos, The (Pound), III, 476

Piscator, Erwin, IV, 394

Pissarro, Camille, I, 478

Pit, The (Norris), III, 314, 322, 326–327, 333, 334

"Pit, The" (Roethke), III, 538

"Pit and the Pendulum, The" (Poe), III, 413, 416

Pitkin, Walter, II, 366

Pittsburgh Daily Leader (newspaper), I, 313

Pittsburgh *Dispatch* (newspaper), I, 499

Pius II, Pope, III, 472

Pius IX, Pope, II, 79

Pixley, Frank, I, 196

Pizer, Donald, I, 424, III, 240–242, 321, 335, 336

Place Called Estherville, A (Caldwell), I, 297, 307

"Place in Fiction" (Welty), IV, 260, 279

Placi, Carlo, IV, 328

"Plagiarist, The" (Singer), IV, 19

Plain Talk (publication), II, 26

Plain Truth: Or, Serious Considerations on the Present State of the City of Philadelphia, and Province of Pennsylvania (Franklin), II, 117–119

Plaint of a Rose, The (Sandburg), III, 579

"Planchette" (London), II, 475–476

Plarr, Victor, III, 459, 477

Plato, I, 224, 279, 383, 389, 485, 523; II, 5, 8, 10, 15 233, 346, 391–392, 591; III, 115, 480, 600, 606, 609, 619–620; IV, 74, 140, 333, 363, 364

"Plato" (Emerson), II, 6

Plautus, Titus Maccius, IV, 155

Playboy (magazine), III, 40

Play Days: A Book of Stories for Children (Jewett), II, 401–402

Plays: Winesburg and Others (Anderson), I, 113

"Plays and Operas Too" (Whitman), IV, 350

"Plea for Captain Brown, A" (Thoreau), IV, 185

"Please Don't Kill Anything (Miller), III, 161

Pleasure Dome (Frankenberg), I, 436

Pleasure of Hope, The (Emerson), II, 8

Plimpton, George, IV, 119

Pliny the Younger, II, 113

"Plot against the Giant, The" (Stevens), IV, 81

Plotinsky, Melvin L., I, 96

Plough and the Stars, The (O'Casey), III, 159

"Ploughing on Sunday" (Stevens), IV, 74

"Plumet Basilisk, The" (Moore), III, 203, 208, 215

Pluralistic Universe, A (James), II, 342, 348, 357–358

Plutarch, II, 5, 8, 16, 555

PM (newspaper), I, 296; IV, 477

Pnin (Nabokov), III, 246

Pocahontas, I, 4; II, 296; III, 584

Pochmann, Henry A., II, 318

Podhoretz, Norman, I, 166; III, 48, 384; IV, 235, 307, 441, 449

Poe, David, III, 409

Poe, Edgar Allan, I, 48, 53, 103, 190, 194, 200, 210, 211, 261, 340, 459; II, 74, 77, 194, 255, 273, 295, 308, 311, 313, 421, 475, 482, 530, 595; III, 259, **409–432**, 485, 507, 593; IV, 123, 129, 133, 141, 187, 261, 345, 350, 432, 438, 439, 453

Poe, Mrs. Edgar Allan (Virginia Clemm), III, 412, 413, 418, 421–422, 428, 429

Poe, Elizabeth Arnold, III, 409, 413, 429

"Poem for Someone Killed in Spain, A" (Jarrell), II, 371

Poems (Berryman), I, 170

Poems (Bryant), II, 311

Poems (Cummings), I, 430, 447

Poems (Eliot), I, 580, 588; IV, 122

Poems (Emerson), II, 7, 8, 12–13, 17

Poems (Moore), III, 194, 205, 215

Poems (Poe), III, 411

Poems (Tate), IV, 121

Poems (Wordsworth), I, 468

Poems of Emily Dickinson, The (ed. Johnson), I, 470

Poems of Emily Dickinson (eds. Todd and Higginson), I, 469, 470

Poems by Emily Dickinson, Secon Series (eds. Todd and Higginson), I, 454

Poems and Essays (Ransom), III, 486, 490, 492

Poems about God (Ransom), III, 484, 486, 491; IV, 121

Poems, 1924–1933 (MacLeish), III, 7, 15

Poems of Places (ed. Longfellow), II, 490

Poems on Slavery (Longfellow), II, 489

Poems of Two Friends (Howells and Piatt), II, 273, 277

"Poet, The" (Emerson), II, 13, 19, 20, 170
"Poet and His Book, The" (Millay), III, 126, 138
"Poet at Seven, The" (Rimbaud), II, 545
"Poète contumace, Le" (Corbière), II, 384–385
Poetic Diction: A Study in Meaning (Barfield), III, 274, 279
"Poetic Principle, The" (Poe), III, 421, 426
Poetics (Aristotle), III, 422
"Poetry" (Moore), III, 204–205, 215
Poetry (publication), I, 51, 103, 109, 235, 384, 393, 475; II, 517; III, 194, 458, 460, 465–466, 469, 581, 586, 592; IV, 76, 370
Poetry and the Age (Jarrell), IV, 352
"Poetry of Barbarism, The" (Santayana), IV, 353
Poetry and Criticism (ed. Nemerov), III, 269
"Poetry and Drama" (Eliot), I, 588
Poetry and Fiction: Essays (Nemerov), III, 269, 281
Poetry of Meditation, The (Martz), IV, 151
Poetry and Poets (Lowell), II, 512
"Poetry and the Public World" (MacLeish), III, 11
Poetry of Stephen Crane, The (Hoffman), I, 405
Poet's Choice (eds. Engle and Langland), III, 277, 542
Poets of the Old Testament, The (Gordon), III, 199
Poets on Poetry (ed. Nemerov), III, 269
Poggioli, Renato, IV, 95
Poincaré, Raymond, IV, 320
"Point of Age, A" (Berryman), I, 173
Point of No Return (Marquand), III, 56, 59–60, 65, 67, 69
Poirier, Richard, I, 136, 143, 166, 239; III, 34, 48
"Pole Star" (MacLeish), III, 16
Politian (Poe), III, 412
Politics (Macdonald), I, 233–234

Polk, James K., I, 17; II, 433–434
Pollin, Burton R., III, 432
Pollock, Jackson, IV, 411, 420
Pollock, Thomas Clark, IV, 472, 473
Polo, Marco, III, 395
"Pomegranate Seed" (Wharton), IV, 316
Pommer, H. E., III, 97
Ponce de Leon, Luis, III, 391
"Pond, The" (Nemerov), III, 272
Ponder Heart, The (Welty), IV, 261, 274–275, 281
Pondrom, Cyrena N., IV, 23
Poole, Ernest, II, 444
Poor Fool (Caldwell), I, 291, 292, 308
"Poor Joanna" (Jewett), II, 394
"Poor Man's Pudding and Rich Man's Crumbs" (Melville), III, 89–90
"Poor Richard" (James), II, 322
Poor Richard's Almanac (undated) (Franklin), II, 112
Poor Richard's Almanac for 1733 (Franklin), II, 108, 110
Poor Richard's Almanac for 1739 (Franklin), II, 112
Poor Richard's Almanac for 1758 (Franklin), II, 101
Poor White (Anderson), I, 110–111
Poore, Charles, III, 364
Poorhouse Fair, The (Updike), IV, 214, 228–229, 232
Pope, Alexander, I, 198, 204; II, 17, 111, 114; III, 263, 267, 288, 517; IV, 145
Popkin, Henry, III, 169
Poplar, Ellen, *see* Wright, Mrs. Richard (Ellen Poplar)
"Poppy Seed" (Lowell), II, 523
Pops, Martin Leonard, III, 97
Popular Mechanics (magazine), II, 589
"Porphyria's Lover" (Browning), II, 522
Port Folio (publication), II, 298, 302
Portable Faulkner (Cowley), II, 57, 59
Porter, Bern, III, 171
Porter, Bernard H., III, 121
Porter, Katherine Anne, I, 97,

385; II, 194, 606; III, **433–455**, 482; IV, 26, 48, 143, 138, 246, 261, 279, 280, 282
Porter, William Sydney (O. Henry), I, 201; III, 5
Portland Gazette (newspaper), II, 493
Portrait of the Artist as a Young Man, A (Joyce), I, 475–476; III, 471, 561
Portrait of Bascom Hawkes, A (Wolfe), IV, 451–452, 456
"Portrait of a Girl in Glass" (Williams), IV, 383
"Portrait of the Intellectual as a Yale Man" (McCarthy), II, 563, 564–565
"Portrait of a Lady" (Eliot), I, 569, 570, 571, 584; III, 4
Portrait of a Lady, The (James), I, 10, 258, 461–462, 464; II, 323, 325, 327, 328–329, 334
Portz, John, III, 384
"Possessions" (Crane), I, 392–393
Pot of Earth, The (MacLeish), III, 5, 6–8, 10, 12, 18
Potter, Jack, I, 496
Potter, Mary Storer, *see* Longfellow, Mrs. Henry Wadsworth (Mary Storer Potter)
Potter, Stephen, IV, 430
"Potpourri, A" (Miller), III, 190
Poulet, Georges, I, 473
Pound, Ezra, I, 49, 58, 60, 66, 68, 69, 105, 236, 243, 256, 384, 403, 428, 429, 475, 476, 482, 487, 521, 578; II, 26, 55, 168, 263, 316, 371, 376, 513, 517, 520, 526, 528, 529, 530; III, 2, 5, 8, 9, 13–14, 17, 174, 194, 196, 217, 278, 430, 453, **456–479**, 492, 504, 511, 523, 524, 527, 575–576, 586, 590; IV, 27, 28, 407, 415, 416, 424, 433, 446
Pound, Mrs. Ezra (Dorothy Shakespear), III, 457, 458, 472
Pound, T. S., I, 428
Powell, Lawrence Clark, III, 189, 191
"Power" (Emerson), II, 2, 3
Power and the Glory, The (Greene), III, 556
Powers, J. F., III, 360

Rougon-Macquart, Les (Zola), II, 175–176

Round Up (Lardner), II, 426, 430, 431

Rourke, Constance, I, 258; IV, 339, 352

Rouse, Blair, II, 195

Rousseau, Jean Jacques, I, 226; II, 8, 343; III, 170, 178, 259; IV, 80, 173, 440

Rover Boys (Winfield), III, 146

Rovit, Earl, I, 143; II, 270; IV, 102

Rowe, H. D., I, 403

Roy, Emil, I, 96

"Royal Palm" (Crane), I, 401

Royce, Josiah, I, 443; III, 303, 600; IV, 26

Royster, Sarah Elmira, III, 410, 429

Rubáiyát (Khayyám), I, 568

Rubin, John D., II, 222

Rubin, Larry, II, 222

Rubin, Louis D., Jr., I, 311; II, 195, 221, 222; III, 360; IV, 116, 119, 259, 284, 462–463, 472, 473

"Ruby Daggett" (Eberhart), I, 539

Rueckert, William, I, 264, 287

Ruihley, G. R., II, 533

Ruland, Richard, I, 263

Rule, Margaret W., I, 96

"Rule of Phase Applied to History, The" (Adams), I, 19

"Rules by Which a Great Empire May Be Reduced to a Small One" (Franklin), II, 120

"Rumpelstiltskin" (Grimm), IV, 266

"Runes" (Nemerov), III, 267, 277–278

Runyan, Harry, II, 76

Rusk, Dean, II, 579

Rusk, Ralph L., II, 22, 23; IV, 189

Ruskin, John, II, 323, 338; IV, 349

Russell, Ada Dwyer, II, 513, 527

Russell, Bertrand, II, 27; III, 605, 606

Russell, Peter, III, 479

Russell, Phillips, II, 124

Russia at War (Caldwell), I, 296

Russian Journal, A (Steinbeck), IV, 52, 63

Ruth (biblical person), IV, 13

Ruth, George Herman ("Babe"), II, 423

Rutledge, Ann, III, 588

Ryan, Pat M., IV, 472

Rymer, Thomas, IV, 122

S.S. Glencairn (O'Neill), III, 387, 388, 405

S.S. San Pedro (Cozzens), I, 360–362, 370, 378, 379

Saadi, II, 19

Sacco, Nicola, I, 482, 486, 490, 494; II, 38–39, 426; III, 139–140

Sacramento Union (newspaper), IV, 196

Sacred Fount, The (James), II, 332–333

Sacred Wood, The (Eliot), IV, 431

Sacrilege of Alan Kent, The (Caldwell), I, 291–292

Sad Heart at the Supermarket, A (Jarrell), II, 386

Sade, Marquis de, III, 259; IV, 437, 442

"Saga of King Olaf, The" (Longfellow), II, 489, 505

Sage, Howard, II, 149

Sahl, Mort, II, 435–436

"Sailing to Byzantium" (Yeats), III, 263

"Sailing after Lunch" (Stevens), IV, 73

"St. Augustine and the Bullfights" (Porter), III, 454

"St. Francis Einstein of the Daffodils" (Williams), IV, 409–411

St. George and the Godfather (Mailer), III, 46

St. Louis *Globe-Democrat* (newspaper), I, 499

St. Louis Post-Dispatch (newspaper), IV, 381

St. Louis *Republic* (newspaper), I, 499

St. Mawr (Lawrence), II, 595

St. Nicholas (magazine), II, 397

"Saint Nicholas" (Moore), III, 215

Sainte-Beuve, Charles Augustin, IV, 432

Saint-Gaudens, Augustus, I, 18, 228; II, 551

Saints' Everlasting Rest, The (Baxter), III, 199; IV, 151, 153

Saintsbury, George, IV, 440

"Sale of the Hessians, The" (Franklin), II, 120

"Salem" (Lowell), II, 550

Salinger, Doris, III, 551

Salinger, J. D., II, 255; III, **551–574**; V, 190, 216, 217

Salmagundi; or, The Whim-Whams and Opinions of Launcelot Langstaff, Esq., and Others (Irving), II, 299, 300, 304

Salome (Strauss), IV, 316

Salt, Henry S., IV, 188, 189

Salt Garden, The (Nemerov), III, 269, 272–275, 277

"Salt Garden, The" (Nemerov), III, 267–268

Saltpeter, Harry, IV, 377

"Salute" (MacLeish), III, 13

Samachson, Dorothy, III, 169

Samachson, Joseph, III, 169

Samain, Albert, II, 528

Same Door, The (Updike), IV, 214, 219, 226

"Sampler, A" (MacLeish), III, 4

Samson (biblical person), IV, 137

Samson Agonistes (Milton), III, 274

Samuels, Charles Thomas, I, 96, 143; IV, 235

Samuels, Ernest, I, 24

San Francisco Call (newspaper), IV, 196

San Francisco *Chronicle* (newspaper), I, 194

San Francisco *Examiner* (newspaper), I, 198, 199, 200, 206, 207, 208

San Francisco *News-Letter* (newspaper), I, 193

San Francisco *Wave* (publication), III, 315, 327

Sanborn, F. B., II, 23; IV, 171, 172, 178, 188, 189

Sanborn, Ralph, III, 406–407

Sanctuary (Faulkner), II, 57, 61–63, 72, 73, 74, 174

"Sanctuary, The" (Nemerov), III, 272, 274

Sanctuary (Wharton), IV, 311

Sand, George, II, 322

Wedekind, Frank, III, 398

Wedge, George F., III, 360

"Weeds, The" (McCarthy), II, 566

Week on the Concord and Merrimack Rivers, A (Thoreau), IV, 168, 169, 177, 182–183

"Weekend at Ellerslie, A" (Wilson), IV, 431

Weekly Spectator (publication), II, 300

Weeks, Edward, III, 64, 73

"Weeping Burgher" (Stevens), IV, 77

Wegelin, Christopher, II, 318

Wegner, Robert E., I, 450

Weigand, Charmion von, III, 408

Weil, Simone, I, 298

Weinberg, Helen, I, 166

Weinstein, Hinda, IV, 285

Weinstein, Lorraine "Laura," *see* Perelman, Mrs. S. J. (Lorraine "Laura" Weinstein)

Weinstein, Max, IV, 285

Weinstein, Mrs. Max (Anna Wallenstein), IV, 285, 287

Weinstein, Nathan, *see* West, Nathanael

Weinstein, Norman, IV, 48

Weird Tales (magazine), IV, 380

Weisenberger, Bernard, I, 427

Weisheit, Rabbi, IV, 76

Weiss, Daniel, I, 427

Weiss, Peter, IV, 117

Weissman, Philip, III, 408

Welcome to Our City (Wolfe), IV, 461

Welded (O'Neill), III, 390

Welker, Robert L., II, 221

Welland, Dennis, III, 169

Wellek, René, I, 253, 261, 263, 282, 287; II, 320

Weller, George, III, 322

Welles, Orson, IV, 476

Wellman, Flora, II, 463–464, 465

Wells, H. G., I, 103, 226, 241, 243, 253, 405, 409, 415; II, 82, 144, 276, 337, 338, 340, 458; III, 456; IV, 340, 455

Wells, Henry W., I, 473; IV, 96

Welsh, Mary, *see* Hemingway, Mrs. Ernest (Mary Welsh)

Welty, Eudora, II, 194, 217, 606; IV, **260–284**

Wendell, Barrett, III, 507

Wept of Wish-ton-Wish, The (Cooper), I, 339, 342, 350

"We're Friends Again" (O'Hara), III, 372–373

"Were the Whole Realm of Nature Mine" (Watts), I, 458

Wescott, Glenway, I, 263, 288; II, 85; III, 448, 454, 455

West, James, II, 562

West, Nathanael, I, 97, 107, 190, 211, 298; II, 436; III, 357, 425; IV, **285–307**

West, Mrs. Nathanael (Eileen McKenney), IV, 288

West, Ray B., Jr., III, 455

West, Rebecca, II, 412, 445; III, 598

Westall, Julia Elizabeth, *see* Wolfe, Mrs. William Oliver (Julia Elizabeth Westall)

Westbrook, Max, I, 427

Westcott, Edward N., II, 102

Westminster Gazette (publication), I, 408

Weston, Jessie L., II, 540; III, 12

West-running Brook (Frost), II, 155

"West-running Brook" (Frost), II, 150, 162–164

Wharton, Edith, I, 12, 375; II, 96, 180, 183, 186, 189–190, 193, 283, 338, 444, 451; III, 69, 175, 576; IV, 8, 53, 58, **302–330**

Wharton, Edward Robbins, IV, 310, 313–314, 319

What Are Masterpieces (Stein), IV, 30–31

What Are Years (Moore), III, 208–209, 210, 215

"What Are Years?" (Moore), III, 211, 213

"What Can I Tell My Bones" (Roethke), III, 546, 549

What Is Art? (Tolstoi), I, 58

"What Is College For?" (Bourne), I, 216

"What Is an Emotion" (James), II, 350

"What Is Exploitation?" (Bourne), I, 216

What Is Man? (Twain), II, 434; IV, 209

What Maisie Knew (James), II, 332

"What Must" (MacLeish), III, 18

What Time Collects (Farrell), II, 46, 47–48

What a Way to Go (Morris), III, 230–232

What's O'Clock (Lowell), II, 511, 527, 528

Wheaton, Mabel Wolfe, IV, 473

Wheel of Life, The (Glasgow), II, 176, 178, 179, 183

Wheeler, John, II, 433

Wheelock, John Hall, IV, 143, 461, 472

When Boyhood Dreams Come True (Farrell), II, 45

"When Death Came April Twelve 1945" (Sandburg), III, 591, 593

"When I Buy Pictures" (Moore), III, 205

"When I Left Business for Literature" (Anderson), I, 101

When Knighthood Was in Flower (Major), III, 320

"[When] Let by rain" (Taylor), IV, 160–161

"When the Light Gets Green" (Warren), IV, 252

"When Lilacs Last in the Dooryard Bloom'd" (Whitman), IV, 347–348, 351

When Time Was Born (Farrell), II, 46, 47

Where the Cross Is Made (O'Neill), III, 388, 391

"Where Is the Voice Coming From?" (Welty), IV, 280

"Where Knock is Open Wide" (Roethke), III, 533–535

"Which Theatre Is the Absurd One?" (Albee), I, 71

Whicher, George F., I, 473; IV, 189

Whicher, Stephen, II, 20, 23, 24

Whilomville Stories (Crane), I, 414

"Whip, The" (Robinson), III, 513

Whipple, T. K., II, 456, 458; IV, 427

"Whispering Leaves" (Glasgow), II, 190

"William Wilson" (Poe), II, 475; III, 410, 412
Williams, Ames W., I, 426
Williams, Blanche C., II, 485
Williams, Cecil, II, 508, 510
Williams, Cratis D., I, 120
Williams, Dakin, IV, 379
Williams, Daniel D., III, 313
Williams, David, II, 149
Williams, Edward, I, 564; IV, 404
Williams, Edwina Dakin, IV, 379, 401
Williams Horace, IV, 453
Williams, John A., IV, 497
Williams, John Sharp, IV, 378
Williams, Miller, III, 502
Williams, Paul, IV, 404
Williams, Raymond, III, 169
Williams, Rose, IV, 379
Williams, Solomon, I, 549
Williams, Stanley T., II, 301, 316, 317, 318, 510
Williams, Stephen, IV, 148
Williams, Ted, IV, 216
Williams, Tennessee, I, 73, 81, 113, 211; II, 190, 194; III, 145, 147; IV, 4, **378–401**
Williams, William, IV, 404, 405
Williams, William Carlos, I, 61, 62, 229, 255, 256, 261, 285, 287, 428, 438, 446, 450, 539; II, 133, 536, 542, 543, 544, 545; III, 194, 196, 198, 214, 217, 269, 409, 453, 457, 458, 464, 465, 591, 598; IV, 30, 74, 75, 76, 94, 95, 96, 286, 287, 307, **402–425**
Williams, Mrs. William Carlos (Florence Herman), IV, 404
Williams family, I, 547, 549
Williamson, George, I, 591
Willingham, Calder, III, 49
Willis, Nathaniel Parker, II, 313; III, 431
Wills, Ridley, IV, 122
Wilshire, Bruce, II, 362, 364, 366
Wilson, Angus, IV, 259, 430, 435
Wilson, Douglas, III, 622
Wilson, Edmund, I, 67, 185, 213, 236, 247, 260, 263, 434, 450, 482; II, 79, 80, 81, 86, 87, 91, 97, 98, 99, 146, 276, 341, 430, 438, 530, 562, 587; III, 144, 455, 588; IV, 48, 72, 307, 308, 310, 330, 377, **426–449**

Wilson, Edmund (father), IV, 441
Wilson, Reuel, II, 562
Wilson, T. C., III, 217; IV, 425
Wilson, Thomas, IV, 153
Wilson, Woodrow, I, 245, 246, 490; II, 183, 253; III, 105, 581
Wilton, David, IV, 147
Windham, Donald, IV, 382, 399
"Windhover" (Hopkins), I, 397; II, 539
"Windows" (Jarrell), II, 388, 389
"Winds, The" (Welty), IV, 265
Windy McPherson's Son (Anderson), I, 101, 102–103, 105, 111
"Wine Menagerie, The" (Crane), I, 389, 391
Wine of the Puritans, The: A Study of Present-Day America (Brooks), I, 240
"Wine of Wizardry, A" (Sterling), I, 208
Winesburg, Ohio: A Group of Tales of Ohio Small Town Life (Anderson), I, 97, 102, 103, 104, 105–108, 111, 112, 113, 114, 116; III, 224, 579
Wing-and-Wing, The (Cooper), I, 350, 355
Wings of the Dove, The (James), I, 436; II, 320, 323, 333, 334–335
Winner, Arthur, IV, 119
Winner Take Nothing (Hemingway), II, 249
Winslow, Devereux, II, 547
Winslow, Harriet, II, 552–553
Winslow, Ola Elizabeth, I, 547, 564
Winslow, Warren, II, 540
Winter Diary, A (Van Doren), I, 168
"Winter Dreams" (Fitzgerald), II, 80, 94
"Winter in Dunbarton" (Lowell), II, 547
"Winter Landscape" (Berryman), I, 174
Winter Lightning (Nemerov), III, 269
Winter of Our Discontent, The (Steinbeck), IV, 52, 65–66, 68
"Winter Remembered" (Ransom), III, 492–493
Winterrowd, Prudence, I, 217, 224

Winters, Yvor, I, 59, 63, 70, 386, 393, 397, 398, 402, 404, 471, 473; II, 246; III, 194, 217, 432, 498, 502, 526, 550; IV, 96, 153, 425
Winterset (Anderson), III, 159
Winther, Sophus Keith, III, 408
Wirt, William, I, 232
Wirth, Louis, IV, 475
Wisdom of the Heart, The (Miller), III, 178, 184
Wise Blood (O'Connor), III, 337, 338, 339–343, 344, 345, 346, 350, 354, 356, 357
"Wish for a Young Wife" (Roethke), III, 548
Wisse, Ruth R., I, 166
Wister, Owen, I, 62
"Witch of Coös, The" (Frost), II, 154–155
With the Empress Dowager of China (Carl), III, 475
Witherington, Paul, I, 96
"Witness, The" (Porter), III, 443–444
Witness Tree, A (Frost), II, 155
Wits Recreations (Mennes and Smith), II, 111
Witt, Grace, III, 49
Wolf, William John, III, 313
Wolfe, Ben, IV, 454
Wolfe, Don M., IV, 117
Wolfe, Mabel, IV, 454
Wolfe, Peter, I, 96
Wolfe, Thomas, I, 119, 288, 289, 374, 478, 495; II, 457; III, 40, 108, 278, 334, 482; IV, 52, 97, 357, **450–473**
Wolfe, William Oliver, IV, 454
Wolfe, Mrs. William Oliver (Julia Elizabeth Westall), IV, 454
Wolfert, Ira, III, 169
Wolfert's Roost (Irving), II, 314
Wolkenfeld, J. S., IV, 24
Wollaston, William, II, 108
Woman of Andros, The (Wilder), IV, 356, 363–364, 367, 368, 374
"Woman in the House, A" (Caldwell), I, 310
Woman on the Porch, The (Gordon), II, 199, 209–211
"Woman on the Stair, The" (MacLeish), III, 15–16

Yeats, William B., I, 69, 172, 384, 389, 403, 434, 478, 494, 532; II, 168–169, 566, 598; III, 4, 5, 8, 18, 19, 20, 23, 29, 40, 205, 249, 269, 270–271, 272, 278, 279, 294, 347, 409, 457, 458–460, 472, 473, 476–477, 521, 523, 524, 527, 528, 533, 540, 541, 542, 543–544, 591–592; IV, 89, 93, 121, 126, 136, 140, 271, 394, 404

Yellow Book (publication), I, 421; III, 508

"Yellow Girl" (Caldwell), I, 310

"Yellow Gown, The" (Anderson), I, 114

"Yellow River" (Tate), IV, 141

"Yentl the Yeshiva Boy" (Singer), IV, 15, 20

Yerkes, Charles E., I, 507, 512

Yet Other Waters (Farrell), II, 29, 38, 39, 40

Yohannan, J. D., II, 20, 24

Yonge, Charlotte, II, 174

"Yore" (Nemerov), III, 283

Yoshe Kalb (Singer), IV, 2

Yost, Karl, III, 144

"You, Andrew Marvell" (MacLeish), III, 12–13

You Can't Go Home Again (Wolfe), IV, 450, 451, 454, 456, 460, 462, 468, 469, 470

You, Emperors, and Others: Poems 1957–1960 (Warren), IV, 245

You Have Seen Their Faces (Caldwell), I, 290, 293–294, 295, 304, 309

You Know Me Al (Lardner), II, 26, 415, 419, 422, 431

You Know Me Al (comic strip), II, 423

You Touched Me! (Williams and Windham), IV, 382, 385, 387, 390, 392–393

Young, Art, IV, 436

Young, Charles L., II, 24

Young, Edward, II, 111; III, 415, 503

Young, Philip, II, 270, 306, 318

Young, Stark, III, 408

Young, Thomas Daniel, III, 502

"Young Folks, The" (Salinger), III, 551

Young Folk's Cyclopaedia of Persons and Places (Champlin), III, 577

"Young Goodman Brown" (Hawthorne), II, 229

Young Immigrants, The (Lardner), II, 426

Young Lonigan: A Boyhood in Chicago Streets (Farrell), II, 31, 41

Young Manhood of Studs Lonigan, The (Farrell), II, 31, 34

"Young Sammy's First Wild Oats" (Santayana), III, 607, 615

Youth and the Bright Medusa (Cather), I, 322

Youth and Life (Bourne), I, 217–222, 232

Youth's Companion, The (magazine), II, 397

Yvernelle: A Legend of Feudal France (Norris), III, 314

Zabel, Morton Dauwen, II, 431; III, 194, 215, 217, 525

Zabriskie, George, IV, 425

Zangwill, Israel, I, 229

Zarathustra, III, 602

Zaturenska, Gregory, I, 404

Zaturenska, Horace, I, 404

Zaturenska, Marya, I, 404; II, 533; III, 144, 217

Zechariah (biblical book), IV, 152

Zeit Ohne Beispiel, Die (Goebbels), III, 560

"Zeitl and Rickel" (Singer), IV, 20

Zend-Avesta (Fechner), II, 358

Zevi, Sabbatai, IV, 6

Ziegfeld, Florenz, II, 427–428

Ziff, Larzer, I, 427; II, 149

Zigrosser, Carl, I, 226, 228, 231

Zimbardo, Rose A., I, 96

Zimmer, Dieter E., III, 266

Zinsser, Hans, I, 251, 385

Zola, Emile, I, 211, 411, 474, 500, 502, 518; II, 174, 175–176, 182, 194, 275, 276, 281, 282, 319, 325, 337, 338; III, 315, 316, 317–318, 319–230, 321, 322, 323, 393, 511, 583; IV, 326

Zolotow, Maurice, III, 161

Zoo Story, The (Albee), I, 71, 72–74, 75, 77, 84, 93, 94; III, 281

"Zooey" (Salinger), III, 564–565, 566, 567, 569, 572

Zorach, William, I, 260

Zukofsky, Louis, IV, 415, 425